I0343108

Tafsīr al-Qurṭubī

Vol. 2

Juz' 2: Sūrat al-Baqarah 142 – 253

# Tafsīr al-Qurṭubī

## The General Judgments of the Qur'an and Clarification of what it contains of the Sunnah and *Āyah*s of Discrimination

Abū 'Abdullāh Muḥammad ibn Aḥmad ibn Abī Bakr ibn Farḥ al-Anṣārī al-Khazrajī al-Andalusī al-Qurṭubī

## Vol. 2

Juz' 2: Sūrat al-Baqarah 142 – 253

translated by
Aisha Bewley

Diwan Press
*Classical and Contemporary Books on Islam and Sufism*

Published by: Diwan Press Ltd.

Website: www.diwanpress.com
E-mail: info@diwanpress.com



| | |
|---|---|
| By: | Abu 'Abdullah Muhammad ibn Ahmad al-Qurtubi |
| Translated by: | Aisha Abdarrahman Bewley |
| Edited by: | Abdalhaqq Bewley |

A catalogue record of this book is available from the British Library.

| | |
|---|---|
| ISBN13: | 978-1-908892-75-1 (Paperback) |
| | 978-1-908892-76-8 (Casebound) |
| | 978-1-908892-74-4 (Hardback) |
| | 978-1-908892-77-5 (ePub & Kindle) |

# Contents

Translator's note vii

2. Sūrat al-Baqarah – The Cow 142 – 253 1

Table of Contents for *Āyat*s 465

Glossary 468

# Table of Transliterations

| | | | |
|---|---|---|---|
| ء | ’ | ض | ḍ |
| ا | a | ط | ṭ |
| ب | b | ظ | ẓ |
| ت | t | ع | ‘ |
| ث | th | غ | gh |
| ج | j | ف | f |
| ح | ḥ | ق | q |
| خ | kh | ك | k |
| د | d | ل | l |
| ذ | dh | م | m |
| ر | r | ن | n |
| ز | z | ه | h |
| س | s | و | w |
| ش | sh | ي | y |
| ص | ṣ | | |

| Long vowel | | Short vowel | |
|---|---|---|---|
| ا | ā | ـَ | a [*fatḥah*] |
| و | ū | ـُ | u [*ḍammah*] |
| ي | ī | ـِ | i [*kasrah*] |
| أَوْ | aw | | |
| أَيْ | ay | | |

# Translator's note

There are minor omissions in the text. Some poems have been omitted which the author quotes to illustrate a point of grammatical usage or as an example of orthography or the usage of a word, often a derivative of the root of the word used in the *āyah*, but not the actual word used. Often it is difficult to convey the sense in English. Occasionally the author explores a grammatical matter or a tangential issue, and some of these may have been shortened. English grammatical terms used to translate Arabic grammatical terms do not have exactly the same meaning, sometimes rendering a precise translation of them problematic and often obscure.

The end of a *juz'* may vary by an *āyah* or two in order to preserve relevant passages.

# 2. Sūrat al-Baqarah – The Cow 142 – 253

سَيَقُولُ ٱلسُّفَهَآءُ مِنَ ٱلنَّاسِ مَا وَلَّىٰهُمْ عَن قِبْلَتِهِمُ ٱلَّتِى كَانُوا۟ عَلَيْهَا ۚ قُل لِّلَّهِ
ٱلْمَشْرِقُ وَٱلْمَغْرِبُ ۚ يَهْدِى مَن يَشَآءُ إِلَىٰ صِرَٰطٍ مُّسْتَقِيمٍ ﴿١٤٢﴾

**142 The fools among the people will ask, 'What has made them turn round from the direction they used to face?' Say, 'Both East and West belong to Allah. He guides whoever He wills to a straight path.'**

**The fools among the people will ask,**

Allah Almighty is giving advance warning of what some people are going to say about the believers changing the direction they face in prayer from Syria to the Ka'bah. The word 'fools' is qualified by 'people' because foolishness is also found in animals. The fools are those who say this. A foolwiht (*safīh*) is someone with a poor intellect. A garment which is *safīh*, the root from which the word comes, is loosely woven. Quṭrub says that they are ignorant wrongdoers. This refers to the Jews in Madīnah, as Mujāhid says. As-Suddī said that it refers to the hypocrites and az-Zajjāj says that it means the unbelievers of Quraysh when they objected to the change of *qiblah*. They said, 'Muḥammad yearns for his homeland and will soon revert to your religion.' The Jews said, 'He is confused about the business.' The hypocrites said, 'What has made them turn around from their *qiblah*?' to mock the Muslims.

**'What has made them turn round from the direction they used to face?'**

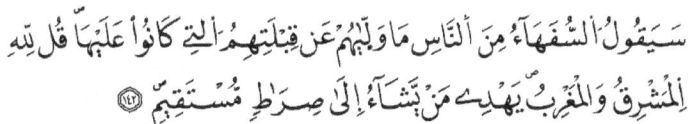

The imams report that Ibn 'Umar said, 'While people were at Qubā' performing the *Ṣubḥ* prayer, someone came to them and said, "The Messenger of Allah ﷺ received Revelation in the night and he has been commanded to face the Ka'bah." They were facing Syria and immediately turned right round to face the Ka'bah.' Al-Bukhārī transmitted from al-Barā' that the Prophet ﷺ was praying towards Jerusalem for sixteen or seventeen months. He wanted his *qiblah* to be towards the Ka'bah. The first prayer he prayed towards it was *'Aṣr*

and people prayed it with him. A man who had prayed with the Prophet ﷺ left and passed by the people of another mosque who were in *rukūʿ*. He said, 'I testify by Allah that I prayed with the Prophet ﷺ towards Makkah.' So they turned round so that they were facing the House. There were men who had died while they were facing the old *qiblah* before the change to the House and they did not know what to say about them. So Allah Almighty revealed: *'Allah would never let your faith go to waste.'* (2:143)

This transmission mentions the *'Aṣr* prayer whereas the transmission of Mālik mentioned the *Ṣubḥ* prayer. It is also said that it was revealed while the Prophet ﷺ was in the mosque of the Banū Salamah performing *Ẓuhr* and he changed *qiblah* after two *rakʿahs* of it. For that reason, it was called the Mosque of the Two *Qiblahs*.

In *at-Tamhīd*, Abū 'Umar mentioned from Nuwaylah bint Aslam, one of the women who gave allegiance: 'We were performing the *Ẓuhr* prayer when 'Abbād ibn Bishr ibn Qayẓī came and said, "The Messenger of Allah ﷺ has faced the *qiblah* (or 'the Sacred House'), so the men moved to where the women were and the women moved to where the men were."' It is also said that the *āyah* was revealed about other than the prayer, and that is more common. *'Aṣr* was the first prayer towards the *qiblah*. Allah knows best.

It is related that the first to pray towards the Kaʿbah, when the *qiblah* was changed from Jerusalem, was Abū Saʿīd ibn al-Muʿallā. That was when he was passing through the mosque and heard the Messenger of Allah ﷺ telling people to change the *qiblah*, reciting this *āyah* while he was on the minbar: *'We have seen you looking up into heaven...'* (2:144) He told his companion, 'Come and let us pray two *rakʿahs* before the Messenger of Allah ﷺ comes down! Then we will be the first to pray and we will be covered in blessings.' They prayed them and then the Messenger of Allah ﷺ descended and led the people in *Ẓuhr*.

There is disagreement about the length of time the Prophet ﷺ was in Madīnah before the *qiblah* was changed. It is said that it was changed after sixteen or seventeen months, as we find in al-Bukhārī. Ad-Dāraquṭnī also reported that al-Barā' said, 'We prayed with the Messenger of Allah ﷺ after he came to Madīnah towards Jerusalem for sixteen months. Then Allah informed the Prophet that He was aware of his desire to change *qiblah* and the Revelation came: *"We have seen you looking into the heaven, turning this way and that."* (2:144) It was sixteen months without doubt.' Mālik related from Yaḥyā ibn Saʿīd that Saʿīd ibn al-Musayyab said that the *qiblah* was changed two months before Badr. Ibrāhīm ibn Isḥāq said that was in Rajab, 2 AH. Al-Bustī said, 'The Muslims prayed towards Jerusalem for seventeen months and three days. He came to Madīnah on Monday, 15 Rabīʿ

al-Awwal, and Allah commanded him to face the Ka'bah on Tuesday, 15 Sha'bān the following year.'

Scholars are of three different opinions concerning the reason why the Prophet ﷺ faced Jerusalem. Al-Ḥasan said, 'It was by opinion and *ijtihād*.' 'Ikrimah and Abū al-'Āliyah agreed with that view. The second opinion is that he had a choice between it and the Ka'bah and chose Jerusalem because he wanted the Jews to believe. Aṭ-Ṭabarī said that. Az-Zajjāj said that it was to test the idolaters because they were used to the Ka'bah. The third opinion and the one which the majority hold – Ibn 'Abbās and others – is that he was obliged to face it by the command of Allah and Revelation from Him. Then Allah abrogated that and commanded him to face the Ka'bah in the prayer. They cite as evidence: *'We only appointed the direction you used to face in order to distinguish those who follow the Messenger from those who turn round on their heels.'* (2:143)

There is also disagreement about when the prayer was first made obligatory for him at Makkah and whether the *qiblah* was then towards Jerusalem or the Ka'bah. There are two positions. One group say that it was towards Jerusalem and remained that way in Madīnah for seventeen months and then Allah changed it to the Ka'bah. Ibn 'Abbās said that. Others say that when the prayer was first made obligatory for him he faced towards the Ka'bah and he continued to pray towards it while he was in Makkah, as Ibrāhīm and Ismā'īl had done. When he went to Madīnah he prayed towards Jerusalem for sixteen or seventeen months and then Allah changed the *qiblah* back to the Ka'bah. Abū 'Umar said, 'I consider this to be the sounder of the two positions.' Another said, 'That was because when the Prophet ﷺ came to Madīnah, he wanted to court the Jews and turned to their *qiblah* so that the Message would be easier for them to accept. When their obstinacy was evident and he despaired of them, he wanted to change back to the Ka'bah and he looked up at the heavens.' His love for Makkah was because it was the *qiblah* of Ibrāhīm, as Ibn 'Abbās said. It is said that it was to call the Arabs to Islam. It is said that it was to be different from the Jews, as Mujāhid said. Abu-l-'Āliyah ar-Riyyāḥī said, 'The mosque and *qiblah* of Ṣāliḥ was towards the Ka'bah. Mūsā used to pray towards the Stone which was in the direction of the Ka'bah and it was the *qiblah* of all the Prophets ﷺ.'

This *āyah* contains clear evidence that the rulings of Allah and His Book can be both abrogating and abrogated and the Community agree on that, except for the rare exception. Scholars agree that the *qiblah* was the first ruling to be abrogated in the Book and that it was abrogated twice, according to one of the positions about the matter. It also indicates that it is permissible for the Sunnah to be abrogated by the Qur'an. That is because the Prophet ﷺ prayed towards Jerusalem and there was no Qur'anic text on that. That was a judgment only from the *Sunnah* and then that was abrogated by the Qur'an.

The *āyah* also contains evidence of the permission to make a ruling based on a single *ḥadīth*. That was because facing Jerusalem was definite in our Sharī'ah, and then when someone came to the people of Qubā' and told them that the *qiblah* had been changed to the Sacred Mosque, they accepted that and turned towards it and abandoned the *mutawātir* in favour of the single report they heard. Scholars disagree about whether it is permitted logically and actually. Abū Ḥātim said, 'What is preferred is that that is permitted logically, if it is part of the worship entailed by the Sharī'ah, and actually in the time of the Prophet ﷺ as is shown in the story of Qubā' and also by the evidence that the Prophet ﷺ sent individual governors to the regions and they conveyed both the abrogating and abrogated. However it became forbidden after the death of the Prophet ﷺ by the consensus of the Companions, and the position then was that the Qur'an and the *mutawātir* are well-known and may not be abrogated by a single *ḥadīth*, and no one believes that to be possible. Those who say that it is forbidden argue by the fact that it would lead to what is impossible, namely removing what is definitive in favour of what is supposition. The story of Qubā' and the governors is based on circumstances that convey knowledge either by transmission and realisation, or by probability and implication. This is a question about the fundamental principles of *fiqh*.

It also contains evidence that if the abrogation has not reached a person, then he should worship according to the first ruling. This differs from those who said that the first ruling is removed by the mere existence of the abrogation, not by knowledge of it. The first view is sounder because the people of Qubā' continued to pray towards Jerusalem until someone came and told them about the abrogation and then they turned towards the *qiblah*. When the abrogation exists, it inevitably removes the prior judgment, but on the proviso that there is knowledge of it, because the abrogation is addressed to people, and if that has not reached someone, he is not addressed by it. The point in this disagreement concerns acts of worship which are performed after the abrogation but before the person performing them has heard about it: should he repeat them or not? This is also the basis for the actions of a deputy after he has been dismissed or the one who appointed him has died before he has learned of that. There are two views.

The same is true of a *qirāḍ* transaction and those appointed by a judge when he dies or is dismissed. What is sound is that the action done by each of those people is carried out and their judgment is not revoked. Qāḍī 'Iyāḍ said, 'There is no disagreement that the judgments of someone who has been freed, when he does not know that he has been freed, are the judgments of a free man in things involving other people. There is no disagreement that someone who has been freed does not repeat, after he was freed, any prayers he prayed with insufficient covering for a free person, when he did not know he had been freed. They disagree about someone who incurs an obligation which changes a ruling in worship while he is performing it which is analogous to the question of the prayer at Qubā'.

So if someone prays in a certain state which then changes before he finishes the prayer, he should complete the prayer and not break it off. What he has done satisfies the requirement. That is the same as someone who prays naked and then finds a garment while he is praying, or starts his prayer while healthy and then becomes ill, or is ill and then recovers, or sitting and then is able to stand, or the case of a slave-girl who is freed while she is praying: she takes a head covering and builds on what she has done. It is like someone who begins the prayer with *tayammum* and then finds water: he does not stop the prayer, as Mālik, ash-Shāfi'ī and others said. Abū Ḥanīfah, however, said that he does stop it.

This contains evidence that a single report is accepted. The Salaf agree on it and there are multiple transmissions about it going back to the Prophet ﷺ sending his governors and messengers singly to all regions to instruct people in their *dīn* and convey to them the Sunnah of their Messenger ﷺ regarding commands and prohibitions. It also makes it very clear that the Qur'an was revealed to the Messenger of Allah ﷺ piece by piece and circumstance after circumstance, according to need, until the *dīn* was complete as Allah says: '*Today I have perfected your* dīn *for you.*' (5:3)

**Say: "Both East and West belong to Allah.**

Since He owns them both, He is entitled to command any direction He wishes.

**He guides whoever He wills to a straight path.'**

This indicates Allah's guidance of this Community to the *qiblah* of Ibrāhīm and Allah knows best. *Ṣirāṭ* is the Path and 'straight' is that in which there are no twists.

وَكَذَٰلِكَ جَعَلْنَٰكُمْ أُمَّةً وَسَطًا لِّتَكُونُوا۟ شُهَدَآءَ عَلَى ٱلنَّاسِ وَيَكُونَ ٱلرَّسُولُ
عَلَيْكُمْ شَهِيدًا ۗ وَمَا جَعَلْنَا ٱلْقِبْلَةَ ٱلَّتِى كُنتَ عَلَيْهَآ إِلَّا لِنَعْلَمَ مَن يَتَّبِعُ
ٱلرَّسُولَ مِمَّن يَنقَلِبُ عَلَىٰ عَقِبَيْهِ ۚ وَإِن كَانَتْ لَكَبِيرَةً إِلَّا عَلَى ٱلَّذِينَ هَدَى
ٱللَّهُ ۗ وَمَا كَانَ ٱللَّهُ لِيُضِيعَ إِيمَٰنَكُمْ ۚ إِنَّ ٱللَّهَ بِٱلنَّاسِ لَرَءُوفٌ رَّحِيمٌ ﴿١٤٣﴾

**143 In this way We have made you a middlemost community, so that you may act as witnesses against mankind and the Messenger as a witness against you. We only appointed the direction you used to face in order to know those who follow the Messenger from those who turn round on their heels. Though in truth it is a very hard thing – except for those Allah has guided. Allah would never let your faith go to waste. Allah is All-Gentle, Most Merciful to mankind.**

**In this way We have made you a middlemost community**

As the Ka'bah is in the middle of the earth, so We made you a middlemost nation, meaning that we made you inferior to the Prophets but superior to other communities. The word *'wasaṭ'* (middlemost) implies being just and balanced. The basis of this is the expression: 'The most praised of things is the middlemost of them.' At-Tirmidhī related from Abū Sa'īd al-Khudrī from the Prophet ﷺ about this *āyah* that it means 'just'. He said that it is a sound *ḥasan ḥadīth*. We find in the Revelation: *'The best* (awsaṭ) *of them said.'* It means the best and most just. The middle part of a valley is the best place in it and has the most plants and water. The middle avoids excess and falling short and is praiseworthy, so this community does not go to excess in elevating their Prophet (like the Christians) nor fall short as the Jews do in respect of their Prophets. In a *ḥadīth* we find, 'The best of matters is the middlemost of them.' 'Alī said, 'You must take the middle way. The high descend to it and the low rise to it.' Someone who is from the middlemost of his people is one of the best of them.

**so that you may act as witnesses against mankind**

This is referring to the Gathering, when the Prophets are joined with their nations, as is established in *Ṣaḥīḥ Bukhārī* when Abū Sa'īd al-Khudrī reported that the Messenger of Allah ﷺ said, 'Nūḥ will be summoned on the Day of Rising and he will say, "At your service and obedience, O Lord!" Allah will say, "Did you convey it?" He will say, "Yes." It will be said to his community, "Did he convey it to you?" They will say, "No warner came to us." Allah will ask Nūḥ, "Who will then testify on your behalf?" He will say, "Muḥammad and his community." They will testify that he conveyed it. That is the meaning of His words: *"In this way We have made you a middlemost community, so that you may act as witnesses against mankind."'* Ibn al-Mubārak mentioned this *ḥadīth* in full. We find in it: 'Those nations will ask, "How will those who did not meet us testify against us?" The Lord will ask them, "How can you testify against those whom you did not meet?" They will answer, "Our Lord, You sent a Messenger to us and sent down Your contract and Book to us and recounted to us that they conveyed it. Therefore we bear witness to what You entrusted to us." The Lord will say, "You spoke the truth." That is the import of His words: "*We have made you a middlemost community,*" and "middlemost" is "just": *"so that you may act as witnesses against mankind and the Messenger as a witness against you."'* Ibn An'am said, 'I heard that on that Day the community of Muḥammad ﷺ will bear witness, except for someone who has sympathy in his heart for his brother.'

One group said that the *āyah* means that they will testify against one another after death as is confirmed in *Ṣaḥīḥ Muslim* from Anas that the Prophet ﷺ said when a funeral passed by him and the deceased was spoken well of: 'It is obliged. It is obliged. It is obliged.' Then another passed him and the deceased was spoken ill of and he said, 'It is obliged. It is obliged. It is obliged.' 'Umar said, 'May my father and mother be your ransom, a funeral passed by and the deceased was spoken well of and you said, "It is obliged. It is obliged. It is obliged." Then a funeral passed by and the deceased was spoken ill of and you said, "It is obliged. It is obliged. It is obliged."' The Messenger of Allah ﷺ said, 'The Garden is obliged for the one you spoke well of and the Fire is obliged for the one you spoke ill of. You are the witnesses of Allah on the earth. You are the witnesses of Allah on the earth. You are the witnesses of Allah on the earth.' Al-Bukhārī transmitted a similar report.

Abān and Layth related from Shahr ibn Ḥawshab that 'Ubādah ibn aṣ-Ṣāmit said that he heard the Messenger of Allah ﷺ say, 'My Community was given three things which no other Prophets were given. Whenever Allah sent a Prophet, He said to him, "Call on Me and I will answer you." He said to this Community, "All of you call on Me and I will answer you." When He sent a Prophet, He said to him, "I have not imposed any hardship on you in the *dīn*." He said to this Community, "I have not imposed any hardship on any of you in the *dīn*." When He sent a Prophet, He made him a witness against his people but He made this Community witnesses against the whole of mankind.' Abū 'Abdullāh at-Tirmidhī al-Ḥakīm transmitted it in *Nawādir al-uṣūl*.

Our scholars say that, in His Book, our Lord has informed us of the preference He has given us by describing us as just and by entrusting us with the important task of bearing witness against all creation. He has given us the first place even if we are the last in time, as the Prophet ﷺ said, 'We are the first who came last.' This is also evidence that only the just may be witnesses, which will be discussed later.

This *āyah* also contains evidence for the soundness of the consensus of the community and the obligation to judge by it because they have been considered just enough to testify against all mankind. Every generation is a witness for those who come after them. The position of the Companions is evidence and testimony for the *Tābi'ūn* and that of the *Tābi'ūn* for those after them. Since the Community have been made witnesses, it is mandatory to accept what they say.

**and the Messenger as a witness against you.**

Meaning about your actions on the Day of Rising. It is also said that this can mean, 'for you', bearing witness that you have faith.

**We only appointed the direction you used to face in order to know those who follow the Messenger**

What is meant here is the first *qiblah* since He says: *'you used to face.'* It is also said that it was, in fact, the second *qiblah*. 'Alī ibn Abī Ṭālib said that 'know' in this context means 'see'. The Arabs used knowledge to mean seeing and seeing to mean knowledge. It is also said to mean 'so that you know that We know.' The hypocrites had doubts about Allah's knowledge of things before they took place. It is said that this distinguishes the people of certainty from the people of doubt, as Ibn Fūrak said. Aṭ -Ṭabarī mentioned the same view from Ibn 'Abbās. It is said that it means: 'so that the Prophet and his followers will know,' when Allah reports that about Himself, as when one says, 'The amīr did such-and-such' whereas it was his followers who did it. Al-Mahdawī mentioned it and it is excellent. It is said that it means: 'so that Muḥammad will know' but He ascribed the knowledge to Himself, exalted is He, to single out and show favour, just as He alluded to Himself ﷻ in His words, 'Son of Adam, I was sick but you didn't visit me...' The best view is that the meaning is that it is direct witnessing which makes recompense mandatory. Allah knows the unseen and the visible and He knows what will come about before it takes place. The circumstances of known things vary but His knowledge does not vary. His knowledge is the same in every instance. *'Follow the Messenger'* here means in respect of the command to change the *qiblah* to the Ka'bah.

**from those who turn round on their heels**

This is referring to those who apostatised from the *dīn*, because when the *qiblah* was changed some of the Muslims reverted to their former belief and some became hypocrites.

**Though in truth it is a very hard thing –**

This means the change of *qiblah* as Ibn 'Abbās, Mujāhid and Qatādah said. *'Except for those Allah has guided'*: He created the guidance which is faith in their hearts as He says: *'Allah has inscribed faith upon such people's hearts.'* (58:22)

**Allah would never let your faith go to waste.**

Scholars agree that this was revealed about those who died having prayed toward Jerusalem as we see in al-Bukhārī from al-Barā' ibn 'Āzib. In at-Tirmidhī, Ibn 'Abbās said, 'When the Prophet ﷺ turned towards the Ka'bah, they asked "Messenger of Allah, what about our brothers who died while they were praying towards Jerusalem?" and Allah revealed this.' The prayer is called 'faith' here because it contains intention, word and action. Mālik said, 'I mention this *āyah* to refute the position of the Murji'ites that the prayer is not part of faith.' Muḥammad ibn Isḥāq said that it means your turning to the *qiblah* and your affirming your Prophet ﷺ. This is the position of most Muslims and those who deal with fundamentals. Ibn Wahb, Ibn al-Qāsim, Ibn 'Abd al-Ḥakam and Ashhab related from Mālik that it means 'your prayer'.

**Allah is All-Gentle, Most Merciful to mankind.**

*'Ra'fah'* (gentleness) is stronger than *'raḥmah'* (mercy). Abū 'Amr ibn al-'Alā' said that gentleness is more frequent than mercy. The meanings are similar.

قَدْ نَرَىٰ تَقَلُّبَ وَجْهِكَ فِي السَّمَآءِ فَلَنُوَلِّيَنَّكَ قِبْلَةً تَرْضَيٰهَا فَوَلِّ وَجْهَكَ
شَطْرَ الْمَسْجِدِ الْحَرَامِ وَحَيْثُ مَا كُنتُمْ فَوَلُّواْ وُجُوهَكُمْ شَطْرَهُۥ
وَإِنَّ الَّذِينَ أُوتُواْ الْكِتَٰبَ لَيَعْلَمُونَ أَنَّهُ الْحَقُّ مِن رَّبِّهِمْ وَمَا اللَّهُ
بِغَٰفِلٍ عَمَّا يَعْمَلُونَ ﴿١٤٤﴾

**144 We have seen you looking up into heaven, turning this way and that, so We will turn you towards a direction which will please you. Turn your face, therefore, towards the Masjid al-Ḥarām. Wherever you all are, turn your faces towards it. Those given the Book know it is the truth from their Lord. Allah is not unaware of what they do.**

**We have seen you looking up into heaven,**

This *āyah* was revealed before 2:282. Aṭ-Ṭabari said that he ﷺ was turning his eyes towards the heaven. Az-Zajjāj said that it is to move the eyes about in the direction of the sky. The meanings are similar. 'Heaven' is mentioned because it was the main direction he looked towards and is the source of things like rain, mercy and revelation. '*Please you*' means that you will love it. As-Suddī said, 'When he prayed towards Jerusalem, he would raise his head towards heaven, waiting to see what he would be commanded to do. He wanted to pray towards the Ka'bah and Allah revealed: "*We have seen you looking up into heaven.*"' Abū Isḥāq related that al-Barā' said, 'The Messenger of Allah ﷺ prayed towards Jerusalem for sixteen or seventeenth months. He wanted to face the Ka'bah and so Allah revealed: "*We have seen you looking up into heaven.*"'

**Turn you face, therefore, towards the Masjid al-Ḥarām.**

It is said to be towards any part of the House as Ibn 'Abbās said while Ibn 'Umar said toward the Mizāb of the Ka'bah as Ibn 'Aṭiyyah related. The Mizāb is the *qiblah* of Madīnah and the people of Syria and Andalusia. Ibn Jurayj related from 'Aṭā' that Ibn 'Abbās reported that the Messenger of Allah ﷺ said, 'The House is the *qiblah* for the people who can see it and the mosque is the *qiblah* for the people of Makkah, and Makkah is the *qiblah* for the rest of the people of my community, wherever they are on the earth, east or west.' The word 'towards' (*shaṭr*) here means 'in the direction of' although the word can mean 'half'.

There is no disagreement among scholars that the Ka'bah itself is the actual *qiblah* of everyone. They agree that it is mandatory for it to be faced by someone who can actually see it, and if he does not do that, then his prayer is invalid and he must repeat it. They agree that all of those who cannot see it face in its direction. If it is hidden from a person, then he must look for evidence for it from the stars, the direction of the wind, location of mountains and the like which will enable him to deduce the direction. If someone is sitting in the Masjid al-Ḥarām, he should face the Ka'bah and look at it with faith and in expectation of the reward. Looking at the Ka'bah is an act of worship as 'Aṭā' and Mujāhid said.

There is disagreement about whether someone not at the Ka'bah must face it exactly or just face in the direction of it. Facing in the direction of it is sound for three reasons. We are only responsible for doing what is possible for us since Allah says: '*Wherever you are, turn your faces towards it.*' That is what we are commanded to do in the Qur'an by this *āyah*. The third reason is that scholars use the long line in the prayer as evidence, since clearly if the line is longer than the side of the Ka'bah not everyone can be facing it directly.

The *āyah* also contains clear evidence in support of what Mālik and those who agree with him hold, which is the ruling that someone praying should look straight ahead and not at the place where he is going to prostrate. Ath-Thawrī, Abū Ḥanīfah, ash-Shāfi'ī and al-Ḥasan ibn Ḥayy said that it is recommended for him to look at the place where he is going to prostrate. Qāḍī Sharīk said, 'While standing, he looks at the place where he is going to prostrate, in bowing he looks at his feet, in prostration he looks at the place of his nose, and in sitting, he looks at his lap.'

**Those given the Book know it is the truth from their Lord.**

This means that the Jews and Christians know that the change of direction has come from Allah. If it is asked, 'How can they know this when it is not part of their *dīn* or in their Book?' there are two answers. One is that since they know from their Book that Muḥammad ﷺ is a Prophet, they know that it follows that he only speaks the truth and only commands it. The second is that they know from their *dīn* that abrogation is permitted, even if some deny it, and so they know that abrogation is permitted in respect of the *qiblah*.

**Allah is not unaware of what they do.**

Ibn 'Āmir, Ḥamzah and al-Kisā'ī recited it with *tā'*, 'what you do', addressed to the community of Muḥammad. Both readings inform us that Allah is not unaware of what His slaves do. It contains a threat. The other reading is with *yā'*: 'what they do'.

وَلَئِنْ أَتَيْتَ ٱلَّذِينَ أُوتُوا۟ ٱلْكِتَٰبَ بِكُلِّ ءَايَةٍ مَّا تَبِعُوا۟ قِبْلَتَكَ
وَمَآ أَنتَ بِتَابِعٍ قِبْلَتَهُمْ وَمَا بَعْضُهُم بِتَابِعٍ قِبْلَةَ بَعْضٍ وَلَئِنِ
ٱتَّبَعْتَ أَهْوَآءَهُم مِّنۢ بَعْدِ مَا جَآءَكَ مِنَ ٱلْعِلْمِ إِنَّكَ إِذًا لَّمِنَ
ٱلظَّٰلِمِينَ ﴿١٤٥﴾

**145 If you were to bring every Sign to those given the Book, they still would not follow your direction. You do not follow their direction. They do not follow each other's direction. If you followed their whims and desires, after the knowledge that has come to you, you would then be one of the wrongdoers.**

**If you were to bring every Sign to those given the Book, they still would not follow your direction.**

This is because they disbelieve even when the truth is clear to them and signs do not help them.

**You do not follow their direction. They do not follow each other's direction.**

You do not incline to anything they face. Then Allah tells us that the Jews do not follow the *qiblah* of the Christians nor the Christians that of the Jews. As-Suddī and Ibn Zayd said that this tells us about their disunity and misguidance. Some people say that it means that those of them who have become Muslim and follow you do not follow the *qiblah* of those who are not Muslim nor do those who are not Muslim follow the *qiblah* of those who are. The first view is more likely, and Allah knows best.

**If you followed their whims and desires,**

This is addressed to the Prophet ﷺ but it is his Community that is meant because it is not permitted for the Prophet to do anything that would entail wrongdoing. It is possible that it means those who disobey the Prophet. The Prophet ﷺ is addressed to give the command more emphasis.

ٱلَّذِينَ ءَاتَيْنَٰهُمُ ٱلْكِتَٰبَ يَعْرِفُونَهُۥ كَمَا يَعْرِفُونَ أَبْنَآءَهُمْ ۖ وَإِنَّ فَرِيقًا
مِّنْهُمْ لَيَكْتُمُونَ ٱلْحَقَّ وَهُمْ يَعْلَمُونَ ﴿١٤٦﴾

**146 Those We have given the Book recognise it as they recognise their own sons. Yet a group of them knowingly conceal the truth.**

**Those We have given the Book recognise it**

The third person pronoun 'it' referring back to the Book can also be read as 'him' referring to the Prophet ﷺ, in which case it means they recognise his Prophethood and affirm his Message, as Mujāhid, Qatādah, as others said. It is also said that what they recognise is that the change of the *qiblah* from Jerusalem to the Ka'bah is true, as Ibn 'Abbās, Ibn Jurayj, ar-Rabī' and Qatādah said.

**as they recognise their own sons.**

'Sons' are mentioned after them 'their own selves' because time may pass for someone in which he does not recognise himself, but he will still recognise his son. It is related that 'Umar asked 'Abdullāh ibn Sallām, 'Did you recognize Muḥammad

ﷺ as you recognise your son?' He answered, 'Yes, and more! Allah sent His trusted one in His heaven to His trusted one on earth with his description and I recognised him. I have doubts about my son.'

**Yet a group of them knowingly conceal the truth.**

The 'truth' they conceal may be their recognition of Muḥammad ﷺ or the change of the *qiblah* and is the result of their obstinacy.

ٱلْحَقُّ مِن رَّبِّكَ فَلَا تَكُونَنَّ مِنَ ٱلْمُمْتَرِينَ ﴿١٤٧﴾

**147 The truth is from your Lord, so on no account be among the doubters.**

**The truth is from your Lord,**

This refers to the change of *qiblah* not what the Jews say about their *qiblah*. According to 'Alī, this is connected to '*they know*' in the previous *āyah* and so it means, 'They know the truth from your Lord.' Or it implies: 'Hold to the truth.'

**so on no account be among the doubters.**

Again, although the Prophet ﷺ is addressed, it is his Community that is meant.

وَلِكُلٍّ وِجْهَةٌ هُوَ مُوَلِّيهَا فَٱسْتَبِقُوا۟ ٱلْخَيْرَٰتِ أَيْنَ مَا تَكُونُوا۟ يَأْتِ بِكُمُ
ٱللَّهُ جَمِيعًا إِنَّ ٱللَّهَ عَلَىٰ كُلِّ شَىْءٍ قَدِيرٌ ﴿١٤٨﴾

**148. Each person faces a particular direction so race each other to the good. Wherever you are, Allah will bring you all together. Truly Allah has power over all things.**

**Each person faces a particular direction**

'*Wijhah*' (direction), *jihah*, and *wajh* mean the same. What is meant is the *qiblah*. It means: 'They do not face your *qiblah* and you do not face theirs.' Each has a *qiblah*, either by the truth or by his own whims and desires. The word 'faces' implies that each person with a religion has a *qiblah* to which he turns. Instead of the reading '*muwallīhā*', Ibn 'Abbās and Ibn 'Āmir recited '*muwallāhā*' without naming the subject, and the pronoun in this reading refers to one, i.e. 'each person has a *qiblah*'. Az-Zajjāj said that. In the majority reading, the pronoun refers to Allah since it is known that Allah is the One Who does that.

**So race each other to the good.**

The primary meaning of the *āyah* is to hasten to what Allah has commanded regarding the facing of the Masjid al-Ḥarām, although the phrase, in fact, contains encouragement to hasten to all acts of obedience in general. What is meant here is facing the *qiblah* because of the context. What is meant by 'racing' is to perform the prayer at the beginning of its time, and Allah knows best. An-Nasā'ī related from Abū Hurayrah that the Prophet ﷺ said, 'The metaphor of the one who goes early to the prayer is that of someone who sacrifices a camel. The one after him is like someone who sacrifices a cow. The one after him is like someone who sacrifices a ram. Then the one after him is like someone who sacrifices a chicken and the one after him is like someone who sacrifices an egg.' Ad-Dāraquṭnī reports from Abū Hurayrah that the Messenger of Allah ﷺ said, 'Each of you should pray the prayer at its time. What is at the beginning of the time is better for him than his family and wealth.' Mālik transmitted it from Yaḥyā ibn Sa'īd. Ad-Dāraquṭnī also transmits from Ibn 'Umar that the Prophet ﷺ said, 'The best of actions is the prayer at the beginning of its time.' He also related from Ibrāhīm ibn 'Abd al-Malik from Abū Maḥdhūrah from his father from his grandfather that the Messenger of Allah ﷺ said, 'The beginning of the time is the pleasure of Allah, the middle of the time is the mercy of Allah, and the end of the time is the pardon of Allah.'

Ibn al-'Arabī said about this, 'Abū Bakr said, "I prefer Allah's pleasure to His pardon. His pleasure is for the good-doers and His pardon is for those who fall short."' That is what ash-Shāfi'ī preferred. Abū Ḥanīfah said, 'The end of the time is better because it is the time of the obligation.'

Mālik made a distinction, saying that in the case of *Ṣubḥ* and *Maghrib*, the beginning of the time is better. In respect of this he goes by the *ḥadīth* of 'Ā'ishah: 'The Messenger of Allah ﷺ used to pray *Ṣubḥ* when it was dark and the women would leave wrapped in their mantles and could not be recognised due to the darkness.' And in the case of *Maghrib*, he goes by the *ḥadīth* of Salamah ibn al-Akwa' that the Messenger of Allah ﷺ prayed *Maghrib* when the sun set. In the case of *'Ishā'*, it is better to delay it if one is able to do so. Ibn 'Umar related, 'We remained that night waiting for the *'Ishā'* prayer with the Messenger of Allah ﷺ. He came out to us when a third of the night or more had has passed and we did not know whether he was doing something with his family or something else. When he came out, he said, "You are waiting for a prayer when none of the people of the *dīn* except you are waiting for it. If it had not been that it would be onerous for this Community, I would always pray at this time with them."' It is related in al-Bukhārī that Anas said, 'The Prophet ﷺ delayed the *'Ishā'* prayer to the middle of the night and then prayed…' Abū Barzah said, 'The Prophet ﷺ preferred to delay it.'

As for *Ẓuhr*, it arrives at a time when people are inattentive and so it is recommended to delay it a little so that people can prepare and gather together. Abu-l-Faraj said that Mālik said, 'The beginning of the time is better for every prayer except for *Ẓuhr* when it is very hot.' Ibn Abī Uways said, 'Mālik disliked praying *Ẓuhr* at midday but did it a little later.' He said that praying exactly at midday is the prayer of the Khārijites. We find in *Ṣaḥīḥ Bukhārī* and the *Ṣaḥīḥ* of at-Tirmidhī that Abū Dharr al-Ghifārī said, 'We were with the Prophet ﷺ on a journey and the *mu'adhdhin* wanted to give the *adhān* for *Ẓuhr*, and the Prophet ﷺ said, "Let it cool." Then again he wanted to give the *adhān* and the Prophet ﷺ said, "Let it cool." When we saw the shadows of the hillocks, the Prophet ﷺ said, "Intense heat is from the exhalation of Hell. When it is very hot, then pray when it is cooler."' We find in *Ṣaḥīḥ Muslim* from Anas that the Messenger of Allah ﷺ used to pray *Ẓuhr* when the sun declined. That on which both *ḥadīth*s from Anas agree is that when it was hot, the prayer was delayed until it was cooler. When it was cool, it was brought forward. Abū 'Īsā at-Tirmidhī said, 'Some of the people of knowledge prefer to delay the *Ẓuhr* prayer when it is very hot. That is the view of Ibn al-Mubārak, Aḥmad and Isḥāq.' Ash-Shāfi'ī said, 'Waiting for the *Ẓuhr* prayer until it is cooler is when its people come from a distance. When someone prays alone or prays in his local mosque, I prefer him not to delay the prayer in intense heat.' Abū 'Īsā said, 'What is meant by those who delay *Ẓuhr* when it is very hot is that it is more appropriate and closer to following [what was done]. As for those who take the position of ash-Shāfi'ī, that the allowance is on account of distance and hardship for people, the *ḥadīth* of Abū Dharr counters ash-Shāfi'ī's opinion. Abū Dharr said, "We were with the Prophet ﷺ on a journey and Bilāl gave the *adhān* for *Ẓuhr*. The Prophet ﷺ said, 'Bilāl, let it cool. Let it cool.'" If the business had been as ash-Shāfi'ī believed, there would have been no point in waiting for it to cool down at that time because they were gathered together in the journey and did not need to come from afar.'

As for *'Aṣr*, it is better to do it early in the time. There is no disagreement in our School that when one hopes for a group, it is better to delay the prayer than to do it early in the time. The excellence of the group prayer is known and the excellence of the beginning of the time is unknown. It is better to obtain what is known. Ibn al-'Arabī said that.

**Wherever you are, Allah will bring you all together.**

This is a reference to the Day of Rising. Then Allah describes Himself as having power over all things since that attribute is appropriate for what was mentioned of being brought back to life after death and decay.

وَمِنْ حَيْثُ خَرَجْتَ فَوَلِّ وَجْهَكَ شَطْرَ ٱلْمَسْجِدِ ٱلْحَرَامِ وَإِنَّهُۥ لَلْحَقُّ مِن رَّبِّكَ
وَمَا ٱللَّهُ بِغَٰفِلٍ عَمَّا تَعْمَلُونَ ﴿١٤٩﴾ وَمِنْ حَيْثُ خَرَجْتَ فَوَلِّ وَجْهَكَ شَطْرَ ٱلْمَسْجِدِ
ٱلْحَرَامِ وَحَيْثُ مَا كُنتُمْ فَوَلُّوا۟ وُجُوهَكُمْ شَطْرَهُۥ لِئَلَّا يَكُونَ لِلنَّاسِ
عَلَيْكُمْ حُجَّةٌ إِلَّا ٱلَّذِينَ ظَلَمُوا۟ مِنْهُمْ فَلَا تَخْشَوْهُمْ وَٱخْشَوْنِى
وَلِأُتِمَّ نِعْمَتِى عَلَيْكُمْ وَلَعَلَّكُمْ تَهْتَدُونَ ﴿١٥٠﴾

**149 Wherever you come from, turn your face to the Masjid al-Ḥarām. This is certainly the truth from your Lord. Allah is not unaware of what you do. 150 Wherever you come from, turn your face to the Masjid al-Ḥarām. Wherever you are, turn your faces towards it so that people will have no argument against you – except for those among them who do wrong and then you should not fear them but rather fear Me – and so that I can complete My blessing to you so that hopefully you will be guided.**

This is stressing the command to face the *qiblah* and the importance of that, because the change was very difficult for them. Therefore the command is repeated so that people will see the importance of it and it will be easier for them. It is said that the first command to turn the face is to look at the Ka'bah when you are praying in front of it. Then 'wherever you are' is for the Muslims in all the mosques in Madīnah and elsewhere. This is a command to face it everywhere and in all circumstances.

This statement is better than the first one because it gives a benefit to each *āyah*. Ad-Dāraquṭnī related that Anas ibn Mālik said, 'When the Prophet ﷺ was on a journey and wanted to pray on his camel, he faced the *qiblah* and said the *takbīr* and then prayed in whatever direction it turned.' Abū Dāwud also transmitted it. Ash-Shāfi'ī, Abū Thawr and Aḥmad said that. Mālik believed that you are not obliged to face Makkah, going by the *ḥadīth* of 'Umar in which he said, 'The Messenger of Allah ﷺ used to pray facing from Makkah towards Madīnah on his camel.' *'Wherever you turn, the Face of Allah is there'* (2:115) was revealed about this.

There is no contradiction between the two *ḥadīths* because this is part of the legal area of texts which are unrestricted or restricted, so the position of ash-Shāfi'ī is more fitting and the *ḥadīth* of Anas is sound. It is related that Ja'far ibn Muḥammad was asked about the meaning of the repetition of stories in the Qur'an. He said, 'Allah knows that all people do not know the Qur'an by heart. If there was no story repeated, then it would be possible that only some people would know the story. It is repeated so that everyone will know it.'

**so that people will have no argument against you –**

Mujāhid said that the 'people' referred to here are the Arab idolaters and their argument is what they said about the *qiblah*. It is said that the meaning of this is: 'So that they will not say to you, "You are commanded to face the Ka'bah yet you cannot see it."' This was removed when He said: '*Wherever you are, turn your faces towards it.*' Abū Isḥāq az-Zajjāj said, 'It means that Allah has acquainted you with the argument about the *qiblah* in His words: *"Each person faces a particular direction." "So that people will have no argument against you"* except for someone who is unjust in his argument when the business is, in fact, clear to him. It is as you say, "You have no argument except being unjust" or "merely in order to wrong me." "You have no definitive argument. You are merely wronging me." So the argument is called "injustice" even though it is invalid.' Quṭrub said that it is possible that it means: 'So that only those who are unjust can argue against you.' Aṭ-Ṭabarī said, 'Allah made it clear that no one has evidence against the Prophet ﷺ and the Companions regarding their facing the *qiblah*.' It means that they only have a baseless argument in their remarks about that.

**and then you should not fear them but rather fear Me –**

'*Khashyah*' (fear) derives from the lack of tranquillity in the heart about what to expect, while *khawf* is the alarm of the heart which makes the limbs tremble. The *āyah* calls attention to the fact that all that is other than Allah is insignificant. The command is for people to cast aside their own affairs and to obey the command of Allah.

**and so that I can complete My blessing to you**

According to az-Zajjāj, this refers to Allah making His chosen *qiblah* known to them. The completion of guidance is being guided to the *qiblah*. It is said to be admitting them into the Garden. Sa'īd ibn Jubayr said, 'Allah's blessing to His slave is not complete until He admits him to the Garden.'

كَمَآ أَرْسَلْنَا فِيكُمْ رَسُولًا مِّنكُمْ يَتْلُوا۟ عَلَيْكُمْ ءَايَٰتِنَا وَيُزَكِّيكُمْ
وَيُعَلِّمُكُمُ ٱلْكِتَٰبَ وَٱلْحِكْمَةَ وَيُعَلِّمُكُم مَّا لَمْ تَكُونُوا۟ تَعْلَمُونَ ﴿١٥١﴾

**151 For this We sent a Messenger to you from among you to recite Our Signs to you and purify you and teach you the Book and Wisdom and teach you things you did not know before.**

Al-Farrā' said that it means: 'So that I can complete My blessing to you by completing the like of what you have been sent with.' Ibn 'Aṭiyyah said that this is the best view, meaning: 'So that I can complete My blessing to you in clarifying that the sunnah of Ibrāhīm is like what We have sent to you.' It is said that it means: 'Perhaps you will be guided to a similar guidance as that We sent previously.' It can also mean: 'I will complete My blessing to you in this state,' and the blessing in respect of the *qiblah* resembles the blessing of the Message, and the remembrance commanded is immense like the blessing. There can also be a change in the normal word order so that it means: 'Remember Me as We sent you...' The view related from 'Alī, which is preferred by az-Zajjāj, is that it means: 'As We sent a Messenger from among you whom you recognise to be truthful, remember Me with *tawḥīd* and affirmation of him.' This is also what at-Tirmidhī al-Ḥakīm preferred: 'As I have given you these blessings that I have enumerated to you, remember Me with gratitude and I will remember you with an increased reward because your remembering that is thanking Me and I have promised an increased reward for thankfulness.' He says: *'If you are grateful, I will certainly give you increase.'* (14:7)

فَٱذْكُرُونِىٓ أَذْكُرْكُمْ وَٱشْكُرُوا۟ لِى وَلَا تَكْفُرُونِ ﴿١٥٢﴾ يَٰٓأَيُّهَا ٱلَّذِينَ ءَامَنُوا۟
ٱسْتَعِينُوا۟ بِٱلصَّبْرِ وَٱلصَّلَوٰةِ ۚ إِنَّ ٱللَّهَ مَعَ ٱلصَّٰبِرِينَ ﴿١٥٣﴾

**152 Remember Me – I will remember you. Give thanks to Me and do not be ungrateful. 153 You who believe! seek help in steadfastness and the prayer. Allah is with the steadfast.**

**Remember Me – I will remember you.**

Allah's remembering of us signifies reward. The root meaning of the word for 'remembering' (*dhikr*) is to be aware with the heart of what is remembered and awake to it. *Dhikr* with the tongue is called *dhikr* because it indicates the remembrance of the heart. It is often used, however, with reference to the spoken words and phrases employed in its performance.

The *āyah* means: 'Remember Me by obeying Me and I will remember you with the reward and forgiveness,' as Sa'īd ibn Jubayr said. He also said, '*Dhikr* is obeying Allah. Anyone who does not obey Him, does not remember Him, even if he does a lot of glorification, *shahādah* and recitation of the Qur'an.' It is related that the Prophet ﷺ said, 'Anyone who obeys Allah has remembered Allah, even if he has not done much prayer, fasting or good action. Anyone who disobeys Allah has forgotten Allah, even if he has done a lot of prayer, fasting and good action,' as Abū 'Abdullāh Muḥammad ibn Khuwayzimandād mentions in *Aḥkām al-Qur'ān*. Abū 'Uthmān an-Nahdī said, 'I know a moment in which Allah remembers us.' He was asked, 'How do you know that?' He answered, 'Allah Almighty says: *"Remember Me – I will remember you."*' As-Suddī said, 'A person does not remember Allah without Allah remembering Him. A believer does not remember Allah without Allah remembering him with mercy. An unbeliever does not remember Allah without Allah remembering him with the punishment.'

Someone said to Abū 'Uthmān an-Nahdī, 'We remember Allah but we do not experience any sweetness in our hearts.' He said, 'Praise Allah Almighty for the fact that He has adorned one of your limbs with obedience!' Dhu-n-Nūn al-Miṣrī said, 'Anyone who really remembers Allah, forgets everything except His remembrance and Allah preserves him from every bad thing and is his redress for everything.' Mu'ādh ibn Jabal said, 'The son of Ādam does not do any action which will be more effective in saving him from the punishment of Allah than *dhikr* of Allah.'

There are many *ḥadīth*s on the virtue of *dhikr* and its reward. Ibn Mājah reports from 'Abdullāh ibn Yūsuf that a Bedouin said to the Messenger of Allah ﷺ, 'The laws of Islam are a lot for me. Tell me something on which I can really concentrate my efforts.' He said, 'Let your tongue remain moist with the remembrance of Allah Almighty.' It is transmitted that Abū Hurayrah reported that the Prophet ﷺ said, 'Allah Almighty says, "I am with My noble slave when he remembers Me and moves his lips with My Name."' This subject will be discussed in greater depth elsewhere.

**Gives thanks to Me**

Thankfulness (*shukr*) is to acknowledge kindness received and to speak of it. The linguistic root of *shukr* means 'to display'. So Allah's slave shows his thankfulness by mentioning Allah's goodness to him and the Real thanks the slave by praising him for obeying Him.

**and do not be ungrateful.**

Do not be ungrateful for Allah's blessings. The word *kufr* here means to cover up the blessing, not total disbelief.

وَلَا تَقُولُوا لِمَن يُقْتَلُ فِي سَبِيلِ اللَّهِ أَمْوَاتٌ بَلْ أَحْيَاءٌ وَلَٰكِن لَّا تَشْعُرُونَ ﴿١٥٤﴾

**154 Do not say that those who are killed in the Way of Allah are dead. On the contrary, they are alive but you are not aware of it.**

This is like another verse: *'Do not suppose those killed in the Way of Allah are dead. No indeed! They are alive and well provided for in the very presence of their Lord.'* (3:169) There we will discuss martyrs and the rulings that apply in their case, Allah willing. Allah will bring them to life after death in order to provide for them and so it is equally possible for the unbelievers to be brought to life in order for them to be punished. This is evidence for the punishment in the grave. The martyrs are alive, as Allah says. It does not mean that they will be brought to life later, since in that case there would be no difference between them and anyone else, because everyone will be brought back to life on the Last Day. The evidence for this is found in His words: '*...but you are not aware of it*', and the believers are certainly aware that they will be brought back to life.

وَلَنَبْلُوَنَّكُم بِشَيْءٍ مِّنَ الْخَوْفِ وَالْجُوعِ وَنَقْصٍ مِّنَ الْأَمْوَالِ وَالْأَنفُسِ
وَالثَّمَرَاتِ وَبَشِّرِ الصَّابِرِينَ ﴿١٥٥﴾

**155 We will test you with a certain amount of fear and hunger and loss of wealth and life and fruits. But give good news to the steadfast:**

**We will test you with a certain amount of fear and hunger and loss of wealth and life and fruits.**

'We will test you so that We know who are the fighters and the steadfast by direct evidence in order that they may be rewarded.' It is said that they will be tested as a sign for those after them and so that they know that if they too are steadfast in this respect, then truth will be clear to them. It is said that He will inform them of this so that they will have certainty that it will befall them as well; then they will be ready for it and will be less likely to be anxious. It advances Allah's reward.

'*Certain amount*' (*shay'*) is in the singular, but has the meaning of a plural. Indeed, aḍ-Ḍaḥḥāk actually recites it in the plural although most have it in the singular. The word 'fear' here refers to fear of the enemy and alarm when fighting as Ibn 'Abbās said. Ash-Shāfi'ī said that it is fear of Allah that is meant. The 'hunger' is that caused by drought and famine according to Ibn 'Abbās. Ash-Shāfi'ī said that it refers to the hunger felt in the month of Ramaḍān. 'Loss of wealth' comes through being occupied with fighting the unbelievers. It is said that it refers to damage done to crops. Ash-Shāfi'ī said that it is the diminishment that comes about through the payment of the obligatory zakat. 'Loss of life', according to Ibn 'Abbās, is by killing and death in *jihād*. Ash-Shāfi'ī said that it is through illnesses. 'Loss of fruits', according to ash-Shāfi'ī means the death of children as they are the fruit of a man's heart as we find in a tradition. Ibn 'Abbās says that it means loss of crops and blessing.

**But give good news to the steadfast:**

Give them the good news of the reward for their steadfastness. The root of the word 'steadfast' (*ṣabr*) means to confine and restrict and its reward is without limit, but that only refers to steadfastness at the first blow. Al-Bukhārī transmitted from Anas that the Prophet ﷺ said, 'Steadfastness is at the first blow.' Muslim transmitted it in a more complete form. The steadfastness which is difficult for the self and which has such an immense reward is that shown when the affliction first strikes since it indicates the strength of the heart and its firmness in the station of steadfastness. When an affliction lessens with time anyone can be steadfast. That is why it is said, 'In an affliction every intelligent person must withstand what a fool can only withstand after three.' Sahl ibn 'Abdullāh at-Tustarī said, 'When the Almighty said: *"give good news to the steadfast"*, steadfastness became a way of life.'

There are two types of steadfastness: steadfastness in not disobeying Allah, and this is that of the *mujāhid*, and steadfastness in obeying Allah, and this is that of the ordinary worshipper. If someone is steadfast in not disobeying Allah and steadfast in obeying Allah, Allah will grant him complete satisfaction with His Decree. The sign of this satisfaction is tranquillity in the heart in the face of everything that happens to you, whether liked or disliked. Al-Khawwāṣ said, 'Steadfastness is firmness in holding to the rulings of the Book and Sunnah.' Ruwaym said, 'Steadfastness is abandoning complaint.' Dhu-n-Nūn al-Miṣrī said, 'Steadfastness is seeking the help of Allah Almighty.'

ٱلَّذِينَ إِذَآ أَصَٰبَتۡهُم مُّصِيبَةٞ قَالُوٓاْ إِنَّا لِلَّهِ وَإِنَّآ إِلَيۡهِ رَٰجِعُونَ ١٥٦
أُوْلَٰٓئِكَ عَلَيۡهِمۡ صَلَوَٰتٞ مِّن رَّبِّهِمۡ وَرَحۡمَةٞۖ وَأُوْلَٰٓئِكَ هُمُ ٱلۡمُهۡتَدُونَ ١٥٧

**156 Those who, when disaster strikes them, say, 'We belong to Allah and to Him we will return. 157 Those are the people who will have blessings and mercy from their Lord; they are the ones who are guided.**

**Those who, when disaster strikes them,**

The word 'disaster' (*muṣībah*) means everything that harms and afflicts a believer, even if it is minor. It is used for any evil. 'Ikrimah related that one night the lamp of the Messenger of Allah ﷺ went out and he said, *'We belong to Allah and to Him we return.'* He was asked, 'Is it a disaster, Messenger of Allah?' He answered, 'Yes, whatever harms a believer is a disaster.' This idea is confirmed in the *Ṣaḥīḥ*. In *Ṣaḥīḥ Muslim* there is a *ḥadīth* transmitted from Abū Sa'īd and Abū Hurayrah in which they heard the Messenger of Allah ﷺ say, 'Whatever afflicts the believer, be it discomfort, fatigue, illness or sorrow, even a care that concerns him, expiates his evil deeds.'

Ibn Mājah in the *Sunan* transmitted from Abū Bakr ibn Abī Shaybah from Wakī' ibn Hishām ibn Ziyād from his mother from Fāṭimah bint al-Husayn from her father that the Messenger of Allah ﷺ said, 'If someone suffers an affliction and remembers his affliction and says, "*We belong to Allah and to Him we will return,*" even after a long time, Allah will write for him a reward the same as if he had said it on the day he was afflicted.'

One of the worst afflictions is an affliction which affects one's *dīn*. 'Aṭā' ibn Abī Rabāḥ reported that the Messenger of Allah ﷺ said, 'When someone suffers an affliction, he should remember his loss of me. That is one of the greatest afflictions.' Abū Muḥammad as-Samarqandī transmitted it in his *Musnad*. Abū Nu'aym reported it from Faṭr and has a similar report which is *mursal* from Makḥūl. Abū 'Umar said, 'The Messenger of Allah ﷺ spoke the truth because the affliction of losing him is greater than any other affliction which a Muslim might suffer after that until the Day of Rising. The Revelation has come to an end and Prophethood has died out.' The first evil to appear was the apostasy of the Arabs. His death was the end of good and the beginning of loss. Abū Sa'īd al-Khudrī said, 'Our hands had not brushed off the dust of the grave of the Messenger of Allah when we found that we did not know our hearts.'

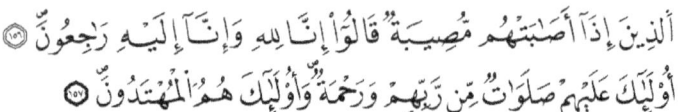

**We belong to Allah and to Him we will return.**

Allah has made these words the refuge of all those overcome by affliction and the resort of all those undergoing trial since it contains many blessed meanings. 'We belong to Allah' is *tawḥīd*, and affirmation of our slavehood and Allah's mastership; '*...and to Him we will return*' is affirmation of the inevitability of death and resurrection from the grave and certainty that the entire affair will return to Allah as it belongs to Him. Sa'īd ibn Jubayr said, 'These words were not given to any Prophet before our Prophet. If Ya'qūb had known them, he would not have said, *"My sorrow for Yūsuf!"* (12:84)'

Abū Sinān said, 'When I buried my son Sinān, Abū Ṭalḥah al-Khawlānī was standing at the edge of the grave. When I was about to leave, he took my hand and tried to cheer me up. He said, "Shall I give you some good news, Abū Sinān? Aḍ-Ḍaḥḥāk reported to me from Abū Mūsā that the Prophet ﷺ said, 'When someone's child dies, Allah says to the angels, "You have taken the child of My slave?" "Yes," they reply. He asks, "You took the apple of his eye?" "Yes," they reply. He asks, "What did My slave say?" They reply, "He praised You and said, 'We belong to Allah and to Him we will return.'" Allah Almighty will say, "Build My slave a house in the Garden and name it the House of Praise."'"'

Muslim related from Umm Salamah that the Messenger of Allah ﷺ said, 'There is no Muslim who is afflicted by a calamity and then says, "We belong to Allah and to Him we return. O Allah, give me a reward for my calamity and give me something better to replace it," without Allah granting him something better in its place.' This is indicated by the words of Allah Almighty: *'Give good news to the steadfast.'* (2:155). The replacement which Allah gave Umm Salamah was the Messenger of Allah ﷺ. He married her when her husband, Abū Salamah, died. Otherwise there is an ample reward in the Next World, as in the *ḥadīth* of Abū Mūsā.

**Those are the people who will have blessings and mercy from their Lord.**

The blessings (*ṣalawāt*) of Allah on His slave are His pardon, mercy, blessing and honour for him in this world and the Next. Az-Zajjāj said, '*Ṣalawāt* from Allah means forgiveness and good praise.' One element of this is the funeral prayer for the dead person which entails praise for him and supplication for him. The word 'mercy' is repeated, when the phrase varies, for emphasis and to expand the meaning. It is said that by 'mercy' Allah means removing grief and fulfilling every need. In al-Bukhārī, "Umar said, "The two sides of the baggage and what is put on it."' The two sides [of the carriers on the camel] mean blessing and mercy, and what is on top is 'those are the guided.' It is said that it means entitlement to the reward and an ample wage. It is also said that it is making disasters easier to bear and alleviating sorrow.

إِنَّ ٱلصَّفَا وَٱلْمَرْوَةَ مِن شَعَآئِرِ ٱللَّهِ فَمَنْ حَجَّ ٱلْبَيْتَ أَوِ ٱعْتَمَرَ فَلَا جُنَاحَ عَلَيْهِ أَن يَطَّوَّفَ بِهِمَا وَمَن تَطَوَّعَ خَيْرًا فَإِنَّ ٱللَّهَ شَاكِرٌ عَلِيمٌ ﴿١٥٨﴾

**158 Ṣafā and Marwah are among the Landmarks of Allah, so anyone who goes on ḥajj to the House or does *'umrah* incurs no wrong in going back and forth between them. If anyone spontaneously does good, Allah is All-Thankful, All-Knowing.**

**Ṣafā and Marwah are among the Landmarks of Allah,**

Al-Bukhārī related that 'Āṣim ibn Sulaymān said, 'I asked Anas ibn Mālik about Ṣafā and Marwah and he said, "We used to think that the observance connected with them was something from the Jāhiliyyah. When Islam came, we kept back from them and then Allah revealed this."' In at-Tirmidhī we find that 'Urwah said, 'I said to 'Ā'ishah, "I do not think that someone who does not go between Ṣafā and Marwah owes any sacrifice and I do not care if I go between them or not." She said, "My nephew, what you say is wrong. The Messenger of Allah ﷺ went between them and so did all the Muslims. Those who previously used to go into *iḥrām* for the idol Manāt, which they used to worship at al-Mushallal, considered it wrong to go between Ṣafā and Marwah, so Allah revealed: '*Ṣafā and Marwah are among the Landmarks of Allah.*' If it was as you say, it would have been: 'incurs no wrong if he does not go between them.'"' Az-Zuhrī said that he mentioned that to Abū Bakr ibn 'Abd ar-Raḥmān ibn al-Ḥārith ibn Hishām and he liked it and remarked, 'There is something I heard men of knowledge say: "Those Arabs who do not go between Ṣafā and Marwah said that our *ṭawāf* between these two stones is something from the Jāhiliyyah and others among the Anṣār said, 'We are commanded to do *ṭawāf* of the House and go between Ṣafā and Marwah.' So Allah revealed: '*Ṣafā and Marwah are among the Landmarks of Allah.*'"' Abū Bakr said, 'I think it was revealed about these groups.' Al-Bukhārī transmitted something to that effect. He said that it is a sound *ḥasan ḥadīth.*

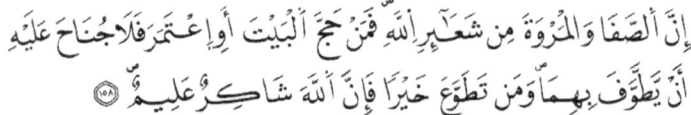

Also in al-Bukhārī there is a *ḥadīth* in which 'Ā'ishah said, 'The Messenger of Allah ﷺ made a sunnah of going between them. No one should abandon going between them.' Then she told Abū Bakr ibn 'Abd ar-Raḥmān and he said, 'This is a piece of knowledge I have not heard. I did hear some of the people of knowledge saying that the people – except for those 'Ā'ishah mentioned who went into *iḥrām* for Manāt – all used to go between Ṣafā and Marwah. When Allah Almighty mentioned *ṭawāf* of the House and did not mention Ṣafā and Marwah in the Qur'an, they said, "Messenger of Allah, we used also do *ṭawāf* of Ṣafā and Marwah and Allah has revealed *ṭawāf* around the House without mentioning Ṣafā. Is it a sin for us to do *ṭawāf* of Ṣafā and Marwah?" Allah Almighty then revealed: *"Ṣafā and Marwah are among the Landmarks of Allah."'* Abū Bakr said, 'I heard that this *āyah* was revealed about both groups – those who used to consider it a sin to do *ṭawāf* of Ṣafā and Marwah in the time of Jāhiliyyah and those who had done *ṭawāf* of them and then considered it a sin to do so in the time of Islam – because Allah Almighty had commanded *ṭawāf* of the House without mentioning Ṣafā, only speaking of it after what He said about *ṭawāf* of the House.'

At-Tirmidhī related that 'Āṣim ibn Sulaymān al-Aḥwal said, 'I asked Mālik about Ṣafā and Marwah and he said, "They were among the Landmarks of the Jāhiliyyah. When Islam came, we refrained from them. Then Allah revealed: *'Ṣafā and Marwah are among the Landmarks of Allah, so anyone who goes on ḥajj to the House or does 'umrah incurs no wrong in going back and forth between them.'"* He said, "They are voluntary. *'If anyone spontaneously does good, Allah is All-Thankful, All-Knowing.'"'* He said that it is a sound *hasan ḥadīth*. Al-Bukhārī also transmitted it.

Ibn 'Abbās said, 'In the time of Jāhiliyyah some *shayṭāns* used to play music the entire night between Ṣafā and Marwah, and there were idols between them. When Islam came, the Muslims said, "Messenger of Allah, we do not go between Ṣafā and Marwah. To do so is *shirk*." Then this was revealed.' Ash-Sha'bī said, 'In the Jāhiliyyah, there was an idol called Isāf on Ṣafā, and an idol called Nā'ilah on Marwah. They used to wipe their hands on the idols when they went between them. So the Muslims refused to go between them. It was because of that that the *āyah* was revealed.'

The root meaning of the name Ṣafā is smooth stone. It is a well known high rock at Makkah and Marwah is another high rock. That is why they take the definite article. Ṣafā gets its name because Ādam, the chosen one (*muṣṭafā*), stopped there, and so it was named after him. Ḥawwā' stopped on Marwah and it was named after the word for 'woman' (*mar'ah*). Allah knows best.

'The Landmarks (*sha'ā'ir*) of Allah' are among His signs and the places of His worship. These are the sites of acts of worship which Allah informs us about, thereby making them signs for people: the standing, *sa'y*, and sacrifice. *Shi'ār* is an identification mark of the kind put on the hump of camels to be sacrificed.

**so anyone who goes on ḥajj to the House or does *'umrah***

He heads for it. The root meaning of the word "ḥajj" means to aim for something. *'Umrah* means a visit.

**incurs no wrong in going back and forth between them**

They do not commit any sin by doing that. The root of the word for '*junāḥ*' (wrong) is *junūḥ*, which means bending and is used for the limbs (*jawāniḥ*) because they bend. To use this expression means to permit the action. 'Urwah thought that it meant that it is permissible to abandon *tawāf* and then he saw that the Sharī'ah confirmed the fact that there is no allowance to abandon it.

At-Tirmidhī transmitted from Jābir that, when the Prophet ﷺ came to Makkah, he went around the House seven times, and recited, '*Take the Maqām of Ibrāhīm as a place of prayer*' (2:125); and he prayed behind the Maqām. Then he went to the Stone and kissed it and then said, 'We begin with what Allah began with.' So he began with Ṣafā. The correct practice, therefore, according to the people of knowledge, is that you begin with Ṣafā. This is a sound *ḥasan ḥadīth*. According to the people of knowledge, the proper action is to begin with Ṣafā. It is not permitted to begin with Marwah.

Scholars disagree about the obligatory nature of *sa'y* between Ṣafā and Marwah. Ash-Shāfi'ī and Ibn Ḥanbal said that it is a pillar of the Ḥajj. This is the well-known position in the school of Mālik, since the Prophet ﷺ said, 'Do *sa'y*. Allah has prescribed *sa'y* for you.' Ad-Dāraquṭnī transmitted it. '*Kataba*' means 'has made obligatory' as we see in the Book and *ḥadīth*s. Ibn Mājah transmitted that an *umm walad* belonging to Shaybah said, 'I saw the Messenger of Allah ﷺ doing *sa'y* between Ṣafā and Marwah. He was saying, "Al-Abṭaḥ should only be crossed quickly."' If someone omits it, or omits even one circuit of it deliberately or out of forgetfulness, he must return from his land, or from wherever he remembers, to Makkah and do *ṭawāf* and *sa'y*, because *sa'y* is only connected to *ṭawāf*.

Mālik said that *sa'y* is the same in ḥajj or *'umrah*, although it is not a *farḍ* in *'umrah*. If someone has sexual contact with a woman, he must perform *'umrah* and sacrifice according to Mālik, but he completes his practices. Ash-Shāfi'ī said that he owes a sacrifice and there is no point in doing *'umrah* if he has gone back and performed *ṭawāf* and *sa'y*. Abū Hanīfah and his people, ath-Thawrī and ash-Sha'bī said that *sa'y* is not mandatory. If someone omits it in the ḥajj and then returns to his homeland without doing it, he owes a sacrifice because it is one of the sunnahs of ḥajj. That is the position of Mālik in *al-'Utibiyyah*. It is, however, related from Ibn 'Abbās, Ibn az-Zubayr, Anas ibn Mālik and Ibn Sīrīn that it is voluntary based on this *āyah*.

**If anyone spontaneously does good, Allah is All-Thankful, All-Knowing**

Ḥamzah and al-Kisā'ī recite *'yaṭṭawwa'*, as with 2:184, while the rest have *'ṭawwa'a'* in the past tense. This refers to any supererogatory good action someone does which is not imposed on them, whether *ṭawāf* or anything else. Allah will show gratitude for the action by rewarding them. What is sound is what ash-Shāfi'ī believed, based on what we mentioned and the fact that the Prophet ﷺ said, 'Take your practices from me.' Therefore it is clear that it is part of the ḥajj and it must be obligatory in the same way as is the case in his making the number of *rak'ahs* clear ﷺ. The same is true of all of that unless it is agreed that it is sunnah or voluntary. Ṭulayb said, 'Ibn 'Abbās saw some people doing *ṭawāf* between Ṣafā and Marwah and said, "This is what your mother, Ismā'īl's mother, bequeathed you."' This is confirmed in *Ṣaḥīḥ Bukhārī* as we will see in *Sūrah Ibrāhīm.*

It is not permitted for anyone to do *ṭawāf* of the House or go between Ṣafā and Marwah riding unless he has an excuse. If he does this with a valid excuse, then he owes a sacrifice. If he does it without an excuse, he must repeat the action as long as he is still at the House. Otherwise he must sacrifice. We say that because the Prophet ﷺ did *ṭawāf* himself and he said, 'Take your practices from me.' We are allowed to do that with an excuse because the Prophet ﷺ did *ṭawāf* on his camel and greeted the Corner with his whip, and when 'Ā'ishah asked him about it, he said, 'I am unwell.' He also told her, 'Do *ṭawāf* riding behind the people.'

Our people differentiate between doing *ṭawāf* on a camel and on a person's back. It is not permitted to do *ṭawāf* on a person's back because then the person being carried is not the one performing *ṭawāf;* the one performing *ṭawāf* is the person who is carrying him. If he does *ṭawāf* on a camel, he is performing *ṭawāf.* Ibn Khuwayzimandād said, 'This is a distinction in choice. It does satisfy the requirement. Do you not see that if someone faints and is carried in the rest of his *ṭawāf* or stops at 'Arafāt while being carried, he has satisfied the requirement.'

إِنَّ ٱلَّذِينَ يَكۡتُمُونَ مَآ أَنزَلۡنَا مِنَ ٱلۡبَيِّنَٰتِ وَٱلۡهُدَىٰ مِنۢ بَعۡدِ مَا بَيَّنَّٰهُ
لِلنَّاسِ فِي ٱلۡكِتَٰبِ أُوْلَٰٓئِكَ يَلۡعَنُهُمُ ٱللَّهُ وَيَلۡعَنُهُمُ ٱللَّٰعِنُونَ ١٥٩

**159 Those who hide the Clear Signs and Guidance We have sent down, after We have made it clear to people in the Book, Allah curses them, and the cursers curse them –**

**Those who hide the Clear Signs and Guidance We have sent down,**

Allah tells us that anyone who hides the Clear Signs and Guidance is cursed. Scholars disagree about what is meant that. It is said that the Jewish rabbis and

Christian monks are the ones who concealed their knowledge of the coming of Muḥammad ﷺ and the Jews concealed the command about stoning. It is said that it means everyone who conceals the truth, and so it is general to all who conceal any knowledge of the *dīn* of Allah which should be made known. That is explained by the words of the Prophet ﷺ, 'If anyone is asked about knowledge which he knows and conceals it, Allah will bridle him with a bridle of Fire on the Day of Rising.' Abū Hurayrah and 'Amr ibn al-'Āṣ related it and Ibn Mājah transmitted it.

That is counterbalanced by the statement of 'Abdullāh ibn Mas'ūd, 'You should not tell people a *ḥadīth* which is beyond the grasp of their intellects lest it be a trial for some of them.' The Prophet ﷺ also said, 'Relate to people according to their ability to understand. Do you want Allah and His Messenger to be denied?' This applies to some areas of knowledge, such as *kalām* and the like which not everyone can grasp. A scholar should transmit what can be grasped and deal with everyone according to their understanding. Allah knows best.

This *āyah* is the one which Abū Hurayrah was referring to when he said, 'If it had not been for an *āyah* in the Book of Allah Almighty, I would not have told you a single *ḥadīth*.' Scholars use it as evidence for the obligation of conveying true knowledge and in general of making knowledge clear without taking a wage for it, since no wage should be received for what it is mandatory to do, just as there is no wage for simply being a Muslim. This has already been discussed in the commentary on *āyah* 41.

The meaning of the *āyah* is that, when a scholar intends to conceal knowledge, he disobeys Allah. When that is not his intention, he is not obliged to convey something if he knows that other people know it. When he is asked, he is obliged by this *āyah* and the *ḥadīth* to convey what he knows. He is not, however, permitted to teach an unbeliever the Qur'an and knowledge of the *dīn* until he becomes Muslim. Similarly he is not permitted to teach an innovator proofs and arguments which he might then use to argue against the people who possess the truth. He should not instruct a litigant in techniques of legal advocacy so that he can use it against his opponent to take his money, nor should he teach a ruler a particular interpretation which he can then use to harm his subjects. He should not inform fools of permissive opinions which they might then use as justification for committing forbidden acts or abandoning their obligations or other such things.

It is related that the Messenger of Allah ﷺ said, 'Do not deny wisdom to those entitled to it and thus wrong them, and do not give it to those not entitled to it and thus wrong it.' It is also reported that he said. 'Do not hang pearls from the necks of swine,' meaning teach *fiqh* to someone who is not able to grasp it. Saḥnūn said, 'The *ḥadīth* of Abū Hurayah and 'Amr ibn al-'Āṣ is about giving testimony.' Ibn al-'Arabī said, 'What is sound is different to that because it says in the *ḥadīth*: "If anyone is asked about knowledge" and not "testimony". One takes the literal meaning unless there is something to alter it.' Allah knows best.

The *'Clear Signs and Guidance'* mentioned in the *āyah* are not specific things. On the contrary, it is a general statement, since guidance includes all knowledge of the *dīn*. The *āyah* is evidence for the obligation of acting by the statement of a single person because clarification would only be mandatory for him if it were mandatory to accept what he says. Allah says: *'except for those who sincerely repent and put things right and make things clear.'* (2:160) So its ruling is that clarification occurs simply by virtue of them reporting it.

If it is said that it is possible that everyone is forbidden to conceal the matter, and commanded to make it clear, so that there will be a great number of people who report it, we reply to those who say this that it is a mistake. That is because they were not forbidden to conceal things because they were among those who might collude in concealing knowledge. If someone is one of those who might collude in concealment, their report is not mandatory, and Allah knows best.

The use of the words *'Clear Signs and Guidance'* also indicates that it is permitted to conceal anything other than that, especially when there is fear of what its misunderstanding might provoke, in which case its concealment is even more emphatically encouraged. Fear of the consequences involved led Abū Hurayrah to do precisely that. He said, 'I preserved two vessels from the Messenger of Allah ﷺ. I have disseminated one of them. If I were to disseminate the other one, my throat would be cut.' Al-Bukhārī transmitted it. Our scholars say that the part which Abū Hurayrah did not disseminate, and on account of which he feared dissension or that he himself might be killed, was knowledge which was connected to seditions, information about apostates and hypocrites, and other such things which are not connected to Clear Signs and Guidance. And Allah knows best.

**after We have made it clear to people in the Book,**

This alludes to the Clear Signs and Guidance which Allah has revealed to the human race. 'The Book' is generic, meaning all the Revealed Books.

**Allah curses them,**

He declares Himself free of them and puts them far from His reward, telling them they are cursed. The root meaning of curse is to put away and drive away.

**and the cursers curse them.**

Qatādah and ar-Rabīʿ said that the 'cursers' are the angels and the believers. Mujāhid and 'Ikrimah say that they are the insects and beasts who curse them because they are afflicted by drought on account of the wrong actions of those evil scholars who conceal knowledge. Az-Zajjāj said that the correct view is that it is the angels and the believers. He says that the truth of the assertion that it is the beasts of the earth would necessarily depend on a text or a report to that effect and none has been found to back it up. There is, however, a *ḥadīth* from al-Barā' ibn 'Āzib in which the Prophet ﷺ said in reference to this fact that it is the beasts of the earth. This *ḥadīth* can be found in Ibn Mājah from Muḥammad ibn aṣ-Ṣabbāḥ from 'Ammār ibn Muḥammad from Abu-l-Minhāl from Zādhān from al-Barā'. It has a good *isnād.*

If it is asked, 'How can the plural reserved for things which have intelligence be used for creatures without intelligence?' the reply is that it is because the action of intelligent beings is ascribed to them. An example of this is when Allah says in *Sūrat Yūsuf*: *'I saw them [the stars] prostrating to me'* (12:4), using the masculine plural. There are many other instances of this and it is something which will be discussed later, Allah willing. Al-Barā' and Ibn 'Abbās said that the 'cursers' are all creatures except for men and jinn. That is because the Prophet ﷺ said, 'When the unbeliever is struck in his grave and shouts out, everything hears him except for men and jinn. All who hear him curse him.' Ibn Mas'ūd and as-Suddī said, 'It is a man who curses his companion and the curse rises to heaven and then descends and does not find the person, about whom it was said, as meriting it and so it returns to the one who said it and does not find him to merit it either. Therefore, it becomes general and falls on the Jews who concealed what Allah revealed.'

إِلَّا ٱلَّذِينَ تَابُوا۟ وَأَصْلَحُوا۟ وَبَيَّنُوا۟ فَأُو۟لَٰٓئِكَ أَتُوبُ عَلَيْهِمْ وَأَنَا ٱلتَّوَّابُ ٱلرَّحِيمُ ﴿١٦٠﴾

**160 except for those who sincerely repent and put things right and make things clear. I turn towards them. I am the Ever-Returning, the Most Merciful.**

**except for those who sincerely repent**

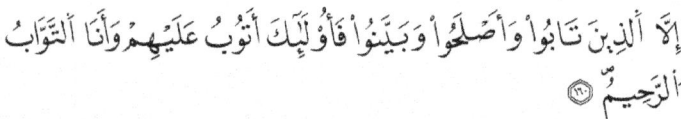

Those who sincerely repent are those who are righteous in their actions and do deeds which make their repentance clear. Simple repentance is not enough according to our scholars; it is necessary for the opposite of someone's original condition to be clearly manifest in him. If he was an apostate and then returns to Islam, he has to be manifestly obeying its laws. If he is one of the people of disobedience, he must become one of the people who perform righteous actions and avoid people immersed in corruption and his former life. If he is an idolater, he must shun the company of other idolaters and mix with the people of Islam. Repentance and its rulings will be explained in *Sūrat an-Nisā'*, Allah willing.

**and put things right and make things clear.**

Some scholars say that '*make things clear*' means, for instance, by breaking wine containers and spilling out their contents and other clear actions connected with breaking with past patterns of behaviour. It is said that it means make clear what is in the Torah about the Prophethood of Muḥammad ﷺ and the obligation to follow him. It is better to take it in the more general sense of displaying the opposite of what people were doing previously. Allah knows best.

إِنَّ الَّذِينَ كَفَرُوا وَمَاتُوا وَهُمْ كُفَّارٌ أُولَٰئِكَ عَلَيْهِمْ لَعْنَةُ اللَّهِ
وَالْمَلَائِكَةِ وَالنَّاسِ أَجْمَعِينَ ﴿١٦١﴾ خَالِدِينَ فِيهَا لَا يُخَفَّفُ عَنْهُمُ الْعَذَابُ
وَلَا هُمْ يُنظَرُونَ ﴿١٦٢﴾

**161 But as for those who are unbelievers and die unbelievers, the curse of Allah is upon them and that of the angels and all mankind. 162 They will be under it for ever. The punishment will not be lightened for them. They will be granted no reprieve.**

Ibn al-'Arabī said, 'Many of my shaykhs told me that it is not permitted to curse a particular unbeliever because his state at the time of his death is not known. Allah Almighty stipulated in this *āyah* that the application of the curse depends on someone actually dying as an unbeliever. As for what is related about the Prophet ﷺ cursing specific unbelievers, that was only because he knew what their fate would be.' Ibn al-'Arabī also said, 'I consider it valid, however, to curse an unbeliever on the basis of his outward state and it is permitted to fight and kill him. It is related that the Prophet ﷺ said, "O Allah, 'Amr ibn al-'Āṣ has satirised me and he knows that I am not a poet, so curse him and satirise him to the extent that he has satirized me." So he cursed him, even though faith, the *dīn* and Islam were to be his end. He was fair when he said, "To the extent that he has satirised me," and no more.'

As for cursing unbelievers in general, without specifying anyone, there is no disagreement about doing that, since Mālik reported with an *isnād* going back to al-A'raj who said, 'People definitely used to curse the unbelievers in Ramaḍān.' Our scholars add, 'Whether or not they are *dhimmīs*.' This is not mandatory but it is permitted if someone does it, because they deny the truth and are hostile towards the *dīn* and its people. The same applies to anyone who commits acts of disobedience openly, like drinking wine and practising usury and other such things.

The point of cursing an unbeliever is not to drive him away from disbelief. It is repayment for his disbelief and his display of it. Some of the Salaf said, 'There is no point in cursing those who are mad or dead among them, either by way of repayment or as a rebuke. It has no effect.'

What is meant by the *āyah*, according to this understanding, is that people will curse them on the Day of Rising so that it has an effect and harms and pains their hearts. That is the repayment for their disbelief as the Almighty says: *'Then on the Day of Rising, they will reject one another and curse one another.'* (29:25) This position inclines to the view that the *āyah* is a simple report from Allah and not a command. Ibn al-'Arabī mentioned that it is not permitted to curse an individual rebel, because it is reported that a man who had drunk wine several times was brought before the Prophet and one of those present said, 'Allah curse him! How often he is brought!' The Prophet ﷺ said, 'Do not help Shayṭān against your brother,' and he called him a brother, which obliges compassion for him. This is a sound *ḥadīth*. Al-Bukhārī and Muslim mentioned it.

One scholar mentioned a disagreement about cursing a specific rebel. He said that the Prophet's words above were about Nu'aymān after the *ḥadd* punishment had been carried out on him. One should not curse someone on whom the *ḥadd* punishment has been carried out. It is, however, permitted to curse someone on whom the *ḥadd* punishment has not been carried out, whether he is named and specific or not, because the Prophet ﷺ only cursed those for whom the curse was obliged as long as they remained in that state which obliged the curse. If someone repents of it, refrains and is purified by the *ḥadd*, then he should not be cursed. This is made evident by the words of the Prophet ﷺ: 'When one of your slave-girls fornicates, carry out the *ḥadd* on her and do not find fault her.' This *ḥadīth*, being sound, indicates that finding fault and cursing are before the *ḥadd* and before repentance. Allah knows best.

Ibn al-'Arabī said, 'It is permitted to curse rebels in general by consensus, based on what is related from the Prophet ﷺ, that he said: 'Allah has cursed a slave who steals a helmet and has his hand cut off.'

Cursed people are far from Allah's mercy. The root meaning of '*la'n*' (curse) is to drive away and put someone far away. The intent of a curse made by people is to drive someone away, and Allah's curse is punishment.

If it is observed that not all mankind curse them because their own people do not, there are three answers to this objection. One is that the curse of most people is applied to them, since it denotes the majority. The second is what as-Suddī said: that everyone curses a wrongdoer and a wrongdoing unbeliever even curses himself. The third is Abu-l-'Āliyah's statement that what is meant is the Day of Rising when his own people will curse him along with everyone else as Allah says: *'But then on the Day of Rising you will reject one another and curse one another.'* (29:25) *'For ever'* refers to the the curse: either in respect of the repayment for it or in respect of its abiding on them for ever. The punishment will not be lightened for them for a single moment.

وَإِلَٰهُكُمْ إِلَٰهٌ وَاحِدٌ لَّآ إِلَٰهَ إِلَّا هُوَ ٱلرَّحْمَٰنُ ٱلرَّحِيمُ ١٦٣

**163 Your God is One God. 'There is no god but Him, the All-Merciful, the Most Merciful.**

**Your God is One God.**

When Allah warned against concealing the truth, He made it clear that the first thing which must be made clear, and which it is not permitted to conceal, is knowledge of Allah's unity. He connected the proof to that and instructed people on how to find out about it: one should reflect on the wonders of creation so as to know that there must be a Unique Doer who is not like anything else. Ibn 'Abbās said, 'Quraysh said, "Muḥammad, describe your Lord for us." Then Allah revealed *Sūrat al-Ikhlāṣ* and this *āyah.* The idolaters had three hundred and sixty idols. Allah made it clear that He is One.'

**There is no god but Him,**

This means that there is nothing worthy of worship except Allah. It is reported that ash-Shiblī used to say the name 'Allah' alone and omit the words '*lā ilāha*' – 'there is no god'. He was asked about that and said, 'I fear that I might die on the word of denial and not reach the word of affirmation.' This is one of the very refined areas of knowledge which has no real substance. Allah mentions this phrase in His Book with both negation and affirmation and repeats it many times and promised, on the tongue of His Prophet ﷺ, an ample reward for whoever says it. *Al-Muwaṭṭā'*, al-Bukhārī, Muslim and others transmitted it. He said ﷺ, 'If someone's last words are "There is no god but Allah", he will enter the Garden.' Muslim transmitted it. What is meant is with the heart, not the tongue alone. If someone says, 'There is no god' and dies before completing the formula but his belief and conscience affirm Allah's unity and His necessary attributes, by the agreement of the people of the Sunnah, he is one of the people of the Garden.

إِنَّ فِي خَلْقِ ٱلسَّمَٰوَٰتِ وَٱلْأَرْضِ وَٱخْتِلَٰفِ ٱلَّيْلِ وَٱلنَّهَارِ وَٱلْفُلْكِ ٱلَّتِي
تَجْرِي فِي ٱلْبَحْرِ بِمَا يَنفَعُ ٱلنَّاسَ وَمَآ أَنزَلَ ٱللَّهُ مِنَ ٱلسَّمَآءِ مِن مَّآءٍ فَأَحْيَا بِهِ
ٱلْأَرْضَ بَعْدَ مَوْتِهَا وَبَثَّ فِيهَا مِن كُلِّ دَآبَّةٍ وَتَصْرِيفِ ٱلرِّيَٰحِ وَٱلسَّحَابِ
ٱلْمُسَخَّرِ بَيْنَ ٱلسَّمَآءِ وَٱلْأَرْضِ لَءَايَٰتٍ لِّقَوْمٍ يَعْقِلُونَ ﴿١٦٤﴾

**164 In the creation of the heavens and earth, and the alternation of the night and day, and the ships which sail the seas to people's benefit, and the water which Allah sends down from the sky – by which He brings the earth to life when it was dead and scatters about in it creatures of every kind – and the varying direction of the winds, and the clouds subservient between heaven and earth, there are Signs for people who use their intellect.**

'Aṭā' said that when the previous *āyah* was revealed, the unbelievers of Quraysh said, 'How can One God be enough for people!' And then this *āyah* was revealed. Sufyān related from his father that Abu-ḍ-Ḍuḥā said that when the previous *āyah* was revealed, they asked, 'What proof is there of this?' and so Allah revealed this *āyah*. It is as if they were asking for a sign to make the oneness of Allah clear to them: this universe and wondrous structure must have a Builder and Maker.

*Samāwāt* (heavens) is in the plural because there are different types of heaven. Each heaven is different from all the other heavens. *Arḍ* (earth) is in the singular because there is only one earth. Allah knows best. The sign of the heavens is that they are elevated without support under them or above them. That indicates incomprehensible power. Then there are the sun, moon and stars which rise and set in them which are yet another sign of Allah's power. The sign of the earth consists of its seas, rivers, mines, trees, gentle terrain and rough terrain.

**and the alternation of the night and day,**

as they come and go from where it is not known. It is said that their differentiation is in respect of the variable intensity of the light and darkness, and the variation in the length and shortness of each. '*layl*' (night) is the plural of '*laylah*'. '*Nahār*' (day) denotes the time of light between dawn and sunset. The beginning of 'day' is sunrise; anything before it is not part of it. Tha'lab said that among the Arabs it begins with sunrise. Az-Zajjāj said in *Kitāb al-Anwā'* that the beginning of the day is the appearance of the sun.

Ibn al-Anbārī said that there are three categories of time. One category is pure night, which extends from sunset to the rising of dawn. A second category is pure day, which extends from sunrise to sunset. The third category is shared between night and day and it is between dawn and sunrise since some of the darkness of night is left with the beginning of the light of day.

What is sound is that 'day' is from the rising of dawn until sunset as is related by Ibn Fāris in *al-Mujmal*. That is indicated by what is confirmed in *Ṣaḥīḥ Muslim* that 'Adī ibn Ḥātim said, 'When it was revealed: *"until you can clearly discern the white thread from the black thread of the dawn"* (2:187), 'Adī said to the Prophet, "Messenger of Allah, I put two strings under my pillow, a white one and a black one, by which I recognise night from day." The Messenger of Allah ﷺ said, "Your pillow is indeed wide! It is the blackness of night and the whiteness of day."' This *ḥadīth* shows that the day is from the rising of dawn until sunset. This *fiqh* is applied in oaths and rulings are connected to it. If someone swears that he will not speak to a person for a day (*nahār*) and then speaks to him before sunrise, he has broken his oath. According to the first view, he has not broken it. What the Prophet ﷺ said is the criterion for that. As for what is part of literal language and derived from the Sunnah is that day begins with whitening of the sky.

**and the ships which sail the seas to people's benefit,**

'*Fulk*' (ships) is a generic term for all watercraft. The meaning of the *āyah* is that Allah controls them so that they move on the surface of the water and float in spite of their weight. The first person to make one was Nūḥ, as Allah reports. Jibrīl showed him how to do it and he bequeathed that to everyone. A ship is like a bird, but it is reversed so that the sea is under it as the bird is in the air above. Ibn al-'Arabī said that.

This *āyah* and those like it indicate the permission to travel on the sea in general, for commerce or for acts of worship such as the ḥajj and *jihād*. In the Sunnah we find the *ḥadīth* of Abū Hurayrah, 'A man came to the Messenger of Allah ﷺ and said, "Messenger of Allah, we travel on the sea and carry a little water with us."' There is the *ḥadīth* of Anas ibn Mālik in the story of Umm Ḥarām transmitted by the imams, Mālik and others. And there are other *ḥadīths* to the same effect such as what is related from him ﷺ by Bundār Muḥammad ibn Bashshār which contains clear evidence for men and women travelling by sea for *jihād*. If it is permitted to travel on it for *jihād*, it is more appropriate for travelling on for the obligatory ḥajj. It is related from 'Umar ibn al-Khaṭṭāb and 'Umar ibn 'Abd al-'Azīz that it is forbidden to travel on it, but the Qur'an and Sunnah refute this view. If travelling on it had been disliked or not permitted, then the Prophet ﷺ would have forbidden it to those who said, 'We travel on the sea.' This *āyah* and what is like it is a text.

As for what the two 'Umars said about that, it is based on being cautious and not endangering oneself in order to seek this world and amass it. That is not the case with obligations. Abū 'Umar said that Mālik disliked women embarking on the sea for ḥajj and even more so for the sake of *jihād*. The Qur'an and the Sunnah refute this although some of the people of Basra said that Mālik disliked that because the ships in the Hijaz were small and people could not conceal themselves when answering the call of nature because of the lack of space and press of people in it. It was possible to travel by land from Madīnah to Makkah, and therefore Mālik disliked going by sea. However, there is nothing wrong in using the large ships that the people of Basra have. He said that the basic principle is that ḥajj is obligatory for all those who can find a way to perform it, men or women, when the route is generally safe. There is no difference between land and sea in that respect.

The Book and the Sunnah both provide evidence that it permitted to travel on the sea for worship and for trade. It is a proof and a model, although the circumstances of people travelling on the sea vary. Many of those who travel on it find it easy and not difficult while others find it difficult and are weakened by it, like those afflicted by extreme seasickness, and are unable thereby to perform the obligation of ḥajj and similar obligations. The first individual is permitted to travel on it and the second is forbidden to do so.

There is no disagreement among the people of knowledge that when the sea is rough, however, it is not permitted for anyone to embark on it nor to do so at times when it is generally unsafe. It is permitted to embark on it when it is generally safe.

The words *'to people's benefit'* in this phrase refer to benefit they have in trade or anything else which is proper for them. If people criticise the Qur'an, saying, 'Allah revealed in the Book: *"We have not omitted anything from the Book"* (6:38), so where do we find food seasonings like salt, pepper and the like?' the reply is, 'They can be found in Allah's words: "*to people's benefit.*"'

**and the water which Allah sends down from the sky –**

This, of course, means the rain which brings the world to life and makes the plants grow and is conserved in it for use at other times. As Allah says: *'We lodged it firmly in the earth.'* (23:18)

**and scatters about in it creatures of every kind –**

This means separates them and spreads them out. The word '*dābbah*' (creatures) includes all animals. Some people say that this *āyah* excludes birds, but this is rejected because they too have feet for walking on the earth.

**and the varying direction of the winds,**

Sending them as sometimes barren sometimes fertilising, sometimes as freezing gales, sometimes helping sometimes destroying, sometimes hot and sometimes cold, sometimes gentle and sometimes tempestuous. It is said that the expression refers to just their direction – north, south, east or west – and the way they veer from one to the other. It is said that it means that they move large ships with full loads as well as small ships and avert what will harm them. It is said to refer to their variation from season to season.

Abū Dāwud related that Abū Hurayrah reported that he heard the Messenger of Allah ﷺ say, 'The wind (*rīḥ*) is part of the solace (*rawḥ*) given by Allah. It brings mercy and brings punishment. When you see it, do not curse it. Ask Allah for its good and seek refuge with Allah from its evil.' Ibn Mājah also transmitted this in his *Sunan* from Abū Bakr ibn Abī Shaybah from Yaḥyā ibn Sa'īd from al-Awzā'ī from az-Zuhrī from Thābit az-Zuraqāi from Abū Hurayrah. It is also related that Prophet ﷺ said, 'Do not curse the wind. It is from the breath of the All-Merciful.' This means that Allah Almighty puts relief, refreshment and comfort in it. We find in *Ṣaḥīḥ Muslim* from Ibn 'Abbās that the Prophet ﷺ said, 'I was helped by the east wind and 'Ād were destroyed by the west wind.' This idea also comes in a report that Allah gave His Prophet ﷺ release with the wind on the day of the Confederates as He says: '*We sent a wind against them and other forces you could not see.*' (33:9) The root of wind (*rīḥ*) comes from *rūḥ* which is why the plural is *arwāḥ*.

Ḥamzah and al-Kisā'ī recited '*rīḥ*' in the singular which is also the case in a number of other *sūrahs*. The rest recite it as '*riyāḥ*' in the plural. If it is in the singular, then it is a generic noun which indicates both a little and a lot. If it is in the plural, then it refers to the different directions in which the winds blow. The plural is with mercy and the singular is with punishment. That is frequent in the Qur'an. It is related that the Messenger of Allah ﷺ used to say when the wind blew: 'O Allah, makes it winds and do not make it a wind.' That is because the wind of punishment is fierce and cohesive like a single body. The wind of mercy is soft and disconnected which is why the plural is used.

Scholars say that the wind moves the air and can be strong or weak. When the movement of the air starts from the direction of the *qiblah*, then the wind called an east wind (*ṣabā*). When the movement begins going towards the *qiblah*, it is a west wind (*dabūr*). When it begins from the right of the *qiblah* going to its left, it is a south wind. When it begins to the left of the *qiblah* going to the right, it is a north wind. Each of these winds has its own nature. Its use is according to its nature. The east wind is hot and dry. The west wind is cold and wet. The south is hot and wet. The north is cold and dry. The difference in their natures is like the difference in seasons.

That is why Allah has made four seasons deriving from the change in the winds. The first season – spring – is hot and wet and growth starts in it, water descends and earth produces its flowers and its plants appear. People begin to cultivate the trees and many crops. Animals reproduce and have abundant milk. When spring ends, it is followed by summer which is like spring in respect of heat but differs from it as it is not wet. The weather in summer is hot and dry. In it fruits ripen and the grain planted in the spring becomes dry. When summer ends, it is followed by autumn which is like summer in being dry, but is not hot like it. Autumn weather is cold and dry. The soundness of fruits ends and they dry up and there is storing. Fruits are plucked, grapes harvested and all the trees emptied. When autumn ends, it is followed by winter which is like autumn in being cold, but is wet rather than dry, because the weather of the winter is cold and wet. There is a lot of rain and snow and the ground is inert like a body at rest. It does not move until Allah makes the heat of spring return to it. When the warmth joins with the moisture, then there is growth by Allah's permission. There are many more winds in addition to what we mentioned, but the bases are these four. Every wind between two falls under the ruling of the one that it is closest to.

**and the clouds subservient between heaven and earth,**

'*Saḥab*' (clouds) take that name because they are dragged (*insiḥāb*) along in the air. *Saḥaba* means to drag along. *Saḥb*, from the same root, means vigorous eating and drinking. They are 'subservient' because they are moved without resistance from one place to another. It is said that their subservience lies in their remaining poised between heaven and earth without any support. The first is more likely. They can bring either water or punishment. In Muslim, Abū Hurayrah reported that the Prophet ﷺ said, 'Once, while a man was walking in the desert, he heard a voice in a cloud saying, "Water the garden of so-and-so," and that cloud went and poured out its water into a rocky area. There was a certain water channel which held all the water and he followed it and found a man standing in his garden directing the water with his spade. He asked him, "Slave of Allah, what is your name?" He said, "So-and-so," giving the same name he had heard from the cloud. The man then said to him, "O slave of Allah, why did you ask me my name?" The first man said, "I heard a voice in the cloud which this water came from say, 'Water the garden of so-and-so' giving your name. What are you doing with it?" He said, "Since you have asked this, I will [reply]. I wait and see what it produces and give a third of it away as *ṣadaqah*, and my family and I eat from a third, and I reinvest a third back into it."' In one version: 'I devote a third of it to the poor, beggars and travellers.'

In the Qur'an we also find: *'It is Allah who sends the winds which raise the clouds which We then drive to a dead land'* (35:9) and *'...when they have lifted up the heavy clouds, We dispatch them to a dead land and send down water to it'* (7:57) and there are many other similar *āyahs*. Ibn Mājah transmitted that 'Ā'ishah said, 'When the Prophet ﷺ saw a cloud coming on the horizon, he left what he was doing, even the prayer, to greet it. He would say, "O Allah we seek refuge with You from the evil of what You have sent." If it rained, he would say, "O Allah, a useful watering" two or three times." If Allah moved it on and it did not rain, he would praise Allah for that.' 'Ā'ishah also said, 'When it was a day of wind and clouds, that could be seen in the face of the Messenger of Allah ﷺ. He paced back and forth. If it rained, he was happy and that state left him.' She said, 'I asked him and he said, "I fear that it will be a punishment sent on My community." When he saw rain, he said, "Mercy."' One variant has: "Ā'ishah, perhaps it will be as the people of 'Ād said: "*When they saw it as a storm cloud advancing on their valleys, they said, 'This is a storm cloud which will give us rain.'* (46:24)"'

These *ḥadīth*s and *āyah*s indicate the soundness of the first view that their subservience is not fixed. Allah knows best. Firmness would indicate that there is no change. If the firmness meant is in the air, it is neither in heaven or earth, and so it is sound since He says 'between'. They are subservient and carry. That shows a greater power, as is the case with birds in the air as the Almighty says: *'Do they not see the birds suspended in mid-air up in the sky? Nothing holds them there except Allah'* (16:79) and *'Have they not looked at the birds above them, with wings outspread and folded back? Nothing holds them up but the All-Merciful.'* (67:19)

Ka'b al-Aḥbar said, 'The clouds are sieves for the rain. Were it not for the clouds, when water descended from heaven, it would ruin the earth on which it fell.' Ibn

'Abbās related that from him. Khaṭīb Abū Bakr Aḥmad ibn 'Alī mentioned that Mu'ādh ibn 'Abdullāh ibn Khubayb al-Juhanī said, 'Once, when I was among the Banū Salamah, I saw Ibn 'Abbās pass by on a mule. Tubay', the son of Ka'b's wife, passed by him and greeted Ibn 'Abbās. Ibn 'Abbās asked him, "Did you hear Ka'b al-Aḥbar say anything about clouds?" "Yes," he replied, "he said, 'The clouds are sieves for the rain. Were it not for the clouds, when water descended from heaven, it would ruin the earth on which it fell.'" He asked, "Did you hear Ka'b say anything about earth that grows plants one year and then again in the following year?" "Yes," he said. "I heard him say, 'Seeds descend from heaven.'" Ibn 'Abbās said, "And I heard that from Ka'b."'

**There are Signs for people who use their intellect.**

Allah's Signs are evidence of His Oneness and Power. That is why these matters are mentioned after the previous *āyah,* which begins *'Your God is One God…'*, in order to demonstrate the truth of that statement about His Oneness and mentioning His mercy and kindness to His creatures. The Prophet ﷺ said, 'Woe to the person who reads this *āyah* and then dismisses it and does not reflect on it or ponder it.'

If someone were to ask, 'What will disprove that the earth engendered itself?', he is told that this is impossible because if it had engendered itself, it must have been existent or non-existent when it did it. If it was non-existent, then it is impossible for it to have done it because that must come from one who is alive, knowing, powerful, and possessing volition. It is not valid to describe something that does not exist with those attributes. If it is existent, then its existence would not require engendering. If this were possible, then it would be possible for a building to build itself, wood to carve itself or wool to weave itself. That is impossible. That which leads to an impossibility is impossible.

Allah does not confine mention of His Oneness to mere reports, but also combines that with investigation and reflection on the *āyah*s of the Qur'an. He instructed His Prophet ﷺ to: *'Say: "Look at what there is in the heavens and on the earth."'* (10:101) This is addressed to the unbelievers since the Almighty says: *'But Signs and warnings are of no avail to people who do not believe.'* He also says: *'Have they not looked into the dominions of the heavens and the earth'* (7:185) and 'dominions' means 'Signs'. He says: *'…and in yourselves as well. Do you not then see?'* (51:21) He is saying, 'Do they not look at themselves with proper reflection and due consideration so that through that they can deduce that it is impossible for events and changes to be self-engendered and that something engendered requires a Maker to make it, and that that Maker must be wise, knowing, powerful, possessing will, hearing, seeing, speaking. That is because if He did not possess these attributes, a human being would be more perfect than Him and that is impossible.

Allah says: '*We created man from the purest kind of clay*' (23:12), meaning Ādam, '*then made him* (meaning his descendants) *a drop in a secure receptacle... you will be raised again.*' (23:13) When a person reflects on the intellect he has been given, he will see that he is managed and moved through various states. He was a drop, then a clot, then a lump, and then flesh and bones. He knows that he did not move himself from being incomplete to being complete because he is not capable of moving himself to the best state, which is full use of his intellect and full strength of limbs. He is not able to add another limb to his limbs. That indicates that he is in a state of incompleteness and weakness and lacks the power to do that. He sees himself as a young man, then a mature man, and then an old man. He did not move himself from being a strong young man to being old and senile. He did not choose it for himself and it is not within his capacity to remove his being old and replace it with restoration of the strength of youth. By that he knows that he is not the one who did those actions on his own and that he has a Maker who accomplished this and moved him from state to state. That had to be the case, for his states could not have changed without there being someone to transfer or manage them.

A wise man said, 'Everything in the macrocosm has its like in the microcosm, which is the body of the human being. That is why the Almighty said: '*We created man in the finest mould*' (95:4) and: '*...and in yourselves as well. Do you not then see?*' (51:21) The sensory faculties of the human being are more noble than the luminous stars. Hearing and sight are in the position of the sun and the moon with regards to perceiving things. His limbs become dust when they decay which is the genus of the earth. He contains water in the form of veins and other fluid components of the body. He contains air in the form of the spirit and respiration. He contains fire in the form of yellow bile. His veins are like the rivers of the earth. His liver is in the position of the springs which supply the rivers as the liver supplies the hepatic veins. His bladder is in the position of the sea since the contents of the body are poured into it as the rivers pour into the sea. His bones are are like trees. As every tree has leaves and fruit, so every limb has an action or effect. The hair on the body is like the plants and insects on the earth. Then the human being can make the sound of every animal with his tongue and his limbs are adapted to the action of every animal. So he is the microcosm within the macrocosm, created and brought about by One Maker. There is no god but Him.'

وَمِنَ ٱلنَّاسِ مَن يَتَّخِذُ مِن دُونِ ٱللَّهِ أَندَادًا يُحِبُّونَهُمْ كَحُبِّ ٱللَّهِ ۖ وَٱلَّذِينَ
ءَامَنُوٓا۟ أَشَدُّ حُبًّا لِّلَّهِ ۗ وَلَوْ تَرَى ٱلَّذِينَ ظَلَمُوٓا۟ إِذْ يَرَوْنَ ٱلْعَذَابَ أَنَّ
ٱلْقُوَّةَ لِلَّهِ جَمِيعًا وَأَنَّ ٱللَّهَ شَدِيدُ ٱلْعَذَابِ ﴿١٦٥﴾

**165 Some people set up equals to Allah, loving them as they should love Allah. But those who believe have greater love for Allah. If only you could see those who do wrong at the time when they see the punishment, and that truly all strength belongs to Allah, and that Allah is severe in punishment.**

**Some people set up equals to Allah,**

In the previous *āyah*, Allah gave evidence of His Oneness, Power and the immensity of His authority and He now adds these cogent *āyahs*, for those with intelligence, about people who set up equals to Him. Mujāhid says that what is meant are the idols which they worshipped in the same way that they worshipped Allah, giving them equal value.

**loving them as they should love Allah.**

They love their false idols as much as the believers love the Truly Real. Al-Mubarrad said that. Az-Zajjāj said, 'In spite of the lack of power of the idols, they love them as the believers love Allah with His real power.' Ibn 'Abbās and as-Suddī said that it refers to their leaders whom they follow in disobeying Allah. Ibn Kaysān and az-Zajjāj said that it means that they have equal love for Allah and the idols.

**But those who believe have greater love for Allah**

Greater than the love that idolaters have for their idols and followers have for those they follow. It is said that they have greater love because Allah loved them first and so they love him. When someone has the one he loves attest to his love, then his love is more complete. Allah says: '*…a people whom He loves and who love Him.*' (5:54) The love that the believers have for Allah and His love of them will be explained in *Sūrat Āl 'Imrān*, Allah willing.

**If only you could see those who do wrong at the time when they see the punishment,**

The reading of the people of Madīnah and Syria is 'you could see' with *ta'* whereas the people of Makkah and Kufa read it as 'they could see' with *yā'*. Abū 'Ubayd said, 'The meaning is, that if those who do wrong in this world were to see the punishment of the Next World, they would know when they see it that all strength belongs to Allah.' 'See' then would mean actual vision. An-Naḥḥās says in his book, *The Meanings of the Qur'an*, 'This position is the one generally held by the people of *tafsīr.*' In *I'rāb al-Qur'ān*, Muḥammad ibn Yazīd said that this explanation of Abū 'Ubayd is unlikely and it is not well expressed because it implies 'if those who did wrong had seen the punishment.' So it is as if he considers it uncertain when Allah has made it mandatory.

**and that truly all strength belongs to Allah,**

Al-Akhfash said that the import of the verb 'see' continues so that the meaning is, 'If those who do wrong could see that strength belongs to Allah…' and that the word 'see' means 'know' in this context so it really means: 'if they knew the reality of the strength of Allah and the severity of His punishment.' Taking the Madinan reading, it is a threat: 'If you, Muḥammad, could see those who do wrong when they see the punishment and are terrified of it, they would affirm that all strength belongs to Allah.' The Prophet ﷺ knew that, but he was addressed when his whole community was intended, as is often the case. It may also mean: 'Say, Muhammad, to the wrongdoer…'

إِذْ تَبَرَّأَ ٱلَّذِينَ ٱتُّبِعُوا۟ مِنَ ٱلَّذِينَ ٱتَّبَعُوا۟ وَرَأَوُا۟ ٱلْعَذَابَ وَتَقَطَّعَتْ
بِهِمُ ٱلْأَسْبَابُ ﴿١٦٦﴾

**166 When those who were followed disown those who followed them, and they see the punishment, and the connection between them is cut,**

**When those who were followed disown those who followed them,**

*'Those who were followed'* are the masters and leaders of the unbelievers. They will declare themselves free of those who followed them in disbelief, as Qatādah, 'Aṭā' and ar-Rabī' said. Qatadah also said, as did as-Suddi, that they were the *shayṭān*s who misguide mankind and who will declare themselves free of them on the Last Day. It is said that it is general to all who are followed in disbelief.

**and they see the punishment,**

'They' are both the followers and the followed. It is said to be through the certainty they will have in this world at the time of their death about the inevitability of punishment and it is said to refer to their being presented before

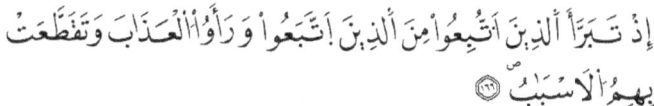

Allah and questioned in the Next World. Both may be true: it can mean at the time of death and it can mean in the Next World when they actually experience the pain of the punishment.

**and the connection between them is cut,**

This refers to their connection in this world through kinship and in other ways, as Mujāhid and others said. The root of the word for 'connection' (*sabab*) is a rope which is tied to a thing so that it can be pulled. So what pulls a thing into existence is a *sabab*, which gives the word its usual meaning of means or cause. As-Suddī and Ibn Zayd said, 'The means are their actions.'

وَقَالَ ٱلَّذِينَ ٱتَّبَعُوا۟ لَوْ أَنَّ لَنَا كَرَّةً فَنَتَبَرَّأَ مِنْهُمْ كَمَا تَبَرَّءُوا۟ مِنَّا ۗ
كَذَٰلِكَ يُرِيهِمُ ٱللَّهُ أَعْمَٰلَهُمْ حَسَرَٰتٍ عَلَيْهِمْ ۖ وَمَا هُم بِخَٰرِجِينَ مِنَ
ٱلنَّارِ ﴿١٦٧﴾

**167 those who followed will say, 'If only we could have another chance, we would disown them just as they have disowned us.' In that way Allah will show them their actions as a cause of anguish and remorse for them. They will never emerge from the Fire.**

**those who followed will say, 'If only we could have another chance,**

The followers claim that they would act righteously if they were given another opportunity. '*Kurrah*' is a return to a previous state.

**In that way Allah will show them their actions as a cause of anguish and remorse for them.**

As Allah will show them the Fire, so He will also show then their actions which are the cause of their entering it. This is actual seeing with the eye. Ar-Rabī' said that these are the corrupt actions which they committed which made the Fire mandatory for them. Ibn Mas'ūd and as-Suddī said that it refers to the righteous actions which they abandoned and thereby forfeited the Garden. There are many *ḥadīth*s to this effect. As-Suddī said, 'They will be shown the Garden and will look at it and at their houses there which they would have had if they had obeyed Allah. Those houses will be divided between the believers.' They are called 'their' actions because they were commanded to do them. '*Ḥasarah*' (anguish) is the highest degree of regret for something forfeited. It is derived from *ḥasīr* (exhausted), which is when something is cut off and its strength gone, like a camel which is completely exhausted. It also means to uncover.

**They will never emerge from the Fire.**

This is an indication that the unbelievers will be in the Fire forever and never leave it, which is the position of the people of the Sunnah. Allah says: *'They will not enter the Garden until a camel goes through a needle's eye.'* (7:40)

يَٰٓأَيُّهَا ٱلنَّاسُ كُلُوا۟ مِمَّا فِى ٱلْأَرْضِ حَلَٰلًا طَيِّبًا وَلَا تَتَّبِعُوا۟
خُطُوَٰتِ ٱلشَّيْطَٰنِ ۚ إِنَّهُۥ لَكُمْ عَدُوٌّ مُّبِينٌ ١٦٨

**168 Mankind! eat what is good and lawful on the earth. And do not follow in the footsteps of Shayṭān. He truly is an outright enemy to you.**

**Mankind!**

It is said that this was revealed about the tribes of Thaqīf, Khuzā'ah and Banū Mudlij about the blessings which they denied themselves, but the words bear a general meaning.

**eat what is good and lawful on the earth.**

'*Ṭayyib*' (good) here means "lawful" and this is emphasised by the use of the actual legal term (*ḥalāl*) immediately after it. This is the position of Mālik about 'good'. Ash-Shāfi'ī said that it means 'pleasant and wholesome' which is why he forbade feeding animals filth. Allah willing, this will be dealt with in greater depth in *Sūrat al-An'ām* and *Sūrat al-A'rāf*.

The term '*ḥalāl*' (lawful) is called that because the bond of prohibition has been released (*inḥilāl*) from it. Sahl ibn 'Abdullāh said, 'Salvation lies in three things: consuming the *ḥalāl*, performing the obligations and imitation of the Prophet ﷺ.' Abū 'Abdullāh as-Sājī, Sa'īd ibn Yazīd, said, 'There are five qualities which complete knowledge: gnosis of Allah Almighty, recognition of the truth, sincere action for Allah, acting according to the Sunnah and consuming the *ḥalāl*. If even one of them is lacking, the action is not complete.' Sahl said, 'Eating the *ḥalāl* is only valid with knowledge, and wealth is not *ḥalāl* until it is free of six things: usury, the *ḥarām*, theft, usurpation, the disliked and the doubtful.'

**And do not follow in the footsteps of Shayṭān.**

It is possible that the word '*khuṭuwāt*' (footsteps) comes from *khaṭī'ah* (error). The majority say that the phrase means: 'Do not follow the actions of Shayṭān.' As-Suddī said that it means: 'do not obey him.' The sound position is that it is general to all customs and laws stemming from innovations and acts of disobedience.

**He truly is an outright enemy to you.**

Allah reports that Shayṭān is an enemy and His report is true. An intelligent person must be cautious about this enemy whose enmity has been clear from the time of Ādam and who has devoted his energy to corrupting the states of mankind. For this reason Allah commanded us to be on our guard against him in many places in the Qur'an. 'Abdullāh ibn 'Umar said, 'Iblīs is confined to the lower earth. When he moves, every evil in the earth between two or more people is set in motion.' At-Tirmidhī transmitted from Abū Mālik al-Ash'arī: 'I command you to remember Allah. An example of that is when a man has an enemy rapidly following his tracks and then reaches a fortified fortress and defends himself from him. Similarly the only thing that protects a person from Shayṭān is remembering Allah.' He said that it is a *gharīb* sound *ḥasan ḥadīth.*

إِنَّمَا يَأْمُرُكُم بِالسُّوٓءِ وَالْفَحْشَآءِ وَأَن تَقُولُوا عَلَى اللَّهِ مَا لَا تَعْلَمُونَ ﴿١٦٩﴾

**169 He only commands you to do evil and indecent acts and to say about Allah what you do not know.**

**He only commands you to do evil and indecent acts**

The word for evil is *sū'* because it is bad for the person who does it and brings evil consequences in its wake. The root of the word for indecent acts (*fahshā'*) means something which is ugly to look at. Sharī'ah is what makes something good or ugly. All that the Sharī'ah forbids is ugly and so it is part of the indecent. Muqātil said, 'Everywhere the Qur'an mentions "indecency" it implies fornication except where Allah says: "*Shayṭān promises you poverty and commands you to avarice* (fahshā')," (2:268) where it means to refuse to pay zakat.'

According to this, there is no *ḥadd* for 'evil', but there is for 'indecency'. That is related from Ibn 'Abbās and others, and Allah knows best.

**and to say about Allah what you do not know.**

Aṭ-Ṭabarī says that this refers to various animals, like *baḥīrah, sā'ibah* and other such animals which the idolaters made unlawful without any basis for doing so.

وَإِذَا قِيلَ لَهُمُ ٱتَّبِعُوا۟ مَآ أَنزَلَ ٱللَّهُ قَالُوا۟ بَلْ نَتَّبِعُ مَآ أَلْفَيْنَا عَلَيْهِ ءَابَآءَنَآ
أَوَلَوْ كَانَ ءَابَآؤُهُمْ لَا يَعْقِلُونَ شَيْـًٔا وَلَا يَهْتَدُونَ ﴿١٧٠﴾

**170 When they are told, 'Follow what Allah has sent down to you,' They say, 'We are following what we found our fathers doing.' What, even though their fathers did not understand a thing and were not guided!**

**When they are told, 'Follow what Allah has sent down on you,'**

It is generally held that it is the unbelieving Arabs who are being addressed here but Ibn 'Abbās said that it was revealed about the Jews. Aṭ-Ṭabarī said that the pronoun refers back to 'mankind' in the last-but-one *āyah*. Following implies both acceptance and action. 'Follow' is to accept and act accordingly.

**They say, 'We are following what we found our fathers doing.'**

The strength of the expression of this *āyah* would seem, on the surface, to challenge the whole matter of *taqlīd*, which is the acceptance of an inherited position without calling it into question, and there are other *āyah*s which have the same import. This *āyah* and the ones like it, however, are connected to what came before them. That is because Allah informs us about the ignorance of the Arabs in judging by their superstitious customs concerning animals like *baḥīrah*, *sā'ibah* and *waṣīlah*, using as evidence the fact that their fathers did that, and the command to abandon such customs was revealed by Allah to His Messenger.

Some people, however, believe that this *āyah* censures taking the position of *taqlīd* since Allah Almighty censures the unbelievers for following their fathers in falsehood and imitating them in disbelief and disobedience. This is sound where falsehood is concerned. As for *taqliḍ* in respect of the truth, it is one of the principles of the *dīn* and is a protection for the Muslims to which unlearned people who are unqualified to make rulings about matters of the *dīn* should have recourse. Scholars disagree about the permissibility of *taqlīd* in matters of *uṣūl* (basic principles), as will be discussed, but it is universally permitted in respect of secondary rulings.

According to scholars, the reality of *taqlīd* is to accept a position without evidence. Accordingly, someone who accepts the Prophet ﷺ without looking at his miracles would be a *muqallid*. Someone who looks into them would not be. It is said that it is believing in the soundness of the fatwas of someone when the soundness of his position is not known. It is derived from the *qilādah* or halter of the camel, which is when a rope is placed around its neck so that it can be led anywhere.

*Taqlīd* is not a means to knowledge nor does it reach it, either in respect of basic principles or secondary rulings. That is the position of the majority of intelligent people and scholars, as opposed to what is related from the ignorant Ḥashwiyyah and Tha'alibiyyah who claim that *taqlīd* is the sole means to recognise the truth and that it is mandatory, and that investigation and consideration are *ḥarām*.

The obligation for the common person, who is not able to deduce rulings from basic principles because he is not qualified to do so on account of his lack of knowledge of the *dīn*, is to head for the person with the most knowledge in his time and his land and ask him about his problem and follow his *fatwā* since Allah says: '*Ask the people of the Reminder if you do not know.*' (16:43) He uses *ijtihād* in finding the most knowledgeable of the people of his time by investigating until he satisfied that he has found the man whom most people agree to be the most learned. A scholar must also imitate a scholar who has a similar standing to him in a case in which he does not find the solution through evidence and his own investigation. Qāḍī Abū Bakr and a group of established scholars believed that.

Ibn 'Aṭiyyah said, 'The Community agrees that *taqlīd* in respect of articles of faith is invalid.' Others, however, stated that there is disagreement about that, like Qāḍī Abū Bakr ibn 'Arabī and Abū 'Amr 'Uthmān Ibn *Dirbās*. In *al-Intiṣār*, Ibn *Dirbās* said, 'Some people permit *taqlīd* in respect of *tawḥīd*, but this is shown to be wrong by the words of Allah: *"We found our fathers following a religion"* (43:23), so He censured their imitation of their fathers and not following the Messenger, and this is just what the followers of sects do when they imitate their great men and do not follow the *dīn* of Muḥammad ﷺ. It is an obligation for every responsible person to learn *tawḥīd* and proper understanding of it. That can only be obtained through the Book and the Sunnah as we made clear. Allah guides whomever He wills.'

Ibn *Dirbās* also said, 'Many of the people who follow sects say that those who cling to the Book and Sunnah are imitators. This is an error on their part. This designation is more applicable to them, and their scholars are less able since they turn to the position of their masters and great men in their deviation from the Book of Allah and the Sunnah of His Messenger and the consensus of the Companions. So they are included among those whom Allah censures when He says: *"Our Lord, we obeyed our masters and great men..."* (33:67) and: *"We found our fathers following a religion and we are simply following in their footsteps."* (43:23) Then He said to His Prophet ﷺ: *"Say: 'What if I have come with better guidance than what you found your fathers following?' They say, 'We reject what you have been sent with.'"* Then He says to His Prophet ﷺ: *"We took revenge on them."* (43:25)

'So Allah made it clear that guidance lies in what His Messengers brought.

It is not what the people of tradition say in their creed: "We found our imams, fathers and people taking the Book, Sunnah and consensus of the righteous Salaf of the community saying, 'We found our fathers and obeyed our leaders and great men on a path.'" That is because these ascribe that to Revelation and following the Messenger, and those ascribe their lies to the people of falsehoods and are increased in misguidance by that. Do you not see that Allah praised Yūsuf in the Qur'an when he said: *"I have left the religion of a people who do not believe in Allah nor do they have faith in the Next World. I have followed the religion of my forebears, Ibrāhīm, Isḥāq and Ya'qūb. We do not associate anything with Allah. That is part of Allah's favour to us and to all mankind."* (12:37-38) That is because his forefathers were Prophets who followed the Revelation, the pure *Dīn* with which Allah is pleased. Their forefathers' following it is praised. In what they brought, there is no mention of 'non-essentials' being connected to 'substances' and being changed in them. It indicates that there is no guidance in them.'

Ibn al-Ḥaṣṣār said, 'This began to be discussed in the reign of al-Ma'mūn, after 200 AH when the early books were translated and there was disagreement in them about the timelessness or contingency of the world. They disagreed about substance (*jawhar*) and its stability and the non-essential (*'araḍ*) and its quiddity. Innovators, those in whose hearts was deviance, hastened to memorise those technical terms and with them they intended to impose foreign terms on the people of the Sunnah and to engender doubts among the weak people of this religion. This continued until innovation appeared and the innovators became a party. The sultan became confused about these matters until it reached the point where the ruler proclaimed that the Qur'an was created and compelled people to adopt that position and Aḥmad ibn Ḥanbal was beaten to force him to accept it.

'Then men from the people of the Sunnah, such as Shaykh Abu-l-Ḥasan al-Ash'arī, Ibn Kullāb, Ibn Mujāhid, al-Muḥāsibī and their likes, were entrusted with the task restoring the Sunnah and entered into in depth discussions with the innovators using their own technical language. They fought and slew them with their own weapons. Muslims of this community went forward, holding to the Book and the Sunnah, and turned away from the doubts of the heretics, not looking into non-essential and substance. Such were the Salaf.'

Now if someone examines the technical terms of the *mutakallimūn* to the point where he uses that to defend the *dīn*, his position is close to that of the Prophets, but as for those among the extreme *mutakallimūn* who scorn the method of taking traditions from the believers, encourage studying the books of *kalām,* and only know the truth through those technical terms, they are censured for not following the path of earlier imams. Allah knows best. As for disputation and arguing with evidence and proof, that is clear in the Qur'an.

وَمَثَلُ الَّذِينَ كَفَرُوا كَمَثَلِ الَّذِي يَنْعِقُ بِمَا لَا يَسْمَعُ إِلَّا دُعَاءً وَنِدَاءً
صُمٌّ بُكْمٌ عُمْيٌ فَهُمْ لَا يَعْقِلُونَ ﴿١٧١﴾

**171 The likeness of those who disbelieve is that of someone who yells out to something which cannot hear it is nothing but a cry and a call. Deaf – dumb – blind. They do not use their intellect.**

One understanding of this *āyah* is that Allah is making a metaphorical allusion to Muhammad ﷺ who is the warner of the unbelievers and the one who calls them to faith. He is saying that he is like a shepherd who calls out to his sheep and camels, but they only hear his call but do not understand what he says. Ibn 'Abbās, 'Ikrimah, as-Suddī, az-Zajjāj, al-Farrā' and Sībuwayh explained it like that, saying that the unbeliever is not the one who calls out but the one called out to. Ibn Zayd said, 'Those who disbelieve are likened in their calling on their inanimate gods, which do not understand, to someone who calls out in the middle of the night and an echo is the only answer they receive. So he shouts to what does not hear or answer and possesses no reality or benefit.'

Qutrub, however, said, 'The metaphor refers to the unbelievers calling out to something which cannot possibly respond, meaning their idols, likening them to a shepherd who calls out to his sheep when he has no idea where they are.' Aṭ-Ṭabarī says it means that the unbelievers, in calling on their idols, are like people who call out to something which is distant and cannot hear. In these latter interpretations those calling out are the unbelievers and the idols are what they are calling out to. '*Na'īq*' is yelling at sheep to keep them back. One uses the term '*nadā*' for what is far and '*du'ā*'' for what is near. That is why the term '*nadā*' is used for the adhan because it calls to those who are far away.

يَا أَيُّهَا الَّذِينَ آمَنُوا كُلُوا مِنْ طَيِّبَاتِ مَا رَزَقْنَاكُمْ وَاشْكُرُوا لِلَّهِ إِنْ
كُنْتُمْ إِيَّاهُ تَعْبُدُونَ ﴿١٧٢﴾

**172 You who believe! eat of the good things We have provided for you and give thanks to Allah if you worship Him alone.**

This confirms the first command (2:68) which was to mankind in general. The believers are singled out here out of preference and what is meant by 'eating' is consuming things and using them in any way. It is also said that it is eating in the usual sense of the word. In *Ṣaḥīḥ Muslim*, the Messenger of Allah ﷺ said, 'People! Allah is good and only accepts the good. Allah gives the same command to the believers that He gives the Messengers. Allah Almighty says: *"O Messengers, eat of the good things and act rightly. I most certainly know what you do"* (23:51) and He says: *"O you who believe! eat of the good things We have provided for you …* (this *āyah*)"' Then he mentioned a man who goes on a long journey, is dishevelled and dusty and stretches out his hands to heaven saying, 'O Lord! O Lord!' and said, 'When his food is unlawful, his drink is unlawful, his clothes are unlawful, and his whole maintenance is unlawful. How could such a man be responded to?'

إِنَّمَا حَرَّمَ عَلَيْكُمُ ٱلْمَيْتَةَ وَٱلدَّمَ وَلَحْمَ ٱلْخِنزِيرِ وَمَآ أُهِلَّ بِهِۦ لِغَيْرِ ٱللَّهِ ۖ
فَمَنِ ٱضْطُرَّ غَيْرَ بَاغٍ وَلَا عَادٍ فَلَآ إِثْمَ عَلَيْهِ ۚ إِنَّ ٱللَّهَ غَفُورٌ رَّحِيمٌ ﴿١٧٣﴾

**173 He has only forbidden you carrion, blood and pork and what has been consecrated to other than Allah But anyone who is forced to eat it – without desiring it or going to excess in it – commits no crime. Allah is Ever-Forgiving, Most Merciful.**

**He has only forbidden you**

The Arabic expression used here implies limitation and restriction, and so Allah moves from the general permission of the previous *āyah* to what is forbidden in this one. There is no food forbidden beyond this. This is a Madinan *āyah* and it is reinforced by another *āyah* revealed at 'Arafah: *'I do not find in what has been revealed to me, any food it is unlawful to eat except for...'* (6:145) So it is completely clear.

'Carrion' applies to animals, which would normally be slaughtered but which have died without being slaughtered, and to animals which may not be eaten even if they have been slaughtered, such as beasts of prey. This will be examined in more detail when we reach the relevant passage in *Sūrat al-An'ām*.

The *āyah* is general and is qualified by the words of the Prophet ﷺ: 'Two kinds of carrion are lawful for us: fish and locusts; and the blood of the liver and spleen is also lawful.' Ad-Dāraquṭnī transmitted it. This is an instance of a *ḥadīth* qualifying a general instruction in the Qur'an. Most of the people of knowledge permit the eating of all the animals of the sea, alive or dead, and this is the school of Mālik. He hesitated about 'sea pigs' (dolphins) and said, 'You said "pig"!' Ibn al-Qāsim said, 'I am cautious about it but do not think that it is unlawful.'

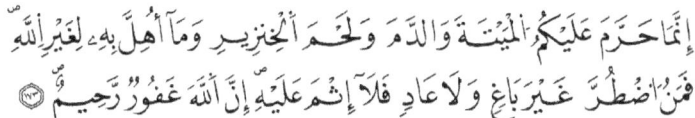

People disagree about the possibility of the Book of Allah being qualified by the Sunnah and they agree that it is not permitted for this to take place if the *ḥadīth* is weak. Ibn al-'Arabī said that. There is evidence that this verse has been qualified by a number of *ḥadīth*s. In *Ṣaḥīḥ Muslim*, 'Abdullāh ibn Abī Wafā said, 'We went on seven expeditions with the Messenger of Allah ﷺ during which we ate locusts.' It is clear that they ate them even though they had died. This is what most scholars including ash-Shāfi'ī and Abū Ḥanīfah say. The Mālikīs say that they should not be eaten if they have been smothered because they are land creatures.

Scholars disagree about using carrion or anything which is impure for purposes other than eating. There are different positions related from Mālik regarding that as well. Once he said that their use was permitted because it is recorded that the Prophet ﷺ passed by a dead sheep and asked, 'Why didn't you take its skin?' Another time he said, 'It is all forbidden and it is not permitted to use any of it nor any other impurity in any way,' so that he did not permit watering crops or animals with impure water or feeding animals things which are impure or even giving them to dogs and other animals. The reason for that is the words of Allah: *'Unlawful for you are carrion and blood.'* (5:3). And the Prophet ﷺ said in another *ḥadīth*, 'Do not use any part of carrion.' According to the *ḥadīth* of 'Abdullāh ibn 'Ukaym, 'Do not use any part of carrion whether the hide or the sinews.'

When a camel, cow or sheep is slaughtered, and there is a foetus inside it, it is permitted to eat the foetus without slaughtering it unless it emerges alive in which case it should be slaughtered. If the foetus emerges dead after the mother has been slaughtered it is considered as one of its limbs. That is clear because it is not permitted to sell an animal excluding her unborn foetus and the foetus follows the mother just as the limbs do. Jābir related that the Prophet ﷺ was asked about a cow, sheep or camel that is slaughtered with a dead foetus inside it. He said, 'Eat it if you wish. Its slaughtering was the slaughtering of its mother.' Abū Dāwud transmitted the same idea from Abū Sa'īd al-Khudrī. It is a definite text.

The transmissions from Mālik vary about whether the skin of carrion is made pure by tanning or not. It is related that it is not, and that is the well-known position of his school, and it is also related that it is pure, based on the words of the Prophet ﷺ, 'Any skin which is tanned is pure.' It is possible that it means that tanning removes external impurities and so it can be used for dry things and for sitting on or for holding water, because water is pure as long as it is not changed in either taste or smell.

The hair and wool of carrion is pure since it is related from Umm Salamah that the Prophet ﷺ said, 'There is no harm in keeping carrion when it is tanned and its wool and hair are washed.' That is because it is pure if it is taken from it while alive, and so the same applies after death, when the flesh is impure, alive or dead. If the flesh is impure when alive, then it is like that after death. So the wool differs in the state of life and death. This is not obliged for milk and the eggs of dead chickens because we believe milk and eggs to be pure after death. They are, however, in an impure vessel and become impure from the proximity of the vessel, not by death.

There are two positions when a mouse falls into something. One position is when the mouse is removed while still alive: then the thing it fell into is pure. If it dies after falling in, there are two possibilities. If it is a liquid, then all of it is impure. If it is solid, then what it is touching is impure. It and what is around it is discarded and the rest can be used since it is pure based on what is related from the Prophet ﷺ when he was asked about a mouse that had fallen into ghee and died. He ﷺ said, 'If it is solid, throw away it and what is around it. If it is liquid, then pour it out.' Scholars disagree about washing such a substance. Some say that it is not purified by washing because it is liquid impurity and so it is like blood, wine, urine and all impurities. Ibn al-Qāsim said that it is purified by washing because it is a substance made impure by proximity to impurity, as is the case with a garment. This is not the case with blood which is impure in itself nor with wine or urine because washing destroys them.

Our ruling that it becomes pure by washing refers to its original state of purity and other aspects of use, but it should not be sold without that being made clear because it is a defect in the eye of people which they dislike. Some believe that it is unlawful and impure and so it is not permitted to sell it until the defect has been made clear as is the case with other defective items. It is not permitted to sell it at all before it has been washed because it is not permitted to sell impure things, and because it is then an impure liquid like wine, and because the Prophet ﷺ was asked about the price for wine and said, 'Allah cursed the Jews. Fat was made unlawful for them and so they collected it and sold it and consulted its price.' When Allah makes something unlawful, He makes its price unlawful. This liquid is unlawful because it is impure and so its price follows the same ruling.

There is disagreement about when something falls into a pot, flying or not, and then dies. Ibn Wahb related that Mālik said that what is in the pot may not be eaten and is impure since it is mixed with what has died in it. It is related from Ibn al-Qāsim that any meat should washed and the broth poured out. Ibn 'Abbās was asked about this and said that the meat is washed and eaten. There is no disagreement among his people about the broth. Ibn Khuwayzimandād mentioned it.

As for the rennet from carrion and milk from carrion, ash-Shāfi'ī says that it is impure because Allah's words are general: *'Unlawful for you are carrion...'* (5:3) Abū Ḥanīfah said that they are pure, saying that the impurity of a source has no effect on what is around it. He said, 'That is why meat is eaten along with its veins in spite of the proximity of blood without requiring purification or washing.' Mālik's view is similar to that of Abū Ḥanīfah: it does not become impure by the fact of its death but by the proximity of the impure vessel. It is something which cannot be washed. The same is true of eggs which emerge from a chicken after death because the egg is soft like a liquid before it comes out and becomes hard by exposure to the air.

Ibn Khuwayzimandād said: 'If it is said that your view leads to what is contrary to consensus, that is because the Prophet ﷺ and the Muslims after him used to eat cheese which was brought to them from foreign lands, and it was known that animals slaughtered by the Magians are carrion, and they did not consider whether it was from carrion or correctly slaughtered animals. Very little of the rennet is used in milk made into cheese and a small amount of impurity is ignored when it is mixed with a lot liquid. This is one answer. The other answer is that that occurred at the beginning of Islam and none of the Companions was able to change the eating of cheese from Persia. Cheese is not part of the food of the Arabs. When the Muslims spread in the territory of the non-Arabs by conquest, they did their own slaughtering. This is why the Prophet ﷺ and the Companions ate cheese brought from the land of the non-Arabs and made from the rennet of their slaughtered animals.'

Abū 'Umar said, 'There is nothing wrong in eating the food of idolaters, Magians and other unbelievers who have no Scripture as long as it is not from their slaughtered animals, except in the case of cheese that may contain the rennet of carrion. We find in the *Sunan* of Ibn Mājah about cheese and ghee from Ismā'īl ibn Mūsā as-Suddī from Sayf ibn Hārūn from Sulaymān at-Taymī from Abū 'Uthmān an-Nahdī that Salmān al-Fārisī said, 'The Messenger of Allah ﷺ was asked about ghee, cheese and wild donkeys. He answered, "The lawful is what Allah has made lawful in His Book. The unlawful is what Allah has made unlawful in His Book. What He remained silent about is excused."'

**blood**

Scholars agree that blood is unlawful and impure and may not be eaten or used. Ibn Khuwayzimandād said, 'Blood is unlawful except what is unavoidable and what is unavoidable is excused. That which is unavoidable is the blood in meat and veins, and a small amount on the body and clothing in which one prays. We have said that because the Almighty says: "*Unlawful for you are carrion, blood...*" (5:3) and elsewhere: "Say: '*I do not find in what has revealed to me, any food it is unlawful to eat except for carrion, flowing blood...*'" (6:145) What is forbidden is blood that is spilled.' 'Ā'ishah said, 'We used to cook a dish in the time of the Messenger of Allah ﷺ and it had a yellow colour from the blood but we ate it without dislike.' Otherwise that would entail undue hardship. This is a basic principle in the Law: whenever the community is harmed and overly burdened by performing an act of worship, that is cancelled for them. Do you not see that someone may eat carrion when forced to out of necessity, a sick person may break the fast and do *tayammum*, and the like?

In this *āyah* Allah forbids blood without qualification and then He qualifies it in *al-An'ām* (6:145) by the word 'flowing' (*masfūḥ*). Scholars agree that this qualifies what is unqualified, and the blood meant is that which is spilled out and not that which is mixed with the flesh which, by consensus, is not forbidden. That is also the case with the liver and spleen. There is disagreement about fish blood which is separated from it. Al-Qābisī related that it is pure and continues to be pure, and that is also said by Ibn al-'Arabī. He said, 'If fish blood had been impure, it would have been prescribed to slaughter them.' Abū Ḥanīfah takes the same view. I heard one of the Ḥanafīs say that the evidence for its purity is that when it is dried, it is white whereas other blood is black. This is a point that they use in their argument against the Shāfi'īs.

**and pork**

Allah mentions the meat of pigs to indicate that it is forbidden, whether slaughtered or not. It includes the fat, gristle and all other parts. The Community agree that the fat of pigs is forbidden. Mālik and his people used as evidence that if someone who swears not to eat fat then eats meat, he has not broken his oath, but if he swears not to eat meat and then eats fat, he has broken his oath because fat is included with meat. Allah made fat unlawful to the tribe of Israel (6:146) but that did not make the meat unlawful. This is the basis for the distinction that Mālik made. According to the view of ash-Shāfi'ī, Abū Thawr and the people of opinion, if someone swears not to eat meat and then eats fat, he has not broken his oath. Aḥmad said that if he swears not to eat meat and then eats fat, there is no harm unless he intended to also avoid fats.

There is no disagreement that all of the pig is forbidden except for the bristles which can be used for stitching. It is reported that a man asked the Messenger of Allah ﷺ about stitching with pig bristle and he said, 'There is no harm in it.' Ibn

Khuwayzimandād mentioned it and said, 'That is because stitching was done in the time of the Messenger of Allah ﷺ and clearly existed after him. We do not know that the Messenger of Allah ﷺ or any of the imams after him objected to it. When the Messenger ﷺ allows something, it is as if it were prescribed from him.

There is no disagreement that pigs on land are unlawful as we mentioned. There is, however, disagreement about 'sea pigs' (dolphins). Mālik refused to give any answer about it and said, 'You said "pigs"!' It will be dealt with in *Sūrat al-Mā'idah*.

**and what has been consecrated to other than Allah.**

This is something over which other than the Name of Allah was mentioned when it was slaughtered. It refers to the slaughtering done by Magians, idol-worshippers and atheists. The idol worshipper sacrifices to an idol, the Magian to the fire, and the atheist, who does not believe anything, slaughters for himself. There is no disagreement among the scholars that whatever a Magian or idol-worshipper slaughters to their idol or fire may not be eaten. According to Mālik, ash-Shāfi'ī and others, what such people sacrifice to the fire or idol may not be eaten at all. Ibn al-Musayyab and Abū Thawr, however, permit that meat be eaten if it is slaughtered for a Muslim at his order. This will explained in more detail in *Sūrat al-Mā'idah*.

The word 'consecration' (*uhilla*) means 'to raise the voice'. It is used for the cry of a newborn baby. Ibn 'Abbās said, 'What is meant is what is sacrificed to idols and stones.' The custom of the Arabs was to shout the name of the one intended by the sacrifice. That was their usual practice and so it is considered to be tantamount to the intention of consecration. Do you not see that when Ghālib, the father of al-Farazdaq, slaughtered camels, 'Alī ibn Abī Ṭālib observed the intention and said, 'It is part of what is consecrated to other than Allah'? People left it. Ibn 'Aṭiyyah said, 'In the reports of al-Ḥasan ibn Abī 'l-Ḥasan, I saw that he was asked about an opulent woman who prepared a wedding for her amusement and slaughtered a camel. Al-Ḥasan said, "It is not lawful to eat it. It was slaughtered to an idol."'

Connected to this is what we related from Yaḥyā ibn Yaḥyā at-Tamīmī, the Shaykh of Muslim, from Jarīr that Qābūs said, 'A woman sent me to 'Ā'ishah and said to greet her and ask her which prayer the Messenger of Allah ﷺ liked best to persevere in. She answered, "He used to pray four *rak'ah*s before *Ẓuhr* in which he stood for a long time and did excellent bowing and prostration. As for what he never omitted, whether healthy or ill, resident or traveling, that was the two *rak'ah*s before the Morning Prayer." At that a woman from the people said, "Mother of the Believers, we have a nurse from the Persians and they give us gifts on their festivals. Can we eat any of it?" She answered, "As for the meat slaughtered in the name of that day, do not eat it, but you can eat of the fruit of their trees."'

**But anyone who is forced to eat it –**

'Anyone who is forced' means 'compelled by need.' It is Form VIII from '*ḍarūrah*' (necessity). Forcing can be either by physical force exerted by a wrongdoer or compulsion due to extreme hunger. That is the position of most *fuqahā'* and scholars regarding the meaning of the *āyah*: that it is someone who is compelled by need and hunger to do that. That is the sound position. It is said that it means that he is forced to eat forbidden things. Mujāhid said, 'Someone can be physically forced when he is captured by the enemy and forced to eat pork and other things in disobedience to Allah. If someone is physically forced by someone to eat something unlawful, that renders it lawful for him for the duration of the time that the force is being applied.'

Hunger can be either persistent or not. If it is persistent, there is no disagreement that it is permitted to eat one's fill of carrion. If someone is suffering from hunger and finds the property of a Muslim, the value of which is not sufficient to cause his hand to be cut off for theft and will cause no annoyance to the owner, such as some dates hanging from a tree, a sheep astray in the mountains and the like, it is not lawful for him to then eat carrion. There is no disagreement about this because of the *ḥadīth* reported by Abū Hurayrah who said, 'Once, when we were with the Messenger of Allah ﷺ on a journey we saw some camels tied to the branches of some trees. We went to them but the Messenger of Allah called to us and we returned to him. He said, "These camels belong to people from a Muslim house. After Allah, it is their strength and fortune. Would you like to return to your bags of provisions and find them gone? Do you think that that would be fair?" "No," we replied. He said, "This is the same situation." We asked, "And if we need food and drink?" He said, "Eat but do not take anything away with you. Drink but do not take anything away with you."' Ibn Mājah transmitted it. Ibn Mājah said, 'I believe this to be the basic principle.'

Ibn al-Mundhir said, 'We asked, "Messenger of Allah, what is lawful for someone to take from his brother's property if he is compelled by hunger?" He replied, "He should eat but not take anything away, and drink but not take anything away."' Ibn al-Mundhir said, 'After that, everyone who disagrees about that is referred to Allah's prohibition of property.'

Abū 'Umar said, 'The predominant position is that it is incumbent on a Muslim to preserve the life of another Muslim. It is an individual obligation for him unless someone else takes care of it. He can fight the one who refuses to allow him to do that, even if that might prove fatal. According to the people of knowledge, that is the case if he is the only one available. Then it is an individual obligation for him. If there are several of them or a group, then that is a group (*kifāyah*) obligation for them. Water in that and other cases is what one can take from another. They do, however, disagree about the obligation of paying for the thing which will save his life. Some make it obligatory and others do not. Both views are found in our School. There is no disagreement among the people of knowledge, past and present, about the obligation of saving life through something insignificant, which is no loss to the owner, when it is feared that someone will die.'

Ibn Mājah transmitted from Abū Bakr ibn Abī Shaybah from Shabbābah, and Muḥammad ibn Bashshār and Muḥammad ibn Ja'far from Shu'bah from Abū Bishr Ja'far ibn Iyās who heard 'Abbād ibn Sharaḥbīl, a man of the Banu Ghubar, say, 'We suffered in the year of the famine and I came to Madīnah and went to one of its gardens and took an ear of corn, ground it, ate some and put some in my garment. The owner came and beat me and took the garment. I went to the Messenger of Allah ﷺ and told him. He told the man, "Why did you not feed him when he was hungry or starving? Why did you not teach him since he was ignorant?" He commanded him to return the man's garment to him and ordered a *wasq* or half a *wasq* of food for him.'

This is a sound *ḥadīth* whose men are agreed upon by Bukhārī and Muslim except for Ibn Abī Shaybah whom only Muslim has. Neither Bukhārī nor Muslim transmit anything from 'Abbād ibn Sharaḥbīl al-Ghubarī al-Yashkurī. The only thing from him is this story from the Prophet ﷺ according to Abū 'Umar. It negates cutting off the hand and demonstrates the proper behavior in case of famine.

Abū Dāwud transmitted from Samurah that the Prophet ﷺ said, 'When one of you comes to a flock and the owner is there, he should ask his permission to milk and drink. If no one is there, he should shout three times. If the person comes, he asks permission. If not, he may milk a ewe and drink but may not take anything with him.' At-TIrmidhī mentioned from Yaḥyā ibn Sulaym from 'Ubaydullāh from Nāfi' from Ibn 'Umar that the Prophet ﷺ said, 'If someone enters a garden, he can eat but not take any food away.' He said that this is a *gharīb ḥadīth* which we only know from Yaḥyā ibn Sulaym. He mentioned from 'Amr ibn Shu'ayb from his father from his grandfather that the Prophet ﷺ was asked about hanging fruit and he said, 'If someone takes what he needs (from hanging fruit) and does not take any away, he has done nothing wrong.' He said that it is a *ḥasan ḥadīth*. 'Umar said, 'When one of you goes past a garden, he can eat but not take any away in a container.' The term used for this refers to something in which a person carries something in but it includes carrying something in one's hands or on one's back. Abū 'Ubayd said, 'This *ḥadīth* means that there is an allowance for someone who is compelled by hunger and has nothing with which to purchase food, but he may only carry away what is in his stomach.'

The fundamental principle which is agreed upon regarding this is that the property of other people is forbidden unless they are content to let it be used. That was a custom that was followed in the beginning of Islam and that now exists in some countries. Then it is permitted. That is also applied in times of hunger and dire need as we already stated. Allah knows best.

If the second case exists at a certain time, scholars have two different views about it. One is that someone may eat carrion until he is full and he is permitted to take provision from it if he fears need ahead in a desert or wasteland. When he later finds enough to eat, he must discard the carrion. That is the sense of what Mālik said in the *Muwaṭṭā'*. Ash-Shāfi'ī and most scholars say that. The proof for that is the principle that necessity removes the prohibition and so that which was forbidden becomes allowed. The extent of what amounts to need is a state of lack of food. That exists until there is food available. The *ḥadīth* about the whale provides textual evidence for that. When the Companions of the Prophet ﷺ returned from a journey and their provision had run out, they went to the sea coast and there rose before them on the coast something like an enormous mound. When they reached it, it was a beast called a whale. Abū 'Ubaydah, the commander, said, 'Carrion.' Then he said, 'No, we are the messengers of the Messenger of Allah ﷺ and are in the Cause of Allah. You are in need. Therefore eat.' He [Jābir] said, 'We, being three hundred, stayed with it for a month until we were plump.' So they ate and were filled from what they believed to be carrion and took provision from it until they reached Madīnah. They mentioned that to the Messenger of Allah ﷺ and he told them that it was lawful. He asked, 'Do you have any of its meat with you so that you can give it to us to eat?' They sent some of it to the Messenger of Allah ﷺ and he ate it.

One group say that you should eat as much as is needed to sustain life. That is the position of Ibn al-Mājishūn and Ibn Ḥabīb. The people of ash-Shāfi'ī distinguish between the state of someone resident and someone travelling. They said that someone resident should eat only that amount that will sustain his life. A traveller, however, may have his fill and take provision. Then, when he finds food, he must discard the carrion. If he finds someone else in need, he should give it to him without seeking recompense. It is not permitted to sell carrion.

If someone is physically forced to drink wine, he may drink it without dispute, but if it is on account of hunger or thirst, he should not do so. That is what Mālik said according to *al-'Utbiyyah*. Wine only increases thirst. That is the position of ash-Shāfi'ī. Allah completely prohibited wine but prohibited carrion provided that there is no dire necessity. Al-Abharī says, 'If wine will remove hunger or thirst from someone, he should drink it because Allah says that pigs are impure but then permits them in case of necessity. Allah calls wine an impurity and it should be included, in necessity, under the same permission as that of pigs, going by the apparent meaning which is stronger than using analogy. There must be quenching, even if only for an instant, and repelling hunger, even if it is only for a short time.'

Aṣbagh related that Ibn al-Qāsim said, 'Someone in dire need may drink blood but not wine. He may eat carrion but not take advantage of lost camels.' Ibn Wahb also said that. He may drink urine but should not go near wine because the *ḥadd* punishment is obliged for it and so, because of this, the prohibition is stronger. That is the correct position for the people of ash-Shāfi'ī.

If someone chokes on food, is drinking wine allowed to relieve it or not? It is said that it is not, out of the fear that people will simply use that as an excuse. Ibn Ḥabīb claims that it is permitted in that instance because it is a case of necessity. Ibn al-'Arabī said, 'Someone who chokes on something is permitted to do that in respect of what is between him and Allah. As for what is between him and us, if we see him the circumstances are not hidden from us, in that we can see that he is choking on something, and so he is believed if he shows those symptoms. If he does not show them, he is given the *ḥadd* punishment outwardly but is safe from the punishment of Allah inwardly if it really was the case.'

If someone who is in dire need finds carrion, pork and human flesh, he may eat the carrion, because it is lawful for him in that one situation, whereas pork and human flesh never are, and so it is better to go for the lesser prohibition. Similarly, if someone is forced to have sexual intercourse with either his sister or an unrelated woman, he should choose the unrelated woman. This is the rule in respect of these judgments. He should never eat human flesh, even if that results in his death. Our scholars said that and Aḥmad ibn Ḥanbal and Dāwud related that. The evidence of Aḥmad is the words of the Prophet ﷺ: 'Breaking the bones of a corpse is like breaking them when the person is alive.' Ash-Shāfi'ī says that he should. It is not permitted to kill a *dhimmī* because his life is respected, or a Muslim or a captive, because he is someone else's property. If he is from the abode of war or a *muḥṣan* fornicator, it is permitted to kill him and eat his flesh. Dāwud objected to al-Muzanī saying that and said, 'He permits eating the flesh of Prophets!' Ibn Shurayḥ overcame him by saying, 'You risk killing Prophets when you forbade them to kill unbelievers.' Ibn al-'Arabī said, 'What I consider to be sound is that a human being may only be eaten when it is absolutely certain that doing that will save a person's life.' Allah knows best.

Mālik was asked about someone compelled to eat carrion, who then finds property belonging to someone else in the form of dates, crops or sheep. He said, 'If he is safe from harm to his body, in that he will not be considered a thief, and he will be believed if he says that he only ate that to assuage his hunger and did not take any of it with him, then I prefer that to eating carrion.' This has already been dealt with. If he fears that he will not believed and that he will be considered to be a thief, then it is more permissible to eat the carrion in my view. In this case there is scope for eating carrion.

Abū Dāwud related from Mūsā ibn Ismā'īl from Ḥammād from Simāk ibn Ḥarb from Jābir ibn Samurah that a man camped in the Ḥarrah with his wife and children. A man said, 'One of my camels has got lost. If you find it, keep it [for me]. He found it but did not find its owner. Then it became ill and his wife said, 'Slaughter it.' He refused and it died. She said, 'Skin it and we can cut its meat and fat into strips and eat it.' He said, 'Not until I ask the Messenger of Allah ﷺ.' He asked him and he said, 'Do you have what is enough for you?' 'No,' he replied. He said, 'Then eat it.' Its owner came and he told him what had happened and he said, 'Why didn't you slaughter it?' He answered, 'I was embarrassed because of what you said to me.'

Ibn Khuwayzimandād said, 'There are two proofs in this *āyah*. One is that someone who is in need can eat carrion, even if he does not fear dying from hunger, because the question is about sufficiency and not about fearing for your life. The second is that he can eat, be filled, store and take provision because there is permission to store it and no stipulation about merely having your fill.'

Abū Dāwud said, 'Hārūn ibn 'Abdullāh related from al-Fadl ibn Dukayn that 'Uqbah ibn Wahb ibn 'Uqbah al-'Āmirī heard his father relate that al-Fukay' al-'Āmirī went to the Messenger of Allah ﷺ and asked, 'What carrion is lawful for us?' He asked, 'What is your usual food?' He said, 'A drink [of milk] in the evening (*ghabūq*) and another in the morning. (*ṣabūḥ*).' Abū Nu'aym said that 'Uqbah explained it as a cup of milk in the morning and one in the evening. The Prophet ﷺ said, 'This does not relieve hunger,' and continued, 'He made carrion lawful for them in this situation.' Abū Dāwud said, '*Gabūq* is at the end of the day and *ṣabūḥ* is at the beginning of the day.' Al-Khaṭṭābī said, '*Gabūq* is evening and *ṣabūḥ* is morning. A cup of milk in the morning and a cup in the evening keep one alive and upright even though the body is not fully nourished or satisfied. In that day they were permitted to use carrion. So it proves that it is permitted to consume carrion until someone has the nourishment they need.' This is what Mālik believed and it is one of the two positions of ash-Shāfi'ī. Ibn Khuwayzimandād said, 'If it is permitted when they have a drink of milk morning and evening, then it is permitted to have one's fill and take provision from it.' Abū Ḥanīfah, and ash-Shāfi'ī in another view, said, 'A person is only permitted to use that amount of carrion that will keep them alive.' That is what al-Muzanī believed. They said: 'That is because if someone was in this state in the first place, he would not be permitted to eat any of it; so that is also the situation after he has obtained it.' Qatādah said, 'He should not carry any of it away.' Muqātil ibn Ḥayyān said, 'He should not seek any provision beyond three morsels.' The sound position differs from this as was already stated.

As for using any of these things for medical treatment, either in their original form or burned, Ibn Ḥabīb says that they are only permitted for medicinal use if they are altered by burning. Ibn al-Mājishūn said that burning purifies since it changes the character of the substance (as in burned bones). It is related in *al-'Utibiyyah* that Mālik said that when *marthak*, which is made from the bones of carrion and then placed on wounds, is used, the person using it should not pray until he has washed it off. Saḥnūn said that carrion or pig should never be used for medicinal purposes since something else which is lawful can be used. This is not the case with hunger. If there is a possible replacement for carrion, when it is to assuage hunger, then the carrion should not be used.

Wine may not be used for medicinal use either, as Mālik stated, and that is also the predominant position of ash-Shāfi'ī. That was preferred by Ibn Abī Hurayrah and his people. Abū Ḥanīfah said that it is permitted to drink it for medicinal purposes but not to assuage thirst. That is preferred by Qāḍī aṭ-Ṭabarī among the people of ash-Shāfi'ī. It is also the view of ath-Thawrī. Some of the Shāfi'ī Baghdādīs say that it is permitted to drink it to assuage thirst but not for medicinal purposes because the harm from thirst is immediate which is not the case with medicinal use. It is also said that it is permitted to drink it for both reasons.

Some of the Shāfi'īs forbid using anything unlawful for medicinal reasons except for camel's urine, whose use is found in the *ḥadīth* of the 'Uranīs. Some people forbid using anything unlawful for medicine, quoting the Prophet's words, 'Allah did not put the treatment of my community in something He made forbidden for them.' When Ṭāriq ibn Suwayd asked the Prophet ﷺ about using wine for medicine and he forbade or disliked the use of it. Ṭāriq said, 'But I am using it for medicine.' His answer was: 'It is not a remedy; it is an illness.' Muslim transmitted this in the *Ṣaḥīḥ*. It is possible that this is limited to necessity and it is permitted to use poison for medicine, but not to drink it. Allah knows best.

**without desiring it or going to excess in it –**

According to Qatādah, al-Ḥasan, ar-Rabī', Ibn Zayd and 'Ikrimah it means: 'without desiring to eat more than what is needed of it' and '*...or going to excess in it'* is eating it in spite of there being a substitute for it. As-Suddī said that it is without having an appetite for it or taking pleasure in it, and excess is by eating beyond taking what is necessary to satisfy one's hunger. Mujāhid, Ibn Jubayr and others said that it means 'not attacking or transgressing against the Muslims and so the *bāghī* and *'ādī* here are considered to be highwaymen, those who rebel against the ruler, travellers who cut off ties of kinship, those who raid the Muslims and others.' This is sound.

The basic linguistic meaning of the word for going to excess, *baghī*, is to aim for and intend corruption. The verb is used of a woman who is dissolute as in 24:33. Sometimes it is used for seeking something other than corruption.

The root of *'ādī* is *'a'id* and it is one of the words in which there has been a reversal. The basic ruling in this matter, as we have made clear, is that Allah permits, in the case of necessity, the consumption of all forbidden things if there is no possibility of obtaining permitted things.

Scholars disagree about what the ruling is if criminal acts of disobedience lead to such a state of necessity, such as highway robbery or causing alarm to people in other ways. Mālik, and ash-Shāfi'ī in one of his positions, forbade using the general permission to cover such acts because Allah made the dispensation in order to help us, and it is not lawful to help a rebel. If he wants to eat, let him repent and eat. Abū Ḥanīfah, and ash-Shāfi'ī in another position, allow it. They consider the permission to be the same. Ibn al-'Arabī said, 'It is a wonder that someone permits that while the person is persisting in disobedience. I do not think that anyone says that. If someone does say it, it is a definite error.'

The sound view differs from this. Destroying a man on a journey in which he is being disobedient to Allah is worse disobedience than that in which he is involved. Allah Almighty says: *'Do not kill yourselves.'* (4:29) This is undefined. Perhaps he may repent later and his repentance will efface what went before. Masrūq said, 'If someone needs to eat carrion, blood, and pork, and then does not eat it and dies as a consequence, he will enter the Fire unless Allah pardons him.'

Abu-l-Ḥasan aṭ-Ṭabarī said, 'Eating carrion in necessity is a dispensation but in his case becomes mandatory. If he refuses to eat the carrion, he becomes a rebel. Using carrion is not a dispensation connected to travelling, but is a consequence of necessity, whether someone is travelling or resident. It is like a rebel who is a resident breaking his fast due to illness or like a rebel who is travelling and who does *tayammum* because of the lack of water.' He said, 'I consider it to be sound.

There are different transmissions from Mālik about that. According to what al-Bājī mentioned in *al-Muntaqā,* it is well known in his school that it is permitted for someone to eat carrion on a journey that entails disobedience to Allah, but it is not permitted for him to shorten the prayer or break the fast. Ibn Khuwayzimandād said, 'In respect of eating carrion due to necessity, those who are obedient and those who are disobedient are the same, because it is permitted to use carrion [out of necessity] both on a journey and while resident. Someone who departs in disobedience does not have the ruling of a resident person cancelled in his case. His situation is worse than being resident. That is not the case with breaking the fast and shortening the prayer since they are indulgences connected to travel. When the journey is one that involves disobedience, then he is not permitted to shorten the prayer in it since the indulgence is particularly connected to the journey itself. That is why we say that he can do *tayammum* when he has no water during a journey of disobedience because *tayammum* is the same for a resident and a traveller. So how can it be possible to forbid him to eat carrion and do *tayammum* on account of disobedience, when not eating it would lead to death, which is the greatest form of disobedience, and not doing *tayammum* would lead to abandoning the prayer? Is it permitted to say that because he has committed disobedience he should commit more disobedience? Is it permitted to tell someone who drinks wine that he should also fornicate, or tell a fornicator that he should also disbelieve? Should one tell them to abandon the prayer?' He mentioned all of this in his *Aḥkām al-Qur'ān* and he did not say anything different from that coming from Mālik or any of his people.

Al-Bājī said, 'Ziyād ibn 'Abd ar-Raḥmān al-Andalusī said that someone who is disobedient on a journey should shorten the prayer and break the fast in Ramadan. He considers all of that to be the same. That is also the position of Abū Ḥanīfah. There is no disagreement that he is not permitted to kill himself by not eating [carrion] and that he is commanded to eat it as an obligation. If someone is on a journey for a disobedient purpose, the obligations and duties of the prayer and fasting are not cancelled for him. He is commanded to perform them. That is as we have mentioned. The meaning behind the first view is that these precepts are permitted on journeys when people are in need of them. One is not, however, permitted to use them to facilitate disobedience. He has a way to avoid killing himself.'

Ibn Ḥabīb said, 'That is so that he can repent. Then he uses the carrion after his repentance.' Ibn Ḥabīb connected that to Allah's words: '*...without desiring it or going to excess in it.*' So he stipulated that the permission to use carrion is dependent on not being *bāghī*. A traveller who is involved in brigandage, highway robbery or severing tires of kingship is '*bāghī*' and going to excess and therefore does not possess the precondition for its being allowed.

This is a deduction based on an understanding which differs from what those who understand fundamental principles believe. The construction of the *āyah* means that the one who is forced does not desire it and is not going to excess and therefore commits no sin in that respect. Allah is silent about others. The basic principle is that it is undefined. If someone claims that a matter is removed then he must offer proof.

**Allah is Ever-Forgiving, Most Merciful.**

Allah forgives acts of disobedience and so He is more likely to forgive something He has given dispensation for. Part of His mercy is to grant dispensations.

إِنَّ الَّذِينَ يَكْتُمُونَ مَا أَنزَلَ اللَّهُ مِنَ الْكِتَابِ وَيَشْتَرُونَ بِهِ ثَمَنًا قَلِيلًا
أُولَٰئِكَ مَا يَأْكُلُونَ فِي بُطُونِهِمْ إِلَّا النَّارَ وَلَا يُكَلِّمُهُمُ اللَّهُ يَوْمَ
الْقِيَامَةِ وَلَا يُزَكِّيهِمْ وَلَهُمْ عَذَابٌ أَلِيمٌ ﴿١٧٤﴾

**174 Those who conceal what Allah has sent down of the Book and sell it cheap, take nothing into their bellies but the Fire. On the Day of Rising Allah will not speak to them or purify them. They will have a painful punishment.**

**Those who conceal what Allah has sent down of the Book**

These are the Jewish scholars who concealed the part of the Torah Allah revealed containing the description of Muḥammad ﷺ and the truth of his Message. The word '*anzala*' (sent down) here means 'disclosed' as in 6:93. It is also said that it means 'revealed', which is its usual meaning.

**and sell it cheap,**

They do this by accepting bribes. The word 'cheap' is used because what they receive will soon disappear and its result is evil. It is also said to mean that the amount of the bribe was small.

**take nothing into their bellies but the Fire.**

This indicates the reality of the consumption since the metaphor of actual eating is used. The use of the word 'bellies' also alludes to their greed and the fact that they have sold the Next World for their portion of food in this one. The fact that they will go to the Fire is because they consumed something which is unlawful and for which Allah will, therefore, punish them. Consuming a bribe is called 'fire' because it leads to the Fire. That is what most commentators say. It is said that it is literally fire in their bellies that they will consume as a punishment.

**On the Day of Rising Allah will not speak to them**

This denotes Allah's anger with them and the removal of His pleasure from them. When someone is angry with someone it is said that he does not speak to him. Aṭ-Ṭabarī said that it means that He will not speak to them saying what they love to hear. We find in the Revelation: *'Slink away into it and do not speak to Me.'* (23:108) It is said that it means He will not send them angels with greeting.

**or purify them.**

This means that Allah will not rectify their wrong actions and so purify them. Az-Zajjāj says, 'He will not praise them or call them pure.' In *Ṣaḥīḥ Muslim*, Abū Hurayrah reported that the Messenger of Allah ﷺ said, 'There are three people that Allah will not speak to on the Day of Rising, or purify, or look at, and they will have a painful punishment: an aged adulterer, a lying ruler and a poor person who is arrogant.' These are singled out for painful punishment and intense torment for pure obstinacy in wrong action and making light of the things which move them to commit these acts of disobedience, since need did not instigate them to do these things nor did necessity bring them to do them, as might be the case with others. In the *ḥadīth* 'He will not look at them,' it means that He will not show them mercy or be kind to them.

أُولَٰئِكَ الَّذِينَ اشْتَرَوُا الضَّلَالَةَ بِالْهُدَىٰ وَالْعَذَابَ
بِالْمَغْفِرَةِ ۚ فَمَا أَصْبَرَهُمْ عَلَى النَّارِ ﴿١٧٥﴾

**175 Those are the ones who have sold guidance for misguidance and forgiveness for punishment. How steadfastly they will endure the Fire!**

Punishment follows misguidance as forgiveness follows the guidance that they have cast aside. 'Selling' is used metaphorically.

#### How steadfastly they will endure the Fire!

Most commentators, including al-Ḥasan and Mujāhid, say that the particle *mā* in this phrase is used to connote wonder and refers to creatures. It is as if Allah were saying, 'They wonder at how steadfast they are in remaining in the Fire!' This is the meaning which Abū 'Alī accepts. Al-Ḥasan Qatādah, Ibn Jubayr and ar-Rabī' said, 'They do not have, by Allah, any steadfastness, but how bold they are towards people!' It is a known Yemeni dialectical form. It is said that it means 'How bold they are in actions which bring them to the Fire!' since they do actions which lead them to the Fire. Az-Zajjāj says that it refers to the great length of time they will remain in the Fire as you say, 'How steadfastly he endures imprisonment!' That means that he remains in it for a long time. It is said that it means: 'How little anxiety they display concerning the Fire!' and so their lack of concern is steadfastness. Al-Kisā'ī and Quṭrub said, 'How long they persist in the actions of the people of the Fire!' It is also said that *mā* is interrogative and rebuke is intended by it. Ibn 'Abbās, as-Suddī, 'Aṭā', and Abū 'Ubaydah Ma'mar ibn al-Muthannā said that. It means: 'What makes them steadfast in doing the actions of the people of the Fire?' It is said that this is to humiliate then and make light of them.

ذَٰلِكَ بِأَنَّ ٱللَّهَ نَزَّلَ ٱلْكِتَٰبَ بِٱلْحَقِّ ۗ وَإِنَّ ٱلَّذِينَ ٱخْتَلَفُوا۟ فِى
ٱلْكِتَٰبِ لَفِى شِقَاقٍۭ بَعِيدٍ ﴿١٧٦﴾

**176 That is because Allah has sent down the Book with truth and those who differ from the Book are entrenched in hostility.**

#### That is because Allah has sent down the Book with truth

'That' means 'that judgment', as if Allah were saying, 'The judgment of the Fire.' Az-Zajjāj said, 'It implies: "The matter is that" or "That is the matter" or "That is the punishment they will have."' The first 'Book' is the Qur'an. 'Truth' here means evidence or truthfulness.

#### and those who differ from the Book

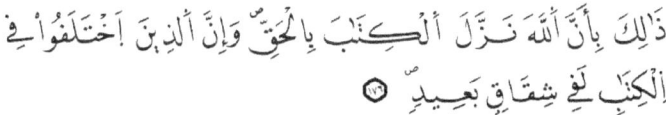

The 'Book' referred to here is the Torah. The Christians claim that it mentioned Jesus and the Jews denied that. It is said that their ancestors disagreed about holding to it. It is said that they disagree about what was in the Torah regarding the description of Muḥammad ﷺ and differed about that. It is said that the Qur'an is meant and those who differed from it were the unbelievers of Quraysh when some of them said that it was magic, others said that it was nothing but ancient myths, and still others said that it was forged. The meaning of 'hostility' was mentioned in the commentary on 2:137.

$$\text{لَيْسَ ٱلْبِرَّ أَن تُوَلُّواْ وُجُوهَكُمْ قِبَلَ ٱلْمَشْرِقِ وَٱلْمَغْرِبِ وَلَٰكِنَّ ٱلْبِرَّ مَنْ ءَامَنَ بِٱللَّهِ وَٱلْيَوْمِ ٱلْءَاخِرِ وَٱلْمَلَٰٓئِكَةِ وَٱلْكِتَٰبِ وَٱلنَّبِيِّـۧنَ وَءَاتَى ٱلْمَالَ عَلَىٰ حُبِّهِۦ ذَوِى ٱلْقُرْبَىٰ وَٱلْيَتَٰمَىٰ وَٱلْمَسَٰكِينَ وَٱبْنَ ٱلسَّبِيلِ وَٱلسَّآئِلِينَ وَفِى ٱلرِّقَابِ وَأَقَامَ ٱلصَّلَوٰةَ وَءَاتَى ٱلزَّكَوٰةَ وَٱلْمُوفُونَ بِعَهْدِهِمْ إِذَا عَٰهَدُواْ وَٱلصَّٰبِرِينَ فِى ٱلْبَأْسَآءِ وَٱلضَّرَّآءِ وَحِينَ ٱلْبَأْسِ أُوْلَٰٓئِكَ ٱلَّذِينَ صَدَقُواْ وَأُوْلَٰٓئِكَ هُمُ ٱلْمُتَّقُونَ ۝}$$

**177 True goodness does not lie in turning your faces to the East or to the West. Rather, those with true goodness are those who believe in Allah and the Last Day, the Angels, the Book and the Prophets, and who, despite their love for it, give away their wealth to their relatives and to orphans and the very poor, and to travellers and beggars and to set slaves free, and who establish the prayer and pay zakat; those who honour their contracts when they make them, and are steadfast in poverty and illness and in battle. Those are the people who are true. They are the people who are godfearing.**

**True goodness does not lie in turning your faces to the East or to the West.**

There is disagreement about who is being addressed by these words. Qatādah said, 'It was mentioned to us that a man asked the Messenger of Allah ﷺ about true goodness (*birr*) and then Allah revealed this *āyah*.' Qatādah continued, 'Before the obligatory acts of worship were prescribed, when a man testified that there is no god but Allah and Muḥammad is His slave and Messenger and then died affirming that, that was sufficient to assure him of the Garden, and so this *āyah* was revealed to redress the balance.' Qatādah and ar-Rabī' said that it is the Jews and Christians who are being addressed because they disagreed about which direction they should turn towards. The Jews faced west towards Jerusalem and the Christians east towards where the sun rose. They spoke about a change of *qiblah* and each group preferred its own direction. They were told that that was not where true goodness lay. Ḥamzah and Ḥafṣ recite *'al-birra'* in the accusative. The rest recite *'al-birru'* in the nominative.

**Rather, those with true goodness are those who believe**

Here '*birr*' (true goodness) is a word which includes all good. Its use on its own here implies: 'But true goodness is the goodness of the one who believes...' but there is an elision. It is said that the meaning is: 'But those with true goodness...' That is because when the Prophet ﷺ emigrated to Madīnah and the obligatory prayers were prescribed, the *qiblah* redirected towards the Ka'bah, and the statutory punishments (*ḥudūd*) were established, Allah revealed this in order to say that true goodness does not lie in praying or doing any other particular action, but rather that a person who is truly good is someone who believes in Allah, and all the other things mentioned in the *āyah*. Ibn 'Abbās, Mujāhid, aḍ-Ḍaḥḥāk, Aṭā', Sufyān and az-Zajjāj held that view. It is possible for *birr* to mean *bārr* and *barr*. *Barr* means kind and benign and filial, while *bārr* also has that meaning, but is a little more restricted.

Our scholars point out that this is an immense *āyah*, one of the matrices of judgment, because it contains sixteen different elements:

- the requirement to have faith in Allah and His Names and Attributes
- the Resurrection
- the Gathering
- the Balance
- the *Sirāṭ*
- the Basin
- the Intercession
- the Garden and the Fire
- the Angels
- the Books revæ...ealed by Allah
- the Prophets
- the duty to spend one's wealth in ways that are both mandatory and recommended
- maintaining ties of kinship and not severing them
- looking after orphans and the poor and not neglecting them
- caring for travellers (or guests) and beggars
- setting slaves free

All these things will be clarified elsewhere. Also included are safeguarding the prayer, paying zakat, fulfilling contracts and showing steadfastness in afflictions. Each of these items would require an entire book to do it justice.

There is disagreement about whether one gives voluntary *ṣadaqah* to an orphan merely because of their being an orphan, in order to maintain ties of kinship, even if the orphan is wealthy, or whether one only gives to the poor. This is about voluntary *ṣadaqah* rather than obligatory zakat.

**and who, despite their love for it, give away their wealth**

This is used as evidence by those who say that there are legal rights on wealth other than just zakat and that they are the means by which true goodness is achieved. It is also said that what is meant here is obligatory zakat. The first opinion is sounder since ad-Dāraquṭnī transmitted from Fāṭimah bint Qays that the Prophet ﷺ said, 'There is a right on wealth over and above zakat,' and he quoted this *āyah* in full. Ibn Mājah and at-Tirmidhī transmit it in their collections as well. He said that the *isnād* of this *ḥadīth* is not that strong because Abū Ḥamzah is weak. Bayān and Ismā'īl ibn Sālim related this *ḥadīth* from ash-Sha'bī, and it is stronger.

The soundness of this *ḥadīth*, even if there is something to be said about the *isnād*, is indicated by the words of Allah later in the same *āyah*: *'establish the prayer and pay zakat'*. He mentions zakat with the prayer. That indicates that what is meant by this phrase is not obligatory zakat because otherwise that would entail an unnecessary repetition, and Allah knows best. Scholars agree that, when an urgent need for the Muslims exists after the payment of zakat, there is a communal obligation to spend money on it. Mālik obliged people to ransom captives, even if it used up all their wealth. There is also consensus on this, and that strengthens what we prefer concerning this matter.

It is said the phrase refers to their love for the wealth they give and the pronoun can also refer to the love the giver has for his relatives. The same applies to Allah's words in *Sūrat al-Insān: 'They give food, despite their love for it, to the poor.'* (76:8) It can have both meanings.

**those who honour their contracts when they make them,**

It is said that this is added to the earlier sentence, i.e. 'Those with true goodness or those who believer and those who honour…' Al-Farrā' and al-Akhfash said that. This refers to contracts between themselves and Allah, and between themselves and other people.

**and are steadfast in poverty and illness and in battle**

'Steadfast' is in the accusative by way of praise or by the effect of an elided verb. The Arabs put the noun in the accusative for both praise and censure as if they were trying to isolate the person praised or blamed.

*Ba'sā'* is hardship and poverty, and *ḍarrā'* is illness. Ibn Mas'ūd said that. The Prophet ﷺ said, 'Allah Almighty says, "When I test any of My slaves in his bed and he does not complain to those who visit him, I will replace his flesh with a better flesh and his blood with a better blood. If I take him, it is to My mercy. If I give him well-being, I give him a well-being in which he has no sin.' He was asked, 'Messenger of Allah, what flesh is better than his flesh?' He answered, 'A flesh without sin.' He was asked, 'What blood is better than his blood?' He answered, 'Blood without sin.' *Ba's* is the time of war.

**Those are the people who are true. They are the people who are godfearing.**

They are described as having integrity and *taqwā* in their affairs and fulfilling them. They are serious regarding the *dīn*. This is great praise. Truthfulness is the opposite of lying. Someone who is *ṣiddīq* is someone who holds closely to the truth. In a *ḥadīth* we find: 'You must have integrity. Integrity guides to goodness and goodness guides to the Garden. A man continues to be true and takes care to remain truthful until he is written with Allah as a true man (*ṣiddīq*).'

يَٰٓأَيُّهَا ٱلَّذِينَ ءَامَنُواْ كُتِبَ عَلَيْكُمُ ٱلْقِصَاصُ فِي ٱلْقَتْلَى ٱلْحُرُّ بِٱلْحُرِّ وَٱلْعَبْدُ
بِٱلْعَبْدِ وَٱلْأُنثَىٰ بِٱلْأُنثَىٰ فَمَنْ عُفِيَ لَهُۥ مِنْ أَخِيهِ شَيْءٌ فَٱتِّبَاعٌ بِٱلْمَعْرُوفِ
وَأَدَآءٌ إِلَيْهِ بِإِحْسَٰنٍ ذَٰلِكَ تَخْفِيفٌ مِّن رَّبِّكُمْ وَرَحْمَةٌ فَمَنِ ٱعْتَدَىٰ بَعْدَ
ذَٰلِكَ فَلَهُۥ عَذَابٌ أَلِيمٌ ﴿١٧٨﴾

**178 You who believe! retaliation is prescribed for you in the case of people killed: free man for free man, slave for slave, female for female. But if someone is absolved the thing by his brother, blood-money should be claimed with correctness and paid with good will. That is an easement and a mercy from your Lord. Anyone who goes beyond the limits after this will receive a painful punishment.**

**You who believe! retaliation is prescribed for you in the case of people killed:**

Al-Bukhārī and ad-Dāraquṭnī related that Ibn 'Abbās said, 'There was retaliation among the tribe of Israel but no blood money. So Allah told this community: *"Retaliation is prescribed for you in the case of people killed: free man for free man, slave for slave, female for female. But if someone is absolved the thing by his brother..."* Absolution is to accept blood money in cases of homicide. *"Blood-money should be claimed with correctness and paid with good will."* By saying it should be claimed with correctness and paid with good will, Allah is making it easier for us than what was imposed on those before us. "Going beyond the limits" refers to killing after having accepted blood money.' This is the wording of al-Bukhārī from al-Ḥumaydī from Sufyān from 'Amr who heard Mujāhid say that he heard Ibn 'Abbās say that.

Ash-Sha'bī said that '*...free man for free man, slave for slave, female for female*' was revealed about two of the Arab tribes that fought each other and would say, 'We will accept so-and-so son of so-and-so for our slave.' Qatādah reported something similar.

The word '*kutiba*' (prescribed) means 'established and made obligatory'. It is also said that this means what was written on the Preserved Tablet and previously decreed. '*Qiṣāṣ*' (retaliation) is from a root meaning someone who follows a trail which has been blazed. A *qāṣṣ* is a storyteller who follows traditions and reports. *Qaṣṣ* also means cutting the hair by following its line. It is as if the killer takes a path with regard to killing, and retaliation is to follow after him and proceed along the same path in that respect. That usage can be seen in 18:64. It is said that *qaṣṣ* is cutting and that is the source of *qiṣāṣ* because the retaliator wounds with the same type of wound or kills in the same way. The verb is also used for mutilation.

The form that retaliation takes is that when the relative (*walī*) wants to kill, the killer is obliged to submit to the command of Allah and to accept the prescribed retaliation. The relative of the murdered man is obliged to stop at the killer of his relative and not to go beyond him and kill someone else as well, which is what the Arabs used to do before Islam. That is the meaning of the words of the Prophet ﷺ, 'On the Day of Rising, the most insolent of people towards Allah will be three men: someone who killed other than the killer, someone who kills in the Ḥaram, and someone who acts by the blood feuds of the Jāhiliyyah.'

Ash-Sha'bī, Qatādah and others said, 'The people of the Jāhiliyyah were excessive and obeyed Shayṭān. When a tribe possessed might and power and a slave of theirs was killed by the slave of another person, they said, "We will only kill a free person for him." If a woman of theirs was killed, they said, "We will only kill a man for her." When a base person among them was killed, they said, "We will only kill a noble for them." They used to say, "Killing safeguards against killing." Allah forbade them such transgression in this *āyah* and others.'

There is no disagreement that retaliation in killing can only be adjudged by those in authority. It is the ruler who imposes retaliation, establishes the *ḥudūd* and other things, because, although Allah Almighty gives all believers the possibility of retaliation, not all believers are ready to agree to it. Therefore the ruler represents them in the matter of carrying out retaliation and imposing other *hudūd*. Retaliation itself is not obligatory. What is obligatory is not to exceed in retaliation or other *ḥudūd*. If there is consent to forgo retaliation and to accept blood money or to pardon, that is permitted.

If it is said that 'prescribed for you' means it is obligatory and necessary, so how, in that case, can *qiṣāṣ* not be mandatory? The reply is that it implies 'if you desire it.' Know that *qiṣāṣ* is the limit for those who want blood. *Qatlā* is the plural of *qatīl*.

**free man for free man, slave for slave, female for female.**

There is disagreement about the interpretation of this. One group say that the *āyah* was revealed to clarify the judgment of the category of those whose blood is forfeit when someone of the same category is killed. So when a free person is killed, someone free is killed in retaliation for him, and when a slave is killed, a slave is killed in retaliation, and a woman is killed in retaliation for a woman. The *āyah* is a firm ruling which is general and explained by the words of Allah: *'…a life for a life'* (5:45) and explained by the Prophet in his Sunnah when he killed a Jew in retaliation for a woman. Mujāhid said that. Ibn 'Abbās said the same, although it is related from him that it is abrogated by the *āyah* in *Sūrat al-Mā'idah*. That is the position of the people of Iraq.

The Kufans and ath-Thawrī said that a free man is killed if he has killed a slave and a Muslim if he has killed a *dhimmī*. Their evidence is the words of Allah here which are general as well as the *āyah* in *Sūrat al-Mā'idah* (5:45). (Mentioned in the previous paragraph). They said that the blood of a *dhimmī* has the same inviolability as that of a Muslim and should be satisfied by retaliation. It is the inviolability of blood which is the principle. Both the Muslim and the *dhimmī* are the people of the Abode of Islam. The thing which verifies that is the fact that a Muslim's hand is cut off for stealing the property of a *dhimmī* which indicates that the property of a *dhimmī* is the same as that of a Muslim. It follows that their blood must be the same since property is respected by respect for its owner. Abū Ḥanīfah and his people, ath-Thawrī, and Ibn Abī Laylā agree that a free man is killed in retaliation for a slave just as a slave is killed in retaliation for him. That is the position of Dāwud. The same is related from 'Alī and Ibn Mas'ūd and is the position of Sa'īd ibn al-Musayyab, Qatādah, Ibrāhīm an-Nakha'ī, and al-Ḥakam ibn 'Uyaynah.

The majority of scholars do not accept killing a free man in retaliation for a slave because of the categories and divisions shown in the *āyah*. Abū Thawr said, 'Since everyone agrees that there is no retaliation between slaves and free people in cases less than homicide, it is even more likely to be the case where homicide is concerned. Those who make a distinction in respect of that are wrong.' Furthermore the consensus, if someone accidentally kills a slave, is that he only owes the price of that slave. Since slaves do not resemble free men where accidental killing is concerned, the same should hold true in cases of intentional homicide. Moreover, a slave is a commodity that is bought and sold and can be disposed of by a free person and so there is no equality between them.

This consensus is sound. The first view is contradictory. Ibn Abī Laylā and Dāwud said that there is retaliation between free men and slaves with regard to life and all limbs. For proof, Dāwud used the words of the Prophet ﷺ: 'The blood of the Muslims is the same.' He did not make a distinction between free men and slaves. This will be explained in *an-Nisā'*, Allah willing.

The majority also agree that a Muslim should not be killed in retaliation for an unbeliever since the Prophet ﷺ said, 'A Muslim is not killed in retaliation for an unbeliever.' Al-Bukhārī transmitted this from 'Alī ibn Abī Ṭālib. They do not consider as sound what is related from Rabī'ah about the Prophet killing a Muslim in retaliation for an unbeliever at Khaybar, because its *isnād* is broken and the *ḥadīth* of Ibn al-Baylamānī, who is weak, from Ibn 'Umar from the Prophet ﷺ is *marfū'*. Ad-Dāraquṭnī said, 'Only Ibrāhīm ibn Abī Yaḥyā has its *isnād*, and his *ḥadīth*s are abandoned. What is correct is that it is from Rabī'ah from Ibn al-Baylamānī *mursal* from the Prophet ﷺ. The *ḥadīth*s of Ibn al-Baylamānī are weak and not used as evidence even when their line of transmission is connected, let alone when it is *mursal*.' The only thing that is sound regarding this topic is the *ḥadīth* of al-Bukhārī which makes the generality of this *āyah* specific.

It is related from 'Alī and al-Ḥasan al-Baṣrī that the *āyah* was revealed to explain the ruling of those mentioned in the *āyah* and to indicate the difference between them and those who would kill a free person in retaliation for a slave or a slave in retaliation for a free person, or male in retaliation for a female or a female in retaliation for a male. They said, 'When a man kills a woman and her relatives want to kill him, they do so and his relatives are paid half of the blood price. If they want to let him live, they accept a woman's blood money from him. If a woman kills a man and his relatives want to kill her, they can kill her and take half the blood money or alternatively they can take the full blood money and let her live.' Ash-Sha'bī related this from 'Alī, but it cannot be sound because ash-

Sha'bī did not meet 'Alī. Al-Ḥakam related that 'Alī and 'Abdullāh said, 'When a man murders a woman with premeditation, he is her retaliation.' This is contrary to the transmission of ash-Sha'bī from 'Alī. Scholars agree that when a one-eyed man or a man with a withered hand kills a man with sound limbs, his relative cannot kill the one-eyed man and take half the blood-money from him because the one-eyed man killed someone with two eyes and the man with the withered hand killed one with two hands. This indicates that blood is equal and it is a life for a life. Children and adults are the same in that respect.

It might be said to those who espouse that position, 'A woman is not equal to a man in that respect and is not included in the words of the Prophet ﷺ about the blood of Muslims being the same. So why should she be killed for a man when she is not equal to him and half the blood-money taken? And yet scholars agree that blood-money and retaliation are not combined and, when blood-money is accepted, the life of the killer is sacrosanct and there is no retaliation. Therefore your position is baseless and not based on any analogy.' Abū 'Umar said that. When a free man kills a slave, the killer is killed if the owner of the slave so wishes and then he pays the blood-money of the free man less the value of the slave. If, instead, he wishes, he can be modest and take the value of the slave. This is mentioned from 'Alī and al-Ḥasan. It is also denied from them.

Scholars agree that a man should be killed in retaliation for killing a woman and a woman in retaliation for killing a man and the majority do not think anything is repaid. One group think that the difference in the blood money is repaid. Mālik, ash-Shāfi'ī, Aḥmad, Isḥāq, ath-Thawrī and Abū Thawr said that is how retaliation proceeds between a man and a woman in respect of what is less than a life. Ḥammād ibn Abī Sulaymān and Abū Ḥanīfah said that there is no retaliation between them in injuries which fall short of killing in which there is a life for a life.

Ibn al-'Arabī said, 'Ignorance leads some people to say that a free man should be killed in retaliation for killing his own slave,' and a *ḥadīth* is related regarding that from Samurah in which the Messenger of Allah ﷺ said, 'We kill the one who kills his slave,' but it is a weak *ḥadīth*. Our evidence is the words of Allah: *'If someone is wrongly killed, We have given authority to his next of kin. But he should not be excessive in taking life.'* (17:33) In this case this refers to the slave's master. All the scholars agree that if a master kills his slave accidentally, the price of the slave is not taken from him for the treasury. 'Amr ibn Shu'ayb related that a man murdered his slave and the Prophet ﷺ flogged him and exiled him for a year and removed his share as a Muslim and did not help him to pay it.

It might be asked, 'If a man kills his wife, why do you not say that marriage sets up a doubt which would avert retaliation from the husband since marriage is a type of slavery?' Al-Layth ibn Sa'd said that. Our reply is that marriage is a contract between him and her with implied restrictions on both sides: he cannot marry her sister or four additional wives (making the total five), and she can demand her right of intercourse from him just as he can demand it from her. He, however, has the merit of guardianship over her, which Allah gave him because he supports her from his wealth, according to what is obligatory for him in terms of the bride-price and maintenance. If a doubt had existed, it would exist for both parties.

This *ḥadīth* which Ibn al-'Arabī says is weak is, in fact, sound. An-Nasā'ī and Abū Dāwud transmitted it and its text is complete: 'If someone amputates a part of someone's body, we amputate that from him. If someone castrates someone, we castrate him.' Al-Bukhārī said that it is sound that 'Alī ibn al-Madīnī heard it from Samurah. Al-Bukhārī said, 'I believe that. If the *ḥadīth* had not been sound, then these two imams would not have believed it. They are enough for you!' A free man is killed for a slave. An-Nakha'ī, and ath-Thawrī in one view, said that al-Ḥasan only heard the *ḥadīth* of the *'aqīqah* from Samurah. Allah knows best. They disagree about retaliation between slaves in cases less than killing. This is the position of 'Umar ibn 'Abd al-'Azīz, Sālim ibn 'Abdullāh, az-Zuhrī, Qurrān, Mālik, ash-Shāfi'ī and Abū Thawr. Ash-Sha'bī, an-Nakha'ī, ath-Thawrī and Abū Ḥanīfah said that there is no retaliation between slaves except with respect to killing. Ibn al-Mundhir said that the first position is sounder.

Ad-Dāraquṭnī and Abū 'Īsā at-Tirmidhī related that Surāqah ibn Mālik said, 'I was present when the Messenger of Allah ﷺ judged that retaliation should be taken from a son for killing his father, but not from a father for killing his son.' Abū 'Īsā said, 'We do not know this *ḥadīth* from Surāqah except by this path and its *isnād* is not sound. Ismā'īl ibn 'Ayyāsh related it from al-Muthannā ibn aṣ-Ṣabbāḥ. Al-Muthannā is weak in *ḥadīth*. This *ḥadīth* is related by Abū Khālid al-Aḥmar from al-Ḥajjāj from 'Amr ibn Shu'ayb from his father from his grandfather from 'Umar from the Prophet ﷺ. The *ḥadīth* is related *mursal* from 'Amr ibn Shu'ayb and contains some muddling. The normative practice among the people of knowledge is that when a father kills his son, he is not killed on that account, and when he slanders him, he does not receive the *ḥadd* punishment.'

Ibn al-Mundhir said, 'The people of knowledge disagree about a man who kills his son deliberately. One group say that no retaliation is taken from him, but he must pay blood-money. This is the view of ash-Shāfi'ī, Aḥmad, Isḥāq and the People of Opinion. That is also related from 'Aṭā' and Mujāhid. Mālik, Ibn Nāfi' and Ibn 'Abd al-Ḥakam said that he is killed in retaliation for him.' Ibn al-Mundhir added, 'This is our view based on the literal meaning of the Book and the Sunnah. The text of the Book is: *"Retaliation is prescribed for you in the case of people killed: free man for free man, slave for slave."* What is confirmed from the Messenger of Allah ﷺ is his words: "The blood of the believers is equal." We do not know of any firm report that makes the father an exception in this regard. Reports which are not firm are related regarding it.' Aṭ-Ṭabarī related from 'Uthmān al-Battī that a father is killed for killing his son since retaliation is general. Something similar is related from Mālik. Perhaps they did not accept single reports defining the general statements of the Qur'an.

There is no disagreement in the school of Mālik that when a man deliberately kills his son, such as when he makes him lie down and slaughters him, or constrains and kills him in a manner which there is no excuse for and there is no way he can claim that it was an accident, he is killed in retaliation for him. If he throws a weapon at him or chokes him while disciplining him, there are two views in the School. One is that he is killed in retaliation for him, and the other is that he is not killed, but made to pay a greater than normal sum in blood-money. That is the position of a group of scholars. A non-relative is killed in a similar case.

Ibn al-'Arabī said, 'I heard our shaykh, Fakhr al-Islām ash-Shāshī, say in debate, "A father is not killed in retaliation for his son because the father is the reason for his existence. How can he be reason for his father's non-existence?" This is invalidated by the fact that a man is stoned if he fornicates with his daughter even though he is the reason for her existence and she is the reason for his non-existence. What sort of understanding comes from this? Why should he not be the reason for his own non-existence since he disobeyed Allah in doing that? There is a report that the Messenger of Allah ﷺ said, "Retaliation is not taken from a father for killing his son," but it is a false *ḥadīth*. They added to this by saying that 'Umar augmented the blood-money in the case of a man who had killed his son and none of the Companions objected to it. The rest of the *fuqahā'* consider the case to be allowable, saying, "Retaliation is not taken from a father for killing his son." Mālik took it as a judgment which is subject to detailed examination of the particular circumstances and said, "If he strikes him with a sword, this is a case in which it is possible that he intended to kill or did not intend to do so. Fatherly compassion provides a doubt which can establish lack of intent and so on that basis retaliation is cancelled. If he lays him down, then the concealed intent is disclosed and the case follows the basic principle."' Ibn al-Mundhir said, 'Mālik, ash-Shāfi'ī, Aḥmad and Isḥāq say that if a son kills his father, he is killed for him.'

Imām Aḥmad ibn Ḥanbal used this *āyah* as evidence that a group should not be killed in retaliation for the death of one person. He said, 'That is because Allah stipulated equality, and there is no equality between a group and one individual.' The answer to this is that retaliation in this *āyah* entails killing the one who did the killing, whoever that may be. This was to refute the Arabs who wanted to kill someone who was not the killer in exchange for someone who had been killed and to kill a hundred innocent people in retaliation for one or to take advantage of rank and power. Therefore Allah commanded fairness and equality so that only those who kill may be killed. 'Umar killed seven men in Sana', and said, 'If all the people of Sana' had participated in the murder, I would have killed them all.'

'Alī killed the Kharijites for killing 'Abdullāh ibn Khabbāb. When they were merely guilty of innovation, he held back from killing them, but when they murdered 'Abdullāh ibn Khabbāb as a sheep would be slaughtered and 'Alī was informed about that, he said, 'Allah is greater!' He called them to bring out the murderers of 'Abdulāh ibn Khabbāb to him. They said, 'All of us killed him' three times. 'Alī told his companions, 'There are the people.' 'Alī and his people did not hesitate to kill them all. Ad-Dāraquṭnī transmits both reports in his *Sunan*.

In at-Tirmidhī Abū Sa'īd and Abū Hurayrah reported that the Messenger of Allah ﷺ said, 'If all the people of heaven and all the people of the earth were to participate in shedding the blood of a believer, Allah would throw them all into the Fire.' It is said that this is a *gharīb ḥadīth*. Furthermore if a group knew that, if they were to kill a person as a group, they would not be killed, then enemies would help one another to kill their enemies by participating in their killing and achieving their desire for revenge. So it is more fitting to follow this rule than the literal words, and Allah knows best. Ibn al-Mundhir said, 'Az-Zuhrī, Ḥabīb ibn Abī Thābit and Ibn Sīrīn said, 'Two are not killed in retaliation for one.' That is also related from Mu'ādh ibn Jabal, Ibn az-Zubayr and 'Abd al-Mālik.' Ibn Mundhir added, 'This is sounder and someone who permits killing a group for the killing of one person has no proof.' What we mentioned is confirmed from Ibn az-Zubayr.

The Imams related from Abū Shurayḥ al-Ka'bī that the Messenger of Allah ﷺ said, 'You company of Khuzā'ah killed this man from Hudhayl and I am responsible for him. Whoever has a relative killed after these words of mine, is entitled to one of two things: taking the blood money or killing in retaliation.' The wording is that of Abū Dāwud. At-Tirmidhī said that it is a sound *ḥasan ḥadīth*. Abū Shurayḥ related that the Prophet ﷺ said, 'The relative of the one killed can take life in retaliation, pardon or take blood money.' This is the position of some of the people of knowledge. It is the position of Aḥmad and Isḥāq.

Scholars disagree about taking blood money from a murderer. One group say that the relative of the murdered man has a choice. If he wishes, he can take retaliation, and if he wishes he can take blood-money, even if the killer does not consent. This is related from Sa'īd ibn al-Musayyab, 'Aṭā' and al-Ḥasan. Ashhab relates this position from Mālik and it is also the position of al-Layth, al-Awzā'ī, ash-Shāfi'ī, Aḥmad, Isḥāq and Abū Thawr. Their proof is the *ḥadīth* of Abū Shurayḥ above and it is a legal text (*naṣṣ*) sufficient to resolve the dispute. It is also deduced by analysis since blood money is imposed on him without his consent because it is an obligation on him to save his own life as Allah says: *'Do not kill yourselves.'* (4:29) He says in this *āyah: 'But if someone is absolved by his brother,'* in other words, he forgoes his right to retaliation in one interpretation and is satisfied with blood money, *'blood-money should be claimed with correctness'*, meaning that the one with right to retaliation follows it by correctly demanding blood money, the killer must pay it with good will without delay.

**But if someone is absolved something by his brother, blood-money should be claimed with correctness and paid with good will.**

Scholars disagree about the interpretation of the words 'someone', 'absolved' and 'something' in this *āyah*. One view is that 'someone' means the killer and 'absolved' refers to what the relative of the deceased does. The 'brother' is the brother of the deceased. The 'something' is his right to retaliation which is absolved and for which he takes blood money. This is the position of Ibn 'Abbās, Qatādah, Mujāhid and a group of scholars. So absolving, in this case, means abandoning the right to retaliation. It means: when the killer is absolved by the relative of the deceased of his right to retaliation and forgoes it, he takes blood-money and follows it with correctness, and the killer pays it with good will.

Another position is that of Mālik which is that 'someone' refers to the relative and 'absolved' is to make easy, not to pardon, and the 'brother' is the killer and the 'something' is the blood money, so the meaning in this case would be that when the relative inclines to foregoing retaliation and taking blood money, the killer can choose between giving it or surrendering himself. Sometimes it is eased and sometimes not. People other than Malik say that if the relatives are satisfied with blood money, the killer has no choice: he has to give it. This is also related from Mālik and many of his people preferred it. Abū Ḥanīfah said that 'absolve' here means to spend. That is known linguistically. So it is as if the meaning was

'Whoever is paid some of the blood money should accept it and pursue it with correctness.' Some people say that the killer should pay it with good will and Allah recommends that the relative of the murder victim should take the money when that is easy for the killer. It is a lightening and a mercy, as He says after mentioning retaliation in *al-Mā'idah*: *'If anyone forgoes that as* ṣadaqah, *it will be expiation for him.'* (5:45) Allah recommends the mercy of absolution and *ṣadaqah,* as in this *āyah* He recommends accepting blood-money when the person pays it. The relative is commanded to claim it with correctness and the perpetrator to pay it with good will.

Some people say that these expressions deal with particular people, about whom the entire *āyah* was revealed, and they paid the blood money to one another in respect of the injuries outstanding between them. The meaning of the *āyah* is about when one group received more than the other group, and so 'absolved' rather means 'has more than'. Ash-Sha'bī said explaining this, 'There was fighting between two tribes of Arabs and several people were killed. One of the tribes said, "We will not be content until a man is killed for a woman and a woman for a man." They went to the Prophet ﷺ and he said, "Killing is the same." They made peace on the basis of the payment of blood money and one of the two tribes received more than the other. That is what this *āyah* refers to. Whoever has more than his brother should pay it correctly.' Ash-Sha'bī said that this was the reason the *āyah* was revealed.

Finally there is the statement of 'Alī about the difference between the blood money of a man and a woman, free person and slave, so the meaning is that the one who has more should demand it correctly.

This *āyah* is encouragement from Allah Almighty for correctness on the part of the person seeking payment and good will on the part of the payer. Is that obligatory or recommended? The recitation in the nominative indicates that it is obligatory, because the meaning is that it must be pursued with correctness.

**That is an easement and a mercy from your Lord.**

This alludes to the fact that Allah did not give those before us any choice in the matter and they had to take a life for a life, whereas Allah has given this Community the advantage of being able to accept blood money when the relative of the deceased is satisfied by it. Others said that the relative of the dead person can only take retaliation and may not take blood money if the killer agrees to that. Ibn al-Qāsim related that from Mālik, and it is well known from him. Ath-Thawrī and the Kufans also said that. Their evidence is the *ḥadīth* of Anas in the story about ar-Rubayya' who broke a woman's tooth. They stated, 'When the Prophet ﷺ judged that there should be retaliation, he said, "Retaliation is the Book of Allah. Retaliation is the Book of Allah."' He did not give the injured woman a choice between retaliation and blood money and so the judgment of the Book of Allah and the Sunnah of the Messenger is that there is retaliation for a deliberate injury. The first position is sounder because of the *ḥadīth* of Abū Shurayḥ.

Ar-Rabī' related that ash-Shāfi'ī said, 'Abū Ḥanīfah ibn Simāk ibn al-Faḍl ash-Shihābī reported to me from Ibn Abī Dhi'b from al-Maqburī from Abū Shurayḥ al-Ka'bī that the Messenger of Allah ﷺ said in the year of the Conquest of Makkah, "If someone is killed, [the relative] has a choice between two courses: if he wishes, he can take the blood-money, and if he wishes, he can take retaliation." Abū Ḥanīfah said, "I asked Ibn Abī Dhi'b, 'Do you take this position, Abu-l-Ḥārith?' He struck my chest, shouted at me and got hold of me, saying, 'I relate to you from the Messenger of Allah ﷺ and then you ask me if I take it? Of course I take it! That is obligatory for me and those who hear it! Allah Almighty chose Muḥammad ﷺ from among people and guided them by him. He chose for them what He chose for him and on his tongue. Therefore people must follow him, willingly and in submission. A Muslim cannot leave that.'"'

This was an easement because the people of Torah only had the choice of killing and nothing else, and the people of the Gospel only had absolution and no retaliation or blood-money. Allah gave this easement to this community and whoever wishes can retaliate by killing, whoever wishes can accept blood-money, and whoever wishes can absolve.

**Anyone who goes beyond the limits after this will receive a painful punishment.**

This refers to someone who kills after taking blood-money and consequently foregoing the blood of the killer. Al-Ḥasan said, 'In the Jāhiliyyah, when someone killed a person he would flee to his own people and the people of the victim would come and negotiate the blood-money. The relative of the victim would say, "I will take the blood-money," and then, when the killer was made secure by this and left, the victim's relative would kill him and throw the blood-money back at the killer's family.'

Scholars disagree about someone who kills after taking blood-money. A group of scholars, including Mālik and ash-Shāfi'ī, said that he is the same as the one who kills in the first place. If the relative wishes, he kills him, and if he wishes, he pardons him and he will be punished in the Next World. Qatādah, 'Ikrimah, as-Suddī and others said that his punishment is to be killed and it is not possible for the relative to pardon him. Abū Dāwud related from Jābir ibn 'Abdullāh that the Messenger of Allah ﷺ said, 'I will not pardon someone who kills after having taken blood-money.' Al-Ḥasan said that his punishment is to return the blood-money and his wrong action remains to be dealt with in the Next World. 'Umar ibn 'Abd al-'Azīz said that his business is left up to the ruler who does whatever he thinks best. We find in the *Sunan* of ad-Dāraquṭnī that Abū Shurayḥ al-Khuzā'ī said, 'I heard the Messenger of Allah ﷺ say, "Whoever is killed or lamed can choose one of three things. If he wants a fourth, then hold him back. He may retaliate, or absolve, or take the blood-money. If he accepts any of those and then attacks after that, he will go to the Fire to be in it forever."'

وَلَكُمْ فِي ٱلْقِصَاصِ حَيَوٰةٌ يَٰٓأُو۟لِى ٱلْأَلْبَٰبِ لَعَلَّكُمْ تَتَّقُونَ ﴿١٧٩﴾

**179 There is life for you in retaliation, people of intelligence, so that hopefully you will be godfearing.**

**There is life for you in retaliation, people of intelligence**

These are succinct and eloquent words which mean: 'You should not kill one another.' Sufyān related that from as-Suddī from Abū Mālik. It means that when retaliation is established and achieved, it will deter the one who wants to kill someone else out of the fear that retaliation will be taken from him, and so both remain alive. It had previously been the case that, when one man killed another, their two tribes would fight and that would lead to many deaths. When Allah prescribed retaliation, it was a deterrent and they stopped fighting. Therefore they had life through that.

The imams who give *fatwā* agree that it is not permitted for anyone to take retaliation from someone without the involvement of the ruler. People cannot do it on their own. The ruler, or someone appointed by him, carry that out. Allah appointed the ruler to restrain people's hands from one another. Scholars agree that the ruler can take retaliation from himself if he transgresses against one of his subjects since he is one of them and has the prerogative of looking after them, like a guardian or trustee. That does not preclude retaliation and so there is no difference between him and anyone else regarding the judgments of Allah in this *āyah*.

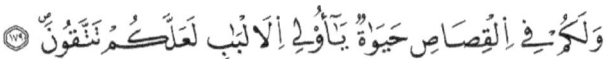

It is confirmed that Abū Bakr aṣ-Ṣiddīq said to a man who complained to him about a governor who had cut off his hand, 'If you are telling the truth, I will take retaliation for you from him.' An-Nasā'ī reported that Abū Sa'īd al-Khudrī said, 'Once, while the Messenger of Allah ﷺ was distributing something, a man bent over him and the Messenger of Allah jabbed him with a stick he had and the man yelled out. The Messenger of Allah ﷺ said to him, "Come, take your retaliation." He said, "I absolve you, Messenger of Allah."' Abū Dāwud aṭ-Ṭayālisī reported from Abū Firās that 'Umar gave a speech in which he said, 'Whoever is wronged by an *amīr* (governor, commander) should present his case to me and I will take retaliation from him.' 'Amr ibn al-'Āṣ stood up and said, 'Amīr al-Mu'minīn, if one of us disciplines a man who is subject to his authority, will you take retaliation from him?' He replied, 'How could I not take retaliation from him when I saw the Messenger of Allah ﷺ take retaliation from himself!' Abū Dāwud as-Sijistānī has: "Umar gave a speech and said, "I have not sent my governors to beat your bodies or take your property. If someone has that done to him, he should present his case to me and I will take retaliation from him.""

**so that hopefully you will be godfearing.**

So that you will be careful to avoid killing and will submit to retaliation. That obedience leads to other types of obedience. Allah makes one firm in obedience through obedience.

كُتِبَ عَلَيْكُمْ إِذَا حَضَرَ أَحَدَكُمُ ٱلْمَوْتُ إِن تَرَكَ خَيْرًا ٱلْوَصِيَّةُ لِلْوَٰلِدَيْنِ
وَٱلْأَقْرَبِينَ بِٱلْمَعْرُوفِ ۖ حَقًّا عَلَى ٱلْمُتَّقِينَ ١٨٠

**180 It is prescribed for you, when death approaches one of you and if he has some goods to leave, to make a will in favour of his parents and relatives, correctly and fairly: a duty for all those who are godfearing.**

This is the '*Āyah* of the Will'. The only *āyah*s in the Qur'an that deal with wills are this one and the ones we find at 4:12 and 5:106. This *āyah* is the most comprehensive of them. It was revealed before the revelation of the statutory shares of inheritance and their laws, as will be explained. There is an 'and' elided in the words: 'And it is prescribed,' because it follows on from the previous *āyah* about retaliation and may well be directed to the one who is about to have retaliation inflicted on him which will clearly cause his death. So he is someone who knows that death is near him and that this is the time when making a will becomes absolutely imperative.

If it is asked why the word '*kutiba*' (prescribed) is in the masculine when the word for will (*waṣiyah*) is feminine, the reply is that the act of making a will (*īṣā'*) is what is meant and that is masculine. It is also said that it is because the verb is considerably separated from its subject.

**and if he has some goods to leave,**

Here '*khayr*' (goods) means wealth. There is no dispute about this but there is disagreement about the amount involved. It is said that it means a lot of wealth, and that is related from 'Alī, 'Ā'ishah and Ibn 'Abbās. They said that seven hundred dinars is a small amount. Qatādah and al-Ḥasan said that it means a thousand dinars or more. Ash-Sha'bī said that the amount intended is from five hundred to a thousand dinars. The word '*waṣiyyah*' (will) can designate anything which someone instructs to be done, whether during his lifetime or after his death. Custom, however, has designated it to be a declaration of what is to be done after death. The plural is *waṣāyā*. *Waṣiy* can be the testator or the executor from the verb *waṣā*, a verb also used to describe dense vegetation and such a land is called '*wāṣiyah*'.

Scholars disagree about whether it is obligatory for those who leave property to make a will, although they agree that it is mandatory for those who hold deposits and have debts. Most scholars believe that a will is not mandatory for those who have neither of these. That is the position of Mālik, ash-Shāfi'ī and ath-Thawrī, whether a person is rich or poor. Another group including az-Zuhrī and Abū Mijlaz say, judging by the literal text of the Qur'an, that making a will is mandatory whether a person has a little or a lot of wealth. Abū Thawr said that making a will is only mandatory for a man who has a debt or wealth belonging to someone else, and then it is mandatory for him to write a will, saying what he owes. As for someone who has no debts or deposits, it is not mandatory for him to make one unless he wishes to do so.

Ibn al-Mundhir said, 'This is good because Allah has made it obligatory to return trusts to their owners but it is not mandatory for someone who holds goods on trust to make a will.' The people with the first view use what is related from Ibn 'Umar as evidence. He said that the Messenger of Allah ﷺ said, 'It is not right for a Muslim man who owes something, which he should specify in a will, to spend two nights without making a written will.' One variant says three nights. 'Abdullāh ibn 'Umar said about it: 'Not a night has passed, since I heard the Messenger of Allah ﷺ say that, without me having my will with me.' Those who argue the opposite say that, if it was mandatory, it would not have been left to the discretion of the one making the will. It would have been necessary for him in every case. Although its literal meaning would make it obligatory, it is refuted that it is obligatory; that is actually only the case for someone who has money that belongs to other people in his possession, which it is feared might be lost, as Abū Thawr said. The same is true if other people owe him money which he fears might be lost to his heir. There is no disagreement that he is obliged to make a will in such a case.

If it is said that Allah's use of the words, 'prescribed for you' means that it is mandatory, the answer to that is found in the previous *āyah*. It is only when you want to make a will, and Allah knows best. An-Nakha'ī said, 'The Messenger of Allah ﷺ died without making a will. Abū Bakr made a will. It is good to make a will but there is nothing wrong in not making one.'

**to make a will in favour of his parents and relatives,**

Allah did not explain in His Book the amount that one should make a will for. He says: '*if he has some goods* (khayr)' and '*khayr*' means 'wealth' as in other *āyah*s such as 2:272 and 100:8. Scholars disagree about the amount constituted by that. It is related that Abū Bakr aṣ-Ṣiddīq left a fifth in bequests. 'Alī said, 'There is a fifth from the booty of the Muslims.' Ma'mar said that Qatādah said that 'Umar left a quarter in bequests. Al-Bukhārī mentioned that from Ibn 'Abbās. It is related that 'Alī said, 'I prefer to make a bequest of a fifth to that of a quarter and I prefer making a bequest of a quarter to that of a third.'

If someone has little wealth and many heirs, one group prefer that he should not make any bequests. That was related from 'Alī, Ibn 'Abbās and 'Ā'ishah ﷺ. Ibn Abī Shaybah related that Ibn Abī Mulaykah said to 'Ā'ishah, 'I want to make a will.' She asked, 'How much do you have?' 'Three thousand,' he replied. She asked, 'How many dependants do you have?' 'Four,' he answered. She said, 'Allah says "*khayr*" and this is something insignificant. It is better for you to leave it to your dependants.'

The majority of scholars believe that it is not permitted for anyone to will away more than a third of their property, except for Abū Ḥanīfah and his followers who said: 'If a person does not have any statutory heirs, he is permitted to will away all his wealth.' They said that on the basis that limiting the legacy to a third is in order to leave the statutory heirs with sufficient property since the Prophet ﷺ said, 'It is better for you to leave your heirs well provided for than to leave them needy, begging from other people.' The imams related it. They say that if he is not someone with an heir, he is not one of those meant by the *ḥadīth*. This view is related from Ibn 'Abbās. It is also the view of Abū 'Ubaydah and Masrūq. Isḥāq believed that and it is one of the two views of Mālik. It is also related from 'Alī. The reason for the disagreement regarding what we mention is the disagreement about whether the Treasury is an heir or a caretaker.

Scholars agree that people who die with statutory heirs should not will away all of their wealth. It is related that when he was dying, 'Amr ibn al-'Āṣ said to his son 'Abdullāh, 'I want to make a bequest,' and his son said to him, 'Go ahead and make a bequest and what you will can be paid from my property.' He called for a paper and dictated. 'Abdullāh said, 'I said to him, "I think that you have exhausted both my property and your property. I will summon my brothers and ask them to permit it."'

They agree that anyone can change his will and retract any part of it if he wishes. They disagree about doing that in respect of a slave who has a specific contract by which he is to be freed after his owner's death (*mudabbar*). Mālik said, 'The position agreed upon among us is that when someone makes a will, whether he is healthy or ill, in which he frees a slave or something else, he can change whatever of it he wants to and add or delete whatever he likes until he dies. If he wants to cancel that will, he can do so – with the exception of a *tadbīr* contract which there is no way to change because the Messenger of Allah ﷺ said, "It is not right for a Muslim who has anything to will to remain for two nights without having a written will in his possession."' Abu-l-Faraj al-Mālikī said, 'A *mudabbar* is analogous to someone who will be set free after a month because it is a term which must come.' They agree that someone cannot make an oath to set free and to set free at a certain term. That is also the case with a *mudabbar*. That is the position of Abū Ḥanīfah. Ash-Shāfi'ī, Aḥmad and Isḥāq said that it is a bequest and it is part of the third like any other bequests. They permit a man to have sex with a female *mudabbar* which nullifies the making of a *mudabbar* analogous to someone set free at a certain term. It is confirmed that the Prophet ﷺ sold a *mudabbar* and that 'Ā'ishah made her slavegirl a *mudabbarah* and then sold her. That is the view of a group of the Tābi'ūn. One group say that a man can change anything he wishes in his will except for emancipation. That is also the position of ash-Sha'bī, Ibn Sīrīn, Ibn Shubrumah and an-Nakha'ī. It is also the view of Sufyān ath-Thawrī.

There is disagreement about what happens when a man tells his slave, 'You are free after I die,' intending to make that a bequest. Mālik says that he can retract it. If he says, 'So-and-so is a *mudabbar* after I die,' he cannot retract that. If he meant a *tadbīr* by his first statement, most of the people of Mālik say that he cannot retract it. Ash-Shāfi'ī, Aḥmad, Isḥāq and Abū Thawr said that he can retract any of that since it is part of the third, and all that is in the third is a bequest. However, ash-Shāfi'ī said, 'The *tadbīr* can only be retracted by the removal of the *mudabbar* from his possession through sale or gift. If the *mudabbar* does not leave his possession until he dies, then he is set free at his death.' In his earlier position, he said that he can retract the *tadbīr* as he can any other bequest. Al-Muzanī preferred that based on their consensus that a person can retract a bequest of emancipation. Abū Thawr said, 'When he says, "I have retracted my *tadbīr,*" then it is invalidated and the slave is not set free when he dies.' Ibn al-Qāsim and Ashhab disagreed about someone who says, 'My slave is free after I die' without intending a bequest or *tadbīr.* Ibn al-Qāsim said that it is a bequest. Ashhab said that he is a *mudabbar* even he did not mean it as a bequest.

Scholars disagree about whether this *āyah* is abrogated or is one which contains an active legal judgment. It is said to be the latter. Its literal expression is general and its meaning is only specific in respect of someone whose parents do not inherit automatically, because they are unbelievers or slaves for instance, and in respect of relatives other than a person's statutory heirs. Aḍ-Ḍaḥḥāk, Ṭāwūs and al-Ḥasan held that view and aṭ-Ṭabari preferred it. Az-Zuhrī said that a will is mandatory whether someone has a little property or a lot. Ibn al-Mundhir said, 'All of those of import among the people of knowledge agree that it is permitted to make a bequest in favour of parents and relatives who do not inherit.'

Ibn 'Abbās, al-Ḥasan and Qatādah said that the *āyah* is general and its judgment was confirmed for a period of time and then abrogated in respect of all those who automatically inherit by virtue of the *āyah*s specifying the statutory shares of inheritance. It is said that the *āyah*s about the shares is not the only thing that abrogates it, but it is also abrogated by the words of the Prophet ﷺ: 'Allah has given everyone with a due his due and there is no bequest in favour of an heir.' Abū Umāmah related it. At-Tirmidhī transmitted it and said that it is a sound *ḥasan ḥadīth.* So the abrogation of the *āyah* is by the firm Sunnah, not only by the *āyah*s explaining the shares of inheritance, according to the sound position of scholars. If it were not for this *ḥadīth*, it would be possible to combine this *āyah* with the *āyah*s specifying the statutory shares of inheritance by receiving property from the testator both by statutory inheritance and by bequest. This *ḥadīth* and the consensus derived from it prevent that happening. Although ash-Shāfi'ī and Abu-l-Faraj deny that the Book can be abrogated by the Sunnah, it is sound that it is permitted by the proof that all is Allah's judgment and comes from Him, even if the name for it differs. This idea was already mentioned. Even if this report has reached us as a single report, the fact that the consensus of the Muslims is added to it – that it is not permitted to make a bequest to an heir – it is evident that the obligation to make bequests to relatives who are heirs is abrogated by the Sunnah and it is agreed upon. Allah knows best.

Ibn 'Abbās and al-Ḥasan say that making a bequest to parents is abrogated by their statutory shares in *Sūrat an-Nisā'*, but that is confirmed in the case relatives who do not inherit automatically. That is the position of ash-Shāfi'ī, most Mālikīs and a group of the people of knowledge. In al-Bukhārī Ibn 'Abbās said, 'It used to be that all the property belonged to the child and the parents only inherited through a will, so Allah abrogated what He wished in respect of that. He gave males the portion of two females and gave each of the parents a sixth. A wife receives an eighth or a quarter, and the husband has half or a quarter.'

Ibn 'Umar, Ibn 'Abbās and Ibn Zayd said that the *āyah* is abrogated while the recommendation to make a bequest remains. That is similar to Mālik's position and an-Naḥḥās mentioned it from ash-Sha'bī and an-Nakha'ī. Ar-Rabī' ibn Khuthaym said that there is no bequest. 'Urwah ibn Thābit said, 'I said to ar-Rabī' ibn Khuthaym, "Make me a bequest of your copy of the Qur'an." He looked at his son and recited: *"Blood relations are closer to one another in the Book of Allah."* (8:75)' Ibn 'Umar did something similar.

*'Aqrabīn* (relatives) is the plural of *qarīb*. Some people say that it is better to make a will in favour of your relatives rather than non-relatives because of this text from Allah regarding them. For this reason aḍ-Ḍaḥḥāk says, 'A person who makes a bequest to other than his relatives ends his actions with disobedience.' It is related that Ibn 'Umar made a bequest of four hundred thousand (dirhams) to each of his slave-girls who bore him children. It is related that 'Ā'ishah willed her household utensils to a freed slave of hers. The like of that is related from Sālim ibn 'Abdullāh. Al-Ḥasan said, 'If a bequest is made to non-relatives, it is returned to the relatives. If it is made to someone completely unrelated, he shares with them. It is not permitted to give to someone other than them while omitting them.'

When Abu-l-'Āliyah died, people said, 'Astonishing! A woman of Riyāḥ freed him but then he leaves his property to the Banū Hāshim!' Ash-Sha'bī said that he could not do that, even for honour. Ṭāwūs said, 'If he makes a bequest to non-relatives, it is returned to relatives and his action is nullified.' Jābir ibn Zayd said that. This is also related from al-Ḥasan. Isḥāq ibn Rāhawayh said that. Mālik, ash-Shāfi'ī, Abū Ḥanīfah, al-Awzā'ī, and Aḥmad ibn Ḥanbal said that if someone leaves a bequest to non-relatives and leaves his relatives in need, he has committed a wrong action. If he does that, however, his bequest stands and is carried out, whether the person receiving it is rich or poor, relative or not, Muslim or unbeliever. It is the meaning of what was related from Ibn 'Umar and 'Ā'ishah. It is the view of Ibn 'Umar and Ibn 'Abbās.

The first view is better. In the case of Abu-l-'Āliyah, it is possible that he thought that the Banū Hāshim were more entitled than the woman who freed him because of him keeping the company of Ibn 'Abbās, him teaching him and joining him to the rank of the scholars in this world and the Next. Although this parenthood is spiritual, it is actual. The purpose of the woman who freed him was to connect him to free men in this world and the reward of emancipation is enough for her. Allah knows best.

The majority of scholars believe that a very sick person is legally debarred from disposing of his property. The Ẓāhirīs have an aberrant view, saying that he is not debarred. Both the *ḥadīth* and the idea refute them. Sa'd said, 'The Messenger of Allah ﷺ visited me during the Farewell Hajj when I was ill and expecting to die and I said, "Messenger of Allah, my illness has reached what you see. I have wealth but only have one daughter as an heir. Can I give two-thirds of my wealth away as *ṣadaqah*?" "No," he said. I said, "A half?" and he said, "No." He then added, "No, but (give) a third, and a third is a lot. It is better for you to leave your heirs wealthy than to leave them in need, begging from people."'

The Ẓāhirīs also forbid leaving more than a third, even if the heirs allow it. All allow it if the heirs agree to it, and it is sound because the sick person is forbidden to make a bequest of more than a third in order to protect the rights of the heirs. When the heirs forgo their right, then that is permitted and it is like a gift from them. Ad-Dāraquṭnī related from Ibn 'Abbās that the Messenger of Allah ﷺ said, 'It is not permitted to make a bequest to an heir unless the heirs want it.' It is related that 'Amr ibn Khārijah said that the Messenger of Allah ﷺ said, 'There is no bequest to an heir unless the heirs allow it.'

They disagree about those who allow a bequest to an heir while the testator was alive rescinding it after his death. One group say that it was permitted by them so they cannot rescind it. This is the view of 'Aṭā' ibn Abī Rabāḥ, Ṭāwūs, Ibn Sīrīn, Ibn Abī Laylā, az-Zuhrī, Rabī'ah and al-Awzā'ī. Another group says that they can rescind it if they wish. That is the view of Ibn Mas'ūd, Shurayḥ, al-Ḥakam, Ṭāwūs, ath-Thawrī, al-Ḥasan ibn Ṣāliḥ, Abū Ḥanīfah, ash-Shāfi'ī, Aḥmad and Abū Thawr. Ibn al-Mundhir preferred it. Mālik made a distinction and said, 'When they allow it when he is healthy, then they can rescind it. When they allow it when he is in his final illness and is, therefore, debarred from acting on his property, that decision is binding on them.' It is the view of Isḥāq. The people who hold the first view argue that the prohibition comes from the heirs, so when they allow it, it is allowed. They agree that when he makes a bequest of more than a third to a non-relative, it is allowed when they allow it. That is the case. The people with the second view argue that they allowed something over which they had no ownership at that moment. The property only came into their possession after his death. The heir whose permission was asked may die before him and then he is no longer an heir; someone else inherits. If someone who has no entitlement gives permission, nothing is obliged. Mālik argued that when a man is healthy, he is more entitled to all his wealth and can do whatever he wishes with it. When they give him permission when he is healthy, they have abandoned something not obliged for them. When they give their permission when he is ill, then they have abandoned that to which they are entitled. Therefore they cannot retract that when he carries it out.

If the sick person does not carry that out, then the heir can rescind it because it has not been achieved. Al-Abharī said that. Ibn al-Mundhir mentioned from Isḥāq ibn Rāhawayh that the position of Mālik in this question is closer than others to the Sunnah. Ibn al-Mundhir said, 'Mālik, ath-Thawrī, the Kufans, ash-Shāfi'ī and Abū Thawr agree that if they allow that after his death, it is binding.'

They disagree about a man who makes a bequest of property to one of his heirs and says in his will: 'If the heirs allow it, it is his. If they do not allow it, it is for the Cause of Allah,' and then they do not allow it. Mālik said, 'If the heirs do not allow it, it reverts to them.' The view of ash-Shāfi'ī, Abū Ḥaniịfah and Ma'mar, the companion of 'Abd ar-Razzāq, say that it is for the Cause of Allah.

There is no disagreement about a will made by a sane adult whose dealings are not legally competent. They disagree about others. Mālik said, 'The generally agreed way of doing things among us is that a simpleton, an idiot, or a lunatic who has moments of recovery can make their wills as long as they are made while they are sound of mind and know what they are doing. The same is true for a child when he understands what he is bequeathing and does not say anything untoward: his will is permitted and carried out.' Abū Ḥanīfah and his people said that a bequest made by a child is not permitted. Al-Muzanī said, 'It is analogous to the view of ash-Shāfi'ī, but I do not find any actual mention or text from ash-Shāfi'ī about that.' His people have two different views. One is like that of Mālik and the other is like that of Abū Ḥanīfah. Their argument is that neither the divorce nor emancipation of such a minor is allowed. Retaliation is not taken from him for an injury and he receives no *ḥadd* punishment for slander. So he is not like a legally incompetent adult. The same is true of his will.

Abū 'Umar said, 'These scholars agree that the will of an adult legally debarred from financial dealings is permitted. It is known that intelligent children can make wills, and therefore his situation is the same as someone who is legally debarred from dealing with his wealth. The reason that he is legally incompetent is that he might squander and destroy it. That reason is removed from him when he dies.

In his incompetency concerning his property he resembles the madman who has no wits. It is mandatory to allow his bequest and this is further supported by what has come regarding it from 'Umar ﷺ. Mālik said, 'It is the generally agreed way of doing things among us in Madīnah. Success is by Allah.' Muḥammad ibn Shurayḥ said, 'When a child or adult makes a bequest, it is a right which Allah has decreed on his tongue. There is no averting the truth.'

**correctly and fairly:**

This means with justice, no more, no less. It is entrusted to the discretion and opinion of the one making the will, and then Allah decided that on the tongue of His Prophet ﷺ who said, 'A third, and a third is a lot,' as we have already mentioned. The Prophet ﷺ said, 'Allah has given you a third of your wealth at your death so that you can increase your good deeds and make it purification for yourself.' Ad-Dāraquṭnī transmitted that from Abū Umāmah from Mu'ādh ibn Jabal from the Prophet ﷺ. Al-Ḥasan said, 'Only a third is permitted in bequests.' Al-Bukhārī believed that and cited as evidence His words: *'Judge between them by what Allah has sent down'* (5:49) and the judgment of the Prophet ﷺ that a third is a lot. That is the ruling that Allah has sent down. Anyone who exceeds the limit of the Messenger of Allah ﷺ and makes it more than a third has done something the Prophet ﷺ forbade. If he knows the judgment of the Messenger of Allah ﷺ and does that, then he becomes a rebel. Ash-Shāfi'ī said that his statement means that a third is not a small amount.

**a duty for all those who are godfearing.**

In other words it is a confirmed and established practice but there is no obligation to do it, since Allah says it is for the godfearing. This indicates that making a will is recommended because if it were obligatory, Allah would have said that it was a duty for all Muslims, not just the godfearing.

Scholars have said that the exhortation to hasten to make a will is not taken from this *āyah* but from the *ḥadīth* of Ibn 'Umar. It is increased security for it to be written and witnessed. That is the will that is agreed upon and used. If reputable witnesses testify orally to it, it should be acted upon, even if not a single line is written down. If a person writes it in his hand without witnesses, the position of Mālik does not vary about not acting on it, unless it contains affirmation of a right which is not suspect and therefore must be carried out.

Ad-Dāraquṭnī related that Anas ibn Mālik said, 'They used to write at the beginning of their wills, "This is the will of so-and-so son of so-and-so who testifies that there is no god but Allah alone with no partner and that Muḥammad is His slave and Messenger. The Hour is coming. There is no doubt about it and Allah will raise up those in the graves.'" A man would command those who survived him to fear Allah as He should be feared, act correctly towards one another and to obey Allah and His Messenger, and would advise them as Ibrāhīm and Ya'qūb had advised their sons: *'My sons! Allah has chosen this* dīn *for you, so do not die except as Muslims.'* (2:132)

فَمَنۢ بَدَّلَهُۥ بَعۡدَ مَا سَمِعَهُۥ فَإِنَّمَآ إِثۡمُهُۥ عَلَى ٱلَّذِينَ يُبَدِّلُونَهُۥٓۚ إِنَّ ٱللَّهَ سَمِيعٌ
عَلِيمٞ ١٨١

**181 Then if anyone alters it after hearing it, the crime is on the part of those who alter it. Allah is All-Hearing, All-Knowing.**

This refers to altering the wording of a will. 'Hearing it' can mean hearing the testator himself or alternatively hearing what is confirmed from him by two witnesses. 'The crime' refers to the alteration, meaning the crime of alteration.

This *āyah* indicates that when a person mentions a debt in his will, it should be paid immediately, since it is his first responsibility, and the executor must produce what is demanded and receives a wage for carrying it out. It is a sin for him to delay paying it.

There is no disagreement that when a person makes a bequest of something which is not permitted, such as wine, pigs or any act of disobedience, it is permitted to change the will and it is not permitted to carry it out, in the same way that it is not permitted to carry out bequests of more than a third.

*'Allah is All-Hearing, All-Knowing.'* By naming these two attributes, it is clear that no bias on the part of the testators or alteration on the part of the witnesses can be hidden from Him.

فَمَنۡ خَافَ مِن مُّوصٖ جَنَفًا أَوۡ إِثۡمٗا فَأَصۡلَحَ بَيۡنَهُمۡ فَلَآ إِثۡمَ عَلَيۡهِۚ إِنَّ ٱللَّهَ غَفُورٞ
رَّحِيمٞ ١٨٢

**182 But if someone fears bias or wrongdoing on the part of the person making the will, and puts things right between the people involved, in that case he has not committed any crime. Allah is Ever-Forgiving, Most Merciful.**

The word '*khāfa*' (fears) can also mean 'knows of' in this instance. The root is *khawf.* 'The person making the will' is recited by Abū Bakr from 'Āṣim, Ḥamzah and al-Kisā'ī as '*muwaṣṣī*' while the rest recite it as '*mūṣī*'. The second reading is clearer because grammarians use the first (Form II) for a more extensive meaning. '*Janaf*' (bias) means 'inclining towards something'. It is related that 'Alī recited '*ḥayf*' rather than *khawf,* meaning 'injustice'. Mujāhid said that this *āyah* means 'someone who fears that the testator will be biased and cut off the inheritance of some people and deliberately cause harm, or even bring that about without doing it deliberately'. This kind of unconscious bias is not necessarily a wrong action, although it is definitely a wrong action if it is deliberate. The *āyah* means that someone who warns a testator about that and averts him from doing it, thereby putting things right between him and his heirs and between the heirs themselves, does nothing wrong. Allah is 'Ever-Forgiving' to the testator when he acts on the warning and retracts the injury he would have inflicted.

Ibn 'Abbās, Qatādah, ar-Rabī' and others say that the meaning of the *āyah* is that anyone who knows the testator was biased and intended injury to some of his heirs should act after his death and put right the disturbance and schism which then arises between the heirs. He does nothing wrong by doing this when the change is in the best interests of the people concerned. The alteration that is sinful is that which arises from inclination to one heir.

The *āyah* is addressed to all Muslims. They are told: if you fear that a testator will be biased in his bequest, turn from what is the right, fall into wrong action and not do what is correct by inclining to his daughter's husband or his daughter's child, for instance, so that the money will go to his daughter, or to the son of his son when he wants it to go to his son, or he wills it to someone distant and neglects his nearer relatives, then they should hasten to put things right between them. Putting things right will remove the wrong action from the one who does it. It is a *farḍ kifāyah* so if no one does it, everyone is guilty of wrong action.

The *āyah* provides evidence for judging based on opinion, because if someone thinks that corruption is intended, he is obliged to strive to put things right. If the corruption is verified, it is no longer considered under the category of putting things right because it becomes a different kind of judgment: one concerned with averting and putting an end to corruption.

There is no disagreement that giving *ṣadaqah* is better when one is alive and healthy than when one is dead since, when the Prophet ﷺ was asked, 'Which *ṣadaqah* is better?' he said, 'That you give *ṣadaqah* when you are desirous of money and healthy.' The people of the *Ṣaḥīḥ* transmitted it. Ad-Dāraquṭnī related from Abū Sa'īd al-Khudrī that the Prophet ﷺ said, 'It is better for a man to give one dirham while he is alive than a hundred when he is dead.' An-Nasā'ī related from Abu-d-Dardā' that he ﷺ said, 'The metaphor of someone who spends or gives *ṣadaqah* after his death is that of someone who gives food after he is full.'

Provided it does not harm anyone, it is permitted for someone to pay any zakat he neglected to pay during his lifetime by means of his will. Ad-Dāraquṭnī related from Mu'āwiyah ibn Qurrah from his father that the Messenger of Allah ﷺ said, 'When someone who is dying makes a will, his will is based on the Book of Allah. It expiates any of his zakat he failed to pay.'

Ad-Dāraquṭnī related from Ibn 'Abbās that the Messenger of Allah ﷺ said, 'Harming people through a bequest is one of the major wrong actions.' Abū Dāwud related that Abū Hurayrah reported that the Messenger of Allah ﷺ said, 'A man or woman can act in obedience to Allah for sixty years and then, when they are about to die, harm someone in their will and end up in the Fire because of it.' An-Nasā'ī speaks about about praying over someone who was biased in his will: 'Alī ibn Ḥajar reported from Hushaym from Manṣūr ibn Zadhān from al-Ḥasan that 'Imrān ibn Ḥusayn said that a man freed six slaves he had when he died and that was the only property he possessed. The Prophet ﷺ heard about that and was angry and stated, 'I wish that I had not prayed over him.' Then he brought the man's slaves and divided them into three parts and then drew lots and freed two and left four as slaves. Muslim transmitted it, but instead of 'I wish that I had not prayed over him', he has, 'He said harsh words about him.'

يَٰٓأَيُّهَا ٱلَّذِينَ ءَامَنُواْ كُتِبَ عَلَيۡكُمُ ٱلصِّيَامُ كَمَا كُتِبَ عَلَى ٱلَّذِينَ مِن قَبۡلِكُمۡ
لَعَلَّكُمۡ تَتَّقُونَ ١٨٣ أَيَّامٗا مَّعۡدُودَٰتٖۚ فَمَن كَانَ مِنكُم مَّرِيضًا
أَوۡ عَلَىٰ سَفَرٖ فَعِدَّةٞ مِّنۡ أَيَّامٍ أُخَرَۚ وَعَلَى ٱلَّذِينَ يُطِيقُونَهُۥ فِدۡيَةٞ طَعَامُ
مِسۡكِينٖۖ فَمَن تَطَوَّعَ خَيۡرٗا فَهُوَ خَيۡرٞ لَّهُۥۚ وَأَن تَصُومُواْ خَيۡرٞ
لَّكُمۡ إِن كُنتُمۡ تَعۡلَمُونَ ١٨٤

**183 You who believe! fasting is prescribed for you, as it was prescribed for those before you – so that hopefully you will become godfearing – 184 for a specified number of days. But any of you who are ill or on a journey should fast a number of other days. For those who are able to fast [only with difficulty and do not fast], their fidyah is to feed the poor. And if someone does good of his own accord, it is better for him. But that you should fast is better for you, If you only knew.**

**You who believe! fasting is prescribed for you,**

Allah mentions two injunctions for Muslims – retaliation and making a will – and then mentions a third, saying that fasting is also prescribed for them and obligatory and mandatory for all. There is no disagreement about this. The Prophet ﷺ said, 'Islam is based on five: the testimony that there is no god but Allah and Muḥammad is the Messenger of Allah, establishing the prayer, paying zakat, fasting Ramadan and ḥajj.' Ibn 'Umar related it. Linguistically '*ṣiyām*' (fasting) means refraining from something and not moving from one state to another. Silence is called fasting because it is refraining from speaking, as we find when Allah says in *Sūrat Maryam*: *'I have made a vow of silence* (ṣawm) *to the All-Merciful.'* (19:26) The verb is also used to refer to the wind being still, to an animal when it goes off its food, and to the day when it reaches its midpoint. *Maṣām* is when the sun reaches midday. In terms of the Sharī'ah, fasting means to refrain from all those things which break the fast, having made the intention to fast, between dawn and sunset, and it is completed and perfected by avoiding all forbidden things and not falling into any prohibited actions, as the Prophet ﷺ said, 'If someone does not abandon lying and acting by it, Allah has no need of him abandoning food and drink.'

The benefits of fasting are huge and its reward enormous. There are many good and excellent reports attesting to that. Sufficient evidence for the excellence of fasting lies in the fact that Allah singled it out for ascription to Himself as is confirmed in the *ḥadīth* in which the Prophet ﷺ reports his Lord as saying, 'Allah Almighty says, "Every action of the son of Ādam is his except for fasting. It is Mine and I reward it."' He singled out fasting as being His, even though all acts of worship are in fact His, for two reasons which make fasting different from other acts of worship. The first is that fasting curtails the enjoyment and appetites of the lower self which other acts of worship do not. The second is that fasting is a secret between the slave and his Lord that only He knows. All other acts of worship are outward and may contain some artifice and showing off, which is not the case with fasting. That is why it is specially for Him. Other things are said as well.

**as it was prescribed for those before you –**

Ash-Sha'bī, Qatādah and others said that the comparison refers to the time of fasting and amount of fasting. Allah had prescribed fasting Ramadan for the people of Mūsā and 'Īsā but they altered it. The priests added ten days due to a vow made by one of them and eventually, due to further oaths, the Christian fast became fifty days and that was too arduous in the heat, so it was moved to the spring. An-Naḥḥās preferred this view and said that it is closer to what is in the *āyah.* There is also a *ḥadīth* which indicates its soundness from Daghfal ibn Ḥanẓalah in which the Prophet ﷺ said, 'The Christians were obliged to fast a month and then one of their men became ill. They said, "If Allah heals him, we will add ten days." Then another ate meat and had a pain in his mouth. They said, "If Allah heals him, we will add seven days." Then a king fell ill and they said, "We will complete the seven days as ten and move our fast to the spring." So it became fifty days.' Mujāhid said, 'Allah prescribed the fast of Ramadan for every nation.' It is said that they took a covenant and fasted a day before the thirty days and a day after it, generation after generation, until their fast reached fifty days. It was difficult for them in the heat and so they moved it to the spring. An-Naqqāsh said, 'There is a *ḥadīth* about that from Daghfal ibn Ḥanẓalah, al-Ḥasan al-Baṣrī and as-Suddī.

Allah knows best, but this is why it is disliked to fast the Day of Doubt and the six days of Shawwāl continuously after the day of the *'Īd.* Ash-Sha'bī said, 'Even if I were to fast all of the six, I would not fast the Day of Doubt. That is because the Christians were obliged to fast the month of Ramadan as we are obliged to fast it. Then they changed it to the spring because it used to coincide with the heat of summer. They did thirty days. Then after them some of them made a covenant imposing on themselves to fast a day before and after the thirty. That continued to be the custom until it reached fifty days. That is the import of His words: *"as it was prescribed for those before you."'*

It is said that the comparison applies to the fact of the obligation to fast, not to the time or amount of fasting. It is said that the comparison is in respect of the description of fasting, as it is denial of food, drink and sexual intercourse. Even if the end of the fast comes and someone is asleep, he does not do any of these things. That is how it was with the Christians and at the beginning of Islam. Then Allah abrogated it by His words: *'On the night of the fast it is lawful for you to have sexual relations with your wives.'* (2:187) As-Suddī, Abu-l-'Āliyah and ar-Rabī' said that.

Mu'ādh ibn Jabal and 'Aṭā' said that the comparison is in respect of fasting, not the manner or the number of days, although the two fasts differ in being more or less in terms of time. Fasting three days of every month and the Day of 'Ashūrā' '... *prescribed for you, as it was prescribed for those before you,'* meaning the Jews. According to Ibn 'Abbās, it was three days of every month and the Day of 'Ashūrā'. This was then abrogated for the Muslims by the prescription of the month of Ramadan. Mu'ādh ibn Jabal said that it was abrogated by *'a specified number of days'* and then by the days of Ramadan.

**so that hopefully you will become godfearing –**

You are weak. When you only eat a little, your appetites are weakened. When the appetites are weakened, acts of disobedience are lessened. This is a good metaphorical interpretation. It is also said it means so that you will be wary of acts of disobedience. It is said that it is general because fasting, as the Prophet ﷺ said, 'is a covering and hope' and a means to becoming godfearing because it subdues appetites.

**for a specified number of days**

This refers to the month of Ramadan. This differs from what is related from Mu'ādh, and Allah knows best.

**But if any of you who are ill or on a journey should fast a number of other days.**

There are two possibilities for someone who is ill. One is that he cannot fast at all and it is obligatory for him to break it. The second is that he is able to fast but only with difficulty. This person is recommended to break his fast and only an ignorant person fasts in that condition. Ibn Sīrīn said, 'When a person is in a state which can be called illness, he can break the fast, analogous with a traveller who does so by reason of travelling, even if he does not have to.' Ṭarīf ibn Tammām said, 'I visited Muḥammad ibn Sīrīn in Ramadan and he was eating, When he finished he said, "I have something wrong with this finger."'

Most scholars, however, say that a person may only break the fast when he has an illness which pains or harms him or when he fears that the illness will last longer or increase if he fasts. Ibn 'Aṭiyyah said, 'This is the position of the people of Mālik who possess extensive knowledge.' Ibn Khuwayzimandād said that there were different transmissions from Mālik about the kind of illness that permits breaking the fast. One view was that the illness had to be one in which there was fear of someone dying if they fasted. Another was that it was a serious illness and there was fear of it getting worse and causing hardship, and this is the sound position of his school. That is based on the literal wording because the 'illness' is unspecified. Therefore it is allowed in the case of any illness except that for which there is specific evidence: headache, fever and minor illness which is unaffected by fasting. Al-Ḥasan said, 'If someone is unable to pray standing due to illness, then he should break the fast.' An-Nakha'ī said that. One group said that you should only break the fast when the illness actually forces you to. When the difficulty accompanying it can be endured, then the fast should not be broken. This is the view of ash-Shāfi'ī.

However, the fairest thing concerning this topic, Allah willing, is what Ibn Sīrīn said, and al-Bukhārī reports a similar position from Isḥāq ibn Rāhawayh. He said, 'I fell ill in Nishapur with a minor illness in the month of Ramadan. Isḥāq ibn Rāhawayh visited me with a group of his companions. He asked me, "Have you broken the fast, Abū 'Abdullāh?" "Yes," I answered. He said, "I feared that you would be too weak to take advantage of the allowance." I said, "'Abdullāh ibn al-Mubārak related to me that Ibn Jurayj asked 'Aṭā', 'For what illness may I break the fast?' He replied, 'For any illness, since Allah Almighty says: "*But if any of you who are ill.*"'""' Al-Bukhārī said that Isḥāq did not have that *ḥadīth*. Abū Ḥanīfah said, 'If a man who is fasting fears that if he does not break the fast his pain or fever will increase, then he should break the fast.'

**or on a journey**

Scholars disagree about the length of journey on which it is permitted to break the fast and shorten the prayer although there is a consensus about the journey being one which is in obedience to Allah, such as ḥajj or *jihād*, or a journey to visit relatives or seeking necessary livelihood. As for journeys for trade and other permitted things, there is disagreement about whether it is forbidden or permitted on these. That it is permitted is more likely. As for a journey for the sake of disobedience, there is also disagreement about whether it is permitted or prohibited to break the fast during it, and prohibited is more likely. Ibn 'Aṭiyyah said that.

According to Mālik, the distance which must be travelled to break the fast is the same as that for which the prayer can be shortened. Scholars disagree about exactly what that is. Mālik said, 'A day and a night,' and then he retracted that and said, 'Forty-eight miles.' Ibn Khuwayzimandād said, 'That appears to be the position of his school.' He is once reported as saying forty-two miles, or thirty-six miles, or a day and night, or two days, which is the position of ash-Shāfi'ī. And there is a difference between land and sea journeys. It is said that a sea journey must be a day and a night whereas on land the stipulation is forty-eight miles. It is said in the School that it is thirty miles, and three miles is said outside the School. Ibn 'Amr, Ibn 'Abbās and ath-Thawrī said that you should break the fast on a journey of three days, as Ibn 'Aṭiyyah also related.

Scholars agree that someone travelling in Ramadan is not permitted to break the fast at home before setting out because a traveller does not become a traveller by intention and remains a resident who is a resident until he becomes a traveller by action and actually setting out. A resident does not need any action because by the intention to remain he immediately becomes a resident. Residency does not need any other action. Therefore the two are different. They say that there is no disagreement about the fact that someone who intends to travel is not permitted to break the fast before he actually leaves. If he does break it, Ibn Ḥabīb says that if he has made preparations to travel and has begun the process, he owes nothing provided that the journey actually takes place. That is also related from Aṣbagh and Ibn al-Mājishūn. If he is then prevented from travelling, he owes *kaffārah*. 'Īsā related from Ibn al-Qāsim, however, that he only has to make up that day because he was following a legal interpretation in breaking the fast. Ashhab says he owes nothing whether he travels or not. Saḥnūn says that he owes *kaffārah* whether he travels or not and that he is like a woman expecting her period who breaks the fast for that reason. Then he reverted to the position of 'Abd l-Malik and Aṣbagh, saying, 'He is not like a woman because a man can start a journey when he wishes and a woman cannot make her period start.'

The position of Ibn al-Qāsim and Ashhab about not owing *kaffārah* in this case is good because it is an action which people are permitted to do and do not incur liability for. Nothing is established about it except by certainty and there is no certainty when there is a disagreement about what is demanded by the words '... *on a journey*'. Abū 'Umar said, 'This is the soundest of their views on this question because it does not intentionally detract from the inviolability of fasting. It is based on a legal interpretation. If someone eats while only intending to travel (and then does not travel), then he must owe *kaffārah* because that which is cancelled after setting out is not cancelled before setting out. If you reflect on that, you will find it to be the case. Allah knows best.'

Ad-Dāraquṭnī related from Abū Bakr an-Naysābūrī from Ismā'īl ibn Isḥāq ibn Sahl in Egypt from Ibn Abī Maryam from Muḥammad ibn Ja'far from Zayd ibn Aslam from Muḥammad ibn al-Munkadir that Muḥammad ibn Ka'b said, 'I went to Anas ibn Mālik in Ramadan when he was intending to travel. His camel was loaded and he had his travel clothes on. It was close to sunset. He called for food, ate, and then mounted. I asked him, 'Sunnah?" "Yes," he replied.' It is also related that Anas said, 'Abū Mūsā said to me, "Have I not informed you that when you leave, you leave fasting, and when you arrive, you arrive fasting? When you leave, leave not fasting and when you arrive, arrive not fasting."' Al-Ḥasan al-Baṣrī said, 'If you wish, you can break it in your house before leaving.' Aḥmad said that someone may break the fast when he goes beyond the houses (of the settlement where he is resident). Isḥāq said, 'No, it is when he puts his foot in the stirrup.'

Ibn al-Mundhir said, 'The view of Aḥmad is sound, because when someone starts the day healthy and then becomes ill, he is told not to fast for the rest of the day. Similarly, when he starts the day at home and then sets out on a journey, he can break the fast.' One group said that he should not break the fast that day, even when he starts a journey. That is what was stated by az-Zuhrī, Makḥūl, Yaḥyā al-Anṣārī, Mālik, al-Awzā'ī, ash-Shāfi'ī, Abū Thawr and the People of Opinion.

They disagree about what happens if he does break it. Most of them say that he makes it up, but does not do *kaffārah*. Mālik said that it was because the journey is an incidental reason and it is similar to when he becomes ill. It is related from some of Mālik's people that he makes it up and does *kaffārah*. That is the view of Ibn Kinānah and al-Makhzūmī. Al-Bājī related that position from ash-Shāfi'ī. Ibn al-'Arabī preferred that and stated it. He said that that is because the journey is something that occurred in his case after the act of worship became binding. Illness and menstruation are different because illness permits breaking the fast and menstruation makes it unlawful to fast. A journey does not authorise that and therefore *kaffārah* is incurred by a person who breaks the fast under those circumstances for violating the inviolability of fasting. Abū 'Umar said, 'This is not the case because Allah has permitted breaking the fast in the Book and the Sunnah. When they say that he should not break it, that is a recommendation for what he has contracted. If he takes up the dispensation that Allah has given, then he must simply make it up. There is no reason for *kaffārah*. Someone who makes it mandatory has made mandatory something which neither Allah nor His Messenger made mandatory.' Regarding this question, it is related that Ibn 'Umar said that he can break it on that day when he sets out on a journey. It is the view of ash-Sha'bī, Aḥmad and Isḥāq.

Al-Bukhārī has a chapter entitled 'Someone breaking his fast on a journey in such a way that people will see him'. He has a *ḥadīth* from Ibn 'Abbās: 'The Messenger of Allah ﷺ went out from Madīnah to Makkah and fasted until he reached 'Usfān. Then he called for water and raised it in his hand so that the people would see him and ceased fasting until he reached Makkah. That was during Ramadan.' Muslim also transmitted that Ibn 'Abbās said in it: 'He called for a vessel which contained something to drink and drank from it in the day so that people would see him. Then he ceased fasting until reached Makkah.' This is a clear text on the topic and so there is no opposition to it. Success is by Allah.

It also contains evidence for those who say that one does not fast on a journey. That is related from 'Umar, Ibn 'Abbās, Abū Hurayrah and Ibn 'Umar. Ibn 'Umar said, 'If someone fasts on a journey, he should still make it up when he becomes resident.' 'Abd ar-Raḥmān ibn 'Awf said, 'Someone who fasts on a journey is like someone who does not fast when resident.' Some of the Ẓāhirīs take that position and cite as evidence *'a number of other days.'* There is also what is related that Ka'b ibn 'Āṣim said, 'I heard the Messenger of Allah ﷺ say, "Fasting on a journey is not part of piety."'

There is also evidence in it for those who say that if someone on a journey intends at night to fast the next day, he can break the fast, even without an excuse. That is the view of Muṭarrif and one of the views of ash-Shāfi'ī. It is held by a group of the people of *ḥadīth*. Mālik said that he must make it up and do *kaffārah* because he has a choice between fasting and not fasting. When he chooses to fast and makes an intention to do so during the night, it is binding on him and he may not break the fast. If he breaks the fast deliberately without an excuse he must make it up and do *kaffārah*. It is also related from him that he does not have to do *kaffārah*. That is the view of most of his people except for 'Abd al-Malik. He said, 'If he breaks his fast through sexual intercourse, then he must do *kaffārah* because doing that does not relate to having sufficient strength for the journey and so he has no excuse. A traveller is permitted to break his fast in order to be strong enough for the journey by doing that. The rest of the *fuqahā'* in Iraq and the Hijaz, including ath-Thawrī, al-Awzā'ī, ash-Shāfi'ī, Abū Ḥanīfah and the rest of the *fuqahā'* of Kufa, say that he owes no *kaffārah*. Abū 'Umar also said that.

Scholars disagree about which is better: breaking the fast or fasting on a journey. Mālik and ash-Shāfi'ī said that fasting is better for the one who is strong enough to do it. The majority opinion in the school of Mālik is that there is a choice, which is also the position in the school of ash-Shāfi'ī. Ash-Shāfi'ī and those who follow him also say that he has a choice, without giving details. That is also the view of Ibn 'Ulayyah based on the *ḥadīth* of Anas who said, 'We travelled with the Prophet ﷺ during Ramadan and those who were fasting did not criticize the non-fasters and the non-fasters did not criticize those who were fasting.' Mālik, al-Bukhārī and others transmitted it. It is related that 'Uthmān ibn Abī 'l-'Āṣ ath-Thaqafī and Anas ibn Mālik, the Companions of the Messenger of Allah ﷺ, said, 'Fasting is better for those who are strong enough to do it.' That is the position of Abū Ḥanīfah and his people. Ibn 'Umar and Ibn 'Abbās said, 'Taking advantage of the dispensation is better,' as did Sa'īd ibn al-Musayyab, ash-Sha'bī, 'Umar ibn 'Abd al-'Azīz, Mujāhid, Qatādah, al-Awzā'ī, Aḥmad and Isḥāq. They say that not fasting is better because of the words of the Almighty: *'Allah desires ease for you. He does not desire difficulty for you.'* (2:185)

**should fast a number of other days.**

There is an elision here, i.e. 'whoever among you is ill or on a journey should break the fast and then make up...' The majority of scholars say that when the people of the land fast twenty-nine days and a man is ill, when he recovers, he makes up twenty-nine days. He makes up the days he missed. Some people, including al-Ḥasan ibn Ṣāliḥ ibn Ḥayy, said, 'He makes up the month without reference to the number of days.' Aṭ-Ṭabarī said, 'This is unlikely because Allah says, *"a number of other days"* and did not say, "a month of other days."' 'Number' (*'iddah*) demands fulfilling the number of days he did not fast. There is no doubt that if he misses some of Ramadan, he must make up the same number of days he missed. It is the number of days that one considers rather than 'the month'.

People disagree about whether it is obligatory for the days to be continuous or not when someone is making them up. Ad-Dāraquṭnī mentioned both in his *Sunan* and related that 'Ā'ishah said that originally the *āyah* said 'fast a continuous number' and then 'continuous' was dropped. This report has a sound *isnād*. Abū Hurayrah reported that the Messenger of Allah ﷺ said, 'Anyone who owes a fast for Ramadan, should do it continuously and not break it.' Its *isnād* contains 'Abd ar-Raḥmān ibn Ibrāhīm who is weak. Ibn 'Abbās, however, says about making up Ramadan, 'Fast it however you wish.' Ibn 'Umar said, 'Fast them as you broke them.' It is traced to Abū 'Ubaydah ibn al-Jarrāḥ, Ibn 'Abbās, Abū Hurayrah, Mu'ādh ibn Jabal and 'Amr ibn al-'Āṣ. Muḥammad ibn al-Munkadir said, 'I heard that the Messenger of Allah ﷺ was asked about breaking up the fast of Ramadan and said, "That is up to you. If someone had a debt and repayment is done in amounts of one or two dirhams, does he not repay it? Allah is more entitled to pardon and forgive."' Its *isnād* is good although it is *mursal* and not confirmed as connected. We find in the *Muwaṭṭā'* from Mālik from Nāfi' that Ibn 'Umar used to say, 'Someone who breaks the fast in Ramadan because he is ill or travelling should make up the days he has missed consecutively.' Al-Bājī said in *al-Muntaqa*: 'It is possible that the report means that it is mandatory, and it is possible that it means that it is recommended. Most *fuqahā'* say that it is recommended. It is allowed to fast them separately. That is the view of Mālik and ash-Shāfi'ī. The evidence for the soundness of this is His words, *"a number of other days"* without specifying whether they are separate or continuous. If he does them separately, he has fasted a number of other days and so it necessarily satisfies it.' Ibn al-'Arabī said that consecutiveness is mandatory during the month since it is specified. It is not specified in making up the days and so it is permitted to break them up.

When Allah says, *'a number of other days'*, it indicates the obligation to make it up without specifying a time for doing it because the phrase applies to times, which are not distinct. We find in the two *Ṣaḥīḥ* collections that 'Ā'ishah said,

'Sometimes I owed fasting for Ramadan and was unable to make the days up until Sha'bān since I was busy with the Messenger of Allah ﷺ.' This is a text and further explanation of the *āyah*. That refutes what Dāwud said about it being obligatory to make it up on the second day of Shawwāl. In his view, someone who dies without having fasted it has sinned. Based on that, if he is obliged to free a slave and finds a slave on sale for eight, he cannot go beyond him and buy another because he was obliged to free the first slave he finds and the obligation is not satisfied by another slave. If the slave the person owns dies, then the emancipation is not invalidated, as it would be invalidated in the case of someone who vows to free a particular slave who then dies. In that case, his vow is invalidated. Some scholars of fundamentals say that if a person dies after the second day of Shawwāl, he is not disobedient provided that he has resolve. What is sound is that he does not sin and is not negligent. That is the majority position, although it is, however, recommended for him to hurry to make them up so that he does not die before having completed them, still owing an obligation.

If someone must make up days of Ramadan and enough days pass after Ramadan in which he could have made them up and he delays doing so until something prevents him from making them until the following Ramadan, he does not have to feed anyone because he was not negligent since he was permitted to delay. This is the position of the Baghdādī Mālikīs and they relate it as the position of Ibn al-Qāsim in the *Mudawwana*.

If someone delays making up the fast until Sha'bān has ended, which is the usual time for making it up, does he owe *fidyah*? Mālik, Aḥmad, ash-Shāfi'ī and Isḥāq said that he does but Abū Ḥanīfah, al-Ḥasan, an-Nakha'ī and Dāwud said he does not. This is what al-Bukhārī believed based on the words he mentioned *mursal* from Abū Hurayrah and Ibn 'Abbās that he should feed people, even though Allah does not mention feeding but fasting a number of days. There is a *ḥadīth* from Abū Hurayrah about the person who neglects to make up the days he owes of Ramadan until the next Ramadan. He said that he fasts it with the people and then fasts what he missed and feeds a poor person for every day. Ad-Dāraquṭnī transmitted it and said that it has a sound *isnād*. It is related from him that the Prophet ﷺ said about a man who breaks the fast in Ramadan due to illness and recovers and does not make it up until the next Ramadan: 'He fasts the month he is in and then fasts the month in which he broke the fast and feeds a poor man for every day.' Ibn Nāfi' and Ibn Wajīh are in the *isnād* and they are weak.

If someone's illness continues and he does not recover until the next Ramadan, ad Dāraquṭnī related from Ibn 'Umar that he should feed a poor person a *mudd* of wheat for every day and does not have to make it up. It is related that Abū Hurayrah said, 'If he does not recover between the two Ramadans, then he fasts for the current one and feeds for the other and does not have to make it up. If he recovers but does not fast until the next Ramadan, he fasts the current one and feeds for the past one. When he breaks the fast, he makes it up.' It has a sound *isnād.*

Our scholars say that the positions of the Companions which use different analogies are also used as evidence. It is related from Ibn 'Abbās that a man came to him and said that he had been ill through two Ramadans. Ibn 'Abbās asked him, 'Was it a continuous illness or did you recover between the two?' He answered, 'I recovered.' He said, 'Fast the two Ramadans and feed sixty poor people.' This replaces his statement that if his illness continues, he does not have to make it up. This is similar to their school about pregnant and nursing women feeding and not making up as we will mention.

There is disagreement about the amount someone is obliged to give in feeding, Abū Hurayrah, al-Qāsim ibn Muḥammad, Mālik and ash-Shāfi'ī say that it is a *mudd* for every day. Ath-Thawrī said that it is half a *ṣā'* for every day.

There is disagreement about what is incurred by someone who breaks the fast or has sex while making up Ramadan. Mālik said, 'Someone who breaks the fast out of forgetfulness during a day when he is making up Ramadan owes nothing except making up. It is recommended that he continue to fast, because of the disagreement about that, and then make it up. If he breaks it intentionally, then he sins, but he only has to make up that day. He does not continue to fast that day because there is no point in refraining from what a faster refrains from since he is not fasting when he deliberately breaks the fast according to a group of scholars. There is no disagreement among Mālik and his people that no *kaffārah* is obliged for that. That is the view of a group of scholars. Mālik said, 'Someone who breaks the fast on a day that he is making up Ramadan, by having sex with his wife or something else, owes no *kaffārah.*' Ibn al-Qāsim related from Mālik that someone who breaks the fast on a day he is making up Ramadan owes two days. Ibn al-Qāsim gave that *fatwā* and then retracted it. Then he said, 'If he breaks the fast deliberately while making up, he must fast two days in its place, in the same way that someone who spoils his *ḥajj* by having sex with his wife and then makes *ḥajj* in the following year and again spoils it by having sex with his wife: he owes two *ḥajj*'s.' Abū 'Umar said, 'Ibn Wahb and 'Abd al-Malik disagreed with him about the *ḥajj.* There is no analogy when something is disputed.' What I believe is correct, and Allah knows best, is that in both cases he only has to make up one day because it is one day that he spoiled twice.

What is demanded by the words is that when someone fasts one day in place of the one in which he broke the fast in Ramadan, he has performed what is obligatory for him and nothing else is obliged. Allah knows best.

Most believe that if someone breaks the fast in Ramadan because of illness and then dies of that illness, or travels and dies on his journey, he owes nothing. Ṭāwūs and Qatādah said that if a sick person dies before he recovers, feeding is done on his behalf.

They disagree about someone who dies owing some days of Ramadan that he has not made up. Mālik, ash-Shāfi'ī and ath-Thawrī said that no one may fast on behalf of someone else. Aḥmad, Isḥāq, Abū Thawr, al-Layth, Abū 'Ubayd and the literalists say that it is possible to fast on behalf of someone else unless the fast is incurred by a specific vow. Something similar is related from ash-Shāfi'ī. Aḥmad and Isḥāq said that feeding can be done on behalf of someone to make up days of Ramadan they missed. Those who say that fasting is possible cite as evidence what Muslim related from 'Ā'ishah that the Messenger of Allah ﷺ said, 'If someone dies owing fasting, then his relative should fast on his behalf.' This is a general statement about fasting which is made specific by Muslim's report that Ibn 'Abbās said, 'A woman went to the Messenger of Allah ﷺ and said, "Messenger of Allah, my mother died while owing a vow to fast (one variant has 'fast for a month'). Can I fast on her behalf?' He answered, 'Do you think that if your mother owed a debt you would pay it for her?' 'Yes,' she answered. He said, 'Fast on behalf of your mother.' Mālik and those who agree with him, however, cite as evidence the words of the Almighty: *'No burden-bearer can bear another's burden'* (6:164), and: *'Man will have nothing but what he strives for'* (53:39) and: *'What each self earns is for itself alone.'* (6:154) They also cite what an-Nasā'ī transmitted from Ibn 'Abbās stating that the Prophet ﷺ said, 'No one may pray on behalf of another and no one may fast on behalf of another, but on their behalf one can feed people with a *mudd* of wheat for every day they owe.'

This *ḥadīth* is general, but his statement that no one may fast on behalf of another might mean the fast of Ramadan whereas it is permitted to do so in the case of unfulfilled vows, as is indicated by the *ḥadīth* of Ibn 'Abbās and others. *Ṣaḥīḥ Muslim* also has a *ḥadīth* from Buraydah similar to that of Ibn 'Abbās. One version has: '...to fast for two months. Can I fast on her behalf?' He replied, 'Fast on her behalf.' She said, 'She did not perform *ḥajj*. Can I perform *ḥajj* on her behalf?' He answered, 'Do not perform *ḥajj* on her behalf.' The fact that she said 'two months' means that it is unlikely that it was for Ramadan. Allah knows best. Mālik's argument is strengthened because it was the practice of the people of Madīnah and is supported by clear analogy. It is a physical act of worship which does not involve any wealth and so she is not doing it for someone who owes something like the prayer. The *ḥajj* does not contradict this because money plays a part in it.

Those who say that you do not fast on a journey and must always make it up use this *āyah* as evidence. Allah says: *'Any of you who are ill or on a journey should fast a number of other days.'* That means that the person concerned owes a number and there is no elision in the words. They also cite the words of the Prophet ﷺ: 'Fasting on a journey is not part of piety.' Something that is not part of piety is sinful. That indicates that it is not permitted to fast on a journey. Most say that there is something elided in it, i.e. '...should not fast and...', as we already mentioned. It is sound based on the *ḥadīth* of Anas already mentioned: 'We travelled with the Prophet ﷺ during Ramadan and those who were fasting did not criticise the non-fasters and the non-fasters did not criticise those who were fasting.'

**For those who are able to fast, their *fidyah* is to feed the poor**

'Poor' (*masākīn*) is a plural. Ibn 'Abbās recited it in the singular: '*miskīn*'. That is related by al-Bukhārī, Abū Dāwud and an-Nasā'ī from 'Aṭā'. It is a good reading because it explains the ruling for each day. Abū 'Ubayd said that. It is the reading of Abū 'Amr, Ḥamzah and al-Kisā'ī. Abū 'Ubayd said that it makes it clear that the ruling is to feed one poor person per day and so the singular can designate the plural while the plural cannot designate the singular. The meaning is that one poor person must be fed for each day. Feeding is *fidyah*.

Scholars disagree about exactly what is meant by this *āyah*. The majority say that it is abrogated. Al-Bukhārī related from Ibn Numayr from [al-A'mash] from 'Amr ibn Murrah from Ibn Abī Laylā from the Companions of Muḥammad ﷺ that Ramadan was sent down and it was difficult for them. Those who fed a poor person for every day left fasting to those who were able to fast. An indulgence was granted to them regarding that and then it was abrogated by: *'But that you should fast is better for you'*. On this basis, the majority reading of '*those who are able to fast*' means 'those who can do it' because that is how the obligation of fasting was: those who wish to do so should fast, and those who wish to do so should feed a poor person. Ibn 'Abbās said that this was revealed about the dispensation for old people and the infirm who do not fast when they are able to do so, which was abrogated by: *'Any of you who are resident for the month should fast it.'* So the dispensation is now only for those who are unable to fast.

Al-Farrā' said that the pronoun in the words can refer to fasting, in which case it means: 'those who cannot fast should feed people when they do not fast' and this was then abrogated. It is also possible that the words apply, not to fasting, but to paying *fidyah*. If the verb in the *āyah* is recited as *'yuṭawwaqūnahu'*, which means those for whom fasting is difficult, such as those who are ill or pregnant, and they can fast but with undue hardship for themselves, they can fast and satisfy the requirement or they can pay *fidyah* instead. Ibn 'Abbās gives that interpretation. Abū Dāwud related from Ibn 'Abbās that that judgment is confirmed for pregnant and nursing women. It is also related from him that it is a dispensation for very old men and women who are nevertheless still capable of fasting: they may feed a poor person for every day they do not fast. If pregnant and nursing women fear for their child, they do not fast and pay *fidyah* instead. Ad-Dāraquṭnī transmitted from him that there is a dispensation for old people to not fast but to feed a poor person for every day and they do not have to make up the days. It has a sound *isnād*. It is also related that he said that the *ayah* is not abrogated and refers to old men and women who cannot fast: they feed a poor person for every day. This is sound. It is related that he told his *umm walad* who was pregnant or nursing: 'You are one of those unable to fast. You must pay *fidyah*, but do not have to make it up.' It also has a sound *isnād*.

It is confirmed with sound *isnād*s from Ibn 'Abbās that the *āyah* is not abrogated, but is one of judgment in respect of those who are mentioned. The first view is also sound although it is possible that the term 'abrogation' can mean the qualification of an earlier judgment and a lot of earlier people used that meaning for the word *naskh*. Allah knows best. Al-Ḥasan al-Baṣrī, 'Aṭā' ibn Abī Rabāḥ, aḍ-Ḍaḥḥāk, an-Nakha'ī, az-Zuhrī, Rabī'ah, al-Awzā'ī and the People of Opinion say that pregnant and nursing women should not fast and do not have to feed anyone, as is the case with a sick person who breaks his fast and then makes it up. Abū 'Ubayd and Abū Thawr said that. Abū 'Ubayd related that from Abū Thawr and Ibn al-Mundhir preferred it. That is the position of Mālik about pregnant women when they do not fast. When nursing women do not fast, however, they must make it up and feed people. Ash-Shāfi'ī and Aḥmad say that both categories should not fast but should feed people as well as making it up. They all agree that old men and women who cannot fast, or who can fast, but only with undue hardship, do not fast.

They do, however, disagree about what they owe in that case. Rabī'ah and Mālik said that they owe nothing, although Mālik did say, 'I prefer for them to feed a poor person for every day.' Anas, Ibn 'Abbās, Qays ibn as-Sā'ib and Abū Hurayrah said that they definitely owe *fidyah*. That is the position of ash-Shāfi'ī, the People of Opinion, Aḥmad and Isḥāq, following the position of the

Companions ﵃ and this *āyah*. Those who are not ill or travelling owe *fidyah*. Mālik's argument is that this category do not fast because of an existing excuse like old age and therefore it is not mandatory for them to feed people, as is the case with those who are travelling or ill. This is also related from ath-Thawrī and Makḥūl. Ibn al-Mundhir preferred it.

There is disagreement about the amount owed by people who have to pay *fidyah*. Mālik said it is a *mudd* of the Prophet ﷺ for every day and ash-Shāfi'ī also said that. Abū Ḥanīfah said that it is a *ṣā'* of dates or half a *ṣā'* of grain. It is related from Ibn 'Abbās that it is a *ṣā'* of grain. Ad-Dāraquṭnī mentioned it. It is related that Abū Hurayrah said, 'If someone becomes elderly and cannot fast, then he owes a *mudd* of wheat for every day. It is related from Anas ibn Mālik that if someone is too weak to fast for a month, he should prepare a bowl of food and invite thirty poor people to it and give them their fill.

**and if someone does good of his own accord, it is better for him.**

Ibn Shihāb said that this refers to anyone who wants to feed as well as fast. Mujāhid said that it is about giving more than a *mudd* when paying *fidyah*. Ibn 'Abbās said that it is to feed another poor person. Ad-Dāraquṭnī mentioned it and said that its *isnād* is sound and firm. 'Īsā ibn 'Amr, Yaḥyā ibn Waththāb, Ḥamzah and al-Kisā'ī recited '*yaṭṭawwa*'' while the rest have '*taṭṭawwa'a*'.

**But that you should fast is better for you if you only knew.**

Fasting is better than breaking the fast. This was before the abrogation. It is said that it refers to travelling and any illness which is not serious. Allah knows best. It is encouragement for fasting, i.e. 'Know that and fast.'

شَهْرُ رَمَضَانَ الَّذِي أُنزِلَ فِيهِ الْقُرْآنُ هُدًى لِّلنَّاسِ
وَبَيِّنَاتٍ مِّنَ الْهُدَىٰ وَالْفُرْقَانِ ۚ فَمَن شَهِدَ مِنكُمُ الشَّهْرَ
فَلْيَصُمْهُ ۖ وَمَن كَانَ مَرِيضًا أَوْ عَلَىٰ سَفَرٍ فَعِدَّةٌ مِّنْ أَيَّامٍ أُخَرَ ۗ
يُرِيدُ اللَّهُ بِكُمُ الْيُسْرَ وَلَا يُرِيدُ بِكُمُ الْعُسْرَ وَلِتُكْمِلُوا الْعِدَّةَ
وَلِتُكَبِّرُوا اللَّهَ عَلَىٰ مَا هَدَاكُمْ وَلَعَلَّكُمْ تَشْكُرُونَ ﴿١٨٥﴾

**185 The month of Ramadan is the one in which the Qur'an was sent down as guidance for mankind, with Clear Signs containing guidance and discrimination. Any of you who are resident for the month should fast it. But any of you who are ill or on a journey**

**should fast a number of other days. Allah desires ease for you; He does not desire difficulty for you. You should complete the number of days and proclaim Allah's greatness for the guidance He has given you so that hopefully you will be thankful.**

### The month of Ramadan

Historians state that the first person to fast Ramadan was the Prophet Nūḥ when he left the Ark. We have already mentioned that Mujāhid said that Allah made fasting the month of Ramadan obligatory for every nation and it is known that there were nations before Nūḥ, and Allah knows best. The word for month, *shahr*, is derived from *ishhār* which means to make something known in such a way that it is not difficult for anyone to know it. The verb is also used for a sword being unsheathed. The name 'Ramadan' is derived from *ramaḍ*, which is burning, because the belly of the faster is burning from thirst. *Ramḍā'* is intense heat. A *ḥadīth* states: 'The prayer of the penitent is like when young camels are burned (*ramiḍat*).' This is when the feet of young camels are burned and they kneel because of the intense heat. It is said the month was named because it was the time of intense heat and so it is derived from *ramḍā'*. Al-Jawharī said that the plural is *ramaḍānāt* and *armiḍā'*. It is said that when the names of the month were transferred from the ancient tongue, they were named after the times in which they occurred and this month coincided with the days of intense heat and that is the source of its name. It is said that it is called that because it burns up wrong actions by means of righteous actions. It comes from *irmāḍ*, which means 'burning', the verb used when one's feet are burned by the heat. The verb can also be used for a matter hurting (literally 'burning') someone. It is said that it is because, in it, the hearts take the heat of admonition and reflection about the Next World as the sand and stones are burned by the heat of the sun. *Ramḍā'* are also burned stones. The verb is also used for putting a blade between two stones and beating it to make it thin. Such a blade is called *ramīḍ* and *marmūḍ*. The month is called that because they used to prepare their weapons in Ramadan so that they could fight with them in Shawwāl before the arrival of the Sacred Months. Al-Māwardī related that its name in the Jāhiliyyah was Nātiq.

The statement implies: 'Obligatory for you is the fasting of the month of Ramadan' or 'part of what has been prescribed for you is the month of Ramadan.' It is also said that this phrase is just descriptive. 'Month' is mentioned a second time in the *āyah* for esteem as occurs elsewhere in the Qur'an.

There is disagreement about whether one can say just 'Ramadan' rather than 'the month of Ramadan.' Mujāhid disliked that and said that it should be said in the manner that Allah said it. We find in a report: 'Do not say "Ramadan". Attribute it as Allah attributed it in the Qur'an. He said, "the month of Ramadan".' He used to say, 'I have heard that it is one of the names of Allah.' That is why he disliked using the plural. He argued from the premise of what he related about it being one of the names of Allah. This is not sound. It comes from the *ḥadīth* of Abū Ma'shar Nujayḥ who is weak. What is sound is that it is permitted to say 'Ramadan' on its own as is confirmed in *aṣ-Ṣiḥāḥ* and elsewhere.

Muslim related from Abū Hurayrah that the Messenger of Allah ﷺ said, 'When Ramadan comes, the gates of mercy are opened, the gates of the Fire are closed and the *shayṭān*s are chained.' We find in the *Ṣaḥīḥ* of al-Bustī that the Messenger of Allah ﷺ said, 'When Ramadan comes, the gates of mercy are opened, the gates of Hell are closed and the *shayṭān*s are chained.' It is related from Ibn Shihāb from Anas ibn Abī Anas from his father that he heard Abū Hurayrah say this. Al-Bustī said that this Anas ibn Abī Anas was the father of Mālik ibn Anas and the name of Abū Anas was Mālik ibn Abī 'Āmir. He was one of the trustworthy people of Madīnah. His full name is Mālik ibn Abī 'Āmir ibn 'Amr ibn al-Ḥārith ibn 'Uthmān ibn Juthayl ibn 'Amr from the Dhū Aṣbagh from the tribes of Yemen.

An-Nasā'ī related from Abū Hurayrah that the Messenger of Allah ﷺ said, 'Ramadan, a blessed month, has come to you. Allah has prescribed that you fast it. In it the gates of heaven are opened, the gates of Hell are closed and the recalcitrant *shayṭān*s are chained. It contains a night better than a thousand months. Anyone who is deprived of its good is truly deprived.' Abū Ḥātim al-Bustī also transmitted it. 'Recalcitrant' defines the '*shayṭān*s'. An-Nasā'ī related from Ibn 'Abbās that the Messenger of Allah ﷺ said to a woman of the Anṣār, 'Perform *'umrah* in Ramadan. An *'umrah* in it is equivalent to a *ḥajj*.' An-Nasā'ī also related from 'Abd ar-Raḥmān ibn 'Awf that he related that the Messenger of Allah ﷺ said, 'Allah Almighty obliged the fast of Ramadan for you and I have made it sunnah for you to pray at night in it. Anyone who fasts and prays at night in it in faith and in expectation of the reward emerges from his wrong actions like the day his mother bore him.' There are many traditions like that, all of which omit the word 'month'.

The excellence of Ramadan is immense and its reward is huge. That is indicated by the meaning of its being derived from being something that burns up wrong actions and as well as the *ḥadīth*s we have mentioned.

Allah imposed fasting from the start of the month of Ramadan, which is when its new moon appears, and that is why the moon is sometimes called a 'month', as in the *ḥadīth*, 'When the month is clouded over for you' meaning the new moon.

If it is cloudy, Sha'bān is counted as thirty days, or, if the end of Ramadan is cloudy, it itself is counted as thirty days so that there will be certainty in respect of worship and certainty that it has ended. Allah says in His Book: *'We have sent down the Reminder to you so that you can make clear to people what has been sent down to them.'* (16:44)

Reliable imams relate that the Prophet ﷺ said, 'Fast by seeing the moon and break the fast by seeing it. If it is cloudy, calculate it.' Muṭarrif ibn 'Abdullāh, one of the great Tābi'ūn, and Ibn Qutaybah, the linguist, said, 'One can rely on reckoning when it is cloudy by observing the stages of the moon, taking the *ḥadīth* of the Prophet ﷺ, "If it is cloudy, calculate it," to mean to use its stages as evidence and complete the month accordingly. The majority, however, say that "calculate" means to complete the number which is elucidated by the *ḥadīth* reported by Abū Hurayrah which says specifically: 'Complete the number.' Ad-Dāwudī mentioned that "calculate" means to calculate the stages of the moon. We do not know of anyone who takes this position except for some Shāfi'īs who say that one can consider the statement of astronomers regarding this matter, but the overwhelming consensus is the argument against them. Ibn Nāfi' related from Mālik that, if a ruler does not fast by sighting the moon or break it by sighting it and fasts and breaks it by calculation, you should not follow him or imitate him.' Ibn al-'Arabī said, 'Some of our people have erred and related that ash-Shāfi'ī said that one can rely on calculation. That is a stumble. May they rise from it!'

Mālik and ash-Shāfi'ī disagree about whether the new moon of Ramadan is confirmed by a single witness or whether it needs two. Mālik says, 'A single testimony is not accepted for it because it is the testimony of a new moon, and not less than two is accepted for it.' The basis is sighting the new moon of Shawwāl and Dhu-l-Ḥijjah. Ash-Shāfi'ī and Abū Ḥanīfah say that one witness is accepted based on what is related by Abū Dāwud that Ibn 'Umar said, 'The people sighted the new moon and so I informed the Messenger of Allah ﷺ and he fasted and ordered the people to fast.' Ad-Dāraquṭnī transmitted it and said that only Marwān ibn Muḥammad has it from Ibn Wahb and he is trustworthy. Ad-Dāraquṭnī related that a man testified that he had seen the new moon in the presence of 'Alī ibn Abī Ṭālib and he fasted. He said, 'I think that he said, "and he ordered the people to fast."' He said, 'I prefer to fast a day of Sha'bān than to not fast a day of Ramadan.' Ash-Shāfi'ī said, 'If most of the people do not see the new moon of the month of Ramadan and one reputable man sees it, I think that he is accepted because of the tradition and out of caution.' Ash-Shāfi'ī later said, 'It is not permitted to fast Ramadan except with two witnesses.' Ash-Shāfi'ī and some of our people say, 'It is only accepted with two witnesses. That is based on an analogy regarding everything which is not present.'

They disagree about someone who sees the new moon of Ramadan or that of Shawwāl when he is alone. Ash-Shāfi'ī is reported as saying, 'If someone sees the new moon of Ramadan on his own, he should fast, and if someone sees the new moon of Shawwāl on his own he should break the fast but conceal it.' Ibn Wahb reported from Mālik that someone who sees the new moon of Ramadan alone should fast because he should not eat knowing that it is one of the days of Ramadan. If someone sees the new moon of Shawwāl on his own, he should not eat on it because the people would suspect anyone among them who broke the fast and he would not be safe unless they say that they have seen the new moon. That is the position of al-Layth ibn Sa'd and Aḥmad ibn Ḥanbal. 'Aṭā' and Isḥāq said, 'He should not fast and break the fast.' Ibn al-Mundhir said, 'He fasts and breaks the fast.'

They disagree about what happens when someone reports about the sighting of the moon in another land. If it is near, their ruling should be followed; if it is far away, then the people of each land should sight it separately. This is related from 'Ikrimah, al-Qāsim and Sālim. It is related from Ibn 'Abbās and Isḥāq also said it. Bukhārī indicated it in a chapter entitled: 'The people of each land sight it.' Others said that when it is established among people that the people of a land have sighted it earlier, then they must make up any days they did not fast. That is what al-Layth and ash-Shāfi'ī said. Ibn al-Mundhir said, 'I only know that to be the position of al-Muzanī and al-Kūfī.'

Aṭ-Ṭabarī mentioned in *Aḥkām al-Qur'ān*: 'The Ḥanafīs agree that when the people of one country fast thirty days by sighting and the people of another land fast only twenty-nine days, those who fasted twenty-nine have to make up one day. The Shāfi'īs do not think that, since the moon rising in different places can vary. The evidence of the Ḥanafīs is the words of the Almighty: *"Complete the number."* It is established by the sighting of the people of a land that the number is thirty and so those people must complete it. Those who differ from them argue by the words of the Prophet ﷺ, "Fast by sighting it and break the fast by sighting it." That necessitates considering the custom of every people in their land.' Abū 'Umar reported the consensus that one does not pay attention to sighting in distant lands, like Andalusia in relation to Khorasan. He said, 'Each land sights it, except for those areas neighbouring large cities.'

Muslim related from Kurayb that Umm al-Faḍl bint al-Ḥārith sent him on a mission to Mu'āwiyah in Syria. He said, 'I came to Syria and did what she asked me to do. Ramadan began while I was in Syria and I saw the new moon on a Friday night. Then I came to Madīnah at the end of the month and 'Abdullāh ibn 'Abbās asked me about when I had seen the new moon. "Friday night," I replied. "You yourself saw it?" he asked. "Yes," I said, "and the people saw it and fasted and Mu'āwiyah fasted." He said, "But we saw it on Saturday night. We will continue to fast until it is the full thirty days or we see it." I asked, "Is it not enough that Mu'āwiyah saw the moon and fasted?" "No," he said, "that is what the Messenger of Allah ﷺ commanded us to do."'

Our scholars said, 'The statement of Ibn 'Abbās, "That is what the Messenger of Allah ﷺ commanded us to do", is a clear statement that goes back to the command of the Prophet ﷺ, and that is evidence that when the lands are far from each other as Syria is far from the Hijaz, the people of each land must act according to their own sighting. If that is confirmed with the overall leader [i.e. the Caliph], he cannot impel people to follow him in that. But if he does, it is not permitted to oppose him.'

Aṭ-Ṭabarī said, 'It is possible to interpret his words, "That is what the Messenger of Allah ﷺ commanded us to do" as referring to the words of the Messenger of Allah ﷺ: "Fast by sighting it and break the fast by sighting it."' Ibn al-'Arabī said, 'There is disagreement about the interpretation of the words of Ibn 'Abbās. It is said that it is refuted because it is a single report. It is said that it is refuted because breaking the fast varies according to different times of moon rising. That is sound because Kurayb did not testify. He merely reported about a ruling that was confirmed by sighting. There is no disagreement that it is permitted to have a firm ruling based on a single report. An example of that is that when it is confirmed with the people of Aghmat that the new moon is seen on Friday and with the people of Seville that it is seen on Saturday, then each acts according to their sighting since the sky was clear in Aghmat but not in Seville. This indicates a difference in risings.'

The position of school of Mālik regarding this question related by Ibn Wahb and Ibn al-Qāsim in *al-Majmū'ah* is that when the people of Basra saw the new moon of Ramadan and then news of it reached the people of Kufa, Madīnah, and Yemen, they had to fast or make it up. Qāḍī Abū Isḥāq related from Ibn al-Mājishūn that if it was confirmed at Basra as a generally known fact which does not require testimony and witnesses (because of the large number of people who had seen it), then it was obligatory for the people of other lands to make it up. If it was confirmed with the ruler only by the testimony of two witnesses then it was not obliged for other countries. It is only obliged for those under that ruler's rule.

But if it was confirmed with the Amīr al-Mu'minīn, then the whole community of Muslims must make it up. That is the position of Mālik.

Most people recite 'month' in the nominative as a *khabar* of an elided *ibtidā'*, meaning 'That is the month' or 'Fasting it, the month of Ramadan, is prescribed for you.' It is said that it is in the accusative as the object of something not named: 'Prescribed for you is the month of Ramadan.'

**is the one in which the Qur'an was sent down as guidance for mankind**

This provides textual evidence that the Qur'an was revealed during the month of Ramadan. It explains the words of the Almighty: *'Ḥā Mīm, by the Book which makes things clear. We sent it down on a blessed night'* (44:1-3), meaning the Night of Power, and: *'We sent it down on the Night of Power'* (97:1). This also indicates that the Night of Power is only in Ramadan. There is no disagreement that the Qur'an was sent down from the Preserved Tablet on the Night of Power all at once. It was then lodged in the House of Might in the lowest heaven. Then Jibrīl brought it down, piece by piece, with commands and prohibitions brought about by different situations over the course of the following twenty years. Ibn 'Abbās said, 'The Qur'an was sent down from the Preserved Tablet all at once to the scribes in the lower heaven. Then Jibrīl brought it down in instalments, meaning as one or two *āyah*s at a time, at different times over twenty-one years.' Muqātil said, 'It was sent down every year from the Preserved Tablet on the Night of Power to the lowest heaven. Then it was sent down from the Preserved Tablet to the scribes over twenty months and Jibrīl brought it over twenty years.' This indicates what al-Ḥasan said about the Night of Power being on the night of the twenty-fourth, as will be mentioned.

The word 'Qur'an' designates the Words of Allah Almighty and means 'recited'. This is a common linguistic usage in Arabic as *'maktūb'* (written) is a book. It is also said that it is a verbal noun.

We find in *Ṣaḥīḥ Muslim* from 'Abdullāh ibn 'Umar that in the sea there are imprisoned *shayṭān*s who were shackled by Sulaymān who are close to emerging and reciting something to people. *Sūrat al-Isrā'* uses the word 'Qur'an' to mean 'recitation' (17:78) The Arabs often use a verbal noun for a passive participle. This common usage is known legally and the Qur'an is a name for the Word of Allah so that it can be said that the Qur'an which is recited is not created. That means what is recited, not the recitation itself. Sometimes the word is also used for the bound book (*muṣḥaf*) in which the words of the Qur'an are written down. The Prophet ﷺ said, 'Do not travel to the land of the enemy with the Qur'an,' meaning a copy of the Qur'an. It is derived from the root *qara'a*, to collect something. It is said that it is a name for the Book of Allah without any derivation, like Torah and Gospel. This is related from ash-Shāfi'ī. What is sound is that all of it is derived.

**as guidance for mankind, with Clear Signs containing guidance and discrimination.**

The Qur'an guides them. It is also clarification, as it makes things clear to them. This refers to the entire Qur'an, its firm judgments and ambiguous expressions, its abrogating and abrogated *āyah*s, and Allah here lays emphasis on the Clear Signs in it, meaning by that the lawful and unlawful, and its warnings and rulings. Its 'discrimination' is that it distinguishes truth from falsehood.

**Any of you who are resident for the month should fast it.**

The verb '*shahida*' means 'to be resident'. It implies: 'Any of you who are resident in a city during the month, sane, adult, healthy and resident should fast it.' This qualifies the command to fast. 'Month' here is not an object, but an adverb of time.

Scholars disagree about the interpretation of this. 'Alī ibn Abī Ṭālib, Ibn 'Abbās, Suwayd ibn Ghafalah and 'Ā'ishah, four Companions, as well as Abū Miljaz Lāḥiq ibn Ḥumayd and 'Abīdah as-Salmānī, said: 'Whoever is resident at the beginning of the month in his town should complete his fast, whether he travels or remains resident after that. He may break his fast on a journey when Ramadan starts while he is travelling.' They think that if Ramadan arrives while someone is travelling, he may not fast and then must make it up with a number of other days. If Ramadan arrives while someone is resident, he should fast. The majority of the community say that whoever is present at the beginning and end of the month should fast as long he is resident. If he travels, then he may break the fast. This is sound and is backed up by firm *ḥadīth*s. Al-Bukhārī has a chapter entitled: 'If someone fasts some days of Ramadan and then sets off on a journey.' 'Abdullāh ibn Yūsuf related from Mālik from Ibn Shihāb from 'Ubaydullāh ibn 'Abdullāh ibn 'Utbah that Ibn 'Abbās reported that the Messenger of Allah ﷺ set off for Makkah in Ramadan and continued fasting. When he reached al-Kadīd, he broke his fast and the rest of the people broke their fast with him.

It is possible that what 'Alī and those who agree with him said means that this is during a recommended journey, such as one for visiting brothers among the righteous, or a permissible one, such as one for seeking provision beyond what is merely sufficient. As for a mandatory journey, such as one for seeking necessary provision or conquering a land when that is certain or to repel enemies, a person can choose, and it is not mandatory for him to fast. Indeed, it is better to not fast so as to increase strength. If the month arrives when he is in his home town, he fasts some of it there based on the *ḥadīth* of Ibn 'Abbās and others. There is no disagreement about this, Allah willing. Allah knows best.

Abū Ḥanīfah and his people say that if Ramadan comes when someone is resident and meets its preconditions and is neither mad nor unconscious, he should fast it. If Ramadan comes when he is in a state of insanity and he continues to be in that condition until the end of the month, then he does not have to make it up because he was not present when the month arrived in a manner which would oblige him to fast. If someone is insane at the beginning and then again at the end of the month, he makes up the days of his insanity.

It is confirmed that the obligation of fasting is made binding by being Muslim, by adulthood, and by having knowledge of the month. When an unbeliever becomes Muslim, or a child becomes an adult, before dawn in Ramadan, they must fast the following day. If it is already dawn, then it is recommended for them not to eat, but they do not have to make up the past days of the month, only the day they became adult or Muslim. Scholars disagree about when an unbeliever becomes Muslim on the last day of Ramadan and whether he is obliged to make up all of that Ramadan or not. Is he obliged to make up the day on which he became Muslim? Imam Mālik and the majority say that he does not have to make up what has passed because he is only present at the month at the time he became Muslim. Mālik said, 'I prefer him to make up the day on which he became Muslim.' 'Aṭā' and al-Ḥasan said, 'He should fast what remains and makes up what has passed.' 'Abd al-Malik ibn al-Mājishūn said, 'He should refrain from eating for that day and then make it up.' Aḥmad and Isḥāq said something similar. Ibn al-Mundhir said, 'He does not have to make up either the rest of the month or that day.' Al-Bājī said, 'Those of our people who say that unbelievers are subject to the laws of Islam, which is what is entailed by the position of Mālik and most of his people, oblige him to fast for the rest of the day.' Ibn Nāfi' related that in the *Mudawannah* from Mālik. Shaykh Abu-l-Qāsim said that. Those of our people who say that unbelievers are not subject to the laws of Islam say that he is not obliged to fast for the rest of the day. That is demanded by what is stated by Ashhab and 'Abd al-Malik ibn al-Mājishūn. Ibn al-Qāsim also said that. It is sound based on Allah's words: '*You who believe!*' So the believers are addressed rather than others. This is clear. Therefore the convert is not obliged to fast for the rest of the day or to make up what has passed. This was discussed in 2:184.

**Allah desires ease for you; He does not desire difficulty for you**

One group recite *yusr* (ease) as *yusur* and *'usr'* (difficulty) as *'usur*. They are dialectic usages. Mujāhid and aḍ-Ḍaḥḥāk said that the word 'ease' refers to not fasting on a journey and the word 'difficulty' to fasting on it. The meaning, however, can be general to all matters of the *dīn* because the Almighty says: *'He has not placed any constraint upon you in the* dīn.' (22:78) The Prophet ﷺ said, 'The *dīn* is ease,' and he further said, 'Make things easy and do not make things difficult.' *'Yusr'* is easiness. An aspect of this is the fact that wealth is sometimes referred to as *yasār*. The left hand (*yusrā*) is used for good fortune because it makes the things easier by helping the right hand.

The *āyah* indicates that Allah wills by His pre-eternal timeless Will which is distinct from His Essence. This is the position of people of the Sunnah, in the same way that He knows by knowledge, has capacity through power, lives by life, hears by hearing, sees by sight and speaks by speech. These are all attributes which exist before time and are distinct from the Essence. The philosophers and the Shi'ah believe these attributes are negated. Allah is greatly exalted above the words of deviants and atheists! That which demolishes the position of the atheists is the fact that it is said: 'If it had not been true that He possesses will, then He would not have will. If that had been true, then everything that lacks a will is inferior to that which has a will. Someone who possesses the qualities of will can make something specific or not make it specific. A sound mind would conclude that that is perfection not imperfection. Were it to be imagined that He is divested of that, then His prior state would have been more perfect than his second state and that which is not described would be more imperfect that what is described. This is clearly impossible. How then can it be imagined that something created is more perfect than the Creator and the Creator more imperfect than something created? That instinctively is rejected and nullified.'

Allah Almighty describes Himself as possessing will. He says: *'He is the Doer of what He wills'* (11:107) and: *'Allah desires ease for you; He does not desire difficulty for you'* (2:185) and: *'Allah desires to make things lighter for you'* (4:28) and: *'...when He desires something, He says to it, "Be!" and it is.'* (36:82) A knower may possess ultimate wisdom, perfection, order and exactitude, but nevertheless it is possible for him to exist or not exist. That which is singled out for existence must possess will, power and knowledge. If a being does not possess knowledge and power, then it is not valid for anything to issue from it. If it does not possess knowledge but does possess power, then what issues from it is not arranged with wisdom and precision. If it does not possess will, then it cannot specify any permissible things with states and times rather than other things since they all have the same relationship to it. So they have said that if it is confirmed that Allah possesses power and will, then He must also have life since life is a precondition for these attributes. Someone who is alive must be hearing, seeing and speaking. If it is not confirmed that something possesses these qualities, then it must be described by their opposites, like being blind, deaf and mute as is known in the visible world. The Almighty Creator is too exalted and pure to be described by something that would oblige His Essence to be imperfect.

**You should complete the number of days**

There are two interpretations of this. One is that someone who breaks the fast on a journey or due to illness must complete the number by fasting the days he missed. The second is that it refers to the number of days in the month, whether it is twenty-nine or thirty. Jābir ibn 'Abdullāh said that the Prophet ﷺ said, 'The month is twenty-nine.' This refutes the interpretation of the one who interprets the words of the Prophet ﷺ: 'The month is counted, and Ramadan and Dhu-l-Ḥijjah are not reduced' to mean that they are not less than thirty days. Abū Dāwud transmitted it. Most scholars interpret that to mean that the reward is not reduced and errors are expiated whether it is twenty-nine or thirty days.

There is no consideration given to a claimed sighting of the new moon of Shawwāl on the 30th of Ramadan during the daytime. That moon belongs to the coming night. This is what is sound. Transmitters from 'Umar differ about his matter. Ad-Dāraquṭnī related that Shaqīq said, "Umar's letter arrived when we were at Khaniqan. It said: "Some new moons are larger than others. When you see the new moon in the day, do not break the fast until there are two witnesses who said that they saw it the day before."' Abū 'Umar mentioned it from the *ḥadīth* of 'Abd ar-Razzāq from Ma'mar from al-A'mash from Abū Wā'il. Abū 'Umar said that 'Alī ibn Abī Ṭālib related the like of what 'Abd ar-Razzāq mentioned. It is also the view of Ibn Mas'ūd, Ibn 'Umar, and Anas ibn Mālik. Mālik, ash-Shāfi'ī, Abū Ḥanīfah, Muḥammad ibn al-Ḥasan, al-Layth and al-Awzā'ī said that. It is also stated by Aḥmad ibn Isḥāq. Sufyān ath-Thawrī and Abū Yūsuf said that if it is seen after midday, it belongs to the coming night, but if it is seen before midday, it belongs to the previous night. Something similar is related from 'Umar. 'Abd ar-Razzāq mentioned from ath-Thawrī from Mughīrah from Shibāk that Ibrāhīm said, "Umar wrote to 'Utbah ibn Farqad: "If you see the new moon in the daytime before midday, the thirty are completed, so break the fast." If you see it after midday, then do not break the fast until evening."' 'Alī related something similar, though nothing is sound regarding this topic in respect of the *isnād* from

'Alī. A similar statement to that of ath-Thawrī is related from Sulaymān ibn Rabī'ah. 'Abd al-Malik ibn Ḥabīb said that. He gave a *fatwā* to that effect in Cordoba.

Different things are reported from 'Umar ibn 'Abd al-'Azīz about this matter. Abū 'Umar said that the meaning contained in the *ḥadīth* from 'Umar is what is believed by Mālik, ash-Shāfi'ī and Abū Ḥanīfah. It is a connected transmission while what is related with the position of ath-Thawrī is broken. It is better to accept what is connected. Those who take the position of ath-Thawrī cite as evidence the *ḥadīth* of al-A'mash which is general and does not mention whether it is before or after midday. The *ḥadīth* of Ibrāhīm has accompanying explanation and so it is better to follow it.

What is related from Umar as connected and *mawqūt* is related *marfū'* by 'A'ishah, the wife of the Prophet ﷺ, who said, 'The Messenger of Allah ﷺ was fasting on the morning of the 30th and saw the new moon of Shawwāl in the daytime. He did not break the fast until evening.' Ad-Dāraquṭnī transmitted from al-Wāqidī that Mu'ādh ibn Muḥammad al-Anṣārī said, 'I asked az-Zuhrī about the new moon of Shawwāl when it is seen in the morning. He said that he heard Sa'īd ibn al-Musayyab say, "When the new moon of Shawwāl is seen after dawn until 'Aṣr, or until sunset, it belongs to the coming night."' Abū 'Abdullāh said, 'This is agreed upon.'

Ad-Dāraqutnī related from Rib'iyy ibn Ḥirāsh that one of the Companions of the Prophet ﷺ said, 'People disagreed about the last day of Ramadan. Two Bedouins came and testified in the presence of the Prophet ﷺ that they had seen the new moon the previous evening. The Messenger of Allah ﷺ commanded people to break the fast and go to their prayer place.' Ad-Dāraqutnī said that this has a sound firm *isnād*. Abū 'Umar said, 'There is no disagreement from Mālik and his people that the *'Īd* prayer may only be performed on the day of the *'Īd* and, even on the day of the *'Īd*, not after midday. That is related from Abū Ḥanīfah. Ash-Shāfi'ī's position on this matter varies. Sometimes he took the view of Mālik. Al-Muzanī preferred that and said, 'If it is not permitted to pray after midday on the day of the *'Īd*, then the second day is even further away, and so it is less fitting to pray then.' There is another transmission from ash-Shāfi'ī' which says that it can be prayed before noon on the second day. Al-Buwayṭī said, 'It may only be prayed if there is a *ḥadīth* established about it.' Abū 'Umar said, 'If the *'Īd* prayer were to be made up after its time has passed, then it would resemble the obligatory prayers but they all agree that the rest of the sunnahs are not made up and this prayer is like them.'

Ath-Thawrī, al-Awzā'ī and Aḥmad ibn Ḥanbal said that people should go out on the following day, and Abū Yūsuf said that in *al-Imlā'*. Al-Ḥasan ibn Sāliḥ Ḥayy said that they do not go out then for the *'Īd of Fiṭr*, but do for the *'Īd al-Aḍḥā*. Abū Yūsuf said that the prayer for the *'Īd al-Aḍḥā* can be performed even on the third day. Abū 'Umar said, 'That is because all the days of *Aḍḥā* are days of *'Īd* and the *'Īd* prayer can be done on any of them. The *'Īd al-Fiṭr* is only one day. If it is not prayed on that day, it is not made up on another day, because it is not one of the obligatory prayers that can be made up.' Al-Layth ibn Sa'd said, 'People go out during the morning on *Fiṭr* and *Aḍḥā*.'

The view about going out is sounder, Allah willing, because of the firm sunnah regarding it. That does not prevent the Lawgiver making any exception he wishes regarding the sunnahs and commanding that the prayer should be made up after its time. At-Tirmidhī related from Abū Hurayrah that the Messenger of Allah ﷺ said, 'If someone does not pray the two *rak'ah*s of *Fajr*, he should pray them after sunrise.' Abū Muḥammad says that it is sound. At-Tirmidhī said, 'Some of the people of knowledge act on this.' It is the position of Sufyān ath-Thawrī, ash-Shāfi'ī, Aḥmad, Isḥāq and Ibn al-Mubārak. It is related that 'Umar did it.

Our scholars say that if the time is short for someone and he prays *Ṣubḥ* and omits the two *rak'ah*s of *Fajr*, he can pray them after sunrise if he wishes. It is also said that he does not pray them then. If we say that he does pray them, is he making them up or performing two two *rak'ah*s whose reward replaces the reward for the *rak'ah*s of *Fajr*? Shaykh Abū Bakr said, 'This follows the basic principle of the School. "Making up" is metaphorical.'

It is not unlikely that the ruling of praying the *Fiṭr* prayer on the second day is based on this source, especially since it is once in the year as is confirmed in the Sunnah. An-Nasā'ī related from 'Amr ibn 'Alī from Yaḥyā from Abū Bishr from Abū 'Umayr from his uncles that some people saw the new moon and went to the Prophet ﷺ and he commanded them to break their fast after it was well into the day and they went out to the *'Īd* on the following day. One variant says: 'they went out to their prayer place the next day.'

Abū Bakr from 'Āṣim, Abū Bakr in part of what was related from him, al-Ḥasan, Qatādah and al-A'raj recited '*li-tukammilū*' in Form II while the rest have '*li-tukmilū*'. Al-Kisā'ī prefers the second since it agrees with 5:30. An-Naḥḥās said that these are two dialectical forms with the same meaning. This is an excellent view.

**and proclaim Allah's greatness**

This is encouragement to say the *takbīr* at the end of Ramadan according to the position of the majority of interpreters. People disagree about its definition. Ash-Shāfi'ī says that it is reported that Sa'īd ibn al-Musayyab, 'Urwah, and Abū Salamah used to say the *takbīr* on the Night of the *'Īd* and praise Allah. He said that that night resembles the Night of Sacrifice. Ibn 'Abbās said, 'It is a duty for the Muslims, when they see the new moon of Shawwāl, to say the *takbīr*.' It is related that he said, 'One says the *takbīr* from the sighting of the moon to the end of the *khuṭbah*, stopping when the imam comes out, and then saying the *takbīr* with his *takbīr* (during the *khutbah*).' Some people say that one says the *takbīr* from the sighting of the moon until the imam comes out for the prayer.' Sufyān said that it is the *takbīr* on the day of *Fiṭr*. Zayd ibn Aslam said, 'They say the *takbīr* when they go out to the place of prayer. When the prayer ends, the *'Īd* ends. This is the school of Mālik.' Mālik said, 'It is said from the time he leaves his house until the imam comes out.'

Ibn al-Qāsim and 'Alī ibn Ziyād said, 'If you go out before sunrise, you do not say the *takbīr* on the way, nor when you sit, until the sun rises. In the morning after sunrise, you say the *takbīr* on the way to the place of prayer and when you sit, until the imam comes out.' According to Mālik, *Fiṭr* and *Aḍḥā* are the same in that respect. That is also the view of ash-Shāfi'ī. Abū Ḥanīfah, however, said that you say the *takbīr* for *Aḍḥā* but not for *Fiṭr*.

The evidence for the [first] position is that Allah says: *'proclaim Allah's greatness'*, and also because this is a day of *'Īd* which does not recur in the year. Therefore the sunnah is to say that *takbīr* when going out to it as is the case with *Aḍḥā*. Ad-Dāraquṭnī related that Abū 'Abd ar-Raḥmān as-Sulamī said, 'They put more weight on doing the *takbīr* for *Fiṭr* than than for *Aḍḥā*.' It is related from Ibn 'Umar that the Messenger of Allah ﷺ used to say the *takbīr* on the Day of *Fiṭr* from when he left his house until he reached the prayer place. It is also related from him that on the morning of *Aḍḥā* and *Fiṭr* he ﷺ would say the *takbīr* aloud until he arrived and then would say that *takbīr* until the imam appeared.

Most of the people of knowledge among the Companions of the Prophet ﷺ and others said the *takbīr* on the *'Īd al-Fiṭr* as Ibn al-Mundhir mentioned, stating that al-Awzā'ī related that from Ilyās. When he saw the new moon of Shawwāl, ash-Shāfi'ī said, 'I like people to say the *takbīr* in groups and alone. They should continue to say it, and do so aloud, until they come to the prayer place up until the imam comes out for the prayer. I also like it on the night of *Aḍḥā* for those not on *ḥajj*.' The ruling of the two *'Īd* prayers and the *takbīr* on them will come in *al-A'lā* and *al-Kawthar*, Allah willing.

The form of the *takbīr* according to Mālik and a group of scholars is to say: *'Allāhu akbar. Allāhu akbar. Allāhu akbar'* three times. That is related from Jābir ibn 'Abdullāh. Some scholars say the *takbīr*, *shahādah* and glorification are all included here in the *takbīr*. Some people say, *'Allāhu akbar kabīran wa-l-ḥamdu lillāhi kathīran wa subḥāna-llāhi bukratan wa aṣīlā.'* (Allah is very much greater. Praise belongs to Allah and glory be to Allah morning and evening.) Ibn al-Mubārak used to say when he left home on the day of *Fiṭr*: *'Allāhu akbar. Allāhu akbar. Lā ilāha illa-llāh. Allāhu akbar lillāhi-l-ḥamd. Allāhu akbar 'alā mā hadānā.'* Ibn al-Mundhir reported that Mālik did not specify any particular form. Aḥmad ibn Ḥanbal said that there is leeway. Ibn al-'Arabī said, 'Our scholars prefer the simple *takbīr*. It is the literal text of the Qur'an, and I incline to that view.'

**for the guidance He has given you**

It is said that this is mentioned because the Christians went astray by altering their fast and it is said that it refers to replacing what was done in the past, because the practice of the Jāhiliyyah involved boasting about ancestors and rivalry based on lineage and titles. It is also said that it means to esteem Allah for the laws He has guided us to, in which case the phrase has a general significance. This was discussed in 2:52.

وَإِذَا سَأَلَكَ عِبَادِي عَنِّي فَإِنِّي قَرِيبٌ أُجِيبُ دَعْوَةَ الدَّاعِ إِذَا
دَعَانِ فَلْيَسْتَجِيبُوا لِي وَلْيُؤْمِنُوا بِي لَعَلَّهُمْ يَرْشُدُونَ ﴿١٨٦﴾

**186 If My slaves ask you about Me, I am near. I answer the call of the caller when he calls on Me. They should therefore respond to Me and believe in Me so that hopefully they will be rightly guided.**

**If My slaves ask you about Me,**

'If they ask you Who it is that they worship, then tell them that I am near and I reward obedience and answer the one who makes supplication to Me.' Allah knows what His slaves do in respect of fasting, prayer and other things. The commentators disagree about the reason this *āyah* was revealed. Muqātil said that 'Umar had sexual intercourse with his wife after he had prayed *'Ishā'* and regretted that and wept. He went to the Messenger of Allah ﷺ and informed him and returned deeply upset. That was before the permission to do so was revealed. Then this *āyah* was revealed.

**I am near.**

This is in respect to the response. It is said to mean 'near by My knowledge', and it is said to mean 'near to My friends through My favour and blessing to them.'

**I answer the call of the caller when he calls on Me.**

This means: 'I accept the worship of the one who worships Me.' The calling means worship and the answer means acceptance. The evidence for that is what Abū Dāwud related from an-Nu'mān ibn Bashīr that the Prophet ﷺ said, 'Supplication is worship. Your Lord says, *"Call on Me and I will answer you."*' So calling (*du'ā'*) is the same as worship. Evidence for that can be found in the words of the Almighty: *'Those who are too proud for My worship will enter Hell abject.'* (40:60) Here it means supplication.

So Allah Almighty commanded us to make *du'ā'* and encouraged it and called it worship and promised that He would answer it. Layth related from Shahr ibn Ḥawshab that 'Ubādah ibn aṣ-Ṣāmit reported that the Prophet ﷺ said, 'My Community have been given three things that only Prophets were given previously. Whenever Allah sent a Prophet, he said, "Call on Me and I will answer you." He told the whole of this community, "Call on Me and I will answer you." When Allah sent a Prophet, he said to him, "I have not placed any constraint on you in the *dīn*." He told the whole of this community, "I have not placed any constraint on you in the *dīn*." When Allah sent a Prophet, He made him a witness against his people, and He made the whole of this community witnesses against mankind.'

Khālid ar-Rib'iyy said, 'I was amazed at this *āyah*: *"Call on Me and I will answer you"* (40:60), in which Allah commands us to make supplication and promises the response without any precondition. Someone asked, "What kind of precondition might there be?" The answer was, "Such as we find in His words: *'Give good news to those who believe and do right actions.'* (2:25) This is a precondition. He says elsewhere: *"Give good news to those who believe that they are on a sure footing."* (10:2) There is no precondition here. He says: *"Call upon Allah, making your* dīn *sincerely His."* (40:14) This is a precondition. He says: *"Call on Me and I will answer you"* (40:60) There is no precondition here. Nations used to resort to their Prophets for their needs so that the Prophets could ask for that for them.'

If it is asked, 'Why would a caller call if he did not expect to be answered?' the reply is that the words of Allah in the two *āyahs*, 'answer' and 'respond' do not absolutely necessitate an answer for every supplicator in detail nor every seeker in detail. Allah says in another *āyah*: *'Call on your Lord humbly and secretly. He does not love those who overstep the limits.'* (7:55) Everyone who persists in a major wrong action, knowingly or ignorantly, is a transgressor and Allah tells us that He does not love transgressors and so how could He answer such a one? The categories of transgression are numerous and, Allah willing, they will be mentioned in *Sūrat al-A'rāf.* Some scholars say: 'He can answer if He wishes as He says: *"If He wills, He will deliver you from whatever it was that made you call on Him."* (6:41)' This is an aspect of the knowledge of what is general and what is defined. The Prophet ﷺ made three supplications and was granted two and denied one as will be made clear in *Sūrat al-An'ām*, Allah willing.

It is said that what is intended by this statement is to acquaint all believers with the fact that their Lord answers the call of those who call in general, and that He is close to His slave and hears his supplication and knows his need and responds to whatever He wishes and in whatever way He wishes. *'Who is further astray than the one who calls other things besides Allah, which will not respond to them?'* (46:5) A master answers his slave and a father his child but may not give them the thing they are asking for. So it is not inevitable that what is asked for will be granted.

It is related through Ibn 'Umar that the Prophet ﷺ said, 'Whoever has the door of supplication opened to him has the doors of the answer opened to him as well.' Allah revealed to Dāwud, 'Tell My wrongdoing slaves not to call on Me for I have made it incumbent on Myself to answer those who call on Me and when I answer wrongdoers, I curse them.' People have said that Allah answers every supplication and that the answer either appears in this world or takes the form of expiation of sins or is stored up in the Next World. Abū Sa'īd al-Khudrī reported that the Prophet ﷺ said, 'There is no Muslim who calls on Allah Almighty with a supplication which does not contain a request for anything wrong or severance from his kin, without Allah giving him one of three things: He either hastens it to him, or stores it up for him or turns away the like of it in evil from him.' They asked, 'What about when we do a lot of supplication?' 'Allah has more,' he replied. Abū 'Umar ibn 'Abd al-Barr transmitted this and Abū Muḥammad said that it is sound. The *Muwaṭṭā'* has it with a severed *isnād.* Abū 'Umar said, 'This *ḥadīth* is transmitted in commentary on the words of the Almighty: *"Call on Me and I will answer you"* (40:60). All of this is part of the answer.' Ibn 'Abbās said, 'Everyone who makes supplication is answered. If someone prays for provision in this world, Allah gives it, and if he does not receive it in this world, then it is stored up for him in the Next World.'

Although the *ḥadīth* of Abū Sa'īd al-Khudrī allows the answer to come in one of three ways, it indicates to you the soundness of what was said about avoiding any transgression that prevents the answer coming by saying: 'which does not contain a request for anything wrong or severance from his kin'. Muslim added, 'As long as he does not seek to hasten it.' It is related from Abū Hurayrah that the Prophet ﷺ said, 'I continue to answer My slave as long as he does not ask for anything wrong or severance from his kin and as long as he does not seek to hasten it.' He was asked, 'Messenger of Allah, what is seeking to hasten it?' He replied, 'It is that he says, "I asked and I asked and have not had any answer." Then he is saddened by that and stops making supplication.' Al-Bukhārī, Muslim and Abū Dāwud related from Abū Hurayrah that the Messenger of Allah ﷺ said, 'You receive an answer as long as you do not seek to hasten it, saying, "I asked and was not answered."'

Our scholars said that it is possible that he is reporting about the obligatory nature of the answer and reporting about how it will occur. So it is a report about the obligation and its occurrence. The answer can come in any of the three ways mentioned above. When someone says, 'I asked and was not answered,' that voids the occurrence of one of these three things and the supplication is then detached from all of them.

The answer to the supplication can also be denied because of consumption of the unlawful and other such things. The Prophet ﷺ said, 'A man is on a long journey with his hair disheveled and covered in dust. He stretches his hands to heaven, saying, "O Lord! O Lord!" But his food is unlawful, his drink is unlawful, his clothing is unlawful and his nourishment is unlawful. How can he be answered when he is in that state?' This question conveys the fact that it is unlikely for his supplication to be accepted when he is like that.

The answer to the supplication is dependent on the necessary preconditions being met in respect of the one making the supplication, the supplication itself, and what he asks for. The preconditions in the case of the one making the supplication is that he knows that only Allah can bring about his need and that the means are in His hand and subject to Him; that he makes the supplication with a sincere intention and with presence of the heart, as Allah does not answer the supplication of someone with a heedless heart; that he avoids unlawful consumption; and that he does not become impatient with respect to his supplication. The precondition regarding what is being asked for is that it is something permissible to seek or lawful to do, confirmed by his words, 'as long as he does not ask for anything wrong or severance from his kin'. 'Wrong' includes all forms of wrong actions, and 'kin' includes all the rights and wrongs of other Muslims.

Sahl ibn 'Abdullāh at-Tustarī said, 'Supplication has seven preconditions: humble entreaty, fear, hope, constancy, humility, universality, and consumption of the lawful.' Ibn 'Aṭā' 'illāh said, 'Supplication has pillars, wings, means and times. When the pillars are in order, it is strong. When its wings are in order, it flies to heaven. When its times are in order, it is successful. When its means are in order, it will succeed. Its pillars are: the presence of the heart, goodness, humility and submission. Its wings are sincerity. Its time is before dawn. Its means is the prayer on the Prophet ﷺ.' It is said that it has four preconditions. They are guarding the heart when alone, guarding the tongue when with people, guarding the eye and keeping it from looking at what is not lawful, and guarding the belly from what is unlawful. It is said that one of its preconditions is that supplication be free of grammatical errors as the poet says:

He calls to his Lord in ungrammatical Arabic.
Perhaps when he supplicates like that it will not be answered.

Ibrāhīm ibn Adham was asked, 'Why do we make supplication and not get an answer?' He answered, 'Because you knew Allah but did not obey Him. You knew the Messenger but did not follow his Sunnah. You knew the Qur'an but did not act by it. You consumed the blessings of Allah but did not thank Him properly for them. You knew of the Garden but did not seek it. You knew of the Fire but did not flee from it. You knew Shayṭān but did not fight him and instead agreed with him. You knew of death but did not prepare for it. You buried the dead but did not reflect on it. You ignored your own faults and busied yourselves with the faults of others.'

'Alī said to Nawf al-Bikālī, 'Nawf, Allah revealed to David, "Tell the tribe of Israel that they should not enter any of My Houses except with pure hearts, lowered eyes and clean hands. I do not answer the supplication of any of them as long as they act unjustly towards any of my creatures." Nawf, do not be a poet, tax-collector, or tax assessor. David rose in at an hour in the night and said, "This is an hour in which no one makes a supplication without it being answered unless he is an appraiser, a policeman, a lute-player or a drummer."'

Our scholars say that no one should say, 'O Allah, give to me if You wish! O Allah, forgive me if You wish! O Allah, show mercy to me if You wish.' His request should be free of saying, 'If You wish.' He makes the request with the full knowledge that Allah will not do it unless He wishes. Furthermore, the expression 'If You wish' contains a degree of not needing His forgiveness, gift and mercy. It is like someone saying, 'If you wish to give me this, then do so.' That form of expression is only used when someone is not really in need of the thing he is asking for. If someone is truly in need of something, then he shows resolve in asking and asks in the manner of someone truly in need of what he is asking for. The imams related from Anas ibn Mālik that the Messenger of Allah ﷺ said, 'When one of you makes supplication, he should be definite in the request and should not say, "O Allah, give to me if You wish." No one can force Him to do anything.' We find [added] in the *Muwaṭṭā'*: 'O Allah, forgive me if You wish. O Allah, show mercy if You wish.'

Our scholars say that the words 'he should be definite in the request' is evidence that a believer must strive in supplication and hope for an positive response. He should not despair of Allah's mercy because he is calling on one who is generous. Sufyān ibn 'Uyaynah said, 'No one should be prevented from making supplication by what he knows about himself. Allah answered the supplication of the worst of creation, Iblīs when he said, "Lord, defer me until the Day they are resurrected." He replied, "You are one of those deferred."'

There are certain times and situations at which supplication is more likely than at others to be answered, such as the time before dawn, the moment of breaking the fast, between the *adhan* and the *iqāmah*, between *Ẓuhr* and *'Aṣr* prayers on Wednesday, at moments of great need, while travelling and while ill, when rain descends and when lining up in the cause of Allah. All of that comes in traditions and they will be explained in the proper place. Shahr ibn Ḥawshab related that Umm ad-Dardā' said, 'Shahr, do you suffer from the shakes?' 'Yes,' he answered. She said, 'Pray to Allah. Supplication for that condition is answered.' Jābir ibn 'Abdullāh said, 'The Messenger of Allah ﷺ made supplication in the Masjid al-Fatḥ on three days: Monday, Tuesday and Wednesday. It was answered for him on Wednesday between the two prayers. I could see the joy in his face.' Jābir added, 'Nothing important happened to me but that I aimed for that time and made supplication in it and had an answer.'

**They should therefore respond to Me...**

Abū Rajā' al-Khurāsānī said: 'They should call on Me.' Ibn 'Aṭiyyah said that this means: 'They should seek for My response.' It is Form X of the verb which is to seek for something. Mujāhid and others said that the meaning is: 'They should respond to Me regarding what I call them to in respect of faith,' in other words, they should obey Allah and act on His commands.

أُحِلَّ لَكُمْ لَيْلَةَ ٱلصِّيَامِ ٱلرَّفَثُ إِلَىٰ نِسَآئِكُمْ هُنَّ لِبَاسٌ لَّكُمْ وَأَنتُمْ لِبَاسٌ
لَّهُنَّ عَلِمَ ٱللَّهُ أَنَّكُمْ كُنتُمْ تَخْتَانُونَ أَنفُسَكُمْ فَتَابَ عَلَيْكُمْ وَعَفَا
عَنكُمْ فَٱلْـَٔـٰنَ بَٰشِرُوهُنَّ وَٱبْتَغُوا۟ مَا كَتَبَ ٱللَّهُ لَكُمْ وَكُلُوا۟
وَٱشْرَبُوا۟ حَتَّىٰ يَتَبَيَّنَ لَكُمُ ٱلْخَيْطُ ٱلْأَبْيَضُ مِنَ ٱلْخَيْطِ ٱلْأَسْوَدِ مِنَ
ٱلْفَجْرِ ثُمَّ أَتِمُّوا۟ ٱلصِّيَامَ إِلَى ٱلَّيْلِ وَلَا تُبَٰشِرُوهُنَّ وَأَنتُمْ عَٰكِفُونَ
فِى ٱلْمَسَٰجِدِ تِلْكَ حُدُودُ ٱللَّهِ فَلَا تَقْرَبُوهَا كَذَٰلِكَ يُبَيِّنُ ٱللَّهُ
ءَايَٰتِهِۦ لِلنَّاسِ لَعَلَّهُمْ يَتَّقُونَ ﴿١٨٧﴾ وَلَا تَأْكُلُوٓا۟

**187 On the night of the fast it is lawful for you to have sexual relations with your wives. They are clothing for you and you for them. Allah knows that you have been betraying yourselves and He has turned towards you and excused you. Now you may have sexual intercourse with them and seek what Allah has written for you. Eat and drink until you can clearly discern the white thread from the black thread of the dawn, then fulfil the fast until the night appears. But do not have sexual intercourse with them while you are in retreat in the mosques. These are Allah's limits, so do not go near them. In this way does Allah make His Signs clear to people so that hopefully they will be godfearing.**

**On the night of the fast it is lawful for you to have sexual relations with your wives.**

The way that this is expressed indicates that it was at first forbidden and then that prohibition was abrogated. Abū Dāwud reported from Ibn Abī Laylā that, when a man broke the fast and then went to sleep before eating again, he would not break his fast until the following morning. One day 'Umar came home and went to his wife and she told him she had already slept. He thought she was making an excuse and had intercourse with her. In another incident a man of the Anṣār wanted to eat and they said, 'We will heat something up for you,' and he fell asleep. In the morning, this *āyah* was revealed.

Al-Bukhārī related that al-Barā' said, 'Among the Companions of Muḥammad ﷺ if ever a man was fasting and the time of fast-breaking came but he went to sleep before he had broken his fast, he would not eat that night or the following day until evening. Qays ibn Ṣirma al-Anṣārī was fasting and when the time of fast-breaking came, he went to his wife and asked her, "Do you have any food?"

She said, "No, but I will go and look for something for you." He worked during the day and sleep overcame him. His wife returned to him and when she saw him, she said, "You are disappointed." In the middle of the day, he fainted and it was mentioned to the Prophet ﷺ. Then this *āyah* was sent down: *"On the night of the fast it is lawful for you to have sexual relations with your wives."* Then they were very happy, and it was revealed: *"Eat and drink until you can clearly discern the white thread from the black thread of the dawn."*'

We find in al-Bukhārī, also from al-Barā': 'When the fast of Ramadan was revealed, they used to not approach their wives through all of Ramadan. Some men betrayed themselves and so Allah revealed: *"Allah knows that you have been betraying yourselves and He had turned towards you and excused you."*' Betrayal here means to have sexual intercourse during the nights of the fast. If someone disobeys Allah, then he has betrayed himself because he has brought down the punishment on himself. Al-Qutabī said, 'The root meaning of betrayal is that a man is entrusted with something and does not fulfil his trust.' Aṭ-Ṭabarī said that one night 'Umar returned after having conversed in the night with the Prophet ﷺ and found that his wife had slept. He desired her and she told him, 'But I have slept!' He said, 'But I have not slept!' and had sex with her. Ka'b ibn Mālik did the same thing. In the morning 'Umar went to the Prophet ﷺ and said, 'I apologise to Allah and to you! My self impelled me and I had sex with my wife. Do you find any indulgence for me?' He said, 'You were not entitled, 'Umar.' When he reached his house, he sent for him and told him about the excuse in the *āyah* of the Qur'an. An-Naḥḥās and Makkī mentioned it.

The word '*rafath*' (sexual relations) is an allusion to sexual intercourse because Allah is noble and prefers to use an allusion. Ibn 'Abbās, as-Suddī and az-Zajjāj said, '*Rafath* is a word which denotes all that a man does with a woman.' Al-Azharī also said that. Ibn 'Arafah said that it is sexual intercourse. It is also said that *rafath* is obscene language.

**They are clothing for you and you for them.**

The metaphor of clothing is used because a married couple are close to one another like garments and garments cling to the body. Someone said that it is because they cover and protect a thing and so each of them protects the other from what is not lawful as we find in a tradition. It is also said that it is because each of them protects the other from the eyes of other people in respect of what occurs between them. Abū 'Ubayd said others said a wife is called one's 'garment', 'bed', and 'waist-wrapper'. Ar-Rabī' said, 'They are a bed for you and you are a cover for them.' Mujāhid said, 'They are a repose for you, i.e. you each find repose in one another.'

**Allah knows that you have been betraying yourselves and He has turned towards you and excused you.**

Betraying yourselves was by having forbidden sexual intercourse and eating after sleeping during the nights of fasting. It is possible that it means each of them betrays himself and it is called that because of the harm that reverts to him. Allah's turning towards them has two possible meanings. One is that He accepts their repentance for having betrayed themselves and the other is that it refers to Him making it easier for them through His indulgence and His allowing them to do what had previously been forbidden, as when He says elsewhere: *'He knows that you will not keep count of it, so He has turned towards you,'* (73:20) meaning He has lightened it for you. There is also His words about accidental killing: *'Anyone who does not find the means should fast two consecutive months. This is a concession* (tawbah) *from Allah.'* (4:92) It means a lightening because the person who did the accidental killing did not do anything for which he should repent. He says: *'Allah has turned towards the Prophet, and the Muhājirūn and the Anṣār, those who followed him at the "time of difficulty".'* (9:117) No repentance was obliged from the Prophet ﷺ.

So the words *'excused you'* can refer to the wrong action or it can mean making things wide and easy, as the Prophet ﷺ said, 'The beginning of the time is the pleasure of Allah and the end of it is the pardon of Allah.' Therefore it means that Allah knew that you would do this and He turned to you after it occurred and lightened things for you. So '*'afā'*' means 'to make easy'. Ibn al-'Arabī said, 'Scholars of asceticism say that that happened so that there could be divine concern and a noble station. 'Umar betrayed himself and Allah made it part of the Sharī'ah and things were made easier for the community. Allah was pleased with him and he was pleased with Allah.'

**Now you may have sexual intercourse with them**

It is lawful for you now to do what was forbidden before. '*Mubāshara*' (sexual intercourse) is so called because of the contact of skin to skin. This is the literal meaning of the word. Ibn al-'Arabī said, 'This indicates that the reason for the revelation of the *āyah* was 'Umar having sex with his wife, not the hunger of Qays, because if the hunger of Qays had been the reason, he would have said, 'Now you may eat' as that would have been the reason for the revelation of the *āyah*.

**and seek what Allah has written for you.**

Ibn 'Abbās, Mujāhid, al-Ḥakam ibn 'Uyaynah, al-Ḥasan, as-Suddī, ar-Rabī', and aḍ-Ḍaḥḥāk said that this refers to seeking to have a child, indicating that it refers directly back to the previous statement about having sexual intercourse. Ibn 'Abbās said, 'What Allah has written for you is the Qur'an.' Az-Zajjāj said, 'It means: "Seek in the Qur'an for what is permitted to you and for what you have been commanded to do."' Ibn 'Abbās and Mu'ādh ibn Jabal reported that it refers to looking for the Night of Power. It is also said that it means: 'Take advantage of the allowance and dispensation Allah has granted you,' and this was what Qatādah and Ibn 'Aṭiyyah said. It is said that it means to seek slavegirls and wives.

**Eat and drink until you can clearly discern the white thread from the black thread of the dawn,**

When it is clear that dawn has arrived it is not lawful for anyone to eat, even if there is still some time until sunrise. There is disagreement about the point at which it becomes clear that one must abstain from things which break the fast. The majority say that dawn is the light which spreads right and left on the horizon and there are *ḥadīth*s to that effect. Muslim related from Samurah ibn Jundub that the Prophet ﷺ said, 'Do not be deluded from your *saḥūr* by the *adhān* of Bilāl nor by the whiteness of the false dawn on the horizon. It is like that until the dawn spreads like that.' Ḥammād related it with his hand open. Ibn Mas'ūd said, 'Dawn is not like this as it is said,' and he put his fingers together and then lowered them to the ground, 'but that which is said to be like this,' and he put his index fingers together and stretched out his hands.' Ad-Dāraquṭnī related from 'Abd ar-Raḥmān from Ibn 'Abbās that the Messenger of Allah ﷺ said, 'There are two dawns. The one that is like a wolf's tail does not permit or forbid anything. As for the one which spreads on the horizon, it makes the prayer permitted and forbids food.' This is a *mursal* report.

One group say that it refers to the time after dawn when it becomes clear in the streets and houses that dawn has arrived. That is related from 'Umar, Ḥudhayfah, Ibn 'Abbās, Ṭalq ibn 'Alī, 'Aṭā' ibn Abī Rabāḥ, al-A'mash, Sulaymān and others. Abstaining becomes obligatory when it is clearly dawn in the streets and on the tops of the mountains. Masrūq said, 'They did not consider it to be their dawn. What they considered to be dawn was that which filled the houses.' An-Nasā'ī related from 'Āṣim that Zirr said, 'We asked Ḥudhayfah, "When did you have *saḥūr* with the Messenger of Allah?" He replied. "It was daytime, although the sun had not yet risen."' Ad-Dāraquṭnī related from Ṭalq ibn 'Alī that the Prophet of Allah ﷺ said, 'Eat and drink. Do not be deceived by the white ascending light.

Eat and drink until the red light spreads horizontally.' Ad-Dāraquṭnī said that Qays ibn Ṭalq is not strong. Abū Dāwud said that this is something that only the people of Yamamah have. Aṭ-Ṭabarī said, 'That which guided them to this fast is that it is during the day and they believe that the day begins with sunrise and ends with sunset.' The disagreement between linguists about that has already been mentioned as well as the explanation of the Messenger of Allah ﷺ: 'It is the darkness of the night and the whiteness of the day.' That is what distinguishes along with *'a specified number of days'*. (2:184)

Ad-Dāraquṭnī related from 'Ā'ishah that the Prophet ﷺ said, 'Whoever does not intend to fast before the rising of dawn has no fast.' 'Abdullāh ibn 'Abbād alone has it from al-Mufaḍḍal ibn Faḍālah with this *isnād*. All of them are trustworthy. It is related from Ḥafṣah that the Prophet ﷺ said, 'Anyone who does not resolve to fast before dawn has no fast.' 'Abdullāh ibn Abī Bakr has it *marfū'* from highly regarded, trustworthy people. It is also related *marfū'* from Ḥafṣah. These two *ḥadīth*s indicate what the majority say about dawn and that someone who does not have an intention before dawn has no fast, differing from the position of Abū Ḥanīfah.

Fasting is one of the acts of worship which is only valid with an intention, and the time to make the intention is before dawn (*fajr*), so how can it be said that eating and drinking is permissible after dawn? Al-Bukhārī and Muslim related that Sahl ibn Sa'd said, 'When *"Eat and drink until you can clearly discern the white thread from the black thread"* was sent down and *"of the dawn"* had not been sent down, some men who wanted to fast would tie a white thread and a black thread to their legs and would continue to eat until they could see them clearly. Allah later revealed *"of the dawn"* and they then knew that it meant night and day.' It is related that 'Adī ibn Abī Ḥātim said, 'I said, "Messenger of Allah, what is the white thread from the black thread? Are they two threads?" He said, "You are a thick-head if you look at the two threads." Then he said, "No, rather it is the blackness of night and the whiteness of day."' Al-Bukhārī transmitted it and said that dawn is called a thread because what appears is a distinct line of white like a thread. A poet said:

> The white thread is the light of morning breaking.
> The black thread is the darkness of night covering.

*'Khayṭ'* (thread) in their language designates colour. *'Fajr'* (dawn) is a verbal noun used for water which gushes up and spreads out. The root meaning is 'cleaving'. It is used for dawn because when the light of the sun begins to appear, it spreads out along the horizon. This is what the Arabs call 'the white thread'. One also says that 'dawn breaks'.

**then fulfil the fast until the night appears.**

Allah made 'night' a time for eating, drinking and sexual intercourse, and 'day' a time for fasting. So the judgments of the two times are clear and distinct from each other. What is allowed in the night is not permitted in the day, except for travellers or ill people as we have already explained. In any other case, if someone breaks the fast he either does it intentionally or out of forgetfulness. If it is the first case, Mālik said, 'Whoever breaks the fast in Ramadan by eating, drinking, or sexual intercourse, must make it up and owes *kaffārah*,' as is reported in the *Muwaṭṭā'* and also in *Ṣaḥīḥ Muslim* where the Prophet ﷺ ordered a man who broke the fast to free a slave, or fast two consecutive months or feed sixty poor people. Ash-Sha'bī said that. Ash-Shāfi'ī and others say that this *kaffārah* is specific to someone who breaks the fast through sexual intercourse based on the *ḥadīth* of Abū Hurayrah who said, 'A man came to the Messenger of Allah ﷺ and said, "I am destroyed, Messenger of Allah!" He asked, "What has destroyed you?" He answered, "I had sex with my wife in Ramadan."' In it he mentioned *kaffārah* and its order. Muslim transmitted it.

They apply this case to the first case and say that it is the same. This is not sound. Rather they are two separate cases because they have two different contexts. *Kaffārah* is connected undefined to someone who breaks the fast and so it is universal. This is the position of Mālik and his people, Al-Awzā'ī, Isḥāq, Abū Thawr, aṭ-Ṭabarī, and Ibn al-Mundhir. That is also related from 'Aṭā' in one transmission as well as from al-Ḥasan and az-Zuhrī. Ash-Shāfi'ī obliges that position and says that there is no distinction in spite of the difference in circumstances. It indicates that the ruling is universal. Ash-Shāfi'ī made the penalty mandatory as well as making up the days because of violating the sanctity of Ramadan.

They also disagree about what is obliged for a woman whose husband has sex with her in the month of Ramadan. Mālik, Abū Yūsuf and the People of Opinion say that she owes the same that her husband owes. Ash-Shāfi'ī says that she only owes one *kaffārah*, whether it was voluntary or forced, because the Prophet ﷺ responded to the questioner with one *kaffārah* without any distinction. It is related from Abū Ḥanīfah that if it is voluntary, then each of them owe one *kaffārah*. If he forced her, then only he owes one *kaffārah*. That is the position of Saḥnūn ibn Sa'īd al-Mālikī. Mālik said that he owes two *kaffārah*s, and that is his final position according to most of his people.

They also disagree about someone who has sex or eats forgetting that he is fasting. Ash-Shāfi'ī, Abū Ḥanīfah and his people and Isḥāq say that he owes nothing in either case, neither making up nor *kaffārah*. Mālik, al-Layth and al-

Awzā'ī say that he must make any such days up but does not owe *kaffārah.* The same is related from 'Aṭā'. It is also related from 'Aṭā' that he owes *kaffārah* if he has sex forgetfully and that it is the same if he does not forget. Some of the Ẓāhirīs say that it is the same whether he has sex forgetfully or deliberately: he must make it up and also owes *kaffārah.* That is the position of 'Abd al-Malik ibn al-Mājishūn. It was the position of Aḥmad ibn Ḥanbal because the *ḥadīth* obliges *kaffārah* and there is no distinction between someone who forgets or someone who does it deliberately. Ibn al-Mundhir says that he owes nothing.

Mālik, ash-Shāfi'ī, Abū Thawr and the People of Opinion said that if someone eats out of forgetfulness and then, thinking that he has broken the fast, has sex deliberately, he must make it up but does not owe *kaffārah.* Ibn al-Mundhir says, 'That is what we say.' It is stated in the School that he must make it up and also owes *kaffārah* if he did it intentionally since he has violated the sanctity of the fast with impudence and lack of esteem. Abū 'Umar said, 'According to the basic principle of Mālik, he does not have to do *kaffārah* because he ate out of forgetfulness and thought that he had broken the fast, he must make up that day. What sanctity has he violated when he was not fasting? Those other than Mālik said that someone who eats forgetting that he is fasting has not broken the fast.

This is sound, and it is the position of the majority: if someone eats or drinks out of forgetfulness, he does not have to make up a day and his fast is complete, based on the *ḥadīth* of Abū Hurayrah who said that the Messenger of Allah ﷺ said, 'If someone fasting eats or drinks out of forgetfulness, it is provision which Allah has given him. He does not have to make it up. (One variant has, 'He should complete his fast.') Allah has fed and watered him.' Ad-Dāraquṭnī related it and said that it has a sound *isnād*, all of whose transmitters are trustworthy. Abū Bakr al-Athram said, 'I heard Abū 'Abdullāh being asked about someone who eats out of forgetfulness in Ramadan. He answered, "He owes nothing based on the *ḥadīth* of Abū Hurayrah.' Then Abū 'Abdullāh Mālik said, "They claim that Mālik says he must make it up!" and laughed.' Ibn al-Mundhir said, 'He owes nothing based on what the Prophet ﷺ said about someone who eats or drinks out of forgetfulness, "He should complete his fast." He completes it and it is a completed full fast.'

When someone breaks the fast out of forgetfulness, he does not have to make it up and his fast is complete, but if he has sexual intercourse deliberately, he makes it up and owes *kaffārah* and Allah knows best. Our scholars cited for evidence of the obligation of making up the fact that he is told to fast a full day without any gaps since He says, *'fulfil the fast until the night appears.'* This day has not been completed, and so it remains for him to fast. Perhaps the *ḥadīth* is actually about voluntary fasting. It is reported in the *Ṣaḥīḥ* collections of al-Bukhārī and Muslim: 'Anyone who forgets while he is fasting and eats or drinks should complete his fast.' It does not mention or allude to making it up.

Our scholars use this as evidence, and it is sound. Were it not sound from the Lawgiver, we would not have mentioned it. There is a sound clear text related by Abū Hurayrah from the Prophet ﷺ: 'If someone breaks his fast in Ramadan out of forgetfulness, he does not have to make it up and owes no *kaffārah*.' Ad-Dāraquṭnī transmitted it and said that Ibn Marzūq has it, and he is trustworthy from al-Anṣārī. The doubt is therefore removed. Praise be to Allah, the Master of Majesty and Perfection!

When Allah mentions the things forbidden by fasting, such as eating, drinking and sexual intercourse, He does not mention other direct physical contact such as kissing, touching and other such things. That indicates the soundness of the fast of someone who kisses or touches because the mention of what is allowed at night indicates its prohibition during the day, and only three things are mentioned. There is no evidence there for anything other than these specific things and therefore one stops at the evidence. This is why there is disagreement about this matter and indeed the Salaf disagreed.

One of those things is the matter of touching. Our scholars say that it is disliked for someone who is not certain that he will be able to control himself in case it becomes a cause leading to something that actually breaks the fast. Mālik related from Nāfi' that 'Abdullāh ibn 'Umar forbade kissing and touching for someone who is fasting. Allah knows best, but this is out of fear for what might happen between the couple. If he kisses and is safe from going further, he does nothing wrong. The same is true of touching. Al-Bukhārī related that 'Ā'ishah said that the Prophet ﷺ used to kiss and touch when he was fasting. 'Abdullāh ibn Mas'ūd and 'Urwah ibn az-Zubayr were among those who disliked kissing by someone fasting. It is related that Ibn Mas'ūd would make up a day to compensate for it. The *ḥadīth* is an argument against them. Abū 'Umar said however, 'I do not know of anyone who grants an indulgence for someone when he knows that it will lead to what will invalidate the fast.'

If someone kisses and ejaculates, then he must make up the day but does not owe *kaffārah*. Abū Ḥanīfah and his people, ath-Thawrī, al-Ḥasan and ash-Shāfi'ī said that. Ibn al-Mundhir preferred it. He said, 'The one who obliges *kaffārah* for it has no argument.' Abū 'Umar said, 'If someone kisses and has a discharge of prostatic fluid, they believe that he does not need to do anything in compensation.' Aḥmad said, 'If someone kisses and has a discharge of prostatic fluid or ejaculates, he must make it up, but owes no *kaffārah*. That is only owed by the one who has sexual intercourse and penetration, whether deliberately or out of forgetfulness.' Ibn al-Qāsim related from Mālik that someone who kisses or touches and is aroused but discharges no fluid at all must make up the day. Ibn Wahb said that he does not have to make up a day unless he has a discharge of prostatic fluid.' Qāḍī Muḥammad said, 'Our people agree that he owes no *kaffārah*.' If it is sperm that is ejaculated, does that oblige *kaffārah* as well as making up? Either it was a single kiss and then discharge, or a kiss which he enjoys and then repeats and has a discharge. If it is a single kiss, or touch, Ashhab and Saḥnūn said that the owes no *kaffārah*, unless he repeats it. Ibn al-Qāsim said that there is *kaffārah* for all of that, except for a glance, for which there is no *kaffārah* unless he repeats it.

Among those who said that someone owes *kaffārah* if he kisses, touches, plays with his wife or has sexual relations short of penetration and then ejaculates were al-Ḥasan al-Baṣrī, 'Aṭā', Abū Thawr, and Isḥāq. That is the position of Mālik in the *Mudawwanah*. The argument behind the view of Ashhab is that touching, kissing and contact do not break the fast in themselves but may lead to a matter which breaks the fast. If he does it once, not intending ejaculation and invalidation of fasting, he does not owe *kaffārah*, as is the case with the glance. If he repeats it, then he has intended to invalidate the fast and he owes *kaffārah*, just as is the case if he looks again. Al-Lakhmī said, 'They all agree that ejaculation brought about by the glance does not entail *kaffārah* unless he continues to do it.'

The fundamental position is that *kaffārah* is only mandatory for someone who intends to break the fast and violate the sanctity of the fast. Since that is the case, one must look at the normal reaction of someone who has a discharge and whether he normally experiences that from a single kiss or touch or whether that varies and sometimes it happens and sometimes not. I think that he should do *kaffārah* because he did that knowing he would violate his fast or to expose himself to that danger. If he is normally safe from that happening, then it is assumed that what happened to him is not normal and he does not owe *kaffārah*. The statement of Mālik about *kaffārah* being mandatory is because that only happens with someone whose nature is like that. Ashhab took the dominant view that they are safe from that and what they say about the glance is evidence of that.

What he related as a basis for the agreement about the glance is not the same. Al-Bājī related in *al-Muntaqā*: 'If someone looks once intending pleasure and then ejaculates, Shaykh Abu-l-Ḥasan said that he must make the day up and owes *kaffārah*.' Al-Bājī said, 'I consider that to be sound because when someone intends pleasure by it, it is the same as a kiss and other types of pleasure. Allah knows best.' Jābir ibn Zayd, Ath-Thawrī, ash-Shāfi'ī, Abū Thawr and the People of Opinion said about someone who continues to look at a woman until he ejaculates that he does not have to make a day up and does not owe *kaffārah.* Ibn al-Mundhir said that. Al-Bājī said, 'In *al-Madaniyyah* Nāfi' related that if someone looks at a naked woman with pleasure and ejaculates, then he must make up the day but does not owe *kaffārah.'*

Most scholars believe that if dawn comes on someone in *janābah*, his fast is still valid. Qāḍī Abū Bakr ibn al-'Arabī said, 'That is permitted by consensus. There was some discussion about it between the Companions. Then it was decided that the fast of someone who is in *janābah* in the morning is sound.' The argument about it is sound and well known and came about from Abū Hurayrah saying, 'Someone who is in *janābah* in the morning has no fast.' This is transmitted in the *Muwaṭṭā'* and elsewhere. We find in an-Nasā'ī that he retracted it. There is disagreement about his retraction. The best known of his two views with the people of knowledge is that the person concerned has no fast as Ibn al-Mundhir related. It is related from al-Ḥasan ibn Ṣāliḥ. Abū Hurayrah also has a third view, which is that when someone knows that he is in *janābah* and goes to sleep until morning has come, he has broken the fast. If he does not know, then he is still fasting. That is related from 'Aṭā', Ṭāwūs, and 'Urwah ibn az-Zubayr. It is related from al-Ḥasan and an-Nakha'ī that it does not matter in the case of voluntary fasting but must be made up where obligatory fasting is concerned.

These are, in fact, four views about someone who finds himself in *janābah* in the morning. What is sound is the position of the majority based on the *ḥadīth* of 'Ā'ishah and Umm Salamah that the Prophet ﷺ would be in *janābah* in the morning after sexual intercourse, not a wet dream, and would still fast. Ā'ishah said, 'In Ramadan, dawn would come while the Messenger of Allah ﷺ was in *janābah* after sexual intercourse, not a wet dream, and he would have a *ghusl* and fast.' Al-Bukhārī and Muslim transmitted it. It is what is necessarily understood from Allah's words: *'Now you may have sexual intercourse with them.'* Since the permission to have sex extends until the rising of dawn, it is necessarily known that dawn might find someone in *janābah* and he would have to have a *ghusl* after dawn. Ash-Shāfi'ī said, 'If his penis is inside his wife at dawn, he does not have to make it up.' Al-Muzanī said, 'He must make it up because it is part of the completion of intercourse.' The first is sounder based on what we mentioned and it is the position of our scholars.

There is disagreement about a menstruating woman who becomes pure before *fajr* but does not purify herself until morning has arrived. Most scholars believe that she is obliged to fast, whether she failed to purify herself deliberately or forgetfully, as is the case with someone in *janābah*. That is the position of Mālik and Ibn al-Qāsim. But 'Abd al-Malik said, 'When a menstruating woman becomes pure before *fajr* but delays *ghusl* until after dawn, then she is not fasting that day because she was impure for part of it. She is not like someone in *janābah* because a wet dream does not break the fast but menstruation does.' That is what Abu-l-Faraj mentioned in his book from 'Abd al-Malik. Al-Awzā'ī said that she makes it up because she neglected *ghusl*. Ibn al-Jallāb mentioned from 'Abd al-Malik that if she becomes pure at a time when it is possible for her to have a *ghusl* before *fajr*, but neglects to do so and does not do it until after morning has arrived, it does not affect her adversely, as is the case with someone in *janābah*. If the time is so short that she would not be able to have a *ghusl* before *fajr*, then her fast is not allowed and she is not fasting that day. Mālik said that. She is the same as someone who is still menstruating at the beginning of the day. Muḥammad ibn Maslamah said that she should fast and make up the day as well, as al-Awzā'ī also said. An aberrant view is related from him that if she becomes pure before *fajr* and then neglects and delays doing a *ghusl* until after the morning has arrived, she owes *kaffārah* as well as making up the day. If a woman becomes pure during the night in Ramadan but does not know whether that was before or after *fajr*, she fasts and also makes up that day out of caution. She owes no *kaffārah*.

It is related that the Prophet ﷺ said, 'The cupper and the one cupped break the fast.' That is related from the *ḥadīth*s of Thawbān, Shaddād ibn Aws and Rāfi' ibn Khadīj. Aḥmad and Isḥāq said that. Aḥmad said that the *ḥadīth* of Shaddād ibn Aws is sound. 'Alī ibn al-Madīnī said that the *ḥadīth* of Rāfi' ibn Khadīj is sound. Mālik, ash-Shāfi'ī and ath-Thawrī said that a person does not have to make it up unless he was forced to do that out of deceit. We find in *Ṣaḥīḥ Muslim* that Anas was asked, 'Do you dislike someone fasting being cupped?' 'No,' he answered, 'unless it results in weakness.' Abū 'Umar said, 'We believe that the *ḥadīth*s of Shaddād, Rāfi' and Thawbān are abrogated by the *ḥadīth* of Ibn 'Abbās who said that the Messenger of Allah ﷺ was cupped while fasting in *iḥrām*. It states in the *ḥadīth* of Shaddād ibn Aws that in the year of the Conquest of Makkah the Prophet ﷺ passed by a man who was being cupped on the 18th of Ramadan and said, 'The cupper and the one cupped break the fast.' Then he himself ﷺ was cupped while he was in *iḥrām* and fasting during the year of the Farewell Hajj. Therefore it must be abrogated because the Prophet ﷺ did not reach another Ramadan after the Farewell Hajj, dying in Rabī' al-Awwal of that year.

*'Fulfil the fast until the night appears'* is an undisputed command. The preposition *'until'* marks its extent in time. In the case of the preposition *ila*, if what is after it and before it are the same, then all is subject to the same ruling, as when you say, 'I have bought from this tree to that tree from you,' so what is sold are trees, and the final tree mentioned is included in the sale. This would not be the case if you said, 'the area up to *(ila)* the house.' The house is not included since it is not the same thing. So here Allah stipulates the completion of the fast when night is clear as it is permitted to eat until day is clear.

Part of the completeness of the fast is that it must be accompanied by an intention which is not removed. According to the *Mudawwanah*, if it is removed at any point during the day by the person intending to break the fast, even if he has not eaten or drunk, he has broken the fast and must make up that day. According to the book of Ibn al-Ḥabīb, however, he is still fasting. He said that he only ceases to fast by breaking it by an action, not by an intention. It is also said that he owes *kaffārah* as well as making it up. Saḥnūn said, 'He does *kaffārah* if he intends not to fast at night, but if he intends it in the day, it does not harm him, even though it is recommended that he make it up.'

When it is clearly night, then you break the fast legally, whether you eat or not. Ibn al-'Arabī said, 'Imam Abū Isḥāq was asked about a man who took an oath, swearing by a treble divorce, that he would not break the fast on anything hot or cold. He answered that he broke the fast when the sun set and so owes nothing. For evidence, he cited the words of the Prophet ﷺ, "When night comes from here and day retreats there, then the faster has broken his fast." Imam Abū Naṣr ibn aṣ-Ṣabbāgh, the author of *ash-Shāmil*, was asked about it and said, "He must break his fast on hot or cold." The response of Imam Abū Isḥāq is more fitting because it is demanded by the Book and Sunnah.'

If someone thinks that the sun has set because of clouds or for some other reason and breaks the fast, and then the sun appears, he must only make up that day according to most *fuqahā'*. We find in al-Bukhārī that Asmā' bint Abī Bakr said, 'Once, during the time of the Messenger of Allah ﷺ, we broke the fast on a cloudy day and then the sun appeared. Hishām said, "We were commanded to make it up."' 'Umar said in the *Muwaṭṭā'* about this, 'That is an easy matter. It was because of our deduction *(ijtihād)* about the time,' meaning making it up. Al-Ḥasan al-Baṣrī said, 'He does not have to make it up,' meaning this view. Allah knows best.

If someone breaks the fast while unsure about whether the sun has set or not, he owes *kaffārah* as well as making it up. Mālik said that, even if the person thinks that it is probable that it has set. If someone is unsure about whether dawn has broken or not, he must refrain from eating. If, in spite of his doubt, he eats, then he must make it up like someone who forgets. There is no disagreement about Malik's position regarding that. Some of the people of Madīnah and others do not think that he owes anything until it is clear to him that dawn really has broken. That is the view of Ibn al-Mundhir. Aṭ-Ṭabarī said, 'Some people think that, since you are permitted to not fast until the beginning of dawn, if someone eats thinking that dawn has not broken, he has eaten with the permission of the Sharī'ah at a time when it is permitted to eat. Therefore he does not have to make it up.' That is also stated by Mujāhid and Jābir ibn Zayd. There is no disagreement that making up a day is obligatory for a person if the new moon is hidden from him by clouds on the first night of Ramadan and he eats, and then it becomes clear that it is Ramadan. We have a similar view. That is also true for a captive in the Abode of War when he eats thinking that it is Sha'bān and then it is clear that that is not the case.

The injunction to '*fast until the night appears*' contains an implicit prohibition against continuous fasting since night marks the end of the fast. 'Ā'ishah said that. It is a subject of dispute as people like 'Abdullāh ibn az-Zubayr, Ibrāhīm at-Taymī, Abu-l-Jawzā', Abu-l-Ḥasan ad-Dīnawāri and others fasted continuously. Ibn az-Zubayr used to fast for seven days at a time. When he broke his fast, he would drink ghee and aloes until his intestines opened. He said, 'It dries the intestines.' Abu-l-Jawzā' used to fast continuously for seven days and seven nights.

The literal text of the Qur'an and Sunnah make it clear that it is forbidden. The Prophet ﷺ said, 'When night comes from here and day retreats there, then the faster has broken his fast.' Muslim transmitted this from 'Abdullāh ibn Abī Awfā. He forbade continuous fasting. When they refused to stop, he fasted day and night continuously with them for a day and then another day. Then they saw the crescent moon and he said, 'If the crescent moon had not appeared, I would have made it longer.' It was like a punishment for them since they would not stop. Muslim transmitted it from Abū Hurayrah. The Prophet ﷺ said, 'Beware of continuous fasting! Beware of continuous fasting!' to stress its prohibition. Al-Bukhārī transmitted it.

Most scholars dislike continuous fasting because it weakens the faculties and exhausts the body. Some of them even made it unlawful since it is contrary to the literal text and imitates the People of the Book. The Prophet ﷺ said, 'The difference between our fast and the fast of the People of the Book is that we eat before dawn.' Muslim and Abū Dāwud transmitted it. We find in al-Bukhārī that

Abū Sa'īd al-Khudrī said that he heard the Messenger of Allah ﷺ say, 'Do not fast continuously. Any of you who wants to fast continuously, fast continuously until before dawn (*saḥar*).' They said, 'But you fast continuously, Messenger of Allah.' He answered, 'I am not like you. In the night I have One Who feeds me and gives me to drink.' They said, 'This is permission to delay breaking the fast until before dawn. It is the limit of someone who wants to fast continuously. It is forbidden to connect the fast of one day to another.' That was stated by Aḥmad, Isḥāq, and Ibn Wahb, the companion of Mālik.

Those who permit continuous fasting argue that the prohibition against continuous fasting was because they were new to Islam and the Messenger of Allah ﷺ feared to burden them with continuous fasting and the highest stations lest they flag or prove too weak to do something that was more beneficial than *jihād* and showing strength against the enemy, in spite of their need at that time. It was something that he imposed on himself: continuous fasting and the highest stations of acts of obedience. When they asked him about continuous fasting, he showed them the difference between him and themselves and informed them that his state in that respect was different to their states. When faith was complete in their hearts and firm in their breasts, and there were many Muslims and they had defeated their enemies, the *awliyā'* of Allah obliged the highest stations for themselves. Allah knows best.

It is better, however, not to fast continuously even though Islam has now been victorious and defeated its enemies. That is the highest degree and station anyone can hope to attain to. The evidence for that is what we mentioned. Night is not a time for legal fasting so that if a person were to start his fast in it with an intention, he would not be rewarded for it. The Prophet ﷺ did not report from himself that he did it, but the Companions thought that he did and said, 'But you fast continuously.' He told them that was given food and drink. The literal meaning of this would be that the Prophet ﷺ was given the food and drink of the Garden. It is said that this can be applied to the meaning of subtleties that came to his heart. When words can be taken both literally and metaphorically, the basis is the literal meaning unless there is evidence that negates it. When they refused to stop continuous fasting, he ﷺ did so with them according to his custom as he had said he did, while they remained doing it in their way until they became weak and lacking in steadfastness. So they ceased to fast continuously. This was a punishment for them so that they would stop their excessive behaviour towards themselves. Success is by Allah.

Breaking the fast with dates or sips of water is recommended based on what is related by Abū Dāwud that Anas said, 'The Messenger of Allah ﷺ used to break the fast with fresh dates before he prayed, and if there were no fresh dates, then with small dry dates. If there were no dry dates, then with a few sips of water.' Ad-Dāraquṭnī transmitted it and said that it has a sound *isnād*. Ad-Dāraquṭnī related that Ibn 'Abbās said, 'When the Messenger of Allah ﷺ broke the fast, he said, "We have fasted for You and broken our fast on Your provision. Accept it from us. You are the All-Hearing, All-Knowing."' Ibn 'Umar said, 'When the Messenger of Allah ﷺ broke the fast, he said, "The thirst has gone, the veins are moist and the wage is confirmed, Allah willing."' Abū Dāwud transmitted it. Ad-Dāraquṭnī said, 'Al-Ḥusayn ibn Wāqid alone has it and its *isnād* is sound. Ibn Mājah related that 'Abdullāh ibn az-Zubayr said, 'The Messenger of Allah ﷺ broke the fast with Sa'd ibn Mu'ādh and said, "The fasters have broken the fast with you, the pious have eaten your food, and the angels have prayed for blessing for you."' It is also related from Zayd ibn Khālid al-Juhanī that the Messenger of Allah ﷺ said, 'All those who provide food for someone to break his fast with have the like of his reward with that decreasing their reward at all.' It is also related from 'Abdullāh ibn 'Amr ibn al-'Āṣ that the Messenger of Allah ﷺ said, 'When the faster breaks his fast, no supplication he makes is rejected.' Ibn Abī Mulaykah said that he heard 'Abdullāh ibn 'Amr say when he broke his fast, 'O Allah, I ask you by Your mercy which encompasses all things to forgive me.' We find in *Ṣaḥīḥ Muslim* that the Prophet ﷺ said, 'A faster has two joys. He has a joy when he breaks his fast and a joy in his fasting when he meets his Lord.'

It is recommended to fast six days of Shawwāl based on what Muslim, at-Tirmidhī, Abū Dāwud, an-Nasā'ī and Ibn Mājah related from Abū Ayyūb al-Anṣārī who said that the Messenger of Allah ﷺ said, 'If someone fasts Ramadan and then follows it with six from Shawwāl, it is as if he had fasted all time.' This is a sound *ḥasan ḥadīth* from Sa'd ibn Sa'īd al-Anṣārī al-Madanī. He is one of those from whom al-Bukhārī did not transmit anything. It has a good *isnād*, explaining the *ḥadīth* of Abū Asmā' ar-Raḥabī from Thawban, the freedman of the Prophet ﷺ, who heard the Messenger of Allah ﷺ say, 'Allah has made a good deed equal to ten like it, and so the month of Ramadan is equal to ten months and the six days of the *Fiṭr* complete the year.' An-Nasā'ī related it.

There is disagreement about fasting these days. In the *Muwaṭṭā'* Mālik disliked it out of fear of the people of ignorance connecting to Ramadan what is not part of it. What he feared actually occurred so that in some towns in Khorasan they rise for the *sahūr* as they do in Ramadan. Muṭarrif related from Mālik that he used to fast it just for himself. Ash-Shāfi'ī recommended fasting them. Abū Yūsuf disliked it.

**But do not have sexual intercourse with them while you are in retreat (*i'tikāf*) in the mosques.**

Allah makes it clear that sexual intercourse invalidates *i'tikāf*. The people of knowledge agree that if someone has sexual intercourse with his wife while he is in *i'tikāf*, that violates his *i'tikāf*. They disagree about what he owes if he does that. Al-Ḥasan al-Baṣrī said that he owes what is owed by someone who has sex with his wife in Ramadan. Pleasures other than intercourse are disliked, even if they were not intended. Touching without lust is not forbidden, because 'Ā'ishah combed the Prophet's hair while he was in *i'tikāf* and that entails touching. This is the position of 'Aṭā', ash-Shāfi'ī and Ibn al-Mundhir. Abū 'Umar said, 'They agree that someone in *i'tikāf* should not touch or kiss, but they disagree about what he owes if he does that. Mālik and ash-Shāfi'ī said, 'If he does any of that, his *i'tikāf* is invalid.' Al-Muzanī also said that. In another place regarding issues concerning *i'tikāf*, he says that his *i'tikāf* is not invalidated by sex unless it is something that would entail the *ḥadd* punishment. Al-Muzanī preferred that based on analogy with fasting during the *ḥajj*.

The word for 'retreat', *i'tikāf*, linguistically means 'to cling to' and someone doing *i'tikāf* clings to good action by obedience to Allah during the period of his *i'tikāf*. In the usage of the Sharī'ah it denotes clinging to a particular act of obedience at a particular time with particular conditions in a particular place. Scholars agree that it is not obligatory but is a supererogatory act of devotion which the Messenger of Allah ﷺ, his Companions and his wives imposed on themselves. It is disliked for someone to begin it if he fears that he will not be able to complete it.

Scholars agree that *i'tikāf* can only be done in mosques, in view of the words of Allah, *'in mosques'*. They disagree about exactly what is meant by mosques in this context. Some people believe that the *āyah* was confined to those mosques which were built by a Prophet, such as the Masjid al-Ḥarām and Jerusalem. This is related from Ḥudhayfah ibn al-Yamān and Sa'īd ibn al-Musayyab, who said that *i'tikāf* can only be done in them. Others say that it can only be done in a mosque in which the *Jumu'ah* prayer is held since they believe that what is indicated in the *āyah* is that category of mosques. This is related from 'Alī ibn Abī Ṭālib and Ibn Mas'ūd. It is the position of 'Urwah, al-Ḥakam, Ḥammād, az-Zuhrī and Abū Ja'far Muḥammad ibn 'Alī, and is one of the positions of Mālik. Still others say that it is permitted in any mosque. This is related from Sa'īd ibn Jubayr, Abū

Qilābah and others. It is the position of ash-Shāfi'ī and Abū Ḥanīfah and his people. Their argument is that *āyah* is general to every mosque with an imam and *mu'adhdhin*. It is another position of Mālik. That is also the view of Ibn 'Ulayyah, Dāwud ibn 'Alī, aṭ-Ṭabarī and Ibn al-Mundhir. Ad-Dāraquṭnī related from aḍ-Ḍaḥḥāk that Ḥudhayfah said that he heard the Messenger of Allah ﷺ say, '*I'tikāf* is proper in any mosque with a *mu'adhdhin* and imam.' Ad-Dāraquṭnī said that aḍ-Ḍaḥḥāk did not listen to Ḥudhayfah.

According to Mālik and Abū Ḥanīfah, the minimum time *of i'tikāf* is a day and a night. If someone vows to do it for a night, he must do it for a day and a night. That is the same if he vows to do it for a day: he must do it for a day and a night. Saḥnūn said that if someone vows to do it for a night, he owes nothing. Abū Ḥanịfah and his people say that if he vows a day, he must do a day without the night. If he vows to do a night, he owes nothing. Ash-Shāfi'ī says that its minimum is an instant and there is not maximum. Some Ḥanafīs say that *i'tikāf* for an hour is valid.

According to this view, fasting is not a precondition for *i'tikāf*. It is related from Aḥmad ibn Ḥanbal in one of his two views, as well as Dāwud ibn 'Alī and Ibn 'Ulayyah. Ibn al-Mundhir and Ibn al-'Arabī also said that. They argued that the Messenger of Allah ﷺ did *i'tikāf* in Ramadan and so it is possible that his fasting was because of its being in Ramadan. According to Mālik and his people, if someone doing *i'tikāf* in Ramadan intends his fast to be both voluntary and obligatory, then his fast is invalid. It is known that in the night someone doing *i'tikāf* must avoid having sex with women as is also the case during the day. The night is included in his *i'tikāf* and the night is not a time for fasting. Therefore the day does not require fasting, but it is good for him to fast.

Mālik, Abū Ḥanīfah and Aḥmad, in his other position, say that *i'tikāf* is not valid without fasting. It is related from Ibn 'Umar, Ibn 'Abbās and 'Ā'ishah. We find in the *Muwaṭṭā'* from al-Qāsim ibn Muḥammad and Nāfi', the freedman of 'Abdullāh ibn 'Umar, that there is no *i'tikāf* without fasting, going by the words of the Almighty in His Book: *'Eat and drink ... in the mosques.'* They said, 'Allah mentions *i'tikāf* together with fasting. Yaḥyā said that Mālik said, 'That is what we go by here.' Their evidence is what 'Abdullāh ibn Budayl related from 'Amr ibn Dīnār from Ibn 'Umar that in the Jāhiliyyah 'Umar imposed on himself that he would do *i'tikāf* for a night or a day at the Ka'bah. He asked the Prophet ﷺ who said, 'Do *i'tikāf* and fast.' Abū Dāwud transmitted it. Ad-Dāraquṭnī said that only 'Abdullāh ibn Budayl has it from 'Amr, and he is weak. 'Ā'ishah said that the Prophet ﷺ said, 'There is no *i'tikāf* without fasting.' Ad-Dāraquṭnī said that only Suwayd ibn 'Abd al-Azīz has it from Sufyān ibn Ḥusayn from az-Zuhrī from 'Urwah from 'Ā'ishah. They said, 'We do not consider fasting to be a precondition for *i'tikāf*. Rather it is sound that fasting can be for it, for Ramadan, for a vow, or something else. If someone makes a vow, it is directed to what it demands in the basis of the Sharī'ah. So if someone vows to pray, he must do it. He does not have to purify himself for it especially, but a previous purification is sufficient.

Someone in *i'tikāf* should only leave it when absolutely necessary based on the imams relating that 'Ā'ishah said, 'When the Messenger of Allah ﷺ did *i'tikāf*, he would put out his head to me and I would comb it. He would not enter the house except for a human need (meaning urine or defecation).' There is no disagreement about this in the community nor among the imams. When someone in *i'tikāf* leaves for a necessary need and returns immediately after the need is fulfilled, he continues with his *i'tikāf* and owes nothing. Clear illness and menstruation are part of need.

They disagree about when someone leaves for some other reason. The position of Mālik is what we have mentioned, and that is also the position of ash-Shāfi'ī and Abū Ḥanifah. Sa'īd ibn Jubayr, al-Ḥasan and an-Nakha'ī said that a person may visit the sick and attend funerals. This is also related from 'Alī, but is not firm from him. Isḥāq made a distinction between mandatory and voluntary *i'tikāf*: in mandatory *i'tikāf* a person may not visit the sick or attend funerals, but in the voluntary, when he begins, he may stipulate that he can visit the sick, attend funerals and attend to other needs. Aḥmad has different positions regarding that: sometimes he forbids it, and sometimes he says, 'I hope that there will be no harm it.' Al-Awzā'ī has the same position as Mālik: no preconditions may be added to *i'tikāf*. Ibn al-Mundhir said, 'A person may not leave his *i'tikāf* except for a necessary need which is that for which the Prophet ﷺ left.'

They disagree about leaving for Jumu'ah. Some say that he should leave for Jumu'ah and return after he says the *salām* because he is leaving for something obligatory and therefore does not break his *i'tikāf*. Ibn al-Jahm related it from Mālik. That is the view of Abū Ḥanifah. Ibn al-'Arabī and Ibn al-Mundhir said that. The well known position of Mālik is that is someone who wants to do *i'tikāf* for ten days, or vows to do that, may only do it in a Jāmi' mosque. If he does it in another mosque, then he must leave for Jumu'ah and his *i'tikāf* is invalidated. 'Abd al-Malik said, 'He goes to Jumu'ah, attends it and then returns and his *i'tikāf* is valid.

That is sound because of Allah's words, *'in the mosques'*, which is general. Scholars agree that *i'tikāf* is not mandatory but sunnah. Most scholars agree that *Jumu'ah* is an individual obligation. When there are two obligations and one is more strongly stressed than the other, then the one that is more strongly stressed is put first. So what is the case when there is something recommended and something mandatory? He did not say that he should fail to go to it, and so that counts as a need.

If someone in *i'tikāf* commits a major sin, his *i'tikāf* is invalidated because a major sin is the opposite of worship in the same way that breaking *wuḍū'* is the opposite of purity. Leaving what Allah has forbidden is the highest of the stations of *i'tikāf* in worship. Ibn Khuwayzimandād stated that.

Muslim related that 'Ā'ishah said, 'When the Messenger of Allah ﷺ wanted to go into *i'tikāf*, he prayed *fajr* and then entered *i'tikāf*. Scholars disagree about the time one enters *i'tikāf*. Al-Awzā'ī took the *ḥadīth* literally. It is related from ath-Thawrī and al-Layth ibn Sa'd in one view, and also stated by Ibn al-Mundhir and a group of Tābi'ūn. Abū Thawr said, 'This is done by someone who makes a vow for ten days. If he adds to it, it is before sunset.' Mālik, ash-Shāfi'ī and Abū Ḥanīfah and his people said: 'When someone imposes on himself to do *i'tikāf* for a month, he should enter the mosque before sunset on that day.' Mālik said, 'That is the case with everyone who wants to do *i'tikāf* for a day or longer.' That was also stated by Abū Ḥanīfah and 'Abd al-Malik ibn al-Mājishūn because the first night of the days of *i'tikāf* is included in them and it is a time of *i'tikāf* and is not divisible. Ash-Shāfi'ī said, 'When someone swears to Allah to do *i'tikāf* for a day, he should enter before dawn and leave after sunset.' This is not his well known position. Al-Layth in one view and Zufar said that he should enter before dawn. They consider a month or a day to be the same. The same is related from Abū Yūsuf and it is also the view of Qāḍī 'Abd al-Wahhāb: night is included in *i'tikāf* as a natural consequence by the evidence that *i'tikāf* is only valid with fasting and night is not a time of fasting. Therefore it is considered that what is meant by *i'tikāf* is the day rather than the night. The *ḥadīth* of 'Ā'ishah refutes these views. It is the proof in case of dispute and is a firm *ḥadīth* which is undisputedly sound.

Mālik recommended that someone doing *i'tikāf* during the last ten nights of Ramadan should spend the night of *Fiṭr* in the mosque and go from there to the prayer. Aḥmad also said that. Ash-Shāfi'ī and al-Awzā'ī said that he should leave at sunset. Saḥnūn related that from Ibn al-Qāsim, because the ten end when the month ends, and the month ends at the sunset of the last day of Ramadan. Saḥnūn said that this is mandatory. If he leaves during the night of *Fiṭr* then his *i'tikāf* is void. Ibn al-Mājishūn said, 'This is invalidated by what we mentioned about the end of the month. If remaining the night of *Fiṭr* had been a precondition of the validity of *i'tikāf*, then no *i'tikāf* is would have been valid unless it was connected to the night of *Fiṭr*. The consensus that this is not the case indicates that it is not a precondition of soundness for someone in *i'tikāf* to stay the night of *Fiṭr*.' This is enough about rulings of fasting and *i'tikāf* connected to these *āyahs*. Success is by Allah.

**These are Allah's limits, so do not go near them.**

'These judgments are the limits of Allah, so do not oppose them.' This indicates these commands and prohibitions. '*Ḥudūd*' (limits) are barriers and *ḥadd* is prevention. Iron is called *ḥadīd* because it prevents the weapon from reaching the body. A doorman and jailer are called *ḥaddād* because they prevent people from entering or going out. The *ḥudūd* of Allah are so called because they prevent the one who commits the crimes from returning to their like.

**In this way does Allah make His Signs clear to people**

Just as He clarifies these limits, He clarifies all the judgments, so that people will be careful not to exceed them. The Signs are the *āyahs* which guide to the truth. Hopefully Allah will ease them to guidance by the direction provided by the Signs.

وَلَا تَأْكُلُوٓا۟ أَمْوَٰلَكُم بَيْنَكُم بِٱلْبَٰطِلِ وَتُدْلُوا۟ بِهَآ إِلَى ٱلْحُكَّامِ
لِتَأْكُلُوا۟ فَرِيقًا مِّنْ أَمْوَٰلِ ٱلنَّاسِ بِٱلْإِثْمِ وَأَنتُمْ تَعْلَمُونَ ۝١٨٨

**188 Do not devour one another's property by false means nor offer it to the judges as a bribe, trying through crime to knowingly usurp a portion of other people's property.**

**Do not devour one another's property by false means**

This was revealed about 'Abdān ibn Ashwa' al-Ḥadramī. He claimed some property from Imru-l-Qays al-Kindī and they went to the Prophet ﷺ and Imru-l-Qays al-Kindī denied 'Abdān's claim and wanted to make an oath. This was revealed and he refrained from making the oath and the Prophet ﷺ ruled in favour of 'Abdān in respect of the disputed property and Imru-l-Qays did not contend against him. But despite the specific cause of the revelation, the *āyah* embraces the entire community of Muḥammad ﷺ. It means: you should not consume one another's property without having the legal right to do so. Things included in this judgment are gambling, fraud, usurpation, denying someone's just rights and anything the owner is not happy about or things which the Sharī'ah forbids, even if the owner is happy about them, such as money from prostitution, fees for soothsaying and money from wine and pigs other such things. 'Property' is ascribed to both parties since the prohibition applies to both of them.

Anyone who obtains someone else's property in a manner other than that permitted by the Sharī'ah has consumed it by false means. One such occasion is if a qāḍī judges in your favour when you know that you are in the wrong. The unlawful does not become lawful by the verdict of a judge because he judges by the outward. This is the consensus concerning property. Umm Salamah transmitted that the Prophet ﷺ said, 'I am but a man to whom you bring your disputes. Perhaps one is more eloquent in his evidence than the other and so I rule according to what I have heard from him. If I make a ruling in his favour about something which is rightfully his brother's, he should not take any of it, for I am awarding him a portion of the Fire.' The position of most scholars and the imams of the *fuqahā'* base their position on this *ḥadīth.*

This is a clear text expressing the fact that the ruling of the judge by the outward does not change the inward judgment, whether it is about property, bloodshed or sexual matters, except for Abū Ḥanīfah's position that judgment does not effect the ruling about private sexual matters. He claimed that if a man gives false witness about divorcing his wife and the judge gives a ruling on the basis of their testimony, since they are reputable in his view, it is lawful for her husband to have sex with her when it is known that the ruling was void after her *'iddah.* That is also the case when one of the witnesses marries her: in his view, it is permitted, because if she is lawful to her new husband outwardly, the witness and others are the same, because the judgment of the qāḍī severed the bond. When that happens, then making lawful or making unlawful occur both outwardly and in private. If that were true, she would not be lawful to past husbands. He argues by the ruling of the *li'ān* and says, 'It is known that a wife can be parted from her husband by a *li'ān* based on lies. If the judge had known her lies, he would have imposed the *ḥadd* on her and not parted them. This has nothing to do with the words of the Prophet ﷺ, "If I give a ruling in his favour about something which is rightfully his brother's, he should not take any of it."'

This *āyah* binds everyone who agrees with or opposes any ruling they ask for themselves which is not permitted. Evidence for this is found in His words: *'Do not consume one another's property by false means.'* (4:29) It could be answered that it is not agreed to be false until there is clear evidence of that being the case. Then it is included in the general statement. It is evidence that false means are not permitted in transactions.

The root of the word for '*by false means*' (*bāṭil*) means literally to go and depart. The plural is *bawāṭil.* One form of it means to follow a diversion. Qatādah says that Allah's words: *'Falsehood cannot reach it"* (41:42), refers to Iblīs. He is not able to add anything or remove anything. In: *'Allah wipes out the false'* (42:24), it means *shirk. Baṭalah* means sorcerers.

**nor offer it to the judges as a bribe,**

It is said that this refers to deposits and things about which there is no evidence, as Ibn 'Abbās and al-Ḥasan said. It is said that it is property belonging to orphans in the possession of their trustees which is presented to the judges when it is demanded, so that some of it can be alienated and apparent evidence given regarding it. Az-Zajjāj said, 'You act according to what the outward rulings demand and leave what you know to be the truth.' *'Adlā bi'l-ḥujja'* is to present something you hope will be successful. It is likened to someone letting down a bucket (*dalw*) into a well. The verb *adlā* is used for releasing it and *dalā* is to pull it out. It means: 'Do not combine consuming wealth by false means with presenting false evidence to judges.' That is like His words: *'Do not mix up truth with falsehood and knowingly hide the truth.'* (2:42) It is said that it means 'Do not cajole judges with your property and give them bribes (*tarshaw*) so that they judge in your favour because judges are rarely free of this.' The two words are similar, as *dalw* means a bucket and the root of the word normally used for bribe (*rashwah*) is *rashā'*, a rope, since people use rope to get what they need. But judges today are likely to take bribes. There is no power nor strength except by Allah!

**trying through crime to knowingly usurp a portion of other people's property.**

*'Farīq'* is a part or portion, and the word is used to denote a sheep that is apart from the greater flock. It means to consume the property of some people. The words 'through crime' mean through injustice and transgression. It is called a 'crime' (*ithm*) because of the wrong action of the doer. *'Knowingly'* means that you know that it is false and a wrong action and this is astonishing audacity and disobedience.

The people of the Sunnah agree that whoever takes any kind of property in this way, no matter whether it is a little or a lot, becomes legally iniquitous by doing that. It is forbidden for him to take it. An exception to that was made by Bishr ibn al-Mu'tamir and the Mu'tazilites who followed him. He said that someone only becomes legally iniquitous by taking ten dinars, not by anything less than that. Ibn Hudhayl that it is five dirhams. Some of the Qadarīs of Basra said that it is one dirham or more, but not less. All of this is rejected by the Qur'an and Sunnah and agreement of the scholars of the community. The Prophet ﷺ said, 'Your blood property and reputations are sacrosanct to you.' This is agreed to be sound.

يَسْـَٔلُونَكَ عَنِ ٱلْأَهِلَّةِ ۖ قُلْ هِىَ مَوَٰقِيتُ لِلنَّاسِ وَٱلْحَجِّ ۗ وَلَيْسَ ٱلْبِرُّ بِأَن تَأْتُوا۟
ٱلْبُيُوتَ مِن ظُهُورِهَا وَلَـٰكِنَّ ٱلْبِرَّ مَنِ ٱتَّقَىٰ ۗ وَأْتُوا۟ ٱلْبُيُوتَ مِنْ
أَبْوَٰبِهَا ۚ وَٱتَّقُوا۟ ٱللَّهَ لَعَلَّكُمْ تُفْلِحُونَ ﴿١٨٩﴾

**189 They will ask you about the crescent moons. Say, 'They are set times for mankind and for the ḥajj.' It is not devoutness for you to enter houses by the back. Rather devoutness is possessed by those who are godfearing. So come to houses by their doors and have fear of Allah, so that hopefully you will be successful.**

**They will ask you about the crescent moons.**

The Jews asked the Prophet ﷺ about this when Mu'ādh was with him and Mu'ādh said, 'Messenger of Allah, the Jews overwhelm us and ask us a lot of questions about the crescent moons. Why does the moon first appear fine and then increase in size until it is round and then get smaller again until it looks like it did at the beginning?' Then Allah revealed this *āyah*. It is also said that the reason for the revelation of this *āyah* was that the Muslims asked the Prophet ﷺ about the new moon and the reason for its waning and fullness and its difference from the sun. Ibn 'Abbās, Qatādah, ar-Rabī' and others said that.

'Crescent moons' (*ahilla*) is the plural of *hilāl*, while it is one in reality since it occurs once in every month, although it also appears at the end. It is a reference to the passing months and the term is used to designate months because the month begins with a crescent moon. The month (*shahr*) takes its name from the fact that people make it known (*tashharu*) by pointing at the new moon with their hands when they see it. The term is used for the two days at the end of the month and the two at the beginning. It is also said to apply to the three at the beginning. Al-Aṣmā'ī says it is called a crescent (*hilāl*) when it is curved like a thin thread. It is also said that it is called *hilāl* until its light is clear in the sky, which is the seventh night. Abu-l-'Abbās said that it is called *hilāl* because the word means to raise the voice and people raise their voices when reporting its sighting. One form of the verb is used for the cry of a newborn baby. Another use is for a face shining with joy.

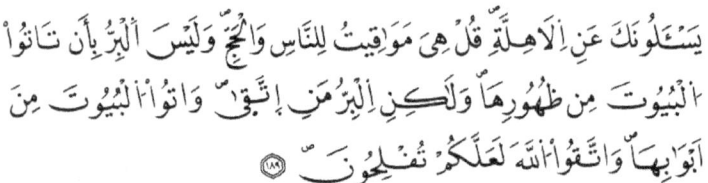

If someone swears that he will settle a debt, or do something else, at the crescent moon or at the beginning of the crescent and does that a day or two after the crescent moon, he has not broken his oath. All the months are valid times for all sorts of acts of worship and transactions.

**Say, 'They are set times for mankind and for the hajj.'**

This explains the legal ruling applied to the waxing and waning of the moon. It removes doubt about the length of set terms and transactions, oaths, *ḥajj*, *'iddah*, fasting and breaking the fast, and the extent of pregnancy, wages and hire and other things. This is referred to in the *ayah*: *'We made the night and day two Signs. We blotted out the Sign of the night and made the Sign of the day a time for seeing so that you can seek favour from your Lord and will know the number of years and the reckoning of time.'* (17:12) Allah also says: *'It is He Who appointed the sun to give radiance and the moon to give light, assigning its phases so you would know the number of years and the reckoning of time.'* (10:5) Counting the new moons is easier than counting days.

What we have affirmed refutes the literalists who say that sharecropping (*musāqāh*) is permitted for an unknown number of years. They argued that the Messenger of Allah ﷺ employed the Jews in return for half the crops and dates without setting a time. This does not constitute evidence because the Prophet ﷺ told the Jews, 'I affirm you in what Allah has affirmed you.' This is the clearest evidence that that was something specifically for him. He was awaiting a judgment concerning that from his Lord. That is not the case with other people. The Sharī'ah deals with ideas of hire and all transactions. Nothing is permitted except what the Book and Sunnah sets out. The imams of the community state that.

'Set times' (*mawāqīt*) is the plural of *mīqāt*. It is also said that *mīqāt* refers to the end of a period, and that *mawāqīt* is not declinable and has no singular form. Hajj is only mentioned because it is something whose time needs to be known and it is not permitted to delay it beyond its time, which differs from what the pre-Islamic Arabs thought because they used to alter the months. Allah nullified what they said and did as will be discussed in *at-Tawbah*, Allah willing.

Mālik and Abū Ḥanīfah used this *āyah* as evidence that *iḥrām* can be validly adopted outside the months of *ḥajj* because Allah Almighty here makes all the crescent moons apply to it. This is contrary to the position taken by ash-Shāfi'ī in view of the words of Allah: *'The ḥajj takes place during certain well-known months'* (2:197), as we will discover when we come to that *āyah*. The meaning of this *āyah*, then, is that some crescent moons are times for people (in general) and some are times for *ḥajj* (specifically).

There is no disagreement between scholars that if someone sells known goods at a known term in the months or days of the customary Arab dating system, that is permitted. That is the same with a sale on credit with a known period of time. They disagree about someone who sells something which is to be paid for at harvest time or the arrivals of stipends or the like. Mālik said, 'That is permitted because it is known.' Abū Thawr said that. Aḥmad said, 'I hope that there is nothing wrong with it.' The same is true when setting a time such as the arrival of an expedition. Ibn 'Umar said that one can sell with payment due at the time of the payment of the stipend. One group said that it is not permitted because Allah Almighty set times and made them the markers for time periods in sales. Ibn 'Abbās said that. Ash-Shāfi'ī and an-Nu'mān stated that. Ibn al-Mundhir said that the view of Ibn 'Abbās is sound.

When the crescent moon is seen to be large, our scholars say that one does not rely on whether it is large or small. It is the product of its night. Muslim related that Abu-l-Bakhtarī said, 'We went out on *'umrah*. When we camped at Baṭn Nakhlah, we saw the new moon. Some of the people said that it was three nights old and some said two nights. We met Ibn 'Abbās and said, "We saw the new moon and some of the people said that it was three nights old and some said two nights." He asked, "Which night did you see it?" We told him and he said, "The Messenger of Allah ﷺ said, 'Allah has extended this for seeing.' It was the night you saw it."'

**It is not devoutness for you to enter houses by the back.**

This is mentioned together with talking about the time of the *ḥajj* because the questions about the crescent moons and entering houses from their backs were asked together and the *āyah* was revealed in answer to both of them.

If the Anṣār set out on *ḥajj* and then returned for something they would not enter the doors of their houses. After they had adopted *iḥrām* for *ḥajj* or *'umrah*, they were not allowed to have anything come between them and the sky, so if one of them returned to get something, he would not go inside his house because the ceiling would come between him and the sky. Instead, he would climb up the outside walls onto the roof and then stand by his room and ask for whatever he needed which would be brought out to him. They used to think that this was piety and devoutness and Allah refuted that, making it clear that piety consists obeying Him.

As transmitted by Abū Ṣāliḥ, Ibn 'Abbās said, 'During the time of the Jāhiliyyah, and also at the beginning of Islam, when someone adopted *iḥrām* for the *ḥajj* and was one of the people who live in houses, he would make a hole in the back of his house and enter and leave through it or put a ladder up and climb up and descend by it. If he lived in a tent, he would enter by the back of the tent unless he was one of the *ḥums*.' Az-Zuhrī related that the Prophet adopted *iḥrām* for *'umrah* in the time of Ḥudaybīyah and entered his room and one of the Anṣār entered after him and made a hole in the wall as was his custom. They asked him, 'Why did you go inside when you are in *iḥrām*?' The man replied, 'You entered and so I entered.' The Prophet ﷺ said, 'I am one of the *ḥums*,' meaning those who do not follow that as a *dīn*. The man said to him, 'I have the same *dīn* as you do,' and the *āyah* was revealed. Ibn 'Abbas, 'Aṭā' and Qatādah said that. It is said that the man was Quṭbah ibn 'Āmir al-Anṣārī. *Ḥums* means the tribes of Quraysh, Kinānah, Khuzā'ah, Thaqif, Jushm, Banū 'Āmir ibn Ṣa'ṣa'ah and the Banū Naṣr ibn Mu'āwiyah. It derives from their zealousness (*ḥamāsah*) in their *dīn*.

There is some disagreement about the interpretation of this phrase. What we have already mentioned is said about it and it is sound. It is said that it is about delaying the *ḥajj*; they would make a month sacred that was not normally sacred by delaying the *ḥajj* so that it took place in it and thereby they also made a sacred month no longer sacred by removing the *ḥajj* from it. According to this, mentioning houses is based on the disagreement about the obligation in respect of the *ḥajj* and its months. Some of this will be mentioned in *at-Tawbah*, Allah willing. Abū 'Ubaydah said that the *āyah* is a metaphor and means: 'It is not devoutness to ask the ignorant, but it is to have fear of Allah and to ask those with knowledge.' This is similar to the words, 'I approached the matter by its door.'

It is related by al-Mahdawī, Makkī from Ibn al-Anbārī and al-Māwardī from Ibn Zayd that the *āyah* is a metaphor for having sex with wives, and men are being instructed to have sex from the front and not the back. Women are called 'houses' because one comes to them as one comes to houses. Ibn 'Aṭiyyah said, 'This is unlikely and alters the form of the words.' Al-Ḥasan said, 'They used to look for omens. If someone went on a journey and did not achieve what he needed, he would come to his house from the back of it because of the ill omen of disappointment. They were told, 'There is no devoutness in omens. Devoutness is to be godfearing and trust in Allah.'

The first view is the soundest one because of what al-Barā' related: 'When the Anṣār went on *ḥajj* and returned, they would not enter the houses by their doors.' He said that one of the Anṣār came and entered his house by the door and was asked about that and so the *āyah* was revealed. This is a text about actual houses. Al-Bukhārī and Muslim transmitted it. The other views are derived from something else in the *āyah*. It is also said that in the *āyah* Allah calls attention to what devoutness is, and it is doing what Allah has commanded. When Allah says to *'come to houses by their doors'*, He is telling people to do things in the manner which Allah has recommended. So the views are sound. 'Houses' is the plural of *bayt*, and it is read as both *buyūt* and *biyūt*.

This *āyah* also makes clear that anything Allah has not prescribed or recommended as an act of devotion is not, in fact, an act of devotion. Ibn Khuwayzimandād said, 'If it is hard to differentiate between what is devoutness and devotion and what is not, examine the action involved. If it is similar in nature to other legal obligations and sunnahs, then it can be that. If that is not the case, then it is not devoutness or devotion.' He added, 'That is found in reports from the Prophet ﷺ.' And he mentioned the *ḥadīth* of Ibn 'Abbās who said, 'Once, when the Messenger of Allah ﷺ was speaking, he saw a man standing in the sun and asked about him. They said, 'He is Abū Isrā'īl. He made a vow to stand and not sit, not to seek shade or speak, and to fast.' The Prophet ﷺ said, 'Tell him to speak, seek shade and sit. He should complete his fast.' So the Prophet ﷺ nullified what was not devotion and had no basis in the Sharī'ah. This confirms that devotion is an action which is somehow similar to other legal obligations and sunnahs.

وَقَٰتِلُوا۟ فِى سَبِيلِ ٱللَّهِ ٱلَّذِينَ يُقَٰتِلُونَكُمْ وَلَا تَعْتَدُوٓا۟ ۚ
إِنَّ ٱللَّهَ لَا يُحِبُّ ٱلْمُعْتَدِينَ ﴿١٩٠﴾

**190 Fight in the Way of Allah against those who fight you, but do not go beyond the limits. Allah does not love those who go beyond the limits.**

#### Fight in the Way of Allah against those who fight you

This was the first *āyah* to be revealed with the command to fight. There is no disagreement that fighting was forbidden before the Hijrah by the words of Allah: *'Repel the bad with something better'* (41:34), *'Pardon them and overlook'* (5:13), *'Cut yourself off from them – but courteously'* (73:10), *'You are not in control of them'* (88:22) and other similar *āyahs* which were revealed in Makkah. When the Prophet ﷺ emigrated to Madīnah, he was commanded to fight and this *āyah* was revealed. Ar-Rabī' ibn Anas and others said this. Abū Bakr aṣ-Ṣiddīq, however, said that the first *āyah* revealed about fighting was the *āyah* in *Sūrat al-Ḥajj*: *'Permission is given to those who are fought against because they have been wronged.'* (22:39). The one in this *sūrah* is more frequently cited as being the first.

The *āyah* for the permission to fight was revealed about fighting in general and the instruction is to fight not only those idolators who fight the Muslims but also those who do not fight. The command refers to the time when the Prophet ﷺ went out with his Companions to Makkah to perform *'umrah.* When he camped at Ḥudaybīyah near Makkah, the idolators prevented him from continuing on into Makkah and he remained there for a month. Ḥudaybīyah is the name of a well and that site is named after the well. They made a treaty stipulating that he could return the following year for three days and that there would be no fighting between them for ten years. After concluding this treaty, he returned to Madīnah. The following year he made preparations for ḥajj and the Muslims feared the treachery of the unbelievers and did not like the idea of fighting in the sacred months and in the Ḥaram.

Then this *āyah* was revealed, meaning that it is lawful for you to fight if the unbelievers fight you. So the *āyah* is connected to the prior mention of ḥajj and entering houses by the back. After this the Prophet ﷺ fought those who fought him and refrained from fighting those who refrained from fighting him until the *āyah* in *Sūrat at-Tawbah* (9:5) was revealed, *'Fight the idolaters,'* and this *āyah* was abrogated. This is the position of the majority of scholars.

Ibn Zayd and ar-Rabī', however, say that this *āyah* was abrogated by Allah's words: *'Fight the idolaters totally'* (9:36) in which he was commanded to fight all the unbelievers. Ibn 'Abbās, 'Umar ibn 'Abd al-'Azīz, and Mujāhid said that it is an *āyah* whose judgment remains operative and means: 'Fight those who fight you and do not transgress by killing women, children, monks and the like' as will be explained. Abū Ja'far an-Naḥḥās said that this is the sounder position in terms of both the Sunnah and in terms of logic. As for the Sunnah, there is a *ḥadīth* reported by Ibn 'Umar that, during one of his expeditions, the Messenger of Allah ﷺ saw a woman who had been killed and he abhorred that and forbade the killing of women and children. As for logic, it applies to children and those like them, such as monks, the chronically ill, old men and hirelings, who clearly should not be killed. When Abū Bakr sent Yazīd ibn Abī Sufyān to Syria, he commanded that he should not do harm to certain groups. Mālik and others transmitted this. Scholars put those who should not be killed into six categories.

– Women. But if they fight, they should be fought. Saḥnūn said, 'In battle and out of it because of the general nature of Allah's words: *"Fight against those who fight you."*' A woman can have an immense effect on the fighting, including supplying assistance and encouraging fighting. Women go out with their hair undone, shouting encouragement and censuring flight. So it is permitted to kill them. If they are captured, however, then enslavement is more beneficial since they are more easily converted and it is difficult for them to run away which is not the case with men.'

– Children. Children should not be killed and that is a firm prohibition. If a child fights, however, then he can be killed.

– Monks. Monks should be neither killed nor enslaved. They are left to live on the property which they own. This is when they live apart from the people of disbelief because of the command which Abū Bakr gave to Yazīd ibn Abī Sufyān, 'You will find some people who claim that they have confined the themselves for the sake of Allah. Leave them with what they claim.' If, however, they are with the unbelievers in churches, they can be killed. As for nuns, Ashhab thinks that they should not be killed. Saḥnūn said, 'Being a nun does not alter the basic ruling about her as a woman.' Qāḍī Abū Bakr ibn al-'Arabī said, 'I think that the sound view is that of Ashhab and nuns are included in the directive of Abū Bakr.'

– The chronically ill. Saḥnūn says that they should be killed. Ibn Ḥabīb says that they should not be killed. The sound position is that we consider their states. If there is potential harm in them, they should be killed. Otherwise, they should be left alone.

– Old men. Mālik says that they should not be killed and that is the position of the majority of *fuqahā'*. If an old man is senile and unable to fight and not consulted for his opinion or taking part in defence, he should not be killed. Mālik and Abū Ḥanīfah say that. Ash-Shāfi'ī has two positions: one is that of the majority and the second is that old men and monks should be killed. The sound position is the first one because of what Abū Bakr said to Yazīd. No one opposes it and there is a consensus to back it up. Also it is not permitted to kill anyone who does not fight or help the enemy, like women. As for those harm is feared in respect of planning, advice or monetary support, if they are captured, the ruler can choose between five options: killing, an act of good will, ransom, enslavement or agreeing to become a *dhimmī* in return for the payment of *jizyah*.

– Hirelings and agricultural workers. Mālik says that they should not be killed. Ash-Shāfi'ī says that agricultural workers, hirelings, and old men should be killed unless they agree to pay the *jizyah*. The first view is sounder because of what the Prophet ﷺ said in the *ḥadīth* reported by Rabāḥ ibn ar-Rabī', 'Join Khālid ibn al-Walīd. He is not to kill children or hirelings.' 'Umar ibn al-Khaṭṭāb said, 'Fear Allah regarding children and agricultural workers who do not fight you.' 'Umar ibn 'Abd al-'Azīz did not kill agricultural workers. Ibn al-Mundhir mentioned that.

Ashhab mentioned that the *āyah* refers to those who were at Ḥudaybīyah who were commanded to fight those who fought them. What is sound is that it is addressed to all Muslims: it commands each of them to fight those who fight them. Do you not see how Allah made the matter clear in *Sūrat at-Tawbah* when He says: *'Fight those of the unbelievers who are near to you.'* (9:123) What was meant first are the people of Makkah and it was specified to begin with them. When Allah conquered Makkah, then it was directed to those nearby who were causing harm until eventually the call became universal and the word reached all areas, no unbeliever remaining. That continues until the Day of Rising, supported by the words of the Prophet ﷺ, 'There is good in the forelocks of horses until the Day of Rising: reward and spoils.' It is said that its end will be the descent of Jesus son of Mary which is in agreement with the previous *ḥadīth* because his descent is one of the signs of the Final Hour.

**But do not go beyond the limits.**

This is a firm judgment. As for the apostates, the only options available concerning them are execution or repentance. The same applies to people involved in deviation and misguidance: the only options afforded them are execution or repentance. If someone conceals a false belief and then it appears in him, as happens with a *zindīq*, he should be killed and is not asked to repent. As for those who rebel against just rulers, they must be fought until they return to the truth.

Some people have said that this phrase means: 'Do not go beyond the limits by fighting for other than the Face of Allah, out of fanaticism, for instance, or to gain fame.' In other words, 'Fight in the Way of Allah against those who fight you. Fight in support of the *dīn* so that Allah's Word is uppermost.' It is said that it means: do not fight those who do not fight. In that case it would be abrogated by the command to fight all the unbelievers, and Allah knows best.

وَاقْتُلُوهُمْ حَيْثُ ثَقِفْتُمُوهُمْ وَأَخْرِجُوهُم مِّنْ حَيْثُ أَخْرَجُوكُمْ وَالْفِتْنَةُ أَشَدُّ مِنَ الْقَتْلِ
وَلَا تُقَاتِلُوهُمْ عِندَ الْمَسْجِدِ الْحَرَامِ حَتَّىٰ يُقَاتِلُوكُمْ فِيهِ فَإِن قَاتَلُوكُمْ فَاقْتُلُوهُمْ كَذَٰلِكَ
جَزَاءُ الْكَافِرِينَ ﴿١٩١﴾ فَإِنِ انتَهَوْا فَإِنَّ اللَّهَ غَفُورٌ رَّحِيمٌ ﴿١٩٢﴾

**191 Kill them wherever you come across them and expel them from where they expelled you. Fitnah is worse than killing. Do not fight them in the Masjid al-Ḥarām until they fight you there. But if they do fight you, then kill them. That is how the unbelievers should be repaid. 192 But if they cease, Allah is Ever-Forgiving, Most Merciful.**

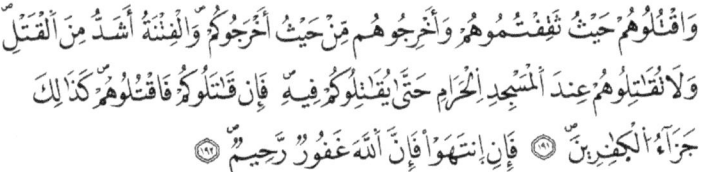

**Kill them wherever you come across them**

This is evidence for killing captives, and that topic will be explained in *Sūrat al-Anfāl*, Allah willing.

**and expel them from where they expelled you**

According to aṭ-Ṭabarī this is addressed to the Muhājirūn and 'they' refers to the unbelievers of Quraysh.

**Fitnah is worse than killing.**

The *fitnah* to which they are subjecting you – trying to make you return to disbelief – is worse than killing. Mujāhid said it refers to the believers, so the meaning is that being killed is better for a believer than being subjected to *fitnah*. Others said that *fitnah* here means their association of others with Allah and their disbelief in Him and it is a great crime and worse than the killing which they criticise you for. There is evidence that the *āyah* was revealed about 'Amr ibn al-Ḥaḍramī when he was killed by Wāqid ibn 'Abdullāh at-Tamīmī at the end of the sacred month of Rajab, an incident which will be explained later. Aṭ-Ṭabarī and others said that.

**Do not fight them in the Masjid al-Ḥarām until they fight you there.**

Scholars take two positions concerning this *āyah*. One is that it is abrogated. The second is that it is an *āyah* containing a firm judgment. Mujāhid says that it is an *āyah* of judgment and that it is not permitted to fight anyone in the Masjid al-Ḥarām unless they fight you there. Ṭāwūs said that as well, and indeed it is what is intimated by the text of the *āyah*. It is a sound position and Abū Ḥanīfah and his people adopted it. In the *Ṣaḥīḥ* Collection, Ibn 'Abbās reported that the Messenger of Allah ﷺ said on the day when Makkah was conquered, 'This land was made sacred on the day Allah created the heavens and the earth and it will remain sacred as Allah has decreed until the Day of Rising. Fighting was not lawful in it for anyone before me and it was only lawful for me for one hour of one day and it will remain sacred until the Day of Rising.'

Qatādah said that the *āyah* is abrogated by Allah's words: *'When the sacred months are over, kill the idolaters wherever you find them.'* (9:5). Muqātil said the same. So this means that it is possible to initiate killing in the Ḥaram and evidence for that position can be found in the fact that *Sūrat at-Tawbah*, where this *āyah* occurs, was revealed about two years after *Sūrat al-Baqarah* and after the Prophet ﷺ entered Makkah and had Ibn Khaṭal, who was clinging to the drapes of the Ka'bah, killed there.

Ibn Khuwayzimandād said that the phrase *'Do not fight them in the Masjid al-*

*Ḥarām'* is abrogated because the consensus is that people should be fought if they attack, even if they occupy Makkah. If they stop people from performing ḥajj, then it is a legal obligation to fight them, even if they do not start the fighting. Makkah is the same as everywhere else in that respect.

It is said that it is a Ḥarām which should be esteemed. Do you not see that the Messenger of Allah ﷺ sent out Khālid ibn al-Walīd in the year of the Conquest, telling him, 'Reap them with your sword until you meet me on Ṣafā.' Al-'Abbās came and said, 'Quraysh are finished! There will be no Quraysh after today!' Do you not see what Allah said about the respect owed to it, that anything found there should not be picked up without it being announced, and yet that is the same with it and other places? It is possible that it is abrogated by His words: *'Fight them until there is no more fitnah.'* (2:193)

Ibn al-'Arabī said, 'I was in Jerusalem on a Friday at the madrasah of Abū 'Uqbah al-Ḥanafī while Qāḍī az-Zanjānī was giving a lesson to us. While we were there, a man with a radiant countenance with rags on his back entered. He gave the greeting of scholars and went to the front of the gathering wearing a shepherd's shirt. Qāḍī az-Zanjānī asked, "Who is the master?" He answered, "A man whom scoundrels looted yesterday while I was making for this sacred Ḥaram. I am a man from the people of Ṣaghān, a seeker of knowledge." The Qāḍī immediately said, "Question him!" It was their custom to honour men of knowledge by immediately questioning them. The lot [for the question posed] that came up was the case of an unbeliever who seeks sanctuary in the Ḥaram: may he be killed or not? The man gave a *fatwā* that he should not be killed. He was asked for his proof and said that it was the words of Allah: *"Do not fight them in the Masjid al-Ḥarām until they fight you there."* It can also be recited as "Do not kill them." If it is recited as that, then it is a clear text forbidding that. If it is recited as "Do not fight them," then it is an admonition because, if Allah forbids fighting which is a cause of killing, it is clear evidence of the prohibition of killing itself. The Qāḍī countered him by supporting ash-Shāfi'ī and Mālik even though he normally did not espouse their school. So he stated, "This *āyah* is abrogated by His words: '*kill the idolaters wherever you find them*' (9:5)." The man from Ṣaghān replied, "This is not fitting for the position and knowledge of the Qāḍī. This *āyah* which you used to counter is general to all places and that which I used for argument is specific. It is not permitted for anyone to say that the generally undefined abrogates the specific." Qāḍī az-Zanjānī was stumped. Ibn al-'Arabī said, 'If an unbeliever seeks sanctuary in the Ḥaram, there is no way to kill him because of the text of the *āyah* and the firm Sunnah that forbids fighting in it. However, the *ḥadd* punishment must be carried out on the fornicator and killer. If, however, the unbeliever initiates fighting, then he is killed according to the text of the Qur'an.'

As for the argument they use about the killing of Ibn Khaṭal and his fellows, that is not a proper argument. That occurred at a time in which Makkah was not a Ḥaram because it was an abode of war and unbelief and so the blood of people could be shed during the time it was not a Ḥaram and in which fighting was permitted. It is confirmed and correct that the first view is sounder, and Allah knows best.

Some scholars say that this *āyah* applies in the case of someone who rebels against the ruler but does not apply to unbelievers. Unbelievers are killed in every case when they fight. Rebels are only fought with defence in mind and should not be pursued if they retreat, or finished off if they are wounded. This will be discussed in *Sūrat al-Ḥujurāt.*

**But if they cease,**

If they stop fighting you because they believe and become Muslims, then Allah will forgive them all that they did before and show mercy to all of them by pardoning them as Allah says elsewhere: *'Say to those who disbelieve that if they stop they will be forgiven what is past.'* (8:38)

وَقَٰتِلُوهُمْ حَتَّىٰ لَا تَكُونَ فِتْنَةٌ وَيَكُونَ ٱلدِّينُ لِلَّهِ ۖ فَإِنِ ٱنتَهَوْا۟ فَلَا عُدْوَٰنَ إِلَّا عَلَى ٱلظَّٰلِمِينَ ﴿١٩٣﴾

**193 Fight them until there is no more fitnah and the dīn belongs to Allah alone. If they cease, there should be no enmity towards any but wrongdoers.**

**Fight them until there is no more fitnah and the dīn belongs to Allah alone.**

This is a command to fight every idolater in every place according to those who say that it abrogates the previous *āyahs*. According to those who say that it does not abrogate other *āyahs*, it means: 'Fight those about whom Allah says: "*if they fight you*".' The former is the more likely meaning. It is an unqualified command to fight without any precondition of hostilities being initiated by the unbelievers. The evidence for that is in the words of Allah: *'and the* dīn *belongs to Allah alone.'* The Prophet ﷺ said, 'I was commanded to fight people until they say, "There is no god but Allah."' The *āyah* and *ḥadīth* both indicate that the reason for fighting is disbelief because Allah says: *'until there is no more fitnah,'* meaning disbelief in this case. So the goal is to abolish disbelief and that is clear.

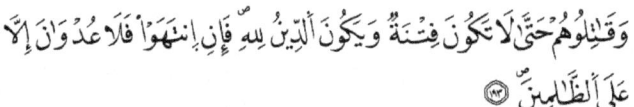

Ibn 'Abbās, Qatādah, ar-Rabī', as-Suddī and others said that *fitnah* here means *shirk* and the subsequent injury to the believers caused by it. The root of *fitnah* is testing and trial, derived from the term for testing silver when it is put in the fire to separate the impurities from the pure metal.

**If they cease, there should be no enmity towards any but wrongdoers.**

If they stop and become Muslim, or submit by paying *jizyah* in the case of the people of the Book. Otherwise they should be fought and they are wrongdoers and only transgress against themselves. What is done to the wrongdoers is called enmity since it is the requital of enmity. Wrongdoing and injustice involve enmity and the requital of enmity is also called enmity. It is as Allah says: *'The repayment of a bad action is one equivalent to it.'* (42:40) The wrongdoers are either those who initiate fighting or those who remain entrenched in disbelief and *fitnah*.

ٱلشَّهۡرُ ٱلۡحَرَامُ بِٱلشَّهۡرِ ٱلۡحَرَامِ وَٱلۡحُرُمَٰتُ قِصَاصٞۚ فَمَنِ ٱعۡتَدَىٰ عَلَيۡكُمۡ فَٱعۡتَدُواْ عَلَيۡهِ
بِمِثۡلِ مَا ٱعۡتَدَىٰ عَلَيۡكُمۡۚ وَٱتَّقُواْ ٱللَّهَ وَٱعۡلَمُوٓاْ أَنَّ ٱللَّهَ مَعَ ٱلۡمُتَّقِينَ ١٩٤

**194 Sacred month in return for sacred month – sacred things are subject to retaliation. So if anyone oversteps the limits against you, overstep against him the same as he did to you. But have fear of Allah. Know that Allah is with those who are godfearing.**

**Sacred month in return for sacred month –**

The reason for this being revealed was reported by Ibn 'Abbās, Qatādah, Mujāhid, Miqsam, as-Suddī, ar-Rabī', aḍ-Ḍaḥḥāk and others. They said that it was revealed during the 'Fulfilled 'Umrah'. When the idolaters prevented the Prophet ﷺ from completing the 'Umra in the Year of al-Ḥudaybīyah, Allah promised him that he would enter Makkah, and he did so in 7 AH and completed the practices of 'umra and the *āyah* was revealed. Al-Hasan related that the idolaters said to the Prophet ﷺ, "Have you ceased fighting in the sacred month, Muḥammad?" "Yes" he replied. They wanted to fight and the *āyah* was revealed by which Allah allowed him to fight against them. The first interpretation, however, is better known.

**Sacred things are subject to retaliation.**

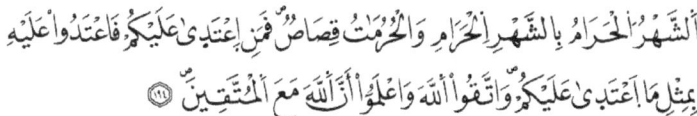

*Ḥurumāt* is the plural of *ḥurmah*. Allah means the sacredness of the sacred month, the sacred land and the sacredness of *iḥrām*. *Ḥurmah* denotes something which is inviolable. Retaliation (*qiṣāṣ*) is to make things equal, so in this instance the compensation for you for when they stopped you in 6 AH is to make up the *'umrah* in 7 AH. So this is connected to what precedes it. It is said that it is separate and that it refers to the state of affairs at the beginning in Islam which was, that if something sacred was violated, they were entitled to the like of the transgression committed against them. Then this was abrogated by the *āyahs* of fighting.

One group say that the *āyah* deals with enmity within the community of Muhammad ﷺ and other crimes and so it is not abrogated. When someone is the victim of transgression in respect of his property or through physical injury, he can retaliate with the like of what was done to him. This is between creatures. There is nothing between the human being and Allah in that respect. Ash-Shāfi'ī and others say that, and there is one transmission to that effect from Mālik. A group of Mālikīs say that matters of retaliation are up to the judges and not the individual. Property is dealt with according to the words of the Prophet ﷺ: 'Surrender trusts to those who entrusted them to you and do not betray those who betrayed you.' Ad-Dāraquṭnī transmitted it. If someone deposits a trust with someone who betrays him, he is not permitted to betray him in return and attain his due from the one he trusted. This is the well known position of their school. Abū Ḥanīfah held that view as well because of this *ḥadīth* as well as the words of the Almighty: *'Allah commands you to return to their owners the things you hold on trust.'* (4:58) That is the position of 'Aṭā' al-Khurāsānī. Qudāmah ibn al-Haytham said, 'I asked 'Aṭā' ibn Maysarah al-Khurāsānī, "A man owes me something. He denies it and denies my proof. Can I retaliate by taking from his property?" He answered, "Do you think that if he had sex with your slave-girl, you would do what he did?"'

What is sound is that it is permitted for him to do that provided that he can obtain his property without being considered to be a thief. That is the school of ash-Shāfi'ī. Ad-Dāwudī related this from Mālik and Ibn al-Mundhir said that as well. Ibn al-'Arabī preferred that and said that it is not treachery, but rather obtaining one's right. The Messenger of Allah ﷺ said, 'Help your brother, wronging or wronged.' Taking what is owed from the wrongdoer is part of helping him. When Hind bint 'Uqbah, the wife of Abū Sufyān, said to the Prophet ﷺ, 'Abū Sufyān is a stingy, mean man. He does not give me and my son enough maintenance unless I take it from his property without his knowledge. Do I do anything wrong?' He ﷺ answered, 'Take what is enough for you and your son in a correct manner.' So he allowed her to take, but only the amount strictly due to her. All of this is confirmed in the *Ṣaḥīḥ*. The words in this *āyah* cut off the dispute.

They disagree about someone taking property which is not of the same sort as the property he is owed. It is said that he can only do that based on the ruling of a judge. Ash-Shāfiʿī has two views. The sounder of the two is that he may take it based on analogy with taking it from the same sort of property. The second view is that he should not take it because it is a different sort of property. Some say that he calculates the value of what he is owed and takes an equivalent amount. This is sound based on what we explained of the proof.

In dealing with taking, does one take into account what someone owes of debts and other things? Ash-Shāfiʿī says that you do not, but simply take what you are owed. Mālik said that a person takes into consideration his position in relation to other debtors when someone is bankrupt. Allah knows best.

**So if anyone oversteps the limits against you, overstep against him the same as he did to you.**

It is agreed that this *āyah* is general and undefined and retaliation can either be done directly, if that is possible, or by obtaining a legal judgment. People disagree about whether ordinary compensation is included under this and whether it can be called 'overstepping' or not. Some say that there are no metaphors in the Qur'an and that this is overstepping, but permitted overstepping (*'udwān*), as that is a normal linguistic usage in Arabic. Others say that there are metaphors in the Qur'an and 'overstepping' here is used in that way. Scholars disagree about someone who destroys or ruins animals or goods which cannot be weighed or measured. Ash-Shāfiʿī, Abū Ḥanīfah and his people and a group of scholars say that he owes the equivalent of that and one pays no attention to price unless there is nothing equivalent available, based on this *āyah* as well as: *'If you want to retaliate, retaliate to the same degree as the injury done to you.'* (16:123)

It is said that this principle should be applied to all things, even broken bowls, since the Prophet ﷺ said, 'A vessel for a vessel and food for food' regarding an incident when one of his wives broke a bowl of food belonging to another wife. Abū Dāwud transmitted from Musaddad from Yaḥyā, and from Muḥammad ibn al-Muthannā from Khālid from Ḥumayd from Anas that the Messenger of Allah ﷺ was with one of his wives when another of the Mothers of the Believers sent a servant with a bowl of food. She struck it with her hand and broke the bowl. The Messenger of Allah ﷺ picked up the two pieces and put them together and began to collect the food in them, saying, 'Your mother is jealous.' He said, 'Eat,' and they ate until a bowl in her house was brought. He kept the messenger and the bowl until they had finished and then gave the unbroken bowl to the messenger and kept the broken one. Abū Dāwud related from Musaddad from Yaḥyā from

Fulayt al-'Āmirī (whom Abū Dāwud says is Aflat ibn Khalīfah) from Jasrah bint Dajājah that 'Ā'ishah said, 'I never saw a woman make food like Ṣafiyyah. She prepared food for the Messenger of Allah ﷺ and sent it to him. I could not keep myself from breaking the vessel. I asked, "Messenger of Allah, what is the expiation for what I did?" He answered, "A vessel like the vessel, and food like the food."' The evidence is that the Prophet ﷺ made a man who freed half of his slave also pay for the half owned by his partner and not just the cost of half of the slave. There is no disagreement between scholars that there is parity in food, drinks and things that are weighed since he ﷺ said, 'Food for food.'

There is no disagreement between scholars that this *āyah* is the basis for parity in retaliation. If someone kills someone, he is killed by the same method he used when he killed, and that is the position of the majority, as long as the victim was not killed by an iniquitous act such as sodomy or drinking wine. In that case, the killer is killed with the sword. One view of the Shāfi'īs is that he is killed in the same way in any case. Ibn al-Mājishūn said that if someone kills by fire or poison, he is not killed by the same method because the Prophet ﷺ said, 'Only Allah punishes with fire.' Poison is internal fire.

As for retaliation with a staff, Mālik said in one transmission that killing with a staff is prolonged and amounts to torture and so he should be killed by the sword. Ibn Wahb related that from him and Ibn al-Qāsim also said that. Another transmission says that he is killed with it, even if it entails that. That is the view of ash-Shāfi'ī. Ashhab and Ibn Nāfi' related that Mālik said that someone who kills with stones or a staff is killed with them provided that the blow will be a fatal one, but not if it requires multiple blows. He should not be shot with arrows or stoned because that entails torture. 'Abd al-Malik said that. Ibn al-'Arabī said, 'What is sound among the views of our scholars is that similarity is mandatory unless that falls under the definition of torture. Then it is abandoned in favour of the sword.' Our scholars agree that when someone cuts off a hand or foot or gouges out an eye, intending torture by that, then that is done to him, as the Prophet ﷺ did to those who killed the herdsmen. But if that occurred through defence or by a striking blow, then he is killed by the sword.

One group take a different view regarding all of this and say that retaliation is only taken by the sword. That is the school of Abū Ḥanīfah, ash-Sha'bī and an-Nakha'ī. Their proof for that is what is related from the Prophet ﷺ: 'There is no retaliation except with iron (i.e. a blade).' There is also the prohibition against mutilation and the words of the Prophet ﷺ, 'Only the Lord of the Fire punishes with fire.'

What is sound is the view of the majority based on what the imams related from

Anas ibn Mālik about a girl who was discovered with her head crushed between two stones. They asked her, 'Who did this to you? So-and-so? So-and-so?' until they mentioned a Jew and she nodded with her head. The Jew was seized and he confessed, so the Messenger of Allah ﷺ ordered that his head be crushed with stones. One version states that the Messenger of Allah ﷺ killed him with two stones. This is a clear explicit text. It is what is demanded by Allah's words: *'If you want to retaliate, retaliate to the same degree as the injury done to you.'* (16:123) As for the evidence used from the *ḥadīth* of Jābir, *ḥadīth* scholars consider it to be weak. It is not related by a sound path. If it had been sound, we would say that it is mandatory. When someone kills with a metal weapon, he is killed with it. This is indicated by the *ḥadīth* of Anas: 'A Jew crushed a girl's head between two stones and so the Messenger of Allah ﷺ had his head crushed between two stones.'

We say that the prohibition against mutilation is applied when the perpetrator does not mutilate. If he mutilates, then we do that to him as is indicated by the *ḥadīth* of the 'Uranīs. It is sound and transmitted by the imams. His words, 'Only the Lord of the Fire punishes with fire' apply when he himself has not burned. If he has burned, then he is burned as is indicated by the generality of the words of the Qur'an. Ash-Shāfi'ī said, 'When a person deliberately throws someone into a fire, then he too is thrown into a fire until he dies.' Al-Waqqār mentioned this in his *Mukhtaṣar* from Mālik. It is also the view of Muḥammad ibn 'Abd al-Ḥakam. Ibn al-Mundhir said, 'Many of the people of knowledge say that there is retaliation against a man who strangles another man. That is opposed by Muḥammad ibn al-Ḥasan. He said, "If he strangles him so that he dies, throws him into a well and he dies, or throws him from a mountain or a roof and he dies, there is no retaliation. His male relatives owe blood-money. If he is known for that and strangles more than one person, then he is killed."' Ibn al-Mundhir said, 'When the Prophet ﷺ took retaliation from the Jew who crushed the girl's head with stones, it was on this basis.'

Someone else related this view from Abū Ḥanīfah and said, 'Abū Ḥanīfah has an aberrant view and stated that if someone kills by strangulation, poison, throwing someone from a mountain or into a well, or with a piece of wood, he is not killed and retaliation is not taken from him unless he killed with a sharpened blade, stone or wood, or is known for strangling and throwing people [to their death]. His male relatives must pay blood-money.' This is contrary to the Book and the Sunnah. It is innovating something which is not the business of the community. It is a means to removing the retaliation which Allah has prescribed for people. This is inevitable.

They disagree about someone who imprisons a man and then another man does the killing. 'Aṭā' said that the killer is killed and the imprisoner imprisoned until he dies. Mālik said, 'If he imprisons him wanting to kill him, then they are both killed.' The view of ash-Shāfi'ī, Abū Thawr and an-Nu'mān said that the one who imprisoned is punished. Ibn al-Mundhir preferred that.

The view of 'Aṭā' is sound and demanded by the Revelation. Ad-Dāraquṭnī related from Ibn 'Umar that the Prophet ﷺ said, 'When one man holds a man while another kills him, then the killer and the one who held him are both killed.' Sufyān ath-Thawrī related it from Ismā'īl ibn Umayyah from Nāfi' from Ibn 'Umar, and Ibn Jurayj from Ismā'īl *mursal.*

'Overstepping' is going beyond the limits as Allah says: *'Those who overstep Allah's limits.'* (2:229) The upshot of the *āyah* is that, if anyone wrongs you, you may take your right according to the way you were wronged, and if someone insults you, you may respond with what he said but may not go beyond what he said. So if someone insults you, you may insult him, but not insult his parents, son or relatives. You are not permitted to lie about him even if he lies about you. Disobedience may not be countered by disobedience. For instance, if someone says to you, 'You unbeliever!' you are permitted to say, 'You are the unbeliever.' But if he says, 'Adulterer!' then your retaliation is to say, 'You liar, bearer of false witness!' If you were to say, 'Adulterer!' then you would be a liar and sin in the lie. About someone who puts you off when he is wealthy without excuse and says, 'Wrongdoer! Consumer of people's wealth!' the Prophet ﷺ said, 'The evasiveness of someone with sufficient means to pay makes his honour forfeit and his punishment lawful.' His honour is by what we explained and his punishment is imprisonment. Ibn 'Abbās said, 'This was revealed before Islam was strong and Muslims who were injured were commanded to repay with the like of the injury received, be patient or pardon. Then that was abrogated by Allah's words: *"Fight the idolators totally."* (9:36)' It is said that it was abrogated by taking it to the ruler and it is not lawful for anyone to take retaliation from anyone without the ruler's permission.

وَأَنفِقُوا۟ فِى سَبِيلِ ٱللَّهِ وَلَا تُلْقُوا۟ بِأَيْدِيكُمْ إِلَى ٱلتَّهْلُكَةِ ۛ وَأَحْسِنُوٓا۟ ۛ إِنَّ ٱللَّهَ يُحِبُّ ٱلْمُحْسِنِينَ ﴿١٩٥﴾

**195 Spend in the Way of Allah. Do not cast yourselves into destruction. And do good: Allah loves good-doers.**

**Spend in the Way of Allah. Do not cast yourselves into destruction.**

Al-Bukhārī related from Ḥudhayfah that this whole *āyah* was revealed about spending. Aslam Abī 'Imrān said, 'We raided Constantinople when 'Abd ar-

Raḥmān ibn al-Walīd was in charge of the group. The Byzantines were keeping their backs to the wall of the city. A man attacked the enemy and the people said, "Easy! Easy! Do not cast yourselves into destruction." Abū Ayyūb said, "Glory be to Allah! This *āyah* was revealed about us, the Anṣār. When Allah gave His Prophet ﷺ victory and made His *dīn* victorious, we said, 'We will stay in our property and put it right.' and then Allah revealed, '*Spend in the Way of Allah.*' The expression '*Do not cast yourselves into destruction*' referred to staying at home to tend to one's property and abandoning *jihād*." Abū Ayyūb continued to do *jihād* in the Way of Allah until he was buried in Constantinople. His tomb is there.' So Abū Ayyūb informed us that casting oneself into destruction is abandoning *jihād* in Allah's cause and that the *āyah* was revealed about that. The like of that is related from Ḥudhayfah, al-Ḥasan, Qatādah, Mujāhid and aḍ-Ḍaḥḥāk.

At-Tirmidhī related this report from Yazīd ibn Abī Ḥabīb from Abū 'Imrān Aslam. He said, 'We were in the city of the Greeks. They came out against us in a single rank. The same number or more of the Muslims went out against them. 'Uqbah ibn 'Āmir was in charge of the Egyptians and Faḍālah ibn 'Ubayd was in charge of the Syrians. A man from the Muslims attacked the Greek ranks until he penetrated them. The people shouted and said, "Glory be to Allah! He is casting himself into destruction!" Abū Ayyūb al-Anṣārī stood and said, "People! You interpret this *āyah* in this way when this *āyah* was revealed about us, the Anṣār! When Allah exalted Islam and its helpers were numerous, we said secretly to one another apart from the Messenger of Allah ﷺ, 'Our property is lost. Allah has exalted Islam and it has many helpers. We should stay in our property and put right what has been lost of it.' So Allah revealed to His Prophet ﷺ that which refuted what we said: '*Spend in the Way of Allah. Do not cast yourselves into destruction.*' The actual destruction was staying in one's property, tending to it, and abandoning expeditions." Abū Ayyūb continued to fight in the Way of Allah until he was buried in Greek territory.' Abū 'Īsā said that it is a sound *gharīb ḥasan ḥadīth*.

Ḥudhayfah ibn al-Yamān, Ibn 'Abbās, 'Ikrimah, 'Aṭā', Mujāhid and the majority of people say that '*do not cast yourselves into destruction*' refers to not spending in the Way of Allah and fearing poverty so that a man says, 'I do not have anything that I can spend.' Al-Bukhārī believed this since he did not mention anything else. Allah knows best. Ibn 'Abbās said, 'Spend in the Way of Allah, even if you do not have a share or portion. No one should say, 'I do not have anything.' The same is reported from as-Suddī: 'Spend, even a hobble. Do not cast yourself into destruction and say, "I have nothing."'

There is a third view stated by Ibn 'Abbās. It is that when the Messenger of Allah ﷺ commanded people to go out in *jihād*, some of the desert Arabs present in Madīnah went to him and said, 'What shall we use for provision? By Allah, we have no provisions and no one will feed us.' So Allah revealed, '*Spend in the Way of Allah,*' i.e. the wealthy should spend in the Way of Allah to obey Allah. '*Do not cast yourselves to destruction,*' i.e. do not refrain from giving *ṣadaqah* so that you are destroyed. That is also what Muqātil said. The meaning of what Ibn 'Abbās said about not refraining from giving *ṣadaqah* is: 'Do not refrain from giving to the weak. If they stay behind you, the enemy will defeat you and you will be destroyed.'

A fourth view is related from al-Barā' ibn 'Āzib about this *āyah*. He was asked, 'Is it a man who attacks a squadron?' He answered, 'No, but it is a man who commits a sin and then says, "I have disobeyed Allah too much. There is no point in repenting," and he despairs of Allah and after that devotes himself to disobedience.' So destruction is despairing of Allah. 'Ubaydah as-Salmānī said that.

Zayd ibn Aslam said that it means: 'Do not travel in *jihād* without provision. People did that and it led to them being cut off on the road or being a burden on the people. This is a fifth view.

The 'Way of Allah' (*sabīlu-llāh*) here means *jihād* and refers to all the ways of doing it. Al-Mubarrad says that 'your hands' [the Arabic is '*bi-aydīkum*', literally 'by your hands'] means 'yourselves'. The part designates the whole. This is a common usage in the Qur'an. It is also said that this is a sort of metaphor. A person puts his hand to something when he undertakes to do it personally, and someone involved in fighting has his weapons in his hand. The expression is also used for something that a person fails to do. 'Destruction' (*tahlukah*) is a verbal noun derived from the verb meaning 'to destroy' (*halaka*). It is also said that it means: 'Do not take what will destroy you.' Az-Zajjāj and others said that. It means: if you do not spend, then you disobey Allah and are destroyed. It is also said that it means: do not hold on to your property as others are certainly going to inherit it and you will be 'destroyed' by being deprived of the use of your property. Another meaning is: do not hold on to your property because, by doing so, you will miss out on its restitution in this world and the reward for giving it away in the Next World. It is also said that it means: do not spend from what is unlawful so that it comes back on you and you are destroyed. Something similar is related from 'Ikrimah. He said that this is like another *āyah*: '*Do not have recourse to bad things when you give.*' (2:267) It is general and includes all that was mentioned since the expression allows that.

Scholars disagree about a man attacking another man in battle and about attacking the enemy on his own. Al-Qāsim ibn Mukhaymarah, al-Qāsim ibn Muḥammad and 'Abd al-Malik among our scholars say that there is no harm in a man attacking a large army alone when he is strong and has a sincere intention. If he is not strong, that is tantamount to suicide. It is said that, when someone seeks martyrdom and has a sincere intention, he is permitted to attack because his aim is to attack the enemy. That is clear in the words of the Almighty: *'Among the people there are some you give up everything, desiring the good pleasure of Allah.'* (2:207) Ibn Khuwayzimandād said, 'If a man attacks a hundred, or an entire army, or a group of thieves and bandits, or Khārijites, there are two possibilities. If he knows and thinks it is probable that he will kill the one he attacks and survive, that is good. If he knows and thinks it probable that he will be killed, but will cause great harm or open a path which the Muslims can use, then it is also permitted.' I have heard that when the Muslim army met the Persians, a group of the Muslim cavalry bolted from the elephants. One of their men made a clay elephant and made his horse familiar with it. In the morning his horse did not shy away from the elephants. He attacked the leading elephant. He was told, 'It will kill you!' He said, 'There is no harm if I am killed and the Muslims are victorious.' The same was true in the Battle of Yamāmah when the Banū Ḥanīfah fortified themselves in the walled garden and one of the Muslims said, 'Put me in the catapult and shoot me at them.' They did that and he fought them alone and opened the gate.

Part of this is what is related that a man said to the Prophet ﷺ: 'What do you think if I am killed in the Way of Allah with steadfastness and in expectation of the reward?' He answered, 'You will have the Garden.' He dived into the enemy until he was killed. We find in *Ṣaḥīḥ Muslim* from Anas ibn Mālik that in the Battle of Uḥud the Messenger of Allah ﷺ was left with only seven of the Anṣār and two men of Quraysh. When the enemy approached, he said, 'Whoever turns them away from us will have the Garden' or 'will be my companion in the Garden.' One of the Anṣār went forward and fought until he was killed. Then they advanced again and again he said, 'Whoever turns them away from us will have the Garden' or 'will be my companion in the Garden.' Another of the Anṣār went forward and fought until he was killed. This continued until all seven were killed and the Prophet ﷺ said, 'We have not done justice to our Companions.'

Muḥammad ibn al-Ḥasan said, 'If one man attacks a thousand idolaters on his own, there is no harm in that provided he hopes to survive or inflict great damage on the enemy. If that is not the case, then it is disliked because he exposes himself to destruction without any benefit for the Muslims. If his intention is to encourage

Muslims to follow him, it may be permitted because of the benefit for the Muslims involved. If he intends to terrify the enemy and show them the resolve of the Muslims, it may also be permitted.'

If that will help the Muslims, strengthen the *dīn* of Allah and weaken the unbelievers, then it is the noble station which Allah praises when He says: *'Allah has bought from the believers their selves and their wealth in return for them having the Garden. They fight in the way of Allah, and they kill and are killed.'* (9:111) There are others *āyahs* in which Allah praises those who expend themselves in that way. The same applies to the ruling of commanding what is correct and forbidding what is bad when one hopes that it will help the *dīn* and a person strives to achieve that until he is killed: he is in the ranks of the martyrs. Allah says: *'Command what is right and forbid what is wrong and be steadfast in the face of all that happens to you. That is certainly the most resolute course to follow.'* (31:17) 'Ikrimah related from Ibn 'Abbās that the Prophet ﷺ said, 'The best of martyrs is Ḥamzah ibn 'Abd al-Muṭṭalib and a man who speaks the truth in the presence of a tyrannical ruler who kills him.' This will be discussed in *Āl 'Imrān*, Allah willing.

**And do good: Allah loves good-doers.**

Spend in obedience and have a good opinion of Allah that He will repay you for doing it. It is said that it means: do good in your actions by obeying Allah. That is related from some Companions.

وَأَتِمُّوا۟ ٱلْحَجَّ وَٱلْعُمْرَةَ لِلَّهِ ۚ فَإِنْ أُحْصِرْتُمْ فَمَا ٱسْتَيْسَرَ مِنَ ٱلْهَدْيِ ۖ وَلَا تَحْلِقُوا۟
رُءُوسَكُمْ حَتَّىٰ يَبْلُغَ ٱلْهَدْىُ مَحِلَّهُۥ ۚ فَمَن كَانَ مِنكُم مَّرِيضًا أَوْ بِهِۦٓ أَذًى مِّن رَّأْسِهِۦ فَفِدْيَةٌ
مِّن صِيَامٍ أَوْ صَدَقَةٍ أَوْ نُسُكٍ ۚ فَإِذَآ أَمِنتُمْ فَمَن تَمَتَّعَ بِٱلْعُمْرَةِ إِلَى ٱلْحَجِّ فَمَا ٱسْتَيْسَرَ
مِنَ ٱلْهَدْيِ ۚ فَمَن لَّمْ يَجِدْ فَصِيَامُ ثَلَٰثَةِ أَيَّامٍ فِى ٱلْحَجِّ وَسَبْعَةٍ إِذَا رَجَعْتُمْ ۗ تِلْكَ
عَشَرَةٌ كَامِلَةٌ ۗ ذَٰلِكَ لِمَن لَّمْ يَكُنْ أَهْلُهُۥ حَاضِرِى ٱلْمَسْجِدِ ٱلْحَرَامِ ۚ وَٱتَّقُوا۟ ٱللَّهَ
وَٱعْلَمُوٓا۟ أَنَّ ٱللَّهَ شَدِيدُ ٱلْعِقَابِ ١٩٦

**196 Perform the Ḥajj and *'umrah* for Allah. If you are forcibly prevented, make whatever sacrifice is feasible. But do not shave your heads until the sacrificial animal has reached the place of sacrifice. If any of you are ill or have a head injury, the expiation is fasting or ṣadaqah or sacrifice when you are safe and well again. Anyone who comes out of *iḥrām* between *'umrah* and**

**ḥajj should make whatever sacrifice is feasible. For any one who cannot, there is three days' fast on ḥajj. and seven on your return – that is ten in all. That is for anyone whose family does not live near the Masjid al-Ḥarām. Be fearful of Allah and know that Allah is fierce in retribution.**

**Perform the ḥajj and *'umrah* for Allah.**

Scholars disagree about what this means [as the verb used normally means 'to complete']. It is said it means: perform them, doing both of them, as the verb is used elsewhere (2:124, 2:187) to mean this. This is according to the position of those who consider *'umrah* to be obligatory. Those who do not consider it to be obligatory say that it means complete them once you have begun them. When someone assumes *iḥrām*, he is obliged to complete the act for which he has entered it and not invalidate it. Ash-Sha'bī and Ibn Zayd stated that. 'Alī ibn Abī Ṭālib said that 'completing them' is to assume *iḥrām* for them from the abode of one's people. That is related from 'Umar ibn al-Khaṭṭāb and Sa'd ibn Abī Waqqāṣ. 'Imrān ibn Ḥuṣayn did that. Sufyān ath-Thawrī said that 'completing them' is to set out intending them and not trade or anything else. That is strengthened by His words, '*for Allah*'. 'Umar said that 'completing them' is to do each of them separately without *tamattu'* or *qirān*. Ibn Ḥabīb said that. Muqātil said that 'completing them' means not to make inappropriate things lawful in them. That was because they used to commit *shirk* in their *iḥrām* and would say, 'At Your service, O Allah! At Your service! You have no partner except a partner that is Yours. You control him and he does not control You.' Therefore He said to complete them without mixing anything else in them.

As for what is related from 'Alī and what 'Imrān ibn Ḥuṣayn did in assuming *iḥrām* before the *mīqāt*s that the Messenger of Allah ﷺ established, 'Abdullāh ibn Mas'ūd and a group of the Salaf supported it. It is confirmed that 'Umar assumed *iḥrām* from Jerusalem and that al-Aswad, 'Alqamah, 'Abd ar-Raḥmān and Abū Isḥāq assumed *iḥrām* from their houses. Ash-Shāfi'ī made an allowance for doing that. Abū Dāwud and ad-Dāraquṭnī related from Umm Salamah said that the Messenger of Allah ﷺ said, 'If someone assumes *iḥrām* for ḥajj or *'umrah* from Jerusalem, he leaves his sins like the day his mother bore it.' One variant has: 'he is forbidden past and future sins.' Abū Dāwud transmitted it and said, 'May Allah show mercy to Wakī'! He assumed *iḥrām* from Jerusalem,' i.e. for Makkah. This contains permission to assume *iḥrām* before the *mīqāt.*

Mālik disliked anyone adopting *iḥrām* before the *mīqāt.* He related that from 'Umar ibn al-Khaṭṭāb who objected to 'Imrān ibn Ḥuṣayn adopting *iḥrām* from

Basra and 'Uthmān objected to Ibn 'Umar adopting *iḥrām* before the *mīqāt*. Aḥmad and Isḥāq said that the correct thing is to start at the *mīqāts*. Part of the argument for this view is that the Messenger of Allah ﷺ established the *mīqāts* and specified them, thereby clarifying something previously undefined about the Hajj. The Prophet ﷺ did not adopt *iḥrām* for *ḥajj* from his house, but did so at the *mīqāt* he established for his community. What the Prophet ﷺ did is the best, Allah willing. That is also what was done by most of the Companions and the Tābi'ūn after them.

The people holding the first view argue that it is better because 'Ā'ishah said, 'The Messenger of Allah ﷺ was not given a choice between two things but that he chose the easier of them,' and the *ḥadīth* of Umm Salamah, along with what was mentioned from the Companions who saw the Messenger of Allah ﷺ adopt *iḥrām* for *ḥajj* from the *mīqāt*. They knew what he intended and knew that his *iḥrām* from the *mīqāt* was to make things easier for his community.

The imams have related that the Messenger of Allah ﷺ set the *mīqāt* for the people of Madīnah at Dhu-l-Ḥulayfah, for the people of Syria at al-Juḥfah, for the people of Najd at Qarn and for the people of Yemen at Yalamlam. Those sites were for them and for other people who came to them intending ḥajj and *'umrah*. Those who were closer to Makkah than them would assume *iḥrām* from where they started so that the people of Makkah did so in Makkah. The people of knowledge agree on the literal meaning of this *ḥadīth* and acting on it. There is absolutely no disagreement about it. They disagree about the *mīqāt* of the people of Iraq and those who take their *mīqāt*. Abū Dāwud and at-Tirmidhī related from Ibn 'Abbās that the Prophet ﷺ set the *mīqāt* for the people of the east at al-'Aqīq. At-Tirmidhī said that it is a *ḥasan ḥadīth*. It is also related that 'Umar set the *mīqāt* for the people of Iraq at Dhat 'Irq. We find in Abū Dāwud from 'Ā'ishah that the Messenger of Allah ﷺ set Dhat 'Irq as the *mīqāt* for the people of Iraq. This is sound. Those who relate that 'Umar set it was because it was conquered in his time and then neglected. It was, in fact, the Messenger of Allah ﷺ who set it as he set al-Juḥfah for the people of Syria although at that time all of Syria was a land of unbelief as was the case with Iraq and other lands at that time. Iraq and Syria were only conquered in the time of 'Umar. That is undisputed. Abū 'Umar said, 'Every Iraqi or easterner adopted *iḥrām* from Dhat 'Irq. All say that *iḥrām* is assumed from the *mīqāt*. They believe, however, that al-'Aqīq is more proper than Dhat 'Irq although Dhat 'Irq is also their *mīqāt*.'

Scholars agree that if someone adopts *iḥrām* before he reaches the *mīqāt* he is in *iḥrām*. Those who forbid that think that adopting *iḥrām* at the *mīqāt* is better out of their dislike of someone making difficult for himself something which Allah has made easier for him, as well as the fact that it might lead to an innovation in respect of *iḥrām*. If he does that, however, all of them confirm his *iḥrām* since he has added something and not decreased it.

This *āyah* is evidence for *'umrah* being obligatory because Allah commands it to be completed as He commands *ḥajj* to be completed. Aṣ-Ṣubayy ibn Ma'bad said, 'I went to 'Umar and said, "I was a Christian and became Muslim. I find that ḥajj and *'umrah* are prescribed for me and so I adopted *iḥrām* for both of them."' 'Umar said to him, 'You have been guided to the Sunnah of the Prophet ﷺ.' Ibn al-Mundhir observed that he did not object to what he said and his assumption that they were obligatory for him. 'Alī ibn Abī Ṭālib, Ibn 'Umar and Ibn 'Abbās all said that they were both obligatory. Ad-Dāraquṭnī related from Ibn Jurayj from Nāfi' that 'Abdullāh ibn 'Umar used to say, 'Allah has not created anyone who does not owe ḥajj and *'umrah* if he is able to find a way to do them. If anyone does more than that, it is good and voluntary.' He said, 'I did not hear him say anything about the people of Makkah.' Ibn Jurayj said that 'Ikrimah reported that Ibn 'Abbās said, '*'Umrah* is obligatory, as is ḥajj, for those who find a way to perform it.'

Among the Tābi'ūn who believed that it was obligatory were 'Aṭā', Ṭāwūs, Mujāhid, al-Ḥasan, Ibn Sīrīn, ash-Sha'bī, Sa'īd ibn Jubayr, Abū Burdah, Masrāuq, 'Abdullāh ibn Shaddād, ash-Shāfi'ī, Aḥmad, Isḥāq, Abū 'Ubayd, and Ibn al-Jahm among the Mālikīs. Ath-Thawrī said, 'We heard that it is mandatory.' Zayd ibn Thābit was asked about doing *'umrah* before ḥajj and said, 'Two prayers: you are not harmed by starting with either of them.' Ad-Dāraquṭnī mentioned it. It is related *marfū'* from Muḥammad ibn Sīrīn from Zayd ibn Thābit that the Messenger of Allah ﷺ said, 'Ḥajj and *'umrah* are two obligations. There is no harm in beginning with either of them.'

Mālik, however, said, '*'Umrah* is sunnah. But we do not know of anyone who made an allowance for abandoning it.' That is also the position of an-Nahka'ī and the People of Opinion (*ra'y*) according to what Ibn al-Mundhir related. Some people of Qazwin and Baghdad report from Abū Ḥanīfah that he considered it obligatory (*wājib*) like the ḥajj, and that it is a confirmed sunnah. lbn Mas'ūd and Jābir ibn 'Abdullāh also said that. Ad-Dāraquṭnī related from Muḥammad ibn Zakariyyā from Abū Kulayb Muḥammad ibn al-'Alā' from 'Abd ar-Raḥīm ibn Sulaymān from Ḥajjāj from Muḥammad ibn al-Munkadir that Jābir ibn 'Abdullāh said, 'A man asked the Messenger of Allah ﷺ about prayer, *zakāh* and ḥajj and whether they were mandatory. He said that they were. Then he asked about whether *'umrah* was mandatory. He answered, "No, but it is better for you to perform *'umrah.*'" Yaḥyā ibn Ayyūb related it *mawqūf* from Ḥajjāj and Ibn Jurayj from Ibn al-Munkadir from Jābir. This is the argument of those who do not make it mandatory in the Sunnah. They said that there is no evidence in the *āyah* of its mandatory nature because Allah connected it to completion, not to initiation, whereas with the prayer and *zakāh* He does by saying: *'Establish the prayer and pay* zakāh' (73:20) and with the ḥajj as well when He says: *'Ḥajj to the House is a duty owed to Allah by all mankind.'* (3:97) When He mentions *'umrah*, He commands that it should be completed. If one were to make ten ḥajj's or ten *'umrah*s, it is obligatory to complete all of them. The *āyah* is about obligation and completion, not obligation and initiation. Allah knows best.

Those who disagree about its mandatory nature say that the pillar of ḥajj is standing at 'Arafah and there is no equivalent standing in *'umrah.* If it had been like the sunnah of the ḥajj, it would be necessary for it to have equivalent actions as is the case with the sunnah prayer which has the same actions as the obligatory prayer.

Ash-Sha'bī and Abū Ḥawyah recite *'al-'umratu',* indicating that it is not mandatory while the main body of the community recite *'al-'umrata',* indicating that it is mandatory. The copy of Ibn Mas'ūd's Qur'an has 'Perform the ḥajj and *'umrah* to the House of Allah' and also 'Establish the ḥajj and *'umrah* to the House of Allah.' The point of mentioning Allah here is that the Arabs used to intend the ḥajj for meeting, public display, vying with one another, disagreement, settling needs and attending markets. None of that involves obeying Allah and there is no intention or act of nearness. Allah therefore commanded that people have the intention to perform the obligation and fulfil the need. After that there is scope for commerce.

There is no disagreement among scholars about the fact that someone who attends the ḥajj or *'umrah* practices must make an intention to do so. Part of the completion of any act of worship is the presence of the intention, which is an obligation in itself. It is an obligation just as *iḥrām* is, since, when the Prophet ﷺ mounted, he said, 'At Your service for both ḥajj and *'umrah.*' Ar-Rabī' mentioned in the book of al-Buwayṭī that ash-Shāfi'ī said, 'If a man says the *talbīyah* and does not intend ḥajj or *'umrah*, he is not performing ḥajj or *'umrah.* If he makes the intention and does not say the *talbīyah* until he has finished the practices, his ḥajj is complete.' The argument is based on the words of the Prophet ﷺ, 'Actions are according to intentions.' If someone does the the same as 'Alī did when he made his *iḥrām* the same as that of the Prophet ﷺ, that intention satisfies the requirement because it was based on the prior intention of someone else, which is not the case in the prayer.

Scholars disagree about adolescents and slaves who perform ḥajj and then become adults or are freed before they stand at 'Arafah. Mālik said, 'There is no way for them to abandon *iḥrām* just as there is no way with anyone else, since Allah says: *'Complete the ḥajj and 'umrah for Allah.'* No one who abandons *iḥrām* completes his ḥajj or *'umrah.* Abū Ḥanīfah said, 'It is permitted for a child who reaches puberty before the standing at 'Arafah to renew his *iḥrām.* If he continues in his original ḥajj, however, it does not satisfy the ḥajj of Islam.' His argument is that since he was not subject to the obligation when he assumed *iḥrām* for the ḥajj, but then ḥajj became obligatory when he reached puberty, it is impossible for him to be distracted from a specific obligation by something supererogatory and neglect his obligation. This is like someone who begins a supererogatory prayer and then the *iqāmah* for a prescribed prayer is given and he fears that he will miss it, so he stops the supererogatory and enters into the prescribed.

Ash-Shāfi'ī says that when a child adopts *iḥrām* and then reaches puberty before standing at 'Arafah, he stands there in *iḥrām* and satisfies the ḥajj of Islam. The same is true of a slave. He said that if a slave is freed at Muzdalifah, or a child reaches puberty there, if they return to 'Arafah after their emancipation or puberty and manage to stand there before dawn, they have satisfied the ḥajj of Islam and they do not owe a sacrifice. I prefer for them to exercise caution and sacrifice. I do not believe that is definitive.

He cited as proof for not renewing *iḥrām* the *ḥadīth* of 'Alī when he arrived from Yemen having adopted *iḥrām* for the ḥajj. The Messenger of Allah ﷺ asked him, 'What did you adopt *iḥrām* for?' He answered, 'I said, "At Your service, O Allah, for an *iḥrām* which is the same as the *iḥrām* of Your Prophet." The Messenger of Allah ﷺ said, "I adopted *iḥrām* for the ḥajj and have driven sacrificial camels."' Ash-Shāfi'ī said, 'The Messenger of Allah ﷺ did not object to what he said nor did he command him to renew his intention for *ifrād*, *tamattu'* or *qirān*.'

Mālik said about a Christian who becomes Muslim on the night of 'Arafah and adopts *iḥrām* for the ḥajj: 'He has satisfied the ḥajj of Islam.' The same is true of a slave who is freed or a child who reaches puberty, when they are not already in *iḥrām* and do not owe a sacrifice. Sacrifice becomes obligatory for someone who wants to go on ḥajj but does not adopt *iḥrām* from the *mīqāt*. Abū Ḥanīfah said that slaves owe a sacrifice. In their view, they are like a free men in respect of going past the *mīqāt*. That is not the case with a child or a Christian. They were not obliged to assume *iḥrām* to enter Makkah because they do not owe the obligation.

When an unbeliever becomes Muslim, or a child reaches puberty, they have the same ruling as the people of Makkah and neither owes anything for missing the *mīqāt*.

**If you are forcibly prevented,**

Ibn al-'Arabī says that this *āyah* is problematical but, in fact, there is nothing problematic about it as we will explain. Being prevented refers to any obstacle which stops you doing what you intended with respect to going on *ḥajj*, whatever that obstacle might be, whether it is an enemy, the injustice of a ruler, illness, highway robbers or anything else that might stop a person from fulfilling his intention. Scholars disagree about the actual obstacle referred to in the *āyah* and have two views. One is stated by 'Alqamah, 'Urwah ibn az-Zubayr and others which is that it refers to illness and not to an enemy. But it is also said that it is only an enemy which is meant, and that is the view of Ibn 'Abbās, Ibn 'Umar, Anas and ash-Shāfi'ī. Ibn al-'Arabī said that that is the opinion our scholars prefer, while linguists prefer illness if the verb *uḥṣira* is used and the enemy if the verb *ḥuṣira* is used.

What Ibn al-'Arabī related as the choice of our scholars is related by Ashhab alone. He is opposed by the rest of the people of Mālik in this case who say that *uḥṣira* is used for illness and *ḥuṣira* for the enemy. Al-Bājī stated that in *al-Muntaqā*. Abū Isḥāq az-Zajjāj related that that is the view of all linguists. Abū 'Ubaydah and al-Kisā'ī said the same, but we find the reverse in Ibn Fāris. One group, including Abū 'Umar, said that *uḥṣira* is used for both. This is the position of Mālik in the *Muwaṭṭā'* where he uses *uḥṣira* for both.

Al-Farrā' said that they both have the same meaning: for illness and the enemy. Abū Naṣr al-Qushayrī said, 'The Shāfi'īs claim that *uḥṣira* is used for the enemy and *ḥuṣira* for illness. What is sound is that they are both used for both.' Al-Khalīl ibn Aḥmad and others state their difference from the Shāfi'īs. Al-Khalīl said, '*Ḥuṣira* is used when a man is detained. *Uḥṣira* is used for someone on ḥajj who is prevented from completing the practices due to illness or the like.' He used *ḥuṣira* for the enemy and *uḥṣira* for illness. This agrees with what Ibn 'Abbās said, in other words that 'forcibly prevented' is by the enemy. Ibn as-Sakkīt said, 'Illness prevents (*uḥṣira*) someone from travelling or from something he needs to do. The enemy prevents (*ḥuṣira*) a person when they restrict and encircle him.' Most linguists say that Form I (*ḥuṣira*) is used for the enemy and Form IV (*uḥṣira*) for illness.

Since the root meaning is to be confined, the Ḥanafīs say that the person who is prevented is someone who is prevented from reaching Makkah after he has adopted *iḥrām*, whether that is due to illness, the enemy, or something else. They cite the general meaning of the word and say, 'The fact that "safety" is mentioned later in the *āyah* indicates that it is not about illness. The Prophet ﷺ said, "A common cold is security from leprosy." He also said, "If someone praises Allah before a sneezer does, he is safe from toothache, earache and colic." Ibn Mājah transmitted that in the *Sunan*.' They said, 'We consider that being detained by the enemy is prevention as it is analogous with illness and has the same ruling. It is not based on the literal meaning of the *āyah*.' Ibn 'Umar, Ibn az-Zubayr, Ibn 'Abbās, ash-Shāfi'ī and the People of Madīnah say that what is meant by the *āyah* is being prevented by the enemy because the *āyah* was revealed in 6 AH during the *'umrah* of Ḥudaybīyah when the idolaters prevented the Messenger of Allah ﷺ from reaching Makkah. Ibn 'Umar said, 'We set out with the Messenger of Allah ﷺ and the unbelievers of Quaysh blocked the way to the House. The Prophet ﷺ sacrificed his animals and shaved his head. This is indicated by His words, *"when you are safe,"* not "when you are free."' Allah knows best.

Most people believe that when someone is prevented by the enemy from continuing, he should come out of *iḥrām* where he is, sacrifice his animals, if he has any, and shave his head. Qatādah and Ibrāhīm said, 'If he is able, he sends his animals on and when they arrive, he comes out of *iḥrām*.' Abū Ḥanīfah said, 'The sacrifices for being prevented from completion do not have to take place on the Day of Sacrifice. It is permitted to sacrifice before the Day of Sacrifice if they have arrived.' His two companions differed from him and said that it is necessary to wait for the Day of Sacrifice and it does not satisfy the requirement if someone slaughters before that. This will be further discussed.

Most scholars say that if someone is stopped by the enemy, be it an unbeliever, Muslim, or ruler who confines him, he owes a sacrifice. That is the position of ash-Shāfi'ī and Ashhab also said that. Ibn al-Qāsim said, 'Someone who is barred from the House in ḥajj or *'umrah* does not have to sacrifice unless he has driven animals with him. That is the view of Mālik.' Part of their argument is that at Ḥudaybīyah the Prophet ﷺ slaughtered the animals he had marked and garlanded when he went into *iḥrām* for *'umrah*. When those animals did not reach their place due to the obstruction, the Messenger of Allah ﷺ commanded that they be slaughtered because they were sacrificial animals obliged as such by garlanding and being marked. They were brought out for Allah and it is not permitted to return them. The Messenger of Allah ﷺ did not slaughter them on account of being barred. That is why someone who is barred from the House is not obliged to sacrifice. The majority use as evidence the fact that the Messenger of Allah ﷺ was not out of *iḥrām* at Ḥudaybīyah and did not shave his head until he had sacrificed. That indicates that one of the preconditions for someone barred from *ḥajj* or 'umra coming out of *iḥrām* is to sacrifice any animals he has with him. If he is poor, then it is when he finds the means to be able to do so. He only leaves *iḥrām* by that. That is demanded by Allah's words here. It is said that he comes out of *iḥrām* and sacrifices if he is able to do so. Both views are related from ash-Shāfi'ī, and there are also two views about someone who does not find a sacrificial animal to purchase.

'Aṭā' and others say that someone prevented from continuing by illness is just like someone prevented by the enemy. Mālik and Shāfi'ī and their people say that someone prevented by illness from continuing does not come of out *iḥrām* until he has done *ṭawāf* of the House, even if it takes years for him to recover. That is the same for someone who makes a mistake in calculating the month or from whom the crescent moon is hidden. Mālik said, 'The people of Makkah are like other people in that respect.' He said, 'If someone ill requires treatment, he is treated and pays *fidyah* and remains in his *iḥrām*. He is not released from his *iḥrām* until he is free of illness and, when he is free of illness, he must continue to the House and do *ṭawāf* of it seven times, run between Ṣafā and Marwah and he then comes out of his *iḥrām* for ḥajj or *'umrah*. This is also the view of ash-Shāfi'ī. Regarding that, he believed what was related from 'Umar, Ibn 'Abbās, 'Ā'ishah, Ibn 'Umar and Ibn az-Zubayr. In the case of someone hindered by illness or miscalculation, they said that he does not come of out *iḥrām* until he has done *ṭawāf* of the House. The same is true of someone who breaks a bone or has an abdominal pain.

The ruling for someone in this situation, according to Mālik and his people is that, if he fears that he will miss standing at 'Arafah due to his illness, he has a choice. If he wishes, when he recovers he can continue on to the House, do *ṭawāf* and come out of *iḥrām* for *'umrah*, or he can instead remain in his *iḥrām* until the next year. If he remains in his *iḥrām* and does not do anything that someone performing ḥajj is forbidden to do, then he owes no sacrifice. A factor in the argument regarding that is the consensus of the Companions that if someone miscalculates the month, his ruling is that he can only come out of *iḥrām* by doing *ṭawāf* of the House.

He said about a Makkan who remains confined until people have finished the ḥajj, that he should go outside the Ḥaram, say the *talbiyyah,* then do what someone performing *'umrah* does, and then he can come out of *iḥrām*. Then the following year he should perform ḥajj and sacrifice. Ibn Shihāb az-Zuhrī said that a Makkan who is barred must stand at 'Arafah, even carried on a bier. This position was preferred by Abū Bakr Muḥammad ibn Aḥmad ibn 'Abdullāh ibn Bukayr al-Mālikī who said: 'Mālik's position about a Makkan who is barred is that what applies to others also applies to him: he should repeat the ḥajj and sacrifice. This differs from the literal wording of the Book where Allah says: "*That is for anyone whose family does not live near the Masjid al-Ḥarām.*"' He added, 'I believe that one takes the position of az-Zuhrī: it is permitted by Allah Almighty for those whose family does not live near the Masjid al-Ḥarām to remain for treatment because of the distance, even if they miss the ḥajj. As for those whose distance from the Masjid al-Ḥarām is not such that one could shorten the prayer when travelling between them, he should attend the practices, even lying on a bier, because he is close to the House.' Abū Ḥanīfah and his people said that if someone is prevented from reaching the House by enemies, illness, lack of money, loss of mount, or being stung by vermin he should remain where he is in *iḥrām* and send ahead his sacrificial animals or their price. When the sacrifice is made, then he comes out of *iḥrām*. That is what is stated by 'Urwah, Qatādah, al-Ḥasan, 'Aṭā', an-Nakha'ī, Mujāhid and the people of Iraq.

Mālik and his people say that someone in *iḥrām* does not benefit from having made a stipulation about his ḥajj if he fears being hindered by illness or the enemy. That is the view of ath-Thawrī and Abū Ḥanīfah and his people. Such a stipulation is that he says when he goes into *iḥrām*: 'At Your service, O Allah, at Your service. I will come out of *iḥrām* if I am prevented in the land.' Aḥmad ibn Ḥanbal, Isḥāq ibn Rāhawayh and Abū Thawr said that there is nothing wrong in making a stipulation if the situation exists. That is stated by more than one of the Companions and the Tābi'ūn. Their argument is the *ḥadīth* of Ḍubā'ah bint az-Zubayr ibn 'Abd al-Muṭṭalib who went to the Messenger of Allah ﷺ and said, 'Messenger of Allah, I want to perform ḥajj. Can I make stipulations?' 'Yes,' he answered. She asked, 'So what should I say?' He said, 'Say: "At Your service, O Allah, at Your service. I will come out of *iḥrām* if I am prevented in the land."' Abū Dāwud, ad-Dāraquṭnī and others transmitted it.' Ash-Shāfi'ī said, 'If the *ḥadīth* of Ḍubā'ah were confirmed, I would not go against it. You come out of *iḥrām* wherever Allah detains you.'

More than one person said that it is sound, including Abū Ḥātim al-Bustī and Ibn al-Mundhir. Ibn al-Mundhir said, 'It is confirmed that the Messenger of Allah ﷺ said to Ḍubā'ah bint az-Zubayr, "Go on ḥajj and make a stipulation."' Ash-Shāfi'ī took that position when he was in Iraq but not when he was in Egypt. Ibn al-Mundhir said, 'I take the first view.' 'Abd ar-Razzāq mentioned it from Ibn Jurayj from Abu-z-Zubayr that Ṭāwūs and 'Ikrimah said that Ibn 'Abbās said,

'Ḍubā'ah bint az-Zubayr went to the Messenger of Allah ﷺ and said, "I am a heavy woman who wants to perform ḥajj. What do you command me to do when I go into *iḥrām*." He said, "Go into *iḥrām* and stipulate that you will come out of *iḥrām* if you are held back."' This is a sound *isnād*.

Scholars disagree about the obligation to make up the ḥajj in the case of someone prevented from completing it. Mālik and ash-Shāfi'ī said that if someone is stopped by the enemy, he does not have to make up either ḥajj or *'umrah* unless he is someone who has not yet performed the ḥajj and still owes it since it is still obligatory for him. That is also the case with those who believe that *'umrah* is a mandatory obligation. Abū Ḥanīfah said, 'Someone barred from completion by illness or the enemy owes both ḥajj and *'umrah.'* That is the view of aṭ-Ṭabarī. The People of Opinion say, 'If someone has adopted *ihrām* for ḥajj, he should make up ḥajj and *'umrah* because his *ihrām* for ḥajj has become *ihrām* for *'umrah.* If he is doing *qirān*, then he should make up ḥajj and two *'umrah*s. If he adopted *ihrām* for *'umrah*, he should make up *'umrah.* That is the same whether he is detained by illness or the enemy.'

They base their argument on the *ḥadīth* of Maymūn ibn Mihrān who said, 'I went out to perform *'umrah* in the year the people of Syria laid siege to Ibn az-Zubayr in Makkah. Some men of my people sent sacrificial animals with me. When I reached the people of Syria, they prevented me from entering the Ḥaram and so I sacrificed my animal where I was and came out of *iḥrām* and went back. The following year I left to complete my *'umrah* and went to Ibn 'Abbās to question him. He said, "Replace the sacrificial animals. The Messenger of Allah ﷺ instructed his Companions to replace the animals that they had sacrificed in the year of Ḥudaybīyah in the Fulfilled *'Umrah.* They did so based on the words of the Prophet ﷺ, 'Anyone who has broken a leg or gone lame should come out of *ihrām* and he owes another ḥajj.'"' 'Ikrimah related that al-Ḥajjāj ibn 'Amr al-Anṣārī also said that he heard the Messenger of Allah ﷺ say, 'Anyone who has broken a leg or gone lame should come out of *ihrām* and he owes another ḥajj.' They stated that the Messenger of Allah ﷺ and his Companions went on *'umrah* in the year after Ḥudaybīyah. That was making up the earlier *'umrah.* They said that is the reason that it is called 'the Fulfilled *'Umrah'*.

Mālik argued by the fact that the Messenger of Allah ﷺ did not instruct any of his Companions or those with him to make up anything or to repeat anything. His doing that is not recorded from him by any path whatsoever. He did not say the following year, 'This *'umrah* is making up for the *'umrah* that I was prevented from completing.' They call it *'Umrat al-Qaḍā'* and *'Umrat al-Qaḍiyyah.* It was called that because the Messenger of Allah ﷺ concluded (*qāḍā*) and made a treaty with Quraysh that year that they would go back from the House that year and come to it to the following year. That is how it gets its name.

None of the *fuqahā'* say that someone who breaks a bone or goes lame has to assume *iḥrām* at the exact place he broke it except for Abū Thawr who follows the literal meaning of the *ḥadīth* of al-Ḥajjāj ibn 'Amr. Dāwud ibn 'Alī and his people corroborate him in that. Scholars agree that someone who breaks a bone should come out of *iḥrām*, but they disagree about what takes him out of *iḥrām*. Mālik and others said that it is only by doing *ṭawāf* of the House. The Kufans who oppose him say that he comes out of *iḥrām* by the intention and does what brings him out of it.

There is no disagreement among the *fuqahā'* of any city that being prevented is general and applies to both ḥajj and *'umrah*. Ibn Sīrīn said, 'There is no prevention in respect of *'umrah* because it has no specific time.' The response to this is that even if it has no specific time, there is harm in waiting until the excuse disappears. The *āyah* was revealed about that. It is related from Ibn az-Zubayr that someone who is prevented from completion by the enemy or illness only comes out of *iḥrām* by doing *ṭawāf* of the House. This is also contrary to the text of the report in the year of Ḥudaybīyah.

The preventing agent may be either an unbeliever or a Muslim. If it is an unbeliever, it is not permitted to fight him, even if the prevented person is confident of defeating him, and comes out of *iḥrām* immediately, since Allah says: *'Do not fight them in the Masjid al-Ḥarām.'* If the unbeliever asks for money, he should not pay it because that would indicate weakness in Islam. If he is Muslim, he is not permitted to fight him in any case and he is obliged to come out of *iḥrām*. If he asks for something in exchange for letting him continue, however, he is permitted to pay it. Fighting is not permitted since it involves destruction of life. There is no obligation to fight where the performance of acts of worship is concerned, even though that is tolerated in the *dīn*. Paying the amount asked for is avoiding the greater of two harms for the lesser. It is also because the ḥajj is something on which one spends money, in any case, and this is counted as part of the expenses.

The enemy who prevents is either someone you are certain, because of his strength and great number, will stay and consolidate, or not. If it is the former, then the one prevented should come out of *iḥrām* immediately where he is. If the latter is the case, and you hope that the enemy concerned will leave, then you are not considered someone who is prevented unless there is not enough time after the time of the departure of the enemy in which to catch the ḥajj. In that case, according to Ibn al-Qāsim and Ibn al-Mājishūn, you should come out of *ihrām*. Ashhab said, 'Someone prevented from completing ḥajj does not come out of *ihrām* until the Day of Sacrifice and does not stop saying the *talbiyyah* until the people go to 'Arafah.' The reason for the position of Ibn al-Qāsim is that this is the moment when he despairs of completing his ḥajj because of the enemy. Therefore he is permitted to come out of *ihrām* then. The day of 'Arafah is the basis for that. The reason for the position of Ashhab is that a person must do the utmost that is possible for him regarding the rules of *ihrām* and so it is obligatory for him until the Day of Sacrifice, which is the moment when those performing ḥajj are permitted to come out of *ihrām*.

**make whatever sacrifice is feasible.**

According to most scholars, this means a sheep. Ibn 'Umar, 'Āishah, and Ibn az-Zubayr said that it is whatever camel or whatever cow is available. Al-Ḥasan said, 'The greatest sacrifice is the camel, the medium one the cow and the least the sheep.' This phrase provides evidence for what Mālik believes, which is that someone stopped by enemy forces does not have to make up his ḥajj, because only the sacrifice is mentioned. Allah knows best.

The word for 'sacrifice' (*hadī*) is used because it refers to camels which are led (*hadā*) to the House of Allah. The Arabs use the term to mean 'camels'. Abū Bakr said that they are called this because they are given (*yuhdā*) to the House of Allah.

**But do not shave your heads until the sacrificial animal has reached the place of sacrifice.**

This is addressed to all Muslims performing the ḥajj, not just those who are prevented from completing their ḥajj. Some scholars think, however, that it only refers to those who have been stopped. So it means: 'Do not come out of *iḥrām* until the sacrifices have been slaughtered'. The 'place of sacrifice' (*maḥillahu*) referred to is the place where it is lawful to slaughter the sacrificial animals. For Mālik and ash-Shāfi'ī, the place to sacrifice is the place where people have been stopped; this is in order to imitate the Messenger of Allah ﷺ at Ḥudaybīyah. Allah says: *'and prevented the sacrifice from reaching its proper place,'* (48:25) which means they are stopped from reaching the Ancient House. Abū Ḥanīfah says that it means the Ḥaram of Makkah since Allah says: '*...and then their place of sacrifice is by the Ancient House.'* (22:33) The response to this is that for this to happen the security necessary to reach the House is essential. Someone who barred fails to meet this condition. The evidence for this lies in the fact that the Prophet ﷺ and his Companions slaughtered their animals at Ḥudaybīyah and not at the Ḥaram. In the Sunnah, the argument advanced is the *ḥadīth* of Nājiyah ibn Jundub, the Companion of the Prophet, who said to the Prophet ﷺ, 'Send the sacrificial camels with me and I will slaughter them at the Ḥaram.' He asked, 'How will you do that?' He said, 'I will lead them through inaccessible wadis and until the point that I can slaughter them in the Ḥaram.' The answer to this is that it is not sound. One slaughters where one comes out of *iḥrām* to imitate what the Prophet ﷺ did at Ḥudaybīyah. This is the sound version related by the imams. Furthermore, the sacrificial animals follow the one who presents them and where he comes out of *iḥrām*.

Scholars disagree about whether someone who is prevented from continuing should shave his head and about the way in which he should come out of *iḥrām* before sacrificing. Mālik said: 'The firm sunnah about which there is no disagreement with us is that it is not permitted for someone to remove any of his hair until he has sacrificed. Allah says: *"Do not shave your heads until the sacrificial animal has reached the place of sacrifice."*' Abū Ḥanīfah and his people say that if he comes out of *iḥrām* before he sacrifices he owes another sacrifice and reverts to being in *iḥrām* until he sacrifices. If he catches game before he slaughters his sacrifice, he owes requital, and the wealthy and poor are the same in that respect. He does not come out of *iḥrām* until he sacrifices or the sacrifice is done for him. They said that the minimum is a sheep which is not blind and does not have its ears cut. For them, that takes the place of fasting.

Abū 'Umar said that the position of the Kufans regarding this matter is weak and contradictory because they do not permit someone barred by illness or the enemy to come out of *iḥrām* until he has sacrificed in the Ḥaram. By permitting the person stopped because of illness to send a sacrificial animal, instructing the person who takes it to slaughter it on a certain day, whereupon he can come out of *iḥrām* and shave his head, they then allow him to assume certainty that the animal has reached the place and has been slaughtered. So they compel him to come out of *iḥrām* based on assumption when scholars agree that it is not permitted for someone obliged to perform one of his obligations to leave it based on assumption. The evidence that it is an assumption is found in their words: 'If that animal dies, is lost or stolen, the one who sent it comes out of *iḥrām* and has sex with his wife and hunts, he reverts to being in *iḥrām* and owes requital for what he hunted.' So they permit him to invalidate the ḥajj and make obligatory him what is binding for someone who has not come out of *iḥrām*. This is an unconcealed contradiction and a weak position. They base all of their school on the position of Ibn Mas'ūd and did not look at anything that disagreed with him.

Ash-Shāfi'ī has two views about someone who is barred when it is difficult for him to sacrifice. One is that he only leaves *iḥrām* by sacrifice, and the other is that he is commanded to do what he is able to do. If he is not able to do something, then he does what he is able to do. Ash-Shāfi'ī said, 'Someone who says this says that he leaves *iḥrām* where he is and slaughters if he is able to do so. If he is able to slaughter in Makkah, then he is only allowed to slaughter there.' He said that his situation is only satisfied by a sacrifice. It is said that if someone cannot find a sacrificial animal, then he should feed people or fast. If he cannot do any of these three, then he does one of them when he is able to. In the case of a slave, it is said that the situation is only satisfied by fasting. The price of a sheep is calculated in dirhams and then the dirhams in terms of food and he should fast a day for every *mudd* so calculated.

There is disagreement about whether someone forced to stop can shave his head or not once he has sacrificed. One group say that he does not have to shave because his rites have ended. Their argument is that all the practices, such as *ṭawāf* and *sa'y*, are cancelled for him when he is barred. That is part of what takes him out of *iḥrām*. Therefore the rest of what brings someone out of *iḥrām* is cancelled for him by the fact of being barred. Among those who argue this are Abū Ḥanīfah and Muḥammad ibn al-Ḥasan who said that someone barred does not have to shave or shorten his hair. Abū Yūsuf said that he should shave, but owes nothing if he does not shave. Ibn 'Imrān related from Ibn Samā'ah from Abū Yūsuf in *an-Nawādir* that he must shave his head or shorten his hair.

Ash-Shāfi'ī has two different view about this matter. One is that the person prevented from finishing the practices shaves his head, which is the view of Mālik, and the other that it is not one of the practices, as is the view of Abū Ḥanīfah. The argument of Mālik is that *ṭawāf* of the House and running between Ṣafā and Marwah are all made impossible for the person who is barred and so what is between him and them is cancelled for him, but there is nothing preventing him from shaving: he is able to do it. When he is able to do something it is not cancelled for him. Part of what indicates that someone barred must still shave their head, in the same way as someone who reaches the House must, is the words of Allah: '*Do not shave your heads until the sacrificial animal has reached the place of sacrifice.*' There is also what is related about the Messenger of Allah ﷺ supplicating three times for those who shave their heads but only once for those who shorten their hair. This is the definitive proof and sound view regarding this matter. It is what Mālik and his people believe. They believe that shaving the head is one of the practices owed by the ḥajjī which complete his ḥajj, and they are also due from someone who misses the ḥajj, someone barred by the enemy or prevented by illness.

The imams related from Nāfi' from 'Abdullāh ibn 'Umar that the Messenger of Allah ﷺ said, 'O Allah, forgive those who shave their heads.' They said, 'And those who shorten their hair, Messenger of Allah!' He said, 'O Allah, forgive those who shave their heads.' They said, 'And those who shorten their hair, Messenger of Allah!' He said, 'and those who shorten their hair.' Our scholars say that this is a supplication by the Messenger of Allah ﷺ three times for those who have shaved and only once for those who shortened their hair. It is evidence that it is better to shave than shorten the hair in the ḥajj and *'umrah*. That is stipulated by Allah's words in the *āyah* where there is no mention of shortening the hair. With the exception of something mentioned by al-Ḥasan about obliging shaving in the first ḥajj that a person makes, scholars are, however, agreed that shortening the hair is permitted for men.

Women do not shave their heads. Their sunnah is to shorten the hair since the Prophet ﷺ said, 'Women do not have to shave off their hair. They shorten it.' Abū Dāwud transmitted it from Ibn 'Abbās. Scholars agree on that position. Some people think that a woman shaving her hair amounts to mutilation. There is disagreement about the amount which should be cut. Ibn 'Umar, ash-Shāfi'ī, Aḥmad, and Isḥāq said that it is a fingertip length from every lock. 'Aṭā' says it is the length of three fingers when put together. Qatādah says a third or a quarter. Ḥafṣah bint Sīrīn says that a woman who is older should cut a quarter and a young woman only a little. Mālik says that it should be cut all round but that whatever a woman removes is adequate; all her locks, however, must be trimmed. Ibn al-Mundhir said that it is anything that can be called 'shortening', but it is more cautious to take a fingertip from every lock.

No one is permitted to shave his head until his sacrifice has been slaughtered. That is because it is sunnah to slaughter before shaving. This *āyah* is the basis for that along with what the Messenger of Allah ﷺ did. He slaughtered first and then shaved after that. If someone reverses this order, he has either done so in error and ignorance or intentionally. If it is the first case, then he owes nothing. Ibn Ḥabīb related that from Ibn al-Qāsim and it is well known in the school of Mālik. Ibn al-Mājishūn said that he owes a sacrifice, and that is what is stated by Abū Ḥanīfah. As for the second case, Qāḍī Abu-l-Ḥasan related that it is permitted to shave the head before sacrificing. Ash-Shāfi'ī also said that. The apparent position in the School is that it is forbidden. What is sound is that it is permitted based on the *ḥadīth* of Ibn 'Abbās in which the Prophet ﷺ was asked about slaughtering, shaving and stoning and a change in the order. He said, 'There is no harm in it.' Muslim related it. Ibn Mājah transmitted from 'Abdullāh ibn 'Amr that the

Prophet ﷺ was asked about someone who slaughtered before shaving or shaving before slaughtering and he said, 'There is no harm in it.'

There is no disagreement that shaving the head in the ḥajj is a recommended practice and permitted in other than the ḥajj, although some disagree and say that in that case it is mutilation. If it had been mutilation it would not have been permitted in the ḥajj or anywhere else because the Messenger of Allah ﷺ forbade mutilation. He shaved the heads of the sons of Ja'far three days after their father was killed. If shaving had not been permitted, he would not have done it. 'Alī ibn Abī Ṭālib used to shave his head. Ibn 'Abd al-Barr said that scholars agree about tying the hair and allowing shaving it. This is enough of a proof. Success is by Allah.

**If any of you are ill or have a head injury, the expiation is fasting or ṣadaqah or sacrifice when you are safe and well again.**

*'If any of you'*: some Shāfi'ī scholars say that this phrase definitely indicates that the one who is *'prevented'* at the beginning of the *āyah* refers to people barred by an enemy and not by illness since, if that was not the case, there would be no need for the repetition here. If someone has something harmful on his head, he must pay *fidyah*. The application of the *āyah* does not necessarily follow in the context. The pronouns at the end refer back to what was mentioned at the beginning. Part of what indicates that is the reason for its revelation. The imams relate about Ka'b ibn 'Ujrah when the Prophet ﷺ saw lice dropping from his hair onto his face and said, 'Perhaps your head is causing you harm?' He commanded him to shave his head at Ḥudaybīyah while they were still hoping to enter Makkah. Then Allah revealed *fidyah* (expiation) and the Prophet ﷺ commanded him to feed six poor people, sacrifice a sheep or fast three days.

Al-Awzā'ī said that if someone in *iḥrām* has something harmful on his head, it is enough for him to expiate it by *fidyah* before shaving his head. According to this, the *āyah* means 'if he wants to shave.' So anyone who shaves owes *fidyah* which he does not pay until he shaves. Allah knows best.

Ibn 'Abd al-Barr says, 'The sacrifice, in this case, is a sheep and there is no disagreement about that. There is disagreement about the amount of fasting and feeding. Most Muslim scholars believe that the fast is for three days, as is found in the sound *ḥadīth* from Ka'b ibn 'Ujrah. Al-Ḥasan. 'Ikrimah and Nāfi' say that it is ten days. None of the *fuqahā'* of the cities or the imams of *ḥadīth* take this position.' It is transmitted by Abu-z-Zubayr from Mujāhid from 'Abd ar-Raḥmān that Ka'b ibn 'Ujrah told him that he went into *iḥrām* in Dhu-l-Qa'dah and his head was full of lice. He went to the Prophet ﷺ who was heating a pot over a fire. He ﷺ said to him, 'It seems that the vermin on your head are causing you harm.' 'Yes,' he answered. He said, 'Shave and make a sacrifice.' He said, 'I do not have the means to sacrifice.' He said, 'Then feed ten poor people.' He replied, 'I do not have the means.' He said, 'Fast for three days.' Abū 'Umar said, 'The *ḥadīth* would give the impression that there is an order in the three alternatives, but is not the case. If this had been sound, it would be first one, then the other, but most of the reports from Ka'b ibn 'Ujrah use the word 'choice'. That is the text of the Qur'an and it is how the scholars in every city acted and that was their *fatwā*. Success is by Allah.

Scholars disagree about how much food is required for the *fidyah* on account of this harm. Mālik, ash-Shāfi'ī, Abū Ḥanīfah and their people said that the feeding required is two *mudd*s measured by the *mudd* of the Prophet ﷺ. That is the view of Abū Thawr and Dāwud. It is related that ath-Thawrī said that *fidyah* is half a *ṣā'* of wheat or a *ṣā'* of dates, barley or raisins. It is also related that Abū Ḥanīfah made half a *ṣā'* of wheat equal to a *ṣā'* of dates. Ibn al-Mundhir said, 'This is an error because in some reports the Prophet ﷺ said to Ka'b, 'Give as *ṣadaqah* three *ṣā'*s of dates to six poor people.' Aḥmad ibn Ḥanbal once said what Mālik and ash-Shāfi'ī said, and another time: 'He should feed each poor person with a *mudd* of wheat or half a *ṣā'* of dates.' Feeding poor people a midday and evening meal does not satisfy the requirement in the expiation for removal of harm. It is necessary to give each poor person two *mudd*s measured by the *mudd* of the Prophet ﷺ. That is what is stated by Mālik, ath-Thawrī, ash-Shāfi'ī, and Muḥammad ibn al-Ḥasan. Abū Yūsuf, however, said that it is enough to feed them a midday and evening meal.

The consensus of the people of knowledge is that someone in *iḥrām* is forbidden to shave his hair or cut it or eliminate it in any way it by shaving or depilation or anything else, except in case of illness as the Qur'an states. They agree that *fidyah* is mandatory for someone who shaves while in *iḥrām* without reason. They disagree about someone who does that or puts on perfume deliberately without an excuse. Mālik said, 'What he has done is bad! He owes *fidyah* and can choose how to pay it. It is the same whether that is deliberate or accidental, due to necessity or not.' Abū Ḥanīfah, ash-Shāfi'ī, their people, and Abū Thawr say that there is no choice except when it was due to necessity, based on this *āyah*. So when he shaves his head deliberately or puts on perfume deliberately without an excuse, then he has no choice and only owes a sacrifice. They disagree about someone who does that out of forgetfulness. Mālik said that the one who does it deliberately or does it forgetfully are the same with respect to the obligation of *fidyah*. That is also the view of Abū Ḥanīfah, ath-Thawrī and al-Layth. Ash-Shāfi'ī has two views about it. One is that he owes no *fidyah* and that is the view of Dāwud and Isḥāq. The second view is that he owes *fidyah*.

Most scholars oblige *fidyah* for a man in *iḥrām* who wears stitched clothing, covers all or part of his head, wears leather socks, cuts his nails, touches perfume, and removes harm. That is also the case if he shaves his body or daubs it, or shaves cupping sites. A woman is like a man in that respect. She must pay *fidyah* for using kohl, even if there is no perfume in it. A man may use kohl if there is no perfume in it. A woman owes *fidyah* if she covers her face or wears gloves. The intentional, forgetful and ignorant are the same regarding that. Some scholars oblige a sacrifice for people who do any of those things. Dāwud said that they owe nothing for shaving body hair.

Scholars disagree about the place where this *fidyah* should take place. 'Aṭā' said, 'Sacrifices should be done in Makkah, while feeding or fasting can be done whenever the person wishes.' The same is stated by the People of Opinion. Al-Ḥasan said that sacrificing must be done in Makkah. Ṭāwūs and ash-Shāfi'ī said that both feeding and sacrificing may only be done in Makkah, while fasting can be done wherever one wishes, because the people of the Ḥaram get no benefit from fasting. Allah Almighty says: *'a sacrifice to reach the Ka'bah.'* (5:95) It is a comfort for poor people in the vicinity of His House. Feeding is beneficial there which is not the case with fasting. Allah knows best. Mālik said, 'He can do that wherever he wishes.' It is a sound view and it is the view of Mujāhid. According to Mālik, slaughtering is a practice but a sacrifice is not, based on the text of the Qur'an and the Sunnah. Practices can be done anywhere but sacrifices may only be done at Makkah. Part of his argument is what is related from Yaḥyā ibn Sa'īd in the *Muwaṭṭā'*: "Alī ibn Abī Ṭālib ordered that Ḥusayn's head should be shaved and then he offered a sacrifice on his behalf, killing a camel for him.' Mālik said that Yaḥyā ibn Sa'īd said, 'Ḥusayn had set out with 'Uthmān on that particular journey to Makkah.'

This is the clearest evidence that *fidyah* for injury can be fulfilled outside of Makkah. If the sacrifice is slaughtered in the Ḥaram, Mālik permits it to be given to people outside of the Ḥaram, since the object of it is to feed poor Muslims. Mālik said, 'Since it is permitted to do the fast outside the Ḥaram, it is also permitted to feed other than the people of the Ḥaram.' Allah's words: *'If any of you are ill…'*, clarify the proof of what we have said. In this *āyah*, He does not mention a specific place. So the literal meaning is that wherever a person does that, it satisfies the requirement. Allah uses '*nusuk*' as a term for what is slaughtered and the Messenger of Allah ﷺ also used that term for it rather than saying '*hady*'. Therefore we are not obliged to treat it as analogous to '*hady*' nor designate it as such in spite of what has come about that from 'Alī. Furthermore, when the Prophet ﷺ commanded Ka'b to do *fidyah*, he was not in the Ḥaram and therefore it is valid for all of that to take place outside of the Ḥaram. The same as this is related from ash-Shāfi'ī.

'*Nusuk*' is the plural of *nasīkah* which is a slaughtered animal that someone offers (*nasaka*) to Allah. *Nusk* is basic worship. An example of that usage is Allah's words: '*Show us our rites* (manāsik)'.' (2:128) It is said that the linguistic root of *nusk* is washing and the verb is used for washing a garment. So it is as if a person washes himself of the filth of sins by worship. It is also said that *nask* are silver ingots, each of which is *nasīkah*.

It is said that the words '*when you are safe*' mean 'when you have recovered from your illness'. It is said that they mean 'safe from fear of the enemy', as Ibn 'Abbās and Qatādah said. That is more in keeping with the expression used, because no one can ever be free from fear of illness to the extent that it is possible to feel entirely safe from it, and Allah knows best.

**Anyone who comes out of *iḥrām* between *'umrah* and ḥajj should make whatever sacrifice is feasible.**

Scholars disagree about who is being referred to in this phrase. 'Abdullāh ibn az-Zubayr, 'Alqamah and Ibrāhīm say that the *āyah* is about those who are forcibly prevented and cannot go on. According to Ibn az-Zubayr the situation referred to is when someone is held up until he misses the ḥajj and then reaches the House after it has passed and assumes *iḥrām* for *'umrah* and then performs ḥajj in the following year to make up for the one he missed. This joins his *'umrah* to the ḥajj of making up. Others say that the situation referred to is when someone is detained and then delays *'umrah* until the following year and does it in the months of ḥajj and performs ḥajj in the same year. Ibn 'Abbās and others said that this *āyah* is about both those who are barred and others who are able to continue.

There is no disagreement among scholars that ḥajj involving a temporary removal of *iḥrām* (*tamattu'*), ḥajj on its own (*ifrād*) and ḥajj and *'umrah* combined (*qirān*) are all permitted because Prophet ﷺ declared himself happy with all of them. He did not object to the ḥajj of any of his Companions, but allowed it for them and was pleased with them. Scholars do, however, disagree about which of them the Messenger of Allah ﷺ adopted when performing his own ḥajj and which is the best, all based on different *hadīths* that have been reported. Some, including Malik, said that *ifrād* is better the *qirān* and *qirān* is better than *tamattu'*, because the Prophet ﷺ did *ifrād*. We find in *Ṣaḥīḥ Muslim* that 'Ā'ishah said, 'We went out with the Messenger of Allah ﷺ and he said, "Whoever among you wants to go into *iḥrām* for ḥajj and *'umrah* should do so. Whoever wants to go into *iḥrām* for ḥajj alone should do so. Whoever wants to go into *iḥrām* for *'umrah* should do so."' 'Ā'ishah said, 'The Messenger of Allah ﷺ went into *iḥrām* for ḥajj and some people did so with him, while others assumed *iḥrām* for ḥajj and *'umrah* and yet others assumed *iḥrām* for *'umrah*. I was one of those who assumed *iḥrām* for *'umrah*.' A group related it from Hishām ibn 'Urwah from his father from 'Ā'ishah. Some of them say that the Messenger of Allah ﷺ said, 'As for myself, I have assumed *iḥrām* for ḥajj.' This is a text used in the topic of this dispute. It is the argument of those who say that *ifrād* is better. Muḥammad ibn al-Ḥasan related that Mālik said, 'Since two different *ḥadīths* have come from the Prophet ﷺ, and we heard that Abū Bakr and 'Umar acted on one of the two *ḥadīths* and left the other, that provides evidence that truth lies in what they did.' Abū Thawr also preferred *ifrād* and thought it better than *tamattu'* and *qirān*. It one of two positions reported from ash-Shāfi'ī and it is well known from him.

Others prefer *tamattu'*, because it is mentioned in the Book, and said that it is better. That is the school of 'Abdullāh ibn 'Umar and 'Abdullāh ibn az-Zubayr and is the view of Aḥmad ibn Ḥanbal and it is the other position of ash-Shāfi'ī. Ad-Dāraquṭnī said, 'Ash-Shāfi'ī said, "I preferred *ifrād*, but *tamattu'* is good and we do not dislike it."' The argument of those who prefer *tamattu'* is found in what Muslim related from 'Imrān ibn Ḥuṣayn who said, 'The *āyah* of *tamattu'* was revealed in the Book of Allah and the Messenger of Allah ﷺ commanded us to do it. Then nothing was revealed to supersede it and the Messenger of Allah ﷺ did not forbid us to do it before he died. Afterwards a man would say whatever he wished about it based on his own opinion.' At-Tirmidhī related from Qutaybah ibn Sa'īd from Mālik ibn Anas from Ibn Shihāb from Muḥammad ibn 'Abdullāh ibn al-Ḥārith ibn Nawfal who, in the year that Mu'āwiyah ibn Abī Sufyān made ḥajj, heard Sa'd ibn Abī Waqqāṣ and aḍ-Ḍaḥḥāk ibn Qays mentioning *tamattu'*, *'umrah* joined to ḥajj. Aḍ-Ḍaḥḥāk ibn Qays said, 'He only did that out of ignorance of Allah's command!' Sa'd retorted. 'What you have said is bad, nephew!' Aḍ-Ḍaḥḥāk said, "Umar ibn al-Khaṭṭāb forbade that!' Sa'd answered, 'The Messenger of Allah ﷺ did it and we did it with him.' This is a sound *ḥadīth*.

Ibn Isḥāq related from az-Zuhrī that Sālim said, 'I was sitting in the mosque with Ibn 'Umar when a man from Syria came and asked him about *tamattu'*. Ibn 'Umar said, "Fine and good." The man said, "Your father used to forbid it." Ibn

'Umar retorted, "Woe to you! If my father forbade it, the Messenger of Allah ﷺ did it and commanded it to be done. Should I take the position of my father or the command of the Messenger of Allah ﷺ? Leave me."' Ad-Dāraquṭnī transmitted it, and Abū 'Īsā at-Tirmidhī transmitted it from the *ḥadīth* of Ṣāliḥ ibn Kaysān from Ibn Shihāb from Sālim. It is related from Layth from Ṭāwūs that Ibn 'Abbās said, 'The Messenger of Allah ﷺ, Abū Bakr, 'Umar and 'Uthmān performed *tamattu'*. Mu'āwiyah was the first to forbid it.' It is a *ḥasan ḥadīth*. Abū 'Umar said that this *ḥadīth* of Layth is *munkar*. He is Layth ibn Abī Sulaym and is weak. What is well known is that 'Umar and 'Uthmān forbade *tamattu'*.

One group of scholars claim that the form of *tamattu'* that 'Umar forbade and nullified was to add ḥajj to *'umrah*. That was not the case in adding *'umrah* to ḥajj. Those who say that it is correct that 'Umar forbade *tamattu'* state that he forbade it so that people would seek their provision at the House twice or more in the same year so that there would be more visitors to it outside the Festival. He wanted to be kind to the people of the Ḥaram in respect of people's visits, to bring about the supplication of Ibrāhīm: *'Make the hearts of mankind incline towards them.'* (14:37) Others say that he forbade it because he saw that people were inclining to *tamattu'* because it was easy and he feared that *ifrād* and *qirān* would be lost when they are two sunnahs of the Prophet ﷺ. In defence of his preference for *tamattu'*, Aḥmad cited the words of the Prophet ﷺ: 'Had I known what I know now, I would not have brought sacrificial camels and I would have made it *'umrah*.' The imams have transmitted it.

Others prefer *qirān*, and they include Abū Ḥanīfah and ath-Thawrī. Al-Muzanī said that the reason for that it is that it is performing two obligations together. That is what Isḥāq said. Isḥāq said, 'The Messenger of Allah ﷺ did *qirān*, and it is the position of 'Alī ibn Abī Ṭālib. The argument for those who recommend and prefer *qirān* is what al-Bukhārī related from 'Umar ibn al-Khaṭṭāb. He said, 'I heard the Messenger of Allah ﷺ say in the valley of 'Aqīq, "In the night someone came to me from my Lord and said, 'Pray in this blessed valley and say, "*'Umrah* in *ḥajj*."'" At-Tirmidhī related that Anas heard the Messenger of Allah ﷺ say, 'At Your service for *'umrah* and ḥajj.' He said that it is a sound *ḥasan ḥadīth*.

Abū 'Umar said, 'Allah willing, *ifrād* is better because the Messenger of Allah ﷺ did *ifrād*. That is why we say that *ifrād* is better. The traditions about his *ifrād* are sounder because *ifrād* has more actions and *'umrah* is another action." Abū Ja'far an-Naḥḥās said, '*Ifrād* has more followers than *tamattu'* because one remains in *iḥrām*. That has a greater reward.' The way that the *ḥadīth*s are brought into agreement with one another is that because the Messenger of Allah ﷺ commanded *ifrād* and *qirān*, it is permitted to say that Messenger of Allah ﷺ did *tamattuʿ* and *qirān* in the same way that Allah says: *'Pharaoh called to his people.'* (43:51) 'Umar ibn al-Khaṭṭāb said, 'We stoned and the Messenger of Allah ﷺ stoned. He commanded stoning.'

What is most evident is that the ḥajj of the Prophet ﷺ was *qirān*. He performed *qirān* according to the *ḥadīth*s of 'Umar ibn al-Khaṭṭāb and Anas that we have mentioned. We find in *Ṣaḥīḥ Muslim* from Bakr that Anas said, 'I heard the Prophet ﷺ say the *talbiyyah* for *ḥajj* and *'umrah* together.' Bakr said, 'I related that to Ibn 'Umar and he said, "He said the *talbiyyah* for ḥajj alone." I met Anas and told him what Ibn 'Umar had said and Anas said, "You are treating us as children! I heard the Messenger of Allah ﷺ say, 'At Your service for *'umrah* and ḥajj!'"' We also find in *Ṣaḥīḥ Muslim* that Ibn 'Abbās said, 'The Prophet ﷺ adopted *iḥrām* for *'umrah* and the people adopted *iḥrām* for ḥajj. Neither the Prophet ﷺ nor his Companions who had brought sacrificial camels came out of *iḥrām* while the rest of them did.' Some of the people of knowledge say that the Messenger of Allah ﷺ did *qirān*. When he did *qirān*, he did ḥajj and *'umrah*. Therefore the *ḥadīth*s agree.

An-Naḥḥās said, 'Part of the best of what is said about this is that the Messenger of Allah ﷺ adopted *iḥrām* for *'umrah* and those who saw him said, "He is performing *tamattuʿ*." Then he adopted *iḥrām* for ḥajj and those who saw him said, "He is performing *ifrād*." Then he said, "At Your service for ḥajj and *'umrah*." Those who heard him said, "*Qirān*." So the *ḥadīth*s agree. The evidence for this is that no one related that the Prophet ﷺ said, "I did ḥajj *ifrād*" or "I did *tamattuʿ*." It is, however, valid that he said, "I did *qirān*," as an-Nasā'ī related from 'Alī. He said, "I went to the Messenger of Allah ﷺ and he asked me, 'What did you do?' I answered, 'I adopted *iḥrām* according to your *iḥrām*.' He said, 'I have brought sacrificial camels and am doing *qirān*.'" He said that he remarked to his Companions, "Had I known what I know now, I would have done what you did, but I have brought sacrificial camels and am performing *qirān*." It is confirmed that Ḥafṣah said, 'I said, "Messenger of Allah, why have people come out of their *iḥrām* when you have not?" He answered, "I matted my hair and drove my sacrificial animals and so I will not come out of *iḥrām* until you slaughter."' This makes it clear that he was doing *qirān* because if he had been doing *tamattuʿ* or *ifrād*, he would not have been prevented from slaughtering the sacrifices.

An-Naḥḥās mentioned that no one related that the Prophet ﷺ said, 'I did ḥajj *ifrād*', while it is related that 'Ā'ishah said that he said, 'I have assumed *iḥrām* for ḥajj.' This means that he was doing *ifrād* although it is possible that he had assumed *iḥrām* for *'umrah* and then said, 'I have assumed *iḥrām* for ḥajj.' Part of what clarifies this is what Muslim related from Ibn 'Umar: 'The Messenger of

Allah ﷺ began and adopted *iḥrām* for *'umrah* and then adopted *iḥrām* for ḥajj.' So his words about adopting *iḥrām* for ḥajj are not evidence for *ifrād*. His words, 'I am doing *qirān*' remain. Anas, his servant, said that he heard him say, 'At Your service for ḥajj and *'umrah* together.' This is a clear text for *qirān* not subject to interpretation. Ad-Dāraquṭnī related from 'Abdullāh ibn Abī Qatādah that his father said, 'The Messenger of Allah ﷺ combined ḥajj and *'umrah* because he knew that he would not perform ḥajj after that.'

As we stated, *ifrād*, *tamattu'* and *qirān* are all permitted by consensus. According to scholars, there are four forms of *tamattu'*. There is agreement about one of them and disagreement about the other three. The one on which there is agreement is the *tamattu'* meant by the words of the Almighty: *'Anyone who comes out of iḥrām between 'umrah and ḥajj should make whatever sacrifice is feasible.'* That is when a man adopts *iḥrām* for *'umrah* in the months of ḥajj, as will be explained, and is not from Makkah. He comes to Makkah and finishes it and then remains in Makkah, not in *iḥrām,* until the ḥajj begins in that year before he has returned home or before he goes to the *mīqāt* of the people of his region. When he does that, he is performing *tamattu'* and owes what Allah has obliged for someone performing *tamattu'*: a feasible sacrifice which he slaughters and gives to the poor at Minā or Makkah. If he cannot do that, then he fasts for three days and seven when he returns home. There is consensus that he does not fast on the Day of Sacrifice. There is disagreement about fasting the days of Tashrīq.

This is the consensus of the people of knowledge, past and present, about *tamattu'*. It has eight preconditions. The first is that someone combines ḥajj and *'umrah.* The second is that it is on the same journey. The third is that is in the same year. The fourth is that it is in the months of ḥajj. The fifth is that *'umrah* is done first. The sixth is that it is not mixed, but the *iḥrām* for ḥajj comes after finishing *'umrah.* The seventh is that both *'umrah* and ḥajj are for the same person, and the eighth is that he is not from Makkah. If you reflect, you will see that these are preconditions for the ruling of *tamattu'*.

The second form of *tamattu'* is basically *qirān.* It is that someone combines them in the same *iḥrām* and assumes *iḥrām* for both of them together in the months of ḥajj or some other time. He says, 'At Your service for both ḥajj and *'umrah.*' When he reaches Makkah, he does one *ṭawāf* for his ḥajj and *'umrah* and one *sa'y* for both according to those who think that it can be done. They are Mālik, ash-Shāfi'ī and their people, Isḥāq and Abū Thawr. It is the school of 'Abdullāh ibn 'Umar, Jābir ibn 'Abdullāh, 'Aṭā' ibn Abī Rabāḥ, al-Ḥasan, Mujāhid and Ṭāwūs, based on the *ḥadīth* of 'Ā'ishah: 'We went out with the Messenger of Allah ﷺ on the Farewell

Ḥajj and we adopted *iḥrām* for *'umrah…'* It says in it, 'Those who combined ḥajj and *'umrah* did one *ṭawāf*.' Al-Bukhārī transmitted it. On the Day of Nafr, he ﷺ said to 'Ā'ishah when she had not done *ṭawāf* of the House and menstruated, 'Your *ṭawāf* and *sa'y* are for both your ḥajj and *'umrah*.' One variant has: 'Your going between Ṣafā and Marwah satisfies both your ḥajj and *'umrah*.' Muslim transmitted it.

Or one does two *ṭawāf*s and two *sa'y*s according to the opinion of those who think that, namely Abū Ḥanīfah and his people, ath-Thawrī, al-Awzā'ī, al-Ḥasan ibn Ṣāliḥ and Ibn Abī Laylā. It is related from 'Alī and Ibn Mas'ūd. That is the view of ash-Sha'bī and Jābir ibn Zayd. They argue by the *ḥadīth*s about 'Alī combining ḥajj and *'umrah* and doing two *ṭawāf*s and two *sa'y*s for them. Then he said, 'That is how I saw the Messenger of Allah ﷺ act.' Ad-Dāraquṭnī transmitted both of them in his *Sunan* and considered them weak. He made *qirān* part of *tamattu'* because the one doing *qirān* is enjoying (*tamatta'a*) lack of fatigue in travelling to perform *'umrah* once and to perform ḥajj once, and enjoying combining them. He does not have to assume *iḥrām* for each of them from his *mīqāt*. By adding ḥajj to *'umrah* he falls under the words of the Almighty: *'Anyone who comes out of iḥrām between 'umrah and ḥajj should make whatever sacrifice is feasible.'*

This is a form of *tamattu'* that is permitted by scholars without any dispute. The people of Madīnah do not permit joining *'umrah* and ḥajj unless the person brings a sacrificial camel with him. They believe that it must be a camel and nothing less. Part of what indicates that *qirān* is *tamattu'* is the view of Ibn 'Umar. He made *tamattu'* exclusively for the people of all regions [outside Makkah] and recited: *'That is for anyone whose family does not live near the Masjid al-Ḥaram.'* Therefore anyone who lives in the vicinity of the Masjid al-Ḥaram and does *tamattu'* or *qirān* does not owe the sacrifice of *tamattu'* or *qirān*. Mālik said, 'I have not heard of a Makkan doing *qirān*. If he were to do it, he would not owe a sacrifice or fasting.' Most *fuqahā'* take Mālik's view regarding that. 'Abd al-Malik ibn al-Mājishūn said, 'When a Makkan does *qirān* of ḥajj with *'umrah*, he does not owe the sacrifice for *qirān* because Allah has cancelled sacrifice and fasting in *tamattu'* for the people of Makkah.'

The third form of *tamattu'* is the one which 'Umar ibn al-Khaṭṭāb threatened. He said, 'I forbid two types of *tamattu'* that were done in the time of the Messenger of Allah ﷺ and I will punish people for them: the *mu'tah* [marriage] with women and the *mu'tah* of ḥajj.' Scholars disagree about the permissibility of this. It is that a man adopts *iḥrām* for ḥajj and then, when he enters Makkah, his ḥajj is changed into *'umrah*. Then he comes out of *iḥrām* and remains so until he adopts *iḥrām* on the Day of Tarwīyah. This is the form which is reported by multiple transmissions from the Prophet ﷺ. In his ḥajj, he ordered those who did not have sacrifices with them and had adopted *iḥrām* for ḥajj to make *it 'umrah.* Scholars agree on the soundness of the traditions that report that from him ﷺ. They did not reject any of them, but they disagree about taking it and acting on it. Most of them believe that it is not acted on because they believe that it was a specific case which the Messenger of Allah ﷺ made for his Companions on that ḥajj. Abū Dharr said, 'The *mut'ah* for us was specifically on that ḥajj.' Muslim transmitted it. One version has: 'Two *mu'tah*s were allowed only to us specifically,' meaning the *mu'tah* with women and the *mu'tah* of ḥajj.

The pretext for its being special and the benefit in it is in what Ibn 'Abbās said: 'They used to think that *'umrah* during the months of ḥajj was one of the most heinous actions anyone could do. They would consider al-Muḥarram to be Ṣafar and would say, 'When the wounds on the back of the camel heal and the scar has gone and Ṣafar has passed, then *'umrah* is lawful for anyone who wants to perform it." The Prophet ﷺ and his Companions arrived on the morning of the fourth of Dhu-l-Ḥijjah, having adopted *iḥrām* for the *ḥajj* and he told them to make it an *'umrah.* They thought that extraordinary and said, "Messenger of Allah, what sort of coming out of *iḥrām* is it?" He said, "A total coming out of *iḥrām.*"' Muslim transmitted it. We find with a sound *isnād* of Abū Ḥātim that Ibn 'Abbās said, 'By Allah, the Messenger of Allah ﷺ told 'Ā'ishah to perform *'umrah* in Dhu-l-Ḥijjah in order by that to cut off the business of the people of *shirk.* This clan of Quraysh and those near them used to say, "When the wounds on the back of the camel heal and the scar has gone and Ṣafar has passed, then *'umrah* is lawful for anyone who wants to perform it." They used to go into *iḥrām* for *'umrah* when Dhu-l-Ḥijjah had passed. The Messenger of Allah ﷺ told 'Ā'ishah to perform *'umrah* to annul that position of theirs.'

This contains proof that the Messenger of Allah ﷺ incorporated the *'umrah* into the ḥajj to show them that there was nothing wrong in performing *'umrah* in the months of ḥajj. That was something specifically for him and those with him because Allah Almighty issued a general command that whoever starts ḥajj or *'umrah* should complete them. One does not oppose the literal text of the Book of Allah, except in favour of something in the Book of Allah or a clarifying sunnah that abrogates it without ambiguity. Their argument is what we mentioned from Abū Dharr as well as the *ḥadīth* of al-Ḥārith ibn Bilāl whose father said, 'We said, "Messenger of Allah, is the casting off of ḥajj something particularly for us or is it for people in general?" He replied, "It is particularly for us."' This is the position of the majority of the *fuqahā'* of the Hijaz, Iraq and Syria except for something related from Ibn 'Abbās, al-Ḥasan and as-Suddī.

Aḥmad ibn Ḥanbal stated it and said, 'I will not deny those sound multiple transmissions of reports which come about casting ḥajj into *'umrah* based on the *ḥadīth* of al-Ḥārith ibn Bilāl from his father and the position of Abū Dharr.' He did not make it particular. Aḥmad argued by the sound long *ḥadīth* of Jābir about the ḥajj. We find in it: 'Had I known what I know now, I would not have brought sacrificial camels and I would have made it *'umrah.*' Surāqah ibn Mālik ibn Ju'shum stood up and said, 'Messenger of Allah, is it specifically for this year or is it forever?' The Messenger of ﷺ intertwined his fingers together and said twice, '*'Umrah* has been incorporated into ḥajj.'

By Allah, I know that it is to this that al-Bukhārī inclined when he entitled a chapter: 'Someone saying *talbiyyah* for ḥajj and specifying it.' He gives the *ḥadīth* of Jābir ibn 'Abdullāh: 'We came with the Messenger of Allah ﷺ saying, "At Your service, O Allah, for the ḥajj." The Messenger of Allah ﷺ instructed us to make it *'umrah.*' Some people said that the command by the Messenger of Allah ﷺ to come out of *iḥrām* came by a different path which Mujāhid mentioned: 'The Companions of the Messenger of Allah ﷺ did not make the ḥajj obligatory first. He commanded them to come completely out of *iḥrām* and to wait for what they were commanded. That is the same with the *iḥrām* of 'Alī in Yemen and the same with the *iḥrām* of the Messenger of Allah ﷺ. It is indicated by his words, 'Had I known what I know now, I would not have brought sacrificial camels and I would have made it *'umrah.*' So it is as if he ﷺ went out waiting for what he was commanded and then commanded his Companions to do that. That is also indicated by his words, 'In the night someone came to me from my Lord and said, "Pray in this blessed valley and say, '*'Umrah* in *ḥajj.*'"'

The fourth form of *tamattu'* is that of someone who is prevented from reaching the House. Ya'qūb ibn Shaybah mentioned from Abū Salamah at-Tabūdhakī from Wuhayb from Isḥāq ibn Suwayd who heard 'Abdullāh ibn az-Zubayr say in a *khuṭbah*: 'People! By Allah, *tamattu'*, joining *'umrah* into ḥajj, is not as you do, but *tamattu'* is that a man sets out on ḥajj and is detained by the enemy until the days of ḥajj have passed. Then he reaches the House and does *ṭawāf* and runs between Ṣafā and Marwah and then enjoys being out of *iḥrām* until the following year when he performs ḥajj and sacrifices.'

Someone hindered by the enemy has already been dealt with. An element of his position is that someone hindered does not come out of *iḥrām*, but rather remains in it until he slaughters the sacrifice on the Day of Sacrifice. Then he shaves but remains in *iḥrām* until he reaches Makkah and then comes out of *iḥrām* for ḥajj by the actions of *'umrah*. What Ibn az-Zubayr mentioned is counter to the undefined nature of this *āyah*. Allah did not make a distinction between ḥajj and *'umrah* in the ruling of someone prevented from completing it. When the Prophet ﷺ and his Companions were stopped at Ḥudaybīyah, they came out *iḥrām* as he did. He commanded them to do so.

Scholars also disagree about the reason for saying that someone is doing *tamattu'*. Ibn al-Qāsim said that he is called that because he can enjoy (*tamatta'a*) all that it is not permitted for someone in *iḥrām* to do from the time he comes out of his *iḥrām* until he starts ḥajj. Others say that he is called that because he enjoys not having to make one of two journeys as it is the due of *'umrah* to be the object of a journey and the same is true of ḥajj. When he enjoys the cancellation of one of them, then he owes a sacrifice to Allah as is also the case with someone doing *qirān* who combines ḥajj and *'umrah* in the same journey. The first position is more universal: he can enjoy all that someone not in *iḥrām* can do and he does not have to make another journey from his land to perform ḥajj, and he does not have to return to his *mīqāt* to adopt *iḥrām* from for ḥajj.

This is what 'Umar and Ibn Mas'ūd disliked. One or both of them said, 'One of you comes to Minā with his penis dripping with semen.' However, the Muslims agree that that is permitted. A group of scholars said that 'Umar disliked it because he preferred to visit the House twice in the year: once on ḥajj and once for *'umrah*. He thought that *ifrād* was better and commanded it and inclined to it. His forbidding other forms of ḥajj was a recommendation. That is why he said, 'Separate your ḥajj and your *'umrah*. It is more complete for your ḥajj to do that; and it is more complete for your *'umrah* to perform it outside of the months of ḥajj.'

Scholars disagree about someone who performs *'umrah* in the month of ḥajj, returns home to his house and then performs ḥajj in the same year. Most scholars say that in that case he is not performing *tamattu'* and does not owe a sacrifice or fasting. Al-Ḥasan al-Baṣrī, however, said that he is performing *tamattu'* if he returns to his family, whether or not he performs ḥajj. He stated that it is because *'umrah* during the months of ḥajj is necessarily *tamattu'*. Hushaym related that from Yūnus from al-Ḥasan. He also related from Yūnus from al-Ḥasan that the person doing that does not owe a sacrifice. The sound position is the first one. That is what was stated by Abū 'Umar: '...whether or not he performs ḥajj.' Ibn al-Mundhir did not mention it, but said that his ḥajj is based on the literal words of the Book: *'Anyone who comes out of iḥrām between 'umrah and ḥajj...'*. There is no exception made for someone who returns to his family or does not return. If Allah had intended that, He would have explained it in His Book or on the tongue of His Messenger ﷺ.

A similar position to that of al-Ḥasan is related from Saʿīd ibn al-Musayyab. Abū ʿUmar said, 'Also related from al-Ḥasan regarding this topic is a position that no one follows and none of the people of knowledge adopt. He said that someone who performs *ʿumrah* on the Day of Sacrifice is doing *tamattuʿ*. Two views are related from Ṭāwūs that are even more aberrant than what we have mentioned from al-Ḥasan. One is that someone who performs *ʿumrah* outside the months of ḥajj, then stays until the time of ḥajj and does ḥajj in the same year, is performing *tamattuʿ*. He is the only scholar to say this and none of the *fuqahā'* of any region believe it. Allah knows best, but that is because the months of ḥajj are more proper for ḥajj than they are for *ʿumrah* because *ʿumrah* is permitted throughout the entire year. The place of the ḥajj is in known months. If someone does *ʿumrah* in the months of ḥajj, he has put it in a place to which ḥajj is more entitled, although in His Book and on the tongue of His Messenger ﷺ Allah made an allowance for doing *ʿumrah* in the months of ḥajj if someone is performing *tamattuʿ* or *qirān*, and for someone who does *ifrād*, out of mercy from Him. He assigned a feasible sacrifice for doing it. The other form is what is said about a Makkan when he does *tamattuʿ* from one the regions: he owes a sacrifice. One does not turn to this because of the literal meaning of His words: *"That is for anyone whose family does not live near the Masjid al-Ḥaram."*' One group of scholars permit *tamattuʿ* with the preconditions we have explained. Success is by Allah.

Scholars agree that if a man, who is not from the people of Makkah, performs *ʿumrah* in the months of ḥajj with the resolve to remain there and then begins ḥajj in that year, that *is tamattuʿ*, and he owes what someone performing *tamattuʿ* owes. They agree that when a Makkan comes from outside the *mīqāt* in *iḥrām* for *ʿumrah* and then begins ḥajj from Makkah while his family is in Makkah and it is his only residence, he owes no sacrifice. That is also the case if he lives elsewhere as well as living there and has family both in Makkah and outside of Makkah. They agree that if he moves with his family from Makkah and then comes performing *ʿumrah* in the months of ḥajj and stays there until ḥajj that year, he is performing *tamattuʿ*.

Mālik, ash-Shāfiʿī, Abū Ḥanīifah and their people, ath-Thawrī and Abū Thawr agree that someone performing *tamattuʿ* does *ṭawāf* of the House for *ʿumrah* and runs between Ṣafā and Marwah and after that does another *ṭawāf* and *saʿy* for ḥajj. It is related from ʿAṭā' and Ṭāwūs that it is enough to do one *saʿy* between Ṣafā and Marwah. They disagree about someone who starts his *ʿumrah* outside the months of ḥajj and then finishes it during the months of ḥajj. Mālik said that his *'umrah* is in the month in which it occurred. He means that if it occurs outside the months of ḥajj, it is not *tamattu'*, but if it occurs in the months of ḥajj, then he is performing *tamattu'* if he does ḥajj in the same year. Ash-Shāfi'ī said, 'If someone does *ṭawāf* of the House in the months of ḥajj, he is performing *tamattu'* if he performs ḥajj in the same year.' That is because *'umrah* is completed by *ṭawāf* of the House. One considers its completion. That is the view of al-Ḥasan al-Baṣrī, al-Ḥakam ibn 'Uyaynah Ibn Shurumah and Sufyān ath-Thawrī.

Qatādah, Aḥmad and Isḥāq said that his *'umrah* is attached to the month in which he assumed *iḥrām*. That idea is also related from Jābir ibn 'Abdullāh. Ṭāwūs said that his *'umrah* is attached to the month in which he enters the Ḥaram. The People of Opinion said that if someone does four circuits of *ṭawāf* in Ramadan and three in Shawwāl, he is not doing *tamattu'*. Abū Thawr said, 'If he starts *'umrah* outside of the months of ḥajj, it is the same whether he does *ṭawāf* in Ramadan or in Shawwāl: he is not doing *tamattu'* in this *'umrah*.' That is the meaning of the statement of Aḥmad and Isḥāq: his *'umrah* is attached to the month in which he assumes *iḥrām*.

The people of knowledge agree that someone who adopts *iḥrām* for *'umrah* in the months of ḥajj and does not add ḥajj to it until he begins *ṭawāf* of the House is by that token doing *qirān*. He is under the same obligation as that of someone who begins ḥajj and *'umrah* together. They disagree about adding ḥajj to *'umrah* after he has begun *ṭawāf*. Mālik said, 'That binds him and he becomes someone performing *qirān* as long as he has not finished *ṭawāf*.' Something similar is related from Abū Ḥanīfah. It is well known from him that it is only permitted to add ḥajj before he begins *ṭawāf*. It was said that he can add ḥajj to *'umrah* as long as he has not prayed the two *rak'ahs* of *ṭawāf*. All of that is the position of Mālik and his people.

If someone performing *'umrah* has done one circuit for his *'umrah* and then adopts *iḥrām* for ḥajj, he is performing *qirān*; the rest of his *'umrah* is cancelled for him and he owes the sacrifice of *qirān*. That is also the case if someone adopts *iḥrām* for ḥajj during *ṭawāf* or after it but before praying the two *rak'ahs*. Some of them say that he can add ḥajj to *'umrah* as long as he has not completed *sa'y* between Ṣafā and Marwah. Abū 'Umar said, 'The people of knowledge consider all of this aberrant.' Ashhab said, 'When he has done one circuit for *'umrah*, he is not obliged to adopt *iḥrām* and he is not doing *qirān*. He continues with his *'umrah* until he finishes it and then adopts *iḥrām* for ḥajj. This is the view of ash-Shāfi'ī and 'Aṭā'. Abū Thawr also said that.'

They disagree about adding *'umrah* to ḥajj. Mālik, Abū Thawr and Isḥāq said that *'umrah* may not be added to ḥajj, and if someone adds *'umrah* to ḥajj, it counts for nothing. Mālik said that and it is one of the views of ash-Shāfi'ī. It was known from him in Egypt. Abū Ḥanīfah and his people and ash-Shāfi'ī in his old school says that he becomes someone performing *qirān* and owes what he owes as long as he has not done one circuit of his *ṭawāf* for ḥajj. He cannot do it if he has done *ṭawāf* because he has done his ḥajj. Ibn al-Mundhir said, 'I take the view of Mālik regarding this question.'

Mālik said, 'If someone has slaughtered an animal for *'umrah* and is performing *tamattu'*, that does not cover what he owes. He owes another sacrifice for *tamattu'* because that is what he is doing when he begins ḥajj after he has come out of *iḥrām* for *'umrah*: a sacrifice is obliged for him. Abū Ḥanīfah, Abū Thawr and Isḥāq said that he should only slaughter his sacrifice on the Day of Sacrifice. Aḥmad said, 'If someone doing *tamattu'* arrives before the tenth, he does *ṭawāf*, *sa'y* and sacrifices. If he comes in the ten days, then he only sacrifices on the Day of Sacrifice.' 'Aṭā' said that. Ash-Shāfi'ī said, 'He comes out of *iḥrām* for *'umrah* when he does *ṭawāf* and *sa'y* whether or not he bas brought a sacrificial animal.'

Mālik and ash-Shāfi'ī disagree about what happens when someone doing *tamattu'* dies. Ash-Shāfi'ī said, 'When he adopts *iḥrām* for ḥajj, then he owes the sacrifice of *tamattu'* if he can afford that.' Az-Za'frānī related it from him. Ibn Wahb related that Mālik was asked whether someone performing *tamattu'*, who dies at 'Arafah or elsewhere after having adopted *iḥrām* for ḥajj, owed a sacrifice. He said, 'If anyone dies before stoning the Jamrat al-'Aqabah, I do not think that he owes a sacrifice. If someone stones the Jamrat al-'Aqabah and then dies, he owes a sacrifice.' He was asked if it was paid from the capital or from the third [for bequests] and said that it was paid from the capital.

**For any one who cannot, there is three days' fast on ḥajj and seven on your return – that is ten in all.**

Anyone who should sacrifice but is unable to do so due to lack of money or lack of animals, must fast for three days during the ḥajj and seven when he returns home. The three days are the three days up to and including the Day of 'Arafah. This is the position of Ṭāwūs and it is related from ash-Sha'bī, 'Aṭā', Mujāhid, al-Ḥasan al-Baṣrī, an-Nakha'ī, Sa'īd ibn Jubayr, 'Alqamah, 'Amr ibn Dīnār and the People of Opinion. Ibn al-Mundhir related it. Abū Thawr reports that Abū Ḥanīfah says that a person may also fast the prescribed days during the time he is in *iḥrām* for *'umrah* because it is one of the two *iḥrām*s of *tamattu'* and so it is permitted to fast these days in the *iḥrām* for *'umrah* in the same way as it is in the *iḥrām* for ḥajj. It is also reported from Abū Ḥanīfah and his people that the day before the day of Tarwiyah (7th Dhu-l-Ḥijjah) should be fasted, then the Day of Tarwiyah and then the Day of 'Arafah.

Ibn 'Abbās and Mālik ibn Anas say that the three days may be fasted at any time from the time someone assumes *iḥrām* for ḥajj until the Day of Sacrifice because Allah says: '*three day's fast on ḥajj*'. If they are fasted on *'umrah*, it is before the time and so it is not allowed. Ash-Shāfi'ī and Ibn Ḥanbal say that the days may be fasted at any time between adopting *iḥrām* for ḥajj up until the day of 'Arafah, which is the position of Ibn 'Umar and 'Ā'ishah. This is also related from Mālik and is stated in the *Muwaṭṭā'*, and it is in order to avoid fasting on the Day of 'Arafah. That is following the Sunnah and more conducive to worship. Aḥmad also said that it is possible to fast the three days before adopting *iḥrām* (but during Dhu-l-Ḥijjah). Ath-Thawrī and al-Awzā'ī said that the days may be fasted from the beginning of the first ten days of Dhu-l-Ḥijjah. 'Aṭā' said that. 'Urwah said that the days may be fasted as long as one remains in Makkah and during the days of Minā, and Mālik and a group of the people of Madīnah also took that view.

The days of Minā are the three days of Tashrīq following the Day of Sacrifice. Mālik related in the *Muwaṭṭā'* that 'Ā'ishah, the Mother of the Believers, said, 'Someone performing *tamattu'*, who does not have a sacrificial animal, should fast [three days] during the period from the time he adopts *iḥrām* for the ḥajj till the Day of 'Arafah, and if he does not fast then, should fast the days of Minā.' These words show that it is good to fast between the time one adopts *iḥrām* for ḥajj *tamattu'* until the Day of 'Arafah. He begins then, either because it is the proper time to do them, and the days of Minā after that are the time of making them up, as the people of ash-Shāfi'ī say, or it is because doing the fasting before the Day of Sacrifice exonerates the person, and that is commanded. What is most apparent in the School is that doing that fulfils the requirement, even though fasting before it is better. It is like the latitude of the time of the prayer: the beginning of the time is better than the end of it. This is the sound position: it is performing the duty, not making it up.

*'Three days fast on ḥajj'* can refer to the locus of the ḥajj or the time of the ḥajj. If it means the actual days, this is a sound view because the last of the days of ḥajj is the Day of Sacrifice. It is also possible, however, that the last of the days are the days of stoning because stoning is one of the actions of the ḥajj in particular even if it is not one of its pillars. If what is meant is the locus of the ḥajj, he may fast the days as long as he is at Makkah during the days of Minā as 'Urwah said and greatly stresses. Some people said that a person may delay starting them until the

days of Tashrīq because fasting only becomes obligatory for him when he does not find a sacrifice on the Day of Sacrifice.

A group of the people of Madīnah and ash-Shāfi'ī in his New School as well as most of his people believe that it is not permitted to fast the days of Minā because the Messenger of Allah ﷺ forbade fasting them. The response to that is that if the prohibition is confirmed, it is general but was qualified by the fact of its permissibility for someone who is performing *tamattu'*, since it is confirmed in al-Bukhārī that 'Ā'ishah fasted them. Ibn 'Umar and 'Ā'ishah both said that there is no allowance to fast the days of Tashrīq unless someone has not brought sacrifices. Ad-Dāraquṭnī said that its *isnād* is sound. It is related *marfū'* from Ibn 'Umar and 'Ā'ishah via three paths of transmission which he considers to be weak. There is an allowance to fast them because only they remain of the days of ḥajj. Therefore it is mandatory for those without sacrificial animals to fast them. Ibn al-Mundhir related that 'Alī ibn Abī Ṭālib said, 'If someone fails to fast before, then he should fast after the days of Tashrīq.' Al-Ḥasan and 'Aṭā' said that. Ibn al-Mundhir said, 'That is what we say.' One group say that if he fails to fast during the ten, then nothing but a sacrifice will satisfy the requirement. That is related from Ibn 'Abbās, Sa'īd ibn Jubayr, Ṭāwūs, and Mujāhid. Abū 'Umar related it from Abū Ḥanīfah and his people. Reflect on it.

Scholars agree that there is no way for someone performing *tamattu'* to fast if he is able to sacrifice. They disagree about what should happen when he does not find a sacrifice and so fasts, but then finds a sacrifice before his fast is complete. Ibn Wahb mentioned that Mālik said, 'When he begins the fast and then finds a sacrifice, I prefer him to sacrifice. If he does not, the fast satisfies the requirement.' Ash-Shāfi'ī said, 'He continues the fast. It is his obligation.' That is also what Abū Thawr says and it is the view of al-Ḥasan and Qatādah. Ibn al-Mundhir preferred it. Abū Ḥanīifah said, 'If it becomes feasible on the third day of the fast, the fast is void and he must sacrifice. If he fasts three days in the ḥajj and then it becomes feasible, he can fast seven days and does not return to sacrifice.' Ath-Thawrī, Ibn Abī Najīḥ and Ḥammād said that.

The words *'your return'* mean when you return to your country as Ibn 'Umar, Qatādah, ar-Rabī', Mujāhid and 'Aṭā' said. Mālik said that in the book of Muḥammad and ash-Shāfi'ī stated that. Qatādah and ar-Rabī' said, 'This is a dispensation from Allah Almighty. No one is obliged to fast the seven until he returns home unless there is a very strong reason, as is the case with someone who fasts while travelling in Ramadan. Aḥmad and Isḥāq said that fasting on the road satisfies the requirement. This is also related from Mujāhid and 'Aṭā'. Mujāhid said, 'If he wishes, he can fast on the road. This is a dispensation.' That is similar to what 'Ikrimah and al-Ḥasan said. However, some linguists say that the the phrase refers to when you leave *iḥrām* and return to the state you were in before. Mālik said, 'When someone has returned from Minā, there is nothing wrong in fasting then.' Ibn al-'Arabī said, 'It is a lightening and allowance. The consensus is that is permitted to bring forward the allowance and abandon the kindness in favour of resolve. If that has a time, there is no text on it and nothing explicit about it meaning a person's own country, although that is what is normally understood.'

There is, however, something evident, which is close to a clarifying text, in Ibn 'Umar's words: 'The Messenger of Allah ﷺ did *tamattu'* in the Farewell Ḥajj, with *'umrah* to ḥajj, and sacrificed. He drove the sacrificial camels with him from Dhu-l-Ḥulayfah. The Messenger of Allah ﷺ first went into *iḥrām* for *'umrah* and then *iḥrām* for ḥajj. People did *tamattu'* with the Messenger of Allah ﷺ. Some people brought sacrificial camels with them and some did not. When the Messenger of Allah ﷺ reached Makkah, he said to the people, "Any of you who have sacrificial camels, should not make lawful anything that was unlawful for you until you finish your ḥajj. Those of you who do not have sacrificial animals should do *ṭawāf* of the House, go between Ṣafā and Marwah, shorten their hair and come out of *iḥrām*. Then they should adopt *iḥrām* for ḥajj and sacrifice. Those who do not find any way to sacrifice should fast for three days on ḥajj and seven when they return to their family."' This is like a text for it not being permitted to fast the seven days except in one's own country and family. Allah knows best.

That is similar to what al-Bukhārī reported from Ibn 'Abbās: 'Then on the eve of Tarwīyah he told us to go into *iḥrām* for ḥajj. When we finished the rites, we came and did *ṭawāf* of the House and did *sa'y* between Ṣafā and Marwah. Our ḥajj was complete and we had to sacrifice, in compliance with the words of Allah Almighty: *"...he should make whatever sacrifice is feasible. For anyone who cannot, there is three days' fast on ḥajj and seven on your return."* (2:196)' An-Naḥḥās said that this is the consensus.

There is disagreement about the meaning of the words *'that is ten in all'*. It is known that it is ten. Az-Zajjāj said, 'Since it is conceivable to imagine that there is a choice between three days on ḥajj or seven when he returns home instead of them since He did not say, "another seven", He removed that possibility by saying, *"that is ten"* and then said "in all" (*kāmilah*). Al-Ḥasan said that he is 'complete' in respect of the reward, just like someone who did not do *tamattu'*. It is said that it is an expression which is in the form of a report while a command is meant. It means: 'Complete them: that is the obligation.' Al Mubarrad said that 'ten' indicates the ten of the number so that it is not imagined that there is anything further after the seven. It is said that it is for stress.

**That is for anyone whose family does not live near the Masjid al-Ḥarām.**

A sacrifice is required from anyone not resident in the Ḥaram who performs *tamattu'*. Al-Bukhārī related that Ibn 'Abbās was asked about ḥajj *tamattu'* and said, 'The Muhājirūn and the Anṣār and the wives of the Prophet went into *iḥrām* for the Farewell Ḥajj and we went into *iḥrām* too. When we reached Makkah, the Messenger of Allah ﷺ said, "Make your *iḥrām* for *ḥajj* an *iḥrām* for *'umrah* – except for those who have garlanded sacrificial animals." We did *ṭawāf* of the House and went between Ṣafā and Marwah, and then went to our wives and put on our (normal) clothes. He said, "Anyone who has garlanded his sacrificial animal should not come out of *iḥrām* until the sacrifice reaches its place." Then, on the eve of Tarwiyah, he told us to go into *iḥrām* for ḥajj. When we had finished the rites, we came and did *ṭawāf* of the House and went between Ṣafā and Marwah. Our ḥajj was complete and we had to sacrifice, in compliance with the words of Allah Almighty: '*...he should make whatever sacrifice is feasible. For any one who cannot, there is three days' fast on ḥajj and seven on your return'* to your cities, a sheep being sufficient. So we combined two practices – ḥajj and *'umrah* – in the same year Allah Almighty sent it down in His Book and it was the Sunnah of His Prophet ﷺ. It was allowed to people other than the people of Makkah. Allah says: "*...that is for anyone whose family does not live near the Masjid al-Ḥaram.*" The months of ḥajj which Allah Almighty mentioned are Shawwāl, Dhu-l-Qa'dah and Dhu-l-Ḥijjah. Whoever performs *tamattu'* in these months must sacrifice or fast.'

The *lām* in *'for anyone'* means the obligation of sacrifice for those who are not from the people of Makkah. That indicates the position of Abū Ḥanīfah and his people that *tamattu'* and *qirān* are only for those who are not from Makkah. They believe that those who live near the Masjid al-Ḥaram cannot do either *tamattu'* or *qirān*, and if someone does that, then he owes the sacrifice for a malpractice, from which he may not eat because it is not the sacrifice of *tamattu'*. Ash-Shāfi' said that they owe the sacrifice of *tamattu'* or *qirān*. What is indicated is sacrifice and fasting and so someone from Makkah does not owe either. 'Abd al-Malik ibn al-Mājishūn made a difference between *tamattu'* and *qirān* and obliged a sacrifice for *qirān* but not *tamattu'*.

People disagree about the definition of those who live near the Masjid al-Ḥaram although they agree that those who live in Makkah and what is directly connected to it are considered to be living near it. At-atabarī said, 'There is consensus that they are the people of the Ḥaram.' Ibn 'Aṭiyyah said, 'It is not as some scholars say about it meaning those who are obliged to attend its *Jumu'ah* prayer and anyone beyond that is a Bedouin, making the expression refer to city people and Bedouins.' Mālik and his people said that they are only the people of Makkah and what is directly connected to it. Abū Ḥanīfah and his people said that they are the people of the *mīqāt*s and those closer than them in all directions. So those who are the people of the *mīqāt*s and those closer than them are considered to be near the Masjid al-Ḥaram. Ash-Shāfi'ī and his people said that they are those who do not have to shorten the prayer when travelling to Makkah. That is the closest *mīqāt*. The positions of the early scholars are based on these views in interpreting the *āyah*.

**Have taqwā of Allah.**

Fear Him in respect of what He has made obligatory for you. This is a general command to be godfearing and a warning about the severity of His punishment.

ٱلْحَجُّ أَشْهُرٌ مَّعْلُومَٰتٌ فَمَن فَرَضَ فِيهِنَّ ٱلْحَجَّ فَلَا رَفَثَ وَلَا
فُسُوقَ وَلَا جِدَالَ فِى ٱلْحَجِّ وَمَا تَفْعَلُوا۟ مِنْ خَيْرٍ يَعْلَمْهُ ٱللَّهُ
وَتَزَوَّدُوا۟ فَإِنَّ خَيْرَ ٱلزَّادِ ٱلتَّقْوَىٰ وَٱتَّقُونِ يَٰٓأُو۟لِى
ٱلْأَلْبَٰبِ ١٩٧

**197 The Ḥajj takes place during certain well-known months. If anyone undertakes the obligation of ḥajj in them, there must be no sexual intercourse, no wrongdoing, nor any quarrelling during hajj. Whatever good you do, Allah knows it. Take provision; but the best provision is fearful awareness of Allah. So be fearful of Me, people of intelligence!**

**The Ḥajj takes place during certain well-known months.**

Allah now explains the difference between the times *of 'umrah* and ḥajj. The period during which *iḥrām* may be assumed for *'umrah* is any time throughout the entire year, but ḥajj is only at one particular time each year. So the *āyah* means that the months when the ḥajj takes place are well-known months, or the time of the ḥajj falls during well-known months, or the time when the actions of the ḥajj take place is well-known, or it may mean simply that the ḥajj occurs in certain months.

There is disagreement about exactly which months are referred to as 'well-known'. Ibn Mas'ūd, Ibn 'Umar, 'Aṭā', ar-Rabī', Mujāhid and az-Zuhrī said that the months of ḥajj are all of Shawwāl, Dhu-l-Qa'dah, and Dhu-l-Ḥijjah. Ibn 'Abbās, as-Suddī, ash-Sha'bī and an-Nakha'ī say that it is Shawwāl, Dhu-l-Qa'dah, and only the first ten days of Dhu-l-Ḥijjah. That is related from Ibn Mas'ūd and is also stated by Ibn az-Zubayr. Both are transmitted from Mālik. Ibn Ḥabīb related the latter and Ibn al-Mundhir the former. The point of the disagreement is specifying when someone owes a sacrifice. Those who say that all of Dhu-l-Ḥijjah is included in the months of Ḥajj do not think that a sacrifice is owed if the actions occur after the Day of Sacrifice, because that is still within the months of ḥajj. According to the second view, ḥajj ends on the Day of Sacrifice, and a sacrifice is owed by anyone who does the actions later than that since he is outside its time.

Allah does not name the months of ḥajj in His Book since they were well-known to the people addressed. It is possible in Arabic for the plural 'months' to be applied to two months and part of a third month.

They disagree about adopting *iḥrām* for ḥajj outside the months of ḥajj. Ibn 'Abbās says that part of the Sunnah is to adopt *iḥrām* during the months of ḥajj. 'Aṭā', Mujāhid, Ṭāwūs and al-Awzā'ī said that if someone adopts *iḥrām* for ḥajj before the months of ḥajj, it can only be considered an *'umrah* and not ḥajj. He is like someone who prays before the time of the prayer. It does not satisfy the obligation, but is supererogatory. Ash-Shāfi'ī and Abū Thawr say that. Al-Awzā'ī says that he adopts *iḥrām* for *'umrah*. Aḥmad ibn Ḥanbal says that it is disliked. Mālik, however, in his well-known position, says that *iḥrām* for ḥajj can be assumed at any time during the entire year and that is also the position of Abū Ḥanīfah. An-Nakha'ī said that a person does not come out of *iḥrām* until he finishes his ḥajj based on the words of Allah: *'They will ask you about the crescent moons, Say: "They are set times for mankind and for the ḥajj."'* (2:189) What ash-Shāfi'ī said is sounder because that is undefined while this *āyah* is specific. It is possible that it is part of the text which is undefined for some people because these months are more excellent than others. On this basis the position of Mālik is sound. Allah knows best.

**If someone undertakes the obligation of ḥajj in them.**

This means if someone obliges himself to do ḥajj by making the inward intention and performing the outward action of setting off and vocalising the *talbīyah* in words. Ibn Ḥabīb and Abū Ḥanīfah say that the *talbīyah* is the definitive action of setting off on ḥajj but ash-Shāfi'ī said that that is not the case because the *talbīyah* is not one of the pillars of ḥajj. That is also the view of al-Ḥasan ibn Ḥayy. Ash-Shāfiʿī says that the intention and the adoption of *iḥrām* is enough.

The literalists and others say that linguistically the root of the word for 'undertakes the obligation' (*faraḍa*) means to make a notch or cut. From that is derived *furḍah*, the notch in an arrow, an inlet in the bank of a river or a crevice in a mountain. So ḥajj is obligatory for the slave of Allah in the same way that the notch is necessary for an arrow. It is also said that *faraḍa* means to make clear, and this goes back to cutting because cutting something makes it distinct from other things. The Arabic particle '*man*' is in the nominative by the *ibtidā'* and has the meaning of the precondition whose *khabar* is '*faraḍa*'.

**there must be no sexual intercourse,**

The word used for sexual intercourse here is *rafath*. Ibn 'Abbās, Jubayr, as-Suddī, Qatādah, al-Ḥasan, 'Ikrimah, az-Zuhrī, Mujāhid and Mālik said that *rafath* means sexual intercourse and that sexual intercourse invalidates the ḥajj. Scholars agree that sexual intercourse before 'Arafah invalidates the ḥajj and makes a new ḥajj obligatory as well as a sacrifice. 'Abdullāh ibn 'Umar, Ṭāwūs, 'Aṭā' and others said that it means obscene speech to a woman, like saying, 'When we come out of *iḥrām*, we will do such-and-such to you' without using an indirect allusion. Ibn 'Abbās said that. He recited while he was in *iḥrām*:

They walk softly with us.
If the birds tell truly, we will have a touch.

His companion, Ḥussayn ibn Qays, said to him, 'Do you speak lewdness (*tarfuthu*) while you are in *iḥrām*?' He answered, '*Rafath* is what is said in the presence of women.' Some people say that it is coarse language mentioning women, whether in their presence or not. It is also said, by some, to apply to all sexual activity which might take place between a man and his wife. Abū 'Ubaydah said that it is foolish talk.

Ibn al-'Arabī said, 'What is meant by *"no rafath"* is a legal prohibition, rather than an existential one. We find and see that which is called *rafath*, and the report of the Almighty cannot be contrary to what it reports. So the words refer to a legal existence rather than a physical one. It is similar to His words: *"Divorced women should wait by themselves for three menstrual cycles."* (2:228) It means legally and not physically because there are divorced women who do not wait. Therefore the negation refers to the legal ruling and not physical existence. The same is true of His words: *"No one may touch it except the purified."* (56:79) If we say that it refers to human beings, which is sound, then it means legally that no one should touch it. If it is touched by someone in this state, it is contrary to the legal ruling. This is a fine point that scholars have missed. They say that a report can mean a prohibition. That does not exist and is not sound. They can differ in reality and description.'

**no wrongdoing,**

*Fusūq* (wrongdoing) in this context means all acts of disobedience according to Ibn 'Abbās, 'Aṭā' and al-Ḥasan. Ibn 'Umar and a group said that, in this context, it means committing those acts of disobedience to Allah which are specific to the state of *iḥrām* for ḥajj, such as killing game, paring nails, cutting hair and the like. Ibn Zayd and Mālik said that it means sacrificing to idols, going by Allah's words: *'Or some deviance* (fisq) *consecrated to other than Allah.'* (6:145) Aḍ-Ḍaḥḥāk said it means exchanging obscene epithets. Indicating that are the words: *'How evil is it to have a name for evil conduct* (fusūq)!' (49:11) Ibn 'Umar also said that it is cursing. That is attested to by the words of the Prophet ﷺ: 'Cursing a Muslim is wrongdoing (*fusūq*) and killing him is unbelief.' The first position is the soundest since it includes all the other possibilities. The Prophet ﷺ said, 'Anyone who makes ḥajj and does not engage in sexual intercourse or wrongdoing returns as he was on the day his mother bore him.' And: 'An accepted ḥajj has no repayment except the Garden.' He also said ﷺ, 'By the One who has my soul in His hand, there is no action between heaven and earth better than *jihād* in the Way of Allah or an accepted ḥajj, in which there is no sexual intercourse, wrongdoing or quarrelling.' The *fuqahā'* state that the accepted ḥajj is one in which one does not disobey Allah while performing it. Al-Farrā' said, 'It is one after which one does not disobey Allah.' An accepted *ḥajj* is one in which, and after which, one does not disobey Allah. Al-Ḥasan said, 'An accepted ḥajj is that a person returns from it abstinent with respect to this world, desiring the Next World.' Other things are said as well.

**nor any quarrelling during ḥajj.**

*Jidāl* (quarrelling) is argumentation and is derived from the word *jadl* which means twisting. A rein which is braided (*majdūl*) is derived from the same root. It is also possible that *jidāl* comes from the word *jadāla* which means the earth. It is as if each of the opponents stands against the other person and one overcomes the other.

Scholars disagree about its exact meaning here and offer six possibilities. Ibn Mas'ūd, Ibn 'Abbās and 'Aṭā' say that *jidāl* here means to argue with a Muslim until you make him angry to the extent that that leads to insults. As for discussing points of knowledge, that is not forbidden. Qatādah said that it means abuse. Ibn Zayd and Mālik ibn Anas said that here it means the disagreements people used to have about which of them was in the authentic places of Ibrāhīm, which used to happen in the Jāhiliyyah when Quraysh stood where the rest of the Arabs did not stand, and so, according to this interpretation, it means that there must be no quarrelling about its sites. One group say that it refers to when one group say. 'The ḥajj is today' and another group say, 'The ḥajj is tomorrow.' Mujāhid and a group said, 'It is to argue about the months according to the Arab reckoning. It used to happen that some would be at 'Arafah while others were at Muzdalifah and they would quarrel about who was in the right.'

According to these two last interpretations, it means that there must be no quarrelling about the time and place of ḥajj. These two positions are the soundest of what is said regarding the interpretation. The Prophet ﷺ said, 'Time revolves as it did on the day that Allah created the heavens and the earth.' It means that the ḥajj has returned to the day and time it used to have. When the Prophet ﷺ performed ḥajj, he said, 'Take your rites from me.' So he clarified the stations and places of ḥajj. Muḥammad ibn Ka'b al-Qurṭubī said, '"Quarrelling" is that one group says, "Our ḥajj was more accepted than your ḥajj," and the others say the same.' It is also said that the quarrelling occurred with respect to boasting about ancestors. Allah knows best.

**Whatever good you do, Allah knows it.**

This means that Allah will repay you for your actions because repayment is only made by the one who has knowledge of the matter concerned. It is also said that this is encouragement to use good words instead of obscenities and to be pious and godfearing rather than wrongdoing and argumentative. It is said that the word 'good' refers to people restraining themselves so that they do not do what is forbidden.

**Take provision;**

This is a command to people to take provisions for their ḥajj. Ibn 'Umar, 'Ikrimah, Mujāhid, Qatādah and Ibn Zayd said, 'The *āyah* was revealed about a group of Arabs who used to go on ḥajj with no provisions. One of them would say, "How could we make ḥajj to the House of Allah and He not feed us?" So they were dependent on other people for their needs. They were forbidden to do that and commanded to take provisions.' 'Abdullāh ibn az-Zubayr said, 'People used to rely on one another and not take provisions, and so they were commanded to take provisions. When the Prophet ﷺ travelled, he took a camel carrying provisions. Three hundred men of Muzaynah came to him and when they were about to leave, he said, "Umar, give the people provisions.' Some people say that the expression refers to a righteous companion, but Ibn 'Aṭiyyah said that this specification is weak. A more fitting meaning of the *āyah* is to store up provision for the Next World in the form of righteous actions.

The first position is sounder because what is meant is actual provision for the ḥajj journey as we mentioned. It is as al-Bukhārī related from Ibn 'Abbās: 'The people of Yemen used to go on ḥajj and not take provisions. They would say, "We are relying on Allah." When they came to Makkah, they begged from people, so Allah Almighty sent down: "*Take provision, but the best provision is fearful awareness* (taqwā) *of Allah.*"' This is what the text suggests and is the position of most commentators. Ash-Sha'bī says that it means specifically dates and *sawīq* (barley mush). Ibn Jubayr says biscuits and *sawīq*.

Ibn al-'Arabī said, 'Allah commands the people of wealth to take provisions. Those who have no money and have a craft by which they support themselves, and those who beg, are not being addressed here. Those addressed are people who have wealth but who leave their wealth and go out without provisions, saying, "We are relying on Allah." Reliance (*tawakkul*) has preconditions. Those who meet those preconditions go out without provision and are not addressed by this. Most people who go out lack the degree of reliance and neglect its realities. Allah knows best.' Abu-l-Faraj al-Jawzī said, 'Iblīs has muddled some people who claim to be relying on Allah, they go out without provision and imagine that this is true reliance on Allah. They are gravely in error. A man said to Aḥmad ibn Ḥanbal, "I want to set out for Makkah based on reliance on Allah without provisions." Aḥmad said to him, "Go out without going in a caravan." "No," he answered, "only with them." He said, "Then you are relying on other people's sacks!"'

**but the best provision is fearful awareness of Allah.**

Allah reports that the best provision is avoiding what is forbidden and so Allah commands us here to add fearful awareness to taking provision. It means to fear Allah by following His command to take provision. It is said that it can mean that the best provision is that by which the traveller is kept safe from destruction or from the need to beg. It is said that it makes it clear that this world is not the abode of permanence. The people with knowledge of subtle indications (*ishārāt*) say that Allah is reminding us of the journey to the Next World and commands us to take fearful awareness of Him as provision. Fearful awareness is the provision of the Next World. Al-A'shā said:

If you do not travel with a provision of fear of Allah,
    you will meet those with provision after you die
And regret that you are not like them
    and that you did not prepare as they prepared.

Someone else said:

Death is a swollen sea
    in which the devices of the swimmer disappear.
Soul! I am speaking, so listen to words
    from a compassionate good counsellor.
In his grave, a man's only companions
    are fear of Allah and righteous deeds.

**So have taqwā of Me, people of intelligence!**

Those with intelligence are singled out, even though the command is to everyone, because they are those through whom the proof of Allah is established. They receive His commands and undertake to carry them out. The word used for intelligent people is the plural of *lubb*, which refers to the core of anything.

لَيْسَ عَلَيْكُمْ جُنَاحٌ أَن تَبْتَغُوا۟ فَضْلًا مِّن رَّبِّكُمْ ۚ فَإِذَآ أَفَضْتُم
مِّنْ عَرَفَـٰتٍ فَٱذْكُرُوا۟ ٱللَّهَ عِندَ ٱلْمَشْعَرِ ٱلْحَرَامِ ۖ وَٱذْكُرُوهُ
كَمَا هَدَىٰكُمْ وَإِن كُنتُم مِّن قَبْلِهِۦ لَمِنَ ٱلضَّآلِّينَ ﴿١٩٨﴾

**198 There is nothing wrong in seeking bounty from your Lord. When you pour down from 'Arafāt, remember Allah at the Sacred Landmark. Remember Him because He has guided you, even though before this you were astray.**

**There is nothing wrong in seeking bounty from your Lord.**

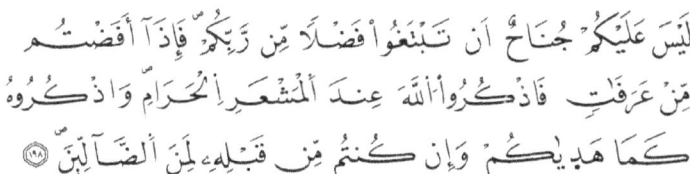

The word used here for 'wrong' (*junāḥ*) means wrong action. After mentioning the things prohibited during ḥajj, namely sexual intercourse, wrongdoing and quarrelling, Allah mentions that trade is allowed. It means that there is nothing wrong in seeking bounty from Allah. In the Qur'an, the phrase 'seeking bounty'

is used for engaging in trade. Allah Almighty says: '*...spread through the earth and seek Allah's bounty...*' (62:10). Evidence for the soundness of this is found in al-Bukhārī where Ibn 'Abbās is reported as observing: "Ukāz, Majinnah and Dhū' l-Majāz were markets in the time of the Jāhiliyyah and people thought it sinful to trade during the festivals; and then this was revealed about the ḥajj festival.' So the *āyah* is evidence that it is permitted for someone on ḥajj to trade during it while performing the rites of ḥajj. Intending to do so is not *shirk* and does not detract from the sincerity of the person concerned.

Nonetheless, performing ḥajj without trade is better since it is free of the impurities of this world and the connection of the heart to something else. Ad-Dāraquṭnī related in the *Sunan* that Abū Umāmah at-Taymī said, 'I said to Ibn 'Umar, "I am a man who hires out in this way. People say that I have no ḥajj." Ibn 'Umar said, "A man came to the Messenger of Allah ﷺ and asked a similar question as you have asked me. He remained silent until this *āyah* was revealed: *'There is nothing wrong in seeking bounty from your Lord.*'"'

**When you pour down from 'Arafat,**

*'Afāda'* (pour down) means to rush on. The verb is used for when you pour liquid into a vessel until it overflows down the sides. A man who is *fayyāḍ* is very munificent. A *ḥadīth* which is *mustafiḍ* is extensively known.

'Arafāt is the name of a place which is in the plural form. It is called that because of what is around it. It is said that the plain is called 'Arafāt because people recognise one another (*yata'ārāfahūna*) there. It is said that when Ādam descended in India and Ḥawwā' at Jiddah, after a long search, they met at 'Arafāt on the Day of 'Arafah, and so the day is called 'Arafah and the place 'Arafāt. Aḍ-Ḍaḥḥāk said that. Other things are said which were mentioned in 2:128.

Ibn 'Aṭiyyah said that it is clear that it is an improvised name as is the case with most names of places. 'Arafah is Na'mān al-Arāk (Na'mān of the Lote-trees).' It is said that it is derived from *'arf*, which means scent. It is a fragrant place as opposed to Minā which is strewn with stomach contents and blood. Hence it is 'Arafāt. Some say that the two names are derived from steadfastness because they are steadfast in supplication, trial and enduring hardships to perform this act of worship, and the *'ārif* is someone who is steadfast and humble. This is found in a saying: 'The soul is steadfast (*'arūf*) and endures what burdens it.' We find in a poem:

I steadfastly (*'ārifah*) endure the heat for that.

Or similarly in Dhū 'r-Rummah:

Steadfast (*'arūf*) in the face of the decrees that are written for it.

So it has this name because of the humility of the person performing ḥajj and his steadfastness in supplication, types of affliction and enduring hardship to carry out this act of worship.

Scholars agree that if someone stands at 'Arafāt on the day of 'Arafah before midday and then goes on before midday, he is not considered to have stood at 'Arafah. They agree that when someone stands at 'Arafah after midday and pours onward before nightfall, his ḥajj is complete, with the exception of Mālik ibn Anas who said that he must have part of the night. If someone stands at 'Arafah in the night, none of the community disagree about his ḥajj being complete. The argument of the majority is based on His words: '*When you pour down from 'Arafāt*', in which He does not specify night or day, and the *ḥadīth* of 'Urwah ibn Muḍarris who said, 'I went to the Prophet ﷺ while he was at the stopping place at Jam'. I said, "Messenger of Allah, I have come to you from the two mountains of Ṭayy'. I have tired my camel out and exhausted myself. By Allah, I have not passed any mountain without standing on it. Do I have a ḥajj, Messenger of Allah?" The Messenger of Allah ﷺ said, "Whoever has prayed the morning prayer with us at Jam', having gone to 'Arafāt before that, either by night or day, has completed his dishevelment and completed his ḥajj."'

More than one of the imams transmitted it, including Abū Dāwud, an-Nasā'ī and ad-Dāraquṭnī. At-Tirmidhī said that it is a sound *ḥasan ḥadīth*. Abū 'Umar said, 'This *ḥadīth* of 'Urwah ibn Muḍarris aṭ-Ṭā'ī is sound and confirmed. It is related by a group of the reliable companions of ash-Sha'bī from ash-Sha'bī, including Ismā'īl ibn Abī Khālid, Dāwud ibn Abī Hind, Zakariyyā ibn Abī Zā'idah, 'Abdullāh ibn Abī 's-Safar and Muṭarrif, all of them from ash-Sha'bī from 'Urwah ibn Muḍarris ibn Aws ibn Ḥārithah ibn Lām.' The argument of Mālik regarding the firm Sunnah is the long *ḥadīth* of Jābir transmitted by Muslim which states: 'He continued to stand until the sun had set, the yellow light had diminished a little and the disc of the sun had disappeared.' His actions ﷺ are mandatory, especially in ḥajj. He said, 'Take your rites from me.'

The majority disagree about someone who leaves before sunset and does not return: what does he owe to make his ḥajj is sound? 'Aṭā', Sufyān ath-Thawrī, ash-Shāfi'ī, Aḥmad, Abū Thawr, the People of Opinion and others said that he owes a sacrifice. Al-Ḥasan al-Baṣrī said that he owes a *hady*. Ibn Jurayj says that he owes a camel. Mālik said that he must do ḥajj again as well as a *hady* that he sacrifices in that ḥajj: he is like someone who has missed ḥajj. If he returns to

'Arafah until he goes on after sunset, ash-Shāfi'ī says that he owes nothing. That is the view of Aḥmad, Isḥāq and Dāwud. Aṭ-Ṭabarī said that. Abū Ḥanīfah and his people and ath-Thawrī said that a sacrifice is not cancelled for him, even if he returns after sunset. That is what Abū Thawr said.

There is no disagreement among scholars that it is better for someone to stop at 'Arafah while mounted because the Prophet ﷺ did that until he went on from it after sunset with Usāmah ibn Zayd riding behind him. This is recorded in the long *ḥadīth* of Jābir and the *ḥadīth* of 'Alī as well as the *ḥadīth* of Ibn 'Abbās. Jābir said, 'Then the Messenger of Allah ﷺ rode to the stopping place and made his she-camel Qaṣwā' turn towards the rocks, with the path of the walkers in front of him. He faced the *qiblah* and continued to stop there until the sun had set, the yellow light had diminished a little and the disc of the sun had disappeared. He had Usāmah ibn Zayd sit behind him.' If someone cannot ride, he stands on foot, making supplication for as long as he is able. There is nothing wrong with a person sitting down if he is unable to stand. Stopping while mounted demonstrates exaltation and honour of the *ḥajj*: *'As for those who honour Allah's sacred rites, that comes from the* taqwā *in their hearts.'* (22:32) Ibn Wahb said in his *Muwaṭṭā'*: 'Mālik said to me, "I prefer stopping at 'Arafah on mounts and camels to standing on foot. There is no harm in someone who stands on foot resting."'

It is confirmed in *Ṣaḥīḥ Muslim* and elsewhere from Usāmah ibn Zayd that when the Prophet ﷺ went on from 'Arafah, he went at a medium pace, but when he found a gap, he sped up. That is what is obliged for the leaders of the ḥajj and those behind them, because hastening the pace to Muzdalifah is hastening to the prayer there. It is known that on that day *Maghrib* and *'Ishā'* must be prayed together at Muzdalifah. That is the Sunnah, as will be made clear, Allah willing.

The literal text of the Qur'an and the Sunnah indicates that the whole of the plain of 'Arafāt is a standing place. The Prophet ﷺ said, 'I stood here and all of 'Arafah is a standing-place.' Muslim and others related it from the long *ḥadīth* of Jābir. We find in the *Muwaṭṭā'* of Mālik that he heard that the Messenger of Allah ﷺ said, 'The whole of 'Arafah is a standing-place, except the middle of 'Uranah, and the whole of Muzdalifah is a standing-place, except for the middle of Muḥassir.' Ibn 'Abd al-Barr said, 'This *ḥadīth* is connected to the *ḥadīth* of Jābir ibn 'Abdullāh, the *ḥadīth* of Ibn 'Abbās, and the *ḥadīth* of 'Alī ibn Abī Ṭālib. Most of the traditions do not exclude the middle of 'Uranah from 'Arafah and the middle of Muḥassir from Muzdalifah. That is how the reliable scholars among the people of *ḥadīth* transmit it in the *ḥadīth* of Ja'far ibn Muḥammad from his father from Jābir.'

Abū 'Umar said that *fuqahā'* disagree about those who stand at 'Uranah on

'Arafah. According to what Ibn al-Mundhir mentioned from him, Mālik said that they should make a sacrifice and then their ḥajj is complete. This is related by Khālid ibn Nizār from Mālik. Abu-l-Muṣ'ab said that a person who stands in the middle of 'Uranah is like someone has not stood and has therefore missed the ḥajj and owes a ḥajj in the following year. It is related that Ibn 'Abbās said, 'If someone pours on from 'Uranah, he has no ḥajj.' That is the view of Ibn al-Qāsim and Sālim. Ibn al-Mundhir mentioned this view from ash-Shāfi'ī. He said, 'That is my view. It is not enough if someone stands in a place where the Messenger of Allah ﷺ commanded that he should not stand.' Ibn 'Abd al-Barr said, 'The exception of 'Uranah from 'Arafah does not come in a manner which would oblige a [new] ḥajj, either by way of transmission or consensus.' The argument of those who take the position of Abu-l-Muṣ'ab is that standing at 'Arafah is an obligation which is agreed upon in a specific place. It is only permitted to perform it with certainty, and there is no certainty when there is disagreement. 'Uranah is to the west of the mosque of 'Arafah. Some scholars said that if the western wall of the 'Arafah mosque were to fall, it would fall in the valley of 'Uranah. Al-Bājī related from Ibn Ḥabīb that 'Arafah is outside of the Ḥaram and 'Uranah is inside it. Abū 'Umar said, 'As for the valley of Muḥassir, Wakī' mentioned from Sufyān from Abu-z-Zubayr from Jābir that the Prophet ﷺ hurried through the valley of Muḥassir.

There is nothing wrong in acknowledging the Day of 'Arafah outside of 'Arafah in such a way as to resemble the people at 'Arafah. Shu'bah related from Qatādah that al-Ḥasan said, 'The first to do that was Ibn 'Abbās in Basra.' It meant people gathering in the mosque at Basra on the Day of 'Arafah. Mūsā ibn Abī 'Ā'ishah said, 'I saw 'Umar ibn Ḥurayth giving a *khuṭbah* on the day of 'Arafah and people had gathered for it.' Al-Athram said, 'I asked Aḥmad ibn Ḥanbal about celebrating 'Arafah in cities by gathering on the Day of 'Arafah. He answered, 'I hope that there is no harm in it. More than one person has done it: al-Ḥasan, Bakr, Thābit and Muḥammad ibn Wāsi'. They used to attend the mosque of the Day of 'Arafah.'

The excellence of the Day of 'Arafah is immense and its reward is immense. On it Allah expiates the worst wrong actions and multiplies good actions. The Prophet ﷺ said, 'The best supplication is supplication on the Day of 'Arafah and the best of what I and the Prophets before have said is: "There is no god but Allah alone with no partner."' Ad-Dāraquṭnī related from 'Ā'ishah that the Messenger of Allah ﷺ said, 'There is no day on which Allah frees a greater number from the Fire than the Day of 'Arafah. On that Day, Allah draws near to the earth and then, showing

His pride in them to the angels, He says, "What do these people want?"' We find in the *Muwaṭṭā'* from 'Ubaydullāh ibn Karīz that the Messenger of Allah ﷺ said, 'Shayṭān is not considered more abased or more cast out or more contemptible on any other day than he is on the day of 'Arafah. That is simply because he sees the descent of mercy and the fact that Allah overlooks great wrong actions. The only exception to that is what he was shown on the Day of Badr.' Someone asked, 'What was he shown on the Day of Badr, Messenger of Allah?' He answered, 'Did he not see Jibrīl arranging the ranks of the angels?' Abū 'Umar said, 'Abu-n-Naḍr Ismā'īl ibn Ibrāhīm al-'Ijlī related this *ḥadīth* from Mālik from Ibrāhīm ibn Abī 'Ablah from Ṭalḥah ibn 'Ubaydullāh ibn Karīz from his father. He did not say in this *ḥadīth* 'from his father'. It is nothing. What is correct is what is in the *Muwaṭṭā'*.

At-Tirmidhī al-Ḥakīm mentioned in *Nawādir al-uṣūl* that it was related from Abū Rawḥ Ḥātim ibn Nu'aym at-Tamīmī from Hishām ibn Abu-l-Walīd 'Abd al-Malik aṭ-Ṭayālisai from 'Abd al-Qāhir ibn as-Sariy as-Sulamī from Ibn Kinānah from 'Abbās ibn Mirdās from his father from his grandfather, 'Abbās ibn Mirdās that, on the evening of 'Arafah, the Messenger of Allah ﷺ made supplication for forgiveness and mercy for his community. He made a lot of supplication and received the reply: 'I have done that, except for when they wrong one another. As for the sins that are between Me and them, I have forgiven them.' He said, 'O Lord, You have the power to reward those wronged with better than the wrong done to them and to forgive those who wronged them.' He did not receive an answer that night. On the following day in the morning at Muzdalifah, he strove in making that supplication and was answered: 'I have forgiven them.' The Messenger of Allah ﷺ smiled and was asked, 'What has made you smile, Messenger of Allah, at a time in which you did not used to smile?' He replied, 'I smiled at the enemy of Allah, Iblīs. When he learned that Allah had answered my supplication for my community, he fell down, crying for woe and destruction and threw dust on his head and then fled.'

Abū 'Abd al-Ghanī al-Ḥasan ibn 'Alī related from 'Abd ar-Razzāq from Mālik from Abu-z-Zinād from al-A'raj from Abū Hurayrah that the Messenger of Allah ﷺ said, 'On the Day of 'Arafah Allah forgives the sincere ḥājjī. On the night of Muzdalifah, Allah forgives the merchants. On the day of Minā, Allah forgives the porters. On the day of the Jamrah 'l-'Aqabah, Allah forgives the beggars. Many are the people among those who say that there is no god but Allah who are not present at that standing who are forgiven.' Abū 'Umar said, 'This is a *gharīb ḥadīth* from Mālik. It is only recorded from him by this path. Abū 'Abd al-Ghanī says that he does not know it. The people of knowledge continue to be indulgent in transmissions about things to be desired and virtues while they are severe about *ḥadīths* that contain judgments.'

The people of knowledge recommend fasting on the Day of 'Arafah, except for the people who are actually there. The imams related from ibn 'Abbās that the Prophet ﷺ did not fast at 'Arafah. Umm al-Faḍl sent some milk to him and he drank it. At-Tirmidhī said that it is a sound *ḥasan ḥadīth*. It is related that Ibn 'Umar said, 'I went on ḥajj with the Prophet ﷺ and he did not fast (the day of 'Arafah). I went with Abū Bakr and he did not fast, and with 'Umar and he did not fast. According to most of the people of knowledge, this is the normal practice. They recommended not fasting at 'Arafah so that a person will strong in supplication. Some of the people of knowledge did fast 'Arafah at 'Arafah.' There is an *isnād* from Ibn 'Umar like the first and he added at the end of it, 'and with 'Uthmān, and he did not fast. So I do not fast it, but I neither command or forbid it.' Ibn al-Mundhir mentioned it.

'Aṭā' said about fasting the day of 'Arafah, 'I fast in the winter and do not fast in the summer.' Yaḥyā al-Anṣārī said, 'One must not fast on the day of 'Arafah.' 'Uthmān ibn Abī 'l-'Āṣ, Ibn az-Zubayr and 'Ā'ishah used to fast the day of 'Arafah.' Ibn al-Mundhir said, 'I prefer to not fast the day of 'Arafah at 'Arafāt to follow the Messenger of Allah ﷺ, but I prefer to fast elsewhere since the Messenger of Allah ﷺ was asked about fasting the day of 'Arafah and said, "It expiates the past year and the coming year."' We were told that 'Aṭā' said, 'If someone does not fast on the day of 'Arafah in order to be strong for supplication, he will have the same reward as someone who fasts.'

**remember Allah at the Sacred Landmark.**

Remember Him by making supplication and reciting the *talbīyah* at the Sacred Landmark. The place is called Jam' because the prayers of *Maghrib* and *'Ishā'* are joined together (*jumi'a*) there. Qatādah said that it is because Ādam met Ḥawwā' there and they joined each other (*jama'a*) there and that is also why it is called Muzdalifah (*izdalafa*, to draw near). It is said that it is called that on account of the actions of the people there, because they draw near (*izdalafa*) to Allah by standing there. The word for Sacred Landmark (*mash'ar*) comes from *shi'ār* which means a sign or landmark, and it is called that because it is a landmark of the ḥajj due to the fact that people are required to pray there and spend the night there in supplication to Allah. It is called a Ḥaram because of its sanctity.

It is confirmed that the Messenger of Allah ﷺ prayed both *Maghrib* and *'Ishā'* at

Muzdalifah. The people of knowledge agree, with no disagreement whatsoever, that the sunnah is to join *Maghrib* and *'Ishā'*. They disagree about someone who prays before reaching Jam'. Mālik said, 'Whoever stands with the imam and goes on when he goes on, does not pray until he reached Jam', where he joins the prayers. Evidence for this is found in the words of the Prophet ﷺ to Usāmah ibn Zayd, 'The prayer is ahead of you.' Ibn Ḥabīb said, 'If someone prays before reaching Muzdalifah without excuse, he repeats it when he knows. He is in the position of someone who prays before midday based on the words of the Prophet ﷺ, "The prayer is ahead of you."' Abū Ḥanīfah said that. Ashhab says that he does not have to repeat them unless he prayed both of them before the disappearance of twilight. And then he only repeats *'Ishā'*. Ash-Shāfi'ī said that. It is what Qāḍī Abu-l-Ḥasan supported. His argument is that that the sunnah is to join these two prayers, but that it is not a precondition for their validity. It is a recommendation, like joining *Ẓuhr* and *'Aṣr* at 'Arafah. Ibn al-Mundhir preferred this position and related it from 'Aṭā' ibn Abī Rabāḥ, 'Urwah ibn az-Zubayr, al-Qāsim ibn Muḥammad, Sa'īd ibn Jubayr, Aḥmad, Isḥāq, Abū Thawr and Ya'qūb. He related that ash-Shāfi'ī said, 'He does not pray until he has reached Muzdalifah. But if the middle of the night comes before he reaches Muzdalifah, he does pray them.'

If someone hurries and reaches Muzdalifah before twilight has disappeared, Ibn Ḥabīb said, 'There is no prayer for someone who hastens to Muzdalifah before twilight has disappeared, either the imam or anyone else, until the twilight has disappeared.' Part of the meaning is that the time of this prayer is after the disappearance of twilight. It is not permitted to pray it before that. If its time had been before the disappearance of twilight, it would not have been delayed.

About someone who reaches 'Arafah after the imam has pressed on, or he is one of those with an excuse who stood with the imam, Ibn al-Mawwāz said: 'If someone stands after the imam, he should pray each prayer at its time.' Mālik said about someone with an excuse that keeps him from being with the imam that he prays both prayers together when the twilight disappears. Ibn al-Qāsim said about those who stand after the imam: 'If he hopes to reach Muzdalifah in the first third of the night, he should delay the prayer until he reaches Muzdalifah. Otherwise he prays each prayer at its time.' So Ibn al-Mawwāz restricted delaying the prayer until Muzdalifah is reached to those who stand with the imam rather than other people. Mālik made it a question of the time rather than the place and Ibn al-Qāsim considers the preferred time for the prayer and the place. If someone fears missing the preferred time, then it is invalid to consider the place. It is more appropriate to observe the preferred time.

Scholars disagree about the form of the prayer at Muzdalifah. There are two possibilities. One is with the adhan and the *iqāmah*. The other is that they are joined together with no action to separate them or action permitted between: setting down baggage and the like. As for the adhan and the *iqāmah*, it is confirmed that the Messenger of Allah ﷺ prayed *Maghrib* and *'Ishā'* at Muzdalifah with one adhan and two *iqāmahs*. The *Ṣaḥīḥ* transmitted that from the long *ḥadīth* of Jābir. That was the view of Aḥmad ibn Ḥanbal, Abū Thawr and Ibn al-Mundhir. Mālik said that they should be prayed with two adhans and two *iqāmahs*. The same is true of *Ẓuhr* and *'Aṣr* at 'Arafah, although the consensus is that that happens at the beginning of the time of *Ẓuhr*. Abū 'Umar said, 'I do not know of any *ḥadīth* regarding what Mālik says that goes back to the Prophet ﷺ by any path, but it is related from 'Umar ibn al-Khaṭṭāb.' Ibn al-Mundhir added Ibn Mas'ūd. Part of the argument of Mālik in respect of this topic is that the Messenger of Allah ﷺ made a sunnah of the two prayers at Muzdalifah and 'Arafah, so arguably the two have the same time since their time is the same. Therefore each of them is prayed in its proper time and neither of them is more entitled to the adhan and *iqāmah* than the other since neither of them is being made up: they are prayers that are being prayed at their time. Each prayer is prayed in its time. Their sunnah is therefore to have an adhan and *iqāmah* for the group. This is clear, and Allah knows best.

The others say that the first one is prayed with an adhan and *iqāmah* and the second is prayed without an adhan and *iqāmah*. They said that 'Umar commanded the second adhan because people had separated for eating and the adhan was to gather them together again. They said, 'That is what we say when the people separate from the imam for eating or any other reason: he can command the *mu'adhdhin* to call in order to gather them. When there is an adhan, there is an *iqāmah*.' They said that this is the meaning of what is related from 'Umar. They mentioned the *ḥadīth* of 'Abd ar-Raḥmān ibn Yazīd in which he said, 'Ibn Mas'ūd used to put the evening meal between the two prayers at Muzdalifah. Another path of transmission states that he prayed every prayer with an adhan and a *iqāmah*. 'Abd ar-Razzāq mentioned it.

Still others said that both prayers are prayed at Muzdalifah with an *iqāmah*, but with no adhan for either of them. It is related from Ibn 'Umar and that is the position of ath-Thawrī. 'Abd ar-Razzāq and 'Abd al-Malik ibn aṣ-Ṣabbāḥ mentioned from ath-Thawrī from Salamah ibn Kuhayl from Sa'īd ibn Jubayr that

Ibn 'Umar said, 'The Messenger of Allah ﷺ joined *Maghrib* and *'Ishā'* at Jam'. He prayed *Maghrib* with three *rak'ah*s and *'Ishā'* with two with one *iqāmah*.'

Others said that both prayers are prayed together between *Maghrib* and *'Ishā'* with one adhan and one *iqāmah*. That was because they believed what Hushaym related from Yaunus ibn 'Ubayd from Sa'īd ibn Jubayr about Ibn 'Umar joining *Maghrib* and *'Ishā'* at Jam' with one adhan and one *iqāmah* with nothing separating them. The same is related *marfū'* from Khuzaymah ibn Thābit. He is not strong. Al-Jūzjānī related from Muḥammad ibn al-Ḥasan from Abū Yūsuf from Abū Ḥanīfah that they are prayed with one adhan and two *iqāmah*s: an adhan for *Maghrib* and only an *iqāmah* for *'Ishā'*. This is the position of aṭ-Ṭaḥāwī based on the *ḥadīth* of Jābir. It is the first view and it is relied on.

Others say that they are prayed with two *iqāmah*s, with no adhan for either of them. Among those with this position are ash-Shāfi'ī and his people, Isḥāq, and it is one of the two positions of Aḥmad ibn Ḥanbal. It is the position of Sālim ibn 'Abdullāh and al-Qāsim ibn Muḥammad. They argue by what 'Abd ar-Razzāq mentioned from Ma'mar from Ibn Shihāb from Sālim from Ibn 'Umar: 'When the Prophet ﷺ came to Muzdalifah, he joined *Maghrib* and *'Ishā'*. He prayed *Maghrib* with three *rak'ah*s and *'Ishā'* with two with one *iqāmah* for each of them. He did not connect them at all.' Abū 'Umar said, 'The reports from Ibn 'Umar about this position are the firmest of what is related regarding this matter, but it is subject to interpretation. There is no disagreement about the *ḥadīth* of Jābir. It is more fitting. There is no scope for speculation regarding this matter. It is something that must be followed.'

As for a separation between the two prayers by some action other than the prayer, it is confirmed from Usāmah ibn Zayd that when the Prophet ﷺ reached Muzdalifah, he dismounted and did *wuḍū'* fully. Then the *iqāmah* for the prayer was made and he prayed *Maghrib*. Then every man made his camel kneel in his camp. Then the *iqāmah* for the prayer was made and he prayed it without praying anything between them. One variant has: 'They did not unpack until the *iqāmah* for *'Ishā'* was given. He prayed and then they unpacked.' We have already mentioned that Ibn Mas'ūd had his evening meal between the two prayers. This is permission to separate the two prayers at Jam'.

Mālik was asked about someone who arrives at Muzdalifah and whether he should begin with the prayer or delay it until he has removed his baggage from his camel. He said, 'If the baggage is light, there is nothing wrong in doing that before the prayer. I do not think that is the case with load-bearers. Then the person begins with the prayer and unloads his camel afterwards.' Ashhab said in his books, 'He can unload his camel before the prayer, although I prefer that he prays *Maghrib* before unloading it unless it is absolutely necessary, because it is heavy for the animal or some other reason.' As for supererogatory prayers between the two prayers, Ibn al-Mundhir said, 'I do not know of any disagreement between them that someone joining prayers does not pray supererogatory prayers between them. According to the *ḥadīth* of Usāmah, "He did not pray anything between them."'

Spending the night at Muzdalifah is not one of the pillars of the ḥajj according to the majority of scholars, but there is disagreement about whether someone who does not spend the night there is obliged to sacrifice. Mālik said that someone who does not spend the night there owes a sacrifice. Someone who stands there for most of the night owes nothing because according to Mālik and his people spending the Night of Sacrifice there is a confirmed sunnah, not an obligation. A similar statement was made by 'Aṭā', az-Zuhrī, Qatādah, Sufyān ath-Thawrī, Aḥmad, Isḥāq, Abū Thawr and the People of Opinion about someone who does not spend the night there. Ash-Shāfi'ī said that if someone leaves it after half the night, he owes nothing, but if he leaves before half the night has passed and does not return to Muzdalifah, he owes *fidyah* of a sheep.

'Ikrimah, ash-Sha'bī, an-Nakha'ī and al-Ḥasan al-Baṣrī said that stopping at Muzdalifah is an obligation and that, if someone misses Jam' and does not stop, he has missed ḥajj and must make his *iḥrām* that of *'umrah*. That is related from Ibn az-Zubayr and it is the position of al-Awzā'ī. The same is related from ath-Thawrī. The soundest transmission from him is that stopping there is a confirmed sunnah. Ḥammād ibn Abī Sulaymān said, 'Someone who misses pouring on from Jam' has missed the ḥajj and should make it an *'umrah* and do ḥajj in the following year. Their argument is based on the literal text of the Book and the Sunnah. In the Book, the basis is the words of the Almighty: *'When you pour down from 'Arafāt, remember Allah at the Sacred Landmark.'* In the Sunnah, it is the words of the Prophet ﷺ: 'Whoever catches Jam' and stands with the people until they pour down has caught it. Whoever does not catch that has no ḥajj.' Ibn al-Mundhir mentioned it. Ad-Dāraquṭnī related that 'Urwah ibn Muḍarris said, 'I went to the Prophet ﷺ while he was at Jam' and said to him, 'Do I have a ḥajj, Messenger of Allah?' The Messenger of Allah ﷺ said, 'Whoever has prayed the morning prayer with us at Jam', having gone to 'Arafat before that, either by night or day, has completed his dishevelment and completed his ḥajj.' Ash-Sha'bī said, 'Anyone who does not stop at Jam' makes it *'umrah*.'

Those who take the majority position answer that the *āyah* does not contain any proof of the obligatory nature of standing or of spending the night there since that is not mentioned in it. All that is mentioned is remembrance (*dhikr*). All agree that if someone stops at Muzdalifah without remembering Allah, his *ḥajj* is complete. If the remembrance commanded is not a primary element of the ḥajj, then it is even more probable that being present at the place is not going to be either. Abū 'Umar said, 'Similarly they agree that, when the sun rises on the Day of Sacrifice, the time of stopping at Jam' has been missed but whoever manages to stop there before sunrise has caught it. Some say that it is an obligation and some say that it is sunnah.' As for the *ḥadīth* of 'Urwah ibn Muḍarris, in some variants it states that it is about stopping at Muzdalifah rather than spending the night there. That is similar to the *ḥadīth* of 'Abd ar-Raḥmān ibn Ya'mar ad-Dīlī who said, 'I saw the Messenger of Allah ﷺ at 'Arafah when some people from Najd came to ask him about the ḥajj. The Messenger of Allah ﷺ said, "The ḥajj is 'Arafah. Whoever catches it before dawn on the night of Jam' has a complete *ḥajj*.' An-Nasā'ī related this from Isḥāq ibn Ibrāhīm from Wakī' from Sufyān ath-Thawrī from Bukayr ibn 'Aṭā' from 'Abd ar-Raḥmān ibn Ya'mar ad-Dīlī. Ibn 'Uyayna related it from Bukayr from 'Abd ar-Raḥmān ibn Ya'mar ad-Dīlī. He said, 'I saw the Messenger of Allah ﷺ say, "The ḥajj is 'Arafah. Whoever catches it before dawn has caught it. The days at Minā are three. There is no sin for someone who hurries on after two and there is no sin for someone who stays longer."' He says in the *ḥadīth* of 'Urwah, 'Whoever prays this prayer of ours,' and he mentioned the prayer at Muzdalifah. Scholars agree that if he spends the night there, stops and then sleeps through the prayer and misses the prayer with the imam, his ḥajj is nevertheless complete. If attending the prayer with the imam is not a primary element of the ḥajj, then stopping at the place where the prayer is held is even less likely to be. They said that this *ḥadīth* only verifies the obligation of 'Arafah.

**Remember Him because He has guided you, even though before this you were astray.**

The command to remember is repeated for emphasis. It is said that the first is a command to remember at the Mash'ar al-Harām and the second is to remember with sincerity. It is said that the second time it means to acknowledge the blessing and show gratitude for it and then to remind them about the time when they were misguided. Remember Him in a good way as He has guided you in a good way. Remember Him as He has taught you what to do and do not turn from it. *'Before this'* refers to before the guidance of Islam came, or before the Qur'an, or before the Prophet ﷺ. The first is the most likely, and Allah knows best.

ثُمَّ أَفِيضُوا۟ مِنْ حَيْثُ أَفَاضَ ٱلنَّاسُ وَٱسْتَغْفِرُوا۟ ٱللَّهَ ۚ إِنَّ ٱللَّهَ غَفُورٌ رَّحِيمٌ ﴿١٩٩﴾

**199 Then press on from where the people press on and ask Allah's forgiveness. Allah is Ever-Forgiving, Most Merciful.**

**Then press on from where the people press on**

The 'people' referred to here are those called Ḥums (Quraysh and others), who did not stop with the people at 'Arafāt, but stopped at Muzdalifah, which is part of the Ḥaram, claiming that they were its servants and must venerate only it. Notwithstanding the fact that they knew that 'Arafāt was where Ibrāhīm had stood, they did not leave the Ḥaram and stood instead at Jam' while the people were at 'Arafāt. They were told to press on with the people. 'Then' in this *āyah* is for order, and it adds one sentence to another. Aḍ-Ḍaḥḥāk says that the entire community is addressed and 'people' means Ibrāhīm as is the case in 3:173. So it has a singular meaning. It is possible that the pressing on here means from 'Arafah or that it means the pressing on from Muzdalifah. Aṭ-Ṭabarī said that it means: 'Press on from where Ibrāhīm pressed on from Muzdalifah Jam',' namely, press on to Minā because the pressing on from 'Arafah is before the pressing on from Muzdalifah.

This is evidence to support those who make it an obligation to stop at Muzdalifah since there is a command to press on from it, and Allah knows best. The sound position regarding the interpretation of this *āyah* is the first one. At-Tirmidhī related that 'Ā'ishah said, 'Quraysh and those following their religion, namely the Ḥums, used to stop at Muzdalifah, saying, "We are the servants of Allah." Other people stood at 'Arafah. Therefore Allah revealed: *"Press on from where the people press on."*' This is a sound *ḥasan ḥadīth.* 'Ā'ishah said in *Ṣaḥīḥ Muslim*, 'The Ḥums were those about whom Allah revealed: *"Press on from where the people press on."*' She added, 'The people used to press on from 'Arafāt while the Ḥums pressed on from Muzdalifah. They said, "We only press on from the Ḥaram." When *"Press on from where the people press on,"* was revealed they returned to 'Arafāt.' This is an explicit text. It is very sound and other views are not relied on. Allah is the One we ask for help.

Sa'īd ibn Jubayr recited '*an-nāsī*' (the forgetter). Its interpretation is that it refers to Adam since Allah says: *'He forgot. We did not find that he had a firm resolve.'* (20:115)

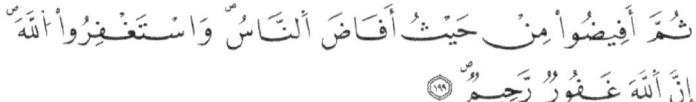

Allah commanded them to ask for forgiveness because this is the place for doing that and a place where it is likely that it will be accepted and that mercy will descend. One group said that it means: 'Ask Allah's forgiveness for any actions you did that are contrary to the sunnah of Ibrāhīm with respect to your standing at Quzaḥ at Muzdalifah rather than 'Arafah.'

Abū Dāwud related that 'Alī said, 'In the morning the Prophet ﷺ stood on Quzaḥ and said, "This is Quzaḥ. It is a place of standing. All of Jam' is a place of standing. I sacrificed here and all of Minā is a place of sacrifice, so sacrifice where your baggage is."' Therefore the ruling for the ḥājjīs when they press on from 'Arafah to Muzdalifah is that they spend the night there. Then the imam leads the people in the *Ṣubḥ* prayer before dawn and they stand at the Sacred Landmark. Quzaḥ is the mountain on which the imam stands. They continue to remember Allah and make supplication until it is close to sunrise. Then they press on before sunrise, differing from the Arabs who used to press on after sunrise, when they would say, '*Ashriq thabīr kaymā nughīr*' (Illuminate Thabīr so that we may hasten)', meaning to approach coming out of *iḥrām*.

Al-Bukhārī related that 'Amr ibn Maymūn said, 'I saw 'Umar pray *Ṣubḥ* at Jam'. Then he stood and said, "The idolaters used not to press on until the sun rose, saying, '*Ashriq thabīr.*' The Prophet ﷺ acted differently to them and pressed on before sunrise."' Ibn 'Uyaynah related from Ibn Jurayj from Muḥammad ibn Makhramah from Ibn Ṭāwūs from his father that the people of the Jāhiliyyah used to press on from 'Arafah before sunset, and press on from Muzdalifah after sunrise. The Messenger of Allah ﷺ delayed one and brought the other forward: he delayed the pressing on from 'Arafah and hastened that of Muzdalifah, acting differently to the idolaters.

When they press on before sunrise, their ruling is to press on in the manner in which they pressed on from 'Arafah, which is that the imam travels with the people at a medium pace, and speeds up slightly when he finds a gap. 'A medium pace' (*'anaq*) is a well known pace taken by mounts. '*Naṣṣ*' is a faster pace than *'anaq*, like *khabab* (a quick amble). We find in *Ṣaḥīḥ Muslim* that Usāmah ibn Zayd was asked, 'How did the Messenger of Allah ﷺ travel when he pressed on from 'Arafah?' He answered, 'He travelled at a medium pace, and when he found a gap, he went quicker (*naṣṣ*).' Hishām said that *naṣṣ* is faster than *'anaq* as we already mentioned. It is recommended to hasten in the valley of Muḥassir for the distance of a stone's throw. There is no harm if one does not do that. It is part of Minā. Ath-Thawrī and others related from Abu-z-Zubayr that Jābir said, 'The Messenger of Allah ﷺ pressed on with tranquillity and told them, "Go gently and quickly in the valley of Muḥassir" and he told them, "Take your rites from me."'

When they reached Minā on the morning of the Day of Sacrifice, they stoned the Jamrat al-'Aqabah in the middle of the morning while mounted, if possible. It is not recommended to ride to the other *jamrahs*. They stone them with seven pebbles, each of them like a pea, as will be explained. When they have stoned them, they leave their *iḥrām* and what was forbidden to them of clothing and other things becomes lawful for them again: except for women, scent and hunting, according to Mālik and Isḥāq in the transmission of Abū Dāwud al-Khaffāf. 'Umar ibn al-Khaṭṭāb and Ibn 'Umar said, 'Everything is lawful to him except women and scent.' According to Mālik, if someone uses scent after stoning and before the *Ṭawāf al-Ifāḍah*, he does not owe *fidyah* because of what has come about that. He believes that if someone hunts after stoning the Jamrah and before the *Ṭawāf al-Ifāḍah*, he owes reparation. Ash-Shāfi'ī, Aḥmad, Isḥāq and Abū Thawr said that everything except women is lawful for him. That is related from Ibn 'Abbās.

The person performing ḥajj stops saying the *talbīyah* with the first pebble he throws at the Jamrat al-'Aqabah. This is the position of most of the people of knowledge in Madīnah and elsewhere. This is permitted and allowed according to Mālik. What is well known from him, however, is that one stops saying it at midday on the day of 'Arafah according to what he mentioned in the *Muwaṭṭā'* from 'Alī. He said, 'That is the way with us.'

The basis for this in the Sunnah is what Muslim related from al-Faḍl ibn 'Abbās. He was riding behind the Messenger of Allah ﷺ who said to the people on the evening of 'Arafah and the morning of Jam', 'You must be calm!' He was holding back his she-camel until he entered Muḥassir (which is part of Minā). He said, 'You must have pea-sized pebbles with which to stone the Jamrah.' He said, 'The Messenger of Allah ﷺ continued to say the *talbīyah* until he had stoned the Jamrat al-'Aqabah.' One variant has: 'The Prophet ﷺ indicated with his hand how someone flicks a pebble.' We find in al-Bukhārī that 'Abdullāh went to the largest Jamrah with the House on his left and Minā on his right. He threw seven pebbles and said, 'That is how the stoning was done by the one to whom *Sūrat al-Baqarah* was revealed.' Ad-Dāraquṭnī related that 'Ā'ishah said that the Messenger of Allah ﷺ said, 'When you have stoned, shaved and sacrificed, then everything except women is lawful for you. Clothing and scent are lawful for you.' We find in *al-Bukhārī* that 'Ā'ishah said, 'I put scent on the Messenger of Allah ﷺ with these two hands when he went into *iḥrām* and when he came out of it before doing *ṭawāf*.' She stretched out her hands. According to scholars, this is the lesser coming out of *iḥrām*. The greater coming out of *iḥrām* is the *Ṭawāf al-Ifāḍah* which makes lawful women and all things that are forbidden in *iḥrām*. More of this will be mentioned in *Sūrat al-Ḥajj*, Allah willing.

فَإِذَا قَضَيْتُم مَّنَاسِكَكُمْ فَاذْكُرُوا اللَّهَ كَذِكْرِكُمْ آبَاءَكُمْ
أَوْ أَشَدَّ ذِكْرًا فَمِنَ النَّاسِ مَن يَقُولُ رَبَّنَا آتِنَا فِي الدُّنْيَا وَمَا لَهُ
فِي الْآخِرَةِ مِنْ خَلَاقٍ ﴿٢٠٠﴾

**200 When you have completed your rites, remember Allah as you used to remember your forefathers, or even more. There are some people who say, 'Our Lord, give us good in this world.' They will have no share in the Next World.**

**When you have completed your rites, remember Allah**

Mujāhid says that the '*manāsik*' (rites) referred to here are the sacrifices and it means the spilling of blood. It is said that it refers to the pillars of ḥājj since the Prophet ﷺ said, 'Take your rites from me.' So the meaning is: 'When you perform the rites of ḥājj, remember Allah, and also remember Him and praise Him for His blessings to you.' '*Qaḍaytum*' means: 'you have performed and finished'. The verb can also be used for performing acts of worship outside of their defined time.

**as you used to remember your forefathers – or even more.**

The custom of the Arabs was that, when they completed the ḥajj, they would stand at the Jamrah and boast of their forefathers and mention the glorious and courageous feats of their ancestors, to the extent that one of them would say, 'O Allah, my father was a great tent with a huge pit and much wealth. Give me the like of what You gave him!' and would only mention his father. This *āyah* was revealed commanding them to remember Allah more than they used to remember their forefathers in the time of the Jāhiliyyah. This is the position of most commentators. Ibn 'Abbās, 'Aṭā', aḍ-Ḍaḥḥāk and ar-Rabī' said that the meaning of the *āyah* is: 'Remember Allah as children remember their fathers and mothers. Seek help from Him and seek refuge with Him as you did with your parents when you were a child.' Another group say that the *āyah* means: 'Remember Allah and esteem Him, defend His sanctity and repel those who desire to introduce *shirk* into His *dīn* and rites just as you would speak well of your parents if someone criticised them, and protect and defend them.'

Abu-l-Jawzā' said to Ibn 'Abbās, 'These days no one mentions his forefathers. So what does the *āyah* mean?' He replied, 'That is not what it is about. Allah is angrier when someone disobeys Him than your parents are angry with you when you abuse them.'

Az-Zajjāj said that *'even more'* means 'with a stronger remembrance.' It is possible that it means: 'Remember Him more.'

**There are some people who say, 'Our Lord, give us good in this world'**

This refers to the idolaters. Abū Wā'il, as-Suddī and Ibn Zayd said, 'In the time of the Jāhiliyyah, the Arabs used only to pray for the good things of this world. They would ask for camels, sheep and victory over their enemies. They would not ask for the Next World since they did not acknowledge it or believe in it. Here they are being forbidden to ask for only this world. The prohibition comes in the form of a report about what they do. It is also possible that this threat refers to the believers when their supplication is confined to this world. They will have no portion in the Next World because they do not ask for it.' *'Khalāq'* is a portion.

وَمِنْهُم مَّن يَقُولُ رَبَّنَآ ءَاتِنَا فِى ٱلدُّنْيَا حَسَنَةً وَفِى ٱلْءَاخِرَةِ
حَسَنَةً وَقِنَا عَذَابَ ٱلنَّارِ ﴿٢٠١﴾

**201 And there are others who say, 'Our Lord, give us good in this world, and good in the Next World, and safeguard us from the punishment of the Fire.'**

The 'others' referred to here are the Muslims who ask for the good of this world and the Next World. There is disagreement about exactly what the two kinds of good entail and there are many things said about this. It is related from 'Alī ibn Abī Ṭālib that the good in this world is a good woman and in the Next World it is the houris, and the *'punishment of the Fire'* refers to a bad woman. This, however, is unlikely and is not a sound transmission from 'Alī because the Fire is, in reality, a burning fire and interpreting it to be a woman would only be metaphorical.

Qatādah said the good of this ephemeral world takes the form of health and adequate wealth. Al-Ḥasan said that the good of this world is knowledge and worship. Other things are said. But what most of the people of knowledge believe is that what is meant by the two kinds of good are the blessings of this world and the Next World. This is sound and the expression entails all of that because the word 'good' in both cases in the supplication has no definite article and so it can be applied to all sorts of good. The good of the Next World is the Garden by consensus. It is also said that it does not mean one particular good, but rather 'Give us the good of this world.'

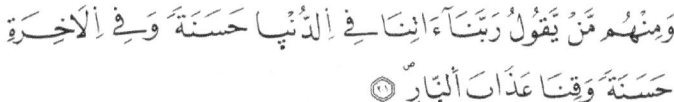

**and safeguard us from the punishment of the Fire.'**

What is meant here is a supplication that the person concerned will not enter the Fire because of his acts of disobedience and that he should be brought out of it by intercession. It is possible that it is a supplication confirming the request to enter the Garden so that it expresses the desire for salvation and success on both fronts. It is as what one of the Companions said to the Prophet ﷺ, 'I say in my supplication, "O Allah, make me enter the Garden and protect me from the Fire." I do not know what it is that you and Mu'ādh mumble.' The Messenger of Allah ﷺ said to him, 'We say that in a low voice.' Abū Dāwud transmitted it in his *Sunan* as did Ibn Mājah.

This *āyah* is a comprehensive supplication, asking for both this world and the Next. Anas was asked, 'Make supplication for us.' He said, 'Give them good in this world and good in the Next World and protect them from the punishment of the Fire.' They said, 'More.' He said, 'What more do you want? I have asked for this world and the Next World!' We find in the *Ṣaḥīḥ* collections that Anas is reported as saying that the Prophet ﷺ frequently used this supplication: 'Give them good in this world and good in the Next World and protect them from punishment of the Fire.' Anas used to use this supplication regularly. It is reported that while 'Umar was doing *ṭawāf*, he said, 'Our Lord, give us good in this world and good in the Next World and protect us from the punishment of the Fire,' and that he said nothing else. Abū 'Ubayd mentioned this. Ibn Jurayj said that he heard that the most frequent supplication of the Muslim when standing at 'Arafāt should be: 'Our Lord, give us good in this world and good in the Next World and protect us from the punishment of the Fire.'

Ibn 'Abbās said, 'There is an angel who has been standing at the [Yemeni] Corner since Allah created the heavens and the earth, saying, "Amen." Therefore say: "Our Lord, give us good in this world and good in the Next World and protect us from the punishment of the Fire."' 'Aṭā' ibn Abī Rabāḥ was asked about the Yemeni corner while he was doing *ṭawāf* of the House and he said, 'Abū Hurayrah related to me that the Prophet ﷺ said, 'Seventy angels have been entrusted to it. If someone says, "O Allah, I ask You for pardon and well-being in this world and the Next! Our Lord, give us good in this world and good in the Next World and protect us from the punishment of the Fire," they say, "Amen."' Ibn Mājah transmitted it in the *Sunān*.

أُوْلَٰٓئِكَ لَهُمْ نَصِيبٌ مِّمَّا كَسَبُواْۚ وَٱللَّهُ سَرِيعُ ٱلْحِسَابِ ۝٢٠٢

**202 They will have a good share from what they have earned. Allah is swift at reckoning.**

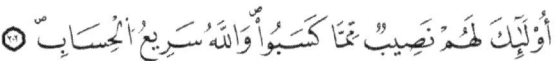

**They will have a good share from what they have earned.**

This refers to the second group, the party of Islam, and informs them that they will have the reward for the ḥajj or the reward for the supplication. A believer's supplication is worship in itself. It is also said that the word 'they' refers to both groups. The believer will receive the reward for his action and his supplication, and the unbeliever will have the punishment for his *shirk* and his confining his outlook to this world. Evidence for that are the words of Allah: *'All have ranks according to what they did.'* (6:132)

**Allah is swift at reckoning.**

'Swift' (*sarīʿ*) comes from the verb *saruʿa*, meaning 'to hasten'. *'Ḥisāb'* (reckoning) is a verbal noun like *muḥāsabah. 'Ḥisāb'* means the same as what is counted (*muḥāsabah*) and so what is counted constitutes the reckoning. *Ḥasab*, meaning noble descent, is what a man counts as one of his glories. One can say that his glory (*ḥasab*) is his *dīn* or his wealth. In a *ḥadīth* we find, '*Ḥasab* is wealth and nobility is piety.' Samurah ibn Jundub related it. Ibn Mājah transmitted it. It is also found in *ash-Shihāb*.

The *āyah* means that Allah is swift in calculating the reckoning and has no need of counting, addition or the action of thought as a human reckoner would. That is why He says: *'We are sufficient as Reckoner.'* (21:47) The Messenger of Allah ﷺ said, 'O Allah, Sender down of the Book, Swift at Reckoning.' Allah knows His slaves and what they do and has no need of memory or reflection since He knows everything to be reckoned for or against them. The purpose of reckoning is ascertaining the truth.

It is said that the phrase means that Allah is swift at repaying people for their actions. It is said that it means that one thing does not distract Him from other things. He reckons them all at the same time as we find in His words: *'Your creation and rising is only like that of a single self.'* (31:28) Al-Ḥasan said, 'His reckoning is swifter than the blink of a eye.' One report says: 'Allah reckons in the amount of time it takes to milk a sheep.' It is said that when He reckons one person, He reckons all creation. 'Alī was asked, 'How can Allah reckon all His slaves in a single day?' He replied, 'In the same way that He provides for them in a single day!' Another possible meaning of reckoning is that Allah acquaints His slaves with the exact repayment they will receive for their actions and reminds them of what they forgot as is seen in His words: *'On the Day Allah raises up all of them together, He will inform them of what they did. Allah has recorded it while they have forgotten it.'* (58:6) It is said that it means that He is swift at bringing about the Day of Reckoning and so the meaning of the *āyah* is to warn about the Day of Rising.

All of these interpretations are possible. The slave of Allah should make the reckoning light for himself through righteous actions. The reckoning will be lighter in the Next World for the one who calls himself to account in this world.

Ibn 'Abbās said, 'The words *"They will have a good share..."* refer to a man who uses money to perform ḥajj for someone else and has a reward.' A *ḥadīth* is reported about that in which a man said, 'O Messenger of Allah, my father died without performing ḥajj. Can I perform ḥajj on his behalf?' The Prophet ﷺ answered, 'If your father had a debt, would you not pay it?' He answered, 'Yes.' He said, 'A debt owed to Allah is more entitled to receive settlement.' He asked, 'Will I have a reward?' and then Allah revealed: *'They will have a good share from what they have earned.'* So the meaning is that the reward for the ḥajj for the dead person is shared between him and the dead person.

Abū 'Abdullāh Muḥammad ibn Khuwayzimandād stated in *al-Aḥkām*, 'The position of Ibn 'Abbās is like that of Mālik because the final position of Mālik is that the one for whom the ḥajj is done has the reward for paying for it and the ḥajj belongs to the one who does it. So it is as if the person doing the ḥajj has the reward of his body and actions and the one who pays for it has the reward of his spending. That is why we say that there is no difference in this ruling between the one who has performed the obligatory ḥajj for himself or one who has not, because in the case of actions in which a proxy is permitted, the ruling of the proxy is the same for someone who has performed it before or has not performed it. This is true of actions which are for this world and those which are for the Next World. Do you not see that someone who owes zakat, *kaffārah* or the like can perform that on behalf of someone else, even if he has not performed it for himself? The same is true of someone who does not attend to his best interests in this world. He can, nonetheless, act as proxy for someone else in such things as that and undertake that for someone else even if he has not undertaken it for himself. He can carry out a marriage for someone else even if he himself has not married.'

وَاذْكُرُوا اللَّهَ فِي أَيَّامٍ مَعْدُودَاتٍ فَمَنْ تَعَجَّلَ فِي يَوْمَيْنِ فَلَا إِثْمَ عَلَيْهِ وَمَنْ تَأَخَّرَ فَلَا إِثْمَ عَلَيْهِ لِمَنِ اتَّقَىٰ وَاتَّقُوا اللَّهَ وَاعْلَمُوا أَنَّكُمْ إِلَيْهِ تُحْشَرُونَ ﴿٢٠٣﴾

**203 Remember Allah on the designated days. Those who hurry on in two days have done no wrong, and those who stay another day have done no wrong – those of them who are fearful of Allah. Be fearful of Allah. And know that you will be gathered back to Him.**

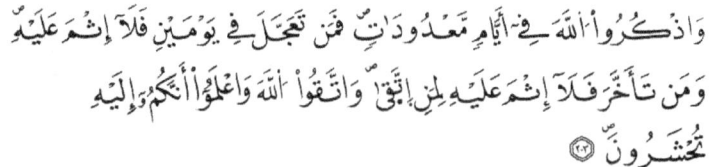

**Remember Allah on the designated days.**

There is no disagreement among scholars that the 'designated days' here refer to the days of Minā. They are the days of *tashrīq*. These three days have various names. They are the days of the stoning of the *jamrah*s which takes place over three days but then it is permitted for someone on ḥajj to hurry and do it in two days after the Day of Sacrifice. Ath-Tha'labī and Ibrāhīm [an-Nakha'ī] said that the 'designated days' are the *'ushar* (10th, 11th and 12th) and the 'specific days' (22:28) are the days of sacrifice. Makkī and al-Mahdawī also said that the 'designated days' are the *'ushar.*

Allah commands His slaves to remember Him on designated days which are the three days after the Day of Sacrifice. The Day of Sacrifice itself is not one of them by the consensus of the people that no one can hurry and leave on the second day. If the Day of Sacrifice had been one of the designated days, then it would be permitted for those who wish to hurry on to leave on the Day of Nafr because he has taken two of the designated days. Ad-Dāraquṭnī, at-Tirmidhī and others transmitted from 'Abd ar-Raḥmān ibn Ya'mar ad-Dīlī that some one of the people of Najd went to the Messenger of Allah ﷺ at 'Arafah to question him and he commanded someone to call out: 'The ḥajj is 'Arafah. Whoever comes on the night of Jam' before dawn has caught it. The days at Minā are three. There is no sin for someone who hurries on after two and there is no sin for someone who stays longer.' It means anyone who hurries on after two of the days at Minā has to stay at Minā for three days including the Day of Sacrifice. His total stoning consists of forty-nine pebbles and he does not have to stone on the third day. Anyone who doesn't leave until the end of the third day stays at Minā for four days because of the Day of Sacrifice and does the full amount of stoning as will be explained. Part of the evidence for staying three days at Minā, as we mentioned, is what al-'Arjī said:

It was only three days at Minā
before Nafr parted us.

The days of stoning are 'designated' and the days of sacrifice are 'specific'. Nāfi' related that Ibn 'Umar said that the 'designated' days and 'specific' days together add up to four days: the Day of Sacrifice and the three days after it. The Day of Sacrifice is 'specific', and not 'designated'; the next two days are both 'specific' and 'designated', and the fourth day is 'designated' and not 'specific'. This is the position in the school of Mālik and others.

That is the case because the first day, the Day of Sacrifice, is not one of the days particular to Minā nor one of those which the Prophet ﷺ specified when he said, 'The days of Minā are three.' So it is 'specific' because Allah says: *'Invoke*

*Allah's name on specific days over livestock He has provided for them.'* (22:28) There is no disagreement that what is meant is the Sacrifice, and the Sacrifice is on the first day. It is the day of Aḍḥā and the two days after it. The consensus of our scholars is that there should be no sacrifice on the fourth day and so the fourth day is not included in His word, 'specific' because there is no sacrifice on it. The stoning on it is 'designated' on account of the stoning, even though it is not 'specific' because of the lack of sacrificing on it. Ibn al-'Arabī said, 'The truth is that the Day of Sacrifice is 'designated' for stoning and 'specific' for slaughtering, but our scholars says that it is not included in His words, *'Remember Allah on designated days.'*

Abū Ḥanīfah and ash-Shāfi'ī said that the 'specific days' are the ten from the 1st of Dhu-l-Ḥijjah to the Day of Sacrifice. Their position on it does not vary and they related that from Ibn 'Abbās. Aṭ-Ṭaḥāwī related from Abū Yūsuf that the 'specific days' are the days of sacrifice and that Abū Yūsuf said, 'That is related from 'Umar and 'Alī and I believe it because Allah says: *"Invoke Allah's name on specific days over livestock He has provided for them."'* Al-Karkhī related from Muḥammad ibn al-Ḥasan that the 'specific days' are the three days of Sacrifice: Aḍḥā and the two days after it. Aṭ-Ṭabarī said, 'According to the view of Abū Yūsuf and Muḥammad there is no difference between the "specific" and "designated" because the "designated days" mentioned in the Qur'an are undisputedly the days of *tashrīq*, and no one doubts that that the "designated days" do not include the ten days, because Allah says: *"Those who hurry on in two days have done no wrong."* The "ten" do not have a ruling connected to two rather than three.' It Is related from Ibn 'Abbās that the 'specific' are the ten and the 'designated' are the days of *tashrīq*. That is the majority position.

Ibn Zayd said that the 'specific days' are the ten days of Dhu-l-Ḥijjah and the days of *tashrīq*. This is unlikely based on what we have mentioned and the literal meaning of the *āyah* refutes it. Allah assigned remembrance in the designated and specific days which indicates something different to what he says, and so there is no need to deal with it.

There is no disagreement that the person addressed here is the person on ḥajj who says the *takbīr* while stoning the *jamrah*s, over the animals he intends to sacrifice during the specific days, and after the prayers without the *talbīyah*. Does it include other than those on ḥajj? The *fuqahā'* of all the regions and the famous Companions and Tābi'ūn agree that everyone is meant to do the *takbīr*, especially at the times of the prayer, and so it is recited, whether you pray alone or in a group, to imitate the Salaf. The *Mukhtasar* of Khalil states that women should not do it but the first position is better known since women follow the rules of *iḥrām* in the same way that men do and the *Mudawwanah* states that.

If someone forgets the *takbīr* after the prayer and not much time has passed since he completed it, he should say it. If, however, a long time has passed, he owes nothing. Ibn al-Jallāb said that. Malik is reported in the *Mukhtaṣar* as saying that you should say it as long as you are still sitting. If you rise before saying it you owe nothing. According to the *Mudawwanah*, Mālik said that if the imam forgets the *takbīr* and remembers soon after, he sits and says it, but if a long time has passed, he owes nothing. If he leaves without saying the *takbīr* and the people are still sitting down, they say it.

Scholars disagree about the end of the time of saying the *takbīr*. 'Umar ibn al-Khaṭṭāb, 'Alī ibn Abī Ṭālib and Ibn 'Abbās said that it is said from the *Ṣubḥ* prayer on the Day of 'Arafah up until *'Aṣr* on the last of the days of *tashrīq*. Ibn Mas'ūd and Abū Ḥanīfah say that it is from the morning of the Day of 'Arafah up until *'Aṣr* of the Day of Sacrifice. His two companions disagree and take the first position. So they agree about its beginning, but not its end. Mālik says that the *takbīr* should be said from *Ẓuhr* on the Day of Sacrifice to the *Ṣubḥ* prayer on the last of the days of *tashrīq*. Ash-Shāfi'ī agrees with that, and it is also the position of Ibn 'Umar and another position of Ibn 'Abbās. Zayd ibn Thābit said that the *takbīr* should be said from *Ẓuhr* on the Day of Sacrifice to the days of *tashrīq*.

Ibn al-'Arabī says that those who say that the *takbīr* is said from the Day of 'Arafah and stopped at *'Aṣr* on the Day of Sacrifice have abandoned the evident text because Allah says: '*on the designated days*', which are three. Those people say that they say the *takbīr* over two days and have therefore abandoned the literal text without any proof. As for those who say that it is said on the Day of 'Arafah and the days of *tashrīq*, their argument is that Allah says: '*When you pour down from 'Arafāt*' (2:198) and so 'Arafāt is included in the days mentioned. So it would be valid for someone to say that the *takbīr* should be said from *Maghrib* on the Day of 'Arafah because that is the time of pouring down. Doing it before that is not demanded by the literal wording of the *ayah*. It is obligatory from the Day of Tarwīyah, when one alights in Minā.

There is disagreement about the wording of the *takbīr*. The well-known position in the school of Mālik is that the *takbīr* is said three times after each prayer. Ziyād ibn Ziyād related it from Mālik. One transmission is that one says after the three *takbīrs*: 'There is no god but Allah. Allah is greater and praise be to Allah.' ('*Lā ilāha illa-llāh, wa-llāhu akbar, wa lillāhi-l-ḥamd.*') In the *Mukhtaṣar* Mālik is reported as saying, 'Allah is greater. Allah is greater. There is no god but Allah and Allah is greater. Allah is greater and praise be to Allah.' (*'Allāhu akbar. Allāhu akbar. Lā ilāha illa-llāh, wa-llāhu akbar. Allāhu akbar, wa lillāhi-l-ḥamd.'*)

**Those who hurry on in two days have done no wrong,**

Hurrying on is only permitted at the end of the second day. The same applies to the third day because the time of stoning during those days is after midday. All agree that on the Day of Sacrifice you only stone the Jamrat al-'Aqabah because the Messenger of Allah ﷺ did not stone the other *jamrah*s on the Day of Sacrifice. The time for stoning on that day is from sunrise to midday. They also agree that the time for stoning the *jamrah*s on the days of *tashrīq* is from after midday up until sunset. They disagree about someone who stones the Jamrat al-'Aqabah before dawn or after dawn but before sunrise. Mālik, Abū Ḥanīfah, Aḥmad and Isḥāq said that it is allowed if it was after dawn, but not before dawn.

Mālik, Abū Ḥanīfah, Aḥmad and Isḥāq said that it is permitted to stone the *jamrahs* after dawn, but before sunrise. Mālik said, 'It has not reached us that the Messenger of Allah ﷺ allowed anyone to stone before dawn.' It is not permitted to stone them before dawn. If someone stones them before dawn, then he must repeat it. Abū Ḥanīfah and his people said similarly that it is not permitted to stone them then. Aḥmad and Isḥāq also said that. One group permit stoning before dawn breaks. It is related that Asmā' bint Abī Bakr used to stone at night. She said, 'We used to do this in the time of the Messenger of Allah ﷺ.' Abū Dāwud transmitted it. This position is related from 'Aṭā', Ibn Abī Mulaykah, and 'Ikrimah ibn Khālid. Ash-Shāfi'ī said that the stoning could occur after the middle of the night. Another group said that there is no stoning until sunrise. Mujāhid, an-Nakha'ī and ath-Thawrī said that. Abū Thawr said, 'If someone stones before sunrise, and they disagree about it, it does not satisfy the requirement. If they agree or there is a sunnah about it, then it does satisfy it.'

Abū 'Umar said, 'As for the view of ath-Thawrī and those who follow him, his argument is that the Messenger of Allah ﷺ stoned the *jamrah* after sunrise and said, "Take your rites from me."' Ibn al-Mundhir said, 'The sunnah is that one does not stone until after sunrise and stoning before sunrise does not satisfy the requirement. If someone does do it, then he must repeat it, since he has acted contrary to the Sunnah that the Messenger of Allah ﷺ laid down for his community.'

Ma'mar related from Hishām ibn 'Urwah that his father said, 'The Messenger of Allah ﷺ commanded Umm Salamah to be in Makkah in the morning of her day…' Abū 'Umar said that this *ḥadīth* varies from Hishām. One group related it *mursal* from Hisham from his father as Ma'mar related it and others related it from Hisham from his father from 'Ā'ishah with an *isnād*. All of them are reliable. The point is that it indicates that she had stoned the *jamrah* at Minā before dawn, since the Messenger of Allah ﷺ commanded her to be in Makkah on the morning of the Day of Sacrifice. This could only happen if she had stoned the *jamrah* at Minā during the night before dawn. Allah knows best.

Abū Dāwud related from Hārūn ibn 'Abdullāh from Ibn Abī Fudayk from aḍ-Ḍaḥḥāk ibn 'Uthmān from Hishām ibn 'Urwah from his father that 'Ā'ishah said, 'The Messenger of Allah ﷺ sent Umm Salamah ahead on the night before the Day of Sacrifice. She stoned the *jamrah* before dawn and then went and performed the *Ṭawāf al-Ifāḍah*. That was the day when the Messenger of Allah ﷺ was going to be with her. If this is confirmed, then stoning at night is permitted, but what is preferred is from sunrise to midday. Abū 'Umar said that they agree that the preferred time for stoning the *Jamrat al-'Aqabah* is between sunrise and midday. All but Mālik agree that if someone stones before sunset on the Day of Sacrifice, it satisfies the requirement and he owes nothing. Mālik said, 'I recommend that if he fails to stone the *Jamrat al-'Aqabah* until evening he should sacrifice an animal that he brought from outside the Ḥaram.

They disagree about someone who does not stone until sunset and then stones in the night or the following morning, Mālik said that he owes a sacrifice. His argument was that the Messenger of Allah ﷺ set a time for stoning the *jamrah*: the Day of Sacrifice. If someone stones after sunset, he has stoned after the end of the time and if someone does something in the ḥajj outside of its time, he owes a sacrifice. Ash-Shāfi'ī said that he owes no sacrifice. That is also the view of Abu Yūsuf and Muḥammad. Abū Thawr said that was because when someone said to the Messenger of Allah ﷺ, 'Messenger of Allah, I stoned after the evening,' he said, 'There is no harm.' Mālik said, 'If someone forgets to stone the *jamrah*s until evening, he should do the stoning at whatever time he remembers, day or night, as someone prays a prayer that he forgot whenever he remembers it. He only stones what he missed. If it is one *jamrah*, he stones it and then stones the *jamrah*s after it. The order of the *jamrah*s in stoning is mandatory. It is not permitted to start stoning the next *jamrah* until he has completed stoning the previous *jamrah*, as is the case with the *rak'ah*s of the prayer.' This is well-known in the School. It is said that the order is not mandatory for the validity of stoning, but all stoning at the correct time of performance satisfies the requirement.

There is no stoning after the end of the days of stoning. If someone remembers failing to do that after he is in Makkah or after he has left it, he owes a sacrifice, whether he omitted all of the stoning or just one *jamrah* or even one pebble of the *jamrah*. If the days of Minā are over, he owes a sacrifice. Abū Ḥanīfah said, 'If someone omits all of the *jamrah*s, he owes a sacrifice. If he omits one *jamrah*, he must feed a poor person half a *ṣā'* of food for every pebble of the *jamrah* he missed until it reaches the level of sacrifice and then he should feed what he wishes, except in the case of the *Jamrat al-'Aqabah* for which he owes a sacrifice. Al-Awzā'ī said that he gives *ṣadaqah* for omitting a pebble. Ath-Thawrī said that he should feed in the case of one, two or three pebbles. If it is four or more, he owes a sacrifice. Al-Layth said that there is a sacrifice for one pebble missed. That is one of the two views of ash-Shāfi'ī. His final position is the well-known one: a *mudd* of food for one pebble, two *mudd*s for two pebbles, and a sacrifice for three pebbles.

The majority say that there is no possibility for anyone to complete anything of the rite of stoning the *jamrah*s on the days of *tashrīq* he has missed once the sun has set on the last day, which is the fourth day from the Day of Sacrifice and the third of the days of *tashrīq*. Such a person must do reparation in the form of sacrifice or feeding the poor according to what we have just mentioned.

It is not permitted to spend the night at Makkah, or elsewhere other than Minā, during the nights of *tashrīq*. All agree that that is not permitted although there is an exception made for herdsmen and those of the family of 'Abbās who bring water. Mālik said, 'A sacrifice is owed by anyone who spends any of the nights of Minā elsewhere, with the exception of herdsmen and those of the family of 'Abbās who bring water.' Al-Bukhārī related from Ibn 'Umar that al-'Abbās asked for permission from the Prophet ﷺ to spend the nights of Minā at Makkah in order to provide water and he gave him permission. Ibn 'Abd al-Barr said, 'Ibn 'Abbās used to oversee the watering and undertook that task. He provided the ḥājjīs with water during the Festival. That is why he had an allowance not to spend the nights at Minā, as did those who herded camels, due to their need to attend to the camels and to take them where they could graze, which was some distance from Minā.

Minā takes its name from the blood shed (*yumnā*) there. Ibn 'Abbās said, 'It is called Minā because Jibrīl said to the Prophet ﷺ: 'Wish (*tamann*).' He said, 'I wish for the Garden.' Therefore it is called Minā. He said that it is called Jam' because Ḥawwā' and Ādam met (*ijtima'a*) there. Jam' is also a name for Muzdalifah which is the Sacred Landmark as we already said.

Fuqahā' agree that spending the nights of Minā at Minā is one of the practices and rites of the ḥajj, except for those we have mentioned who are given a dispensation. Logic demands that any omission of its practices calls for a sacrifice, based on analogy with the rest of the ḥajj and its rites. We find in the *Muwaṭṭā'*: 'From Mālik from Nāfi' from Ibn 'Umar is that 'Umar said, "No one performing ḥajj should spend the nights of Minā beyond al-'Aqabah."' The area of 'Aqabah beyond which 'Umar forbade anyone to spend the night is that which is at the *jamrah* that people stone on the Day of Sacrifice, which is closer to Makkah. Ibn Nāfi' related it from Mālik in *al-Mabsūṭ*. He said that Mālik said, 'Anyone who spends the nights of Minā beyond it owes *fidyah*. That is because he spent the nights of Minā other than at Minā.' Spending those nights there is prescribed in the ḥajj and therefore a sacrifice is owed by someone who does not spend the night there, as is the case if someone does not spend the night at Muzdalifah. According to Mālik, *fidyah* means a *hady*. He said, 'It is a *hady* driven from outside the Ḥaram into the Ḥaram.'

Mālik related from 'Abdullāh ibn Abī Bakr ibn Muḥammad ibn 'Amr ibn Ḥazm from his father that Abu-l-Baddāḥ ibn 'Āṣim ibn 'Adī reported that the Messenger of Allah ﷺ allowed those herding the camels, who spend the nights away from Minā, to stone on the Day of Sacrifice, then to stone on the following day and the day after it. Then they stone on the Day of Nafr.

Abū 'Umar said, 'Mālik's view does not accord with this *ḥadīth*. He used to say that they stone the *Jamrat al-'Aqabah* on the Day of Sacrifice and then do not stone on the following day, which is the second of the days of *tashrīq*, and the day when those who want to hurry on do so or when those who are permitted to hurry on stone on the two days – that day and the day before it – because they perform what they owe. In his view no one pays anything except after it is obligatory for him. This is the meaning of Mālik's interpretation of this *ḥadīth* in the *Muwaṭṭā'*.'

Others say that there is nothing wrong in any of that, based on what is in the *ḥadīth* of Mālik, because they are all days of stoning. In Mālik's view, it is not permitted for herdsmen to bring forward the stoning because those other than the herdsmen are not permitted to stone the *jamrah*s on the days of *tashrīq* before midday. If someone stones them before midday, he must repeat it. They cannot bring it forward. They do have an allowance for that on the second to the third day. Ibn 'Abd al-Barr said, 'What Mālik says regarding this question exists in the transmission of Ibn Jurayj from Muḥammad ibn Abī Bakr ibn Muḥammad ibn 'Amr ibn Ḥazm from his father, saying that Abu-l-Baddāḥ ibn 'Āṣim ibn 'Adī reported that the Messenger of Allah ﷺ allowed those herding the camels, who spend the nights away from Minā, to alternate so that they would stone on the Day of Sacrifice, leave the second day and night and then stone on the following day. Our scholars say that stoning the third *jamrah* is cancelled for those who hurry on. Ibn Abī Zaminīn said, 'One stones it on the first day of Nafr when he wants to hurry on.' Ibn al-Mawwāz said, 'The one who hurries on stops with twenty-one pebbles in the two days, seven pebbles for each *jamrah.* That makes his total stoning forty-nine pebbles because he stoned the *Jamrat al-'Aqabah* with seven on the Day of Sacrifice.' Ibn al-Mundhir said that the stoning for the third day is cancelled.

Mālik related from Yaḥyā ibn Sa'īd that he heard 'Aṭā' ibn Abī Rabāḥ mention that there was a dispensation for the herdsmen to stone in the night at first. Al-Bājī said, '"At first" means that it was during the time of the Prophet ﷺ, because it is the first period of this Sharī'ah.' According to this it is *mursal.* It is possible that he means the time that 'Aṭā' heard it. Then it would be a *mawqūf isnād.*' Allah knows best. It has an *isnād* from 'Amr ibn Shu'ayb from his father from his grandfather from the Prophet ﷺ that ad-Dāraquṭnī and others transmitted. We mentioned it in *al-Muqtabis fī sharḥ Muwaṭṭā' Mālik ibn Anas.* They were permitted to stone at night because it is easier for them and shows more concern for their efforts to herd the camels, because night is a time when they do no graze or wander off. That is why they stone at that time.

There is disagreement about someone who misses doing the stoning until the sun has set. 'Aṭā' said, 'The only people who are permitted to stone at night are the herdsmen. Merchants may not do that.' It is related that Ibn 'Umar said, 'If someone fails to stone until the sun has set, he should not stone until the sun has risen on the following day.' Aḥmad and Isḥāq said that. Mālik said, as transmitted by Ibn al-Qāsim, 'If he fails to do it in the day he should stone at night and owes a sacrifice.' The *Muwaṭṭā'* does not mention owing a sacrifice. Ash-Shāfi'ī, Abū Thawr, Ya'qūb and Muḥammad said that if someone fails to stone until evening, he stones and does not owe a sacrifice. Al-Ḥasan al-Baṣri makes an allowance for stoning the *jamrah*s at night. Abū Ḥanīfah said that he stones and owes nothing, even though he did not mention it as being in the night. If he waits until the following day, then he owes a sacrifice. Ath-Thawrī said that if he delays the stoning until night, out of forgetfulness or deliberately, he must sacrifice.

As for the camel-herders or the people who get water (*siqāyah*) stoning at night, they owe no sacrifice based on the *ḥadīth.* However, if it is done by other people, then logic demands that they sacrifice. That is when it is deliberate, and Allah knows best.

It is confirmed that the Messenger of Allah ﷺ stoned the *Jamrat al-'Aqabah* on the Day of Sacrifice while mounted. Mālik and others recommended stoning it while mounted. Ibn 'Umar, Ibn az-Zubayr, and Sālim used to stone it on foot.

The stoning consists of twenty-one pebbles on each of the three days and the *takbīr* is said with each pebble. The person should face towards the Ka'bah when he stones and do the *jamrah*s in the correct order, doing them all without stopping and without separating them or reversing them. He starts with the first *jamrah* and throws seven pebbles at it and does not set them down. That is what was stated by Mālik, ash-Shāfi'ī, Abū Thawr, and the People of Opinion. If he simply tosses them, that is permitted by the People of Opinion.

Ibn al-Qāsim said, 'It is not permitted to throw them all together.' That is sound because the Prophet ﷺ used to stone them and he did not throw two or more stones at the same time. When he did the stoning, he did it with one pebble at a time. When he had finished throwing them, he stood in front of the *jamrah* for a long time making such supplication as was feasible. Then he stoned the second one, which is the middle one and left it going to the left in the bottom of the river-bed and stood for a long time at that one making supplication. Then he stoned the third one, the *Jamrat al-'Aqabah*, with seven pebbles from below it, but he did not stop beside it. It is satisfactory to stone them from above. The *takbīr* should be said with every pebble thrown.' The Sunnah of remembrance when stoning the *jamrahs* is to say the *takbīr* and nothing else. They should be stoned on foot which is not the case with the *jamrah* on the Day of Sacrifice.

All this is related by an-Nasā'ī and ad-Dāraquṭnī from az-Zuhrī from the Messenger of Allah ﷺ. He used to stone the *jamrah* that is next to the mosque of Minā with seven pebbles, saying the *takbīr* with every pebble. Then he went forward and stood for a long time facing the *qiblah*, raising his hands in supplication. Then he went to the second *jamrah* and stoned it with seven pebbles, saying the *takbīr* with every pebble. Then he went down to the left opposite the wadi and stood facing the *qiblah*, raising his hands in supplication. Then he went to the *jamrah* at al-'Aqabah and stoned it with seven pebbles, saying the *takbīr* with every pebble. Then he left without standing there. Az-Zuhrī said that he heard Sālim ibn 'Abdullāh relate this from his father from the Prophet ﷺ. He said that Ibn 'Umar used to do it like this.

The ruling of the *jamrah*s is that they are considered pure and are are not affected by anything used to stone them. If someone stones them with what has already been used to stone them, Mālik believes that it does not satisfy the requirement. Ibn al-Qāsim said that he said that if that is only a matter of a single pebble, it satisfies the requirement. Ibn al-Qāsim gave that *fatwā*. The people of knowledge recommend taking the stones from Muzdalifah, not from the mosque. If someone takes more than he needs and still has some in his possession after stoning, he should bury them and not just throw them away. Aḥmad ibn Ḥanbal and others said that.

Most, with the exception of Ṭāwūs, say that they should not be washed. He related that it is not good if the *jamrah*s and what is thrown are not washed free of impurity but, if they are not, it still satisfies the requirement. Ibn al-Mundhir said that it is disliked to throw what has already been thrown but, nonetheless, it still satisfies the requirement since he did not know of anyone who obliges someone who does that to repeat it. We do not know of any reports stating that the Prophet ﷺ washed the pebbles or commanded that they be washed. Ṭāwūs, as we stated, did wash them.

Throwing bits of mud at the *jamrah*s does not satisfy the requirement nor does anything except stone. That is the position of ash-Shāfiʿī, Aḥmad and Isḥāq. The People of Opinion say that it is permitted with dry clay. The same applies to anything that is part of the earth: it satisfies the requirement. Ath-Thawrī said that if someone throws date-stones or mud, that does not satisfy the requirement. The Messenger of Allah ﷺ threw pebbles.

There is disagreement about the size of what is thrown. Ash-Shāfiʿī said that the pebbles should be smaller in both length and width than a fingertip. Abū Thawr and the People of Opinion said that they should be like the pebbles used for flicking. We related that Ibn ʿUmar used to stone the *jamrah* with something the size of sheep pellets. There is no sense in Mālik's statement, 'I prefer them being larger than that' because the Prophet ﷺ made a sunnah of stoning with something similar in size to date-stones. It is permitted to stone with anything that can be called a pebble, but it is better to follow the Sunnah. Ibn al-Mundhir said that.

This is the sound position which cannot be opposed by anyone who is guided and follows. An-Nasā'ī related that Ibn 'Abbās said, 'The Messenger of Allah ﷺ said to me on the morning of al-ʿAqabah while he was on his camel, "Pick up some pebbles for me." I picked up seven pebbles the size of peas. When I put them in his hand, he said, "Something like these. Beware of excess in the *dīn*. Those before you were destroyed by excess in the *dīn*."' His words about 'excess in the *dīn* indicate dislike of stoning of the *jamrah*s with large stones and the fact that doing that is part of excess. Allah knows best.

If someone has a pebble left in his hand and he does not know which of the *jamrah*s it was for, he stones the first and the middle and the last one after it. If it has been a long time, he starts over again.

Mālik, ash-Shāfiʿī, 'Abd al-Malik, Abū Thawr, and the People of Opinion said that if someone puts one *jamrah* ahead of another, it does not satisfy the requirement unless he stones them in order. Al-Ḥasan, 'Aṭā' and some people say that it does satisfy it. Some people cite as evidence the statement of the Prophet ﷺ: 'There is no harm in someone putting one rite before another.' He said, 'This is not more than a man who combines the prayer and fasting and makes up one of them before the other.' The first shows more caution. Allah knows best.

They disagree about the stoning done by someone who is ill and someone stoning on his behalf. Mālik said that one may stone on behalf of someone ill or a child who cannot stone. The ill person takes care when he stones and says seven *takbīr*s for each *jamrah* and he owes a *hady*. When a sick person recovers during the days of stoning, he stones for himself. According to Mālik, he owes a sacrifice in addition to that. Al-Ḥasan al-Baṣrī, ash-Shāfi'ī, Aḥmad, Isḥāq and the People of Opinion say that one can stone on behalf of a sick person and they do not mention a sacrifice. There is no disagreement about stoning on behalf of a child who is unable to stone. Ibn 'Umar used to do that. Ad-Dāraquṭnī related that Abū Sa'īd al-Khudrī said, 'We said, "Messenger of Allah, we reckon that these *jamrah*s that are stoned decrease in size." He said, "What is accepted of it is taken up. If it were not for that, you would see them like mountains."'

Ibn al-Mundhir said that scholars agree that if someone wants to leave Minā to return to his country and come out of *iḥrām* without staying at Makkah, he can depart after midday when he has stoned during the day after the Day of Sacrifice. That is because Allah says, *'Those who hurry on in two days have done no wrong.'* He can go as long as there is some of the day left. We related that an-Nakha'ī and al-Ḥasan said that someone who catches *'Aṣr* at Minā on the second day of *tashrīq* should not leave until the following day. Ibn al-Mundhir said, 'It is possible that they both said that as a recommendation. We take the first view based on the literal text of the Book and the Sunnah.'

They disagree about whether the people of Makkah can leave in the first departure. We related that 'Umar ibn al-Khaṭṭāb said, 'Any of the people who wish can leave in the first departure except for Khuzaymah. They may only leave in the final leaving.' Aḥmad ibn Ḥanbal used to say, 'I do not like those who leave in the first departure to be resident in Makkah.' He said, 'It is making light for the people of Makkah.' Aḥmad and Isḥāq took the meaning of 'Umar's words 'except Khuzaymah' to mean the people of Makkah. Mālik used to say about the people of Makkah, 'Anyone with an excuse can hurry on in two days, but if someone merely wants to lighten the business of the ḥajj for himself, that is not permitted.' So he thought that hurrying was for those who lived far away.

One group said that the *āyah* is general and the allowance is for all people: the people of Makkah as well as others. It is for those who want to leave Minā either to reside in Makkah or to return to their homeland. 'Aṭā' agreed that it is for people in general. Ibn al-Mundhir said, 'It accords with the school of ash-Shāfi'ī, and we take that position.' Ibn 'Abbās, al-Ḥasan, 'Ikrimah, Mujāhid, Qatādah and an-Nakha'ī said that there is nothing wrong with leaving on the second of the designated days and there is nothing wrong in remaining to the third day. So the *āyah* means that all of that is permitted. This division is given attention since some Arabs criticised those who hurried on and some criticised those who did not. Therefore this *āyah* was revealed to remove any consideration of harm from either position.

'Alī ibn Abī Ṭālib, Ibn 'Abbās, Ibn Mas'ūd, and Ibrāhīm an-Nakha'ī said that it means that anyone who hurries on is forgiven and whoever stays is forgiven. Their argument is based on the *ḥadīth* of the Prophet ﷺ: 'Anyone who makes ḥajj to this House and does not engage in sexual activity or wrongdoing emerges from his errors like the day his mother bore him.' So Allah's words *'have done no wrong'* is a general negation and absolution. Mujāhid said that the *āyah* means: there is no wrongdoing for those who hurry on or stay until the following year. This report has an *isnād*. Abu-l-'Āliyah said about the *āyah*, 'There is no wrongdoing for someone who remains godfearing for the rest of his life. The ḥājjī is absolutely forgiven,' meaning that all his sins have departed provided he remains godfearing for the rest of his life. Abū Ṣāliḥ and others said that the *āyah* means that there is no wrongdoing for someone who is fearful of killing game and avoiding that which must be avoided in the ḥajj. He also said, 'Someone who is godfearing in his ḥajj and performs it fully is accepted.'

**those of them who are fearful of Allah.**

This statement is connected to forgiveness. It implies that there is forgiveness for those who are fearful of Allah. This is the interpretation of Ibn Mas'ūd and 'Alī. Qatādah said, 'Ibn Mas'ūd mentioned to us that forgiveness is reserved for those who remain fearful of Allah after finishing the ḥajj and avoid all acts of disobedience.' Al-Akhfash said that it implies: 'Forgiveness is for those who are fearful of Allah.' One of them said that it refers to not killing game in *iḥrām* or in the Ḥaram. It is said that there is safety for anyone who is fearful of Allah. This is related from Ibn 'Umar. It is also said that it means safety for those who are godfearing. It is also said that it is connected to the remembrance inherent in the word, *'Remember'* which begins the *ayah*, meaning that remembrance is confined to those who are fearful of Allah. Allah commands us to be fearful of Him and reminds us of the Gathering and Standing.

وَمِنَ ٱلنَّاسِ مَن يُعْجِبُكَ قَوْلُهُۥ فِى ٱلْحَيَوٰةِ ٱلدُّنْيَا وَيُشْهِدُ ٱللَّهَ عَلَىٰ
مَا فِى قَلْبِهِۦ وَهُوَ أَلَدُّ ٱلْخِصَامِ ﴿٢٠٤﴾

**204 Among the people there is someone whose words about the life of this world excite your admiration, and he calls Allah to witness what is in his heart, while he is in fact the most hostile of adversaries.**

**Among the people there is someone whose words about the life of this world excite your admiration,**

This *āyah* is here because Allah has just mentioned in His words a little earlier that the aspiration of some people is confined to this world: *'Our Lord, give us good in this world.'* The believers are those who ask for the good of both the worlds. Hypocrites are mentioned because hypocrites make a display of faith while concealing disbelief. As-Suddī and other commentators say that it was revealed about al-Akhnas ibn Sharīq. His name was actually Ubayy and al-Akhnas was a nickname for him because on the day of the Battle of Badr, he withdrew (*khanasa*) from fighting the Messenger of Allah ﷺ with three hundred men of his allies of the Banū Zuhrah. This will be explained in *Āl 'Imrān*. He was a man of sweet words and good appearance. He came to the Prophet ﷺ and made a display of Islam and said, 'Allah knows that I am telling the truth,' and then after that he ran away. On his way he passed some crops and animals belonging to some Muslims and burned the crops and hamstrung the donkeys. Al-Mahdawī said that Allah's words: *'But do not obey any vile swearer of oaths, and backbiter, slandermonger'* (68:10-11), were also revealed about him as were the words: *'Woe to every fault-finding slanderer.'* (104:1)

Ibn 'Aṭiyyah said, 'It is not established that al-Akhnas became Muslim.' Ibn 'Abbās says that it was revealed about some hypocrites who spoke about those killed in the Rajī' expedition, saying that they should have stayed at home. Then this was revealed to describe the hypocrites while those who were martyred in Rajī' are referred to in the words: *'And among the people there are some who give up everything.'* (2:207).

Qatādah, Mujāhid and a group of scholars said that the *āyah* was revealed about anyone who conceals disbelief, hypocrisy, lying or vindictiveness while displaying the opposite of that in what he says. Therefore the meaning is general and unrestricted. This is akin to something at-Tirmidhī quotes as being contained in one of the books of Allah, which goes: 'There are some slaves of Allah whose tongues are sweeter than honey while their hearts are more bitter than aloes. They appear to people to be like gentle sheep while they use the *dīn* to buy this world. Allah Almighty says: "Do they attempt to delude Me? Are they bold towards Me? I swear by My Self that I will destine for them a trial that will leave someone forbearing bewildered!"'

**and he calls Allah to witness what is in his heart,**

He does this by saying, 'Allah knows that I am telling the truth,' whereas Allah knows that he is different to what he says. As Allah says: *'Allah bears witness that the hypocrites are certainly liars'* (63:1).

The reading of Ibn Mas'ūd reverses the position of *'Allāhu'* and *'yashhadu'* in the *āyah*, (which would mean 'Allah bears witness to…') but the majority reading is stronger in censure because he remains adamant in holding to good words while something other than that is manifesting itself inside him.

Our scholars say that this *āyah* calls attention to the necessity of caution in dealing with both matters of the *dīn* and matters of the material world, and the need to verify the states of witnesses and qāḍīs. It points out that a judge should not base his judgment merely on the outward states of people and any display of faith and rectitude they make, without investigating their inward, because Allah will make the inward states of people clear. Some people can speak sweetly while intending evil.

If it is said that this is contradicted by the words of the Prophet ﷺ, 'I was commanded to fight people until they say, "There is no god but Allah"...' the answer is that that was at the beginning of Islam when people's Islam was sound, before corruption became widespread. That is what Ibn al-'Arabī said. The sound position, however, is that a judge should judge by the outward until something contrary to it becomes clear, going by the statement of 'Umar ibn al-Khaṭṭāb in al-Bukhārī, 'O people, Revelation has come to an end. We now judge according to what appears to us of your actions. If someone exhibits good, we consider him trustworthy and bring him near. We know nothing of what is concealed within him; Allah will call him to account for what is in his heart. If someone exhibits bad to us, we do not consider him trustworthy or believe him, even if it happens to be that his heart is good.'

**while he is in fact the most hostile of adversaries.**

The word '*aladd*' (hostile) is derived from the word *ladīdān*, meaning both sides of the neck so that the implication is that his hostility is deeply rooted. The word '*khiṣām*' (adversaries) is a verbal noun from *khāṣama*, and it is also said to be the plural of *khaṣm*. Az-Zajjāj said that. It means that he is the most vehement in argumentation when he speaks to you and replies to you and you find his words sweet, even though what he says is inwardly false. This indicates that argumentation is only permitted when the inward and outward are the same. We read in *Ṣaḥīḥ Muslim* that 'Ā'ishah reported that the Messenger of Allah ﷺ said, 'The man Allah most hates is "*the most hostile of adversaries*".'

وَإِذَا تَوَلَّىٰ سَعَىٰ فِي الْأَرْضِ لِيُفْسِدَ فِيهَا وَيُهْلِكَ الْحَرْثَ وَالنَّسْلَ
وَاللَّهُ لَا يُحِبُّ الْفَسَادَ ﴿٢٠٥﴾

**205 When he leaves you, he goes about the earth corrupting it, destroying crops and animals Allah does not love corruption.**

**When he leaves you, he goes about the earth corrupting it,**

The verb '*tawallā*' (leaves) is said to imply being misguided, angry and arrogant and '*sa'y*' (goes about) to imply scheming and striving to bring about reverses for Islam and its people, as Ibn Jurayj and others have said. It is also said that it is the action of a single person, so he turns his back and leaves you. *Sa'y* is to go about on his feet, cutting off the road and corrupting it as Ibn 'Abbās and others say. Both forms of *sa'y* are corruption.

**destroying**

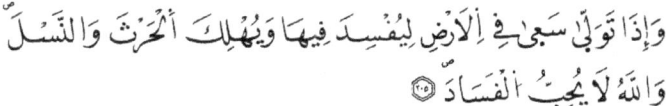

This is added to 'corrupting'. Although the *āyah* is held to refer specifically to al-Akhnas burning crops and killing camels, aṭ-Ṭabarī said that its meaning is general and should be extended to all who fit its description and merit the curse and punishment. Some scholars said that if someone kills a donkey or burns a haystack, he must be blameworthy and shame is attached to him until the Day of Rising. Mujāhid said, 'What is meant is that wrongdoers work corruption in the earth so that Allah withholds the rain from it, causing crops and animals to die.' It is said that 'crops' are wives and 'animals' are children. The reason for this is that hypocrisy leads to disunity and fighting and that causes people to be killed. Az-Zajjāj expressed that idea. *Sa'y* in the land is 'running' and this is an expression for causing sedition and contention between people. Allah knows best. We find in a *ḥadīth*: 'When people see an oppressor and do not take hold of his hands [to stop him], Allah is about to envelop them with a punishment from Him.'

**crops and animals.**

The root of the word '*ḥarth*' (crops) linguistically means splitting and the word for plough (*miḥrāth*) comes from it since it splits the earth. By extension *ḥarth* comes to mean gaining and amassing wealth. We find in a *ḥadīth*, 'Cultivate (*aḥrith*) for this world as if you are going to live forever.' *Ḥarth* is agriculture. *Ḥarrāth* is a ploughman. Other uses of the verb are *aḥratha* mean to study thoroughly, to ride an animal until it is exhausted, and to poke the fire. *Miḥrāth* is also a poker according to al-Jawharī.

The word '*nasl*' (animals) denotes any progeny of a female. Its root meaning is 'to leave and fall'. The verb is used for hair falling out and feathers moulting. We find it used in the *ayah*: *'they will be sliding* (yansilūna) *from their graves towards their Lord'* (36:51) and: *'rush down* (yansilūna) *from every slope.'* (21:96) So the words in the *āyah* indicate planting and cultivating the earth, planting trees to bear fruit, and seeking increase in livestock which provide livelihood for a person. This refutes those who espouse abandoning secondary means.

**Allah does not love corruption.**

Al-'Abbās ibn al-Faḍl said that '*fasād*' (corruption) means ruin. Sa'īd ibn al-Musayyab said that clipping dirhams forms part of corruption in the land. 'Aṭā' said, 'A man called 'Aṭā' ibn Munabbih assumed *iḥrām* in a jubbah and the Prophet ﷺ told him to remove it.' Qatādah said to 'Aṭā', 'We heard that he tore it in half.' 'Aṭā' said, 'Allah does not love corruption.'

The *āyah* is general to all kinds of corruption in the land, in respect of either property or the *dīn*, and that is the sound position, Allah willing. It is said that He does not love corruption in people of righteousness, or He does not love it as a *dīn*.

وَإِذَا قِيلَ لَهُ ٱتَّقِ ٱللَّهَ أَخَذَتْهُ ٱلْعِزَّةُ بِٱلْإِثْمِ فَحَسْبُهُۥ جَهَنَّمُ وَلَبِئْسَ
ٱلْمِهَادُ ﴿٢٠٦﴾

**206 When he is told to be fearful of Allah, he is seized by a feeling of might which drives him to wrongdoing. Hell will be enough for him! What an evil resting-place!**

This describes the chief attribute of the unbeliever and the hypocrite: arrogance.

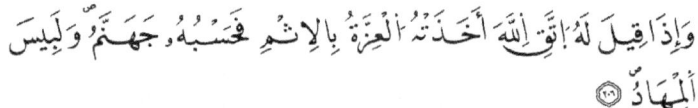

It is disliked for a believer to fall into this. 'Abdullāh said, 'It is enough wrong action for a man that he says to his brother, "Fear Allah," and he retorts, "Mind your own business! Someone like you advises me!"' The word '*'izzah*' (might) denotes strength and dominance, as it is used in 38:23. It is also said to mean zeal. It is said that it means unapproachable self-esteem. He exalts himself and when that arrogance takes hold of him, that leads him to commit wrong action. Qatādah said, 'It means that when he is told to slow down, he is increased in his advancing towards disobedience. It means that his pride leads him to commit wrong action, so that he falls into disbelief for the sake of might and the zeal of the Jāhiliyyah. It is like the *ayah*: *'Those who disbelieve are full of vainglory and entrenched in hostility.'* (38:2) It is said that it means that arrogance and zeal make him refuse to accept the warning about the wrong action that is in his heart, which constitutes hypocrisy.

It is mentioned that a Jew needed something from Hārūn ar-Rashīd and he kept going to his door for a year without his need being met. So he stood at his door and when Hārūn came out, he ran and stood in front of him. He said, 'Fear Allah, *Amīr al-Mu'minīn*!' Hārūn dismounted and went down into prostration. When he raised his head. He commanded that his need be met. When he returned, it was said to him, '*Amīr al-Mu'minīn*! Do you dismount from your animal for the words of a Jew!' 'No,' he answered, 'but I remembered the words of Allah: *"When he is told to have* taqwā *of Allah, he is seized by pride which drives him to wrongdoing. Hell will be enough for him! What an evil resting-place!"* That is enough of a consequence and repayment.'

The usual meaning of the word 'resting place' (*mihād*) is a place prepared for sleep. It is also used for a child's cradle. Jahannam (Hell) is referred to as one because it is where the unbelievers will remain. It is also said that here 'Hell' is an appositive for 'resting-place'.

وَمِنَ ٱلنَّاسِ مَن يَشْرِى نَفْسَهُ ٱبْتِغَآءَ مَرْضَاتِ ٱللَّهِ وَٱللَّهُ
رَءُوفٌۢ بِٱلْعِبَادِ ﴿٢٠٧﴾

**207 And among the people there are some who give up everything, desiring the good pleasure of Allah. Allah is Ever-Gentle with His slaves.**

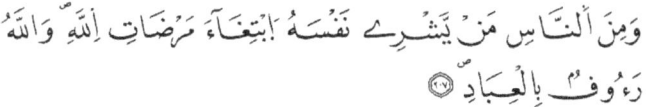

After speaking of the actions of the hypocrites, Allah talks about the behaviour of the believers. It is said that the *āyah* was actually revealed about Ṣuhayb. He emigrated to the Messenger of Allah ﷺ and some people of Quraysh followed him. He dismounted, took out what was in his quiver and took up his bow and said, 'You know that I am the best shot among you. By Allah you will not reach me until I have shot what is in my quiver and struck with my sword until nothing remains in my hands and then do what you wish.' They said, 'We will not let you leave us as a wealthy man when you came to us with nothing. Direct us to your property in Makkah and we will let you go.' They made an agreement with him to that effect and he did that. When he came to the Messenger of Allah ﷺ, this *āyah* was revealed and the Prophet ﷺ said to him, 'A profitable sale, Abū Yaḥyā!' and recited it to him. Razīn transmitted it. Sa'īd ibn al-Musayyab said that.

Commentators say that the idolaters took Ṣuhayb and tortured him and Ṣuhayb said to them, 'I am an old man. Your security will not be prejudiced if I am with other than you. Will you not take my wealth and leave me with my *dīn*?' They did that and he stipulated a camel and provision for himself and went to Madīnah where Abū Bakr, 'Umar and some men met him. Abū Bakr told him, 'A profitable sale, Abū Yaḥyā!' Ṣuhayb asked what he meant and he told him about the revelation of the *āyah*.

Al-Ḥasan said, 'Do you know about whom this *āyah* was revealed? It was revealed about a Muslim who met an unbeliever and told him, "Say: 'There is no god but Allah'. If you say it, your property and life are safe." He refused to say it. The Muslim said, "By Allah, I will sell my self to Allah" and he advanced and fought until he was killed.' It is said that it was revealed about all those who command what is known to be right and forbid what is recognised as wrong and that is the way it was interpreted by 'Umar, 'Alī and Ibn 'Abbās. 'Alī and Ibn 'Abbās said, 'Two men fought and the one who was trying to make the corrupter change his ways said, "Be fearful of Allah!" The corrupter refused and pride took hold of him. So the one who was trying to change him sold himself to Allah and fought him. So the two fought.'

Al-Khalīl said, "Umar ibn al-Khaṭṭāb heard a man reciting this *āyah* and said, "We belong to Allah and to Him we return. A man stood commanding what is known to be right and forbidding what is recognised as wrong and was killed.' It is said that 'Umar heard Ibn 'Abbās say, 'Two men fought,' when the reciter recited this *āyah*. He asked him about what he had said and he explained it to him in this way. 'Umar said to him, 'May Allah bless you, Ibn 'Abbās!'

It is also said that it was revealed about someone who leaps into the fight. Hishām ibn 'Āmir attacked the ranks at Constantinople and fought until he was slain and Abū Hurayrah recited: *'And among the people there are some who give up everything, desiring the good pleasure of Allah.'* Something similar is related from Abū Ayyūb.

It is also said that it was revealed about those martyred in the Rajī' expedition. Qatādah said that it refers to the Muhājirūn and Anṣār. It is said that it was revealed about 'Alī when the Prophet ﷺ left him on his bed on the night he went out to the cave as we will deal with in *Sūrat at-Tawbah.* It is said that the *āyah* is general and applies to everyone striving in the way of martyrdom for Allah's sake or changing something wrong. We have already mentioned the ruling on someone who attacks the ranks of the enemy. The rulings of someone who changes something wrong will come in *Āl 'Imrān.*

*'Yashrī'* means 'to sell'. 'Selling the self' means to expend it in obeying Allah's commands. The verb can also mean 'to purchase'. We see this interpretation of the *āyah* in the story of Ṣuhayb because he purchased himself with his property and did not sell it, unless it is said that Ṣuhayb offering to fight them was selling himself to Allah, in which case the word bears its normal meaning.

يَٰٓأَيُّهَا ٱلَّذِينَ ءَامَنُوا۟ ٱدْخُلُوا۟ فِى ٱلسِّلْمِ كَآفَّةً وَلَا تَتَّبِعُوا۟
خُطُوَٰتِ ٱلشَّيْطَٰنِ إِنَّهُۥ لَكُمْ عَدُوٌّ مُّبِينٌ ﴿٢٠٨﴾

**208 You who believe! enter Islam totally. Do not follow in the footsteps of Shayṭān. He is an outright enemy to you.**

**You who believe! enter Islam totally.**

After Allah made it clear that people are either believers, unbelievers or hypocrites, He says, "Follow only one religion and agree on Islam and remain firm in it." Here the word *salm* means Islam as Mujāhid said and as is related from Ibn 'Abbās. Part of that is seen in the words of the Kindī poet:

I called my tribe to Islam (*salm*) when I saw them turn their backs on us.

This is calling them to Islam when Kindah apostasised after the death of the Prophet ﷺ under al-Ash'ath ibn Qays al-Kindī. Another reason that it cannot mean 'truce or a peace treaty' here is because the Muslims were never commanded to enter into a truce in this way. Rather the Prophet ﷺ was told to incline to peace if the enemy inclined to it, but not to initiate it. Aṭ-Ṭabarī said that. It is said that Allah is here commanding those who articulate belief with their tongues to enter into it with their hearts as well. Ṭāwus and Mujāhid said that it means, 'Enter under the authority of the *dīn*.' Sufyān ath-Thawrī says that it refers to all types of piety.

It is read both as *salm* (Warsh) and *silm* (Ḥafṣ) and they mean the same. This is the position of most of the Basrans and they use both to signify Islam and to signify 'truce'. Abū 'Amr ibn al-'Alā' distinguished between them and here he recited *'as-silm'* meaning Islam, and recited *'as-salm'* in *al-Anfāl* and *Muḥammad* where he said that it means 'truce'. Al-Mubarrad denied this difference. 'Āṣim al-Jaḥdarī said that *silm* is Islam, *salm* is truce and *salam* is submission. Muḥammad ibn Yazīd disliked this distinction and said, 'Language is not defined like this. Language is defined by oral transmission, not on the basis of analogy. Someone who makes a distinction like this requires some evidence.' The Basrans said that *silm*, *salm* and *salam* are employed with the same meaning. Al-Jawharī said that *silm* and *salm* mean truce, derived from the root meaning of submission. Aṭ-Ṭabarī says that the word means Islam.

Regarding this *āyah*, Ḥudhayfah ibn al-Yamān said, 'Islam is divided into eight parts. The prayer is one part, zakat is one part, fasting is one part, ḥajj is one part, *'umrah* is one part, *jihād* is one part, commanding what is known to be right is one part, and forbidding what is recognised as wrong is one part. Disappointed is he who has no part of Islam.'

Ibn Abbas said that it was revealed about the People of the Book and the meaning is: 'You who believe in Mūsā and 'Īsā, enter into Islam totally through Muḥammad ﷺ.' It is reported in *Ṣaḥīḥ Muslim* from Abū Hurayrah that the Prophet ﷺ said, 'By the One who has the soul of Muḥammad in His hand, any Jew or Christian who hears this and then dies without believing in what I was sent with will be one of the people of the Fire.'

*'Kāffatan'* means 'totally' and it is an adverb modifying 'Islam' or 'believers'. It is derived from the expression, *'kafaftu'* meaning 'I prevented'. So none of you should be prevented from entering Islam. *Kaff* is stoppage. The hem (*kuffah*) of a sleeve stops it from unravelling just as the scale (*kiffah*) of a balance collects what is weighed and keeps it from spreading. The hand (*kaff*) of a person is that which collects the things that benefit and harm him. The eyes of a blind (*makfūf*) man are prevented from seeing. The communal group is called *kāffah* because it prevents separation.

**Do not follow in the footsteps of Shayṭān.**

Muqātil said, "Abdullāh ibn Salām and his people asked for permission to recite the Torah in the prayer and to do some of what is in the Torah and this was revealed. It means: "It is better to follow the Sunnah now that Muhammad ﷺ has been sent than to follow the footsteps of Shayṭān."' It is also said that it means: 'Do not follow the path that Shayṭān calls you to.'

فَإِن زَلَلْتُم مِّن بَعْدِ مَا جَآءَتْكُمُ ٱلْبَيِّنَٰتُ فَٱعْلَمُوٓا۟ أَنَّ ٱللَّهَ
عَزِيزٌ حَكِيمٌ ﴿٢٠٩﴾

**209 If you backslide after the Clear Signs have come to you, know that Allah is Almighty, All-Wise.**

**If you backslide**

In other words, if you turn back from the path of righteousness. The root of '*zalal*' (backslide) relates to the foot slipping and so it is used metaphorically for reverting from beliefs, opinions and other such things.

**after the Clear Signs have come to you,**

This may refer to the miracles of the Prophet ﷺ or to the *āyah*s of the Qur'an if it is addressed to the believers. If it is addressed to the people of the Book, the Clear Signs are what came in their Books telling them about Muhammad ﷺ. The *āyah* contains evidence that the punishment of a man of knowledge for a wrong action is greater than the punishment of an ignorant person and is also evidence that someone who has not heard the call of Islam is not an unbeliever by the fact of not observing its laws. An-Naqqāsh related that when Ka'b al-Aḥbar became Muslim, he used to study the Qur'an. The one who was teaching him recited to him: 'Know that Allah is Ever-Forgiving, Forbearing.' Ka'b said, 'I do not think that that is how it is.' A man passed by them and Ka'b asked, 'How do you recite this *āyah*?' The man answered, '*Know that Allah is Almighty, All-Wise.*' Ka'b said, 'That is correct.' The Name *'Azīz* signifies the One Who cannot be stopped from doing anything He wills, and the Name *Ḥakīm* signifies the One Who is wise in what He does.

هَلْ يَنظُرُونَ إِلَّآ أَن يَأْتِيَهُمُ ٱللَّهُ فِى ظُلَلٍ مِّنَ ٱلْغَمَامِ وَٱلْمَلَٰٓئِكَةُ
وَقُضِىَ ٱلْأَمْرُ ۚ وَإِلَى ٱللَّهِ تُرْجَعُ ٱلْأُمُورُ ﴿٢١٠﴾

**210 What are they waiting for but for Allah to come to them in the shadows of the clouds, together with the angels, in which case the matter will have been settled? All matters return to Allah.**

**What are they waiting for but for Allah to come to them in the shadows of the clouds**

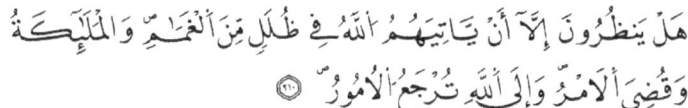

This is referring to those who do not enter into Islam and implies obstinacy on their part. Qatadah, Abu Ja'far Yazīd ibn al-Qa'qā' and aḍ-Ḍaḥḥāk recited '*ẓilāl*'

instead of '*zulal*'. Abū Ja'far recited 'angels' in the genitive, as being in apposition to 'clouds'. It implies 'with the angels'. This is an Arabic usage. *Zulal* is the plural of *zullah*. Al-Akhfash says that if it is in the genitive, it means 'in the angels'. He says that the nominative reading is better as is evidenced in other *āyahs* like 6:158 and 89:22. The reading of 'Abdullāh has: 'What are they waiting for but for Allah and the angels to come to them'. Qatādah says that it refers to the angels coming to take their souls. It is also said to refer to the Day of Rising, and that is more likely.

Abu-l-'Āliyah and ar-Rabī' said that the angels will come to them in the shadows of the clouds and Allah will come to them in whatever way He wishes. Az-Zajjāj said, 'It implies "in the shadows of the clouds and among the angels".' It is said that the words should not be taken literally in respect of Allah. It means for the command and judgment of Allah to come to them. It is said that it means that the reckoning and punishment that Allah has promised them is lying in wait for them in the shadows, as we find in the *ayah*: '*Then Allah came upon them from where they least expected it.*' (59:2) This means that He will cause them disappointment. This is what az-Zajjāj said. The first is the view of al-Akhfash. It is also possible that what is being referred to is the repayment they will receive for their wrong actions and that this particular usage is employed to intensify the threat and to convey alarm. This is also the case elsewhere in the story of the approach of Nebuchadnezzar (16:26).

The word 'coming' can entail all these ideas because its root linguistically means to aim for something and so the *āyah* means: 'What are they waiting for but for Allah to show them something by means of one of His created forms, with the aim of repaying them and judging their affairs?'

Allah also has the capability to originate an event to which He refers by the words 'coming' or 'settling'. So here He can originate an action which He calls 'coming'. But His actions are without any cause or instrument. Glory be to Him! As transmitted by Abū Ṣāliḥ, Ibn 'Abbās said, 'This is part of what is unknowable and should not be explained.' So some people were silent about its interpretation and others interpreted it as we have mentioned. It is said that '*fī*" (in) here means '*bā*" (through), so He comes to them through clouds. There is also the *ḥadīth* which states: 'Allah will come to them in a form…', meaning a form which is to test them. It is not permitted to take this and similar things which come in the Qur'an and in reports as meaning movement in a place, movement in general, or disappearance, because such things are attributes of physical bodies. Allah is greatly exalted and elevated, the Master of Majesty and Nobility. He is far beyond being anything like physical bodies.

The word for 'clouds' (*ghamām*) in this *āyah* means 'thin fine white clouds'. They are called that because they cover, for the verb *ghamma* means 'to cover'.

**in which case the matter will have been settled**

Mu'ādh ibn Jabal recited, *'qaḍā'u-l-amr'*. Yaḥyā ibn Ya'mar recited *'quḍiyy' 'l-umūr'* in the plural. Most have: *'quḍiya-l-amr'*. It means that the matter being settled is a reference to the repayment and the punishment of the people of disobedience. Although most readings have *'turja'u-l-umūr'* ('All matters return to Allah'), Ibn 'Āmir, Ḥamzah and al-Kisā'ī have *'tarji'u-l-umūr'*. Both readings are good and have the same meaning. All affairs return to Allah, before and after. He calls attention to remembering that on the Day of Rising things that belonged to the kings of this world will disappear.

سَلْ بَنِىٓ إِسْرَٰٓءِيلَ كَمْ ءَاتَيْنَٰهُم مِّنْ ءَايَةٍۭ بَيِّنَةٍ ۗ وَمَن يُبَدِّلْ نِعْمَةَ ٱللَّهِ مِنۢ
بَعْدِ مَا جَآءَتْهُ فَإِنَّ ٱللَّهَ شَدِيدُ ٱلْعِقَابِ ﴿٢١١﴾

**211 Ask the tribe of Israel how many Clear Signs We gave to them. If anyone alters Allah's blessing after it has come to him, Allah is fierce in retribution.**

**Ask the tribe of Israel how many Clear Signs We gave to them.**

What is being referred to in this *āyah* is the great number of signs which came to them making the coming Prophethood of Muḥammad ﷺ clear to them and directing them to him. Mujāhid, al-Ḥasan and others said that it refers to the miraculous signs which Mūsā manifested such as the splitting of the sea, the shading by the clouds, his staff turning into a snake, his hand turning white and other things. The command present in the *āyah* is to His Prophet to ask them by way of rebuking them.

**If anyone alters Allah's blessing after it has come to him,**

This is a general expression applying to everyone, even if it is the tribe of Israel who are mentioned in this instance. They changed things in their Books and denied the Prophethood of Muhammad ﷺ. But the expression applies to all those who alter the blessing of Allah. Aṭ-Ṭabarī said that the blessing here is Islam and this is close to the first statement. The expression also includes the unbelievers of Quraysh since the fact that Muḥammad ﷺ was sent to them was a blessing to them and instead of being thankful they rejected him.

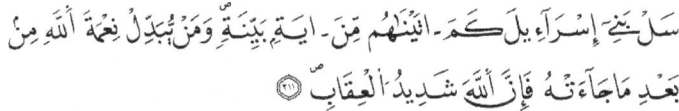

**Allah is fierce in retribution.**

This is a threat. *'Iqāb* (retribution) is derived from *'aqib* which means the last part or heel of something and so it is as if the one being punished has retribution following at his heels. Also from the same root is *'uqbah*, used for the 'turn of the person riding' (when people take it in tums to ride an animal) and someone's turn to get water (when a water source is being shared). *'Iqāb* and *'uqūbah* are punishment, because they follow after the wrong action and punishment is a consequence of a wrong action.

زُيِّنَ لِلَّذِينَ كَفَرُوا الْحَيَوٰةُ الدُّنْيَا وَيَسْخَرُونَ مِنَ الَّذِينَ ءَامَنُوا وَالَّذِينَ
اتَّقَوْا فَوْقَهُمْ يَوْمَ الْقِيَٰمَةِ وَاللَّهُ يَرْزُقُ مَن يَشَاءُ بِغَيْرِ حِسَابٍ ﴿٢١٢﴾

**212 To those who disbelieve, the life of this world is painted in glowing colours and they laugh at those who believe. But on the Day of Rising those who fear Allah will be over them. Allah provides for whomever He wills without any reckoning.**

**To those who disbelieve, the life of this world is painted in glowing colours.**

Although no one is named, those intended here are the leaders of Quraysh. The One Who adorns it is its Creator and Originator. Shayṭān also makes it seem attractive by his whispering and causing people to err. Those who disbelieve are singled out for mention because they are totally taken in by the adornment of this world and turn to it and tum away from the Next World because of it. Allah has made what is on the earth its adornment in order to test His creatures to see who will perform the best actions. The believers who follow the norms of the Sharī'ah are not tempted by worldly adornment but it dominates the minds of the unbelievers because they do not believe in anything but it. Abū Bakr aṣ-Ṣiddīq said when he was offered wealth, 'O Allah we cannot do other than rejoice in what You have made seem attractive to us.'

**and they laugh at those who believe.**

This indicates the unbelievers of Quraysh. So it is as if the unbelievers of Quraysh thought highly of their state in this world and delighted in it and scoffed at the followers of Muḥammad ﷺ. Ibn Jurayj said that they scoffed at their seeking the Next World. It is said that they mocked their poverty and those who were poor among them like Bilāl, Ṣuhayb, Ibn Mas'ūd and others.

**But on the Day of Rising those who fear Allah will be over them.**

Allah calls attention to the lowering of their position because of their ugly behaviour: *'On the Day of Rising those who fear Allah will be over them.'* 'Alī reported that the Prophet ﷺ said, 'If anyone demeans a believing man or woman, or disdains them on account of their poverty and lack of possessions, Allah will make him known on the Day of Rising and will disgrace him. If anyone slanders a believing man or woman or says something about them that is not true, Allah Almighty will make him stand on a hill of fire on the Day of Rising until he produces what he said about them. If someone esteems a believer, Allah will esteem and honour him more than one of the angels near to Him. There is nothing which Allah loves better than a repentant believing man or repentant believing woman. A believer is acknowledged in heaven as a man is acknowledged in this world among his family and children.'

It is said that this expression refers to their ranks because they will be in the Garden while the unbelievers are in the Fire. It is possible that 'over' actually does have a kind of spatial meaning since heaven is high and the Fire is the lowest of the low. It is also possible that it means that what they will have is better than what the unbelievers claim to have. Connected to that is the *ḥadīth* of Khabbāb with al-'Āṣ ibn Wā'il. Khabbāb said, 'Al-'Āṣ owed me a debt and I went to ask him to settle it. He told me, "I will not settle it until you reject Muḥammad ﷺ." I told him, "I will not reject him until you die and are resurrected." He asked, 'Will I be resurrected after death? Then I will pay you when I return to my wealth and children."'

The verb for 'laughing at' is *sakhira* and the nouns for it are *sukhrīyah*, *sukhrī* and *sikhrī*.

**Allah provides for whomever He wills without any reckoning**

Aḍ-Ḍaḥḥāk says that this means without being subject to accountability in the Next World. It is said that it refers to those who are being victimised, meaning that Allah will provide them with a high station. The *āyah* calls attention to the great blessing they will receive and says their provision is without reckoning because it will last forever and never end and so the amount of it cannot be calculated. It is said that '*without any reckoning*' refers to Allah's provision which He dispenses as He wishes and His bounty is beyond reckoning. What is based on a reckoning is dependent on a person's prior actions. Allah says, *'a recompense from your Lord, a commensurate gift.'* (78:36) Allah knows best. It is also possible that it means without the reckoning of those who receive the provision as evinced by His words: *'He will provide from him from where he does not expect.'* (65:3)

كَانَ ٱلنَّاسُ أُمَّةً وَٰحِدَةً فَبَعَثَ ٱللَّهُ ٱلنَّبِيِّـۧنَ مُبَشِّرِينَ وَمُنذِرِينَ وَأَنزَلَ مَعَهُمُ
ٱلْكِتَٰبَ بِٱلْحَقِّ لِيَحْكُمَ بَيْنَ ٱلنَّاسِ فِيمَا ٱخْتَلَفُوا۟ فِيهِ ۚ وَمَا ٱخْتَلَفَ فِيهِ إِلَّا ٱلَّذِينَ
أُوتُوهُ مِنۢ بَعْدِ مَا جَآءَتْهُمُ ٱلْبَيِّنَٰتُ بَغْيًۢا بَيْنَهُمْ ۖ فَهَدَى ٱللَّهُ ٱلَّذِينَ ءَامَنُوا۟ لِمَا
ٱخْتَلَفُوا۟ فِيهِ مِنَ ٱلْحَقِّ بِإِذْنِهِۦ ۗ وَٱللَّهُ يَهْدِى مَن يَشَآءُ إِلَىٰ صِرَٰطٍ
مُّسْتَقِيمٍ ﴿٢١٣﴾

**213 Mankind was a single community. Then Allah sent out Prophets, bringing good news and giving warning, and with them He sent down the Book with truth to decide between people regarding their differences. Only those who were given it differed about it, after the Clear Signs had come to them, envying one another. Then, by His permission, Allah guided those who believed to the truth of that about which they had differed. Allah guides whoever He wills to a straight path.**

**Mankind was a single community.**

This means that they had one *dīn*. Ubayy ibn Ka'b and Ibn Zayd said that what is meant by 'mankind' here are all the sons of Ādam when Allah brought out their souls from the back of Ādam and they affirmed His oneness. Muhājid said that 'mankind' refers to Ādam alone. A singular noun can be used for a plural because he is the source of his offspring. It is said that it means Ādam and Ḥawwā'. Ibn 'Abbās and Qatādah said that what is meant are the generations between Ādam and Nūḥ, which were ten, who followed the truth until they differed, and then Allah sent Nūḥ and the Prophets after him. Ibn Abī Khaythamah said that the length of time which passed from the time Allah created Ādam until He sent Muḥammad ﷺ is fifteen thousand eight hundred years. It is said that it is more than that. There were twelve hundred years between him and Nūḥ and Ādam lived to the age of nine hundred and sixty. People in his time had one religion and held to the *dīn* and the angels shook hands with them. They remained like that until Idrīs was taken up and then they differed.

This is unclear because it is known that Idrīs came after Nūḥ. Some people, including al-Wāqidī and al-Kalbī, say that what is meant is Nūḥ and those with him in the Ark. They were Muslims and then after the death of Nūḥ they differed. Ibn 'Abbās said, 'They were one community in disbelief, meaning in the time of Nūḥ until Allah sent Nūḥ.' He also said, 'People in the time of Ibrāhīm were one community: all unbelievers. Ibrāhīm was born in a time of ignorance and then Allah sent Ibrāhīm and other Prophets.'

According to these statements, the verb '*kāna*' (was) actually means the past. So mankind were believers for the time mentioned and then they disagreed and then the Prophets came. This indicates an elision. *'Only those who were given it differed about it'* means that people based themselves on the truth and followed it, and then they differed and so Allah sent the Prophets to give good news to those who obey and warn those who disobey. Prophets were sent to all of those whom Allah decreed would become unbelievers. But it is also possible that *kāna* has a continuous meaning and that what is meant is to inform us that mankind as a species would all be one community in respect of their failure to follow Allah's laws and their ignorance of the truth if it were not for Allah's grace to them and His favour in granting them Messengers. In this case *kāna* does not actually refer to the past.

The word '*ummah*' (community) is taken from *amma*, meaning to aim for. So an *ummah* has one focus. One person can be called an *ummah*, when what is meant is that his aim is not the same as that of other people. An example of that is what the Prophet ﷺ said about Quss ibn Sā'idah, 'He will be gathered on the Day of Rising as a whole *ummah*.' That was also said about Zayd ibn 'Amr ibn Nufayl. *Ummah* also means 'stature because it is as if it is the aim of the entire body. *Imma* means blessing because people aim for it. *Imām* is used because people aim in the same direction as him. An-Naḥḥās said that.

**Then Allah sent out Prophets**

There were twenty-four thousand Prophets and three hundred and thirteen of them were Messengers. There are eighteen mentioned by name in the Qur'an. The first Messenger was Ādam as we find in the *ḥadīth* of Abū Dharr, which was transmitted by al-Ājurrī and Abū Ḥātim al-Bustī. It is also said that it was Nūḥ going by the *ḥadīth* of intercession where people say to him, 'You are the first of the Messengers.' It is also said that the first was Idrīs. This will be dealt with in *Sūrat al-A'rāf*, Allah willing.

**and with them He sent down the Book with truth**

Here 'Book' is generic and means all the Books. Aṭ-Ṭabarī says that it means the Torah.

**to decide between people regarding their differences.**

Most scholars say that it is 'the Book' which is the deciding factor since every

Prophet judges according to his Book. When he judges by the Book it is as if the Book itself does the judging. 'Āṣim al-Jaḥdarī recites it as '*li-yuḥkama*' in the passive. That is an aberrant reading because 'Book' was already mentioned. It is said that the meaning is that Allah judges.

**Only those who were given it differed about it,**

The 'it' can also be understood as 'him' in which case it refers to the one it has been revealed to, meaning Muḥammad ﷺ. Az-Zajjāj said that. They disagreed about the Prophet ﷺ only after they were given knowledge of him.

**envying one another.**

Their failure to accept him was only due to envy. This calls attention to the foolishness of what they did and its ugliness.

**Then, by His permission, Allah guided those who believed**

Allah guided the community of Muḥammad ﷺ to the truth since He clarified the matters about which those before them had disagreed. One group says that it means that the previous communities denied each other's Books and so Allah guided the community of Muḥammad ﷺ to what was true in all of them. Another group says that Allah guided the believers to the truth regarding the disagreements of the People of the Book about whether Ibrāhīm was a Jew or a Christian. Ibn Zayd and Zayd ibn Aslam said that it is about their *qiblah*: the Jews faced Jerusalem and the Christians the east. Or it may be about the Day of Jumu'ah. The Prophet ﷺ said, 'This is the day about which they differed and Allah guided us to it. The Jews have tomorrow and the Christians the day after it.' It is also said to be about fasting or about all their differences. Ibn Zayd said, 'They disagree about Jesus; the Jews say he was a fraud and the Christians say he was a Lord. So Allah guided the believers to consider him to be a slave of Allah.'

Al-Farrā' said that there is an inversion here, and that is what aṭ-Ṭabarī prefers. He said that the meaning is: 'So Allah guided those who believe to the truth regarding that about which they differed.' Ibn 'Aṭiyyah said that he claimed this implication lest the words give rise to the impression that they disagreed about the truth and so Allah guided the believers to part of that about which they disagreed which may not have actually been the truth. Aṭ-Ṭabarī inclined to this in what he recounted from al-Farrā'. Claiming inversion in the Qur'an without necessity could lead to having a bad opinion. The words should be taken as they are because the word 'guided' implies that they got the truth. The words conclude at '*fīhi*'. What is made clear by Allah's words '*to the truth*' is that it was a matter about which there was disagreement. Al-Mahdawī said that the idea of disagreement is mentioned before mentioning the truth out of concern for it, since what one is concerned with is the mention disagreement. Ibn 'Aṭiyyah said that he does not consider this to be strong.

The words '*by His permission*' mean 'by His knowledge' according to az-Zajjāj. An-Naḥḥās says that this is not correct and that it means 'by His command'. When He gives permission for something, it is commanded. Allah guided those who believe by commanding them to do what they were obliged to do.

**Allah guides whomever He wills to a straight path.**

This is another refutation of the rationalist Mu'tazilite position that maintains that the human being is his own guide.

أَمْ حَسِبْتُمْ أَن تَدْخُلُوا الْجَنَّةَ وَلَمَّا يَأْتِكُم مَّثَلُ الَّذِينَ خَلَوْا مِن قَبْلِكُم
مَّسَّتْهُمُ الْبَأْسَاءُ وَالضَّرَّاءُ وَزُلْزِلُوا حَتَّىٰ يَقُولَ الرَّسُولُ وَالَّذِينَ
آمَنُوا مَعَهُ مَتَىٰ نَصْرُ اللَّهِ أَلَا إِنَّ نَصْرَ اللَّهِ قَرِيبٌ ﴿٢١٤﴾

**214 Or did you suppose that you would enter the Garden without facing the same as those who came before you? Poverty and illness afflicted them and they were shaken to the point that the Messenger and those who believed with him said, 'When is Allah's help coming?' Be assured that Allah's help is very near.**

**Or did you suppose that you would enter the Garden**

Qatādah, as-Suddī and most commentators say that this *āyah* was revealed about the Battle of the Ditch [in 5/627] when the Muslims suffered from overtiredness, stress, heat and cold, poor food and various other difficulties. As Allah says, it was a time when: '*your hearts rose to your throats*' (33:10). It is also said that it was revealed about the Battle of Uḥud and is similar to what Allah says in *Āl 'Imrān*: '*Or did you reckon that you were going to enter the Garden without Allah knowing those among you who had struggled?*' (3:142) One group say that it was revealed to console the Muhājirūn when they were forced to leave their homes and wealth in the hands of the idolaters in Makkah, preferring the pleasure of Allah and His Messenger, and then the Jews showed animosity to the Prophet ﷺ and some of the wealthy Madinans concealed hypocrisy in their hearts. This was revealed to cheer the hearts of the Muhājirūn.

**without facing the same as those who came before you?**

This means that they would be tried to the same degree that those before them were tried so that they could be steadfast in the same way as those before them had been steadfast. An-Naḍr ibn Shumayl said that *'mathal'* has an adjectival meaning and so the meaning can be: what afflicts you is the like of what afflicted those before you. This refers to trial. Wahb said 'There were seventy dead Prophets between Makkah and Ta'if. They died of hunger and fleas.' This is like another *āyah*: *'Do people imagine that they will be left to say, "We believe," and will not be tested? We tested those before them.'* (29:1-3) Allah calls on them to be steadfast and promises them that they will be helped if they are, saying, *'Allah's help is very near.'*

**Poverty and illness afflicted them and they were shaken to the point...**

The word 'shaken' (*zulzilū*) refers to great turbulence. It can be applied to both individuals and situations. The noun *zalzalah* means "earthquake" and its plural *zalāzil* is used for hardships. Az-Zajjāj said the root of the word is *zalla*, which is used when a thing slips from its place.

**...that the Messenger and those who believed with him, said, 'When is Allah's help coming?' Be assured that Allah that Allah's help is very near.**

The verb 'said' is recited by Nāfi' as *'yaqūlu'* while the rest have *'yaqūla'*. The position of Sībuwayh is that each reading has two aspects. You say, 'I travelled until I entered the city' with a *fatḥah*, and it means that both the journey and the entry are in the past. The other aspect with a *fatḥah,* which is used elsewhere, is 'I travelled to it in order to enter it.' One of the two aspects when it is read with a *ḍammah* is: 'I travelled and entered it,' and both are in the past. An-Naḥḥās thinks that the reading with *ḍammah* is sounder and clearer in meaning, i.e. 'they were shaken until the Messenger said...' because the statement is not separate from the shaking. According to Muqātil, the Messenger here is Shu'ayb. He is al-Yasa'. Al-Kalbī said that this is about every Messenger sent to his nation who strives in fulfilling his mission to the point that he says, 'When is Allah's help coming?" It is related that aḍ-Ḍaḥḥāk said that it means Muḥammad ﷺ and the revelation of the *āyah* indicates him. Allah knows best. The other aspect with a *ḍammah*, which is used elsewhere: 'I travelled so that I might enter it' where the journey is in the past and the entry in the present. Mujāhid, al-A'raj, Ibn Muḥayṣin and Shaybah preferred the *ḍammah.* Al-Ḥasan, Abū Ja'far, Ibn Abī Isḥāq, Shibl and others recited it with a *fatḥah.* Makkī said that he preferred it because most reciters have that.

The question is part of the words of the Prophet ﷺ in which he asks for help to come quickly, without that expressing doubt or uncertainty about its arrival in any way. The word *'rasūl'* (Messenger) is generic here. One group said that there is a reversal of normal order here. The implied meaning is that those who believed said, 'When is Allah's help coming?' and the Messenger said. 'Be assured that Allah's help is very near.' The Messenger ﷺ is mentioned first because of his high rank. The words of the believers are put first because they occurred earlier in time. Ibn 'Aṭiyyah said this is an arbitrary interpretation and it is probable that the words *'Be assured that Allah's help is very near'* is simply a report from Allah.

يَسْـَٔلُونَكَ مَاذَا يُنفِقُونَ قُلْ مَآ أَنفَقْتُم مِّنْ خَيْرٍ فَلِلْوَٰلِدَيْنِ وَٱلْأَقْرَبِينَ
وَٱلْيَتَـٰمَىٰ وَٱلْمَسَـٰكِينِ وَٱبْنِ ٱلسَّبِيلِ وَمَا تَفْعَلُوا۟ مِنْ خَيْرٍ فَإِنَّ ٱللَّهَ بِهِۦ
عَلِيمٌ ٢١٥

**215 They will ask you what they should give away. Say, 'Any wealth you give away should go to your parents and relatives and to orphans and the very poor and travellers.' Whatever good you do, Allah knows it.**

This was revealed about 'Amr ibn al-Jamūḥ who was a very old man. He said, 'Messenger of Allah, I have a lot of wealth. What *ṣadaqah* should l give and to whom should I give it?' and this was revealed.

It is said that the askers are the believers in general, and it means: 'They will ask you about the ways in which to spend and whether to spend.' As-Suddī said that this *āyah* was revealed before zakat became obligatory and that the imposition of zakat abrogated it. Ibn 'Aṭiyyah said that al-Mahdawī thinks this statement to be weak. He stated that the *āyah* was about the obligatory zakat. It was at a later time that parents ceased to be recipients of it. Ibn Jurayj and others said that it refers to recommended spending and that zakat is something else and so this *āyah* is not abrogated.

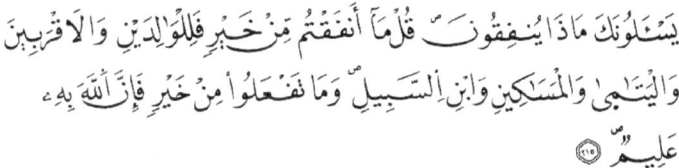

It clarifies the channels of voluntary *ṣadaqah*. A rich man must spend on his needy parents to the point that their standard of living is brought up to the level of his own in respect of food, clothing and other such things. Mālik said that a son is not obliged to go as far as procuring a wife for his father but he should spend on his father's wife, whether she is his mother or not. Mālik said that he does not have to procure a wife for his father because he thinks that, in general, there is no real need for him to marry. If, however, his father does really need a wife, then he should procure one for him. As for expenses connected to worship, the son does not have to pay for his father to perform ḥajj or go on *jihād* but he does have to pay his *zakat al-fiṭr.* The other channels – orphans, the poor and travellers – have already been discussed. This *āyah* is similar to His words: *'Give relatives their due, and the poor and travellers.'* (30:38)

كُتِبَ عَلَيْكُمُ الْقِتَالُ وَهُوَ كُرْهٌ لَّكُمْ وَعَسَىٰٓ أَن تَكْرَهُوا۟ شَيْـًٔا وَهُوَ خَيْرٌ لَّكُمْ وَعَسَىٰٓ
أَن تُحِبُّوا۟ شَيْـًٔا وَهُوَ شَرٌّ لَّكُمْ وَاللَّهُ يَعْلَمُ وَأَنتُمْ لَا تَعْلَمُونَ ﴿٢١٦﴾

**216 Fighting is prescribed for you even if it is hateful to you. It may be that you hate something when it is good for you and it may be that you love something when it is bad for you. Allah knows and you do not know.**

### Fighting is prescribed for you

'*Kutiba*' (prescribed) means 'made obligatory'. This means that fighting is obligatory and refers to the obligation of *jihād.* Allah makes it clear that He has made the trial of fighting a means of reaching the Garden. What is meant by fighting is fighting enemies among the unbelievers. This is known from the context. The Prophet ﷺ was not given permission to fight while he was in Makkah. When he emigrated, he was given permission to fight those idolaters who fought him when Allah said: *'Permission to fight is given to those who are fought against'* (22:39), and then he was given permission to fight idolaters in general.

There is disagreement about who is meant by the *āyah.* It is said that it refers to the Companions of the Prophet in particular, and so fighting with the Prophet is an obligation for each of them individually. When the Sharī'ah was established, it became a *farḍ kifāyah,* an obligation for the community as a whole but not for every individual in it. 'Aṭā' and al-Awzā'ī stated that. Ibn Jurayj said, 'I asked 'Aṭā', "Is *jihād* made obligatory for everyone by this *āyah*?" He replied, "No, it was prescribed for those people in particular."'

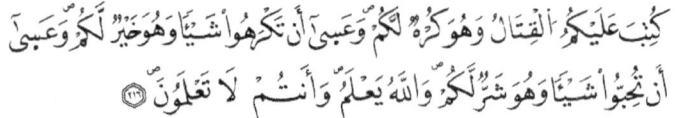

The majority say that, at first, it was a *kifāyah* obligation, not specific to all of them, but when the Prophet ﷺ called them out, it was incumbent on them to obey him. Sa'īd ibn al-Musayyab said, 'Jihād will remain an obligation forever for every single Muslim.' Al-Māwardī related that. Ibn 'Aṭiyyah said, 'That on which there is consensus is that *jihād* is a *farḍ kifāyah* for the entire community of Muhammad ﷺ. If some undertake it, the obligation falls from the rest, unless the enemy arrives in a Muslim land and then it is an obligation for every individual.' This will be explained in *Sūrat at-Tawbah,* Allah willing. Ath-Thawrī said that *jihād* is voluntary. Ibn 'Aṭiyyah remarked that he thought that these words were in response to a question put by someone who had already performed *jihād* and he was told that it was voluntary.

**even it is hateful to you.**

It is natural to dislike it. Ibn 'Arafah said about the word '*kurh*' (hateful) that, when it is pronounced with a *ḍammah*, *kurh*, as it is here, it means hardship and when it is pronounced with a *fatḥah*, *karh*, it means hateful. It is also possible that *kurh* has the same meaning as *karh*. The verb is *kariha*. Jihād is hateful because it involves spending money, leaving one's homeland and family, exposing one's body to head fractures and wounds, loss of limbs and death. So people find that aspect of it hateful, not the fact that it is an obligation from Allah. 'Ikrimah mentioned that they first hated it and then came to love it because, even though obeying the command entails hardship, the knowledge of the reward made it easy.

It is similar to the removal of things which cause people pain and which they fear, like the amputation of limbs, the extraction of teeth, venesection, cupping and other such things which people undergo to improve their health. Knowledge of the eventual benefit makes people keen to undergo these things in spite of the temporary hardship they entail. There could be no benefit greater than everlasting life in the Abode of Eternity: *'on seats of honour in the Presence of an all-powerful King'* (54:55).

**It may be that you hate something when it is good for you and it may be that you love something when it is bad for you.**

The word "*asā*' (may be) can mean that it is actually the case. Al-Aṣamm said that it has the meaning of *qad* [indicating that something certain has taken place]. It is said that it means that it is mandatory. When the word is used by Allah, it means that that is the case everywhere in the Qur'an except 66:5. It means, in other words: 'You do hate the hardship in *jihād* but it is good for you in that you conquer, have victory, take booty and are rewarded and whoever perishes dies a martyr. You do love peace and not fighting but it is evil for you since you will be overcome and abased and your authority lost.' This is absolutely true and it happened in Andalusia when they abandoned *jihād* and avoided fighting and many fled. The enemy took the land and captured, killed and enslaved the Muslims. We belong to Allah and to Him we return! That was because of what they did and earned! Al-Ḥasan said that the meaning of this *āyah* is: 'Do not hate vicissitudes that occur. Your success may lie in many a matter that you hate and your perdition in many a matter that you love.' Abū Sa'īd aḍ-Ḍarīr composed:

Many a thing you fear
may bring something that pleases you.
What is loved is hidden from you
while what is hated appears openly.

يَسْـَٔلُونَكَ عَنِ ٱلشَّهْرِ ٱلْحَرَامِ قِتَالٍ فِيهِ قُلْ قِتَالٌ فِيهِ كَبِيرٌ وَصَدٌّ عَن سَبِيلِ ٱللَّهِ
وَكُفْرٌۢ بِهِۦ وَٱلْمَسْجِدِ ٱلْحَرَامِ وَإِخْرَاجُ أَهْلِهِۦ مِنْهُ أَكْبَرُ عِندَ ٱللَّهِ وَٱلْفِتْنَةُ أَكْبَرُ مِنَ ٱلْقَتْلِ
وَلَا يَزَالُونَ يُقَـٰتِلُونَكُمْ حَتَّىٰ يَرُدُّوكُمْ عَن دِينِكُمْ إِنِ ٱسْتَطَـٰعُوا۟ وَمَن يَرْتَدِدْ مِنكُمْ
عَن دِينِهِۦ فَيَمُتْ وَهُوَ كَافِرٌ فَأُو۟لَـٰٓئِكَ حَبِطَتْ أَعْمَـٰلُهُمْ فِى ٱلدُّنْيَا وَٱلْـَٔاخِرَةِ وَأُو۟لَـٰٓئِكَ
أَصْحَـٰبُ ٱلنَّارِ هُمْ فِيهَا خَـٰلِدُونَ ﴿٢١٧﴾ إِنَّ ٱلَّذِينَ ءَامَنُوا۟ وَٱلَّذِينَ هَاجَرُوا۟ وَجَـٰهَدُوا۟ فِى
سَبِيلِ ٱللَّهِ أُو۟لَـٰٓئِكَ يَرْجُونَ رَحْمَتَ ٱللَّهِ وَٱللَّهُ غَفُورٌ رَّحِيمٌ ﴿٢١٨﴾

**217 They will ask you about the Sacred Month and fighting in it. Say, 'Fighting in it is a serious matter; but barring access to the Way of Allah and rejecting Him and barring access to the Masjid al-Ḥarām and expelling its people from it are far more serious in the sight of Allah. Fitnah is worse than killing.' They will not stop fighting you until they make you revert from your dīn, if they are able. As for any of you who revert from their dīn and die unbelievers, their actions will come to nothing in this world and the Next. They are the Companions of the Fire, remaining in it timelessly, for ever. 218 Those who believe and make hijrah and do *jihād* in the Way of Allah can expect Allah's mercy. Allah is Ever-Forgiving, Most Merciful.**

**They will ask you about the Sacred Month**

Jarīr ibn 'Abd al-Ḥamīd and Muḥammad ibn Fuḍayl related from 'Aṭā' ibn as-Sā'ib from Sa'īd ibn Jubayr that Ibn 'Abbās said, 'I have not seen any people better than the Companions of Muhammad ﷺ. They only asked him about thirteen matters, all of which are in the Qur'an. *"They will ask you about menstruation," "they will ask you about the Sacred Month," "they will ask you about orphans."* They only asked him about what would benefit them.' Ibn 'Abd al-Barr said, 'There are only three of the thirteen in the *ḥadīth*.'

Abū-l-Yasār reported from Jundub ibn 'Abdullāh that the Prophet ﷺ sent out a party led by 'Abdullāh ibn Jaḥsh and wrote a letter for him and instructed him not to read the letter until he reached a certain place. He said, 'Do not force your companions to go on.' When he reached the place, he read the letter and said, 'We belong to Allah and return to Him. We hear and obey His Messenger.' Two men returned while the rest continued. They met Ibn al-Ḥadramī and killed him, not knowing that it was the month of Rajab. The idolaters said, "You have killed in the Sacred Month!" and Allah revealed this.

It is related that the reason for its revelation was that two men of the Banū Kilāb met 'Amr ibn Umayyah aḍ-Ḍamrī on the first day of Rajab and he killed them. Quraysh said, 'You killed them during the Sacred Month,' and Allah revealed the *āyah*. The most commonly accepted version, however, is that of 'Abdullāh ibn Jaḥsh. The Prophet ﷺ sent him with eight or nine men in the month of Jumādā al-Ākhirah two months before the Battle of Badr. It is also said that it was in the month of Rajab. In *Kitāb ad-Durar*, Abū 'Amr said, 'When the Messenger of Allah ﷺ returned from pursuing Kurz ibn Jābir, which is called the First Expedition of Badr, he stayed in Madīnah for the rest of Jumādā al-Ākhirah and Rajab. During Rajab, he sent out 'Abdullāh ibn Jaḥsh ibn Ri'āb al-Asadī with eight of the Muhājirūn: Abū Ḥudhayfah ibn 'Utbah, 'Ukkāshah ibn Miḥṣan, 'Utbah ibn Ghazwān, Suhayl ibn Bayḍā' al-Fihrī, Sa'd ibn Abī Waqqāṣ, 'Āmir ibn Rabī'ah, Wāqid ibn 'Abdullāh at-Tamīmī, and Khālid ibn Bukayr al-Laythī. He wrote a letter to 'Abdullāh ibn Jaḥsh and told him not to look at it until he had travelled for two days. Then he was to open it and do what he was commanded to do, but he was not force any of his companions. He was their commander.

'Abdullāh ibn Jaḥsh did what he was commanded. When he opened the letter, he found in it: 'When you read this letter, proceed to Nakhlah between Makkah and Ta'if. Lie in wait for Quraysh there and find out for us what they are doing.' When he read the letter, he said, 'We hear and obey.' Then he informed his companions about that and the fact that he was not to force any of them to go and whoever wanted to rise and go for his sake should obey him, and if no one obeyed him, he would go alone. Anyone who desired martyrdom should go forward and anyone who disliked death should go back. They answered, 'We want what you want. There is none of us who does not hear and obey the Messenger of Allah ﷺ.' So they went forward with him. They travelled through the Hijaz. Then the camel on which Sa'd ibn Abī Waqqāṣ and 'Utbah ibn Ghazwān were alternating on went astray and they fell behind to look for it. 'Abdullāh ibn Jaḥsh and the rest of them pressed on until they stopped at Nakhlah. A caravan of Quraysh carrying raisins and other goods passed by them. The caravan included 'Amr ibn al-Ḥaḍramī (whose name was 'Abdullāh ibn 'Abbād, one of Ṣadif, a sub-tribe of

Hadramawt), 'Uthmān ibn 'Abdullāh ibn al-Mughīrah and his brother, Nawfal ibn 'Abdullāh ibn al-Mughīrah al-Makhzūmī, and al-Ḥakam ibn Kaysān, the freedman of the Banū 'l-Mughīrah.

The Muslims held a council and said, 'We are in the last day of the sacred month of Rajab. If we fight them, we will violate the sanctity of the sacred month. If we leave them until nightfall, they will enter the Ḥaram.' They agreed to engage them. Wāqid ibn 'Abdullāh at-Tamīmī shot 'Amr ibn al-Ḥaḍramī and killed him. 'Uthmān and al-Ḥakam were captured and Nawfal ibn 'Abdullāh slipped away. Then they took the caravan and the two captives. 'Abdullāh ibn Jaḥsh said to them, 'Leave the fifth of our booty for the Messenger of Allah ﷺ.' They did that. It was the first *khums* in Islam.

Then the Qur'an was revealed: *'Know that when you take any booty, a fifth of it belongs to Allah.'* (8:41) So Allah and His Messenger affirmed what 'Abdullāh ibn Jaḥsh had done. Allah was pleased with it and made it a sunnah for the community until the Day of Rising. They were the first spoils to be taken in Islam and 'Abdullāh was the first commander. 'Amr ibn al-Ḥaḍramī was the first to be killed.

The Messenger of Allah ﷺ disapproved of killing Ibn al-Ḥaḍramī in the sacred month and the group were in despair. Then Allah revealed: *'They will ask you about the Sacred Month and fighting in it… …remaining in it timelessly, forever.'* The Messenger of Allah ﷺ accepted ransom for the two captives. 'Uthmān ibn 'Abdullāh died an unbeliever in Makkah. Al-Ḥakam ibn Kaysān became a Muslim and remained with the Messenger of Allah ﷺ until he was martyred at Bi'r Ma'ūna. Sa'd and 'Utbah returned to Makkah in safety.

It is said that Sa'd ibn Abī Waqqāṣ and 'Utbah went to look for their camel with the permission of 'Abdullāh ibn Jaḥsh. When 'Amr ibn al-Ḥaḍramī and his fellows saw the Companions of the Messenger of Allah ﷺ, they were frightened of them. 'Abdullāh ibn Jaḥsh said, 'The people are alarmed by you.' One of the men shaved his head and showed himself to them. When they saw his shaved head, they felt safe and said, 'People performing *'umrah*. There is nothing for you to worry about.' Then they discussed fighting them.

The Jews took this as a bad omen and said, 'Wāqid: war is kindled (*waqadat*). 'Amr: war has come to life (*'amarat*). Al-Ḥaḍramī: war is present (*ḥaḍarat*).' The Makkans sent the ransom for the captives and he ﷺ said, 'We will not let them be ransomed until Sa'd and 'Utbah return. If they do not return, we will kill the two of them in exchange.' When they appeared, he let them ransom them. Al-Ḥakam became Muslim and stayed in Madīnah until he was killed as a martyr at Bi'r Ma'ūnah. 'Uthmān returned to Makkah and died there as an unbeliever. Nawfal struck the belly of his horse in the Battle of the Confederates in order to enter the Trench to attack the Muslims. He fell into the trench with his horse and they were both crushed. Allah killed him, and the idolaters asked to pay for his corpse. The Messenger of Allah ﷺ said, 'Take it. A foul corpse, foul blood-money.' This was the reason for the revelation of the *āyah*.

Ibn Isḥāq mentioned that 'Amr ibn al-Ḥaḍramī was killed on the last day of Rajab as we already mentioned. Aṭ-Ṭabarī mentioned from as-Suddī and others that it was on the last day of Jumādā al-Ākhirah. The first is more famous, although Ibn 'Abbās mentioned that it was on the first night of Rajab while the Muslims thought that it was still Jumādā al-Ākhirah. Ibn 'Aṭiyyah said, 'Aṣ-Ṣāḥib ibn 'Abbād said in his *Risālah* known as *al-Asadiyyah* that 'Abdullāh ibn Jaḥsh was called the 'Amīr al-Mu'minīn' at this time because he was in command of a group of Muslims

Scholars disagree about whether the *āyah* was abrogated. The majority say that it was abrogated and that it is permitted to fight the idolaters in the Sacred Months. They disagree about what abrogated it. Az-Zuhrī said that it was abrogated by: '*fight the idolaters totally.*' (9:36) It is said that it was abrogated by the expedition of the Prophet ﷺ against Thaqīf in the Sacred month and his sending 'Āmir against Awṭās in the Sacred Month. It is said that it was abrogated by the Pledge of Riḍwān to allow fighting in Dhu-l-Ḥijjah. This is weak. When the Prophet ﷺ heard that 'Uthmān had been killed in Makkah and that they were resolved on fighting him, he accepted allegiance from the Muslims to defend themselves, not to initiate the fighting.

Al-Bayhaqī mentioned from 'Urwah ibn az-Zubayr from other than the account of Muḥammad ibn Isḥāq after the story of al-Ḥaḍramī, 'Allah revealed the *āyah*: *"They will ask you about the Sacred Month and fighting in it."* So Allah informed them in His Book that fighting in the Sacred Month was still as unlawful as it always had been, but what had been made lawful against the believers was far worse than that: barring access to the Way of Allah by imprisoning the Muslims, torturing them and keeping them from emigrating to the Messenger of Allah ﷺ, their denial of Allah, and preventing the Muslims from reaching the Masjid al-Ḥarām for ḥajj and *'umrah* and preventing them from praying in it, expelling the people of the Masjid al-Ḥarām from it when they were its Muslim inhabitants, and trying to make them revert from their *dīn*. We heard that the Prophet ﷺ paid the blood money of Ibn al-Ḥaḍramī and considered the Sacred Month to be sacred as they did until Allah revealed: *"Allah and His Messenger are free of them."* (9:1)'

'Aṭā' said that the *āyah* is one of judgment and that it is not permitted to fight in the Sacred Months. He swore to that because the *āyahs* which come after it are general with respect to times while this one is specific. It is agreed that the general does not abrogate the specific. Abu-z-Zubayr related that Jābir said, 'The Messenger of Allah ﷺ did not fight in the Sacred Months unless he was attacked.'

**and fighting in it.**

Sībuwayh says that '*fighting in it*' is grammatically an inclusive substitute because the question asked includes both the months and fighting. It means that the unbelievers will ask you in wonder at the violation of the sanctity of the month and the reason they asked was because of the fighting in it. Az-Zajjāj said they ask you about fighting in the Sacred Month. Al-Qutaybī said, 'They are asking whether it is permitted to fight in the sacred month.'

**Say, 'Fighting in it is a serious matter;**

It was objectionable because the prohibition against fighting in the Sacred Month was still in place at that time if the Muslims initiated it. The word '*shahr*' (month) here is generic. The Arabs made it a principle that was equal to all. Blood was not shed during those months and there was no change in the Sacred Months which are Rajab, Dhu-l-Qa'dah, Dhu-l-Ḥijjah and Muḥarram. Three are together and one is separate. This will be further explained in *al-Mā'idah*, Allah willing.

**but barring access to the Way of Allah and rejecting Him**

This is a greater wrong action than fighting in the Sacred Month. Al-Mubarrad and others said that and it is sound since they prevented people from doing *ṭawāf* of the Ka'bah. The words "*kufrun bihi*" (rejecting Him) are generally taken to be referring to rejecting Allah though it is also said that they refer to the ḥajj and the Sacred Months.

**and expelling its people from it are far more serious in the sight of Allah.**

This means that, in the sight of Allah, these things merit a far greater punishment than fighting in the Sacred Month. Most say that the *āyah* means: 'O unbelievers of Quraysh! you think that it is terrible for us to fight in the Sacred Month yet what you do to us in barring access to the Way of Allah, your rejection of Allah, and your expelling the people of the Mosque from it as you did to the Messenger of Allah ﷺ and His Companions is a far more grievous sin in the sight of Allah.' 'Abdullāh ibn Jaḥsh said:

> You count killing in the Sacred Month as something terrible,
> but far graver than it, if you are properly guided,

Is your barring them from what Muḥammad says
and disbelief in it which Allah sees and witnesses,
And your expelling its people from the mosque of Allah
So that none is seen prostrating to Allah in His House.
If you criticise us for killing him,
oppressors and enviers are more perilous to Islam.
Our spears drank the blood of Ibn al-Ḥaḍramī
at Nakhlah when Wāqid lit the flames of war.
'Uthmān ibn 'Abdullāh is with us:
a bloody leather collar restrains him.

Az-Zuhrī, Mujāhid and others said that *'Fighting in it is a serious matter'* is abrogated by *'...fight the idolaters totally.'* (9:36) and *'...fight the idolaters.'* (9:5) 'Aṭā' said that it is not abrogated and that there should not be fighting in the Sacred Months as we already mentioned.

**Fitnah is worse than killing.**

Mujāhid and others said that *fitnah* in this instance means disbelief so their disbelief is worse than our killing them. Most say that *fitnah* here means their tempting the Muslims away from their *dīn* so that they would be destroyed. That is a worse crime than killing people in the Sacred Month.

**They will not stop fighting you until they make you revert from your dīn,**

This warns the believers of the nature of the evil of the unbelievers. Mujāhid said that it is the unbelievers of Quraysh who are meant here.

**As for any of you who revert from their *dīn* and die unbelievers, their actions will come to nothing in this world and the Next.**

So if anyone apostasises and returns to disbelief their actions are nullified and useless. The root of the word for "come to nothing" is *ḥabaṭ*, which is a word denoting what happens to livestock when they eat too much herbage and their bellies swell. This sometimes causes them to die. This is a threat to the Muslims, warning them to stay firm in Islam.

Scholars disagree about whether or not apostates are asked to repent. One group say that they are asked to repent and, if they do not, they are killed. Some say they are given an hour and others a month. Others say that they are asked to repent three times. That is related from 'Umar and 'Uthmān and that is the view of Mālik. Ibn al-Qāsim related it from him. Al-Ḥasan said they are asked a hundred times. It is also said that they are killed without being asked to repent. Ash-Shāfi'ī says that in one of his two views and it is one of the positions of Ṭāwūs and 'Ubayd ibn 'Umayr. Saḥnūn mentioned that 'Abd al-'Azīz ibn Abī Salmah al-Mājishūn said that apostates are killed without being asked to repent. He argues that based on the *ḥadīth* of Mu'ādh and Abū Mūsā. It says: 'When the Prophet ﷺ sent Abū Mūsā to Yemen, he sent Mu'ādh ibn Jabal after him. When he came to him, he dismounted and Abū Mūsā gave him a cushion. There was a man in shackles beside him. Mu'ādh asked, "Who is this?" He replied, "He is a Jew who became Muslim and reverted and returned to Judaism." He stated, "I will not sit down until he is killed. This is the judgment of Allah and His Messenger." "Sit," Abū Mūsā said. He repeated, "No, I will not sit down until he is killed. This is the judgment of Allah and His Messenger." He said it three times and he commanded that he be killed.' Muslim and others transmitted it.

Abū Yūsuf mentioned from Abū Ḥanīfah that an apostate is offered Islam. If he does not accept Islam, he is killed immediately unless he requests a delay. If he requests a delay, he is given three days. What is well known from him and his people is that an apostate is not killed without being asked to repent. He considered an apostate and *zindīq* to be the same in that respect. Mālik, however, said that *zindīq*s are killed without being asked to repent. This was mentioned at the beginning of *al-Baqarah*.

They disagree about someone who goes from one form of unbelief to another. Mālik and most *fuqahā'* say that he is not interfered with because he has moved to what would have originally be confirmed for him. Ibn 'Abd al-Ḥakam related from ash-Shāfi'ī that he is killed based on the words of the Prophet ﷺ, 'If someone changes his religion, kill him,' without specifying Muslims rather than unbelievers. Mālik said that the *ḥadīth* means someone who leaves Islam for unbelief and that those who leave unbelief for unbelief are not meant by the *ḥadīth*. That is the view of a large group of *fuqahā'*. What is well known from ash-Shāfi'ī is what al-Muzanī and ar-Rabī' mentioned about one of the people of the *dhimmah* changing his religion: the ruler sends him to the Abode of War and expels him from his territory; his property is fair game along with the rest of the property of the people of war if their territory is conquered, because he was given his *dhimmī* status based on the religion he was following at the time of the contract.

They disagree about female apostates. Mālik, al-Awzā'ī, ash-Shāfi'ī and al-Layth ibn Sa'd said that a female apostate is killed just as a male apostate is killed, based on the literal words of the *ḥadīth*: 'If someone changes his religion, kill him.'

'Someone' can be male or female. Ath-Thawrī and Abū Ḥanīfah and his people said that a woman is not killed. That is the position of Ibn Shubrumah and it was what Ibn 'Ulayyah believed. It is also the position of 'Aṭā' and al-Ḥasan. Their argument is that Ibn 'Abbās related that *ḥadīth* from the Prophet ﷺ and then said, 'A female apostate is not killed.' The one who related the *ḥadīth* has a better knowledge of its interpretation. Something similar is related from 'Alī. The Prophet ﷺ forbade killing women and children. The people with the first view argue by the words of the Prophet ﷺ: 'The life of a Muslim is only lawful by one of three things: unbelief after belief...' Therefore it is general to those who disbelieve after having believed. It is sounder.

There is also discussion about whether people's actions are considered to have been invalidated by apostasy or not if they later return to the *dīn*. Ash-Shāfi'ī says that an apostate who returns to Islam does not have his actions or his ḥajj invalidated. His actions come to nothing if he dies an apostate. Mālik says that they are invalidated by apostasy. There is disagreement about a Muslim's ḥajj when he apostatises and then returns to Islam. Mālik said that he must perform ḥajj again because the first was cancelled by apostasy. Ash-Shāfi'ī says that he does not have to repeat it because the action remains. Our scholars cite as evidence Allah's words: *'If you associate others with Allah, your actions will come to nothing.'* (39:65) It is addressed to the Prophet ﷺ while his community is meant because apostasy is legally impossible for him. The people of ash-Shāfi'ī said, 'It is addressed to the Prophet ﷺ to make it more severe for the community. It is clear that, in spite of his noble position, had the Prophet ﷺ committed *shirk*, his actions would have come to nothing, so what then is the case with you! But, of course, he did not do so because of his excellent rank as Allah says: "*Wives of the Prophet! if any of you commits an obvious act of indecency she will receive double the punishment.*" (33:30) That is because of the nobility of their status. It is not conceivable that any of them would violate the honour of their noble, esteemed husband.'

Ibn al-'Arabī said, 'Our scholars say that Allah mentioned compliance here as a precondition because it is connected to eternity in the Fire as a repayment. So if someone complies with unbelief, Allah will put him in the Fire forever according to this *āyah*. If someone commits *shirk*, Allah will cancel his deeds based on the other *āyah*. So these are two useful *āyah*s with two meanings and two different wisdoms. That which was addressed to the Prophet ﷺ was meant for his community to confirm his special status. What was said about his wives was said to explain that, had it been conceivable, the one who did so would be violating the sanctity of the *dīn* as well as the sanctity of the Prophet ﷺ. There would be a punishment for each violation of sanctity. That is in the position of someone who disobeys Allah in the Sacred Month, the Sacred Land or the Masjid al-Ḥarām. The punishment is multiplied because of multiple violations. Allah knows best.'

Another question is whether apostates are inherited from and there is disagreement about that. 'Alī ibn Abī Ṭālib, al-Ḥasan, ash-Sha'bī, al-Ḥakam, al-Layth, Abū Ḥanīfah and Isḥāq ibn Rāhawayh said that their property reverts to their Muslim heirs. Malik, Rabī'ah, Ibn Abī Laylā, ash-Shāfi'ī and Abū Thawr said that their property goes to the treasury. Ibn Shubrumah, Abū Yūsuf, Muḥammad and al-Awzā'ī, in one of two transmissions, say that what an apostate earned after his apostasy goes to his Muslim heirs. Abū Ḥanīfah said that whatever an apostate earns while an apostate is spoils, but what he earned while a Muslim before his apostasy is inherited by his Muslim heirs. Ibn Shubrumah, Abū Yūsuf, and Muḥammad do not make a distinction between the two. The general nature of the words of the Prophet ﷺ, 'There is no inheritance between the people of two religions', indicate that their position is false. They agree that someone's unbelieving heirs do not inherit from him with the exception of 'Umar ibn 'Abd al-'Azīz who says that they do inherit.

### Those who believe and make hijrah

Jundub ibn 'Abdullāh, 'Urwah ibn az-Zubayr and others said that when Wāqid ibn 'Abdullāh at-Tamīmī killed 'Amr ibn al-Ḥadramī in the sacred month, the Messenger of Allah ﷺ hesitated to take the *khums*, which was his rightful share of the booty, from 'Abdullāh ibn Jaḥsh and the captives. The Muslims rebuked 'Abdullāh ibn Jaḥsh and his companions until it became hard for them and then Allah revealed this *āyah* about the Sacred Month, relieved them, and informed them that they had the reward of those who emigrated and fought. They are indicated in His words: "*Those who believe...*" and that quality remains for those who do what Allah mentioned. It was said that if they if did not have a burden, they would not have a reward, and so Allah revealed this *āyah*.

To make *hijrah* means to move from one place to another, and the aim is to leave one out of preference for the other. *Hajr* means separation, the opposite of connection. A *muhājir* is someone who emigrates from one land to another, leaving the first for the second. *Tahājur* is mutual severance. Some say that *muhājarah* is to move from the desert to the city. This is weak because that was normal among the Arabs and also because the people of Makkah would, in that case, not be Muhājirūn.

**and do *jihād* in the Way of Allah can expect Allah's mercy**

'*Jāhada*' is Form III of the verb, which means to strive by exerting effort and to struggle (*jahd*, *mujāhadah*, *jihād*). *Ijtihād* and *tahājud* is expending effort and exertion). *Jahād* means 'hard land'. The word 'expect' implies hope and also trying to bring near. It is said that this is praise of them because no one in this world knows if he will go to the Garden, no matter how many good actions he does. There are two reasons for this. The first is that he does not know what his seal will be and the second is that he should not rely on his actions. Hope delights and hope is always accompanied by fear and fear is always accompanied by hope. Hope derives from a desire for a good outcome.

يَسْـَٔلُونَكَ عَنِ ٱلْخَمْرِ وَٱلْمَيْسِرِ قُلْ فِيهِمَآ إِثْمٌ كَبِيرٌ وَمَنَـٰفِعُ لِلنَّاسِ وَإِثْمُهُمَآ
أَكْبَرُ مِن نَّفْعِهِمَا وَيَسْـَٔلُونَكَ مَاذَا يُنفِقُونَ قُلِ ٱلْعَفْوُ كَذَٰلِكَ يُبَيِّنُ ٱللَّهُ
لَكُمُ ٱلْـَٔايَـٰتِ لَعَلَّكُمْ تَتَفَكَّرُونَ ٢١٩

**219 They will ask you about alcoholic drinks and gambling. Say, 'There is great wrong in both of them and also certain benefits for mankind. But the wrong in them is greater than the benefit.' They will ask you what they should give away. Say, 'Whatever is surplus to your needs.' In this way Allah makes the Signs clear to you, so that hopefully you will reflect.**

**They will ask you about alcoholic drinks and gambling**

Those who ask are the believers. The word for 'alcoholic drinks' (*khamr*) comes from *khamara*, to cover, and the *khimār* (veil) of a woman comes from the same root. The verb is used for anything that covers something, as in the expression, 'Cover your vessels.' So wine covers the intellect and obscures it. *Khamar* is also used for a covert of trees because it conceals what is under it, so that wolves and other animals are able to conceal themselves there. It is also used for hiding oneself in a crowd when a person is in a situation that causes him to feel alarm. *Khumār* describes disappearing into a crowd of people so that one is hidden. It is said that it is called *khamr* because it obscures the mind. It is also said that it is called that because it is left until it becomes intoxicating as Form VIII of the verb is used for dough rising. It is also used to describe having a concealed suspicion until the matter is made clear. It is said that wine is called *khamr* because it muddles the intellect. *Mukhāmirah* is become mixed and muddled. The meanings are close together, but the true linguistic root means covering.

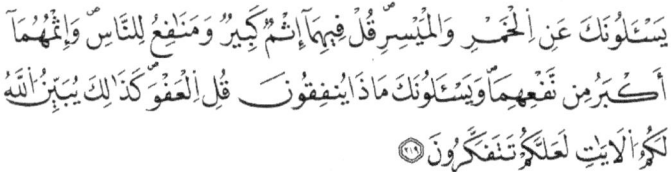

The word *khamr* is generally used for the juice of grapes which has become fermented. However any other substance which intoxicates the mind carries the same ruling, just as there is a consensus among scholars that all types of gambling are unlawful even though only *maysir* is mentioned here. All other kinds of types of gambling follow the same ruling by analogy. *Maysir* is, in fact, the act of drawing arrows to determine the distribution of meat. By the same process every alcoholic drink that intoxicates like wine falls under the same ruling.

The majority of the Community believe that when a lot of something intoxicates, then drinking either a little or a lot of it is unlawful and the *ḥadd* punishment is obliged for doing it. Abū Ḥanīfah, ath-Thawrī, Ibn Abī Laylā, Ibn Shubrumah and a group of the scholars of Kufa say that when a lot of something, other than actual wine made from grapes, intoxicates, it is lawful and if someone becomes intoxicated by it without intending to then the *ḥadd* punishment is not applicable. This is weak and refuted both by logic and by reports as will come in the commentary about it in *Sūrat al-Mā'idah* and *Sūrat an-Naḥl*, Allah willing.

Some commentators say that there is no honour or kindness which Allah failed to bestow on this Community. Part of His generosity and kindness was that He did not impose laws on them all at once, but little by little. This was the case with the prohibition of wine. This is the first *āyah* revealed about it, and then after it comes 4:43, then 5:91 and finally 5:90 as will be explained in those places, Allah willing.

The 'gambling' (*maysir*) referred to here, as mentioned above, is a particular type of gambling which the Arabs did with arrows. Ibn 'Abbās said, 'In the Jāhiliyyah, a man would stake his wealth and family with another man and then this *āyah* was revealed.' Mujāhid, Muḥammad ibn Sīrīn, al-Ḥasan Ibn al-Musayyab, 'Aṭā', Mu'āwiyah ibn Ṣāliḥ, Ṭāwūs, 'Alī and Ibn 'Abbās say that everything in which there is an element of gambling, such as backgammon and chess, is considered to be *maysir*, even children playing with walnuts and dice. An exception is made in the case of permitted wagers in respect of horses and drawing lots to sort out rights. Mālik said that there are two types of *maysir*: one constitutes simple amusement and the other is gambling. The kind which constitutes amusement includes chess, backgammon and other games. Gambling is when people bet against one another. 'Alī ibn Abī Ṭālib said that chess is the *maysir* of the non-Arabs. According to Mālik and other scholars any form of gambling is *maysir*. This will be further clarified in *Sūrat Yūnus*.

The word *maysir* is derived from *yasar*, which is when something is imposed on a person. *Yāsir* is the person who casts the divining arrows. Al-Azharī said that *maysir* is the slaughtered camel for which they are betting. It is called *maysir* because it is divided into parts and the *yāsir* is the slaughterer because he divides the meat into portions. He said that this is the original root of *yāsir* and then it was used for those who cast arrows and gamble for animals. The *yāsirūn* are slaughterers because the *maysir* is the reason for the slaughtering taking place. The verb *yasara* is used for the people who slaughter the camel and divide up its joints.

Mālik related in the *Muwaṭṭā'* that Dāwud ibn Ḥuṣayn heard Sa'īd ibn al-Musayyab say, 'One form of the gambling of the people of Jāhiliyyah was bartering live animals for slaughtered meat, for instance, one live sheep for two slaughtered sheep.' This is applied by Mālik and most of his people to the same category, i.e. selling an animal in exchange for meat of the same type. He considered it part of *muzābanah*, chance and gambling because it is not known whether the live animal will have the same amount of meat or not. It is not permitted to sell meat for meat when there is a disparity, and selling a live animal for meat is like selling meat for other meat of the same kind which is still in its skin. He considers one category to be camels, cattle, sheep, gazelles, mountain goats and other wild beasts. He considers all four-legged edible animals to be a single category and does not permit selling any animal of this category for the meat of another of the same category in any manner whatsoever because he considers it to be *muzābanah*: like selling raisins for grapes, olives for olive oil, sesame oil for sesame seeds, and the like. He also considers birds to all be a single category and fish to be a single category as well.

Ash-Shāfi'ī and his people and al-Layth ibn Sa'd said that it is not permitted to sell meat for the animal in any case whatsoever, whether they are the same category or two different categories because the *ḥadīth* is general. It is related from Ibn 'Abbās that a camel was slaughtered in the time of Abū Bakr aṣ-Ṣiddīq and divided into ten parts. A man said, 'Give me a portion in exchange for a sheep.' Abū Bakr, 'This is not correct.' Ash-Shāfi'ī said, 'I do not know that any of the Companions disagreed with Abū Bakr about that.' Abū 'Umar said that it was related that Ibn 'Abbās permitted selling sheep for meat, but it is not a strong transmission. 'Abd ar-Razzāq related from ath-Thawrī from Yaḥyā ibn Sa'īd that Sa'īd ibn al-Musayyab disliked selling something living for something dead, meaning a slaughtered sheep for a standing one. Sufyān said, 'We do not see any harm in it.' Al-Muzanī said, 'If the *ḥadīth* about selling a live animal for meat is not sound, then by analogy it is permitted. If it is sound, the analogy is false and the tradition should be followed.' Abū 'Umar said, 'The Kufans have many proofs about permitting selling meat for an animal based on analogy and reflection. However, if the tradition is sound, analogy and investigation are false.'

Mālik related from Zayd ibn Aslam from Sa'īd ibn al-Musayyab that the

Messenger of Allah ﷺ forbade selling an animal for meat. Abū 'Umar said, 'I do not know that its transmission is directly connected to the Prophet ﷺ by a sound path. The best of its *isnād*s are *mursal* from Sa'īd ibn al-Musayyab according to what Mālik mentioned in the *Muwaṭṭā'*. That is what ash-Shāfi'ī believed. His fundamental principle is that he does not accept *mursal ḥadīth*s although he claimed that he dismissed the *mursal ḥadīth*s of Sa'īd and then found them – or most of them – to be sound. Therefore he disliked selling categories of animals for categories of meat based on the literal and undefined words of the *ḥadīth* because there is no report that makes it specific and there is also no consensus about it. He does not permit a text to be made specific through analogy. He believes that 'animals' includes all living creatures on land or in water, even if they are different species, just as 'food' is a noun for all that is eaten or drunk.

**Say, 'There is great wrong in both of them**

'*Both of them'* refers to wine and gambling. The wrong in wine is the evil which issues from the drinker: quarrelling, cursing, foul language, lies, loss of the intellect and, therefore, of the obligations owed to the Creator, the invalidation of the prayer, turning from remembering Allah and other such things. In an-Nasā'ī, 'Uthmān is reported as saying, 'Avoid wine. It is the mother of all foul things. There was a man before you who used to worship Allah. Then a seductive woman became attached to him and sent her female servant to him to invite him to act as a witness. He went with her servant and whenever they went through a door she locked it behind them until he reached a beautiful woman who had with her a slave-boy and a vessel of wine. She said, "By Allah, I did not invite you to act as a witness! I invite you to have sex with me, drink a cup of this wine or kill the boy." He said, "Let me drink a cup of this wine." So she gave him a cup to drink and he said, "Give me more." He did not stop until he had sex with her and took a life. Therefore avoid wine. By Allah, Allah does not combine faith and inveterate drinking without one being on the point of expelling the other.' Abū 'Umar mentioned it in *al-Isti'āb*.

It is related that when al-A'shā went to Madina to become Muslim, some idolaters met him on the road and asked him, 'Where are you going?' He said that he was going to Muḥammad ﷺ. They said, 'Do not go to him. He will command you to pray.' He replied, 'It is obligatory to worship the Lord.' They said, 'He will command you to give wealth to the poor.' He answered, 'Giving charity is also obligatory.' He was told, 'He forbids fornication.' He replied, 'It is foul and ugly and, in any case, I have become old and have no need of it.' He was then told,

'He forbids drinking wine.' He said, 'This is something I cannot endure!' So he went back. He said, 'I will drink wine for a year and then go back to him.' Before reaching his house, he fell from his camel, broke his neck and died.

Qays ibn 'Āṣim al-Minqarī used to drink in the Jāhiliyyah and then forbade it to himself. The reason for that is that while he was drunk he insulted his parents and saw the moon and said something. He gave the wine-merchant a great deal of his money. When he recovered, he was told what he had done and forbade himself wine. He said:

I thought that wine was good
while it contain things that corrupt a patient man.
No, by Allah! I will not drink it while healthy
and I will never use it to treat illness!
As long as I live, I will not pay for it
nor invite anyone to drink with me at night.
Wine disgraces the one who drinks it.
It makes those who drink do terrible things.

Abū 'Umar said that Ibn al-A'rābī related from al-Mufaḍḍal aḍ-Ḍabbī related these verses spoken Abū Miḥjan ath-Thaqafī when he gave up wine:

If I die, bury me beside a vine
whose roots will give my bones a drink after my death.
Do not bury me in the desert.
I fear that when I die, I will not taste it again.

'Umar flogged Abū Miḥjan several times for drinking and exiled him to an island in the sea. Sa'd met him and 'Umar wrote, telling him to imprison him and he did so. He was a bold and brave warrior. Sa'd released his chains in the Battle of al-Qādisiyyah and said, 'We will never flog you again for drinking wine.' Abū Miḥjan said, 'And I, by Allah, will never drink again!' and he never drank after that. One version adds, 'I used to drink and then the *ḥadd* punishment would be imposed on me and so I would be purified of it. Since you have granted me immunity, by Allah, I will never drink again!' Al-Haytham ibn 'Adī mentioned that someone told him that he had seen the grave of Abū Miḥjan in Azerbaijan or in the region of Jurjān and the roots of three grapevines grew from it. They were tall and bore fruit on a trellis over his grave. Written on his grave was 'This is the grave of Abū Miḥjan.'

Someone who drinks becomes a laughing-stock in the eyes of those who are sober. He may play with his urine and filth and may wipe his face with his urine while saying, 'O Allah, make me one of the penitent! Make me one of those who purify themselves!' One of them was seen with a dog licking his face while he was saying, 'Make Allah honour you!'

Gambling brings about enmity and hatred because it is consuming someone's property falsely.

**and also certain benefits for mankind.**

Wine has the benefit of producing profitable trade. They used to bring it from Syria for a cheap price and sell it in the Hijaz for a profit. They could not store it and the wine sold for a high price. This is the soundest of what is related about its benefit. It is said that it helps to digest food, strengthens the weak, increases sexual energy, makes the miser generous, the coward brave, brightens colour and gives other kinds of pleasure. Ḥassān ibn Thābit said:

We drink it and it turns us into kings and fearless lions.
Many poems have been written in praise of it.

The benefit of gambling is that by it a man can obtain something without toil or work. They used to buy a camel carcass and divide it into shares. Whoever had a share drawn took his share of the meat without paying anything, whereas the others would pay the full price and not get any of the meat. It is said that its benefit is expansion for the poor. The one who gambled did not eat any of its meat, but divided it among the poor.

There were eleven arrows in *maysir*, seven of which had shares according to the number of portions. They are: *fadhdh*, which has one notch and one share, *taw'am*, which has two notches and two shares, *raqīb*, which has three notches, *ḥils*, which has four, *nāfiz* or *nāfis* which has five, *musbil*, which has six, and *mu'allī*, which has seven. That adds up to twenty-eight shares. The shares of the camel were like that according to al-Aṣmā'ī. There remain four arrows which are blanks with no shares or portions. They are: *muṣaddar*, *muḍa''if*, *manīḥ* and *safīḥ*. It is also said that there are three blanks called *safīḥ*, *manīḥ* and *waghd*. They added these three to increase the shares on what is allowed so that the one shuffles them would have no bias to anyone. The one who shuffles the arrows is called *mujīl*, *mufīḍ*, *ḍārib* or *ḍarīb*, the plural of which is *ḍurabā'*. It is said that a watcher was put behind him to ensure that there is no bias towards anyone. The shuffler kneels and wraps them with a cloth and then puts his hand in the bag and draws out the arrow. The custom of the Arabs was to use these arrows to draw lots for the poor in winter, times of scarcity and extreme cold. A camel would be purchased and the wealthy would guarantee its price and satisfy its owner. They used to boast about that and criticize those who did not do it. They called such a person '*baram*' (niggardly). Mutammim ibn Nuwayrah said:

He was not niggardly, a man to whose wife women bring gifts,
when the tent flaps in the bitter cold of winter.

Then it would be slaughtered and divided into ten parts. Ibn 'Aṭiyyah said, 'Al-Aṣmā'ī erred about the division of the camel when he mentioned it there were twenty-eight portions. That was not the case. They drew for ten portions. Whoever had his arrow come out of the bag first took his share and gave it to the poor. The 'bag' (*rabābah*) was like a quiver. The arrows were put into it. It may also the name for all the arrows.

Sometimes they gambled for themselves and then the one whose arrow did not come out was liable for the whole cost as was already stated. The poor of the time subsisted on this custom. Al-A'shā said:

Those who feed a guest in the winter
and make the gambler give to the poor.

**But the wrong in them is greater than the benefit.'**

Allah tells us that the wrong in these things is greater than the benefit and will incur harm in the Next World and so the great wrong action is after the prohibition and the benefits before it. Ḥamzah and al-Kisā'ī recited '*kathīr*' (more). Their argument is that the Prophet ﷺ cursed wine and cursed ten along with it: the one who sells it, the one who buys it, the one for whom it is bought, the one who presses it, the one who has it pressed, the one who serves it, the one who drinks it, the one who conveys it, the one for whom it is conveyed, and the one who benefits from its price. With the sum of its benefits, then it is good to have the sum of its sins and '*kathīr*' conveys that. The rest of the reciters and most people recite '*kabīr*' (greater). Their argument is that the wrong action in gambling and drinking wine is among the major wrong actions and so it is more fitting to call it 'greater'. It also agrees with '*akbar*' as they agree that it is not '*akthar*' except in the copy of 'Abdullāh ibn Mas'ūd.

Some people say that wine is forbidden by this *āyah* because Allah said, '*My Lord has forbidden indecency, both open and hidden, and wrong action*' (7:33) and here He reports that there is wrong in both of them. Therefore it is forbidden. Ibn 'Aṭiyyah said that this view is not good because the wrong in it is the unlawful that stems from it, not the thing itself as this view would demand. Some people say that this *āyah* prohibits wine because it is called 'wrong' and 'wrong' is unlawful in the other *āyah* and some people said that 'wrong' means wine. This is also not good because Allah did not call wine 'wrong' in this *āyah*. He says: '*There is great wrong in both of them*' not, 'They are wrong.' The *āyah* in *al-A'rāf* explains this. Qatādah said that this *āyah* censures wine. The actual prohibition comes in *al-Mā'idah* according to most commentators.

**They will ask you what they should give away. Say, 'Whatever is surplus to your needs.'**

Most recite "*afw*' in the accusative while Abū 'Amr recites it in the nominative. There is disagreement from Ibn Kathīr. Al-Ḥasan, Qatādah and Ibn Abī Isḥāq recite it in the nominative. An-Naḥḥās and others said that if '*dhā*' means 'which', then it is better to have the nominative as it means: 'That which you give away is surplus.' The accusative is permissible. If '*mā*' and '*dhā*' are one word, then the accusative is preferable and it means: 'Say: 'Give away whatever is surplus,' although the nominative is permissible.

Scholars say that since the first question mentioned previously in *āyah* 215 above is a question of whom to spend on, as we made clear, the answer is appropriate to the question. The second question here is about the amount to give, and it is still connected with the question asked by 'Amr ibn al-Jamūḥ. When: '*Any wealth you give away should go to your parents...*' (2:215) was revealed, he asked, 'How much?' and was told, 'Your surplus' (*'afw*), which means 'what is easy, feasible and superfluous and is not hard to give.' It is as the poet said:

Take what is surplus from me and continue to love me.
Do not speak about my outburst when I am angry.

It means spend what is surplus to your needs so that you will not harm yourselves by it and thus become needy. This is the most fitting of what is said regarding the interpretation of this phrase, and it is what al-Ḥasan, Qatādah, 'Aṭā', as-Suddī, al-Quraẓī, Muḥammad ibn Ka'b, Ibn Abī Laylā and others said. They said 'surplus to poverty', and Ibn 'Abbās said the same. Mujāhid said, 'Giving *ṣadaqah* when you are wealthy.' The Prophet ﷺ said, 'The best *ṣadaqah* is what you give when you are wealthy.' A similar *ḥadīth* has: 'The best *ṣadaqah* comes from the wealthy.'

Qays ibn Sa'd said. 'This means obligatory zakat.' But the majority of scholars said that it refers to voluntary spending. It is said that it is abrogated. Al-Kalbī said, 'After the revelation of this *āyah*, when a man had gold, silver, crops or animals, he would work out what would satisfy him and his dependants for a year and keep that and give the rest as *ṣadaqah*. If he was someone who earned his living from manual work, he kept what was adequate for the day and gave the rest away. This was the case until the *āyah* of obligatory zakat was revealed and this was abrogated.' Some people say that this *āyah* is one of judgment and that there is a right on property over and above zakat. The first position is the most evident.

**In this way Allah makes the Signs clear to you,**

Al-Mufaḍḍal ibn Salamah said that it is by the command to spend.

**so that hopefully you will reflect...**

You will reflect and work out how much of your property is needed for you in the life of this world and spend the rest on what will benefit you in the Next World. It is said that there is a change in the word order: that is how Allah makes the Signs clear to you in this world and the Next World so that you will reflect about this world and how it will vanish so that you are abstinent in it and about the Next World and its permanence so that you desire it.

فِي الدُّنْيَا وَالْآخِرَةِ ۗ وَيَسْأَلُونَكَ عَنِ الْيَتَامَىٰ ۖ قُلْ إِصْلَاحٌ لَّهُمْ خَيْرٌ ۖ وَإِن تُخَالِطُوهُمْ
فَإِخْوَانُكُمْ ۚ وَاللَّهُ يَعْلَمُ الْمُفْسِدَ مِنَ الْمُصْلِحِ ۚ وَلَوْ شَاءَ اللَّهُ لَأَعْنَتَكُمْ ۚ إِنَّ اللَّهَ عَزِيزٌ حَكِيمٌ ﴿٢٢٠﴾

**220 ...on this world and the Next. They will ask you about the property of orphans. Say, 'Managing it in their best interests is best.' If you mix your property with theirs, they are your brothers. Allah knows a squanderer from a good manager. If Allah had wanted, He could have been hard on you. Allah is Almighty, All-Wise.**

**They will ask you about the property of orphans.**

Abū Dāwud and an-Nasā'ī related that Ibn 'Abbās said: 'When Allah revealed: *"Do not go near the property of orphans except in a good way..."* (6:152), and: *"...those who consume the property of orphans wrongfully..."* (4:10), everyone who had an orphan in their care separated their food and drink from that of any orphans in their care and began to keep their food aside for them until they ate it or it went bad. That was hard for people. They mentioned that to the Messenger of Allah ﷺ and then Allah revealed this. So they shared their food and drink.'

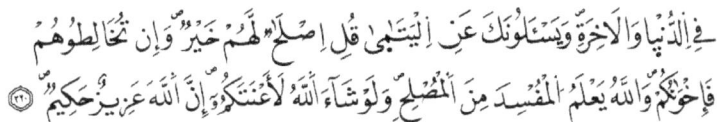

This *āyah* is connected to what came before it because the command to preserve the property of orphans is connected to the discussion about property. It is said that the asker was 'Abdullāh ibn Rawāḥah and it is said that it was the Arabs who thought it bad luck to resort to the property of orphans in what they ate. When Allah gave permission for dealing with orphans with the intention of making things right for them, that indicated the permission to utilise the property of orphans. The executor deals with selling, division and other things since this *āyah* is general. It is not transmitted that any of the caliphs put anyone in charge of an orphan even though they existed at that time.

There are many *ḥadīths* about making use of an orphan's property in *muḍārabah* and trade. The permission for a guardian to mix his property with that of an orphan in his charge is evidence that it is permitted to utilise an orphan's property in buying and selling and other such things when that is beneficial. There is disagreement about using an orphan's money for a *qirāḍ*. Ashhab forbade it, based on analogy with the guardian being forbidden to buy or sell from them for himself. Someone else said that if the guardian takes a share of the profit of the *qirāḍ*, then the *qirāḍ* is acceptable, it being comparable to the guardian selling something on behalf of an orphan, subject to investigation. Muḥammad ibn 'Abd al-Ḥakam said, 'If the guardian of an orphan buys something on credit, that is questionable.'

Ibn Kinānah says that a guardian may spend on an orphan's wedding and perfume and other things required for it and other matters which are in his best interests. That depends on the orphan's social standing as well as that of the person he marries, and the extent of his wealth. The same applies to his circumcision. If someone fears that he might fall under suspicion of misusing an orphan's wealth, he should tell the ruler what he wants to do, who can then command him according what is intended. It is, however, permitted for him to do that if he thinks that correct. The exchange of gifts to curry favour is not permitted nor is bad management of an orphan's wealth. The literal meaning of the *āyah* indicates that guardians should teach the orphans in their care about this world and the Next and pay for someone to teach them a craft. When an orphan is given something, the guardian can take it and use it in the orphan's best interests. This will be further explained in *an-Nisā'*, Allah willing.

There are two situations regarding what an executor and guardian spend out of an orphan's property. One is when there is testimony to the transaction. Then his word is only accepted when he provides evidence. The second is when it is not possible to have witnesses to it. In that case, his word is accepted without evidence. When he buys real estate and that which customarily is secured, then his word is not accepted without evidence. Ibn Khuwayzimandād said, 'That is why our people make a distinction between two cases. The first is an orphan who lives in the house of the executor who spends on him, and who is not required to bring witnesses for his expenditure and clothing because it is impossible to have witnesses to what he eats and wears at every moment. Instead he says, "I spent these expenses for a year," and that is accepted from him. The second case is when the orphan is with his mother or nurse and the executor claims that he spent on him or gave the expenses and clothing to his mother or nurse. His word about giving it to the mother or nurse is not accepted except with proof that she took it either monthly or yearly.

Scholars disagree about a man who gives an orphan in his care in marriage and whether he can buy for himself from the property of his orphan. Mālik said, that matrimonial guardianship (*wilāyah*) by actual guardianship (*kafālah*) and custody is stronger than it by kinship, so that he said about the desert Arabs who handed over their children in times of famine, that they could marry them. A marriage by a guardian will be mentioned in *an-Nisā'*, Allah willing.

Mālik says in his best known position that a guardian may buy from the orphan in his care. That is also what Abū Ḥanīfah says: he may buy the orphan's property for himself for a greater than normal price because that is putting right as indicated by the words of the Qur'an. Ash-Shāfi'ī said that he is not permitted to do that either in respect of marriage or sales, because disposal of assets is not mentioned in the *āyah*.

**Say, 'Managing it in their best interests is best.'**

No specifics are mentioned. Abū Ḥanīfah said, 'Since welfare is good, it is permitted to arrange a marriage for them.' Ash-Shāfi'ī does not think that marriage should be considered a best interest unless there is a real need for it and there is no real need before puberty. Ibn Hanbal permits arranging marriage because it may be in someone's best interest. Ash-Shāfi'ī permits a grandfather to arrange marriage with the executor and by the right that a father has for a child whose mother has died, not by the ruling of this *āyah*. Abū Ḥanīfah permits a qāḍī to carry out a marriage of an orphan based on the literal text of the *āyah*. These positions all originate from this *āyah*. If it is confirmed that marriage is a benefit, then the literal text of the Qur'an demands that it be permitted. It is possible that the phrase: '*They will ask you about orphans…*' means about their sustenance for their guardians.

**If you mix your property with theirs, they are your brothers. Allah knows a squanderer from a good manager.**

If it is said that the property of an orphan should be left alone because buying it might lead to suspicion, the response is that that is not necessary. The blocking of means is employed because forbidden actions may lead to what is forbidden by the text. Here Allah permits a certain level of the mixing of an orphan's property with that of his guardian and enjoins on guardians to be true to their trusts regarding that, saying: *'Allah knows a squanderer from a good manager.'* It is not said about other risky matters which Allah has entrusted to people, that they are a means to something unlawful and so must be forbidden. For instance, Allah has entrusted Muslim women with protecting their private parts, even though there are immense judgments that arise from sexual behaviour which are connected to lawfulness, unlawfulness and lineage, and even though it is possible that the women concerned may lie.

When Ṭāwūs was asked about orphans, he would recite, *'Allah knows a squanderer from a good manager.'* Ibn Sīrīn said that it is preferable, concerning the property of orphans, that their advisors meet and see what would be best for the orphans concerned. Al-Bukhārī quotes it. This is evidence for the fact that a guardian is permitted to buy from an orphan in his care for himself, as was mentioned earlier. The other view is that a guardian should not buy anything which is under his management since that might give rise to suspicion, unless that sale is made by the ruler in a community. Muḥammad ibn 'Abd al-Ḥakam said, 'He should not buy from an inheritance. There is no harm if someone who is buying on his behalf includes some of it without his prior knowledge.'

The mixing of property is like mixing like with like, like dates with dates. Abū 'Ubayd said, 'This mixing is when an orphan has money and it is difficult for his guardian to isolate his food. He has no alternative to mixing the orphan's property with that of his own dependants, so he takes what is adequate from the orphan's property after due investigation and includes it in with his family's maintenance. This may increase and decrease. This abrogating *āyah* brought the allowance to do this.' Abū 'Ubayd also said, 'I consider this to be the basis for what fellow travellers do on a journey. They distribute their provisions equally between themselves even though the amount of food each brings may vary. Not everyone who eats a little food is happy about giving the surplus to his companion. Since there is leeway in the property of orphans, that applies even more to others. Otherwise I fear that things would be oppressive for people.'

The second phrase is a warning. Allah knows those who squander the property of orphans from those who look after it and will repay each of them.

**If Allah had wanted, He could have been hard on you.**

Al-Ḥakam ibn Miqsam related that Ibn 'Abbās said, 'If Allah had wanted to He could have made what you took of the property of orphans a crime.' The expression *'hard on you'* means: 'He could have destroyed you' according to az-Zajjāj and Abū 'Ubaydah. Al-Qutaybī says that it means: 'He could have constricted things for you and been harsh, but He only desired ease for you.' It is said that it means that Allah could have obliged you to repay what you used when you mixed your property with theirs as was the case with those before you, but He made things easier for you.

*"Anat'* (hardship) is a word used for the breaking of a bone when it has been previously broken and then mended. It is used for an animal that re-breaks a bone so that it cannot walk. *'Anūt* is used for a mountain which is hard to climb. Ibn al-Anbārī says that the root of the word means to make something hard and difficult, to force someone to do something which is difficult to perform, and the meaning is extended to the sense of destruction.

**Allah is Almighty, All-Wise.**

There is nothing impossible for Him. He is 'Wise' in disposing of His kingdom as He wishes and nothing can stop Him doing so.

وَلَا تَنكِحُوا۟ ٱلْمُشْرِكَٰتِ حَتَّىٰ يُؤْمِنَّ ۚ وَلَأَمَةٌ مُّؤْمِنَةٌ خَيْرٌ مِّن مُّشْرِكَةٍ
وَلَوْ أَعْجَبَتْكُمْ ۗ وَلَا تُنكِحُوا۟ ٱلْمُشْرِكِينَ حَتَّىٰ يُؤْمِنُوا۟ ۚ وَلَعَبْدٌ مُّؤْمِنٌ خَيْرٌ
مِّن مُّشْرِكٍ وَلَوْ أَعْجَبَكُمْ ۗ أُو۟لَٰٓئِكَ يَدْعُونَ إِلَى ٱلنَّارِ ۖ وَٱللَّهُ يَدْعُوٓا۟ إِلَى
ٱلْجَنَّةِ وَٱلْمَغْفِرَةِ بِإِذْنِهِۦ ۖ وَيُبَيِّنُ ءَايَٰتِهِۦ لِلنَّاسِ لَعَلَّهُمْ يَتَذَكَّرُونَ ﴿٢٢١﴾

**221 Do not marry women of the idolaters until they believe. A slavegirl who is one of the believers is better for you than a woman of the idolaters, even though she may attract you. And do not give [your women] in marriage to men of the idolaters until they believe. A slave who is one of the believers is better for you than a man of the idolaters, even though he may attract you. Such people call you to the Fire whereas Allah calls you, with His permission, to the Garden and forgiveness. He makes His Signs clear to people so that hopefully they will pay heed.**

**Do not marry women of the idolaters until they believe.**

The root of the word used for 'marry' here – *nakaḥa* – means to have sexual intercourse and it is used metaphorically to mean marriage.

After Allah has given permission for using an orphan's property in a beneficial manner and for arranging their marriage, He makes it clear that marriage with idolaters is not permitted. Muqātil said, 'This *āyah* was revealed about Abū Mirthad al-Ghanawī or Kannāz ibn Ḥusayn. The Messenger of Allah ﷺ sent him secretly to Makkah to bring out one of his Companions. There was a woman in Makkah called 'Anaq whom he had loved in the time of the Jāhiliyyah. She came to him and he told her, "Islam forbids what used to happen in the time of Jāhiliyyah." "So marry me," she said. He replied, "Not until I ask permission from the Prophet ﷺ." He asked for permission and he forbade him to marry her because he was a Muslim and she was an idolater.' This will be further explained in *an-Nūr*, Allah willing

Scholars disagree about the interpretation of this *āyah*. One group says that Allah forbade marrying all women idolaters in *Sūrat al-Baqarah*, including women of the Book (Jews and Christians), and then allowed marriage with them in *Sūrat al-Mā'idah*. This position is related from Ibn 'Abbās and was related by Mālik ibn Anas, Sufyān ibn Sa'īd ath-Thawrī and 'Abd ar-Raḥmān ibn 'Amr al-Awzā'ī. Qatādah and Sa'īd ibn Jubayr said that the *āyah* is general to every female unbeliever and there is a special case for women of the Book [Jews and Christians], which is explained in *Sūrat al-Mā'idah*, and so the general statement never included women of People of the Book. This is one of the positions of ash-Shāfi'ī. According to the first view, the *āyah* is taken to be general and then some of that generality was abrogated by *al-Mā'idah*. The first position is that of Mālik; and Ibn Ḥabīb mentioned it and said, 'Marrying a Jewish or Christian woman, even though it is allowed by Allah Almighty, is disliked and blameworthy.'

Isḥāq ibn Ibrāhīm al-Ḥarbī said, 'Some people say that the *āyah* in *Sūrat al-Baqarah* is the abrogating one and the one in *Sūrat al-Mā'idah* is abrogated, and so they forbid any woman idolater, whether she is of the Book or not.' An-Naḥḥās said, 'This has a sound *isnād* from Muḥammad ibn Rayyān from Muḥammad ibn Rumḥ from al-Layth from Nāfi' saying that 'Abdullāh ibn 'Umar was asked about a man marrying a Christian or Jewish woman and said, 'Allah forbade idolatrous women to the believers and I do not know of any *shirk* greater than for a woman to say, "My Lord is Jesus" or any of the slaves of Allah!' An-Naḥḥās observes that the prohibition against marrying Christian or Jewish women is contrary to the position of the majority because some of the Companions and Tābi'ūn married women of the Book, including, among the Companions, 'Uthmān, Ṭalḥah, Ibn

'Abbās, Jābir and Ḥudhayfah, and among the Tābi'ūn, Sa'īd ibn al-Musayyab, Sa'īd ibn Jubayr, al-Ḥasan, Mujāhid, Ṭāwūs, 'Ikrimah, ash-Sha'bī, and aḍ-Ḍaḥḥāk. That is the position of the *fuqahā'* of all regions. It is also impossible for this *āyah* to abrogate the one in *Sūrat al-Mā'idah* because *Sūrat al-Baqarah* was one of the first *sūrah*s to be revealed in Madīnah and *Sūrat al-Mā'idah* was one of the last, and the later clearly abrogates the earlier. There is no evidence in the *ḥadīth* of Ibn 'Umar because Ibn 'Umar was a man who hesitated on the side of caution. When he heard one *āyah* that made it lawful and the other that made it unlawful, and he had not heard about the abrogation, he hesitated and did not take the abrogation, but interpreted it. One does not use interpretation in respect of the abrogating and abrogated.

Ibn 'Aṭiyyah mentioned that Ibn 'Abbās said in part of what is related from him that the *āyah* is general, including pagans, Magians and Kitābīs. All of those who are following other than Islam are unlawful. According to this, it abrogates the *āyah* in *al-Mā'idah*. The position of Ibn 'Umar in the *Muwaṭṭā'* takes this view: 'I do not know of any *shirk* greater than for a woman to say, "My Lord is Jesus."'

It is related that 'Umar parted Ṭalḥah ibn 'Ubaydullāh and Ḥudhayfah ibn al-Yamān from their Kitābī wives. They said, 'We will divorce, Amīr al-Mu'minīn. Do not be angry!' He replied, 'If it were permitted to divorce them, it would be permitted to marry them. I will part you.' Ibn 'Aṭiyyah mentioned that its *isnād* is good and it is also reported that 'Umar wanted to separate them and Ḥudhayfah said to him, 'Do you claim that it is unlawful so that I should let go, Amīr al-Mu'minīn?' He answered, 'I do not claim that it is unlawful, but I fear that you will engage with prostitutes from them.' Something similar is related from Ibn 'Abbās.

Ibn al-Mundhir mentioned from 'Umar ibn al-Khaṭṭāb that it is permitted to marry Kitābī women and he mentioned the Companions and Tābi'ūn in connection with this view. Ibn an-Naḥḥās said that at the end of his words that it is not valid that any of the early people said that it was unlawful.

Some scholars said that there is no conflict between the two *āyah*s. The literal meaning of the term '*shirk*' does not include the People of the Book since the Almighty says: '*Those of the People of the Book who disbelieve and the idolaters do not like anything good to be sent down to you from your Lord*' (2:105) and: '*The People of the Book who disbelieved and the idolaters.*' (98:1) So He distinguished between them in His words. The use of the conjunction 'and' means that there must be a difference between the two. Furthermore the term '*shirk*' is undefined and not a text. Allah says: '*Free women of those given the Book*' (5:5) and: '*free women from among the believers.*' So there is no contradiction between what is implied and what is not implied. If it is said that

His words: '*free women of those given the Book before you*' mean 'who were given the Book before you and then became Muslims,' as He says: '*Among the People of the Book there are some who believe in Allah*' (3:199) and: '*There is a community among the People of the Book who are upright*' (3:113), the answer is that this is different to the text of the *āyah* when He says: '*free women of those given the Book before you*' and the position of the majority. It is not unclear to anyone that it is permitted to marry someone who has become Muslim and become one of the Muslims. If they remark that He says: '*Such people call you to the Fire,*' then the reason for the prohibition of marrying them is because they invite to the Fire. The answer is that that is based on His words: '*A slavegirl who is a believer is better for you than a woman of the idolaters,*' because idolaters call to the Fire. This reason is the same for all unbelievers and there is no dispute that a Muslim is better than an unbeliever. This is clear.

It is not lawful to marry people of the Book when they are people who are fighting the Muslims. Ibn 'Abbās was asked about that and said, 'It is not lawful.' He recited: '*Fight those of the people who were given the Book who do not believe in Allah and the Last Day…*' (9:29) The *ḥadīth* transmitter said that Ibrāhīm an-Nakha'ī related that and approved of it. Mālik disliked marrying such women because of leaving children in the Dār al-Ḥarb and because of their consumption of wine and pork.

**A slavegirl who is one of the believers is better for you than a woman of the idolaters, even though she may attract you.**

A believing slavegirl is better than an idolatress, even though she may attract you by her lineage, wealth or beauty. This is what aṭ-Ṭabarī and others said. It was revealed about Khansā', a black girl who belonged to Ḥudhayfah ibn al-Yamān. Ḥudhayfah said, to her, 'Khansā', you were mentioned in the Highest Assembly in spite of the fact that you are black and ugly. Allah mentioned you in His Book.' So Ḥudhayfah freed her and married her.

As-Suddī said that it was revealed about 'Abdullāh ibn Rawāḥah. He had a black slavegirl whom he slapped in anger and then regretted doing so. He went to the Prophet ﷺ and told him and the Prophet asked, 'What kind of girl is she, 'Abdullāh?' He replied, 'She fasts, prays, does *wuḍū'* well, and testifies to the *shahādah.*' The Messenger of Allah ﷺ said, 'She is a believer.' Ibn Rawāḥah said, 'I will free her and marry her.' He did so and he was attacked by some of the Muslims who said, 'He has married a slavegirl!' They thought that they could marry idolatrous women out of the desire for their lineage, and so this *āyah* was revealed. Allah knows best.

Scholars disagree about the permissibility of marrying Christian or Jewish slavegirls. In the book of Muḥammad, Ashhab said about someone who became Muslim and was married to a Kitābī slavegirl that they should not be parted. Abū Ḥanīfah and his people said that it is permitted to marry slavegirls from the People of the Book. Ibn al-'Arabī said, 'Shaykh Abū Bakr ash-Shāshī taught us in Madīnat as-Salam, "As evidence for the permissibility of marrying a Kitābī slavegirl, the people of Abū Ḥanīfah cite the *āyah*: *"a slavegirl who is a believer is better for you than a woman of the idolaters"*. The way the *āyah* supports this evidentially is that Allah gives a choice between marrying a believing slavegirl and an idolatress. Were it not permissible to marry an idolatrous slavegirl, Allah would not have given a choice between them because choice is between two permissible matters, not between something permissible and something forbidden nor between two opposite matters. The answer to this objection is that linguistically and in the Qur'an it is possible to have a choice between two opposites because Allah says: *'The Companions of the Garden on that Day will have better lodging and a better resting-place.'* (25:24) And 'Umar said in his letter to Abū Mūsā, 'Returning to the truth is better than remaining in falsehood.' Another answer is that His words, 'slavegirl' (*amah*) does not mean slavehood by virtue of ownership. Rather it simply means a human being, all human beings being the slaves of Allah. Qāḍī Abu-l-'Abbās al-Jurjānī said that in Basra.

There is also disagreement about the permissibility of marrying Magian women. Mālik, ash-Shāfi'ī, Abū Ḥanīfah, al-Awzā'ī and Isḥāq forbid it. Ibn Ḥanbal says, 'I do not like it.' It is related that Ḥudhayfah ibn al-Yamān married a Magian woman and 'Umar told him to divorce her. Ibn al-Qaṣṣār said, 'Some of our fellows said that according to one of two views, it is mandatory that they have a Scripture which permits marriage with them.' Ibn Wahb related from Mālik that it is not permitted to have sexual intercourse with a Magian slavegirl by virtue of ownership. The same is true for pagans and other unbelieving women. That is the view of a group of scholars, except for what Yaḥyā ibn Ayyūb related from Ibn Jurayj that 'Aṭā' and 'Amr ibn Dīnār were asked about marrying Magian slavegirls and they said that there is no harm in it. They interpreted the *āyah* as referring to the marriage contract, not the purchased slavegirl. They used as evidence the captives of Awṭās and the fact that the Companions married the slavegirls from them by virtue of ownership. An-Naḥḥās said that this is an aberrant view, and it is possible that the slavegirls from Awṭās became Muslim and therefore it was permitted to marry them. Arguing by Allah's words: *'Do not marry women of the idolaters until they believe'* is an error since they took '*nikāḥ*' to mean the contract, while linguistically it can refer to both the contract and to sexual intercourse, and so when He says: *'Do not marry women of the idolators'*, He forbade every form of *nikāḥ* with women idolaters, whether actual marriage or sexual intercourse.

Abū 'Umar ibn 'Abd al-Barr said that al-Awzā'ī said, 'I asked az-Zuhrī about whether a man who buys a Magian woman can have sexual intercourse with her. He answered, "When she testifies that there is no god but Allah, he can have sexual relations with her."' Yūnus related that Ibn Shihāb said that it is not lawful for him to have sexual intercourse with her until she becomes Muslim. Abū 'Umar said, 'In view of the fact that he was the most knowledgeable of people regarding expeditions and biographies, Ibn Shihāb's statement, that it is not lawful for him to have sex with her until she becomes Muslim, is proof of the falsity of the statement of those who claim that the Companions had sexual relations with the captives of Awṭās before they became Muslim. That is related from a group of them, including 'Aṭā' and 'Amr ibn Dīnār who said that there is nothing wrong in having sexual intercourse with a Magian woman. None of the *fuqahā'* pay any attention to this.

It has come from al-Ḥasan al-Baṣrī, who was one of those who did not go on that expedition and only engaged in expeditions to Persia and beyond as far as Khorasan, and none of those people were People of the Book. It was not clear how they behaved in respect of their captured women. 'Abdullāh ibn Muḥammad ibn Asad reported from Ibrāhīm ibn Aḥmad ibn Firās from 'Alī ibn 'Abd al-'Azīz from Abū 'Ubayd from Hishām from Yūnus that al-Ḥasan said, 'A man asked him, "Abū Sa'īd, what do you do when they are captured?" He answered, "We used to turn her to the *qiblah* and command her to become Muslim and testify that there is no god but Allah and that Muḥammad is the Messenger of Allah. Then we would command her to have a *ghusl*. If her owner wants to have sexual intercourse with her, he does not do so until she has done *istibrā'*."' A group follow this interpretation, taking Allah's words as meaning that they are pagans and Magians because Allah has made women of the Book lawful by His words: *'free women of those given the Book before you'*. This means chaste women, not known for fornication. Some dislike marrying them or having sexual intercourse with them by virtue of ownership since that corrupts lineage.

**And do not give [your women] in marriage to men of the idolaters until they believe. A slave who is one of the believers is better for you than a man of the idolaters, even though he may attract you.**

A Muslim woman may not marry an idolatrous man. The Community agree that an idolater may not marry a believing woman in any case. That is shame towards Islam.

This *āyah* provides textual evidence of the fact that marriage is only possible with the presence of a *walī*. Muḥammad ibn 'Alī said, 'Marriage with a *walī* is found in the Book,' and he recited this *āyah*. Ibn al-Mundhir said, 'It is confirmed that the Messenger of Allah ﷺ said, "There is no marriage except by a *walī*."' Scholars disagree about marriage without a *walī*. Most scholars say that there is no marriage without a *walī*. This is related from 'Umar ibn al-Khaṭṭāb, 'Alī ibn Abī Ṭālib, Ibn Mas'ūd, Ibn 'Abbās and Abū Hurayrah. It is also the position of Sa'īd ibn al-Musayyab, al-Ḥasan al-Baṣrī, 'Umar ibn 'Abd al-'Azīz, Jābir ibn Zayd, Sufyān ath-Thawrī, Ibn Abī Laylā, Ibn Shubrumah, Ibn al-Mubārak, ash-Shāfi'ī, 'Ubaydullāh ibn al-Ḥasan, Aḥmad ibn Ḥanbal and Abū 'Ubayd.

It is the position of Mālik, Abū Thawr and aṭ-Ṭabarī. Abū 'Umar said, 'The argument of those who say that there is no marriage without a *walī* is that the Prophet ﷺ affirmed that position in the *ḥadīth* which was related *mursal* by Shu'bah and ath-Thawrī from Abū Isḥāq from Abū Burdah from the Prophet ﷺ. Those who accept *mursal ḥadīth*s must accept it, but those who do not accept *mursal* reports must also accept it, because those who connected its transmission are people of memorisation and trustworthiness. Among those who connected its transmission were Isrā'īl and Abū 'Awānah from Abū Isḥāq from Abū Burdah from Abū Mūsā from the Prophet ﷺ. Isrā'īl and those who corroborated him are *ḥuffāẓ*. Something added by a *ḥāfiẓ* is accepted and this addition is supported by fundamental principles. Allah Almighty says: *'Do not prevent them from marrying their first husbands.'* (2:232) This *āyah* was revealed about Ma'qil ibn Yasār when he prevented his sister from returning to her husband. Al-Bukhārī has it. Were it not that he had a right concerning her marriage, he would not have been forbidden from preventing it.

One thing that indicates this in the Book is Allah's words: *'Marry them with their owners' permission'* (4:32) and: *'Marry of those among you who are unmarried…'* (24:32) Allah only addresses men with respect to marrying. If women had that right, He would have mentioned them. This will be explained in *an-Nūr*. Allah says relating from Shu'ayb in the story of Mūsā: *'I would like to marry you to one of these two daughters…'* (28:27) as will be explained in *al-Qaṣaṣ*. Allah also says, *'Men have charge of women.'* (4:34) Both the Book and the Sunnah confirm that there is no marriage without a *walī*. Aṭ-Ṭabarī said, 'We find in the *ḥadīth* about Ḥafṣah, when she was widowed, that 'Umar carried out her marriage rather than her doing it herself. This invalidates the position of those who say that an adult woman has power over herself and can give herself in marriage and make the contract without her *walī*. If that had been true, then the Messenger of Allah ﷺ would have proposed to Ḥafṣah herself, since she would have been more entitled to that than her father was, and the proposal would have been being made to someone who had no power to carry out the contract on her behalf.' This also provides clarification of the words of the Prophet ﷺ: 'A widow is more entitled to herself than her *walī*.' It means that she is more entitled to herself so that he cannot make a contract for her marriage without her consent, not that she is more entitled to make a contract a marriage for herself without her *walī* being involved.

Ad-Dāraquṭnī related from Abū Hurayrah that the Messenger of Allah ﷺ said, 'A woman may not give another woman in marriage nor may she give herself in marriage. A fornicatress is someone who gives herself in marriage.' He said that it is a sound *ḥadīth*. Abū Dāwud related from Sufyān from az-Zuhrī from 'Urwah that 'Ā'ishah said that the Messenger of Allah ﷺ said three times, 'If any woman is married without the consent of her *walī*, her marriage is invalid.' Then he continued, 'If he consummates it with her, then she has the dower because of what he has got from her. If they quarrel, then the ruler is the *walī* of those with no *walī*.' This is a sound *ḥadīth*. No attention should be paid to the statement of Ibn 'Ulayyah from Ibn Jurayj: 'I asked az-Zuhrī about it and he did not recognise it.' No one but Ibn 'Ulayyah says that Ibn Jurayj said this. A group who related from az-Zuhrī did not mention it. If it had been confirmed from az-Zuhrī, it would still not be a proof because trustworthy men transmitted it from him, including Sulaymān ibn Mūsā, a trustworthy imam, and Ja'far ibn Rabī'ah. If az-Zuhrī forgot it that does not harm him because no human being is safe from forgetfulness. The Prophet ﷺ said, 'Ādam forgot and so his descendants forgot.' The Prophet himself ﷺ forgot, so it is more fitting that others should suffer from forgetfulness. The one who remembers is an argument against the one who forgets. When someone trustworthy relates a report, the forgetfulness of someone who forgets does not harm him. This is the case if what Ibn 'Ulayyah related from Ibn Jurayj is sound, so what then is the situation if the people of knowledge deny that story?

Abū Ḥātim Muḥammad ibn Ḥibbān at-Tamīmī al-Bustī transmitted this *ḥadīth* in his sound *Musnad* without a break in its *isnād*. No detraction is confirmed in respect of the one who transmitted from Ḥafṣ ibn Ghiyāth from Ibn Jurayj from Sulaymān ibn Mūsā from az-Zuhrī from 'Urwah from 'Ā'ishah that the Messenger of Allah ﷺ said, 'Marriage can only take place with a *walī* and two reputable witnesses. Any marriage without that is invalid. If they quarrel, then the ruler is the *walī* of someone without a *walī*.' Abū Ḥātim said, 'Only three people add "and two reputable witnesses" in the report of Ibn Jurayj from Sulaymān ibn Mūsā from az-Zuhrī: Suwayd ibn Yaḥyā al-Umawī from Ḥafṣ ibn Ghiyāth, 'Abdullāh ibn 'Abd al-Wahhāb al-Jumaḥī from Khālid ibn al-Ḥārith, and 'Abd ar-Raḥmān ibn Yūnus ar-Raqqī from 'Īsā ibn Yūnus.'

The stipulation of two witnesses is only found in this report. If this report is sound, the Book and Sunnah explicitly state that there is no marriage without a *walī*. There is no sense in opposing it. Az-Zuhrī and ash-Sha'bī said that when a woman gives herself in marriage to an equal with two witnesses, the marriage is permitted. That is what Abū Ḥanīfah said. That is the position of Zufar. When she marries herself to someone who is not her equal, the marriage is permitted, but the relatives can separate them. Ibn al-Mundhir said, 'What an-Nu'mān said is contrary to the Sunnah and not part of the position of most of the people of knowledge. We take the report of the Messenger of Allah ﷺ.'

Abū Yūsuf said, 'Marriage is only permitted provided there is a *walī*. If the *walī* accepts it, it is allowed. If he refuses to accept it and the husband is an equal, then the qāḍī allows it. The marriage is achieved when the qāḍī allows it. If he does not do that, then there must be a new contract.' There is no disagreement between Abū Ḥanīfah and his people that when a woman's *walī* allows her to carry out the marriage herself, it is allowed. Al-Awzā'ī said, 'When she assigns the matter to a man who gives her in marriage to an equal, the marriage is allowed and her *walī* cannot part them unless she is an Arab who marries a client (*mawlā*).' This is similar to the school of Mālik as will be mentioned.

Some of those who take the school of az-Zuhrī, Abū Ḥanīfah and ash-Sha'bī take the *ḥadīth* of the Prophet ﷺ about there being no marriage except with a *walī* as applying to perfection rather than completion. This is similar to the words of the Prophet ﷺ: 'The neighbour of a mosque has no prayer except in the mosque,' and 'There is no portion of Islam for anyone who abandons the prayer.' They cite as evidence the words of Allah: *'Do not prevent them from marrying their first husbands…'* (2:232) and: *'…you are not to blame for anything they do with themselves with correctness and courtesy.'* (2:234) They also cite what ad-Dāraquṭnī related about Simāk ibn Ḥarb saying, 'A man came to 'Alī and said, "A woman, of whom I am the *walī*, married without my permission." 'Alī said, "Investigate what she has done. If she married an equal, we allow that for her. If she has married someone who is not her equal, we assign that to you."' We find in the *Muwaṭṭā'* that 'Ā'ishah gave her niece by her brother 'Abd ar-Raḥmān in marriage while he was absent. Ibn Jurayj related from 'Abd ar-Raḥmān ibn al-Qāsim ibn Muḥammad ibn Abī Bakr from his father that 'Ā'ishah said that the man to whom she married her brother's daughter was al-Mundhir ibn az-Zubayr. A curtain was set up between them and then she spoke until nothing remained but the contract. She commanded a man to carry out the marriage. Then she said, 'Women cannot perform marriage.' The point of the *ḥadīth* of Mālik from 'Ā'ishah is that she set (the amount of) the dower and the terms of the marriage. Although one of her male relatives in fact carried out the marriage, the contract was attributed to 'Ā'ishah because she arranged it.

Ibn Khuwayzimandād mentioned that what is transmitted from Mālik about guardians varies as to who they are. Sometimes he says that whoever represents the best interests of a woman is her *walī*, whether he is from the paternal or maternal relatives, unrelated men, ruler or guardian (*waṣī*). At other times he says that guardians should be paternal relatives and whichever of them represents her best interests is her *walī*. Abū 'Umar said that Mālik said in what Ibn al-Qāsim related from him that when a woman is given in marriage by someone other than her *walī* with her permission, if she is noble and has a position among people, then her *walī* has a choice between invalidating or affirming the marriage. If she is lowly like a freed woman, black woman, or prostitute or someone with no position, her marriage is allowed. Then her *walī* has no choice because they are equals. It is related from Mālik that neither a noble or lowly woman may be given in marriage except by her *walī* or the ruler. Ibn al-Mundhir chose this position. He said, 'As for the difference Mālik makes between a poor woman and one with no worth, it is not valid because the Prophet ﷺ made judgments the same in respect of blood, saying, 'The blood of all Muslims is equal in value.' Since they are the same in respect of blood, they are the same in respect of other things as well.

Ismā'īl ibn Isḥāq said, 'When Allah commanded marriage, He made the believers guardians of one another. Allah says: *"The men and women of the believers are friends (*awliyā'*) of one another."* (9:71) The believers in that sentence inherit from one another. If a man dies without having an heir, his inheritance goes to the Muslims. If a Muslim inflicts an injury, then the blood money is paid by the Muslims. So one guardianship is closer than another and one kinship is closer than another. If a woman is in a position where there is no ruler or *walī* to represent her, her affair is handed over to one of her neighbours who is trusted who gives her in marriage and acts as her *walī* in this case, because people must marry and so they do the best that they can in order to bring that about. This is the basis of the view of Mālik concerning a woman in a weak situation: she is given in marriage by the one to whom she entrusts her business because she is too insignificant to have the ruler act on her behalf and so, in that respect, she is like someone without a ruler. Therefore in general it reverts to the totality of Muslims being guardians for her. If she gives her affair to a man and abandons her relatives, she has proceeded improperly in the business and he does something the judge and Muslims dislike him doing and that marriage is invalidated without it being announced that it is unlawful since we have described the Muslims as being guardians of each other and since there is some disagreement about that. The marriage is, however, invalidated because it has been carried out improperly and that is more cautious in respect of protecting private parts. If the marriage has been consummated, a long time has passed and children have been born, then invalidation is not permitted because when matters are dissimilar, then only the undoubtedly unlawful with respect to them is rejected. It resembles something that has been misapplied because of the ruling of a judge; the ruling of a judge is only invalidated by an undoubted error.'

Ash-Shāfi'ī and his people believe that a marriage without a *walī* is always invalid, both before and after consummation, and that the couple do not inherit from one another when one of them dies. They believe that having a *walī* is one of the obligatory elements of marriage because of the evidence in the Book and Sunnah. Allah says: *'Marry off those among you who are unmarried'* (24:32): *'Marry them with their owners' permission'* (4:25) and He addresses guardians with the words: *'...do not prevent them...'* (2:232). The Prophet ﷺ said, 'There is no marriage without a *walī*.' There is no differentiation between lowly and noble women based on the consensus of scholars that there is no difference between them in respect of blood since the Prophet ﷺ said, 'The blood of the Muslims is equal in value.' That is true of other rulings. There is no distinction between noble and lowly in the Book and Sunnah.

There is disagreement about a marriage that happens without a *walī* and then is allowed by the *walī* before consummation. Mālik and his people said that that is only valid for a slave. That is permitted when he allows it soon afterwards, whether or not it has been consummated. This is when the contract of marriage is without a *walī* and the woman did not contract herself. If the woman contracted herself and makes a marriage contract without a *walī* among the Muslims, this marriage is never affirmed even if a long time has passed and children have been born, but the paternity of any child is attached to the father and there is no *ḥadd* punishment. That marriage must be annulled in any case. Ibn Nāfi' said that Mālik said that it is annulment rather than a divorce.

Scholars disagree about the position and rank of guardians. Mālik used to say, 'The first in line are sons, however far removed, (i.e. sons of sons) then fathers, then full brothers, then paternal half-brothers, then sons of full brothers, then sons of the father's brothers, then grandfathers on the father's side, however far removed, then uncles in the order of the brothers, then their sons in the order of the sons of the brothers, however far removed, then clients, and then the ruler or the qāḍī. An executor is put ahead of relatives in giving orphans in marriage. He is the deputy and representative of the father and so his position is that which the father would have had if he were still alive.

Ash-Shāfi'ī said that no one else has guardianship when the father is available, and if he dies, then it is the grandfather, then the father of the father's father because they are all fathers. After the grandfather, it goes to the brothers and then to other relatives. Al-Muzanī said in the new School that when there is only a mother, the grandfather is more entitled to conduct the marriage as is the case with inheritance. In the old School ash-Shāfi'ī said that they are the same.

The Madinans related from Mālik something similar to the view of ash-Shāfi'ī and that the father is more entitled than the son. That is one of the two views of Abū Ḥanīfah related by al-Bājī. It is related that al-Mughīrah said, 'The grandfather is more entitled than the brothers.' What is well-known in his school is what we have already mentioned. Aḥmad said that the father is the most entitled to give a woman in marriage; then the son, then the brother, then his son, then the paternal uncle. Isḥāq said that the son is more entitled than the father as Mālik already stated. Ibn al-Mundhir preferred that because 'Umar ibn Abī Salamah married Umm Salamah to the Messenger of Allah ﷺ. An-Nasā'ī transmitted that from Umm Salamah and has a chapter entitled 'A son giving his mother in marriage'.

Our scholars often cite this as proof, but it counts for nothing. The evidence for it is what is confirmed in sound collections that 'Umar ibn Abī Salamah said, 'I was a boy in the care of the Messenger of Allah ﷺ and my hand would go around the platter. He said, "Boy, say the Name of Allah, eat with your right hand, and eat from what is in front of you."' Abū 'Umar said in *Kitāb al-Isti'āb*, 'The *kunyah* of 'Umar ibn Abī Salamah was Abū Ḥafṣ. He was born in 2 AH in Abyssinia.' It is said that he was nine years old when the Messenger of Allah ﷺ died. It is not possible for someone of this age to act as a *walī*. However, Abū 'Umar mentioned that Abū Salamah and Umm Salamah had two sons, the other being called Salamah. He is the one who carried out the contract between the Messenger of Allah ﷺ and his mother, Umm Salamah. Salamah was older than his brother 'Umar. Nothing is transmitted by him from the Prophet ﷺ, only from 'Umar.

They disagree about a woman being given in marriage by a more distant guardian when a nearer relative is available. Ash-Shāfi'ī said that the marriage is void and Mālik said that it is allowed. Ibn 'Abd al-Barr said, 'If the closer relative does not object to anything in the contract or reject it, then it is carried out. If he objects, and the woman has been previously married or is an adult orphan virgin with no executor, the position of Mālik and his people and a group of the people of Madīnah varies about it. Some say that it is not rejected and is carried out because the marriage was contracted with the permission of a *walī* from the tribe. Others among them say that it should not be carried out and say that rank must be observed in guardians according who is the best and most proper. However, that is recommended and not mandatory. This is a summary of the school of Mālik according to most of his people. Ismā'īl ibn Isḥāq and his followers preferred that. It is also said that the ruler looks into it and questions the closer relative regarding what he disagrees about. Then if he thinks that it should be carried out, it is carried out, and if he thinks that it should be rejected, it is rejected. It is said that the nearer guardian can reject it in any case because he has the right to do so. It is said that he can reject it or allow it as long as a long time has not passed and there are no children. All of these are positions of the people of Madīnah.

If the closest guardian is a Magian or a fool, then the next closest relative gives her in marriage, and the former is considered to be like someone who is deceased. The same is true if the closest guardian is absent at a great distance or absent so that it is not expected that he will return soon: then the next closest relative gives her in marriage. It is also said that if the closest guardian is absent, then the next one does not give her in marriage, rather the judge does. The former is the view of Mālik.

If two relatives are equal in their closeness and one of them is absent, then the woman entrusts the contract of her marriage to the one who is present and the absent one has no grounds for objection. If they are both present, then she entrusts the contract to one of them and he only gives her in marriage with the other's permission. If the two disagree, then the judge looks into it and allows it if he thinks that it is best for her. Ibn Wahb related that from Mālik.

Having witnesses to the marriage is not one of the pillars of marriage in the view of Mālik and his people. It is enough that it be made known and announced and not kept secret. As for keeping a marriage secret, Ibn al-Qāsim reports that Mālik stated, 'If someone marries with witnesses and then orders them to keep that secret, the marriage is not allowed because it is a secret marriage. If someone marries without witnesses, not seeking to conceal it, it is allowed. They bear witness in the future.' Ibn Wahb related from Mālik about a man who marries a woman with the testimony of two men and asks them to conceal it, that the couple are separated by a divorce and the marriage is not allowed. The woman has her dower if he has consummated the marriage and the witnesses are not punished.

Abū Ḥanīfah and ash-Shāfi'ī say that it is permitted if there were two witnesses, even if he has asked them to conceal it. Abū 'Umar said, 'This is the position of our man, Yaḥyā ibn Yaḥyā al-Laythī al-Andalusī, who said, 'Every marriage that has been witnessed by two men is no longer secret.' I think that he related it from al-Layth ibn Sa'd. As for secret marriage, ash-Shāfi'ī and the Kufans and those who follow them say that any marriage without two or more male witnesses is invalid in every case.

The position of ash-Shāfi'ī is sounder because of the *ḥadīth* we mentioned. It is related that Ibn 'Abbās said: 'There is no marriage without witnesses and a sensible *walī*.' As far as I know, none of the Companions disagreed with that. The evidence for Mālik and his School is that the sales transactions that Allah mentioned have witnesses to the contract. There is evidence that that is not one of the requirements of a sale, so it is even more fitting that, since Allah did not mention witnesses to marriage, witnesses are not one of its preconditions and mandatory elements. The goal is to make it known and public in order to preserve lineage. Witnesses are good after the contract when there are conflicting claims and disagreement about what was contracted between the two parties. It is related that the Prophet ﷺ said, 'Make marriage public.' This position of Mālik is the position of Ibn Shihāb and most of the people of Madīnah.

A believing slave is better than a noble and wealthy idolater. The Prophet ﷺ said, 'All of your men are slaves of Allah and all of your women are slaves of Allah.' He also said, 'Do not bar the female slaves of Allah from the mosques of Allah.' Allah says: *'What an excellent slave! He truly turned to His Lord.'* (38:30, 44) This is the best interpretation of this this *āyah*. It removes dispute and disagreement. Allah is the One Who gives success.

**Such people call you to the Fire**

Meaning the men and women who are idolaters. They call you to actions which make the Fire inevitable. Keeping their company and being intimate with them means that you yourself are bound to participate in many of their deviances quite apart from what they will teach your children.

**whereas Allah calls you, with His permission, to the Garden and forgiveness.**

He calls you to the actions of the People of the Garden. Az-Zajjāj said that *'with His permission'* means 'by His command'.

وَيَسْأَلُونَكَ عَنِ الْمَحِيضِ قُلْ هُوَ أَذًى فَاعْتَزِلُوا النِّسَاءَ فِي الْمَحِيضِ وَلَا
تَقْرَبُوهُنَّ حَتَّىٰ يَطْهُرْنَ فَإِذَا تَطَهَّرْنَ فَأْتُوهُنَّ مِنْ حَيْثُ أَمَرَكُمُ اللَّهُ
إِنَّ اللَّهَ يُحِبُّ التَّوَّابِينَ وَيُحِبُّ الْمُتَطَهِّرِينَ ﴿٢٢٢﴾

**222 They will ask you about menstruation. Say, 'It is an impurity, so keep apart from women during menstruation and do not approach them until they have purified themselves. But once they have purified themselves, then go to them in the way that Allah has enjoined on you.' Allah loves those who turn back from wrongdoing and He loves those who purify themselves.**

**They will ask you about menstruation.**

At-Ṭabarī mentioned from as-Suddī that the askers referred to in this *āyah* were Thābit ibn ad-Daḥdāḥ or Usayd ibn Ḥuḍayr and 'Abbād ibn Bishr, which is the position of the majority. The reason for the question, according to Qatādah and others, was that the Arabs in Madīnah and around it had adopted the custom of the Jews with respect to avoiding menstruating women and so this was revealed. Mujāhid said, 'They used to avoid normal intercourse with women when they were menstruating and they would have anal intercourse with them during their period of menstruation and then this was revealed.'

We find in *Ṣaḥīḥ Muslim* that Anas said, 'When Jewish women menstruated, the Jews would not eat with them or go to them in their rooms. The Companions asked the Prophet ﷺ about this and Allah revealed: *"They will ask you about menstruation."* The Messenger of Allah ﷺ said, "Do everything short of actual intercourse." The Jews heard this and they said, "This man will not leave any practice we do without opposing us in it!" Usayd and 'Abbad told the Prophet ﷺ what they were saying and asked, "Messenger of Allah, the Jews say such-and-such. Should we not have sex with women?" They said, "The face of the Messenger of Allah ﷺ changed colour until we thought that he was angry with them. They left. The Messenger of Allah had been given a gift of buttermilk and so he sent for those two men and gave them it to drink. So they knew that he was not angry with them.' Our scholars say that Jews and Magians shunned menstruating women while the Christians did not avoid them at all, and this was a middle way.

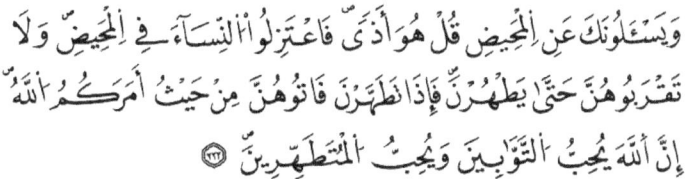

The root of the word for menstruation (*maḥīḍ*) means to flow and overflow. It is used for a torrent which overflows or a tree whose sap or gum flows out. The forms of the verbal noun also include *ḥayḍ* and *maḥāḍ*. A menstruating woman is described as *ḥā'iḍ* or *ḥā'iḍah*, the plurals being *ḥuyyaḍ* and *ḥawā'iḍ*. *Ḥīḍah* is a rag used by a woman during menstruation as is *maḥīḍah*. It is also said that *maḥīḍ* designates time and place. *Ḥawḍ* meaning a basin or reservoir is from the same root because water flows into it. The Arabs can use the *wāw* and *yā'* interchangeably. Ibn al-'Arabī said that there are eight names for a menstruating woman: *ḥā'iḍ*, *'ārik*, *fārik*, *ṭāmis*, *dāris*, *kābir*, *ḍaḥik* and *ṭāmith*.

Scholars agree that there are three rulings which concern a woman when she sees evident vaginal flowing blood. One of those is normal menstruation whose blood is thick and darker than red. Then she does not pray or fast. There is no disagreement about that. It may be either continuous or with breaks. If it is continuous, then the ruling about it is firm. If it has breaks and she sees blood one day and none one day, or she sees blood for two days and none for one or two days, she does not pray in the days of bleeding and has a *ghusl* when it stops and then prays. Then she puts together the days of bleeding and cancels the intervening pure days and does not count them as pure in either *'iddah* or *istibrā'*. Menstruation is part of a woman's natural constitution and nature.

Al-Bukhārī related that Abū Sa'īd al-Khudrī said, 'The Messenger of Allah ﷺ set out to the place of prayer on the Day of *Aḍḥā* or *Fiṭr* and passed by the women. He said, "O company of women! Give *ṣadaqah* for I have seen that you make up the majority of the inhabitants of the Fire!" They asked, "Why, Messenger of Allah?" He replied, "You call down too many curses and show ingratitude to your husbands. I have not seen anyone more deficient in intellect or *dīn*. Yet the mind of even a resolute man might be swept away by one of you." They asked, "In what way is our *dīn* and intellect deficient, Messenger of Allah?" He asked, "Is not the testimony of a woman worth only half that of a man?" "Yes," they answered. He said, "That is how your intellect is deficient. Is it not so that when a woman is menstruating, she neither prays nor fasts?" They said, "Yes, Messenger of Allah." He said, "That is how her *dīn* is deficient."'

Scholars agree that menstruating women do not pray or fast and that they must make up days of fasting missed but not missed prayers. That is based on the *ḥadīth* of Mu'ādhah who said, 'I asked 'Ā'ishah, "Does a menstruating women make up the fast but not make up the prayers?" She said, "Are you a Ḥarūrī (Khārijite)?" I replied, "I am not a Ḥarūrī, but I am just asking." She said, "We experienced that and were commanded to make up the fast but not commanded to make up the prayers."' Muslim transmitted it. When it ends, she purifies herself with a *ghusl* as will be dealt with later.

Scholars disagree about the length of a menstrual period. The *fuqahā'* of

Madīnah said that it cannot be longer than fifteen days. So it can be fifteen days or less. What goes beyond fifteen days is not menstruation but rather false menstruation (*istiḥāḍah*). That is the school of Mālik and his people. It is related from Mālik that there is no time for the minimum or maximum of menstruation except that which exists in women. It is as if he abandoned the first position and referred to the custom of women.

Muḥammad ibn Salamah said that the minimum period of purity is fifteen days. Most of the Baghdādī Mālikīs prefer that and it is also the view of ash-Shāfi'ī, Abū Ḥanīfah and their people, and ath-Thawrī. That is sound in respect of this topic because Allah Almighty made the *'iddah* of women with periods three menstrual cycles and the *'iddah* of those who do not menstruate due to old age or youth three months. So it is as if every period is equal to a month and the month includes purity and menstruation. If the period of menstruation is less, that of purity is increased. If the period of menstruation is more, then that of purity is less. So when menstruation is more than fifteen days, then the minimum period of purity opposite it must be fifteen days to complete the month of menstruation and purity. It is what is normally customary in the constitution of women as well as being reinforced by the evidence of the Book and Sunnah.

Ash-Shāfi'ī said that the minimum period of menstruation is a day and a night and its maximum period is fifteen days. A similar position to that of Mālik is related from him about referring the matter to the custom of women. Abū Ḥanīfah and his people said that the minimum period of menstruation is three days and its maximum period is ten days. Ibn 'Abd al-Barr said, 'According to them, what is less than three days is *istiḥāḍah* and it only prevents the prayer when it first appears because it is not known how long it will last. Then the woman must make up the prayers she missed. That is also the case, according to the Kufans, if it is more than ten days. According to the Hijazīs, what is more than fifteen days is *istiḥāḍah*. According to ash-Shāfi'ī, what is less than a day and a night is *istiḥāḍah*. That is the view of al-Awzā'ī and aṭ-Ṭabarī. Among those who said that the minimum length of menstruation was a day and a night and its maximum fifteen days were 'Aṭā' ibn Abī Rabāḥ, Abū Thawr and Aḥmad ibn Ḥanbal. Al-Awzā'ī said, 'We believe that a woman can menstruate in the morning and be pure in the evening.'

We have seen what scholars say regarding this topic about the maximum and minimum periods of menstruation and the minimum period of purity in *al-Istiẓhār* and the argument in *al-Muqtabis fī sharḥ Muwaṭṭā' Mālik ibn Anas*. According to ash-Shāfi'ī, if a woman is a virgin experiencing her first period, she starts the fifteen days as soon as she sees blood. Then she has a *ghusl* and makes up the prayers for fourteen days. Mālik said that she does not have to make up the prayer and her husband should refrain from sexual intercourse with her. Ibn Ḥanbal says that she should wait for a day and a night and then have a *ghusl* and her husband may not approach her. Abū Ḥanīfah and Abū Yūsuf said that she leaves the prayer for ten days, then has a *ghusl* and prays for ten days and then after that stops praying for ten days. This is her state when the bleeding stops. If she has known days, then Mālik says that she adds three days through *istiẓhār* to the known days, as long as it does not exceed fifteen days. Ash-Shāfi'ī says that she has a *ghusl* at the end of her days without adding anything.

The second type of bleeding is lochia (*nifās*) after childbirth. Scholars also disagree about its length. It is said that it is two months, which is the view of Mālik. It is said that it is forty days, which is the view of ash-Shāfi'ī. Other things are said. She is pure when it ends. The *ghusl* for it is the same as the *ghusl* for *janābah*. Qāḍī Abū Muḥammad 'Abd al-Wahhāb said, 'Bleeding for menstruation and lochia prevent eleven things: the obligation of the prayer and the soundness of performing it, fasting which is not mandatory (and the difference between the two is that the fast must be made up but not the prayer), vaginal intercourse, *'iddah*, divorce, *ṭawāf*, touching a copy of the Qur'an, entering a mosque and doing *i'tikāf* in it, and there are two transmissions about reciting the Qur'an.

The third type of bleeding is that which is neither normal nor part of the natural constitution. It is from a vein which bleeds red blood and does not stop until it is healed. Its ruling is that a woman suffering from it is pure and is not prevented from praying or fasting. This is based on the consensus of scholars and *marfū'* reports that agree on that since it is known that it is blood from a vein, not menstrual blood. Mālik related from Hishām ibn 'Urwah from his father that 'Ā'ishah said, 'Fāṭimah bint Abī Ḥubaysh said, "Messenger of Allah, I never become pure. Should I abandon the prayer?" The Messenger of Allah ﷺ said, "That is a vein, not menstruation. So when your period approaches, stop praying. When its normal length ends, wash the blood from yourself and pray."'

This *ḥadīth*, which is sound and has few words, explains the rulings of menstruation and false menstruation. It is the soundest of what is related regarding this matter. It refutes what is related from 'Uqbah ibn 'Āmir and Makḥūl about a menstruating woman doing *ghusl* and *wuḍū'* for every prayer and facing the *qiblah* sitting while remembering Allah. It says that a menstruating woman does not pray. That is the consensus of the great majority of scholars, with the exception of a few of the Khārijites who say that a menstruating women owes the prayer. It also indicates that a woman suffering from *istiḥāḍah* is not obliged to do other than a *ghusl* for her period. If she had been obliged to do anything else, he ﷺ would have commanded her to do it. It also refutes the view of those who think that she must do a *ghusl* for every prayer, those who think that she does one *ghusl* for the day prayers, one for the two night prayers and one for *Ṣubḥ*, those who say that she does a *ghusl* for one purity to another, and the view of Sa'īd ibn al-Musayyab that it is from one purity to another, because the Prophet ﷺ did not command any of that. It refutes those who espouse *istiẓhār* because the Prophet ﷺ commanded her to do *ghusl* and pray when she knew that her period had ended and he did not command her to leave the prayer for three days to wait and see whether menstruation was coming or not. The cautiousness is respect of performing the prayer, not leaving it.

**Say, 'It is an impurity,**

It is something by which women and others are discommoded, referring to the smell of menstrual blood. The word *'adhā'* (impurity) alludes to impurity in general and is also applied to disliked words. Part of that is the words of Allah: *'Do not nullify your* ṣadaqah *by demands or gratitude or insulting words* (adhā)' (2:265) where it is disliked words, and: *'Disregard their abuse* (adhā)' (33:48), meaning to ignore the abuse of the hypocrites. A *ḥadīth* states, 'Remove *'adhā'* from him,' meaning, the hair on the head of the newborn child. It is shaved on the seventh day which is the *'aqīqah*. There is also the *ḥadīth* on faith: 'The least of it is removing something harmful (*adhā*) from the road.' This is stones, thorns and the like which might harm a passerby. Allah also says: *'There is nothing wrong, if you are bothered (adhā) by rain.'* (4:102)

This *āyah* is used as evidence by those who forbid sexual intercourse with a woman experiencing *istiḥādah* (false menstruation) when blood is flowing since all blood is impurity and must be washed from the clothes and body. All such blood, whether menstrual or resulting from *istiḥādah* is still an impurity. Permission to pray is an allowance brought by the Sunnah just as someone with incontinence can also pray. This is the position of Ibrāhīm an-Nakha'ī, Sulaymān ibn Yasār, al-Ḥakam ibn 'Uyaynah, 'Āmir ash-Sha'bī, Ibn Sīrīn and az-Zuhrī. There are different positions from al-Ḥasan. 'Ā'ishah also said that a woman's husband should not come to her at that time. That is the position of Ibn 'Ulayyah, al-Mughīrah ibn 'Abd ar-Raḥmān, the most elevated of Mālik's companions, and Abū Muṣ'ab who gave a *fatwā* to that effect.

The majority of scholars, however, say that a woman experiencing *istiḥādah* can pray, fast, do *ṭawāf* and recite Qur'an. Her husband can come to her as well.

Mālik said, 'The position of the people of *fiqh* and knowledge is this, even if the bleeding is considerable.' Ibn Wahb related it from him. Aḥmad said, 'I prefer that a husband should not have intercourse with such a woman unless her condition persists for a long time.' Ibn 'Abbās said about a woman suffering from *istiḥādah*, 'There is no harm in her husband having intercourse with her, even if the blood is flowing onto her heels.' Mālik said, 'The Messenger of Allah ﷺ said, "That is a vein, not menstruation." If it were menstruation, what would prevent him having sex with her when she is praying?' Ibn 'Abd al-Barr said, 'When Allah judged that the blood of a woman experiencing *istiḥādah* does not prevent the prayer and other acts of worship done by a woman who is not menstruating, then it is mandatory that none of the rulings of a menstruating women apply to her except for the consensus of having a *ghusl* as is the case with all sorts of bleeding.'

**so keep apart from women during menstruation**

This can either mean 'during' the time of menstruation if it is a verbal noun or it may refer to the place of menstruation itself in which case it would merely mean avoiding the actual act of sexual intercourse. Scholars disagree about other kinds of sexual contact with a menstruating woman and what is permitted in that respect. Ibn 'Abbās and 'Abīdah as-Salmānī said that a man must leave his wife's bed when she menstruates. This is an aberrant position, outside the position of most scholars. Even if the general words of the *āyah* may suggest that, the Sunnah is contrary to it. Ibn 'Abbās's aunt, Maymūnah, went to him and said, 'Do you turn away from the Sunnah of the Messenger of Allah ﷺ!'

Mālik, ash-Shāfi'ī, al-Awzā'ī, Abū Ḥanīfah, Abū Yūsuf and the vast majority of scholars say that a man can enjoy everything above the waist-wrapper because that is what the Prophet ﷺ said about this. When someone asked him, 'What is lawful to me of my wife when she is menstruating?' He replied, 'She should tie on her waist-wrapper, and then your business is what is above that.' The Prophet ﷺ said to 'Ā'ishah when she was menstruating, 'Tie on your waist-wrapper and then return to bed.' Ath-Thawrī, ash-Shaybānī and some Shāfi'īs say that a man should avoid the actual site of the blood, since the Prophet ﷺ said, 'Do everything except sexual intercourse.' That is the position of Dāwud and it is the sound view from ash-Shāfi'ī. Abū Ma'shar related from Ibrāhīm that Masrūq said, 'I asked 'Ā'ishah what is lawful to me of my wife while she is menstruating and she answered, "Everything except the genitals."' Scholars say that the reason a woman wears a waist wrapper is to cut off the means because a man might otherwise exceed what is allowed. That agrees with the reports and is not contradictory. Success is by Allah.

They disagree about what someone who does have sexual intercourse with his wife while she is menstruating should do. Mālik, ash-Shāfiʿī and Abū Ḥanīfah say that he should ask for Allah's forgiveness and owes nothing. That is the position of Rabīʿah and Yaḥyā ibn Saʿīd. Dāwud also said that. It is related from Muḥammad ibn al-Ḥasan that he should give half a dinar as *ṣadaqah*. Aḥmad ibn Ḥanbal said, 'The most excellent remedy is the *ḥadīth* of 'Abd al-Ḥamīd from Miqsam from Ibn 'Abbās in which the Prophet ﷺ said, 'He should give a dinar or half a dinar as *ṣadaqah*.' Abū Dāwud transmitted it and he said that this is a sound transmission: '...a dinar or half a dinar.' Aṭ-Ṭabarī recommended that, but if someone does not do it, he owes nothing. That is the view of ash-Shāfiʿī in Baghdad. One group of the People of Hadith said, 'If he has intercourse during bleeding, he owes a dinar. If he has intercourse after it has ended, he owes half a dinar.' Al-Awzāʿī said, 'If someone has intercourse with his wife while she is menstruating, he should give five dinars as *ṣadaqah*.' The paths of transmission of all of this is found in the *Sunan* of Abū Dāwud, ad-Dāraquṭnī and elsewhere. At-Tirmidhī transmitted from Ibn 'Abbās that the Prophet ﷺ said, 'If it is red blood, he owes a dinar. If it is yellow, then half a dinar.' Abū 'Umar said, 'The argument that he owes no expiation except asking for forgiveness and repentance is the weakness in the *isnād* from Ibn 'Abbās. Something like that is not used as a proof. He remains free of liability. It is not mandatory to confirm anything in it for a poor person or anything else except by an undisputed proof, and that does not exist with respect to this matter.'

**and do not approach them until they are pure.**

Ibn al-'Arabī said that he heard ash-Shāshī say in an assembly of debate, 'When it says, "Do not approach (*taqrab*)", it means "Do not touch." If it is "*tuqrib*", it means "Do not go near". Nāfiʿ, Abū 'Amr. Ibn Kathīr and 'Āṣim in the transmission of Ḥafṣ recite '*yaṭhurna*' while Ḥamzah, al-Kisā'ī, 'Āṣim in the transmission of Abū Bakr and al-Mufaḍḍal recite '*yaṭṭahharna*'. The copies of the Qur'an of Ubayy and 'Abdullāh have '*yataṭahharna*'. The copy of Anas ibn Mālik has 'do not approach women while they are menstruating and withdraw from them until they have purified themselves.' Aṭ-Ṭabarī preferred a double *ṭā'*, saying that it means 'they have washed' since the consensus of all is that it is unlawful for a man to approach his wife after the bleeding has stopped until she has had a *ghusl*.' The disagreement is about the type of purification required. Some say it is *ghusl*, some say it is *wuḍū'* and some say it is merely washing the genitals. That makes her lawful to her husband, even if she has not had a *ghusl* on account of menstruation.

**But once they have purified themselves,**

This is generally understood to refer to a full *ghusl* with water. That is the position of Mālik and most scholars. They say that the purification by which sexual intercourse with a woman who has been menstruating becomes lawful is by washing the whole body with water like you do for *janābah*. Neither *tayammum* nor anything else is adequate. That is the position of Mālik, ash-Shāfi'ī, aṭ-Ṭabarī, Muḥammad ibn Maslamah, the people of Madīnah and others. Yaḥyā ibn Bukayr and Muḥammad ibn Ka'b al-Qurṭubī said, 'When the period of a menstruating woman has completely finished and she does *tayammum* in a situation when there is no water, she is lawful for her husband without doing *ghusl*.' Mujāhid, 'Ikrimah and Ṭāwūs said that the end of bleeding makes her lawful for her husband, but she should perform *wuḍū'*. Abū Ḥanīfah, Abū Yūsuf and ash-Shaybānī said that when the blood has stopped for ten days, he can have sexual intercourse with her before she does *ghusl*. If it is before that time, he is not permitted to do so unless she has a *ghusl* or it becomes obligatory for her to do the prayer. This is arbitrary and without logic. That judgment would mean that after the end of bleeding, the woman would still be in her *'iddah* and her husband would be able to take her back as long as she has not had a *ghusl* for her third period.'

Our evidence is that Allah connected the ruling about this to two preconditions. The first is the end of bleeding which is in His words: *'until they are pure.'* The second is having a *ghusl*, which is in His words: '*once they have purified themselves*,' i.e. done a *ghusl* with water. This is like His words, *'Keep a close check on orphans until they reach a marriageable age…'* (4:6) where He connected the ruling, which is giving them their wealth, to two preconditions. The first is reaching the age of marriage and the second is recognition of their good sense. Another example is His words about a divorced woman: *'She is not lawful to him after that until she has married another husband'* (2:230) and then the Sunnah brings in sexual relations [with the new husband]. Therefore making the woman lawful to her first husband is based on two things today: a marriage contract and sexual intercourse with the new husband.

Abū Ḥanīfah argued that the *āyah* means that the end [of impurity] in the precondition is the same as the end which is mentioned before it, and so the two uses of *'yaṭhurna'* has the same meaning as *'yaṭṭahharna'*, and so both linguistic usages must be acted on and we must we take each of them to have its own meaning, so the first is about the end of bleeding which is the lesser end, and we do not permit having sex with her until she has had a *ghusl* because there is always the possibility of its resuming. We take the other *āyah* to mean when her bleeding stops at the maximum length, and so it is permitted to have sex with her, even if she has not had a *ghusl*. Ibn al-'Arabī says that this is the strongest position that they have.

The answer to the first is that it is not the language of those eloquent in Arabic. If that were the case, it would entail a repetition counting. When it is possible to apply the same words to a single thing, then no repetition is used by people, so how could that not be the case with the words of the All-Wise, All-Knowing? The answer to the second is that each of them can be taken to have a meaning that the other does not have, and so when the bleeding stops, she still has the ruling of being menstruating until she has a *ghusl*. They do not say that, as we made clear. It is agreed that she is still menstruating, and it is not permitted to have sex with a menstruating women. Furthermore, if they said that it demands that it is permitted to have sex when the bleeding ends at the maximum length, what we said demands prohibition. When there is a conflict between what demands prohibition and what demands permissibility, then prohibition takes precedence as was stated by 'Alī and 'Uthmān in respect of having two sisters by virtue of ownership: one *āyah* makes them lawful and the other *āyah* makes then unlawful. The prohibition takes precedence. Allah knows best.

Scholars disagree about whether a woman of the People of the Book should be forced to have a *ghusl* or not. In the transmission of Ibn al-Qāsim, Mālik said that she is compelled to have one in order to make intercourse with her husband lawful. Allah says: *'Do not approach them until they have purified themselves.'* He says that she should do it with water and that the instruction does not single out just Muslim women. Ashhab, however, relates from Mālik that she is not compelled to do so because she does not believe in that instruction. Since Allah says: *'It is not lawful for them to conceal what Allah has created in their wombs if they believe in Allah and the Last day.'* (2:228) That refers to menstruation and pregnancy. The instruction is addressed to believing women. Allah says: *'There is no compulsion where the* dīn *is concerned.'* (2:256) This is stated by Maḥmūd ibn 'Abd al-Ḥakam.

The *ghusl* that a menstruating woman performs is the same as that performed on account of *janābah*. She does not have to undo her braids when doing it, based on Muslim's relation that Umm Salamah said, 'I said, "Messenger of Allah, I have tight braids on my head. Do I have to undo them for the *ghusl* for *janābah*?" He answered, "No, it is enough for you to pour three handfuls of water on your head, then water over yourself, and you will be purified."' One variant has: 'undo them on account of menstruation and *janābah*.'

**then go to them in the way that Allah has enjoined on you.'**

This means to have sexual intercourse with them. It is a command which gives permission. 'Go to' is a euphemism for sexual intercourse. This is strengthened by the mention of purification with water since that is a form of command from Allah which is only complete. Allah knows best. The particle *'min'* here means 'in', namely where Allah has commanded which is the vagina. *'Min'* is used to mean 'in' in other *āyahs*. It is said that it means 'in the manner in which He has permitted you,' so not while fasting, in *iḥrām* or while in *i'tikāf*. Al-Aṣamm said that. Ibn 'Abbās and Abū Razīn said that it means in a state of purity, not during menstruation. Aḍ-Ḍaḥḥāk said that. Muḥammad ibn al-Ḥanafiyyah said that it means lawfully and not in fornication.

**Allah loves those who turn back from wrongdoing and He loves those who purify themselves.**

There is disagreement about what this means. It is said that it refers to those who turn back from wrong action and *shirk* and those who purify themselves with water from *janābah* and minor impurities. 'Aṭā' and others said that. Mujāhid said that it is turning back from wrong actions and also from anal intercourse with women. Ibn 'Aṭiyyah said, 'It appears to be a reference to the words about the people of Lūṭ in 7:82.' It is said that those purify themselves are those who have not committed wrong actions. Someone who repents is someone who does not despair of gaining Allah's mercy and is not arrogant as we see in another *āyah*: *'But some of them wrong themselves; some are ambivalent; and some outdo each other in good.'* (35:32)

نِسَآؤُكُمْ حَرْثٌ لَّكُمْ فَأْتُوا۟ حَرْثَكُمْ أَنَّىٰ شِئْتُمْ
وَقَدِّمُوا۟ لِأَنفُسِكُمْ وَٱتَّقُوا۟ ٱللَّهَ وَٱعْلَمُوٓا۟ أَنَّكُم مُّلَٰقُوهُ
وَبَشِّرِ ٱلْمُؤْمِنِينَ ﴿٢٢٣﴾

**223 Your women are fertile fields for you, so come to your fertile fields however you like. Send good ahead for yourselves and be fearful of Allah. Know that you are going to meet Him. And give good news to the believers.**

**Your women are fertile fields for you,**

It is related in Muslim from Jābir ibn 'Abdullāh: 'The Jews used to say, "If a man has intercourse with a woman from the rear, the child will be squint-eyed."' Then this *āyah* was revealed. The transmission from az-Zuhrī adds, 'If he wishes, when she is lying on her front, and if he wishes, when she is not lying on her front, as long as it is only the one opening.' At-Tirmidhī mentioned it.

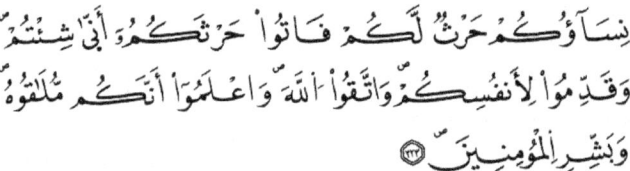

Al-Bukhārī related that Nāfi' said, 'When Ibn 'Umar recited the Qur'an, he would not speak until he finished it. I came to him one day and he recited *Sūrat al-Baqarah* until he reached a place whereupon he asked, "Do you know about what this was revealed?" "No," I answered. He said, "It was revealed about such-and-such." Then he continued. It is related by 'Abd aṣ-Ṣamad from his father from Ayyūb from Nāfi' that Ibn 'Umar said that this *āyah* means '*however you like*'. Al-Ḥumaydī says that the word refers to the vagina. Abū Dāwud related that Ibn 'Abbās said, 'Ibn 'Umar (may Allah forgive him!) misunderstood something. There was this tribe of the Anṣār, who had been idolaters, and the tribe of the Jews, who were People of the Book, and they [the Anṣār] used to think that the Jews were superior to them in knowledge. Therefore they used to imitate much of what they did. They had commanded the People of the Book not to have intercourse with women except on one side [i.e. lying on their backs] as that was more concealing for the woman. This tribe of the Anṣār adopted this from them. The tribe of Quraysh used to uncover women completely and enjoy them coming to them from in front and behind and lying on their backs. When the Muhājirūn came to Madīnah and a man married a woman of the Anṣār, he would act with her in that way and she disliked it and told him, "We are approached on one side! Do that or keep away from me!" This business spread and it reached the Prophet ﷺ. Then Allah Almighty revealed: *"Come to your fertile fields however you like,"* meaning from in front and behind and lying on the back, referring to the place where the child is born [i.e. the vagina].'

At-Tirmidhī related that Ibn 'Abbās said, "Umar went to the Messenger of Allah ﷺ and said, "Messenger of Allah, I am destroyed!" "What has destroyed you?" he asked. He said, "Last night I changed my direction." The Messenger of Allah ﷺ did not say anything. Then Allah revealed this *āyah* to the Messenger of Allah ﷺ: *"Your women are fertile fields for you, so come to your fertile fields however you like."* [He said,] "Approach from the front or the back, but avoid the anus and menstruation."' He said that this is a sound *ḥasan ḥadīth.*

An-Nasā'ī related that Abu-n-Naḍr said that he said to Nāfi', the freedman of Ibn 'Umar, 'It is often said that you say that Ibn 'Umar gave a *fatwā* that one can have anal intercourse with women.' Nāfi' exclaimed, 'They have lied about me! I will tell you how the business is. Ibn 'Umar read the Qur'an to me one day while I was with him until we reached: *"Your women are fertile fields for you."* Do you know what this *āyah* commands? We, the Quraysh, used to have women lie on their backs. When we arrived in Madīnah and married the women of the Anṣār, we wanted from them what men want from their wives and they disliked that and thought it terrible. The women of the Anṣār used to have sex on their sides. Then Allah revealed: "*Your women are fertile fields for you, so come to your fertile fields however you like.*'"

These *ḥadīths* provide a text about the permission for all forms when it is vaginal intercourse, i.e. whatever position you wish, front or back, reclining or lying on the back. As for sex in that part which is not permitted, it is not permitted! The *āyah* uses the word "*ḥarth*" (fields) and so this must apply to the vagina, because that entails fertility. Metaphorically, a woman is like the earth, the sperm is like the seed and the child is like the plants

**So come to your fertile fields however you like.**

The majority of the Companions, the Tābi'ūn and the imams qualified to give *fatwā* say that it means whatever position, front or back. The word for 'however' (*annā*) has various meanings in Arabic: however, whenever, and wherever. 'However' refers to the manner of joining. One group who say it means 'wherever' say that it is permitted to penetrate the anus. Among those to whom this view is ascribed are Sa'īd ibn al-Musayyab, Nāfi', Ibn 'Umar, Muḥammad ibn Ka'b al-Quraẓī and 'Abd al-Malik ibn al-Mājishūn. It is also related from Mālik in a book called *Kitāb as-Sirr*. However, the astute Mālikīs and their shaykhs reject that book. Mālik is too esteemed to have a '*Kitāb as-Sirr*'. This view is found in *al-'Utbiyyah*. Ibn al-'Arabī mentioned that Ibn Sha'bān ascribes this view to a large group of the Companions and Tābi'ūn. There are many transmissions ascribed to Mālik in *Kitāb Jimā' an-Niswān wa-l-Aḥkām al-Qur'ān*. Aṭ-Ṭabarī said, 'It is related that Muḥammad ibn Ka'b al-Quraẓī saw nothing wrong with that. In that he interpreted the following words of Allah: *"Of all beings, do you lie with males, leaving the wives your Lord has created for you?"* (26:165) He said that it implies: "You leave the like of that with your wives and if the like of that had not been permitted with wives, that would not be sound." It is not the site which is permitted so that you say, "You do that and leave its like which is permitted."' Aṭ-Ṭabarī said, 'This is debatable since it means: "You leave what your Lord created for you of your wives in which you still your appetite and the pleasure of intercourse is obtained by the two of them together." According to this, the rebuke is permitted. His words: *"Once they have purified themselves, then go to them in the way that Allah has enjoined on you"* and *"Come to your fertile fields"* indicate that it is one site in particular, and it is confined to the site of childbirth.'

This is what is true regarding this matter. Abū 'Umar ibn 'Abd al-Barr mentioned that scholars do not disagree that a woman whose vagina is closed so that there is no way to have sexual intercourse with her has a defect for which she can be rejected, with the exception of something that has come from 'Umar ibn 'Abd al-'Azīz by a path that is not sound that there can be no rejection on account of a closed vagina or anything else. All the *fuqahā'* take a different view because touching is what is desired in marriage. Their consensus about this is evidence that an old woman who cannot bear children is not rejected. What is sound in respect of this matter is what we explained.

What is ascribed to Mālik and his people regarding this is false and they are innocent of that because the permission is particularly connected to the place of the field because of His words and because the wisdom in creating couples is the bringing about of progeny. The power of marriage is only obtained by the site of procreation. This is the truth. Ibn al-'Arabī said, 'Shaykh Fakhru 'd-dīn Abū Bakr Muḥammad ibn Aḥmad ibn al-Ḥusayn, the *faqīh* and imam of his time, said, "The vagina is the thing most like thirty-five things," and he made a fist with his hand then said, "The urinary passage has thirty. The passage of the penis and vagina contain five. Allah has made the vagina unlawful during menstruation because of the impurity arriving. So it even more proper for the anus to be unlawful because of the inevitable impurity."' Mālik said to Ibn Wahb and 'Alī ibn Ziyad when they informed him that some people in Egypt claimed that he allowed anal intercourse, that he objected to that and rebuked the one who told him: 'They have lied about me! They have lied about me! They have lied about me!' Then he asked, 'Are they not an Arab people? Did not Allah say: *"Come to your fertile fields"?* Is a fertile field other than a place capable of growth?'

What opponents cite about the phrase '*...however you like*' including all passages, because it is undefined, is not a true argument since it is specific to what we mentioned. There are also numerous *ḥadīth*s which are excellent, sound and well-known, related from twelve Companions with different texts, all of which forbid anal intercourse with women. Aḥmad ibn Ḥanbal mentioned them in his *Musnad* as did Abū Dāwud, an-Nasā'ī, at-Tirmidhī and others. Abu-l-Faraj ibn al-Jawzī compiled them, along with their paths of transmission, in a section entitled: 'Prohibition of the disliked place'. Our Shaykh, Abu-l-'Abbās has a section entitled 'Exposition on turning away from those who allow anal intercourse.'

This is the truth which is followed and what is sound regarding this matter. Someone who believes in Allah and the Last Day must not be turned, in this calamity, to a scholastic error after having it rectified. We should be cautious about scholastic errors. Something different is related from Ibn 'Umar in which he said that someone who does it is an unbeliever. That is what he held to. May

Allah be pleased with him. Similarly Nāfi' said that the one who reported the previous transmission from him was lying, as an-Nasā'ī mentioned. Mālik denied it and thought it terrible and said that those who ascribed it to him were lying. Abū Muḥammad ad-Dārimī related in his *Musnad* from Abu-l-Ḥubāb that Sa'īd ibn Yasār said, 'I asked Ibn 'Umar, "What do you say about slavegirls when one 'pastures' with them?" He asked, "What is 'pasturing'?" I mentioned to him that it was anal intercourse. He exclaimed, "Do any of the Muslims do that!"' It is transmitted that Khuzaymah ibn Thābit said, 'I heard the Messenger of Allah ﷺ say, "People! Allah is not shy of the truth. Do not go women from their rear."' Something similar is reported from 'Alī ibn Ṭalq. Abū Hurayrah reported that the Prophet ﷺ said, 'If someone has anal sex with a woman, Allah will not look at him on the Day of Rising.' Abū Dāwud aṭ-Ṭayālisī related in his *Musnad* from Qatādah from 'Amr ibn Shu'ayb from his father from 'Abdullāh ibn 'Amr that the Prophet ﷺ said, 'That is the lesser sodomy.' It is related that Ṭāwūs said. 'The actions of the people of Lūṭ started with committing sodomy with women.' Ibn al-Mundhir said, 'The fact that something is confirmed from the Prophet ﷺ dispenses with the need for any further evidence.'

**Send good ahead for yourselves and be fearful of Allah**

Do what will be of benefit to you on the Last Day. Allah says elsewhere: *"Any good you send ahead for yourselves you will find with Allah."* (2:110) So it means obedience and righteous actions. It is also said that it means seeking children and progeny since a child is good for you in this world and the Next. He may be an intercessor and protection for you. It is said it means marriage with a chaste woman so that the ensuing child will be pure and righteous. It is said that it is excess as the Prophet ﷺ said, 'Anyone who has three of his children die before reaching the age of [accountable] sin will not be touched by the Fire except that which will fulfill an oath.' This will be dealt with in *Maryam*, Allah willing. Ibn 'Abbās and 'Aṭā' said that it means to mention Allah before sexual intercourse as the Prophet ﷺ said, 'If, when he goes to his wife, one of you were to say, "In the Name of Allah. O Allah, keep Shayṭān away from us and keep Shayṭān away from what You provide us with" and a child is decreed for them, Shayṭān will never harm him.' Muslim transmitted it.

**Know that you are going to meet Him.**

This is a far-reaching threat, because Allah will repay people both for their piety and for any wrong actions they commit. Ibn 'Uyaynah related that 'Amr ibn Dīnār heard Sa'īd ibn Jubayr say that Ibn 'Abbās said, 'I heard the Messenger of Allah ﷺ say while he was giving an address, "You will meet Allah barefooted, naked, on foot and uncircumcised." Then the Messenger of Allah ﷺ recited: *"Have* taqwā *of Allah and know that you are going to meet Him."'* Muslim transmitted it.

*'Give good news to the believers'* is to make it easy to do good actions and seek the paths of guidance.

وَلَا تَجْعَلُوا۟ ٱللَّهَ عُرْضَةً لِّأَيْمَٰنِكُمْ أَن تَبَرُّوا۟ وَتَتَّقُوا۟ وَتُصْلِحُوا۟ بَيْنَ
ٱلنَّاسِ وَٱللَّهُ سَمِيعٌ عَلِيمٌ ﴿٢٢٤﴾

**224 Do not, by your oaths, make Allah a pretext to avoid good action and being fearful of Him and putting things right between people. Allah is All-Hearing, All-Knowing.**

**Do not, by your oaths, make Allah a pretext**

Scholars say that Allah commands people to spend on, and behave well towards, orphans and women and, as a corollary, He is saying, 'Do not reject anything of noble character, using as an excuse, "I took an oath that I would not do such-and-such a thing."' That is what Ibn 'Abbās, an-Nakha'ī, Mujāhid ar-Rabī' and others said that the *āyah* means. Sa'īd ibn Jubayr said, 'It is about a man refusing to be pious, or to maintain contact with his kin, or to put things right between people, all of which constitute goodness, saying that he took an oath not to.' Some commentators say that it means 'Do not swear falsely by Allah if you truly desire good and that things be put right.' It is said that it simply means to make an excessive number of oaths by Allah because such oaths are more likely to move people. That is why Allah says, *'Keep your oaths.'* (5:89) He censured making an excessive number of oaths: *'Do not obey any vile swearer of oaths.'* (68:10) The Arabs praise making a small number of oaths as one says:

Having few oaths, he keeps his oaths.
If he makes an oath, he fulfils it.

This means that making few oaths comes from piety and *taqwā*. If someone makes many oaths, then he also breaks them and rarely guards the right of Allah Almighty. This is a good interpretation. Mālik ibn Anas said, 'I have heard that people swear by Allah to everything.' It is said that it means: 'Do not make oaths commonplace in respect of everything, both true and false.' Az-Zajjāj and others said that the *āyah* means that when a person is asked to do a good action, he uses

Allah as an excuse and says, 'I have sworn an oath' which he has not, in fact, sworn. Al-Qutabī said that it means: 'When you swear not to maintain ties with your kin, not to give *ṣadaqah* and not to put things right and similar good deeds, then you should expiate your oath.' This is an excellent position, and it is also what is indicated by the reason for the revelation as we will make clear.

It is said that it was revealed about the time when Abū Bakr made an oath not to give any more money to his poor kinsman Miṣṭaḥ, when he gossiped about 'Ā'ishah, as we shall read in the story of the Lie which will be discussed in *Sūrat an-Nūr* (24). It is also said that it was revealed because of Abū Bakr aṣ-Ṣiddīq when he swore that he would not eat with his guests. It is also said that it was revealed about 'Abdullāh ibn Rawāḥah when he swore not to speak to Bashīr ibn an-Nu'mān who was his son-in-law. Allah knows best.

The word "'*urḍah*" (pretext) means a target, intention, obstacle, or something which strengthens and supports something, in this case, the oath. The term is used of a woman being a 'target' for marriage since it is good for her and strengthens her. It is also used for strength to travel and fight. It means: 'Do not use your oaths to make Allah reinforce yourselves and as a means to refuse to do good.'

**To avoid good action and being fearful of Him**

It is more appropriate to do good, like *'More fitting for them would be obedience and honourable words.'* (47:21) Az-Zajjāj and an-Naḥḥās said that.

لَّا يُؤَاخِذُكُمُ ٱللَّهُ بِٱللَّغْوِ فِىٓ أَيْمَٰنِكُمْ وَلَٰكِن يُؤَاخِذُكُم
بِمَا كَسَبَتْ قُلُوبُكُمْ وَٱللَّهُ غَفُورٌ حَلِيمٌ ﴿٢٢٥﴾

**225 Allah will not take you to task for careless statements in your oaths, but He will take you to task for the intention your hearts have made. Allah is Ever-Forgiving, All-Forbearing.**

**Allah will not take you to task for careless statements in your oaths,**

The expression '*laghw*' (careless statements) is a verbal noun that means making use of unnecessary words or things which are not good but which do not actually involve wrongdoing. It is used in a *ḥadīth* to describe someone else speaking while the imam is speaking on the minbar.

Scholars disagree about exactly what is meant by a careless or ineffective oath. Ibn 'Abbās said that it refers to those oaths that people make while speaking or arguing when they say, 'No, by Allah' and 'Yes, by Allah' without really intending to make an actual oath. Al-Marwazī says, 'The ineffective oath, about which scholars agree, are the careless words of a man, "No, by Allah" and "Yes, by Allah", when an actual oath is not intended.' Ibn Wahb related from Yūnus from Ibn Shihāb from 'Urwah that 'Ā'ishah said, 'A careless oath is one made when arguing or joking and words which the heart does not intend.' We find in al-Bukhārī that 'Ā'ishah said, 'The words of Allah, *"Allah will not take you to task for careless statements in your oaths"* was revealed about when a man says, "No, by Allah" and "Yes, by Allah."'

It is said that a careless oath is one which is based on speculation and so the truth may tum out to be different. Mālik said that and Ibn al-Qāsim related it from him. A group of the Salaf also said that. Abū Hurayrah said, 'When a man swears to something, thinking that it is true, and then it turns out that it is not true, that is a careless oath and there is no expiation owed for it.' Something similar is related from Ibn 'Abbās. It is related that some people exchanged words in the presence of the Messenger of Allah ﷺ while they were shooting. One of them swore, "I hit it and you missed!" It turned out that the business was different and the man said, "He broke his oath, Messenger of Allah!" The Prophet ﷺ said, "The oaths of archers are ineffective oaths. There is no breaking them and no expiation owed for them."' Mālik stated in the *Muwaṭṭā'*, 'The best of what I have heard on the matter is that carelessness in oaths is when a man makes an oath about something which he feels certain is like he said, only to find that it is other than what he said. There is no *kaffārah* owed for it.'

If someone swears to something while knowing that he is lying and sinning, in order to please someone or to make an excuse to someone or to get some wealth, this is worse than an oath for which *kaffārah* is due. *Kaffārah* is due from someone who swears that he will not do something that it is permitted to do and then does it, or he that he will do something and then does not do it, as happens when he swears that he will not sell a garment for ten dirhams and then sells it for that amount, or he swears that he will beat his boy and then does not beat him.

If it is a sound transmission, Ibn 'Abbās said, 'A careless oath is what you swear when you are angry.' Ṭāwūs said that. Ibn 'Abbās related that the Messenger of Allah ﷺ said, 'There is no oath while someone is angry.' Muslim transmitted it. Sa'īd ibn Jubayr said that it is making what is lawful unlawful, as when someone says, 'My property is unlawful to me if I do such-and-such,' or 'the unlawful is lawful to me.' Makḥūl ad-Dimishqī said that. Mālik said that this excludes oaths about his wife where the prohibition is binding unless he excludes her in his heart.

It is said that it is an oath to do something in which one disobeys Allah, as was stated by Sa'īd ibn al-Musayyab, Abū Bakr ibn 'Abd ar-Raḥmān, and 'Urwah and 'Abdullāh, the sons of az-Zubayr. That is like when someone swears to drink wine or sever ties with his kin. His keeping of his oath in that instance is to abandon that action, and he owes no *kaffārah*. Their argument is found in the *ḥadīth* of 'Amr ibn Shu'ayb from his father from his grandfather that the Prophet ﷺ said, 'If someone swears an oath and sees something else better than it, he should abandon it. His abandoning it is its *kaffārah*.' Ibn Mājah transmitted it in the *Sunan*. It will be discussed in *al-Mā'idah*.

Zayd ibn Aslam said, 'A careless oath is when someone invokes Allah against himself like, "May Allah blind me," "May Allah remove my wealth," "I am a Jew" or "I am an idolater." This is a careless oath if he says that.' Mujāhid said, 'It is like when there are two men involved in a sale and one of them says, "By Allah, I will not sell it to you for that," and the other says, "By Allah, I will not buy it for this."' An-Nakha'ī said that it is a man swearing that he will not do something and then he forgets about having said that and does it. Ibn 'Abbās and aḍ-Ḍaḥḥāk said that an ineffective oath is one that is expiated, i.e. when the oath is expiated, it is cancelled and becomes of no note and Allah does not take him to task for its expiation and returning to what is better.

Ibn 'Abd al-Barr related a position that ineffective oaths are those which are forced. Ibn al-'Arabī said, 'As for an oath which is forgotten, there is no doubt that it is ineffective because it is different to his intention and so it is absolutely of no note. The oath of someone forced is of this sort, and the ruling of someone who is forced will be dealt with in *an-Naḥl*, Allah willing.

Ibn al-'Arabī said, 'As for those who say that an ineffective oath is an oath entailing disobedience to Allah, that is false because someone who swears to abandon an act entailing disobedience makes his oath an act of worship, and someone who swears to commit disobedience makes his oath disobedience and is told, "Do not do it. Expiate it." If he does the action, he sins in advancing to do it to fulfil his oath.' As for someone who says that it entails a man invoking against himself that something will happen to him if he does not do a certain thing, it is careless words in the path of *kaffārah*, but it is binding when it is intentional, but disliked. He may be punished for it because the Prophet ﷺ said, 'None of you should invoke against himself. It is possible that it will coincide with a moment in which Allah grants anything that He is asked.' As for someone who says that it is an oath in anger, he is refuted by the oath of the Prophet ﷺ in anger that he would not give camels to ride to the Ash'arīs and then he did so and expiated his oath as will be explained in *at-Tawbah*.

Ibn al-'Arabī said, 'As for those who say that it is an expiated oath, it is not pertinent to what is related.' Ibn 'Aṭiyyah also says that it is weak. He said, 'Generally speaking, Allah removed any calling to task for a careless oath. The reality is that it is not a sin and there is no expiation required for it. Taking to task for oaths is punishment in the Next World for a deliberately false oath and for those whose *kaffārah* has not been done when it is something for which there should be *kaffārah*, and taking to task in this world is by making *kaffārah* necessary. Therefore the statement that it is an expiated oath is weak because there is censure for it and censure is for its being in the Next World.'

*'Aymān'* (oaths) is the plural of *'yamīn'* which literally means 'right hand,' and the basis for that is that among the Arabs, when they made a contract or alliance, they would shake each other's right hands and so an oath became termed *yamīn*. It is said that it is because it contains blessing (*yumn*). Allah called it that because it preserves rights.

**but He will take you to task for the intention your hearts have made.**

This is an adjunct to Allah's words: *'Allah does not take you to task for your inadvertent oaths.'* (5:89) Zayd ibn Aslam said that His words are about someone who says, 'He is an idolater if he does it.' This is careless unless he believes in *shirk* in his heart and acquires it. *'Ever-Forgiving, All-Forbearing'* are two attributes appropriate to what was mentioned about not taking to task since they are aspects of compassion and leniency.

لِّلَّذِينَ يُؤْلُونَ مِن نِّسَآئِهِمْ تَرَبُّصُ أَرْبَعَةِ أَشْهُرٍ فَإِن فَآءُو فَإِنَّ ٱللَّهَ
غَفُورٌ رَّحِيمٌ ﴿٢٢٦﴾ وَإِنْ عَزَمُوا۟ ٱلطَّلَٰقَ فَإِنَّ ٱللَّهَ سَمِيعٌ عَلِيمٌ ﴿٢٢٧﴾

**226 Those who swear to abstain from sexual relations with their wives can wait for a period of up to four months. If they then retract their oath, Allah is Ever-Forgiving, Most Merciful. 227 If they are determined to divorce, Allah is All-Hearing, All-Knowing.**

**Those who swear to abstain from sexual relations with their wives**

This kind of oath is called *īlā'* in Arabic. There are other forms of the verbal noun from the verb: *aliyyah*, *alwah* and *ilwah*. 'Abdullāh ibn 'Abbās said that the *īlā'* in the days of Jāhiliyyah could be for one, two or even more years. Men intended by that to harm their wives and so a maximum time of four months was set for it. If someone vows less than that it is not considered an *īlā'*. According to *Saḥīḥ Muslim,* it is said that the Prophet ﷺ pronounced an *īlā'* because his wives asked him for maintenance which he did not have. It is said that it is because Zaynab returned his gift to him and he became angry with his wives. This is what we find in Ibn Mājah.

*Īlā'* has the same legal conditions as a pronouncement of divorce and a free person, slave or drunk person can invoke it, as can a simpleton and one under a guardian, provided that he is adult and not insane. The same is true of a hermaphrodite if he is not mad and an elderly man as long as he is still alive and active. The position of ash-Shāfi'ī varies regarding an *īlā'* by a eunuch. One view says that he cannot make an *īlā'* and another says that it is sound. The first is more correct and closer to the Book and the Sunnah. Sexual intercourse is what cancels the oath and a verbal statement about it does not cancel it. As long as the oath remains unbroken the ruling of *īlā'* remains.

Scholars disagree about the kind of oath by which *īlā'* occurs. Some say it only occurs with an oath by Allah alone since the Prophet ﷺ said, 'Whoever swears should swear by Allah or be silent.' Ash-Shāfi'ī said that in his new school. Ibn 'Abbās says that any oath that prevents sexual intercourse is sufficient for it. That is what is said by ash-Sha'bī, an-Nakha'ī, Mālik, the people of Hijaz, Sufyān ath-Thawrī and the people of Iraq, ash-Shāfi'ī in his first view, Abū Thawr, Abū 'Ubayd, Ibn al-Mundhir and Qāḍī Abū Bakr ibn al-'Arabī. Ibn 'Abd al-Barr said that it applies to every oath because of which a man cannot have intercourse with his wife. Unless he breaks it, he is carrying out an *īlā'* when the oath goes more than four months. So it is all a person can swear by: by Allah, by one of His attributes, by saying, 'I swear by Allah' or 'I bear witness by Allah', or 'I have a promise or pact or pledge with Allah'. In all these cases it is an *īlā'*. If, however, a man says, 'I swear' and does not mention Allah, it is said that it is not an *īlā'* unless he means 'by Allah' and intends that. This will be further explained in *al-Mā'idah.* If he swears that he will fast if he has sexual intercourse with his wife and says, 'If I have sex with my wife, I will fast for a month or a year,' that is an *īlā'*. That same is true if it involves divorce, emancipation, prayer or *ṣadaqah.* The basis for this is the generality of Allah's words: '*Those who swear to abstain.*' He made no distinction about what makes it obligatory.

If a man makes an oath not to have intercourse and says '*inshā'llāh*', it can still be an *īlā'*, but if, in that instance, he has intercourse with his wife, he owes no *kaffārah* in the transmission of Ibn al-Qāsim from Mālik. Ibn al-Mājishūn said in *al-Mabsūṭ* that in that case it is not an *īlā'* and that is sounder because of the "*inshā'llāh*" which undoes the oath. That is the position of the people of all regions because he makes it clear by saying '*inshā'llāh*' that he is not resolved on the action. The reason for what Ibn al-Qāsim related is based on the fact that '*inshā'llāh*' does not undo the oath, but has an effect on cancelling *kaffārah* as will be explained *in al-Mā'idah*. When the oath remains, then the ruling of *īlā'* is obliged for him, even if *kaffārah* is not obliged.

If a man swears by the Prophet, the angels, or the Ka'bah not to have intercourse or says that he is a Jew or a Christian or fornicator if he does, this is not an *īlā'*. Mālik and others said that. Al-Bājī said, 'I believe that it means it is not a form of the oath unless he meant by what he said for it to be an *īlā'*.' According to *al-Mabsūṭ*: 'Ibn al-Qāsim was asked about whether a man who tells his wife, "You are not welcome," means an *īlā'* by that. He said that Mālik said, "All words by which divorce are intended are divorce. This is divorce in any case."'

Scholars disagree about the *īlā'* mentioned in the Qur'an. Ibn 'Abbās said that it is not an *īlā'* unless he swears that he will never touch her. One group said that if he swears that he will not go near his wife for a day, or more or less than that, and then does not have sex with her for four months, she is free from him by *īlā'*. This is related from Ibn Mas'ūd, an-Nakha'ī, Ibn Abī Laylā, al-Ḥakam, Ḥammād ibn Abī Sulaymān and Qatādah, and Isḥāq said that. Ibn al-Mundhir said that many of the people of knowledge deny this view. Most say that an *īlā'* is that a man swears not to have sex with is wife for more than four months. If he swears that for four months or less, it is not an *īlā'*. They consider it to be a simple oath. If he has sex with her in this period he owes nothing as is the case with other oaths. This is the view of Mālik, ash-Shāfi'ī, Aḥmad and Abū Thawr. Ath-Thawrī and the Kufans said that an *īlā'* is that a man swears to four months or more. That is the view of 'Aṭā'.

The Kufans said that Allah made the waiting period in the *īlā'* four months as He made the '*iddah* of a widow four months and ten days. There are three menstrual cycles in the '*iddah* and there is no waiting after it. They said that it is mandatory that the *īlā'* is cancelled after that period, and it is only cancelled by intercourse within the period. There is a divorce after four months. Mālik and ash-Shāfi'ī argued that Allah assigned four months for the *īlā'* and so he can have it in full without any protest from his wife in it, just as happens in the case of a deferred debt where the one owed it cannot demand it until the end of the stipulated period. The approach of Isḥāq about a short period in which a person is doing *īlā'* when he does not have sex is based on someone making an oath to do more than four months: he is doing an *īlā'* because he intended harm by the oath. This idea exists in a short period.

They disagree about someone who swears not to have sex with his wife for more than four months and then the four months comes to an end without his wife requesting it or presenting the case to the ruler to enforce a stop. According to Mālik and most of the people of Madīnah nothing is obliged for him. Some of our scholars say that after the end of four months a revocable divorce has taken place. Some of them and others said that he has a final divorce at the end of four months. The sound position is that of Mālik and his people: a divorce is not obliged for the person with the *īlā'* until the ruler asks him to stop at the request of his wife to have sex. Then he can take his wife back through sexual intercourse and expiate his oath or divorce her. He must either have intercourse or divorce her. Sulaymān ibn Yasār said, 'Nine of the Companions of the Prophet ﷺ detained people on account of an *īlā'*.' Mālik said, 'That is what is done with us.' Al-Layth, ash-Shāfi'ī, Aḥmad, Isḥāq and Abū Thawr said that. Ibn al-Mundhir preferred it.

The term of the *īlā'* starts from the day of the oath, not from the day the woman argues with him and presents the case to the judge. If she argues with him and is not content with his refusal of sex, the ruler sets for him a term of four months from the day he swore the oath. If he has sex with her, he has fulfilled the wife's right and then he expiates his oath. If he does not have sex, then a revocable divorce is carried out. Mālik said, 'If he takes her back, it is not validated until he has had sex with her during the *'iddah*.' Al-Abhurī said, 'That is because divorce occurs to avert harm. When he does not have sex with her, the harm continues. There is no sense in taking her back without that unless he has a reason that prevents sexual intercourse. If there is, then his taking her back is validated because the harm has disappeared since his refusal to have sex is not about causing harm, but comes from a valid excuse.'

Scholars disagree about an *īlā'* when one is not angry. Ibn 'Abbās said that an *īlā'* is only possible in anger. That is related from 'Alī ibn Abī Ṭālib in the well-known position reported from him. Al-Layth, ash-Sha'bī, al-Ḥasan and 'Aṭā' all said that the *īlā'* is only made in a state of anger, harshness and desire to cause trouble. It is the same whether that upholds the best interests of a child or not. If it does not come from anger, it is not *īlā'*. Ibn Sīrīn said, 'It is the same whether the oath is done in anger or not: it is still *īlā'*.' Ibn Mas'ūd, ath-Thawrī, Mālik, the people of Iraq, ash-Shāfi'ī and his people and Aḥmad said that. Mālik, however, said, 'as long as the best interests of a child is not intended by it.' Ibn al-Mundhir said, 'This is sounder because they agree that *ẓihār*, divorce and other oaths are the same in both anger and pleasure. So the *īlā'* is like that.' This is indicated by the general nature of the Qur'an. Making it is specific to anger would require a proof. Allah knows best.

Our scholars have said that if a man refuses to have intercourse with his wife without making an oath in order to harm her, he is ordered to have intercourse with her. If he refuses to do so, then they are divorced without a term being set. It is also said that the term of the *īlā'* is set. It is said that it is not *īlā'* when a man shuns his wife, even if that lasts for years and he does not have sex with her. However, he is admonished and commanded to have *taqwā* of Allah by not causing her harm.

They disagree about someone who swears not to have sex with his wife until he weans her child so that the child does not become squint-eyed, without intending harm to her, until the end of the period of suckling. During that period the wife cannot make a demand of the husband according to Mālik because he is intending the best interests of the child. Mālik said, 'I heard that 'Alī ibn Abī Ṭālib was asked about that and did not consider it to be *īlā'*. Ash-Shāfi'ī said that in one of his views. The other view is that it is *īlā'*. He does not take the suckling of the child into account. Abū Ḥanīfah said that.

Mālik, ash-Shāfi'ī, Abū Ḥanīfah and his people, al-Awzā'ī and Aḥmad ibn Ḥanbal believed that he is not making an *īlā'* when he swears not to have sex with his wife in this house or this land because he has a way to have sex with her elsewhere. Ibn Abī Laylā and Isḥāq said that if he leaves her for four months, she is clear of him by *īlā'*. Do you not see that he is detained for four months? If he swears not to have sex with her in his city or land, according to Mālik, it is considered to be an *īlā'*. This is when a journey would entail hardship rather than in a garden or cultivated land nearby.

The words 'their wives' include free women, *dhimmī* women and slavegirls when they are married. An *īlā'* made by a slave is binding. Ash-Shāfi'ī, Aḥmad and Abū Thawr said that his *īlā'* is the same as that of a free man. Their argument is the literal text of the Qur'an in this *āyah* which is general to all. Ibn al-Mundhir said, 'That is what I say.' Mālik, az-Zuhrī, 'Aṭā' ibn Abī Rabāḥ and Isḥāq said that the length of a slave's *īlā'* is two months. Al-Ḥasan and an-Nakha'ī said that an *īlā'* with a slavegirl is two months and that with a free woman is four months. Abū Ḥanīfah said that. Ash-Sha'bī said that the *īlā'* of a slavegirl is half that of a free woman.

Mālik and his people, Abū Ḥanīfah and his people, al-Awzā'ī, an-Nakha'ī and others said that the binding nature of an *īlā'* is the same in a consummated and unconsummated marriage. Az-Zuhrī, 'Aṭā' and ath-Thawrī said that there can only be an *īlā'* after consummation. Mālik said that there can be no *īlā'* with a girl who has not yet reached puberty. If the husband pronounces the *īlā'* and then the girl reaches puberty, the *īlā'* becomes binding from the day she reaches puberty.

An *īlā'* made by a *dhimmī* man is not valid. The same is true of his *ẓihār* and divorce. That is because we do not consider the marriages of the people of *shirk* to be valid. They do have a quasi-authority. Since *dhimmī*s are not bound by the Sharī'ah, they owe no *kaffārah*. If they were to present themselves to us in a case of *īlā'*, it is not proper for our judges to render judgment. They should be sent to their own judges. If that occurs in the form of mutual injustice towards each other, then the ruling is that of Islam, as when a Muslim refuses to have sex with his wife in order to harm her, but without an oath.

**can wait for a period of up to four months.**

The word *tarabbuṣ* means being patient and waiting. The reason for this period of time. according to Ibn 'Abbās, has already been mentioned in what he said about the people of the Jāhiliyyah. Allah forbade that and allowed a husband four months in which to discipline his wife by shunning her since Allah says: '… *refuse to sleep with them'* (4:34) The Prophet ﷺ parted from his wives in this manner for a month to rectify their behaviour. It is said that this is the maximum which a woman can endure. It is related that 'Umar ibn al-Khaṭṭāb used to go around Madīnah at night and heard a woman saying:

'This night is long and dark
    and it pains me that I have no beloved with whom to play.
By Allah – were it not for Allah, there would be nothing but Him –
    the sides of this bed would shake!
Fear of Allah and modesty restrain me
    as well as the honour of my husband from doing it!'

In the morning 'Umar sent for that woman and asked her, 'Where is your husband?' She replied, 'You sent him to Iraq!' Then he summoned the women and asked them about the length of time a wife could endure being without her husband. 'Two months,' they answered. 'Her patience becomes stretched after three months, and disappears after four.' Therefore 'Umar made four months the maximum length of time for a man to be absent on a military expedition. Then they would be replaced by others. Allah knows best, but this makes it clearer why four months is singled out here.

**If they then retract their oath,**

This means retract it or go back on it. We see its usage in 49:9. The word '*fay*'' is also used for the shadow after midday because it returns from the west to the east. Ibn al-Mundhir said that all scholars, who are recorded, agree that retraction consists in having sexual intercourse unless someone has a valid excuse. If he has an excuse in the form of illness or imprisonment or the like, his simple statement of retraction is valid and she remains his wife. If the excuse ends, as when he returns from a journey, recovers from illness or is released from prison, and he still refuses to have sexual intercourse, the couple are separated if the end of the time has been reached. Mālik stated that in the *Mudawwanah* and the *Mabsūṭ*. 'Abd al-Malik said, 'She is parted from him the day that the period ends. If he has a valid excuse for retraction which is possible, his truthfulness is judged retrospectively. If what he claims about retraction being impossible when, in fact, he was able to do so, then he is taken to be lying about it and stubborn. Rulings are carried out according to what is in force at the time.'

One group said that when there is proof of retraction at a time when an excuse exists, then it is allowed. Al-Ḥasan, 'Ikrimah and an-Nakha'ī said that. Al-Awzā'ī said that. An-Nakhā'ī said, 'Retraction is only validated by a statement and witnesses. The ruling of *īlā'* is cancelled. So what do you think if he does not rise to intercourse?' Ibn 'Aṭiyyah said, 'If he does not have sex, then this statement amounts to causing harm.' Aḥmad ibn Ḥanbal said, 'If he has an excuse, he retracts in his heart.' Abū Qilābah said that. Abū Ḥanīfah said, 'If he is unable to have sex, he says, "I have taken her back."' Aṭ-Ṭabarī said, 'Abū Ḥanīfah says that if someone pronounces an *īlā'* while he is ill and a period of four months passes when the wife has a blockage that prevents intercourse or is too young, and he retracts that verbally when the period has passed and the excuse remains, that is a sound retraction. Ash-Shāfi'ī opposes him in one of his positions. One group said that retraction only takes place by sexual intercourse, whether it is at a time of valid excuse or not. That is what Sa'īd ibn Jubayr said and he said that it is the case when he is on a journey or in prison.

Mālik, ash-Shāfi'ī, Abū Ḥanīfah and his people, and most scholars say that a man must do *kaffārah* if he retracts his oath. Al-Ḥasan said that there is no *kaffārah*. An-Nakha'ī said that, stating: 'They used to say that when he retracts it, he owes no *kaffārah*.' Isḥāq said, 'Some commentators say that "*If they then retract*" means "if they then break the oath."' That is the position about oaths, in the view of some of the Tābi'ūn, about someone who swears an oath to do good, have *taqwā* or some area of good if he does not do it. If he does it, then he owes no *kaffārah*. Their argument is found in Allah's words: '*If they then retract their oath, Allah is Ever-*

*Forgiving, All-Forbearing.'* There is no mention of expiation here. This is also based on the ineffectiveness of an oath sworn to disobey Allah. Abandoning sex with one's wife is an act of disobedience. There is evidence for this position in the Sunnah in the *ḥadīth* that 'Amr ibn Shu'ayb reported from his father from his grandfather that the Prophet ﷺ said, 'If someone swears an oath and then sees something better than it, he should abandon it. His abandoning it is its expiation.' Ibn Mājah transmitted it in the *Sunan*. This is further explained in the *āyah* on oaths. The argument of the majority is in accordance with the words of the Prophet ﷺ: 'If someone swears an oath and then sees something better than it, he should do what is better and expiate his oath.'

When he expiates his oath, the *īlā'* is cancelled. Our scholars said that. That contains evidence for putting *kaffārah* ahead of breaking the oath in the School. That is the consensus about the *īlā'*. The evidence is against Abū Ḥanīfah in the question of oaths since he does not think it is permissible to do *kaffārah* ahead of breaking the oath. Ibn al-'Arabī said that. Muḥammad ibn al-Ḥasan used this *āyah* as evidence that it is not permitted to do *kaffārah* ahead of breaking the oath. He said, 'Then Allah judged that the person doing an *īlā'* is subject to one of two rulings, retraction or resolving on divorce, because if he breaks the oath, nothing is incumbent on him for breaking it. When the one who breaks the oath is not obliged to do anything, he is not in an *īlā'*. The permission to do *kaffārah* first cancels the ruling of *īlā'* in a way other than how Allah mentions. That is contrary to the Book.'

**If they are determined to divorce,**

Determination (*'azima*) means to conclude a contract on something. It comes from the verb *'azama*. It is also to adjure someone to do something. Shamr said, '*'Azīmah and 'azm* is resolving to do something. *Ṭalāq* is divorce. A divorced women is both *ṭāliq* and *ṭāliqah*. *Ṭalāq* is to undo the marriage contract. The root meaning is to release and let go. Divorced women are let go and divorce is letting go. A released camel is called '*ṭāliq*', meaning that it is left to graze without a lead or herdsman. The plural is *aṭlāq*. A woman who is divorced is free to go her own way. It is also said that it is derived from the running free (*ṭalaq*) of a horse.

The *āyah* is evidence that the wife is not divorced simply by the conclusion of the period of four months. As Mālik says, 'The divorce does not occur automatically after the time is up.'

**Allah is All-Hearing, All-Knowing.**

Allah is referred to as 'All-Hearing' meaning that the pronouncement is heard after the time. Abū Ḥanīfah said that He hears the *īlā'* and 'knows' the resolve. Suhayl ibn Abī Ṣāliḥ relates that his father said, 'I asked twelve of the Companions of the Messenger of Allah ﷺ about a man who does an *īlā'* from his wife. All of them said that nothing is obliged for him until the end of four months. Then he is detained. If he does not retract, he is divorced.' Qāḍī Ibn al-'Arabī said, 'The truth of the matter is that we think that the *āyah* means that the retraction is at the end. The divorce is by failing to retract it at the end of the period of waiting. This is an equal possibility.'

If the two possibilities are equal, then the position of the Kufans is stronger in analogy based on a woman in *'iddah* counting months and menstrual cycles since Allah has established that term. At the end of it, the bond is severed completely without dispute. Then her husband has no way to return to her without her permission. That is how it is with the *īlā'*. So if he forgets to retract it and the term ends, the divorce occurs. Allah knows best.

*'If they are determined on divorce"* is evidence that there is no *īlā'* with a slave-girl with whom he has relations based on ownership since there is divorce. Allah knows best.

وَٱلۡمُطَلَّقَٰتُ يَتَرَبَّصۡنَ بِأَنفُسِهِنَّ ثَلَٰثَةَ قُرُوٓءٖۚ وَلَا يَحِلُّ لَهُنَّ أَن يَكۡتُمۡنَ
مَا خَلَقَ ٱللَّهُ فِيٓ أَرۡحَامِهِنَّ إِن كُنَّ يُؤۡمِنَّ بِٱللَّهِ وَٱلۡيَوۡمِ ٱلۡأٓخِرِۚ وَبُعُولَتُهُنَّ
أَحَقُّ بِرَدِّهِنَّ فِي ذَٰلِكَ إِنۡ أَرَادُوٓاْ إِصۡلَٰحٗاۚ وَلَهُنَّ مِثۡلُ ٱلَّذِي عَلَيۡهِنَّ
بِٱلۡمَعۡرُوفِۚ وَلِلرِّجَالِ عَلَيۡهِنَّ دَرَجَةٞۗ وَٱللَّهُ عَزِيزٌ حَكِيمٌ ٢٢٨

**228 Divorced women should wait by themselves for three menstrual cycles; and it is not lawful for them to conceal what Allah has created in their wombs if they believe in Allah and the Last Day. Their husbands have the right to take them back within that time, if they desire to be reconciled. Women possess rights similar to those held over them to be honoured with fairness; but men have a degree above them. Allah is Almighty, All-Wise.**

**Divorced women should wait by themselves for three menstrual cycles;**

Allah follows the mention of *īlā'* by talking about women who have been divorced and clarifies the rulings applying to women after divorce has taken place. We find in Abū Dāwud and an-Nasā'ī from Ibn 'Abbās about Allah's words: *'Divorced women should wait by themselves for three menstrual cycles;'* 'That is because when a man divorces a woman, he is still entitled to her, but if he divorces her three times, that is superseded when He says: *'Divorce is twice...'*. 'Divorced women' is general but what is meant here specifically are those in a consummated marriage. This excludes those divorced before consummation which is dealt with in the *āyah* in *al-Aḥzāb*: *'...there is no* 'iddah *for you to calculate for them.'* (33:49) The same is true of pregnant women, about whom Allah says: *'The time for women who are pregnant is when they give birth.'* (65:4) The purpose of the menstrual cycles is to ascertain whether or not the woman is pregnant, whereas the waiting period at the time of bereavement is for worship. If the woman does not menstruate due to youth or age, then the time is counted in months rather than menstrual cycles. Some people say that the generality of the term '*divorced women*' first included all of these and was then abrogated. That is weak. The *āyah* is about menstruating women in particular. It is the most common state of women.

'*Tarabbuṣ*' means waiting as we already stated. Although it is phrased as a report, the waiting referred to here is in fact a command. This is the undoubted position of linguists according to what Ibn ash-Shajarī. Ibn al-'Arabī said that this is false and that it is simply a report about a ruling of the Sharī'ah. That must be a report from Allah Almighty. It is said that there is an implied '*li*' omitted at the beginning of '*tarrabuṣ*'.

Most people recite 'menstrual cycles' as *qurū'* with a *hamzah* while Nāfi' has *quruw*. It is the plural of *aqru'* and *aqrā'* which is, in turn, the plural of *qur'*. Al-Aṣma'ī said that. Abū Zayd said that it is *qar'*. The word also can mean the end of menstruation. Some of them say that it is the time between two menstrual periods. Abū 'Amr ibn al-'Alā' said, 'Some Arabs call menstruation *qur'* and some use that term for purity and some use it for both.' An-Naḥḥās mentioned that.

Scholars disagree about which of them is meant here. The people of Kufa say that it is the time of menstruation which is meant, based on what 'Umar, 'Alī, Ibn Mas'ūd, Abū Mūsā, Mujāhid, Qatādah, aḍ-Ḍaḥḥāk, 'Ikrimah and as-Suddī said, while the people of the Hijaz say that it is the period of purity which is meant, which is the position of 'Ā'ishah, Ibn 'Umar, Zayd ibn Thābit, az-Zuhrī, Abān ibn 'Uthmān, and ash-Shāfi'ī. Those who consider it to be menstruation do so because the blood collects (*qara'a*) in the womb and those who consider it to be purity do so because the blood collects in the body. That which is precise about the matter is that the term is about time as one says, 'The wind blew in its time (*li-qur'ihā*).'' It is said that menstruation has a time and purity has a time since they both refer to a known time.

Some people say that the word is derived from the settling (*qur'*) of water in a basin where it collects. The Qur'an takes its name from the fact that it collects meanings or is collection of letters. The womb collects blood at the time of menstruation and the body collects it in the period of purity. Abū 'Umar ibn 'Abd al-Barr said, 'The view of those who say that *qur'* is derived from the word for water collecting in a basin amounts to nothing because *qur'* has a *hamzah* and that word does not.' This is sound as it is transmitted by linguists like al-Jawharī and others: the noun for water settling is *qirā* and *qur'* is moving from purity to menstruation or menstruation to purity. That is what ash-Shāfi'ī said: it is moving from purity to menstruation. He did not think that it is moving from menstruation to purity. This demands that it is *qur'*, based on derivation, and the *āyah* means three cycles or three movements.

A divorced woman is described by both states – sometimes she is moving from purity to menstruation and sometimes from menstruation to purity – and so the meaning of the words is in order. It directs to the movement of menstruation and purity and so it is a shared word. It is said that if it is confirmed that *qur'* is movement, then her moving from purity to menstruation is not meant at all by the *āyah*. That is by the sunnah commanding that divorce does not take place during menstruation. That is a divorce with an *'iddah*. If it is a divorce with an *'iddah*, then it is done in a state of purity. That indicates that *qur'* is derived from the movement.

Since divorce in a state of purity is sunnah, the words imply that their *'iddah* is three changes. The first is from the purity in which the divorce occurred and which the change from menstruation to purity does not make a *qur'* because the language indicates that. However, we recognise another proof. Allah did not mean the change from menstruation to purity. When one of them is removed, then what is meant is the other, which is the change from purity to menstruation. On this basis, there are three changes, the first of which is purity. According to this, it is possible to fulfil three full cycles when divorce is done in a state of purity. It is not used metaphorically in any way. Aṭ-Ṭabarī said, 'This is a fine inspection at the end of the direction taken by ash-Shāfi'ī. It is possible that in that we mention a secret that it is not hard to understand in the fine points of the Sharī'ah. It is that the change from purity to menstruation is a *qur'* since it indicates that the womb is clear. Normally, a pregnant woman does not menstruate and so menstruation indicates that the womb is empty.'

The change from menstruation to purity is different to this. A menstruating woman can become pregnant at the end of her menstrual period. When pregnancy continues and the child is strong, then the bleeding stops. That is why Arab women become pregnant while pure.

This is how scholars and linguists interpret *qur'*. They use the verb for a woman when she menstruates, when she is pure and when she becomes pregnant and agree *qur'* refers to a time. If you were to say, 'Divorced women should wait by themselves for three times,' the *āyah* would explain the probable number in what is counted and so clarification must be sought elsewhere. Our evidence is found in Allah's words: *'...divorce them during their period of purity (*'iddah*)'* (65:1), There is no disagreement about the fact that one is commanded to divorce during purity and it is necessary that it is what is considered in the *'iddah*. When He says: *'...divorce them,'* He means in a time in which she can do *'iddah*. Then He says: *'calculate their* 'iddah,*'* meaning what the divorced woman observes which is the state of purity in which she is divorced. The Prophet ﷺ said to 'Umar, 'Order him to take her back and then keep her until she is pure and then to wait until she menstruates and then becomes pure again. That is the *'iddah* which Allah has commanded for divorced women.' Muslim and others transmitted it. It is a text about the time of purity being called *'iddah* which is the time in which women are divorced.

There is no disagreement that a woman who is divorced while menstruating does not count that menstruation, but when she is divorced while pure, that period of purity is counted in the *'iddah* by the majority. That is more appropriate. Abū Bakr ibn 'Abd ar-Raḥmān said, 'We did not meet any of our *fuqahā'* who did not take the position of 'Ā'ishah about *'aqrā'* being periods of purity. When a man divorces a woman in a period of purity, during which he did not have sex with her, she observes *'iddah* for the rest of it, whether it is only an hour or an instant. Then she starts another period of purity after her menstruation and then a third after the second menstruation. When she sees the blood of the third menstruation, she is lawful to marry and leaves her *'iddah*. If someone divorces a woman during a period of purity, during which he has had sex with her, the divorce is binding, but he has behaved badly and she observes *'iddah* for the rest of that period of purity. Az-Zuhrī said that when a woman is divorced in a state of purity, her *'iddah* is three periods of purity other than the rest of that period. Abū 'Umar said, 'I do not know of anyone who says that *'aqrā'* are periods of purity and then takes this view other than Ibn Shihāb az-Zuhrī. He said that the period of purity in which she is divorced does not count. Then she must observe three periods of purity because of Allah's words in the *āyah*.'

According to this view, a divorced woman is not lawful until after the fourth menstrual period. The position of Ibn al-Qāsim, Mālik and most of his people, ash-Shāfi'ī and the scholars of Madīnah is that when a divorced women sees the first drop of the third period, she is free of the bond. That is the school of Zayd ibn Thābit, 'Ā'ishah and Ibn 'Umar. Aḥmad ibn Ḥanbal also said that and it is what Dāwud ibn 'Alī and his people said. The argument against az-Zuhrī is that the Prophet ﷺ gave permission to divorce a woman in a state of purity without intercourse and did not stipulate the beginning or end of the period. Ashhab said, 'The bond and inheritance are not severed until it is certain that it is menstrual blood to ensure that it is not a single gush which is not menstrual blood. The Kufans argue by what the Prophet ﷺ said to Fāṭimah bint Abī Ḥubaysh when she complained of bleeding to him, 'That is a vein. Wait and when you see your menstrual period, do not pray. When the period passes, then purify yourself and then pray from one period to another.'

The Almighty says: *'In the case of those of your wives who are past the age of menstruation, if you have any doubt, their 'iddah should be three months.'* (65:4) This indicates that, in the case of the *'iddah* of a woman beyond the age of menstruation, the time is counted in months. 'Umar said in the presence of the Companions, 'A slavegirl's *'iddah* is two months, half that of a free woman. If you are able to make it one and a half months, do so.' No one objected to that. That indicates that it is their consensus. It is also the view of the Companions, including the first four caliphs. What they have said is enough for you! Allah's words: *'Divorced women should wait by themselves for three menstrual cycles,'* indicate that because it means to wait for three full cycles. This is only possible based on saying that they are menstrual cycles because if someone says that they are periods of purity, then it is possible to do an *'iddah* of two periods of purity and part of another because when she is divorced in a period of purity, she counts the rest of that period as a cycle. We believe that she starts from the beginning of menstruation so that the name holds true. When a man divorces her in a period of purity without having had sex during that time, she turns to a menstrual period, then another and then another. When she has a *ghusl* after the third period, she leaves the *'iddah.*

This is refuted by the words of the Almighty: *'Allah subjected them to it for seven whole nights and eight whole days'* (69:6). 'Eight' is feminine because *'yawm* (day)' is masculine. The same is true of *qur'*. This indicates that it is meant. Abū Ḥanīfah agreed with us that when a woman is divorced while menstruating, she does not count the menstrual period in which she is divorced nor the purity after it; she starts the *'iddah* with the menstruation after purity. We count by periods of purity as we already made clear. Linguists permit designating a part of something by the noun for the whole of it.

Some of those who say that it is menstruation say that when she is pure after the third menstrual period, the *'iddah* ends after *ghusl* and there is no right then for the husband to take her back. Sa'īd ibn Jubayr, Ṭāwūs, Ibn Shurbrumah and al-Awzā'ī said that. Sharīk said, 'When a woman delays the *ghusl* for twenty years, her husband can still take her back as long as she has not had a *ghusl*.' It is related that Isḥāq ibn Rāhawayh said, 'When a woman starts her third menstrual period, she is clear of the husband and he no longer has a right to take her back although it is not lawful for her to marry another until she has had a *ghusl* after menstruation.' Something similar is related from Ibn 'Abbās, but it is a weak position because of the evidence in the words of the Almighty: *'When their 'iddah comes to an end, you are not to blame for anything they do with themselves.'* (2:234) As for what ash-Shāfi'ī mentioned about the change from purity to menstruation being called *qur'*, the point of it is to shorten the *'iddah* for the woman. So when a woman is divorced in the last hour of purity and then starts to menstruate, she counts it as a cycle and at the change from the third period of purity, the bond is severed and she is lawful. Allah knows best.

Most scholars say that the *'iddah* of a slavegirl who menstruates is two menstrual cycles after her husband divorces her. It is related that Ibn Sīrīn said, 'I only think that the *'iddah* of a slavegirl is the same as that of a free woman although there is a past sunnah on that. It is more appropriate to follow the Sunnah.' 'Abd ar-Raḥmān ibn Kaysān al-Aṣamm, Dāwud ibn 'Alī and a group of the Ẓāhirīs said that the *āyah*s about the *'iddah* for divorce and widowhood in months and cycles are general to slavegirls and free women. So the *'iddāh* of a free woman and slavegirl is the same. The majority argue by the words of the Prophet ﷺ: 'Divorce of a slavegirl is two times and her *'iddah* is two menstrual cycles.' Ibn Jurayj related that from 'Aṭā' from Muẓāhir ibn Aslam from his father from al-Qāsim ibn Muḥammad that 'Ā'ishah said that the Messenger of Allah ﷺ said, 'Divorce of a slavegirl is twice and her cycles are two menstrual cycles.' Both divorce and *'iddah* are ascribed to her. However, only Muẓāhir ibn Aslam has this *ḥadīth*, and he is weak.

**and it is not lawful for them to conceal what Allah has created in their wombs**

'Ikrimah, az-Zuhrī, and an-Nakha'ī said that this refers to the concealment of menstruation. 'Umar and Ibn 'Abbās said that it is pregnancy. Mujāhid said that it is menstruation and pregnancy. This is on the basis that a pregnant woman can menstruate. The idea that is meant in the *āyah* is that the length of the waiting period (*'iddah*) depends on the statement of the women concerned and their word is accepted about whether the *'iddah* has ended or not. They are entrusted with that and it is what is meant by this *āyah*. Sulaymān ibn Yasār said, 'We were not commanded to investigate women and examine their private parts. That is up to them since they are entrusted with it.'

The reason for prohibiting concealment is to prevent harm to the husband and taking away his right. If a woman says, 'I have menstruated' when she has not, then she takes away his right to take her back. When she says, 'I have not menstruated' when she has, he is obliged to pay maintenance to which she is not entitled and she thereby harms him. Or she may intend by her lie in denying menstruation that he may not take her back until the *'iddah* is over and so cuts off his right. The same is true of a pregnant woman who conceals her pregnancy to cut off his right to take her back. Qatādah also mentions that it was the custom in the time of Jāhiliyyah for women to conceal their pregnancy so that the child could be ascribed to a new husband and that is the reason that the *āyah* was revealed. It is related that a man of the tribe of Ashja' went to the Messenger of Allah ﷺ and said, 'Messenger of Allah, I divorced my wife while she was pregnant. I do not feel safe that she will not marry again and my child will be attributed to another.' Then this *āyah* was revealed and his wife was returned to him.

Ibn al-Mundhir said, 'All that I remember from scholars is that when a woman says after ten days, "I have had three periods and my waiting period is over," her words are not believed or accepted unless she says that she had a miscarriage and that is clear.' They disagree about the time when the woman's statement is accepted. Mālik says that what she says is accepted if the period of time is reasonable for someone like her. There are two views when what she says is something that rarely occurs. We find in the *Mudawannah*: 'If she says she has had three periods in a single month and other women confirm it, she is believed.' That is what Shurayḥ said. 'Alī ibn Abī Ṭālib said to him, 'You are right and have done well!' He said in the book of Muḥammad, 'She is only believed after a month and a half has passed.' Abū Thawr said something similar. He said, 'The minimum for that is forty-seven days. That is the minimum fifteen days of purity and the single day for the minimum of menstruation.' An-Nu'mān said, 'She is not believed about less than sixty days.' Ash-Shāfi'ī said that.

**if they believe in Allah and the Last Day.**

This is a strong threat to emphasise the prohibition against concealment and to encourage women to fulfil the trust placed in them by telling the truth about what is in their wombs. It makes concealment tantamount to not believing in Allah. This is not the action of someone who believes.

**Their husbands have the right to take them back within that time, if they desire to be reconciled.**

The word used for 'husbands' here is the plural of the word *ba'l*. This word is used because of a husband's position in respect of his wife. We find in 37:125: *'Do you call on Baal?'* Baal means a lord or someone in a high position. *Bi'āl* means sexual intercourse and this is found in the words of the Prophet ﷺ about the days of *Tashrīq*: 'They are the days of eating, drinking and sexual intercourse.' The word *ba'l* can in fact be used for husband or wife.

The *'right to take them back'* can be exercised in two ways: one is during the waiting period, according to the *ḥadīth* of Ibn 'Umar, and the other is after the waiting period has come to an end, according to the *ḥadīth* of Ma'qil. If that is the case, then the *āyah* is evidence that the generality regarding those named has become specific. *'Divorced women should wait by themselves for three menstrual cycles'* is general in respect of women divorced three times and those divorced less times than that without disagreement. Then Allah says: *'Their husbands have the right to take them back.'* That is a specific ruling about someone whose divorce is less than three times.

Scholars agree that when a free man divorces his free wife, whose marriage has been consummated once or twice, he is entitled to take her back as long as her *'iddah* is not over, even if she dislikes him doing that. If the man does not take her back until the *'iddah* is over, then she is more entitled to herself and is not related to him. She is only lawful to him by a proposal of a new marriage with a *walī* and witnesses. This is not part of the sunnah of taking back a wife. This is the consensus of the scholars.

Al-Muhallab said, 'If the man takes his wife back during the *'iddah*, none of the rulings of marriage are necessary for him except for witnessing to the taking back. This is the consensus of scholars because Allah says: *'Then when they have reached the end of their* 'iddah, *either retain them with correctness and courtesy or part from them with correctness and courtesy. Call two upright men from among yourselves as witnesses.'* (65:2) He mentions witnesses in taking back but not in marriage or divorce. Ibn al-Mundhir said, 'What we mentioned from the Book of Allah and the consensus of scholars is enough in this area. Allah knows best.'

They disagree about what constitutes a man taking back his wife during the *'iddah*. Mālik said, 'When he has sex with her during the *'iddah*, intending to take her back, while being ignorant of having to declare that he has done that, that is taking her back. If the man has not made his intention clear, the woman should refuse intercourse until he declares that he has taken her back. Isḥāq said that. It is because the Prophet ﷺ said, 'Actions are by intentions, and a man has what he intends.' If he has sex with her during the *'iddah* without having intended to take her back, Mālik says, 'He takes her back in the *'iddah* and does not have sex with her until she is free of his false sperm.' Ibn al-Qāsim added, 'Even if her *'iddah* ends and neither he nor anyone else has had sex with her in the rest of the period of *istibrā'*. If he does that, his marriage is void but the prohibition between them is not perpetual because it was his sperm.' One group said that if he has sex with her, that constitutes taking her back. That is what Sa'īd ibn Jubayr, al-Ḥasan al-Baṣrī, Ibn Sīrīn, az-Zuhrī, 'Aṭā', Ṭāwūs and ath-Thawrī said. It is said that he should make a declaration. That is what is stated by the People of Opinion, al-Awzā'ī and Ibn Abī Laylā. Ibn al-Mundhir related it. Abū 'Umar said, 'It is said that his having sex with her is taking her back in any case, whether he intended it or not.' That is related from a group of the people of Mālik and al-Layth believed that. They do not disagree about someone who sells a slavegirl with an option of return that he can have sex with her during the period of the option. He takes back her ownership by that and chooses to break the sale by doing that.

If someone kisses or touches his wife with the intention of taking her back by that, it is a retraction. If he did not intend retraction by that, he sins and does not take her back. The Sunnah is that he should testify before having sex and before kissing or touching. Abū Ḥanīfah and his people said that if he has sex with her or touches her with lust, that constitutes a retraction. That is the view of ath-Thawrī. He should testify. In the view of Mālik, ash-Shāfi'ī, Isḥāq, Abū 'Ubayd and Abū Thawr, it is not a retraction. Ibn al-Mundhir said that. He said in *al-Muntaqā*: 'There is no disagreement about the validity of verbal retraction. As for action, like sexual intercourse and a kiss, Qāḍī Abū Muḥammad said that it is valid by this and any sort of pleasurable enjoyment.' Ibn al-Mawwāz said, 'It is like a touch for pleasure, or looking at her private parts or similar beauties when he intends retraction by that. This differs from the position of ash-Shāfi'ī that retraction can only be done verbally. Ibn al-Mundhir related it from Abū Thawr, Jābir ibn Zayd and Abū Qilābah.

Ash-Shāfi'ī said, 'If he has sex with her, whether or not he intends retraction, it is not a retraction and she receives an appropriate dower. Mālik said that she has nothing because if he takes her back, he does not owe any dower. There is no sex without retraction and no dower for retraction. Abū 'Umar said, 'I do not know of anyone who obliges him to pay an appropriate dower other than ash-Shāfi'ī. His position is not strong because she falls under the ruling of a wife and they inherit from each other. So how can a suitable dower be obliged for having sex with a woman when most of her rulings are those of a wife.' However, the judicial error in the view of ash-Shāfi'ī is strong because she is unlawful to him unless he takes her back. They agree that when someone has sex with a woman based on a judicial error, she is obliged a dower. That is enough!

They disagree about travelling with her before taking her back. Mālik and ash-Shāfi'ī said that he should not travel with her until he has taken her back. That is also the position of Abū Ḥanifah and his people except for Zufar. Al-Ḥasan ibn Ziyād related from him that he can travel with her before taking her back. 'Amr ibn Khālid related from him that he should not travel with her until he has taken her back.

They disagree about when he visits her without seeing any of her beauties and whether she can adorn herself for him. Mālik said that he should not be alone with her and only visit her with permission. He should not look at her unless she is fully dressed. He should not look at her hair. There is nothing wrong with him eating with her when there is someone else with them. He should not spend the night with her. Ibn al-Qāsim said, 'Mālik retracted that and said that he should not visit her or look at her hair. Abū Ḥanīfah and his people did not disagree that she can adorn herself, perfume herself, and wear jewellery. Sa'īd ibn al-Musayyab said, 'When a man divorces his wife once, he must ask permission to visit her and she can wear whatever clothes and jewellery he likes. If they only have one room, they put a curtain between them and give the greeting when they enter. Something similar is related from Qatādah. When he enters, he makes her aware by clearing his throat. Ash-Shāfi'ī said, 'A divorced woman who can be taken back is unlawful to her husband until he takes her back and that can only be by declaration.'

Scholars agree that when the man says after the *'iddah* is over, 'I took you back inside the *'iddah'* and she denies it, one takes her statement with her oath and he has no way to her. However, an-Nu'mān did not think that there was any question of an oath in marriage or retraction. His two companions disagreed with him and took a similar view to that of most scholars. The same is true when the wife is a slavegirl and the master and slavegirl disagree and the husband claims that he took her back in the *'iddah* after the end of the *'iddah* and she denies it. One takes the statement of the wife, even if the master says that she is lying. This is the view of ash-Shāfiʿī, Abū Thawr and an-Nuʿmān. Yaʿqāub and Muḥammad said that the statement of the master is taken and he is more entitled to her.

Rejection demands the removal of the bond although scholars say that a revocable divorce makes intercourse forbidden and the rejection refers to being lawful. Al-Layth ibn Saʿd and Abū Ḥanīfah and those who take their position that the retraction makes intercourse lawful: the point of the divorce decreases the number he has. The rulings of being married remain and none of them are dissolved. They said that even if the rulings of being a wife remain, as long as she is in her *ʿiddah* the woman is on course for their removal when the *ʿiddah* ends. Retraction turns away from this path that the woman is travelling. This is a metaphorical rejection and the rejection by which we judge is real. There is an achieved removal, which is the prohibition of sex and the rejection of it is real. Allah knows best.

The word 'right' is used in the comparative form here, '*aḥaqq*' (literally 'more right') because there are two rights in any conflict and one has to be preferred. So the husband has the right during the waiting period to take his wife back, which is not the case when the waiting period has ended. This is similar to the words of the Prophet ﷺ: 'A widow is more entitled to herself than her guardian (*walī*).' A husband is recommended to take his wife back, but that is provided that he puts things right between himself and her and removes the alienation between them. If he just desires to harm her more and to prolong her waiting period and to prevent her being free from the marriage, it is forbidden and the man concerned does wrong. Allah says: *'Do not retain them by force, thus overstepping the bounds.'* (2:231) If someone does do that, the retraction is nevertheless valid even though he does something forbidden and wrongs himself.

#### Women possess rights similar to those held over them

Women have rights over men just as men have rights over women. This is why Ibn 'Abbās said, 'I adorn myself for my wife as she adorns herself for me. I do not want to take from her all the rights she owes me for then I would be obliged to give her all the rights I owe her because the Almighty says: *"Women possess rights similar to those held over them to be honoured with fairness,"* in other words for their husbands to make themselves attractive as long as it does not involve something wrongful.' He also said, 'They are entitled to good company from and intimate relations with their husbands and they must obey their husbands.' It is said that their right is that their husbands should not cause them any harm and in return they should not cause any harm to their husbands. Aṭ-Ṭabarī said that. Ibn Zayd said, 'Fear Allah in respect of them as they should fear Allah in respect of you.' The meanings are close and the *āyah* is general to all marital rights.

Ibn 'Abbās said, 'I adorn myself for my wife.' Scholars say that a man's adornment is dependent on his state. Men do that according to what is seemly and appropriate. Sometimes adornment is proper at one time but not at another, and some adornment suits young men but not old men, and some suits old men but not young men. Do you not see that when old men and mature men trim their moustaches, it is seemly and adorns them, but when young men do that, it is ugly and unseemly because their beard is not yet full. If someone trims his moustache as soon as the hair appears on his face, it is silly. If his beard is full and he trims his moustache, that adorns him. It is related that the Prophet ﷺ said, 'My Lord commanded me to leave my beard and trim my moustache.' The same principle applies to dress.

This applies to all seeking of rights. A man acts according to what is seemly and appropriate with his wife in respect of adornment so that it delights her and makes her abstain from other men. The same is true of mature men: one type of adornment may be appropriate for some but not others. As for wearing perfume, using siwak and toothpicks, removing dirt, excess hair, washing and clipping the nails, that is clearly appropriate for everyone. Henna is for old men, and rings are adornment for all, young and old. That is the adornment of men, as will be made clear in *Sūrat an-Naḥl.* A husband must bear in mind the times when a wife needs a man to satisfy her so that she has no need to look elsewhere. If a man sees that he is unable to carry out his wife's right to sexual satisfaction from him, he should take medicines to increase his potency.

**but men have a degree above them.**

The root of the word *darajah* (degree) means 'to roll up'. A *darajah* is a step which one steps on to ascend. *Rijlah* means 'strength' and a horse that is '*rajīl*' is strong in walking. The extra degree of a man is on account of intelligence, power to spend and maintain, paying blood money, larger shares of inheritance, and *jihād.* Ḥumayd said that the degree referred to is the beard, but even if this is sound from him, it is weak because it is not implied by the *āyah* nor does the *āyah* mean it. Ibn al-'Arabī said, 'Bliss to the slave who refrains from what he does not know, especially when it concerns the Book of Allah! The superiority of men over women is not hidden from someone who is intelligent, even if it were not that woman is created from man, and so he is her root. He can prevent her going out without his permission and she may only fast with his permission and only make *ḥajj* with him.'

It is said that the degree is the dower as ash-Sha'bī said. It is said that it is the permission to discipline. Thus the degree entails preference. You should be aware that the right she owes to her husband obliges the right that he owes to her. That is why the Prophet ﷺ said, 'If I were to command anyone to prostrate to other than Allah, I would have commanded a woman to prostrate to her husband.' Ibn 'Abbās said, 'The degree indicates encouragement for men to be good company and expansive to women in money and character, because the one preferred must make greater efforts.' Ibn 'Aṭiyyah said that this is an outstanding and excellent opinion. Al-Māwardī said that it is possible that it is about marital rights because he can initiate divorce but she cannot and he can call her to bed while she cannot force him to respond. Related to that are the words of the Prophet ﷺ, 'If a woman is called to her husband's bed and refuses, the angels curse her until morning.'

*'Allah is Almighty'* with power that none can resist, and *'All-Wise'*, knowing what is correct in His actions.

ٱلطَّلَٰقُ مَرَّتَانِ ۖ فَإِمْسَاكٌۢ بِمَعْرُوفٍ أَوْ تَسْرِيحٌۢ بِإِحْسَٰنٍ ۗ وَلَا يَحِلُّ لَكُمْ أَن
تَأْخُذُوا۟ مِمَّآ ءَاتَيْتُمُوهُنَّ شَيْـًٔا إِلَّآ أَن يَخَافَآ أَلَّا يُقِيمَا حُدُودَ ٱللَّهِ ۖ فَإِنْ خِفْتُمْ
أَلَّا يُقِيمَا حُدُودَ ٱللَّهِ فَلَا جُنَاحَ عَلَيْهِمَا فِيمَا ٱفْتَدَتْ بِهِۦ ۗ تِلْكَ حُدُودُ
ٱللَّهِ فَلَا تَعْتَدُوهَا ۚ وَمَن يَتَعَدَّ حُدُودَ ٱللَّهِ فَأُو۟لَٰٓئِكَ هُمُ ٱلظَّٰلِمُونَ ﴿٢٢٩﴾

**229 Divorce can be pronounced two times; in which case wives may be retained with correctness and courtesy or released with good will. It is not lawful for you to keep anything you have given them unless a couple fear that they will not remain within Allah's limits. If you fear that they will not remain within Allah's limits, there is nothing wrong in the wife ransoming herself with some of what she received. These are Allah's limits so do not overstep them. Those who overstep Allah's limits are wrongdoers.**

**Divorce can be pronounced two times;**

It is confirmed that people in the time of Jāhiliyyah had no limit to the number of divorces they could pronounce although they did have a known waiting period (*'iddah*). It was the same at the beginning of Islam: a man would divorce his wife as often as he wished. Then when she was almost free he would take her back. Then during the time of the Prophet ﷺ a man said to his wife, 'I will not house you nor will I let you go.' 'How can you do that?' she asked. He said, 'I will divorce you and when your *'iddah* is almost up, take you back.' The woman complained about that to 'Ā'ishah and she mentioned it to the Prophet ﷺ and then Allah revealed this *āyah*, which clarifies the number of divorces a man can pronounce and then retract without having a new marriage with dower and *walī*. It superseded what they were doing. This was said by 'Urwah ibn az-Zubayr, Qatādah, Ibn Zayd and others. Ibn Mas'ūd, Ibn 'Abbās, Mujāhid and others said that the *āyah* is simply meant to establish the sunnah of divorce: anyone who divorces twice should fear Allah in the third and either leave her without wronging any of her right or keep her correctly. The *āyah* includes both possibilities.

Divorce is accomplished by the removal of the contractual bond between a husband and wife by means of the pronouncement of certain words. It is permitted by this *āyah* and others and by the words of the Prophet ﷺ in the *ḥadīth* of Ibn 'Umar, 'If he wishes, he may keep her, and if he wishes, he may divorce her.' The Prophet ﷺ divorced Ḥafṣah and then took her back. Ibn Mājah transmitted it. Scholars agree that it is sunnah to divorce when the woman concerned is free of menstruation in a period of purity in which he has not had sex with her. Then he follows the sunnah in the divorce and the *'iddah* which Allah has commanded. He retracts that if he has sex with her before the end of *the 'iddah*. If it has ended, then he becomes a suitor like any other. The Book, Sunnah and consensus of the community is that divorce is permitted and not prohibited. Ibn al-Mundhir said that there is no report that confirms a prohibition of it.

Ad-Dāraquṭnī related from Abu-l-'Abbās Muḥammad ibn Mūsā ibn 'Alī ad-Dūlābī and Ya'qāub ibn Ibrāhīm from al-Ḥasan ibn 'Arafah from Ismā'īl ibn 'Ayyāsh ibn Ḥumayd ibn Mālik al-Lakhmī from Makḥūl that Mu'ādh ibn Jabal said, 'The Messenger of Allah ﷺ said, "Mu'ādh, Allah has not created on the face of the earth anything dearer to Him than setting free a slave and Allah has not created anything on the face of the earth more hateful to Him than divorce. When a man says to his slave, 'You are free, Allah willing,' he is free without exception. When a man says to his wife, 'You are divorced, Allah willing,' his exception holds good and there is no divorce."'' Muḥammad ibn Mūsā ibn 'Alī related from Ḥumayd ibn ar-Rabī' from Yazīd ibn Hārūn from Ismā'īl ibn 'Ayyāsh with a similar *isnād*. Ḥumayd said, 'Yazīd ibn Hārūn said to me, "What a *ḥadīth* that would be if only Ḥumayd ibn Mālik al-Lakhmī were recognised!" I answered, "He is my grandfather!" Yazīd said, "You have delighted me, Now it is a *ḥadīth*!"' Ibn al-Mundhir said, 'Among those who believed that the exception "Allah willing" applied in divorce were Ṭāwūs, Ḥumayd, ash-Shāfi'ī, Abū Thawr and the People of Opinion. According to the position of Mālik and al-Awzā'ī, the exception is not permitted in divorce. That is the view of al-Ḥasan and Qatādah about divorce in particular.

**in which case wives may be retained with correctness and courtesy or released with good will.**

This means that you must do that or that it is obligatory for you to retain them correctly. '*With good will*' means without wronging her in any way with respect to her rights or overstepping in words. '*Imsāk*' (retaining) is the opposite of divorce. '*Tasrīḥ*' (releasing) means to let something go. It is used for combing the hair since the hairs are released from one another. It is also used for releasing livestock. The releasing referred to here either means to leave the woman until the waiting period of the second divorce has ended so that she has control of herself, as as-Suddī and aḍ-Ḍaḥḥāk said, or to divorce her a third time and let her go as Mujāhid, 'Aṭā' and others said.

The latter is more likely for three reasons. One is a *ḥadīth* in ad-Dāraquṭnī, reported by Anas that a man said, 'Messenger of Allah, Allah says, *"Divorce is twice."* Why does it become three?' He replied, 'Retaining with correctness or releasing with good will is the third.' Ibn al-Mundhir mentioned it. The second possibility is that the word 'release' is one of the expressions used for divorce. The third is that it is allowed by the verbal form of 'release' which is causative. Abū 'Umar said that scholars agree that Allah's words: '*...or released with good will*' is the third divorce after the second. It is also meant by His words: *'But if a man divorces his wife a third time, she is not lawful for him until she has married another husband.'* (2:230) They agree that someone who divorces his wife once or twice can take her back. After the third divorce, she is not then lawful to him until she has married another man. This is a firm ruling of the Qur'an about whose interpretation there is no disagreement. The same is also related from reputable people. Sa'īd ibn Naṣr related from Qāsim ibn Aṣbagh from Muḥammad ibn Waḍḍāḥ from Abū Bakr ibn Shaybah from Abū Mu'āwiyah from Ismā'īl ibn Sumay' that Abū Razīn said, 'A man came to the Prophet ﷺ and said, "Messenger of Allah, have you seen that Allah says, *'Divorce is twice.'* Where is the third?" The Messenger of Allah ﷺ said, *"Wives may be retained with correctness and courtesy or released with good will."*"' Ath-Thawrī and others related the like from Ismā'īl ibn Sumay' from Abū Razīn.

Aṭ-Ṭabarī mentioned this report and said that it is confirmed in its transmission.

He preferred the statement of aḍ-Ḍaḥḥāk and as-Suddī that the third divorce is mentioned in the course of His words: *'If a man divorces his wife a third time.'* (2:230) The third is mentioned in these words with the obliged separation and the prohibition only removed by another husband. So His words, *'released with good will'*, are a renewed point: the separation at the end of the *'iddah*. The goal of the *āyah* is to explain the number of divorces which oblige making her unlawful and superseding what was permitted of an unlimited number of divorces. If *'released with good will'* was the third divorce, the goal of causing the prohibition by three would not be clear since stopping at that would not indicate the separation which makes her prohibited without marriage to another. The prohibition is known from Allah's words: *'If a man divorces his wife a third time…'* and there the earlier words do not mean the third. If it had meant the third, then the following words would mean a fourth divorce because the *fā'* entails consequence.

Al-Bukhārī has a section on 'The one who allowed a triple divorce by the words of the Almighty: *"Divorce can be pronounced two times; in which case wives can be retained with correctness and courtesy or released with good will"*'. This indicates that this is the maximum number allowed. It is binding for the one who has constricted himself. Our scholars said that the imams of *fatwā* agree that a triple divorce can take place in a single statement. That is the position of the majority of the Salaf with the exception of Ṭāwūs and some of the Ẓāhirīs who believe that saying it three times in one statement is only a single divorce. This is related from Muḥammad ibn Isḥāq and al-Ḥajjāj ibn Arṭa'ah who said that nothing is obliged for him. It is the position of Muqātil. It is related from Dāwud that it does not occur. What is famous from al-Ḥajjāj ibn Arṭa'ah, the majority of the Salaf and the imams is that three must occur and there is no difference between saying the three together or separately.

Those who believe that nothing is obliged cite Allah's words: *'Divorced women should wait by themselves for three menstrual cycles.'* (2:228) This is general and includes every divorced woman except for certain specific ones. Allah also says: *'Divorce can be pronounced two times'* and: '*…wives can be retained with correctness and courtesy or released with good will.'* It is not binding for someone who divorces three times in one statement because it is not mentioned in the Qur'an.

Those who believe that it is a single divorce cite three *ḥadīth*s. One is the *ḥadīth* of Ibn 'Abbās transmitted by Ṭāwūs, Abu-ṣ-Ṣahbā' and 'Ikrimah. The second is the *ḥadīth* of Ibn 'Umar as transmitted by those who related that he divorced his wife three times in a single statement and the Prophet ﷺ ordered him to take her back and count it as a single divorce. The third is that Rukānah divorced his wife like that and the Messenger of Allah ﷺ ordered him to take her back. The retraction makes clear that it was considered as a single divorce. The answer to the *ḥadīth*s is what aṭ-Ṭaḥāwī mentioned that Sa'īd ibn Jubayr, Mujāhid, 'Aṭā', 'Amr ibn Dīnār, Mālik ibn al-Ḥuwayrith, Muḥammad ibn Iyās ibn al-Bukhayr and an-Nu'mān ibn Abī 'Ayyāsh related from Ibn 'Abbās that someone who divorces his wife three times in a single statement has disobeyed his Lord and his wife is parted from him and he can only marry her after she has married another husband.

Those imams related from Ibn 'Abbās that which agrees with the general consensus and indicates the weakness of what Ṭāwūs and others related. Ibn 'Abbās would not adopt his own opinion if it disagreed with that of the Companions as a whole. Ibn 'Abd al-Barr said, 'The transmission of Ṭāwūs is weak and an error which is not used as a basis by any of the *fuqahā'* of the regions in the Hijaz, Syria, Iraq or the east and the west. It was said that Abu-ṣ-Ṣahbā' is not known among the freemen of Ibn 'Abbās.' Qāḍī Abu-l-Walīd al-Bājī said, 'I think that the transmission of Ibn Ṭāwūs about that is sound. Imams have related it from him: Ma'mar, Ibn Jurayj and others. Ibn Ṭāwūs is an imam. The *ḥadīth* which they indicate is that which Ibn Ṭāwūs related from his father from Ibn 'Abbās: "In the time of the Messenger of Allah ﷺ, Abū Bakr and two years of the caliphate of 'Umar ibn al-Khaṭṭāb, divorce was three divorces in one. 'Umar said, 'People are hasty in a matter about which they should be slow. We should carry out something on them!' and he did so." The account means that they used to carry out a single divorce instead of what people do now with three divorces. The soundness of this interpretation is indicated by what 'Umar said, "People are hasty in a matter about which they should be slow." He disliked them innovating haste in divorce when they should be slow about it. If their state had been that in the time of the Prophet ﷺ, he would not have said it and there would have been nothing wrong in them being hasty about a matter in which they should be slow. The soundness of this interpretation is indicated by what is related from Ibn 'Abbās by a different path: he gave a *fatwā* that the triple divorce was binding when someone did it all at once. If this is the meaning of the *ḥadīth* of Ibn Ṭāwūs, then it is what we said. If the *ḥadīth* of Ibn 'Abbās is applied to the interpretation, no attention is paid to that statement. Ibn 'Abbās went back to the position of the majority and the consensus. Our evidence by way of analogy is that this divorce was carried out by someone with the power to do so and so it must be binding, the same as is the case if it is a single one.'

The interpretation of al-Bājī is what aṭ-Ṭabarī mentioned from the scholars of *ḥadīth*, that they used this single divorce which became three: they did not divorce in one go, but did so once in the entire *'iddah* so that the woman was clear and the *'iddah* ended. Qāḍī Abū Muḥammad 'Abd al-Wahhāb said, 'It means that people used to confine themselves to one divorce. Then in the time of 'Umar, they increased it to three.' The Qāḍī said, 'This is the closest to what the transmitter said: in the time of 'Umar people used to hasten to do three, so he hastened that for them, i.e. obliged the ruling on them.'

As for the *ḥadīth* of Ibn 'Umar, ad-Dāraquṭnī related from Aḥmad ibn Ṣubayḥ from Ṭarīf ibn Nāṣiḥ from Mu'āwiyah ibn 'Ammār adh-Dhahabī that Abu-z-Zubayr said, 'I asked Ibn 'Umar about a man who divorced his wife three times while she was menstruating. He said, "Do you know Ibn 'Umar?" "Yes," I answered. He said, "I divorced my wife three times in a single statement in the time of the Messenger of Allah ﷺ while she was menstruating. The Messenger of Allah ﷺ returned it to the Sunnah."' Ad-Dāraquṭnī said, 'All of them are Shi'ah. It is recorded that Ibn 'Umar divorced his wife once while she was menstruating.' 'Ubaydullāh said, 'The only thing contrary to the Sunnah is his divorcing her during menstruation.' Similarly Ṣāliḥ ibn Kaysān, Mūsā ibn 'Uqbah, Ismā'īl ibn Umayyah, Layth ibn Sa'd, Ibn Abī Dhi'b, Ibn Jurayj, Jābir. Ismā'īl ibn Ibrāhīm ibn 'Uqbah said that Nāfi' said that Ibn 'Umar did a single divorce. That is also what az-Zuhrī said from Sālim from his father, Yūnus ibn Jubayr, ash-Sha'bī and al-Ḥasan.

It is said that the *ḥadīth* of Rukānah is a muddled, severed *ḥadīth*. It has no authoritative *isnād*. Abū Dāwud related it from Ibn Jurayj from one of the Banū Abī Rāfi', among whom there is no one authoritative, from 'Ikrimah from Ibn 'Abbās. It says: Rukānah ibn 'Abd Yazīd divorced his wife three times. The Messenger of Allah ﷺ told him, 'Take her back.' It is also related by various paths from Nāfi' ibn 'Ujayr that Rukānah ibn 'Abd Yazīd divorced his wife with a triple divorce and the Messenger of Allah ﷺ asked him to swear to what he meant by it. He swore that he had only intended a single divorce and so he returned her to him. There is confusion regarding the name and the action. No one uses something like this as an argument.

Ad-Dāraquṭnī transmitted this *ḥadīth* by various paths in the *Sunan*. In one of them Muḥammad ibn Yaḥyā ibn Mirdās related from Abū Dāwud as-Sijistānī from Aḥmad ibn 'Amr ibn as-Sarḥ, Abū Thawr, Ibrāhīm ibn Khālid al-Kalbī, and another that Muḥammad ibn Idrīs ash-Shāfi'ī related from his uncle Muḥammad ibn 'Alī ibn Shāfi' from 'Abdullāh ibn 'Alī ibn as-Sā'ib from Nāfi' ibn 'Abd Yazīd that Rukānah ibn 'Abd Yazīd divorced his wife Suhaymah al-Muzaniyyah with a final divorce. He informed the Messenger of Allah ﷺ about that and said, 'By Allah, I only meant one!' The Messenger of Allah ﷺ asked, 'By

Allah, did you only mean one?' Rukānah said, 'By Allah, I only meant one by it!' So the Messenger of Allah ﷺ returned her to him. He divorced her a second time during the caliphate of 'Umar ibn al-Khaṭṭāb and a third time during the caliphate of 'Uthmān. Abū Dāwud said that it is a sound *ḥadīth*. What is sound in the *ḥadīth* of Rukānah is that he divorced his wife finally, not three times. There is disagreement about a final divorce as we will explain. So there is no argument. Allah knows best. Abū 'Umar said that the transmission of ash-Shāfi'ī from his uncle is more complete. The addition is not refuted by the sources and so it is obligatory to accept it because of the trustworthiness of its transmitters. Ash-Shāfi'ī, his uncle and grandfather were from the household of Rukānah. All of them were from the Banū 'Abd al-Muṭṭalib ibn 'Abd Manāf. They were people who knew the story.

Aḥmad ibn Muḥammad ibn Mughīth aṭ-Ṭulayṭilī mentioned this matter in *al-Wathā'iq*. He said, 'There are two types of divorce: the sunnah divorce and the innovated divorce. The sunnah divorce occurs in the manner that the Sharī'ah recommended. The innovated divorce is the opposite. It is to divorce a wife while she is menstrual or in post-natal lochia and to do three in one statement. If he does it, then the divorce is nevertheless binding.'

Then after the consensus that she is divorced, scholars disagree about what is obliged for someone after the divorce. 'Alī ibn Abī Ṭālib and Ibn Mas'ūd said that one divorce is obliged. Ibn 'Abbās said that. He observed that his word triple has no sense because he did not divorce three times. The word 'three' is allowed if he is reporting about the past and says, 'I divorced three times,' reporting about three actions that he did three times. It is as when a man says, 'Yesterday I recited the *sūrah* three times.' That is sound. If he recited it once and says, 'I recited it three times,' he is lying. That is also the case if he swears by Allah three times to repeat the oath: that is three oaths. If, however, he says, 'I swear by Allah trebly,' that is one oath. That is the case with divorce. That was stated by az-Zubayr ibn al-'Awwām and 'Abd ar-Raḥmān ibn 'Awf. We related all of that from Ibn Waḍḍāḥ and it is the position of the shaykhs of Cordoba: Ibn Zinbā', Muḥammad ibn Taqiyy ibn Mukhallad, Muḥammad ibn 'Abd as-Salām al-Ḥasanī, the unique scholar and *faqīh* of his time, Aṣbagh ibn al-Ḥubāb and a group of others.

Part of the argument of Ibn 'Abbās is that Allah separated the word 'divorce' in His Book. He said: *'Divorce can be pronounced two times,'* meaning the maximum number after which there must be either retaining with correctness during the waiting period or releasing. Releasing means to leave her without returning to her until the end of the waiting period. That is being good to her if there is regret between them. Allah says: *'You never know, it may well be that after that Allah will cause a new situation to develop'* (65:1), which means regret about separation and the desire to return. The pronouncement of three in one go is not good because it is abandoning what is recommended in something Allah has allowed. Allah mentioned divorce separated [in the *āyahs*] to indicate that when someone combines it in one phrase, he has left what is analogous in other recommended matters that indicate that. An example of that is when a person says, 'My property is *ṣadaqah* for the poor': a third satisfies that. In the *Ishrāf*, Ibn al-Mundhir says, 'Sa'īd ibn Jubayr, Ṭāwūs, Abu-sh-Sha'thā', 'Aṭā', and 'Umar ibn Dīnār said that if someone divorces a virgin three times in one statement, it is one divorce.' Sometimes they make an exception for a woman whose marriage is unconsummated and has no *'iddah* when he says, 'You are divorced three times.' Then she is clear of him as soon as he says, 'You are divorced,' before the 'three times'.

The same verb for 'release' is used in 33:49: *'Let them go.'* So this expression amounts to explicit divorce, according to ash-Shāfi'ī. Scholars disagree about the meaning of this and whether it is tantamount to divorce. Qāḍī Abū Muḥammad believed that an explicit expression must contain some form of the word 'divorce' like 'You are divorced,' 'I have divorced you,' 'Divorce is binding on you,' and other similar expressions which are used to allude to divorce. Abū Ḥanīfah said that. Qāḍī Abu-l-Ḥasan said, 'There are many explicit statements of divorce, some of which are clearer than others: *ṭalāq* (divorce), *sarāḥ* (release), separation, being unlawful, letting go and cut off. Ash-Shāfi'ī said, 'There are three explicit phrases which come in the Qur'an: divorce, release and separation. Allah says: "*...part from them with correctness*" (65:2), "*...released with good will*" and "*...divorce them during their period of purity*" (65:1)."

If this is affirmed, then there are two types of divorce: explicit and allusory. We have mentioned the explicit. That in which divorce alluded to is the other. The difference between them is that the explicit form does not require an intention. Divorce occurs by the mere articulation of the words. That which is alluded to requires an intention. The argument of those who say that 'unlawful', 'letting go' and 'cutting off' are explicit divorce is because they are so frequently used in divorce, to the point that it is common knowledge. Therefore the intention about divorcing is clear. Then 'Umar ibn 'Abd al-'Azīz said, 'If divorce is a thousand, nothing of it remains clear. If someone says, "Finally," then that is the furthest end.' Mālik transmitted it. Ad-Dāraquṭnī related that 'Alī said, 'The statements about letting go, being cut off, clear and unlawful constitute a triple divorce. The woman is not lawful to him until she has married another.' It has come from the

Prophet ﷺ that use of the word 'finally' constitutes a triple divorce. It comes from a path of transmission with some weakness in it which ad-Dāraquṭnī transmitted. It will be discussed in 2:231.

Scholars do not disagree that if someone tells his wife, 'I have divorced you,' it is an explicit divorce whether or not the marriage has been consummated. If someone tells his wife, 'You are divorced,' it is one unless he intends more than that. If he intends two or three, it is as he intended. If he does not intend anything, it is one divorce and he can take her back. If he says, 'You are divorced (*ṭāliq*),' and then says, 'I meant to say "fetter (*wathāq*)",' his statement is not accepted and it is binding for him unless there is some evidence that he is telling the truth. If someone says, 'You are divorced once and I will not take you back,' the words, 'I will not take you back' are baseless. He can take her back because he said 'once', not 'three times'.

They disagree about someone who tells his wife, 'I have parted from you,' 'You are let go', 'cut off', or 'clear,' 'Your rope is on your withers,' 'You are unlawful to me,' 'Rejoin your family,' 'I have given you to your family,' 'I have let you go,' or 'I have no way to you.' Abū Ḥanīfah and Abū Yūsuf said that they constitute a final divorce. It is related that Ibn Mas'ūd said, 'When a man tells his wife, "You are in charge of your business," "I give command to you," or "Rejoin your family," they accept it and it is one final divorce.' It is related from Mālik that if someone says to his wife, 'I have parted from you' or 'I have released you,' it is an explicit divorce, just as when you say, 'You are divorced.' It is related from him that it is an allusion that refers to the intention of the one who says it and he is asked about the number he meant, whether or not the marriage was consummated. Ibn al-Mawwāz said, 'The sounder of his two views is that it is one for an unconsummated marriage unless he intends more. Ibn al-Qāsim and Ibn 'Abd al-Ḥakam said that. Abū Yūsuf said that it is three and is like, 'I have slipped you off' or 'I have no authority over you.'

As for other allusions, Mālik considers them, when the speaker has no particular intention, to constitute a triple divorce in every consummated marriage and, in the case of an unconsummated marriage, only if there is a specific intention. If he swears that he only meant one, he is the same as any other suitor because he let go the wife with whom he had a consummated marriage and he only is free or cut off from her by three divorces. In the case of an unconsummated marriage, he is free and parted from her by one divorce. Mālik and a group of his people and a group of the people of Madīnah maintain that in all these expressions he has what he intends and divorce is obliged. It is related from him that it is only when the expression 'final divorce' in particular is used, rather than other allusions in which he does not intend that, whether or not it is consummated. If a man intends three, it is three. If he intends one, it is a final one and she has control over herself. If he intends two, it is one. Zufar said that if he intends two, it is two. Ash-Shāfi'ī said, 'He is not divorcing in any of those instances until he says, "The words I spoke meant divorce." He has what he intended. If he intends less than three, it is revocable. If he divorces with a final one, it is revocable.' Isḥāq said, 'All that resembles divorce is what he intends of divorce.' Abū Thawr said, 'It is a revocable divorce and he is not asked about his intention.' It is related that Ibn Mas'ūd did not think that there was a final divorce except in the case the *khul'* or *ilā'*. That is recorded from him. Abū 'Ubayd said that.

Al-Bukhārī has a chapter entitled: 'Chapter on if a man says, "I have parted from you," "I have let you go," or other expressions which indicate leaving or freeing, or that by which divorce was meant, it is according to what he intended.' This indicates the position of the Kufans, ash-Shāfi'ī and Isḥāq when he says, 'or that by which divorce is meant.' The argument in that is that any statement that can be construed as being divorce or not being divorce does not necessitate divorce unless the one who said it says that he meant divorce by it. Then it is binding on him by his affirmation. It is not permitted to nullify a marriage because they agree that it is sound. Abū 'Umar said, 'The position of Mālik about the meaning of a man's words to his wife, 'Go out,' 'I have released you,' or 'Your rope is on your withers,' varies. Once he said that intention concerning such statements is not taken into account and it constitutes a triple divorce and another time he said, 'He has what he intends in all of that, whether or not it is consummated.' I say that.

What the majority believe and what is related from Mālik is that intention in using these expressions is pivotal and the ruling is based on that. That is sound because of the evidence we have mentioned and the sound *ḥadīth* that Abū Dāwud, Ibn Mājah, ad-Dāraquṭnī and others transmitted from Yazīd ibn Rukānah: Rukānah ibn 'Abd Yazīd divorced his wife Suhaymah and informed the Prophet ﷺ about that and said, 'By Allah, I only meant one!' The Prophet ﷺ asked, 'By Allah, did you only mean one?' Rukānah said, 'By Allah, I only meant one!' So the Messenger of Allah ﷺ returned her him. Ibn Mājah said that he heard Abu-l-Ḥasan aṭ-Ṭanāfisī say, 'How noble this *ḥadīth* is!' Mālik said about a man who tells his wife, 'You are like carrion, blood and pork to me!': 'I think that it is final even if he had no intention. She is not lawful to him until she has married another husband.' Ash-Shāfi'ī thought that if he meant a divorce, then it was a divorce and whatever number of divorces he meant, and if he did not mean a divorce, it is nothing after he takes an oath to that effect.

Abū 'Umar said, 'The basis of this topic regarding every allusion to divorce is what is related about the Prophet ﷺ saying to a woman he married when she said, "I seek refuge with Allah from you", "You have sought refuge with One Who gives refuge. Rejoin your family." That was a divorce. When the Prophet ﷺ told Ka'b ibn Mālik to withdraw from his wife, he told her, "Rejoin your family," but it was not a divorce. This indicates that the expression requires an intention and the only ruling is according to what a man intended by what he said. It is like that with all allusions that can possibly give rise to separation and others.' Allah knows best. Most scholars say that there is no divorce on account of it unless that is what is intended by the speaker. Mālik said, 'Divorce is obliged by whoever intends divorce by any expression he uses.'

**It is not lawful for you to keep anything you have given them**

This is addressed to husbands. They are forbidden to take anything from their wives which might cause them harm. The *khul'* divorce is only valid when it is the man alone who has not done anything which would constitute grounds for divorce. Husbands are mentioned because the custom among people is that, in separation, a man seeks what he has given his wife as a dower and support. That is why men are mentioned.

The majority agree that taking a payment for divorce is allowed and they agree that it is forbidden to take anything belonging to the wife unless it is a case of disobedience and bad behaviour on her part. Ibn al-Mundhir related that an-Nu'mān said, 'If the disobedience or injustice comes from him and she asks for a *khul'*, it is allowed and he is a wrongdoer. What he did is not lawful but he cannot be forced to return what he has taken.' Ibn al-Mundhir says that this is contrary to the text of the Book of Allah and contrary to a firm report from the Prophet ﷺ, and contrary to what most scholars agree on. I do not think that if someone were told to exert himself to look for an error, he would find something worse that someone saying that the Book forbids something and then, having had that countered by a text, still saying that his view is permitted. Abu-l-Ḥasan ibn Baṭṭāl said that Ibn al-Qāsim related the like from Mālik. This position is contrary to the literal text of the Book of Allah and contrary to the *ḥadīth* about the wife of Thābit which will be dealt with.

**unless a couple fear that they will not remain within Allah's limits.**

In this *āyah* Allah forbids a man to take anything unless there is fear they will not establish the limits of Allah and he stresses the prohibition by a threat issued to the one who exceeds the limits. It means that each of them thinks that they will not be able to endure giving the obligatory rights to his or her companion due to the dislike she has for him or vice versa. This is not an objection to her ransoming herself, nor is there any objection to the husband taking what she pays. The *āyah* is addressed to the couple and the dual is used. 'Fear' here implies knowledge, so the inference is that they know that they will not be able to remain within the limits, and that is true fear. It is apprehension that something disliked is bound to happen. It is close to the meaning of supposition. Then it is said that 'unless they fear' is an exceptive severed from the general sentence. It means: if there is antipathy on their part, there is nothing wrong in them accepting *fidyah*. Ḥamzah recited '*yukhāfā*' [instead of *yakhāfā*] in the passive with the subject elided. The subject in that case is guardians and judges. Abū 'Ubayd preferred that since He said '*if you fear*' and so the fear comes from other than the couple. If the couple had been meant, Allah would have said '*khāfā*'. This is evidence for those who say that the *khul'* should be referred to the ruler.

This is the view of Sa'īd ibn Jubayr and Ibn Sīrīn. Shu'bah said, 'I asked Qatādah, "From whom did al-Ḥasan take the idea of presenting a *khul'* to the ruler?" He answered, "Ziyād. He was the governor of 'Umar and 'Alī."' An-Naḥḥās said, 'This is known from Ziyād. There is no sense in this position because when a man does a *khul'* from his wife, it is based on what they both consent to. The ruler cannot make him to do that. Therefore there is no sense in saying that it is up to the ruler.'

Abū 'Ubayd denied that he had a choice. I do not know that anything regarding a choice is more unlikely than the particle '*illā*' because that is not obliged by the inflection, the word, or the meaning. As far as the inflection is concerned, Ibn Mas'ūd recited '*illā an yakhāfa*' as '*takhāfā*'. In Arabic, when reference is made to someone where the subject is not named, it is said, '*illā an yukhāf*'. If the expression is '*yakhāfā*', then it must be recited '*khīfa*'. If it is based on the expression, '*in khiftum*', then it must be said '*takhāfū*'. As far as the meaning is concerned, it is not unlikely for someone to say: 'It is not lawful for you to take anything of what you have given them unless others fear...' So the *khul'* can be taken to the ruler. Aṭ-Ṭaḥāwī said, 'It is true that 'Umar, 'Uthmān and Ibn 'Umar allowed it to be carried out by other than the ruler. Just as divorce and marriage are permitted without a ruler, the same is true of the *khul'*. That is the view of most scholars.'

**If you fear that they will not remain within Allah's limits,**

The limits of Allah consists of what is obliged for them in respect of good company and affectionate fellowship. This is addressed to rulers, and mediators in this matter, even if they are not rulers. Not remaining within Allah's limits is when a woman makes light of her husband's due and does not obey him. Ibn 'Abbās, Mālik Ibn Anas and most *fuqahā'* say that. Al-Ḥasan ibn Abī 'l-Ḥasan and some people said that when a woman says, 'I will never obey anything you order, I will not have a *ghusl* on account of *janābah*, and I will not fulfill any oath to you,' then a *khul'* is lawful. Ash-Sha'bī said that it means 'if they fear they will not obey Allah.' That is due to anger with one another which makes them stop obeying. 'Aṭā' ibn Abī Rabāḥ said, 'The *khul'* is lawful as is taking property in cases where the woman tells her husband, "I hate you and will never love you." This is like: "*there is nothing wrong with a wife ransoming herself.*"'

**there is nothing wrong in the wife ransoming herself**

Al-Bukhārī reports a *ḥadīth* from Ayyūb from 'Ikrimah from Ibn 'Abbās that the wife of Thābit ibn Qays came to the Prophet ﷺ and said, 'Messenger of Allah, I do not fault him in respect of the *dīn* or his character, but I will not obey him!' The Messenger of Allah ﷺ said, 'Will you return his garden to him?' 'Yes,' she replied. Ibn Mājah transmitted from Qatādah from 'Ikrimah from Ibn 'Abbās that Jamīlah bint Salūl came to the Prophet and said, 'By Allah, I do not fault Thābit in respect of his *dīn* or his character, but I dislike ingratitude in Islam and I will not obey him due to my hatred of him.' The Prophet ﷺ asked, 'Will you return his garden to him?' 'Yes,'" she replied, and he commanded him to take his garden from her and no more. It is said that she hated him intensely and he loved her fervently. The Messenger of Allah ﷺ separated them by means of the *khul'* divorce and it was the first *khul'* divorce in Islam.

Ibn 'Abbās is also reported as saying that the first person to have a *khul'* divorce in Islam was the sister of 'Abdullāh ibn Ubayy. She came to the Prophet ﷺ and said, 'Messenger of Allah, my head and his head will never be joined. I lifted the side of the tent and saw him in a group and he was the ugliest and shortest of them and had the ugliest face.' He asked, 'Will you return his garden to him?' 'Yes,' she replied, 'and if he wishes, I will give more.' He separated them. This is the basis of the *khul'* divorce and it is accepted by the majority of *fuqahā'*. Mālik said, 'That is what I have heard from those who possess knowledge, and it is what is done among us. If a man does not harm his wife and is not bad to her and she wants to leave him, it is lawful for him to take whatever she pays to ransom herself as the Prophet ﷺ did with the wife of Thābit ibn Qays.'

If the antipathy is on his side, as it is when he oppresses her and harms her, he should return to her anything he has taken from her. 'Uqbah ibn Abī 'ṣ-Ṣahbā' said. 'I asked Bakr ibn 'Abdullāh al-Muzanī about a man who wanted his wife to pronounce a *khul'* divorce and he said, "It is not lawful for him to take anything from her." I asked, "So where are the words of Allah: *'If you fear that you will not remain within Allah's limits, there is nothing wrong in the wife ransoming herself'*?" "It was abrogated," he replied. "Where?" I asked. He said, "In *Sūrat an-Nisā'*: *'If you desire to exchange one wife for another, and have given your original wife a large amount, do not take any of it. Would you take it by means of slander and downright crime'*" (4:20)"' An-Naḥḥās said, 'This is an aberrant view outside of the general consensus. Neither of the two contradicts the other so that there is abrogation because *"If you fear..."* does not cancel the other *āyah* because, when they fear thus, the husband does not fall into the category designated by the words *"If you desire to exchange..."* because the latter is addressed to men alone.' Aṭ-Tabarī said, 'This *āyah* is one of judgment and what Bakr said is nonsense.'

Those who think that *khul'* is specific to the state of schism and harm use this *āyah*, and say that it is a precondition for *khul'*. They support this by what Abū Dāwud related from 'Ā'ishah to the effect that Ḥabībah bint Sahl was married to Thābit ibn Qays and he hit her and broke her jaw. She went to the Messenger of Allah ﷺ after the *Ṣubḥ* prayer and complained to him. The Prophet ﷺ summoned Thābit and said, 'Take some of her property and separate from her.' He asked, 'Is that proper, Messenger of Allah?' 'Yes,' he said. He said, 'I gave her the two gardens she has as a dower.' The Prophet said, 'Take them and separate from her.' He took them and separated from her. However, the position of the majority is that *khul'* is permitted without any complaint of harm as we see in the *ḥadīth* of al-Bukhārī and other *ḥadīth*s. The *āyah* is not a proof for it since Allah did not mention it as a precondition, but rather mentioned it because it is the usual case in the *khul'*.

The *āyah* also indicates the permission for taking, in a *khul'* divorce, more than a husband gave to his wife. Scholars disagree about this. Mālik, ash-Shāfi'ī, Abū Ḥanīfah and his people and Abū Thawr say that it is permitted to do whatever they agree on, whether that is less or more that he gave her. This is reported from 'Uthmān ibn 'Affān, Ibn 'Umar, Qabīṣah and an-Nakha'ī. Qabīṣah recited as proof: '*...there is nothing wrong in the wife ransoming herself.*' Mālik said, 'Doing that is not part of noble character, but I have not seen any of the people of knowledge express dislike of it.'

Ad-Dāraquṭnī related that Abū Sa'īd al-Khudrī said, 'My sister was married to a man of the Anṣār who married her in return for a garden he gave her. There were some words between the two of them and they took it to the Messenger of Allah ﷺ who said, "Will you return the garden he gave you and then he will divorce you?" "Yes," she answered, "and I will give him more." He said, "Return his garden to him and give him more."' We find in the *ḥadīth* of Ibn 'Abbās: 'If he wishes, I will give him more,' and he did not object to it.

One group said that he should not take from her more than he gave her. That is what was stated by Ṭāwūs, 'Aṭā', and al-Awzā'ī. Al-Awzā'ī said, 'Judges do not permit anyone to take other than what he gave his wife.' Aḥmad and Isḥāq said that. They argue by what Ibn Jurayj related from Abu-z-Zubayr that Thābit ibn Qays ibn Shammās was married to Zaynab bint 'Abdullāh ibn Ubayy ibn Salūl. He gave her a dower of a garden. The Prophet ﷺ said, 'Not more, but his garden.' 'Yes,' she said. He took it and let her go. When Thābit ibn Qays heard that, he said, 'I have accepted the judgment of the Messenger of Allah ﷺ.' Abu-z-Zubayr and others heard it. Ad-Dāraquṭnī transmitted it. It is related *mursal* from 'Aṭā' that the Prophet ﷺ said, 'The man does not take from a woman in a *khul'* more than what he gave her.'

In the view of Mālik, a *khul'* can be carried in exchange for unripe fruit, for a stray camel or runaway slave, an unborn child of a slavegirl and the like that and other unsure things which is not the case in sales and marriage. He can make a demand for all that. If it is sound, it is given to him and if it is not sound, he gets nothing. Divorce is carried out based on its ruling. Ash-Shāfi'ī said, 'The *khul'* is allowed [in this case] but he receives the appropriate dower.' Ibn Khuwayzimandād related that Mālik said, 'That is because when contracts involving mutual exchange contain an unsound reimbursement and have passed, then one refers to what is necessary in similar substitutes.' Abū Thawr said, 'The *khul'* is invalid.' The People of Opinion said, 'The *khul'* is allowed and he has the unborn child of the slavegirl. If there is no child, then he has nothing.'

In *al-Mabsūṭ,* Ibn al-Qāsim reported that he said: 'It is permitted in exchange for the fruits of his palm trees for a year or for what his sheep produce in a year.' This differs from the position of Abū Ḥanīfah and ash-Shāfi'ī. The proof for what Mālik and Ibn al-Qāsim say is the general nature of the words of the Almighty: '*...there is nothing wrong in the wife ransoming herself.*' By way of analogy, it is part of what he owns by gift or bequest and so it is permitted for it to be an exchange in the *khul'*, just as is the case with something known. Furthermore, *khul'* is a form of divorce, and divorce is valid without any recompense whatsoever. Since it is valid without any such recompense, then it is even more likely to be valid with unsound goods because the worst state of that which is spent is that about which one is silent. It is also true because marriage, a contract which makes something lawful, is not rendered unsound by unsound goods and so that is even more the case in divorce which destroys the lawfulness of a contract.

If she is given a *khul'* provided that she nurse her son for two years, that is also permitted. There are two views about the basis of the *khul'* being that she support her son after the two years for a known period. One is that it is permitted and that is the view of al-Makhzūmī and the view preferred by Saḥnūn. The second is that it is not permitted. Ibn al-Qāsim related that from Mālik and said that if the husband stipulated it, it is void and removed from the wife. Abū 'Umar said, 'Those who permit a *khul'* in exchange for a stray camel, runaway slave and the like of uncertain things make this permitted as well.' Other scholars of the Qarawīn say that Mālik did not forbid a *khul'* in exchange for maintenance for more than two years because of the uncertainty; he forbade it because it is a duty specifically for the father in every case and therefore he cannot transfer it to someone else. The difference between this and maintenance for two years is that the maintenance, which is for suckling, may be imposed on the mother while she is married and after the divorce if the father is in straitened circumstances. Therefore it is permitted to transfer this maintenance to the mother because she is subject to it. In *al-Mabsūṭ*, Mālik cited as evidence the words of the Almighty: *'Mothers should nurse their children for two full years – for those who wish to complete the full term of nursing.'* (2:233)

If a *khul'* occurs in a permitted manner, based on providing for the son, and then the child dies before the end of the period, does the husband have recourse to her for payment of the rest of the maintenance? Ibn al-Mawwāz related from Mālik that he cannot pursue her for anything. Abu-l-Faraj related from him that he can pursue her because it is his confirmed due which is the responsibility of the wife by *khul'* and it is not cancelled by the death of the child. That is also the case if he does a *khul'* for money: she is liable for it. The reasoning behind the first view is that he did not stipulate for himself any wealth with which to enrich himself, but the duty of the support of his child. Then if the child dies, he has no right of restitution from her at all. That is like a case in which a man voluntarily supports a child for a year and then the child dies: he owes no restitution at all because he intended to take on his support. Allah knows best. Mālik said, 'I do not think that anyone should be pursued for something like this. If he does pursue it, he can make a statement regarding that.' They agree that if she dies, then the child is supported from her money because it was a right established before her death and is not removed by her death.

If in the *khul'* a man stipulates the maintenance of her unborn child and that she will have nothing, he must support the child if she has no wealth to spend on the child. If she then later becomes wealthy, he can pursue her for what he spent and take it from her. Mālik said, 'It is part of the duty of the man to maintain his child, even if he stipulates that the mother will support it, when she does not have the wherewithal to do so.'

Scholars disagree about whether the *khul'* is a divorce or annulment. It is related from 'Uthmān, 'Alī, Ibn Mas'ūd and a group of Tābi'ūn that it is a divorce. That was stated by Mālik, ath-Thawrī, al-Awzā'ī, Abū Ḥanīfah and his people and ash-Shāfi'ī in one position. If someone intends two or three divorces by the *khul'*, that is binding for him according to Mālik. The People of Opinion said that if he intends three divorces, it is three, and if he intends two, it is one final one because it is one statement. Ash-Shāfi'ī said in his other view that if he intends divorce by the *khul'* and calls it divorce, then it is divorce, and if he did not intend divorce and did not call it such, that separation does not occur.' He said that in his Old School. I prefer his first position. Al-Muzanī said, 'It is the soundest in my view.' Abū Thawr said, 'When divorce is not named, then *khul'* is separation and not divorce. If it is called divorce, then it is divorce and the husband has the power to take her back as long as she is in her '*iddah*.'

Among those who said that *khul'* is annulment and not divorce unless it is intended are Ibn 'Abbās, Ṭāwūs, 'Ikrimah, Isḥāq and Aḥmad. For evidence they cite the *ḥadīth* of Ibn 'Uyaynah from 'Amr ibn Ṭāwūs from Ibn 'Abbās that Ibrāhīm ibn Sa'd ibn Abī Waqqāṣ asked him about when a man has divorced his wife two times and then does a *khul'* to part from her. Can he remarry her? He said, 'Yes, he can remarry her. The *khul'* is not a divorce. Allah mentioned divorce at the beginning and end of the *āyah*, and the *khul'* is between that and so the *khul'* is not divorce.' Then he quoted, *'Divorce can be pronounced two times; in which case wives may be retained with correctness and courtesy or released with good will.'* (2:229) Then he recited, *'If a man divorces his wife a third time, she is not lawful to him after that until she has married another husband.'* (2:230) He said, 'That is because if *khul'* had been a divorce, it would have been the third after the two divorces. And His words after that *"If a man divorces"* would indicate a fourth divorce. Then the prohibition would be connected to a fourth divorce.'

They also use as evidence what at-Tirmidhī, Abū Dāwud and ad-Dāraquṭnī cited from Ibn 'Abbās that the wife of Thābit ibn Qays obtained a *khul'* from her husband in the time of the Messenger of Allah ﷺ and the Messenger of Allah ﷺ ordered her to observe an *'iddah* of one menstruation. At Tirmidhī said that it is a *ḥasan gharīb ḥadīth.* Ar-Rubayyi' bint Mu'awwidh ibn 'Afrā' reported that she had a *khul'* in the time of the Prophet ﷺ and he told her to observe an *'iddah* of one menstruation. At-Tirmidhī said that the *ḥadīth* of ar-Rubayyi' is sound about her being ordered to observe an *'iddah* of one menstruation. He said that it indicates that *khul'* is annulment, not divorce because Allah says: *'Divorced women should wait by themselves for three menstrual cycles.'* (2:228) If it had been a divorce, it would not have been confined to one cycle.

If someone divorces his wife twice and then does a *khul'* from her and then wants to marry her, he can do that, as Ibn 'Abbās said, even if she had not married another husband, because he has only done two divorces and the *khul'* does not count. Someone who considers the *khul'* to be a divorce says that he is not permitted to take her back until she has married another husband because the three divorces are complete by the *khul'*. That is sound, Allah willing. Qāḍī Ismā'īl ibn Isḥāq said, 'How can it be permitted for a man whose wife has told him, "Divorce me for a sum" which he then does, to say that it is not a divorce? If he had put her authority in her hands without anything else and then she divorced herself, it would be divorce.' He says that Allah's words: *'If a man divorces his wife a third time, she is not lawful to him after that until she has married another husband'* are added to His words: *'Divorce can be pronounced two times'* because the words *'released with good will'* mean 'or divorced'. If *khul'* had been added to the two divorces, it would only be permitted to have a *khul'* after two divorces. No one says this.

Someone else said that their interpretation of this *āyah* is a mistake. *'Divorce can be pronounced twice'* gives the ruling of two times when it occurs other than in a *khul'*. It is confirmed that he can still take her back when Allah says: *'...retained with correctness and courtesy'*. Then He mentioned their ruling when it is by way of *khul'*. So the *khul'* refers to the two already mentioned since what is meant by them is to explain divorce in general, divorce in exchange for recompense, and a triple divorce with or without recompense after which the woman is only lawful after another husband.

This is the answer to the evidence of the *āyah*. As for the *ḥadīth*, when mentioning the *ḥadīth* of Ibn 'Abbās about one menstrual period, Abū Dāwud said that the *ḥadīth* was related by 'Abd ar-Razzāq from Ma'mar from 'Amr ibn Muslim from 'Ikrimah *mursal* from the Prophet ﷺ. Al-Qa'nabī related from Nāfi' that Ibn 'Umar said, 'The *'iddah* of a woman separated by a *khul'* is the same as that for divorce.' Abū Dāwud said, 'We believe that our action is based on this.' It is the school of Mālik, ash-Shāfi'ī, Aḥmad, Isḥāq, ath-Thawrī and the people of Kufa.

At-Tirmidhī said, 'That is the view of most of the people of knowledge among the Companions of the Prophet and others.'

The *ḥadīth* of Ibn 'Abbās about a single menstruation is *gharīb* according to at-Tirmidhī and *mursal* according to what Abū Dāwud mentioned about it being said that the Prophet ﷺ made her *'iddah* one and a half menstrual cycles. Ad-Dāraquṭnī transmitted from Ma'mar from 'Amr ibn Muslim from 'Ikrimah from Ibn 'Abbās that the wife of Thābit ibn Qays got a *khul'* from her husband and the Prophet ﷺ made her *'iddah* one and a half menstrual cycles. Here a cycle and a half is mentioned by Ma'mar while one menstrual cycle is also related from him. The transmitter was Abū 'Abd ar-Raḥmān Hishām ibn Yūsuf aṣ-Ṣan'ānī al-Yamānī. Only al-Bukhārī transmitted from him. The *ḥadīth* is unsettled in both its *isnād* and its text. It is not used to argue that the *'iddah* for *khul'* is one menstrual cycle. So the words of the Almighty: *'Divorced women should wait by themselves for three menstrual cycle,'* remain for every divorced woman whose marriage has been consummated except for special cases. At-Tirmidhī said, 'Some of the Companions of the Messenger of Allah ﷺ said that the *'iddah* for a *khul'* is one menstruation.' Isḥāq said, 'If someone believes this, it is a strong position.' Ibn al-Mundhir said, "Uthmān ibn 'Affān and Ibn 'Umar said that her *'iddah* is one menstrual cycle. That was stated by Abān ibn 'Uthmān and Isḥāq.' 'Alī ibn Abī Ṭālib said that her *'iddah* is that of a divorced woman. I take the position of 'Uthmān and Ibn 'Umar. The *ḥadīth* of 'Alī is not firm. We already mentioned from Ibn 'Umar that the *'iddah* for a *khul'* is the same as that for a divorce. It is sound.

The position of Mālik varies about the case of someone who intends to carry out a *khul'* without any recompense. 'Abd al-Wahhāb said, 'Mālik considers it to be a *khul'* and the divorce is final.' It also is reported that he said that it is not final unless there is recompense. Ashhab and ash-Shāfi'ī said that because it is a divorce divested of recompense and the number must be observed. It is revocable as it would be if he had said 'divorce'. Ibn 'Abd al-Barr said, 'I and the people of knowledge believe this to be the soundest of his views.' The reason behind the first is the lack of recompense in the *khul'* does not remove it from what is demanded. The basis for that is if the *khul'* is based on wine or pigs.

The woman with a *khul'* is the one divested of all she has received and the woman who ransoms herself does so with some of it and takes some of it. A woman who frees herself is the one who frees herself from her husband before consummation, saying, 'I am free of you, so be free of me.' This is the view of Mālik. 'Īsā ibn Dīnār related that Mālik said, 'The freed woman is the one who does not take anything or give anything. The woman with a *khul'* is the woman who gives what she was given and may give more. The woman who ransoms herself is the one who ransoms herself with some of what she was given while keeping some. All of this is whether or not the marriage has been consummated. If it is before consummation, then she has no *'iddah*. A woman who conciliates is like the woman who frees herself.'

Qāḍī Abū Muḥammad and others said that these four expressions refer to the same idea, even if their qualities differ in respect of occurrence. It is a final divorce whether or not it is named. She cannot be taken back in the *'iddah* but she can be married in the *'iddah* or after it with her consent and with a *walī* and dower, before or after having another husband. This is not the view of Abū Thawr because of the fact that she gave him something in exchange for control over herself. If the *khul'* divorce had been revocable, she would not have control over herself. In that case, the husband would have both the recompense and that for which it was given.

This is in spite of the fact that the contract is usually carried out. If she gives him recompense and he stipulates the right of retraction, there are two transmissions about that which Ibn Wahb related from Mālik. One is that it is affirmed, which is the view of Saḥnūn. The other is that it is denied. Saḥnūn said that the reason for the first transmission is that they both agreed on the recompense in compensation for dropping the number of divorces. This is permitted. The reason for the second is that he made a stipulation in the contract which precludes the aim of the contract, and therefore it is not confirmed as would be the case if he stipulated in the marriage contract that he would not have sex with her.

**These are Allah's limits so do not overstep them.**

After Allah has clarified the judgments of marriage and divorce, He says: *'These are Allah's limits...'* which you are commanded to obey, just as He explains those matters which are prohibited during the fast in another *āyah* and says: *'Those are Allah's limits, so do not go near them.'* (2:187) So He divided the limits into two categories: limits which one is commanded to obey and limits which one is commanded to avoid. Then He ends with the threat: *'Those who overstep Allah's limits are wrongdoers.'*

فَإِن طَلَّقَهَا فَلَا تَحِلُّ لَهُۥ مِنۢ بَعۡدُ حَتَّىٰ تَنكِحَ زَوۡجًا غَيۡرَهُۥۗ فَإِن طَلَّقَهَا فَلَا
جُنَاحَ عَلَيۡهِمَآ أَن يَتَرَاجَعَآ إِن ظَنَّآ أَن يُقِيمَا حُدُودَ ٱللَّهِۗ وَتِلۡكَ حُدُودُ
ٱللَّهِ يُبَيِّنُهَا لِقَوۡمٖ يَعۡلَمُونَ ٢٣٠

**230 But if a man divorces his wife a third time, she is not lawful for him after that until she has married another husband. Then if he divorces her, there is nothing wrong in the original couple getting back together provided they think they will remain within Allah's limits. These are Allah's limits which he has made clear to people who know.**

**But if a man divorces his wife a third time,**

Some of the Khorasanī Ḥanafī shaykhs used this *āyah* as evidence that the *khul'* should be followed by normal divorce. They said, 'Allah prescribed an explicit divorce after she has ransomed herself through *khul'* because the use of the particle *fā'* here is sequential. It is unlikely for it to refer back to: *"Divorce can be pronounced twice"* because the intervening words prevent: *"If he divorces her"* being based on it. It is more likely to refer to the exception close to it and it would only refer to something before that with some evidence as we see in 4:23.'

Scholars disagree about the divorce after the *khul'* during the *'iddah.* One group say that if a wife frees herself from her husband by *khul'* and then he divorces her again during the waiting period, the new divorce applies rather than the *khul'*. That was stated by Sa'īd ibn al-Musayyab, Shurayḥ, Ṭāwūs, an-Nakha'ī, az-Zuhrī, al-Ḥakam, Ḥammād, ath-Thawrī and the People of Opinion. There is a second view and that is that the second divorce bears no legal weight and is not considered. Ibn 'Abbās, Ibn az-Zubayr, 'Ikrimah, al-Ḥasan, Jābir ibn Zayd, ash-Shāfi'ī, Aḥmad, Isḥāq and Abū Thawr take this position. It is also the position of Mālik, although Mālik says, 'If she ransoms herself from him on the condition that he gives her a triple divorce consecutively, when he pronounces the divorce, then the full divorce has taken place. If there is a silence between that, what follows the silence is nothing. That is because the sequential and connected nature of the words demands one ruling. That is also the case when "Allah willing" is connected to the oath by Allah: it is preferred and the ruling of the exception is confirmed. When it is separated from it, then it is not connected to the previous words.'

**she is not lawful for him after that until she has married another husband.**

This is agreed upon and there is no disagreement about it. But there is disagreement about exactly what constitutes an intervening marriage and what it is permitted to be. Sa'īd ibn al-Musayyab and those who agree with him said that the contract itself is enough. Al-Ḥasan ibn Abī 'l-Ḥasan said that there must be ejaculation as well as sexual intercourse. A group of scholars and *fuqahā'* agree that sexual intercourse is enough, and that consists of the meeting of the private parts in the manner which would necessitate the *ḥadd* and *ghusl*, which would invalidate fasting and ḥajj, and which would make the payment of a full dowry obligatory. Ibn al-'Arabī said, 'I have not come across a question in *fiqh* more difficult than this one. That is because the basis of the legal position is contingent on what the ruling is connected to: the minimum to which it is possible to apply the term "marriage" or the full meaning of the term "marriage". If we say the minimum, then we take the position of Sa'īd ibn al-Musayyab. If it is connected to the latter, then there must be ejaculation and penetration, as al-Ḥasan said.'

Ibn al-Mundhir said that the term used in the *ḥadīth*, 'taste sweetness', means sexual intercourse and that is the position of the majority of scholars with the exception of Sa'īd ibn al-Musayyab who said, 'People say that she is not lawful to her first husband until she has had sex with the second husband. I, however, say that when he marries her in a sound marriage which is only intended to make her lawful, there is nothing wrong in her marrying the first husband.' We do not know of anyone who agrees with this statement except a group of the Khārijites. The Sunnah spares the need for anything else. Sa'īd ibn Jubayr took the position of Sa'īd ibn al-Musayyab. An-Naḥḥās mentioned it in *Kitāb ma'ānī al-Qur'an*. He said, 'The people of knowledge say that marriage here entails sexual intercourse because Allah says, *"another husband"*. Being a spouse was already mentioned, and so "marriage" must mean sexual intercourse. Sa'īd ibn Jubayr, however, said that marriage here is sound marriage when it is not with the simple intention of making her lawful.'

I think that what is most likely is that they had not heard the *ḥadīth* about 'sweetness' or believed that it was not sound and took the literal text of the Qur'an when Allah says: *'until she has married another husband'*. Allah knows best.

The imams like ad-Dāraquṭnī related that 'Ā'ishah said that the Messenger of Allah ﷺ said, 'When a man divorces his wife three times, then she is not lawful to him until she has married another husband and each of them has tasted the sweetness of the other.' Some of the Ḥanafī scholars said, 'If someone makes a marriage contract based on the position of Sa'īd ibn al-Musayyab, the qāḍī can nullify it. Disagreement regarding it is not considered because it deviates from the consensus of scholars.' Our scholars said that his words ﷺ, '...each of them has tasted the sweetness of the other,' means that they are equal in enjoying the pleasure of sexual intercourse. It is the proof of one two views. We believe that if he has sex with her while she is asleep or unconscious, she still is not lawful to the man who divorced her because she has not tasted 'sweetness'.

An-Nasā'ī related from 'Abdullāh that the Messenger of Allah ﷺ cursed those women who tattoo and are tattooed, those who add hairpieces and those to whose hair they are added, those who consume and pay usury and those who facilitate re-marriage and those for whom that facilitation is done. At-Tirmidhī related that 'Abdullāh ibn Mas'ūd said, 'The Messenger of Allah ﷺ cursed those who facilitate re-marriage and those for whom that facilitation is done.' He said that this is a sound *ḥasan ḥadīth*. This *ḥadīth* is also related from the Messenger of Allah ﷺ by a different path. It was the normative position among the people of knowledge among the Companions of the Prophet ﷺ, including 'Umar ibn al-Khaṭṭāb, 'Uthmān ibn 'Affān, 'Abdullāh ibn 'Umar and others. It is the position of the *fuqahā'* among the Tābi'ūn. It was also the position of Sufyān ath-Thawrī, Ibn al-Mubārak, ash-Shāfi'ī, Mālik, Aḥmad and Isḥāq. I heard al-Jārūd mention that Wakī' said, 'One must remove this topic from the People of Opinion.' Sufyān said, 'When a man marries a woman to make her lawful and then decides to keep her, she is not lawful to him until he marries her with a new marriage.'

Abū 'Umar ibn 'Abd al-Barr said, 'Scholars disagree about a marriage to facilitate remarriage. Mālik said, "A man who married to facilitate remarriage does not remain in his marriage until he has a new marriage. If he has sex with her, then she receives an appropriate dower. It is not lawful for her first husband to have sex with her, whether or not they know that he has married her to make her lawful for her first husband. He is not confirmed in the marriage and it is nullified." Ath-Thawrī and al-Awzā'ī said that.'

There is a second view about it related from ath-Thawrī about a marriage which is incorrect, or to facilitate remarriage, that the marriage is sound but the precondition is void. That is the view of Ibn Abī Laylā about that matter and the temporary (*mu'tah*) marriage. Al-Awzā'ī said that the marriage for facilitation is a bad action but the marriage is allowed. Abū Ḥanīfah, Yūsuf and Muḥammad said that the marriage is allowed if it is consummated and he can keep her if he wishes. Once Abū Ḥanīfah and his people said that she is not lawful to the first husband if someone married her just to facilitate that, and another time they said that he is lawful to her by this marriage provided he has sex with her and then divorces her. They do not disagree that a marriage of this kind is sound and he can maintain it.

There is a third view. Ash-Shāfi'ī said that when a man says, 'I will marry you to make you lawful,' then there is no marriage between them after that. This is a sort of temporary marriage. It is unsound and not confirmed. It is annulled. If he has sex with her on this basis it does not legalise re-marriage. If he marries her with a simple marriage in which there is no stipulation and he does not stipulate that it is to legalise re-marriage, ash-Shāfi'ī has two views on that in his old book:

one is like the view of Mālik and the other is like that of Abū Ḥanīfah. His view in his new Egyptian book does not vary: the marriage is sound if he makes no stipulation. That is the view of Dāwud as well.

Al-Māwardī related from ash-Shāfi'ī that if a man stipulates that legalisation is the object before the contract, the marriage is sound and he makes her lawful for the first husband. If they stipulate that in the contract, however, then the marriage is invalid and she is not lawful for the first husband. He said that it is the view of ash-Shāfi'ī. Al-Ḥasan and Ibrāhīm said that if any one of the three people intends legalisation by it, then the marriage is invalid. This is stricter. Sālim and al-Qāsim said that there is nothing wrong in a man marrying a woman to legalise her when the couple do not know about it and he is paid. Rabī'ah and Yaḥyā ibn Sa'īd said that. Dāwud ibn 'Alī said that: provided that it does not appear as a stipulation when the contract is made.

According to scholars, a marriage arranged with the ostensible purpose of legalising remarriage is permitted for the [second] husband who marries [the woman]. It is the same whether that was stipulated or intended [before the marriage], but when that actually occurs [for that sole purpose], then the marriage is unsound and not confirmed. His having sex with the woman does not make her lawful for her first husband. It is the same whether the first husband knows that or is ignorant of that. It is said that when he learns that the man married her for that purpose, he should not take her back. According to Mālik, she is only made lawful by a marriage in which he desires and has need of her and does not intend to legalise her. The new husband having sex with her [in that marriage] is permissible as long as she is not fasting, in *iḥrām* or menstruating, and he is an adult Muslim.

Ash-Shāfi'ī, on the other hand, said, 'If the new husband has sex with her on the basis of a valid marriage and fully consummates it, then they have tasted "sweetness". It is the same whether it is a strong or weak marriage and whether the consummation was achieved by his or her hand, and whether he was a child, adolescent or eunuch as long as he still has part of his penis, and whether the woman is fasting or in *iḥrām*.' This entire description of ash-Shāfi'ī is also the position of Abū Ḥanīfah and his people, ath-Thawrī, al-Awzā'ī, and al-Ḥasan ibn Ṣāliḥ, and it is also the position of some of the people of Mālik. Ibn Ḥabīb said that if he marries her and likes her, he can keep her. If he expects payment for making her legal, it is not permitted since he mixed marriage with the intention of legalisation. In that case she is not lawful for the first husband.

When a master has sex with his slavegirl who has been finally divorced by her husband, she does not become lawful for the first husband since the master is not a husband. That is related from 'Alī ibn Abī Ṭālib and is the view of 'Ubaydah, Masrūq, ash-Sha'bī, Ibrāhīm, Jābir ibn Zayd, Sulaymān ibn Yasār, Ḥammād ibn Abī Sulaymān and Abu-z-Zinād. That is also the position of most of the *fuqahā'* of the different regions. The opposite of that, however, is related from 'Uthmān, Zayd ibn Thābit and az-Zubayr. They said that when her master has sex with her in a manner by which he does not intend deceit or legalisation, she may remarry her husband with a proposal and dower. The first view is sounder because the Almighty says: '*...until she has married another husband*'. A master has control by virtue of ownership not marriage. This is clearer.

We find in the *Muwaṭṭā'* of Mālik that Sa'īd ibn al-Musayyab and Sulaymān ibn Yasār were both asked whether, if a man married a slave of his to a slavegirl who then divorced her finally and then her master gave her to him, she was lawful to the slave by virtue of ownership. They said that she was not lawful to him until she had married another husband.

Mālik related that he asked Ibn Shihāb about a man who was married to a slavegirl owned by someone else and then bought her and divorced her with a single divorce. He said, 'She is lawful to him by virtue of ownership as long as it was not a final divorce. If it was a final divorce, she is not lawful to him by virtue of ownership until she has married another husband.' Abū 'Umar said, 'This is the position of the bulk of scholars and imams of *fatwā*: Mālik, ath-Thawrī, al-Awzā'ī, ash-Shāfi'ī, Abū Ḥanīfah, Aḥmad, Isḥāq, and Abū Thawr. Ibn 'Abbās, 'Aṭā', Ṭāwūs, and al-Ḥasan said that if the one who finally divorced her buys her, then she is lawful to him by virtue of ownership based on the general nature of Allah's words: '*...those you own as slaves*'. (4:3) Abū 'Umar said, 'This is an erroneous view because Allah's statement: '*...those you own as slaves*' does not permit mothers or sisters or the rest of those forbidden by kinship.'

When a Muslim divorces his *dhimmī* wife three times and she then marries a *dhimmī* who consummates the marriage and then divorces her, one group say that the *dhimmī* is a proper husband for her and she can remarry the first husband. That is what al-Ḥasan, az-Zuhrī, Sufyān ath-Thawrī, ash-Shāfi'ī, Abū 'Ubayd and the People of Opinion said. Ibn al-Mundhir said, 'That is what we say because Allah says: '*...until she has married another husband*' and the Christian man is a husband. Mālik and Rabī'ah said that he does not make her lawful.

An invalid marriage does not permit a woman who has been divorced three times to remarry her first husband according to the majority position. Mālik, ath-Thawrī, ash-Shāfi'ī, al-Awzā'ī, the People of Opinion, Aḥmad, Isḥāq and Abū

'Ubayd said that she is only lawful for the first husband if she has entered into a valid intervening marriage. Al-Ḥakam said that this refers to the husband. Ibn al-Mundhir said that it does not refer to the husband because the spousal rulings of *ẓihār*, *īlā'* and *li'ān* are not confirmed between them. All of those scholars who are regarded say that if a woman says to the first husband, 'I have married and it was consummated,' and he believes her, she is lawful to him. Ash-Shāfi'ī said that it is scrupulous not to do it if he suspects that she is lying.

'Umar ibn al-Khaṭṭāb strongly condemned this practice of false marriage and said, 'If I am brought someone who makes remarriage legal or someone for whom it was done, I will stone them.' Ibn 'Umar said, 'False marriage in order to legalise re-marriage (*taḥlīl*) is fornication and people who do it are fornicators, even if they remain together for twenty years.' Abū 'Umar said, "Umar's words are only taken to indicate the severity of his position because it is clear that the *ḥadd* punishment is removed from someone who has unlawful sexual intercourse when he is ignorant that it is unlawful and has the excuse of ignorance. This is a more appropriate interpretation. There is no dispute that he is not stoned for it.'

**Then if he divorces her, there is nothing wrong in the original couple getting back together**

The word 'he' here refers to the second husband. If he divorces the woman concerned there is nothing wrong if she and her first husband remarry. Ibn 'Abbās said that there is no disagreement about this. Ibn al-Mundhir said that scholars agree that when a free man divorces his wife three times and her waiting period comes to an end and then she marries another husband who is free and the marriage is consummated and then he divorces her and her waiting period for that divorce ends, then she can re-marry the first husband.

They disagree about what happens when a man divorces his wife once or twice and then she marries someone else and then later remarries her first husband. One group say that she only has the number of divorces which remain from the time she was previously married to the man, as was stated by the great Companions of the Messenger of Allah: 'Umar ibn al-Khaṭṭāb, 'Alī ibn Abī Ṭālib, Ubayy ibn Ka'b, 'Imrān ibn Ḥuṣayn and Abū Hurayrah. That is also related from Zayd ibn Thābit, Mu'ādh ibn Jabal and 'Abdullāh ibn 'Amr ibn al-'Āṣ. It is also the position of 'Abīdah as-Sulmānī, Sa'īd ibn al-Musayyab, al-Ḥasan al-Baṣrī, Mālik, Sufyān ath-Thawrī, Ibn Abī Laylā, ash-Shāfi'ī, Aḥmad, Isḥāq, Abū 'Ubayd, Abū Thawr, Muḥammad ibn al-Ḥasan and Ibn Naṣr.

There is a second position that the marriage is new and divorce starts afresh.

That was the position of Ibn 'Umar and Ibn 'Abbās. That was also the position of 'Aṭā', an-Nakha'ī, Shurayḥ, an-Nu'mān and Ya'qūb. Abū Bakr ibn Abī Shaybah mentioned from Abū Mu'āwiyah and Wakī' from al-A'mash that Ibrāhīm said, 'The companions of 'Abdullāh used to say, "Is a marriage destroyed by three and not destroyed by one or two?"' Ḥafṣ related from Ḥajjāj from Ṭalḥah from Ibrāhīm that the companions of 'Abdullāh used to say that a single or double divorce annuls as is the case with three, except for 'Abīdah who said that a wife remains with the remaining unused divorces. Abū 'Umar mentioned it. Ibn al-Mundhir said, 'I take the first view.' There is a third view which is that if there was consummation in the last one, it is a new divorce and new marriage, and if there was no consummation, the number remains as it was. This was the view of Ibrāhīm an-Nakha'ī.

**provided they think they will remain within Allah's limits**

Ṭāwūs said, 'If they think that each of them will treat the other well.' It is said that the limits of Allah refer to what He has made obligatory, so it means when they know that there will be correctness between them in the second marriage. If the husband knows that he is unable to support his wife or pay her dowry or provide for any of her obligatory rights, it is not lawful for him to marry her until he makes that clear to her and knows that he will, in fact, be able to fulfil her rights. It is the same if he has a defect which prevents sexual enjoyment. This is so that he does not deceive the woman regarding himself. Similarly he must not deceive her about his lineage or wealth or work by lying about that. Similarly if the woman knows that she will be unable to carry out the duties owed by her to the husband or has a defect which prevents sexual intercourse such as insanity, leprosy or genital defects, she is not permitted to deceive him and must make that clear to him. This same principle applies to those who sell goods: they must make any faults clear. If one of the couple discovers a defect in their partner, they can reject him or her. If it is the man who has the fault, the woman keeps her complete dower if the marriage is consummated and half the dower if it has not been consummated. If the fault is with the woman, the husband returns her and takes back the dower he has given her. It is related that the Prophet ﷺ married a woman from the Banū Bayāḍah and discovered that she had leprosy. He returned her saying, 'You deceived me.'

There are varying views from Mālik about a woman who is frigid and refuses sex and whose marriage is ended because of that. Sometimes he says that she keeps all of her dower and sometimes that she only keeps half of it. This is because of the difference in his view about whether the entitlement to the dower is based on acceptance or consummation.

Ibn Khuwayzimandād said, 'Our companions disagree about whether the wife has to serve or not. Some say that a man cannot oblige his wife to serve and that is because the contract specifies enjoyment, not service. Do you not see that it is not a contract of hire or slavery? It is a contract of pleasure and what is entailed by the contract is enjoyment and nothing more and so more than that may not be demanded of her. Do you not see the words of Allah Almighty: *"But if they obey you do not look for a way to punish them"* (4:34)? Others among our companions say that she owes the service of a woman of her standing. If she is noble due to the wealth or lineage of her parents, she must manage the house and direct the servants. If she is middle-class, she must make the bed and the like. If she is less than that, she should attend to the house, cooking and washing. If she is a woman from the Kurds, Daylam and the mountains, she is obliged to do what their women are normally obliged to do. That is because Allah says: *"Women possess rights similar to those held over them to be honoured with fairness."* (2:228) The custom of Muslims in their lands, ancient and modern, is as we have mentioned it. Do you not see that the wives of the Prophet ﷺ and his Companions used to undertake grinding, bread-making, baking, making beds, serving food and the like? We do not know of any woman who refused to do that. She could not refuse and they used to beat their wives when they fell short in doing that and oblige them to serve. Had that not been an entitlement [at that time], they would not have asked for it.'

**These are Allah's limits which he has made clear to people who know.**

The '*ḥudūd*' (limits) are what He has forbidden. The root of the verb is used for confining and denying good. A man who is *maḥdūd* is deprived of good. The verb is used for a woman in mourning who is forbidden adornment. A doorkeeper can be called *ḥaddād*, because he prevents people from entering. The words *'a people who know'* are used because when someone ignorant is subject to a lot of commands and prohibitions, he will not observe them or abide by them. The one who knows will do so. This is why those who know are addressed and not the ignorant.

وَإِذَا طَلَّقْتُمُ النِّسَاءَ فَبَلَغْنَ أَجَلَهُنَّ فَأَمْسِكُوهُنَّ بِمَعْرُوفٍ أَوْ سَرِّحُوهُنَّ
بِمَعْرُوفٍ وَلَا تُمْسِكُوهُنَّ ضِرَارًا لِّتَعْتَدُوا وَمَن يَفْعَلْ ذَٰلِكَ فَقَدْ ظَلَمَ نَفْسَهُ وَلَا
تَتَّخِذُوا آيَاتِ اللَّهِ هُزُوًا وَاذْكُرُوا نِعْمَتَ اللَّهِ عَلَيْكُمْ وَمَا أَنزَلَ عَلَيْكُم مِّنَ الْكِتَابِ وَالْحِكْمَةِ
يَعِظُكُم بِهِ وَاتَّقُوا اللَّهَ وَاعْلَمُوا أَنَّ اللَّهَ بِكُلِّ شَيْءٍ عَلِيمٌ ﴿٢٣١﴾

**231 When you divorce women and they reach the end of their waiting period, then either retain them with correctness and courtesy or release them with correctness and courtesy. Do not retain them by force, thus overstepping the limits. Anyone who does that has wronged himself. Do not make a mockery of Allah's Signs. Remember Allah's blessing to you and the Book and Wisdom He has sent down to you to admonish you. Be fearful of Allah and know that Allah has knowledge of all things.**

**When you divorce women and they reach the end of their waiting period,**

The word '*balagha*' (reach) here means 'to draw near to' according to the consensus of scholars, because, if she actually reaches the end, her husband no longer has a choice about keeping her. It is a mutual prohibition in the *āyah* after it because the idea demands that.

**then either retain them with correctness and courtesy**

This means the husband must undertake to fulfil his legal obligations towards his wife. That is why a group of scholars said that an aspect of retaining with correctness is that if the husband does not have what is necessary for the maintenance of his wife, he must divorce her. If he does not do so, he is no longer in the right and the divorce can be forced upon him by the judge due to the harm she would suffer by remaining with someone who cannot support her. That was the position of Mālik, ash-Shāfi'ī, Aḥmad, Isḥāq, Abū Thawr, Abū 'Ubayd, Yaḥyā al-Qaṭṭān, and 'Abd ar-Raḥmān ibn Mahdī. It was stated by 'Umar, 'Alī and Abū Hurayrah among the Companions, and Sa'īd ibn al-Musayyab among the Tābi'ūn. He said that it is sunnah. Abū Hurayrah related that from the Prophet ﷺ.

Another group say that the couple are not separated in that situation and she must put up with that. Maintenance is made his responsibility by the ruling of a judge. That is the position of 'Aṭā' and az-Zuhrī and it is the position which is taken by the Kufans and ath-Thawrī. Their evidence is found in the *āyahs*: '*If someone is in difficult circumstances, there should be a deferral until things are easier*' (2:280) and: '*Marry off those among you who are unmarried.*' (24:32). So Allah recommends that poor people marry and so poverty cannot be a reason for separation. It is, however, recommended along with marriage. Also marriage between a couple is established by consensus and there is no separation except by consensus or an irrefutable sunnah from the Prophet ﷺ. The evidence for the first position is in *Ṣaḥīḥ Bukhārī*: 'The woman says, "Either feed me or divorce me."' This provides a text in case of dispute. We consider separation due to hardship to constitute a revocable divorce, differing from ash-Shāfi'ī who thinks it is final. This is because it is a separation after consummation when the number of divorces has not been used up, not in exchange for compensation nor due to harm on the part of the husband. Therefore it is revocable.

**or release them with correctness and courtesy.**

This means to divorce them as was already mentioned.

**Do not retain them by force, thus overstepping the limits.**

Mālik related from Thawr ibn Zayd ad-Dīlī that a man would divorce his wife and then take her back, having no need for her and not intending to keep her, but simply to make the waiting period longer for her and to thereby hurt her more, and so Allah revealed this.

**Anyone who does that has wronged himself.**

Az-Zajjāj says that 'wrongs himself' here means that he exposes himself to punishment by doing what Allah has forbidden. This report agrees with the report which was revealed about abandoning what the people of the Jāhiliyyah used to do in divorce and taking wives back as we mentioned earlier. These two reports tell us that the revelation of these two *āyahs* was about the same idea of a man keeping a woman and taking her back in order to cause harm to her. This is evident.

**Do not make a mockery of Allah's Signs.**

This means 'Do not mock Allah's judgments'. They are all serious. If someone mocks them, they are still binding on him. Abu-d-Dardā' said that in the time of Jāhiliyyah a man used to pronounce a divorce by saying, 'You are divorced and I am joking,' as he would do in marriage and emancipation. So Allah revealed this *āyah* and the Prophet ﷺ said, 'If anyone divorces, emancipates, marries or gives in marriage and then says, "I was only joking," what he said is taken seriously.' Ma'mar related it from 'Īsā from 'Amr from al-Ḥasan from Abu-d-Dardā'. We find in the *Muwaṭṭā'* that a man said to Ibn 'Abbās, 'I divorced my wife a hundred times. What do you think?' Ibn 'Abbās said, 'She was divorced from you by three, and you made a mockery of Allah's Signs in the ninety-seven.' Ad-Dāraquṭnī transmitted from Ismā'īl ibn Umayyah al-Qurashī that 'Alī said, 'The Prophet ﷺ heard a man do a final divorce and he became angry and said, "Do you make a mockery of Allah's Signs or the *dīn* of Allah and make a game of final divorce? We obliged that it is three and she is not lawful to you until she marries another husband."' This Ismā'īl ibn Umayyah is Kufan and weak in *ḥadīth*.

It is related that 'Ā'ishah said, 'A man used to divorce his wife and say, "By Allah, I will neither let you inherit nor will I let you go."' "How is that?" she asked. He said, "When you are about to finish your *'iddah*, I will take you back."' So the *āyah* was revealed. Our scholars say that all such expressions are included in what is said in this *āyah* because it is said of someone who mocks the Signs of Allah as well as someone who rejects them and someone who discards them and acts on another basis. Thus all are included in this *āyah*. The Signs of Allah are His proofs, commands and prohibitions.

There is no disagreement between scholars that, if someone divorces in jest, the divorce is binding but they disagree about other matters as will be dealt with in *Sūrat at-Tawbah*, Allah willing. Abū Dāwud related from Abū Hurayrah that the Messenger of Allah ﷺ said, 'Three matters are serious and jests about them are taken seriously: marriage, divorce and taking back in marriage.' It is related from 'Alī ibn Abī Ṭālib, Ibn Mas'ūd and Abu-d-Dardā': 'There is no jest in three matters and someone who plays with them is serious: marriage, divorce and emancipation.' It is said that it means: 'Do not abandon Allah's commands so that you fall short and are playing.' This *āyah* includes verbally asking for forgiveness while persisting in the deed. That is the case with everything of this sort, so know that.

**Remember Allah's blessing to you and the Book and Wisdom He has sent down to you to admonish you.**

The blessing is Islam and Allah making His judgments clear. 'Wisdom' refers to the Sunnah which makes things clear on the tongue of the Messenger of Allah ﷺ in respect of things about which there is no text in the Qur'an. He admonishes you to frighten you.

وَإِذَا طَلَّقْتُمُ النِّسَاءَ فَبَلَغْنَ أَجَلَهُنَّ فَلَا تَعْضُلُوهُنَّ أَن يَنكِحْنَ أَزْوَاجَهُنَّ إِذَا تَرَاضَوْا
بَيْنَهُم بِالْمَعْرُوفِ ذَٰلِكَ يُوعَظُ بِهِ مَن كَانَ مِنكُمْ يُؤْمِنُ بِاللَّهِ وَالْيَوْمِ الْآخِرِ ذَٰلِكُمْ
أَزْكَىٰ لَكُمْ وَأَطْهَرُ وَاللَّهُ يَعْلَمُ وَأَنتُمْ لَا تَعْلَمُونَ ﴿٢٣٢﴾

**232 When you divorce women and they reach the end of their waiting period, do not prevent them from marrying their first husbands if they have mutually agreed to it with correctness and courtesy. This is an admonition for those of you who believe in Allah and the Last Day. That is better and purer for you. Allah knows and you do not know.**

When you divorce women and they reach the end of their waiting period, do not prevent them from marrying their first husbands

Ma'qil ibn Yasār related that his sister was married to Abu-l-Baddāḥ and he divorced her and left her until after the end of her waiting period and then regretted it and proposed and she agreed to remarry him. Her brother refused to give her in marriage. He said, 'It will be unlawful for us to see one another if you marry him,' and the *āyah* was revealed. Muqātil said that the Prophet ﷺ summoned Ma'qil and said, 'If you are a believer, you will not prevent your sister from remarrying Abu-l-Baddāḥ.' He said, 'I believe in Allah and give her in marriage to him.' Al-Bukhārī related from al-Ḥasan that the sister of Ma'qil ibn Yasār was divorced by her husband. Her *'iddah* ended and he proposed to her. Ma'qil refused him and the *āyah* was revealed. Ad-Dāraquṭnī also transmitted from al-Ḥasan that Ma'qil ibn Yasār told him, 'I had a sister and proposals were made to me and I used to refuse her to people. A cousin of mine came and proposed and I married her to him. They were together for as long as Allah wished and he divorced her with a revocable divorce and left her until her *'iddah* had ended. Then he proposed together with other suitors. I said, "I kept her from people and married her to you and then you divorced her with a revocable divorce and left her until her *'iddah* had ended. Now you propose to me and come to me along with other suitors! I will never marry her to you!" So Allah revealed: *"When you divorce women and they are near the end of their 'iddah, do not prevent them from marrying their first husbands."* So I expiated my oath.' The variant of al-Bukhārī has: 'Ma'qil was angry out of pride and said, "He kept away from her when he could keep her and now he proposes to her again!" Allah revealed the *āyah* and the Messenger of Allah ﷺ summoned him and recited it to him and so he set aside his anger and obeyed Allah's command.' He was Ma'qil ibn Sinān. An-Naḥḥās said, 'Ash-Shāfi'ī related it in his books from Ma'qil ibn Yasār or ibn Sinān.' Aṭ-Ṭaḥāwī said that it is Ma'qil ibn Sinān.

If this is true it indicates that it is not permitted for any woman to marry without a *walī* because the sister of Ma'qil had clearly previously been married. If the matter had been left to her and not to her guardian, she would have married by herself and would have had no need of Ma'qil. So the words *'do not prevent'* are addressed to guardians. They are commanded to give the women concerned in marriage with their consent. It is also said that it is addressed to the husbands, because taking the woman back to cause her harm keeps her from marrying another and makes her waiting period longer. The people of Abū Ḥanīfah use it as evidence that a woman can give herself in marriage. They said that that is because Allah Almighty ascribes that to her as He says: *'She is not lawful to him after that until she has married another husband.'* (2:230) He did not mention a *walī*. This has already been discussed. The first position is sounder since we mentioned the reason for the revelation. Allah knows best.

The word *'reach'* in this instance really means that the *'iddah* has actually ended because initiating marriage is only conceivable after the end of the *'iddah*. The verb for *"prevent"* is *'aḍala*, meaning to restrain them. Al-Khalīl said that a *mu'ḍil* is a hen which cannot lay eggs. It is said that *'aḍl* is to constrict and prevent, from the meaning of confinement. The verb is used for being prevented from doing something. The verb *a'ḍala* is used for a matter when one cannot solve it. Al-Azharī said, 'The root of *'aḍl* comes from the verb used for a she-camel when the foetus is stuck and hard to get out, just as is the case with a chicken which cannot lay its eggs.

**That is better and purer for you.**

If you do that you will be righteous.

وَٱلْوَٰلِدَٰتُ يُرْضِعْنَ أَوْلَٰدَهُنَّ حَوْلَيْنِ كَامِلَيْنِ لِمَنْ أَرَادَ أَن يُتِمَّ ٱلرَّضَاعَةَ وَعَلَى
ٱلْمَوْلُودِ لَهُۥ رِزْقُهُنَّ وَكِسْوَتُهُنَّ بِٱلْمَعْرُوفِ لَا تُكَلَّفُ نَفْسٌ إِلَّا وُسْعَهَا
لَا تُضَآرَّ وَٰلِدَةٌۢ بِوَلَدِهَا وَلَا مَوْلُودٌ لَّهُۥ بِوَلَدِهِۦ وَعَلَى ٱلْوَارِثِ مِثْلُ ذَٰلِكَ
فَإِنْ أَرَادَا فِصَالًا عَن تَرَاضٍ مِّنْهُمَا وَتَشَاوُرٍ فَلَا جُنَاحَ عَلَيْهِمَا وَإِنْ
أَرَدتُّمْ أَن تَسْتَرْضِعُوٓا۟ أَوْلَٰدَكُمْ فَلَا جُنَاحَ عَلَيْكُمْ إِذَا سَلَّمْتُم
مَّآ ءَاتَيْتُم بِٱلْمَعْرُوفِ وَٱتَّقُوا۟ ٱللَّهَ وَٱعْلَمُوٓا۟ أَنَّ ٱللَّهَ بِمَا تَعْمَلُونَ بَصِيرٌ ﴿٢٣٣﴾

**233 Mothers should nurse their children for two full years – those who wish to complete the full term of nursing. It is the duty of the fathers to feed and clothe them with correctness and courtesy – no self is charged with more than it can bear. No mother should be put under pressure in respect of her child nor any father in respect of his child. The same duty is incumbent on the heir. If the couple both wish weaning to take place after mutual agreement and consultation, there is nothing wrong in their doing that. If you wish to find wet-nurses for your children, there is nothing wrong in your doing that provided you hand over to them what you have agreed to give with correctness and courtesy. Be fearful of Allah and know that Allah sees what you do.**

**Mothers should nurse their children for two full years – those who wish to complete the full term of nursing.**

After Allah has spoken of marriage and divorce He then speaks about children, since a couple may have children when they separate. So the *āyah* is about divorced women who have children by their ex-husbands. As-Suddī, aḍ-Ḍaḥḥāk and others said that, meaning that they are more entitled to nurse their children than other women because they will be more compassionate towards them and it is harmful to both mother and child to remove a small child from her. This also indicates that, even if the child is weaned, the mother is still more entitled to custody because of her compassion for it. She remains more entitled unless she remarries as will be mentioned.

This renders problematic the words: *'It is the duty of the fathers to feed and clothe them'*, because, if it is not a revocable divorce, divorced women are not entitled to clothing. They are entitled to a wage. Noble character, however, would ensure that the wage was adequate for both her food and her clothing. It is said that the *āyah* is general to both divorced women who have children and to wives. The most evident position is that it is about wives while the marriage remains, because they are entitled to maintenance and clothing, whether they nurse or not. Maintenance and clothing are according to the man's ability. If she is busy with nursing and he lacks ability, it might be imagined that maintenance is cancelled. To remove that idea, the Almighty says: *'It is the duty of fathers* – referring to the husband – *to feed and clothe them'* while they are nursing because, in doing it, they are occupied with the interests of the husband. So if she were to travel for what the husband needs with his permission, maintenance is not cancelled.

Nursing is mandatory for some and recommended for some. It is said that it is reporting about what is prescribed. People disagree about whether nursing is a right for or against the mother. The expression can mean either because, taken literally, it means that it is obligatory for mothers to nurse their children just as fathers are obliged to maintain them. But that is only while she is married and also only when custom demands it. If she is noble and wealthy, the custom is for her not to nurse. That is like a stipulation. If the child will not, however, accept another woman, then nursing becomes mandatory for her. This is also the case if no one else is available. If the father dies and the child has no property, the position of Mālik in the *Mudawwanah* is that the mother is still obliged to nurse without being paid a wage. Ibn al-Jallāb said that the wage should be paid from the Treasury. 'Abd al-Wahhāb said that that only applies when the father is a Muslim who is poor.

When a woman has been trebly divorced, she does not have to nurse and only does so if she wishes to. If she does so, she is entitled to a suitable wage if the husband is wealthy. If he does not have wealth, he cannot oblige her to nurse unless she is the only one the child will accept. If she is obliged to nurse and some excuse arises which prevents her from doing so, nursing then becomes the father's responsibility. It is related from Mālik that if he is poor and the child has no property the mother must nurse. If she has no milk and has wealth, the child is nursed at her expense. Ash-Shāfi'ī said that paying for nursing is only mandatory for the father or grandfather. This will be further discussed later.

The words *'two full years'* denote a measure of time that revolves in a full cycle. The word for 'year,' *ḥawl*, comes from the verb *ḥāla*, which means 'to be transferred, so a 'year' is transferred from one moment to another. It is also said that it is called that because it is normal period for the transformation of things. The word 'full' is added because the word 'year' by itself can be used for less than a complete year, so 'two years' can actually be a year and part of another year. Allah says: *'those who hurry on in two days'* (2:203) and that is actually in a day and part of another day. Allah's words: *'those who wish to complete the full term of nursing'* indicates that the two full years is not a definitive term. Weaning can take place before the two years are up. A limit is set merely to eliminate any dispute between the couple about the length of nursing. The father does not have to pay for more than two years and, if the father wants the child to be weaned before two years and the mother does not consent, he cannot enforce that. An increase or decrease in the two years can be made provided that the child is not harmed and that the parents agree.

Mālik and those who follow him and another group of scholars deduce from this *āyah* that the nursing which creates a milk relationship only occurs within this first two year period and ends when those two years end, so that any nursing after that is not considered. He states that in the *Muwaṭṭā'*. Muḥammad ibn 'Abd al-Ḥakam related it from him. It is the position of Ibn 'Umar and Ibn 'Abbās. It is related from Ibn Mas'ūd and was also stated by az-Zuhrī, Qatādah, ash-Sha'bī, Sufyān ath-Thawrī, al-Awzā'ī, ash-Shāfi'ī, Aḥmad, Isḥāq, Abū Yūsuf, Muḥammad and Abū Thawr. Ibn 'Abd al-Ḥakam related from him that it is two years and a few days more. 'Abd al-Malik said that it is like a month or so more. Ibn al-Qāsim related that saying, 'Nursing is two years, and two months after the two years.' Al-Walīd ibn Muslim related that he said, 'A month or two or three after the two years is part of the two years. What is after that is of no consequence.' It is related that an-Nu'mān said, 'Nursing up to six months after the two years is still considered nursing. The first view is the sound one since Allah says: *"Mothers should nurse their children for two full years."* This indicates that no ruling is attached to it when the child is nursed after the two years.' Sufyān related from 'Amr ibn Dīnār from Ibn 'Abbās that the Messenger of Allah ﷺ said, 'Suckling is only in the first two years.' Ad-Dāraquṭnī said that only al-Haytham ibn Jamīl has it from Ibn 'Uyaynah. He is trustworthy with good memory.

This report, the *āyah* and the meaning make it clear that an adult cannot be suckled. It has no standing. The statement that they can was related from 'Ā'ishah. Among scholars, al-Layth ibn Sa'd said that. It is related that Abū Mūsā al-Ash'arī thought that an adult could receive suckling, and then it is related that he retracted that. This will be explained in *Sūrat an-Nisā'*.

A group of commentators say that the period of suckling is two years for each child. It is related from Ibn 'Abbās that that is when the child is in the womb for six months. If it remains for seven months, the nursing period is twenty-three months. If it is nine months, the nursing is twenty-one months going by Allah's words: *'His bearing and weaning is thirty months.'* (46:15) So the period of pregnancy and the period of nursing are interconnected and one reduces the length of the other.

**It is the duty of the fathers to feed and clothe them with correctness and courtesy – no self is charged with more than it can bear.**

'*Rizq*' in this ruling is adequate food. This is evidence for the obligation of the father to maintain the child since it is weak. The feeding referred to is the nourishment which reaches the child by means of the mother through nursing. Scholars agree that a man must support all his children who have no money. When Hind bint 'Utbah told the Prophet ﷺ, 'Abū Sufyān is miserly and does not give me adequate maintenance and what is enough for my son. If I take from his property without his knowledge, do I do anything wrong?' he told her, 'Take what is adequate for you and your child in a correct manner.' '*Kiswah*' is clothing. '*Ma'rūf*' (correctness) means what is customary in the usage of the Sharī'ah without excess or negligence. Then Allah made it clear that a man's duty of maintenance is according to his wealth and position, and that no specific amount is stipulated, by His words: '*no self is charged with more than it can bear.*' This will be clarified later. It is said that it means that a woman should not made to endure stinting in her wage and a husband should not be forced to be extravagant. Rather the basic aim should be taken into account.

Mālik thought that this *āyah* indicates that a mother should have custody of her sons until puberty and of her daughters until marriage. That is her right, and Abū Ḥanīfah stated the same. Ash-Shāfi'ī said that when the child is eight years old, which is the age of discrimination, it is given a choice between his parents. At that stage its interest and desire should be stimulated to learn the Qur'an, manners and the duties of worship. That is the same for both boys and girls.

An-Nasā'ī and others reported from Abū Hurayrah that a woman came to the Prophet ﷺ and said, 'My husband wants to take my son.' The Prophet ﷺ said to him, 'This is your father and this is your mother: choose whichever of them you want,' and he took his mother's hand. We find in Abū Dāwud that Abū Hurayrah said, 'A woman went to the Messenger of Allah ﷺ while I was sitting with him and she said, "Messenger of Allah, my husband wants to take my son. He brings me water from the well of Abū 'Inabah and helps me." The Prophet ﷺ said, "Draw lots for him." Her husband exclaimed, "Who contends with me for my son?" The Prophet ﷺ said, "This is your father and this is your mother: choose whichever of them you want," and he took his mother's hand and went with her.' Our evidence is what Abū Dāwud related, that al-Awzā'ī related from 'Amr ibn Shu'ayb from his father from his grandfather 'Abdullāh ibn 'Amr that a woman came to the Prophet ﷺ and said, 'Messenger of Allah, my womb was a vessel for this son of mine, my breasts a source of drink for him, and my lap a protection for him. His father has divorced me and wants to take him away from me.' The Messenger of Allah ﷺ said, 'You are more entitled to him as long as you do not marry.' Ibn al-Mundhir said, 'The consensus of eminent scholars is that when a couple separate and have a child, the mother is more entitled to it as long as she does not remarry.' Abū 'Umar said, 'I do not know of any disagreement among scholars that a divorced woman, as long as she does not marry again, is more entitled to her child than the father, while he is still young and lacking discrimination; this is when he is safe with her and sufficiently supported and no dissoluteness or ostentation is confirmed about her.'

They disagree about the child being given a choice when he understands the situation and who is most entitled to look after the child then. Ibn al-Mundhir said, 'It is confirmed that the Prophet ﷺ judged that the daughter of Ḥamzah should go to her maternal aunt. The Prophet did not give a choice to Ḥamzah's daughter.' Abū Dāwud reports that when Zayd ibn Ḥārithah went to Makkah and brought Ḥamzah's daughter, Ja'far said, 'I am more entitled to her. She is my uncle's daughter and her maternal aunt is married to me, and that maternal aunt is also a mother.' 'Alī said, 'I am more entitled to care for her. She is my uncle's daughter and I am married to the daughter of the Messenger of Allah ﷺ and she is more entitled to her.' Zayd said, 'I am more entitled to her. I went and travelled to get her and brought her!' The Prophet ﷺ said, 'I judge the girl to go to Ja'far so she can be with her maternal aunt. The maternal aunt is in the position of the mother.'

Ibn al-Mundhir said, 'The esteemed people of knowledge agree that a mother does not have the right to the child when she remarries.' That is what he states in *Kitāb al-Ashrāf*. Qāḍī 'Abd al-Wahhāb mentioned in his commentary on the *Risālah* from al-Ḥasan that her right to custody is not cancelled simply by marriage. Mālik, ash-Shāfi'ī, an-Nu'mān and Abū Thawr agree that the mother's mother is most entitled to the custody of the child [after the mother]. They disagree about when she has no mother but the father's mother is available. Mālik said, 'The father's mother is more entitled when the child has no maternal aunt.' Ibn al-Qāsim said that Mālik said, 'I have heard that the maternal aunt is more entitled to custody than the father's mother.' In the view of ash-Shāfi'ī and an-Nu'mān the father's mother is more entitled than the maternal aunt. It is said that the father is more entitled to his son than the father's mother. Abū 'Umar said, 'I believe that this is the case when he does not have another wife.'

Then the sister is next after the father and then the paternal aunt. This is when each of those can be trusted with the child and it is in a state of security and adequacy with them. When that is not the case, there is no right to custody. In awarding custody one investigates who will protect the child, be good to him in preserving him and teaching him good. This is the position of those who say that custody is the right of the child. That is related from Mālik and a group of his people also said that. They also do not think that custody should be granted to a reprobate woman or one who is too weak to look after the child's right due to illness or chronic illness.

Ibn Ḥabīb mentioned from Muṭarrif and Ibn al-Mājishūn from Mālik that custody goes first to the mother, then the mother's mother, then the maternal aunt, then the father's mother, then the child's sister, then the child's paternal aunt, then the daughter of the child's brother, then the father. The father's mother is more entitled than the sister. The sister is more entitled than the paternal aunt. The paternal aunt is more entitled than those who come after her. The most entitled of men are the guardians. There is no right to custody for an aunt's daughter or the daughters of the child's sister.

When it is not feared that the guardian may cause the death of the child or cause corruption to him, he remains his guardian until he reaches puberty. It is also said that it only lasts until the child looses his milk-teeth. In the case of a girl, it is until she marries. This is the case unless the father wants to travel and resettle somewhere else. In that case, he is more entitled to the child than the mother and others if they do not wish to move. If he wants to leave for the sake of trading, he does not have the right to the child's custody. The same is true of the relatives of the child, to whom he has been allotted, when they move with the intention of resettling. The mother cannot move her child from the place where the father resides except for a short distance, such that it would not entail shortening the prayer. When the father moves from the mother's land and stipulates that he will not leave his child with her unless she is responsible for his maintenance and support for a number of known years and she takes that on, it is binding on her. If she dies, however, her heirs are not pursued for that maintenance and support from her estate. It is also said, however, that it does constitute a debt that should be taken from her estate. The first view is sounder, Allah willing. That is also the case if the father dies, or if he made an agreement with her for the support of pregnancy and nursing: it is cancelled and she is not pursued for any of that.

According to Mālik, if the mother remarries, the child is not removed from her until the marriage is consummated. Ash-Shāfi'ī said, 'When she marries, her right is severed.' If her husband then divorces her, according to what we think is the best known position of Mālik in his school, custody does not then revert to her. Qāḍī Ismā'īl and Ibn Khuwayzimandād mentioned that Mālik's position about that varied. Sometimes he said that the child is returned to her and sometimes he said that it is not. Ibn al-Mundhir said, 'If the mother leaves the land where her child is and then returns to it, she is more entitled to her child according to ash-Shāfi'ī, Abū Thawr and the People of Opinion. That is also the case if she marries and then is divorced or widowed: her right to the child is restored.' That is like the position of Qāḍī Abū Muḥammad 'Abd al-Wahhāb. If she is divorced or widowed, she can take the child back since the pretext for removing it no longer exists.

When a mother forgoes the right to custody and she is not married to another man and then later wants to take the child back, she can only do so if she had a legitimate excuse for what she did. If she left it out of dislike for the child, then she cannot take it back.

They disagree about what happens to a couple who are divorced when the wife is a *dhimmī*. One group say that there is no difference between a *dhimmī* and Muslim mother: they are both entitled to their child. This is the position of Abū Thawr, the People of Opinion, and Ibn al-Qāsim, the follower of Mālik. Ibn al-Mundhir says that there is a *marfū' ḥadīth* which states this, although there is some dispute about its *isnād*. The other position is that the child remains with the Muslim parent. This is the position of Mālik, Sawwār, and Ibn al-Qāsim, and is reported from ash-Shāfi'ī. There is the same disagreement when one of the couple is free and the other a slave. One group said that the free parent is more entitled to custody. This is the view of 'Aṭā', ath-Thawrī, ash-Shāfi'ī, and People of Opinion. Mālik said, 'If the father is free, the child is free, and the mother is a slave, then the mother is more entitled to custody unless she is sold and moves. Then the father is more entitled.

**No mother should be put under pressure in respect of her child nor any father in respect of his child.**

The mother should not refuse to nurse her child in order to harm the father or ask for more than an appropriate wage and it is not lawful for the father to refuse to let the mother nurse when she wants to. This is the position of the majority of commentators. Nāfi', 'Āṣim, Ḥamzah and al-Kisā'ī recited '*tuḍārra*' ('put under pressure') in the jussive because it is a firm prohibition. It means: 'Do not remove the child from her if she is content to nurse and the child is fond of her.' Abū 'Amr, Ibn Kathīr, Abān ibn 'Āṣim and a group recite '*taḍārru*' added to His words, '*no self is charged*'. So it is a report by which the command is meant. Yūnus related that al-Ḥasan said, 'She should not harm her husband by saying, "I will not nurse him," and he should not harm her by removing the child from her if she says that she will nurse him.'

**The same duty is incumbent on the heir.**

There is disagreement about the interpretation of this phrase. Qatādah, as-Suddī, al-Ḥasan, and 'Umar ibn al-Khaṭṭāb said that the heir referred to is the heir of the child if he dies. Some said that it is only the male heirs who must pay the nurse, as the father of the child would have that duty if he were alive. Mujāhid and 'Aṭā' said that. Qatādah and others said that the heirs of the child can be both men and women and they must have it nursed paying in proportion with their shares of inheritance. Aḥmad and Isḥāq said that. Qāḍī Abū Isḥāq Ismā'īl ibn Isḥāq said in his book, *Meanings of the Qur'an*, 'Abū Ḥanīfah said that the maintenance and nursing of the child is incumbent on every relative. For instance, in the case of the young son of a sister who is needy and the young son of an uncle when he is his heir: maintenance is incumbent on the maternal uncle if his sister's son becomes fatherless even though he does not inherit from him. The responsibility is removed from the son of an uncle if there is another son of an uncle who is an heir.' Abū Isḥāq said that those who say this are taking a position which is not in the Book of Allah and we do not know of anyone who says it.

Aṭ-Ṭabarī reported that Abū Ḥanīfah and his adherents said that the heir who must pay for the nurse is the child's heir who is a close relative. As for nephews and those who are not close relatives, they are free of that responsibility. It is said that what is meant is that the paternal relatives of the father must maintain and clothe the child. Aḍ-Ḍaḥḥāk said, 'If the child's father dies and the child has property, his nursing is paid for from his own property. If he has no property, it is taken from the paternal relatives. If they have no money, then the mother is compelled to nurse him.' Qabīṣah ibn Dhu'ayb, aḍ-Ḍaḥḥāk and Bashīr ibn Naṣr, the Qāḍī of 'Umar ibn 'Abd al-'Azīz, said, 'The "heir" means the child himself. It means that he must pay for nursing from his own property since he was his father's heir.'

Sufyān said, 'The heir here is the remaining parent of the child after the death of one of them. If the father dies, then the mother must care for the child if he has no property. The paternal kin share with her in payment for nursing the child according to their share of the estate. Ibn Khuwayzimandād said, 'If an orphan is poor and has no money, the ruler must support him from the Treasury. If the ruler does not do it, then the Muslims must do it, starting with those specified in order. The mother is the first specified and it is obliged for her to nurse him and sustain him. She does not resort to him or anyone else.'

Nursing is mandatory and maintenance is recommended. Husbands are obliged to maintain the women who nurse their children. If the husband is unable to pay what is due owing to death or hardship, the duty is not cancelled for the mothers. A waiting period is mandatory for them, as is maintenance and lodging by their husbands. If maintenance is impossible, their waiting period is not thereby cancelled. In al-*Asadiyyah* 'Abd ar-Rahmān ibn al-Qāsim reported that Mālik ibn Anas said, 'A man is not obliged to maintain a sister or a relative.' He said that Allah's words: *'The same duty is incumbent on the heir'* are abrogated. An-Naḥḥās said, 'This is what Mālik said. Neither he nor 'Abd ar-Rahmān ibn al-Qāsim explained what abrogated it. I do not know of any of their people who made that clear. Allah knows best, but it seems that he believes that what abrogates it is that at first Allah made it obligatory for the widow to receive maintenance for a year and lodging from the property of the deceased and then that was abrogated and removed and it was also abrogated for the heir.' According to this, the child is obliged to pay for his upkeep from his property and not his heir.

Ibn al-'Arabī said, 'Ibn al-Qāsim said that Mālik said that the instruction: "*the same duty is incumbent on the heir*", is abrogated. These are words which the hearts of the heedless abhor and which bewilder the minds of the isolated. But the business is close! The early *fuqaha'* and commentators used to refer to specification (*takhṣīṣ*) as abrogation because it removes part of what was entailed by the generality of the *āyah*. They used that language and what they meant became unclear to later people. The verification of that is that Allah's words: *"The same duty is incumbent on the heir"*, indicate what was before. Some people refer it to all of the obligation of maintenance and prohibition of harm, including Abū Ḥanīfah among the *fuqahā'* and Qatādah and al-Ḥasan among the Salaf, deriving it from 'Umar.

One group of scholars said that the *āyah* does not refer to all of that, but means that the heir is forbidden to harm the mother by withholding what is due from the father. This is the basic principle. Whoever claims that that it refers to all must provide the proof. 'This is the basic principle' means to refer the pronoun to closest person mentioned. That is sound. If it had meant all, which is nursing, spending and lack of harm, Allah would have said, '*The same duties* – using the plural – *are incumbent...*'. This indicates that it is added to the prohibition to harm. All commentators interpret in that way according to what is related from Qāḍī 'Abd al-Wahhāb. What is meant by it is that mother may not harm her child by not nursing him when the father pays her a suitable wage, and the father may not harm the mother when she is paid to nurse him for an appropriate wage, because the mother is kinder and gentler towards the child and her milk is better for him than the milk of other women.

Ibn 'Aṭiyyah said, 'Mālik and all his adherents, ash-Sha'bī, az-Zuhrī, aḍ-Ḍaḥḥāk and all scholars, say that what is meant by *"the same duty"* is that she should not be harmed. He is not obliged to give anything in respect of food and clothing.' Ibn al-Qāsim related from Mālik that the *āyah* includes the fact that the heir owes food and clothing, but then the consensus of the community is that this was abrogated by the heir not being put under pressure. The disagreement is about whether or not he owes food and clothing. Yaḥyā ibn Ma'mar recited 'heirs' in the plural. That would demand the generality of the *āyah*. They took as evidence the words of the Prophet ﷺ: 'Allah does not accept *ṣadaqah* when there are relatives in need.' The answer to them is that 'relatives' is general and includes every relative, *maḥram* or not. There is no doubt that giving *ṣadaqah* to relatives is better because the Prophet ﷺ said, 'Give it to your relatives.' The *ḥadīth* is taken in that manner and there is no proof in it for what they claim. Allah knows best.

An-Naḥḥās said that the opinion of those who say that *'the same duty is incumbent on the heir'* means not to harm is a good opinion because people's property is protected and so none of it taken except by decisive evidence. As for the position of those who say that it refers to the heirs of the father, their argument is that maintenance is the responsibility of the father and so his heirs are more suitable to provide it than the heirs of the son. The argument of those who say that it is the responsibility of the son's heirs is that as they inherit from him, so they should support him.

An-Naḥḥās said, 'Muḥammad ibn Jarīr preferred the position of those who say that the heir here is the son. It is an odd position. Deduction by it is sound and the argument based on it is evident because he is more entitled to his own property. With the exception of the odd aberrant position, *fuqahā'* agree that if a man has a child who is a minor and the child has property and the father is in straitened circumstances, neither maintenance nor nursing are obliged from the father but rather they are taken from the child's property. If it is said that Allah says: *"It is the duty of the fathers to feed and clothe them with correctness and courtesy,"* then it is answered that it is a feminine pronoun. Nonetheless, the consensus defines and explains the *āyah* and no Muslim can depart from it. As for those who say that it is owed by the remaining parent, their argument is that it is not permitted for a mother to let her child perish, given that the one who supported her and the child has died.'

Al-Bukhārī has a chapter that refutes that entitled '"*The same duty is incumbent on the heir.*" Does a woman owe any support?' He provides the *ḥadīth*s about Umm Salamah and Hind. Umm Salamah had sons by Abū Salamah who had no property. She asked the Prophet ﷺ who told her that she would have a reward for that. This *ḥadīth* indicated that she was not obliged to spend on her sons. If she had been obliged to do so, then she would not have said to the Prophet ﷺ, 'I would not leave them.' In the *ḥadīth* of Hind, the Prophet ﷺ allowed her to take the maintenance for her and her son from the father's property and he did not oblige her to spend from herself as he obliged it for the father. Al-Bukhārī deduced from this that since mothers are not obliged to support their children while their father is alive, neither are they obliged to support them after their father's death.

As for the view of those who say that the spending and clothing is the duty of every *maḥram* relative, their argument is that a man must spend on all *maḥram* relatives if they are poor. An-Naḥḥās said, 'This view is countered by the fact that it is not taken from the Book of Allah, consensus, or sound Sunnah. It is only known from what we mentioned. The Qur'an, however, says: *"The same duty is incumbent on the heir,"* so the heir owes maintenance and clothing. They differ from that and said, "If he leaves a maternal uncle and a son of a paternal uncle, then maintenance is owed by his uncle and the cousin owes nothing." This differs from the text of the Qur'an because the maternal uncle does not inherit with the son of a paternal uncle according to one view, and he does not inherit alone according to the view of most scholars. Most scholars take a different view than the one they hold about owing maintenance to every relative.'

**If the couple both wish weaning to take place**

The dual pronoun refers to the parents. Weaning is the child leaving nourishment by the mother's milk for other foods. The root meaning of the noun *fiṣāl* (weaning) means 'separation'. It is called weaning because the child is separated from the mother's breast. This *āyah* refers to it happening before the two years are up. In that case '*there is nothing wrong in*' weaning him. That is because when Allah set two years as the period of nursing, He made it clear that no one can dispute the time of weaning unless the parents agree on less than that amount of time, as long as that does not harm the child. That is permitted based on this clarification. Qatādah said, 'Nursing was mandatory for the two years and weaning before that time was forbidden, and then it was lightened and it was allowed to nurse less than two years when Allah said: "*If the couple both wish weaning to that place.*"' This indicates that Allah has allowed *ijtihād* in the rulings on that, when the parents consult one another, about the course which will be in the best interests of the child. That is based on their predominant opinions, not on reality and certainty. *Tashāwur* is joint consultation. *Mashūrah* and *mushāwarah* mean the same. The verb *shāra* is used for extracting honey and it is also used for making a horse run before buying it. *Shawār* are household utensils because they are evident to someone who looks. *Shārah* is a man's shape and *ishārah* is bring out something from inside yourself and reveal it.

**If you wish to find wet-nurses for your children,**

This means other than the mother. Az-Zajjāj said that. An-Naḥḥās said, 'In Arabic it implies looking for other women to nurse your children.' This is evidence for hiring a wet-nurse when the parents agree to that. 'Ikrimah said that the words: '*No mother should be put under pressure*', refer to getting a wet-nurse. Ibn 'Aṭiyyah says that the basic position is that every mother is obliged to nurse her child as Allah mentions and their husbands are obliged to give them maintenance and clothing while they are married. If nursing had been a requirement of the father, Allah would have mentioned it with the requirements of maintenance and clothing. Mālik, however, excepted noble women and said that they are not obliged to nurse. He removed them from the general category by the legal principle of custom. This is a principle which only Mālik understands. This splendid principle is that the matter existed in the Jāhiliyyah, regarding those of noble birth, and then Islam came and did not alter it. So those of wealth and high birth continued to free the mothers among them for enjoyment by giving suckling infants to wet-nurses for a period of time. He stated that position and it continues until now and so it is part of the Sharī'ah.

**provided you hand over to them what you have agreed to give**

This means that the father is responsible for paying the wages of the wet-nurse. Sufyān said that. Mujāhid said that it means to hand over the wages to the mothers for their nursing until the time they wish to find a wet-nurse. Six of the seven readings has *'ātaykum'*, meaning 'give' and Ibn Kathīr has *'ataykum'* meaning 'bring and do'. Qatādah and az-Zuhrī said that it means: 'you hand over what you have done in desiring to seek a wet-nurse', which means that both parents submit and are satisfied. That is based on their agreement, good intention and seeking what is correct regarding the matter. According to this possibility, 'hand over' is addressed to men and women. According to the first two views, it is only addressed to men. Abū 'Alī said that it means 'when you hand over what you have given of money or gift and there is some elision. According to this interpretation, it refers to men because they are the one who pay the wages of the wet-nurses.' Abū 'Alī also said that it is possible that *'mā'* acts as a verbal noun and has the same meaning as the first view.

وَالَّذِينَ يُتَوَفَّوْنَ مِنكُمْ وَيَذَرُونَ أَزْوَاجًا يَتَرَبَّصْنَ بِأَنفُسِهِنَّ أَرْبَعَةَ أَشْهُرٍ
وَعَشْرًا فَإِذَا بَلَغْنَ أَجَلَهُنَّ فَلَا جُنَاحَ عَلَيْكُمْ فِيمَا فَعَلْنَ فِي أَنفُسِهِنَّ بِالْمَعْرُوفِ
وَاللَّهُ بِمَا تَعْمَلُونَ خَبِيرٌ ﴿٢٣٤﴾

**234 Those of you who die leaving wives behind: they should wait by themselves for four months and ten nights. When their waiting period comes to an end, you are not to blame for anything they do with themselves with correctness and courtesy. Allah is aware of what you do.**

**Those of you who die leaving wives behind: they should wait by themselves for four months and ten nights.**

After Allah has mentioned the waiting period of divorce followed by nursing, He speaks about the waiting period for widowhood as well so that it is not assumed that the waiting period for widows is the same as the waiting period for divorce. The words *'those of you'* refer to husbands and *'they'* to widows. Az-Zajjāj said that and an-Naḥḥās also mentioned that. 'Abū 'Alī al-Fārisī said, 'It implies: "those of you who die and leave wives: they should wait after them."' The expression is extremely succinct. Al-Mahdawī said that Sībuwayh said that it means: 'In what is recited to you: those of you who die…'

This *āyah* is about the waiting period of widows. Its literal meaning is general while its actual meaning is specific. Al-Mahdawī related from one scholar that the *āyah* concerned pregnant women and that it was abrogated by: *'The time for those who are pregnant is when they give birth.'* (65:4) Most scholars say that this *āyah* abrogates: *'Those of you who die leaving wives behind should make a bequest to their wives...'* (2:240) because, in the beginning of Islam, when a man died and left a pregnant wife, he would make a bequest for her of maintenance for a year and provide lodging for her until she left and remarried. Then this was abrogated by four months and ten days and a share of inheritance. Other people have said that there is no abrogation in this and that it constitutes a reduction from the original year in the same way that the travelling prayer was reduced from four to two *rak'ah*s. This is not abrogation.

This view is a clear error because the ruling was a waiting period for a year provided the widow did not go out. If she went out, she was not prevented from doing so but the maintenance would thereby be brought to an end. Then this was removed and a waiting period of four months and ten days was imposed. This is an abrogation, and it has nothing to do with the case of the travelling prayer. In any case, 'Ā'ishah said, 'The prayer was prescribed as two *rak'ah*s each, and then the resident prayer was increased and the travel prayer remained the same.' That will be dealt with in due course.

The waiting period of a pregnant widow lasts until she gives birth according to the majority of scholars. It is related from 'Alī and Ibn 'Abbās that the end of the waiting period is whichever of the two terms is longer. Among our scholars Saḥnūn chose this view. It is also related that Ibn 'Abbās retracted his statement. Their reasoning is that they prefer to combine both *āyah*s (2:234 and 65:4) and maintain acting on them by taking the longer term. If her *'iddah* ends by giving birth, then she has not acted on the *āyah* containing the waiting period of the widow. According to the people of fundamentals, joining them is better than giving preference to one of them. This view would be good were it not for the fact that it is overturned by the *ḥadīth* of Subay'ah al-Aslamiyyah. She gave birth some days after the death of her husband and she mentioned that to the Messenger of Allah ﷺ and he told her to marry. It is transmitted in the *Ṣaḥīḥ*. So the *ḥadīth* makes it clear that this ruling applies both to widows and divorced women when they are pregnant, and the waiting period of a widow is specifically for one who is not pregnant. This is reinforced by the view of Ibn Mas'ūd: 'The relationship between the two is that the short "*Āyah* of Women" was revealed after the *āyah* dealing with the waiting period of widows.'

Our scholars say that the apparent meaning of the words is that abrogation has taken place. That is not what is meant, and Allah knows best. What is actually meant is that it is specific to her. Certain circumstances have removed her from the ruling. The incident involving Subay'ah took place after the revelation of the *āyah* about the waiting period of widowhood because it occurred after the Farewell Hajj. Her husband was Sa'd ibn Khawlah, one of the Banū 'Āmir ibn Lu'ayy, who had been present at the Battle of Badr. He died in Makkah while she was pregnant. The Messenger of Allah ﷺ told her that he had died in Makkah, and she gave birth after about half a month. Al-Bukhārī said that it was forty days. Muslim related from 'Umar ibn 'Abdullāh ibn al-Arqam that Subay'ah asked the Messenger of Allah ﷺ about that and he gave her a *fatwā* that she was lawful for remarriage when she gave birth and told her that she could marry if that seemed proper for her.

Ibn Shihāb said, 'I do not think that there is anything wrong in her marrying after she gives birth, even if she is still bleeding, but her husband should not approach her until she is pure.' This is the position of the majority of scholars and imams of the *fuqahā'*. Al-Ḥasan, ash-Sha'bī, an-Nakha'ī and Ḥammād said that a woman should not marry in the period of lochia. They had two stipulations: giving birth and purity after the bleeding of lochia. The *ḥadīth* provides the argument against them. They have no argument in his words ﷺ, 'When she finished her lochia, she beautified herself for suitors', as we find in *Ṣaḥīḥ Muslim* and Abū Dāwud, because although the root of the word 'finished' means to be pure of the blood of lochia, according to what al-Khalīl says, it is possible that what is meant here is that she is finished with the pains of lochia. If we accept that it means what al-Khalīl said, there is no argument in it. The proof lies in what the Prophet ﷺ said to Subay'ah: 'You are lawful when you give birth.' So she becomes lawful when she gives birth. He ﷺ did not say that it is at the end of bleeding or when she has purified herself. What is sound then is what the majority stated.

There is no disagreement that the end of the waiting period of every pregnant divorced woman ends when she gives birth, whether that was a revocable divorce or not, and whether she is free, a slave, a *mudabbarah* or *mukātabah*. There is some disagreement about the end of the waiting period of a pregnant widow, as we have stated. All of them agree, without any disagreement, that if a man dies leaving a pregnant widow, even after the period of four months and ten days she is still not lawful until she has given birth. Therefore it is known that what is meant is giving birth.

The word 'wait' here means to refrain from remarrying and leaving the marital home. That means not leaving it at night. Allah did not mention the residence of widows in His Book as He did that of divorced woman when He says: *'let them live...'* (65:6). There is nothing in the term *'iddah* that indicates mourning. He says, *'wait'* and the Sunnah clarifies that and there are many *ḥadīth*s from the Prophet ﷺ indicating that the waiting period of widowhood is a period of mourning, which should be marked by not wearing jewelry, beautiful dyed garments, perfume and the like. This is the statement of the majority of scholars. Al-Ḥasan said that it has nothing to do with mourning and it is only about not marrying, and so a widow is free to adorn herself and use perfume. This is weak because it is contrary to the Sunnah as we will make clear.

It is confirmed that the Prophet ﷺ said to Furay'ah bint Mālik when she was widowed, 'Remain in your house until the term is reached.' She said, 'My waiting period was for four months and ten days.' This is a confirmed *ḥadīth* transmitted by Mālik from Sa'īd ibn Isḥāq ibn Ka'b ibn 'Ujrah. It was related from him by Mālik, ath-Thawrī, Wuhayb ibn Khālid, Ḥammād ibn Zayd, 'Īsā ibn Yūnus and a great number of others. Ibn 'Uyaynah, al-Qaṭṭān and Shu'bah. Mālik related it from Ibn Sha'bān. That is enough for you! Al-Bājī said that no one else related it from him. 'Uthmān ibn 'Affān accepted it. Abū 'Umar says that it contains the judgment for the widow spending the waiting period in her house. It is a famous *ḥadīth* among scholars of the Hijaz and Iraq who maintain the widow should spend the waiting-period in her house and not leave. It is the position of a group of the *fuqahā'* of the cities in the Hijaz, Syria, Iraq and Egypt.

Dāwud, however, said that a widow may spend the waiting period wherever she wishes because, in the Qur'an, lodging is only mentioned in the case of divorced women. He argues that it is a disputed question. They said that this *ḥadīth* was related by a woman not known for conveying knowledge. Lodging and other rulings are only obliged by a text of the Qur'an, Sunnah or consensus. Abū 'Umar said, 'The Sunnah is confirmed. Praise be to Allah. There is no need for consensus when the Sunnah exists, because when a disagreement occurs about a question, the argument goes in favour of the position that agrees with the Sunnah. Success is by Allah.' What has come from 'Alī, Ibn 'Abbās, Jābir, and 'Ā'ishah supports the opinion of Dāwud and that position was taken by Jābir ibn Zayd, 'Aṭā' and al-Ḥasan al-Baṣrī. Ibn 'Abbās said that it is because Allah says: *'...they should wait by themselves for four months and ten days'* and did not say, 'wait in their houses'. So she does the *'iddah* wherever she wishes. It is also reported from Abū Ḥanīfah.

'Abd ar-Razzāq related from Ma'mar from az-Zuhrī that 'Urwah reported that when 'Ā'ishah's sister, Umm Kulthum, was widowed when her husband, Ṭalḥah ibn 'Ubaydullāh, was killed, 'Ā'ishah took her to Makkah on *'umrah*. Her judgment was that a widow could go out during her waiting period. Ath-Thawrī related that 'Ubaydullāh ibn 'Umar heard al-Qāsim ibn Muḥammad remark that some people rejected that position of hers. Ma'mar related that az-Zuhrī said, 'Those who make allowances for widows take the position of 'Ā'ishah and those who are scrupulous and firm take that of Ibn 'Umar.' It states in the *Muwaṭṭā'* that 'Umar ibn al-Khaṭṭāb sent back some widows from al-Bayḍā' when they were on their way to *ḥajj* and prevented them from doing it. This was based on his *ijtihād* because he thought that widows must stay in their husbands' houses and that that is demanded by the Qur'an and the Sunnah. A widow is not permitted to go on a *ḥajj* or *'umrah* until her *'iddah* is over. Mālik said that she is sent back as long as she has not adopted *iḥrām*.

If the husband owns the dwelling, his widow observes her waiting period in it according to most *fuqahā'* – Mālik, Abū Ḥanīfah, ash-Shāfi'ī and Aḥmad among them – based on the *ḥadīth* of Furay'ah. But can the house then be sold if it belonged to the deceased and the heirs want to sell it? Most of our people say that the sale is permitted but a precondition of the sale must be that the widow can observe her waiting period there. Ibn al-Qāsim said that is because she is entitled to her lodging as a creditor. Muḥammad ibn al-Ḥakam said that the sale is invalid until the end of the widow's waiting period. The reasoning behind the view of Ibn al-Qāsim is that soundness is predominant and doubt is rare and so that does not cause the contract to be invalid. If the sale occurs with this precondition, that causes uncertainty. Mālik said in the book of Muḥammad, that the widow is entitled to reside until the doubt ends. He said that he preferred the buyer to have the option to cancel the sale or carry it out and not retract anything, because it is based on a known amount of time. If the sale has the precondition of the removal of doubt, it is unsound. Saḥnūn said, 'The buyer has no argument, even if the doubt lasts for five years. The like of that is related by Abū Yazīd from Ibn al-Qāsim.

If the husband has a dwelling that is not owned, she can live in it for the waiting period. Abū Ḥanīfah and ash-Shāfi'ī disagree since the Prophet ﷺ said to Furay'ah, knowing that her husband did not own the house, 'Stay in your house until the period is concluded.' It is not said that the house was hers. That is why he said to her, 'Stay in your house.' Ma'mar related from az-Zuhrī that she mentioned to the Prophet ﷺ that her husband had been killed and he had left her in a house which was hers and she sought his permission. He mentioned the *ḥadīth*. We take it to mean that he left a house in which she could live and would not be pursued for. So the wife had to do the waiting period in it. The basis of that is owning the right to live in it.

This is when her deceased husband paid the rent. If he has not paid it, the

*Mudawwanah* states that she has no right of lodging from the property of the deceased, even if he was wealthy, because her right was contingent on what he owned completely. She has only what she receives by inheritance and that is property and not lodging. Muḥammad reported that Mālik said that renting a lodging for the widow is an obligation and must be paid for from the property of the deceased.

The words of the Prophet ﷺ to Furay'ah, 'Stay in your house until the term is concluded' may mean that he commanded her to do that since her husband had paid the rent or had provided for her lodging in his will or that the owner of the house allowed her to spend her waiting period there with or without rent. It is whatever Allah meant by that, in view of the fact that it is necessary for her to have somewhere to live until the end of her waiting period.

They disagree about a woman who is informed of her husband's death while she is in a house other than that of her husband. Some relate that she should return to his house and Mālik ibn Anas said that. He related it from 'Umar ibn 'Abd al-Azīz. Sa'īd ibn al-Musayyab and an-Nakha'ī said that she does the waiting period where the news reaches her and does not leave until the end of her waiting period. Ibn al-Mundhir says that the sound position of Mālik is that she should return to the deceased husband's house unless he himself had moved her to her current location. In that case, she stays at that place.

She is permitted to go out for her needs and her work, at the time when people normally go out for such things, up until the time of the *'Ishā'* prayer. She should, however, spend the night in that house alone. We find in al-Bukhārī and Muslim from Umm 'Aṭiyyah that the Messenger of Allah ﷺ said, 'A woman should not mourn for a dead person more than three days, except in the case of a husband, when the mourning period is four months and ten days. A widow should not wear a dyed garment except for one made of pre-dyed yarn. She should not wear eye make-up (kohl) or perfume until her waiting period has ended, except for costus or aẓfar (types of aromatic wood).' Umm Ḥabībah said, 'It is not lawful for a woman who believes in Allah and the Last Day to mourn for a dead person more than three days unless it is her husband. She should mourn him for four months and ten days.' Mourning consists of abandoning all adornment in respect of clothing, perfume, jewellery, make-up and henna during the waiting period, because adornment is a sign of seeking a husband and so it is forbidden as a protection and in order to make sure that that does not happen. Oiling the hair is not considered as adornment but henna is. The Arabic for a woman in mourning is *ḥādd* and *muḥidd*.

We believe that the fact that the Prophet ﷺ described a woman with faith indicates the soundness of one of the two views about a widowed Kitābī woman not having to observe mourning. That is the view of Ibn Kinānah and Ibn Nāfi'. Ashhab related it from Mālik. That is also what is stated by Abū Ḥanīfah and Ibn al-Mundhir. It is related from Ibn al-Qāsim that she must mourn like a Muslim. That is the view of al-Layth, ash-Shāfi'ī, Abū Thawr and most of our people because it is one of the rulings about the *'iddah* and so it is obliged for the Kitābī wife of a Muslim just as lodging and *'iddah* are also obliged.

The words of the Prophet ﷺ, 'more than three days' indicate that it is unlawful for Muslim women to observe mourning for other than their husbands for more than three days, and the fact that it is definitely permitted to mourn them for three days, starting the number with the night before to the end of the third day. If her close friend dies at the end of a day or night, it is not counted and the number starts from the following night.

This *ḥadīth* indicates a general ruling which applies to all widows and it included slave-girls and young and old free women. That is the position of the majority of scholars. Abū Ḥanīfah believed that neither a slave-girl nor a young girl have to observe mourning. Qāḍī Abu-l-Walīd al-Bājī related it from him. Ibn al-Mundhir said that a married slave-girl is included with wives in general since the reports are non-specific. That is the view of Mālik, ash-Shāfi'ī, Abū Thawr and the People of Opinion. I do not recall any disagreement about that from anyone and I do not know that they disagree about mourning in respect of an *umm walad* if her master dies because she is not a wife and the *ḥadīth*s are about wives. Al-Bājī said, 'When the young girl is one of those who understands commands and prohibitions, she is obliged to observe the mourning period prescribed for her, but if she does not grasp any of that because of her youth, Ibn Muzayn related from 'Īsā that her family should make her avoid what an adult woman would avoid. She must do that. The evidence for the obligation of mourning for a young girl is something related from the Prophet ﷺ. A woman asked him about a daughter of hers who was widowed and had something wrong with her eye. Could she treat it with kohl? The Prophet ﷺ answered, 'No,' saying it two or three times. He did not ask about her age. If there had been a separate judgment about young and old, he would have asked about her age to make the ruling clear. It is not permitted to delay clarification about something like this. All who are obliged to observe the waiting period of a widow must observe mourning as is the case with an adult woman.

Ibn al-Mundhir said, 'I do not know of any disagreement about dyeing being part of the forbidden adornment. They agree that she is not permitted to wear dyed clothing except for that made with black. There is an allowance for it from 'Urwah ibn az-Zubayr, Mālik and ash-Shāfi'ī. Az-Zuhrī said that she should not wear a black head-scarf. That differs from the *ḥadīth*. In the *Mudawwanah* Mālik said, 'She should not wear fine black Yemenī fabric,' but he makes an allowance if it is coarse. Ibn al-Qāsim said that the reason for that is that fine fabric is like dyed garments. She can wear fine garments of silk, linen and cotton. Ibn al-Mundhir said, 'Everyone from whom I have reported makes an allowance for white clothing.' Qāḍī 'Iyāḍ said, 'Ash-Shāfi'ī said that every dye is adornment and the woman in mourning should not touch it, whether it is fine or coarse. Qāḍī 'Abd al-Wahhāb says something similar. He said, 'A mourning woman is forbidden from enjoying any colour that women use to adorn themselves for their husbands.' Some of our later shaykhs forbid fine white cloth that is used for adornment. The same is true of fine black cloth. Ibn al-Mawwāz related from Mālik that a woman should not wear jewellery if she is in mourning. In general, any kind of jewellery that a woman wears for adornment should not be worn by a woman in mourning. There is no specific text on gems, rubies, emeralds and things of that sort. Allah knows best.

The people agree that Muslim widows should go into mourning – with the exception of al-Ḥasan who says that it is not mandatory. He based that on the *ḥadīth* of 'Abdullāh ibn Shaddād ibn al-Hādi about Asmā' bint 'Umays when Ja'far ibn Abī Ṭālib was killed. She said that the Messenger of Allah ﷺ told her, 'Withdraw for three and then do what you wish.' Ibn al-Mundhir said, 'It is only al-Ḥasan al-Baṣrī among scholars who did not think that there was mourning. He said that a divorced woman and a widow observe three days. They may then wear kohl, dye and do whatever they like.' Reports from the Prophet ﷺ confirm mourning. No one who heard those reports did not accept them. Perhaps they did not reach al-Ḥasan, or they reached him, but he interpreted them by the *ḥadīth* of Asmā' bint 'Umays who asked the Prophet ﷺ for permission to mourn for her husband, Ja'far. He gave her permission for three days and then after three days he sent word to her to purify herself and wear kohl. Ibn al-Mundhir said that the people of knowledge present this *ḥadīth* with various aspects. Aḥmad ibn Ḥanbal said. 'This is aberrant in the *ḥadīth* and not taken.' Isḥāq said it.

Mālik and ash-Shāfi'ī believed that a woman divorced finally, once, or more, or revocably, does not have to mourn. That is the view of Rabī'ah and 'Aṭā'. The Kufans, namely Abū Ḥanīfah and his people, ath-Thawrī, al-Ḥasan ibn Ḥayy, Abū Thawr and Abū 'Ubayd said that a woman divorced trebly must mourn.

That is also the view of Sa'īd ibn al-Musayyab, Sulaymān ibn Yasār, Ibn Sīrīn, and al-Ḥakam ibn 'Uyaynah. Al-Ḥakam said, 'It is more stressed for her than a widow. Part of the idea is that they both observe a waiting period by which lineage is protected.' Ash-Shāfi'ī, Aḥmad and Isḥāq said that part of caution is that a divorced woman avoids adornment. Ibn al-Mundhir said, 'The words of the Prophet ﷺ, "It is not lawful for a woman who believes in Allah and the Last Day to mourn for a deceased person other than her husband for more than three days. For a husband it is four months and ten days," are evidence that a woman who is divorced three times and whose husband is alive does not mourn.'

Scholars agree that if someone divorces his wife in a manner in which he can take her back and then dies before the end of the waiting period, she must observe the waiting period of a widow and she inherits from him. They disagree about the *'iddah* of a woman triply divorced while the husband is ill. One group said that she observes the waiting period for a divorce. This is the view of Mālik, ash-Shāfi'ī, Ya'qūb, Abū 'Ubayd and Abū Thawr. Ibn al-Mundhir said, 'That is what I say because Allah Almighty made the waiting period of divorced women three menstrual cycles. They agree that if the husband of a woman who has been divorced three times dies, she does not inherit from him because she is not his wife. If she is not his wife, he is not her husband. Ath-Thawrī said that she should observe the longer of the two waiting periods. An-Nu'mān and Muḥammad said that she must observe four months and ten days in which the three menstrual cycles are completed.

They disagree about a woman who hears that her husband has died or has divorced her. One group say that the waiting period for both begins from the day he dies or she was divorced. This is the position of Ibn 'Umar, Ibn Mas'ūd and Ibn 'Abbās. That is also stated by Masrūq, 'Aṭā', and a group of Tābi'ūn. It was the position of Mālik, ash-Shāfi'ī, Aḥmad, Isḥāq, Abū 'Ubayd, ath-Thawrī, Abū Thawr, the People of Opinion and Ibn al-Mundhir. There is a second view regarding her, which is that it starts from the day the news reaches her. This view was related from 'Alī. That is the view of al-Ḥasan al-Baṣrī, Qatādah, 'Aṭā' al-Khurāsānī and Jullās ibn 'Amr. Sa'īd ibn al-Musayyab and 'Umar ibn 'Abd al-'Azīz said, 'If there is evidence, her waiting period starts from the death or divorce. If there is no evidence, then it starts from the day the news reaches her.' The first is the sound position because Allah Almighty connected the waiting period to death or divorce and because, had she known of his death, she would have finished mourning and the *'iddah* would have ended. It is easier for her to have left it when she did not know. Do you not see that a young girl finishes her waiting period and does not observe mourning? Scholars also agree that if the woman is pregnant and does not know that her husband has divorced her or died and then gives birth, her *'iddah* is over. There is no difference between this question and the disputed one. The reasoning of those who say that her waiting period begins from the day the news reaches her is that it is an act of worship by abandoning adornment which is only valid by aim and intention. There is only an intention after knowledge. Allah knows best.

The waiting period for widowhood must be observed by both free women and slaves, young and old, those who have not reached the age of menstruation, those who menstruate, those past the age of menstruation and Kitābī women, whether or not the marriage has been consummated, when the woman is not pregnant. Except for slave-girls, the waiting period of all of them is four months and ten days since the *āyah* is general. The waiting period of a slave-girl is two months and five days. Ibn al-'Arabī said that the consensus is that it is half of that of a free woman except for what is related from al-Aṣamm that it is the same for a slave-girl and free woman. The consensus of the community preceded that, but perhaps he had not heard it because of his deafness. Al-Bājī said, 'We do not know of any disagreement except what is related from Ibn Sīrīn, which is not actually confirmed from him, about slave-girls having the same *'iddah* as free women.'

The position of al-Aṣamm is sound from the point of view of reflection as the *āyahs* which deal with the waiting person for widowhood and divorce mention months and menstrual cycles and have general application to both slave-girls and free women. Therefore their waiting period is the same, based on this consideration. Generalities do not make a distinction between free and slave and, as the free woman and slave-girl are the same in respect of marriage, so they should be the same in respect of waiting period. Allah knows best. Ibn al-'Arabī said, 'It is related from Mālik that a *kitābī* woman should observe an *'iddah* for three menstruations when she is not pregnant. This is very unsound because it removes her from the generality of the *āyah* of widowhood when she is in fact part of it and includes her in the generality of the *āyah* of divorce when she is actually not part of it.' This is the basis for what is found in the *Mudawwanah* about her not having to observe a waiting period if the marriage has not been consummated because it is known that she is not pregnant. This entails the fact that she can marry a Muslim or someone else after her husband's death because she does not have to observe an *'iddah* for widowhood nor wait to see if she is pregnant. Therefore she is lawful for marriage.

They disagree about the *'iddah* of an *umm walad* whose master has died. One group said that it is four months and ten days as was stated by a group of Tābi'ūn, including Sa'īd, az-Zuhrī, al-Ḥasan al-Baṣrī and others. Al-Awzā'ī and Isḥāq said that. Abū Dāwud and ad-Dāraquṭnī related from Qabīṣah ibn Dhu'ayb that 'Amr ibn al-'Āṣ said, 'Do not muddle up the Sunnah of our Prophet ﷺ for us. The waiting period of an *umm walad* is four months and ten days.' Ad-Dāraquṭnī said that this is *mawqūf.* That is correct: it is *mursal* because Qabīṣah did not listen to 'Amr. Ibn al-Mundhir said that Aḥmad and Abū 'Ubayd said that this *ḥadīth* is weak. It is related from 'Alī and Ibn Mas'ūd that her waiting period is three menstrual periods. This is the position of 'Aṭā', Ibrāhīm an-Nakha'ī, Sufyān ath-Thawrī and the People of Opinion who said that it is because the *'iddah is* obliged when the woman is free and so it must be a full *'iddah.* The basis of the *'iddah* is that of a free woman. Mālik, ash-Shāfi'ī, Aḥmad and Abū Thawr said that her *'iddah* is one menstrual period. That is the view of Ibn 'Umar. It is related from Ṭāwūs that her *'iddah* is half that of a widowed free woman. Qatādah said that. Ibn al-Mundhir said, 'I take the position of Ibn 'Umar because it is the minimum of what is said about it and there is no sunnah which is followed nor any consensus which is relied on.' He mentioned their disagreement about her waiting period when she is freed as well as when she is widowed. Al-Awzā'ī, however, said that her *'iddah* when she is freed is three menstrual periods.

The soundest position is that of Mālik since Allah says: *'Divorced women should wait by themselves for three menstrual cycles.'* (2:228) So the precondition for waiting based on menstrual cycles is that it is on account of divorce. So he said that it is not for other things. Allah says: *'Those of you who die leaving wives behind: they should wait by themselves for four months and ten days,'* and He connected that to the woman being a widow. This indicates that a slave-girl is different; and also a slave-girl with whom the master has had sex based on ownership observes *istibrā'* of one menstrual period. That is the basic principle.

If this is confirmed, then the question about the waiting period of an *umm walad* is whether it is *'iddah* or *istibrā'*. Abū Muḥammad mentioned in *al-Ma'ūnah* that one menstrual period is *istibrā'* and it is not *'iddah*. According to the *Mudawwanah*, an *umm walad* must observe an *'iddah* and her *'iddah* is one menstrual period as that of a free woman is three menstrual periods. The point of the difference lies in calling it '*'iddah*'. Mālik said, 'I do not like anyone promising to marry her until she has had one menstrual period.' Ibn al-Qāsim said, 'I heard that he said that she should only spend the night in her house.' He confirmed that the period of her *istibrā'* has the same ruling as *'iddah*.

Scholars agree that the husband must support a trebly divorced woman and a revocably divorced woman while she is pregnant since Allah says: *'If they are pregnant, maintain them until they give birth.'* (65:6)

They disagreed about the obligation of the maintenance of a pregnant widow. One group said that she has no maintenance, as was stated by Jābir ibn 'Abdullāh, Ibn 'Abbās, Sa'īd ibn al-Musayyab, 'Aṭā', al-Ḥasan, 'Abd al-Malik ibn Ya'lā, Yaḥyā al-Anṣārī, Rabī'ah, Mālik, Aḥmad and Isḥāq. Abū 'Ubayd also related that from the People of Opinion. The second view is that she receives maintenance from the entire estate. This position is related from 'Alī and 'Abdullāh. It was affirmed by Ibn 'Umar, Shurayḥ, Ibn Sīrīn, ash-Sha'bī, Abū 'Āliyah, an-Nakha'ī, Jullās ibn 'Amr, Ḥammād ibn Abī Sulaymān, Ayyūb as-Sijistānī, Sufyan ath-Thawrī and Abū 'Ubayd. Ibn al-Mundhir said, 'I take the first view because they agree that if someone is obliged to maintain someone while he is alive, like his young children, wife and parents, it is cancelled for him in death. The same is true of maintenance for his pregnant wives ceasing.' Qāḍī Abū Muḥammad said, 'That is because maintenance of a pregnant widow is not a confirmed debt, so it is attached to his property after his death with the evidence that it is cancelled for him in case of hardship. So it is more likely that it would be cancelled for him after his death.'

Scholars disagree about the period of *'four months and ten nights'* which Allah set for the waiting period of a widow and whether it requires menstruation to take place in it or not. Some say that a widow with whom the deceased husband has had sex must have at least one menstrual period within the four months and ten days. Otherwise there is the possibility that she is pregnant. Others state that she does not owe more than the four months and ten days in any circumstance unless she herself is uncertain, because this is a period of time in which a woman normally has a period, unless she is a woman who does not menstruate or she is a woman who knows that her menstrual period will occur in a longer period than this.

Wakī' related from Abū Ja'far ar-Rāzī from ar-Rabī' ibn Anas that Abu-l-'Āliyah was asked why the ten days were added to the four months. He said, 'Because the spirit is breathed in during that time.' This will be explained in *al-Ḥajj,* Allah willing. Al-Aṣma'ī said, 'It is said that the foetus of every pregnant woman moves halfway through the pregnancy.'

Al-Khaṭṭābī said, 'Allah knows best, but "ten" means the days with the nights.' Al-Mubarrad said that 'ten' is feminine because it means the period (*muddah*). The 'ten' means every period of a day and a night. The night and day is a known period. It is said that Allah does not say "*ashrah'* in the feminine because the night predominates, since night comes before day and the day is included in it. Also "*ashr'* is easier to say. Night take precedence over day when they are together in dating because the months begin with the night when the new moon is sighted. Since the month begins with a night, it takes precedence. Mālik, ash-Shāfi'ī and the Kufans believe that what is meant are days and nights. Some *fuqahā'* believe that when four months and ten nights have passed, the widow can lawfully remarry. That is because *'iddah* is undefined and so the feminine takes preference and it is interpreted as meaning nights. This is the view of al-Awzā'ī among the *fuqahā'* and Abū Bakr al-Aṣamm among the *mutakallimūn*. It is related that Ibn 'Abbās recited 'ten nights'.

**When their waiting period comes to an end, you are not to blame for anything they do with themselves with correctness and courtesy.**

The waiting period referred to is that of women whose husbands have died. The words *'you are not to blame'* are addressed to people in general, but particularly to judges and relatives. What widows do with respect to marriage and adornment once they leave mourning is their own business. 'Correctness' refers to what is permitted regarding choosing husbands and determining dowry without actually making a contract, because it is the guardian who makes the contract. But this does provide evidence that relatives have the right to prevent widows from adorning themselves and seeking a husband during the time of their waiting period. This refutes Isḥāq's view that a divorced woman can do that once she starts her third menstrual period. She is not completely free until she has had a *ghusl*. Sharīk said that a divorced woman's husband can take her back as long as she has not had a *ghusl*, even if twenty years have passed. However, Allah's words in this *āyah* mean that the waiting period ends with the blood of the third menstrual period. Allah did not mention *ghusl*. When the waiting period ends, then it is lawful for her to remarry and there is no blame for anything she does of that then. If the *ḥadīth* from Ibn 'Abbās is sound, then it may simply be a recommendation.

وَلَا جُنَاحَ عَلَيْكُمْ فِيمَا عَرَّضْتُم بِهِۦ مِنْ خِطْبَةِ ٱلنِّسَآءِ أَوْ أَكْنَنتُمْ فِىٓ
أَنفُسِكُمْ ۚ عَلِمَ ٱللَّهُ أَنَّكُمْ سَتَذْكُرُونَهُنَّ وَلَٰكِن لَّا تُوَاعِدُوهُنَّ سِرًّا إِلَّآ أَن تَقُولُوا۟
قَوْلًا مَّعْرُوفًا ۚ وَلَا تَعْزِمُوا۟ عُقْدَةَ ٱلنِّكَاحِ حَتَّىٰ يَبْلُغَ ٱلْكِتَٰبُ أَجَلَهُۥ ۚ وَٱعْلَمُوٓا۟
أَنَّ ٱللَّهَ يَعْلَمُ مَا فِىٓ أَنفُسِكُمْ فَٱحْذَرُوهُ ۚ وَٱعْلَمُوٓا۟ أَنَّ ٱللَّهَ غَفُورٌ
حَلِيمٌ ٢٣٥

**235 Nor is there anything wrong in any allusion to marriage you make to a woman, nor for any you keep to yourself. Allah knows that you will say things to them. But do not make secret arrangements with them, rather only speak with correctness and courtesy. Do not finally decide on the marriage contract until the prescribed period has come to its end. Know that Allah knows what is in your selves, so beware of Him! And know that Allah is Ever-Forgiving, All-Forbearing.**

**Nor is there anything wrong in any allusion to marriage you make to a woman,**

'Wrong' (*junāḥ*) in this context means sin. That is sounder in the Sharī'ah. It is said that it means something difficult. The *āyah* is addressed in particular to any man who wants to marry a woman who is still in her waiting period, saying that there is no sin in alluding to marriage during that time. An allusion is not an explicit statement. It produces understanding of what is alluded to in words whose expression is not explicit. It is like circling around something without actually saying it. It is said that it means 'to offer' as in offering someone a present and we find that usage of the verb in *ḥadīth*. Alluding to something in words connects a person to something whose meaning is understood.

Ibn 'Aṭiyyah said that the Community is agreed that speaking to a woman in her waiting period about marriage in an explicit way is not permitted. They agree that speaking to her mentioning sex or its encouragement or anything like that is not permitted. Other than that is permitted. The closest to that which is explicit is found in the words of the Prophet ﷺ to Fāṭimah bint Qays, 'Stay with Umm Sharīk. Do not advance yourself too quickly.' There is a consensus that it is not permitted to allude to marriage with a woman who is in her waiting period following a revocable divorce, because, in that, case, she is still in fact a wife. It is, however, permitted in the case of a woman who is in her waiting period after a final divorce. Allah knows best.

It is related that there are many such allusions and they fall into two categories. The first is to mention her to her guardian to tell him not to give her in marriage before his offer. The second category is to indicate that to her without an intermediary by saying to her things like, 'I'm intending to marry,' 'You're very beautiful,' 'Allah will bring you good,' 'I desire you and who could not?' 'I am in need of a wife' or 'Allah will decree good for you.' Mālik and Ibn Shihāb used these as examples. Ibn 'Abbās said, 'There is nothing wrong in saying, 'Do not be hasty with yourself.' There is nothing wrong in a man giving her a present or doing some work for her while she in the waiting period when it is part of his business. Ibrāhīm said that. He is permitted to praise himself and mention his deeds as part of an allusion to marriage. Abū Ja'far Muḥammad ibn 'Alī ibn al-Ḥusayn is mentioned as doing that.

Sukaynah bint Ḥanẓalah said, 'Muḥammad ibn 'Alī asked for permission to visit while I was still in my waiting period after the death of my husband. He said, "You know my kinship to the Messenger of Allah ﷺ and my kinship to 'Alī and my place among the Arabs." I said, "May Allah forgive you, Abū Ja'far! You are a man from whom people take knowledge and yet you propose to me while I am in my *'iddah*!" He answered, "I have informed you of my kinship to the Messenger of Allah ﷺ and 'Alī. The Messenger of Allah ﷺ visited Umm Salamah when she became the widow of Abū Salamah and said, 'You know that I am the Messenger of Allah and know my goodness and position among my people.' That was a proposal."' Ad-Dāraquṭnī transmitted it.

It is permitted to give a gift to a woman in her *'iddah*. That is part of making an allusion. Saḥnūn and many scholars said that. Ibrāhīm also stated it. Mujāhid disliked anyone saying, 'Do not hasten to offer yourself to anyone before me.' He thought that it amounted to a secret arrangement. Qāḍī Abū Muḥammad ibn 'Aṭiyyah said, 'I consider this to be an interpretation of the words of the Prophet ﷺ to Umm Salamah as a sort of opinion about who should marry her, not that he meant to marry her himself.

*Khiṭbah* (proposal) is the action of a suitor with an intention either by word or deed. *Khaṭṭāb* is a man who frequently proposes to women. *Khaṭīb* and *khāṭib* mean 'suitor' as does *khiṭb*. *Khuṭbah* means words that can be about marriage or something else.

**not for any (allusion) you keep to yourself.**

This means what you conceal during a woman's waiting period when you want to marry her after it has finished. *Iknān* is covering and concealment. *Kunnu* and *ikanna* both mean 'to conceal'. It means to protect something from disaster whether or not it is concealed. *Maknūn* is therefore used of eggs and pearls. It can be concealed by a garment, a house, land or something else. It can also be concealed in oneself although the Arabs do not use it in that way. So Allah removed any wrong action from a man who wants to marry a woman who is still in her waiting period and conceals it. He forbade any arrangements which involve a clear statement of desire for marriage, such as a proposal. Allah made this dispensation because He knows people have human weaknesses.

Shāfi'īs use this as evidence that the *ḥadd* punishment is not required in the case of a slanderous allusion. They say that, since Allah said that allusion is not wrong in this case, an allusion implying slander should not incur the *ḥadd* either, because Allah makes it clear here that an allusion is not the same as an explicit statement. We disagree and say that this is an invalid analogy because Allah did not allow explicit marriage proposals, but an allusion by which marriage is understood. An allusion to slander acts in the same way and so the *ḥadd* punishment is required because the slander is in fact clearly understood just as the allusion to marriage was.

**Allah knows that you will say things to them.**

He knows, whether that is secretly or openly, in yourselves or on your tongues. There is an allowance in respect of allusions but not explicit statements. Al-Ḥasan said that it means, 'He knows that you will propose to them.'

**But do not make secret arrangements with them,**

Scholars disagree about what is meant by 'secret' here. It is said that it means to actually arrange a marriage, in other words a man should not say to a woman during her waiting period, 'Will you marry me?' He should merely allude to what he intends and not secretly make an agreement whereby she will not marry someone else. This is the position of Ibn 'Abbās, Ibn Jubayr, Mālik and his people, Mujāhid, 'Ikrimah, as-Suddī and most of the people of knowledge. It is also said that 'secret' in this context implies fornication, in other words 'do not agree to fornicate during the waiting period'. Jābir ibn Zayd, Abū Miljaz Lāḥiq ibn Ḥumayd, al-Ḥasan, Qatādah, an-Nakha'ī and aḍ-Ḍaḥḥāk said that and that 'secret' in this *āyah* refers to fornication. So it means: 'Do not make secret arrangement to fornicate with them.' Aṭ-Ṭabarī preferred that. It is also said that 'secret' refers to sexual intercourse, meaning, 'Do not describe yourselves to them as being someone who likes a lot of sexual intercourse to make them desire to marry you.' Mentioning that to other than one's spouse is lewdness. Ash-Shāfi'ī said that. It could also be that the secret is the marriage contract, whether it is secret or public. Ibn Zayd says that it means to not marry them secretly. If it is lawful, then make it public and consummate it with them. This is the same as the first view. According to this, Ibn Zayd took the first view, but it is very odd to call the contract 'an arrangement'. That is unsettled. Makkī and ath-Tha'labī said that it is abrogated by Allah's words in this ayah: *'Do not finally decide on the marriage contract…'*.

Abū Muḥammad ibn 'Aṭiyyah said, 'The Community agree that it is disliked to arrange a marriage with a woman during her waiting period or for her father to do so for his virgin daughter or a master for his slave-girl.' Ibn al-Mawwāz said, 'I dislike a *walī*, who does not have the power of compulsion, doing it but if it happens, I do not invalidate it.' Malik said, 'If they make an arrangement during the waiting period and then marry afterwards, I prefer them to separate, whether or not the marriage has been consummated, and it is one divorce. When she can lawfully marry, then he is just one among other suitors.' This is what is transmitted from Ibn Wahb. Ashhab related from Mālik that they must be separated. Ibn al-Qāsim said that as well. Ibn al-Ḥārith related the same thing from Ibn al-Mājishūn. He added that it obliges a perpetual prohibition of marriage between the two. Ash-Shāfi'ī said, 'If someone makes an explicit proposal and the woman explicitly consents but the marriage does not take place until after the waiting period has ended, the marriage is valid and it was the explicit proposal which was disliked.' Ibn al-Mundhir said that.

**rather only speak with correctness and courtesy.**

This refers to those allusions which are permitted. Aḍ-Ḍaḥḥāk mentioned that such courteous words might be to say to a woman in *'iddah*, 'Keep yourself for me. I desire you,' to which she replies, 'The same applies here.' This is a sort of arrangement.

**Do not finally decide on the marriage contract until the prescribed period has come to its end.**

The meaning of *'azm*, to resolve or decide on something, has already been discussed. Here it means: 'Do not resolve on the marriage contract.' It is clear that the Qur'an uses the most eloquent language. What it brings cannot be opposed and its soundness and eloquence is undoubted. Allah says: *'If they are determined* ('azamū) *to divorce'* (2:227) and here He uses the same verb. It means: 'Do not decide on the contract of marriage during the time of the waiting period.' An-Naḥḥās said that it means 'make the contract'.

'*Kitāb*' (prescribed period) literally means 'book' and here denotes the limit which is set and the length of the period. It is called a 'book' since it is defined and imposed in the Book of Allah. The same word is used elsewhere in reference to the prayer, as in 4:103. So '*kitāb*' is the obligation, and it means 'until the obligation reaches its end.' The term is also used of the fast in 2:183. It is said that there is some elision in the words, i.e. until the prescribed obligation reaches its end. According to this, '*kitāb*' here means the Qur'an and there is no elision. That is more appropriate.

Allah has definitively forbidden marriage during the waiting period. This is firmly agreed on. It is not allowed until the waiting period is finished although indirect allusions to marriage are permitted during the waiting period. As we have mentioned, there is disagreement about which forms of expression are allowed. There is disagreement about a man who proposes to a woman during her waiting period out of ignorance, or who makes an arrangement and then concludes the contract after its end. We have already discussed this.

There is also disagreement about deciding on marriage while a woman is in her waiting period and when that is discovered and declared invalid by a judge. 'Umar ibn al-Khaṭṭāb and a group of scholars say that it does not create a perpetual ban and the man concerned simply becomes one of the suitors. Mālik and Ibn al-Qāsim said that in the *Mudawannah* at the end of the chapter after 'Setting a term for a missing person'. Ibn al-Jallāb related from Mālik that there is a perpetual ban against marriage, even if the marriage is declared invalid before it takes place. His reasoning is that it is marriage within the waiting period and therefore there is a perpetual ban. This is based on the marriage being consummated. If the contract is made within the waiting period and then the marriage consummated afterwards, some scholars say that it is the same as when it is consummated inside the waiting period – there is a perpetual ban between them – whereas other scholars said that there is not a perpetual ban. Mālik said that it does bring about a perpetual ban. Once he stated that the perpetual ban is based on clear evidence. Both views are found in the *Mudawwanah* in the section on the sunnah divorce.

If the union is consummated in the waiting period, Mālik, al-Layth and al-Awzā'ī said that they must be parted and she will never be lawful to him. Mālik and al-Layth said that that includes ownership, although they do not permit marriage with someone with whom she has fornicated. Their argument is that 'Umar ibn al-Khaṭṭāb said, 'They may never be joined together.' Sa'īd said, 'She receives her dower because he was allowed to have sex with her.' Mālik transmitted that in the *Muwaṭṭā'*. Ath-Thawrī, the Kufans and ash-Shāfi'ī said that they are separated but the prohibition is not perpetual. The marriage is invalidated and she observes a waiting period and then he is one of the suitors. Their argument is based on the consensus that, if he commits fornication with her, she is not unlawful for him to marry. Therefore the same must be true if he has sex with her while she is in the waiting period. They stated that that is the view of 'Alī. 'Abd ar-Razzāq mentioned it. Something similar is mentioned from Ibn Mas'ūd and al-Ḥasan. 'Abd ar-Razzāq mentioned from ath-Thawrī from Ash'ath from ash-Sha'bī from Masrāuq that 'Umar retracted that and permitted them to be joined.

Qāḍī Abu-l-Walīd al-Bājī mentioned in *al-Muntaqā*: 'When someone marries a woman in *'iddah*, then he must consummate it either within or after the end of the *'iddah*. If he consummates it within the *'iddah*, then the well-known position of the school is that the ban is perpetual. Aḥmad ibn Ḥanbal said that.' Shaykh Abū l-Qāsim related in *at-Tafrī'* that there are two transmissions about a man who knowingly marries a woman who is in *'iddah* on account of divorce or becoming a widow. One is that she is perpetually unlawful to him as we already stated. The second view is that he commits fornication and receives the *ḥadd* punishment and the child is not attached to him. He can marry her at the conclusion of the *'iddah*. That is the view of ash-Shāfi'ī and Abū Ḥanīfah.

The reasoning behind the first view, which is the well-known one, is based on what is confirmed of the judgment 'Umar gave regarding that and his establishing that among the people. His judgments have travelled and spread throughout the regions and no one is known to dispute them. It is confirmed that it is the consensus. Qaḍī Abū Muḥammad said, 'The same thing is related from 'Alī ibn Abī Ṭālib and no one opposes them in spite of that being well known and widespread, and so this has the ruling of consensus.'

The reasoning behind the second view is that this is forbidden sexual intercourse and so her prohibition is not perpetual, as would be the case if she had given herself in marriage, done a *mu'tah* marriage or fornicated. Qaḍī Abu-l-Ḥasan said that the well-known school of Mālik regarding that matter is weak in respect of logical thought. Allah knows best.

Abū 'Umar related from 'Abd al-Wārith ibn Sufyān from Qāsim ibn Aṣbagh from Muḥammad ibn Ismā'īl from Nu'aym ibn Ḥammād from Ibn al-Mubārak from Ash'ath from ash-Sha'bī that Masrūq said, "Umar ibn al-Khaṭṭāb heard that a woman of Quraysh had married a man of Thaqīf during her *'iddah* and he sent to them and separated them and punished them. He said, "You will never marry her!" He put her dower in the treasury. The news of that spread among people and the news reached 'Alī. He said, "May Allah have mercy on the Amīr al-Mu'minīn! What business does the treasury have with dowries? They were ignorant and the leader must return them to the sunnah." He was asked, "Then what do you say about them?" He answered, "She has her dower which makes sex lawful. They are separated but not flogged. She completes her first *'iddah* and then does a second full *'iddah* of three menstrual cycles. Then he can propose to her if he wishes to do so." 'Umar heard that and he addressed the people and said, "People! Prefer ignorance to the Sunnah!"'

Aṭ-Ṭabarī said, 'There is no disagreement among *fuqahā'* that if someone makes a marriage contract with a woman during her waiting period for another marriage, that marriage is invalid. The fact that 'Umar and 'Alī agreed that they are not subject to the *ḥadd* punishment indicates that an invalid marriage does not necessitate the *ḥadd* punishment. That is agreed upon if they are ignorant of the fact that it is forbidden, but there is disagreement when they do know about it.

They also disagree about whether she does an *'iddah* for both of them. This is the question about two *'iddah*s. The Madinans related from Mālik that she completes the rest of the first *'iddah* and then starts a new one for the other. That is the position of al-Layth, al-Ḥasan ibn Ḥayy, ash-Shāfi'ī, Aḥmad and Isḥāq. It is also related from 'Alī as we mentioned, and also from 'Umar. Muḥammad ibn al-Qāsim and Ibn Wahb related from Mālik that her *'iddah* for the second is enough from the day they are parted, whether by pregnancy, menstrual cycles or months. That is the view of ath-Thawrī, al-Awzā'ī, and Abū Ḥanīfah. Their argument is the consensus that the first husband may not marry her in the rest of the waiting period and so that indicates that she is in the waiting period for the second husband. Were it not for that, he would have married her in her waiting period for his marriage. The people with the first view reply that that is not necessary and that, because the first husband refused to marry her in the rest of the waiting period, it is mandatory when it is followed by the waiting period for the second. These are two duties which she owes two husbands, just like rights and duties owed to other human beings. One does not diminish the other.

Mālik transmitted from Ibn Shihāb from Sa'īd ibn al-Musayyab and Sulaymān ibn Yasār that Ṭulayḥah al-Asadiyyah was married to Rashīd ath-Thaqafī. He divorced her and she remarried during her *'iddah.* 'Umar ibn al-Khaṭṭāb beat her and beat her new husband with a scourge and separated them. Then 'Umar ibn al-Khaṭṭāb said, 'If any woman marries during her *'iddah* and the new husband has not consummated the marriage, separate them. Then she finishes her *'iddah* from her first husband and the new husband becomes one of the suitors. If he has consummated the marriage, separate them. Then she finishes her *'iddah* from her first husband and then observes another *'iddah* for the new husband and they are never united.' Mālik added that Sa'īd ibn al-Musayyab said, 'She has her dower because sex was made lawful.' Abū 'Umar said, 'This Ṭulayḥah is Ṭulayḥah bint 'Ubaydullāh, the sister of Ṭalḥah ibn 'Ubaydullāh at-Taymī. Some copies of the *Muwaṭṭā'* in the transmission of Yaḥyā have Ṭulayḥah al-Asadiyyah. That is an ignorant error and I do not know of anyone who said that.'

When he said that he beat them with a scourge, it means as a punishment for committing something forbidden, which is marriage during the waiting period. Az-Zuhrī said, 'I do not think that it reached the level of flogging.' He said, "Abd al-Malik flogged both of them with forty lashes for that.' He said, 'Qabīṣah ibn Dhu'ayb was asked about that and said, "You should have been lighter and given them twenty!"' Ibn Ḥabīb said about when a woman marries in the waiting period and then the new husband touches her, kisses her, winks or looks with a look of pleasure, then the couple should be punished as well as the *walī*, the two witnesses and anyone who knew that she was still in her *'iddah*. There is no punishment for any of them who did not know that. Ibn al-Mawwāz said that if they did that deliberately, the couple are flogged with the *ḥadd* punishment. It is possible that the position of Ibn Ḥabīb is about the one who knows about the *'iddah*. It is possible that he was ignorant of the prohibition and did not intend to commit something prohibited. That is the one who is merely punished. Accordingly, 'Umar beat the woman and her husband with a scourge. The punishment and discipline for that is according to the circumstances of the one punished. The statement of Ibn al-Mawwāz can be taken to mean that they knew of the prohibition and committed what was forbidden out of boldness. Shaykh Abu-l-Qāsim said that these are two transmissions about doing it deliberately: one is that there is the *ḥadd* and the other that there is punishment and no *ḥadd*.

**Know that Allah knows what is in yourselves, so beware of Him!**

This is an extreme warning against falling into what is forbidden.

لَّا جُنَاحَ عَلَيْكُمْ إِن طَلَّقْتُمُ ٱلنِّسَآءَ مَا لَمْ تَمَسُّوهُنَّ أَوْ تَفْرِضُوا۟ لَهُنَّ
فَرِيضَةً وَمَتِّعُوهُنَّ عَلَى ٱلْمُوسِعِ قَدْرُهُۥ وَعَلَى ٱلْمُقْتِرِ قَدْرُهُۥ مَتَٰعًۢا
بِٱلْمَعْرُوفِ حَقًّا عَلَى ٱلْمُحْسِنِينَ ٢٣٦

**236 There is nothing wrong in your divorcing women before you have touched them or allotted a dower to them. But give them a gift – he who is wealthy according to his means and he who is less well off according to his means – a gift to be given with correctness and courtesy: a duty for all good-doers.**

**There is nothing wrong in your divorcing women before you have touched them or allotted a dower to them.**

This is another of the rulings which deal with divorced women. It deals with removing any aspersion of wrongdoing from a man who divorces before the consummation of a marriage, whether or not a dower has been stipulated. So the Messenger of Allah ﷺ forbade marriage merely for the sake of gratification and sexual indulgence and instructed people to marry for the sake of protection and in order to obtain Allah's reward, and with the intention of having a constant companion. The believers did not like divorcing before a marriage had been consummated, as they believed that it was disliked and so this *āyah* was revealed to remove their prejudice against it, since the basis of marriage lies in the good intention behind it. Some people said that '*nothing wrong*' means that you should not ask for the return of the entire dower. You are only entitled to get back half of what has been allotted to her and you should give a gift to the woman if the amount of the dower has not been stipulated. It is said that when the command to pay the dower was confirmed in the Sharī'ah, it was thought that a dower was obligatory, either stipulated or appropriate. In this *āyah* the wrong was removed from someone who divorces before any dower has been stipulated. Some people have said that it refers to those who pronounce divorce during menstruation when the marriage has not been consummated since in that case the woman does not have to observe a waiting period.

There are four types of divorced women:

- Women in a consummated marriage with an allotted dower and Allah has mentioned before this *āyah* that the ruling in respect of their *'iddah* is three menstrual periods. They are not asked to return any of their dower.
- Women without an allotted dower whose marriage has not been consummated and this *āyah* is about them. They are not allotted a dower but Allah says that they should be given a gift. And it is made clear in *Sūrat al-Aḥzāb* (33) that a woman whose marriage has not been consummated and who is divorced has no *'iddah*.
- Women who have been allotted a dower whose marriage has not been consummated who will be mentioned after this *āyah* in 2:237.
- Women without a dower whose marriage has been consummated. They will be mentioned in *Sūrat an-Nisā'* (4:24).

This *āyah* is about women divorced before either consummation or the allotment of a dower, and the next is about women who are divorced before consummation but after the allotment of dower. The first receives a gift and the second receives half of the dower because of the specification of the contract.

Allah divided divorced women into two groups: those with an allotted dower and those without. He indicated that *tafwīḍ* marriage is permitted. This is a marriage in which the dower is not mentioned. It is not disputed and in it the woman is allotted a dower after the contract. If it is allotted, it is connected to the contract and permitted. If it is not allotted to her and there is a divorce, the consensus is that the dower is not obliged. Qāḍī Abū Bakr ibn al-'Arabī said that. Al-Mahdawī related from Ḥammād ibn Abī Sulaymān that when a man divorces a wife without having consummated the marriage, and has not allotted her a dower, he is compelled to give half of a suitable dower. If the dower has been allotted after the marriage contract and before divorce, Abū Ḥanīfah said that it is not made half by divorce because it was not obliged by the contract. This is contrary to the literal meaning of the text of His words: *'If you divorce them before you have touched them but have already allotted them a dower.'* (2:237) It is also contrary to analogy. The allotment after the contract is connected to the contract and so it is obliged to be halved by divorce. The basic position is that the allotment is connected to the contract.

Concerning what happens if death occurs before allotment, at-Tirmidhī mentioned that Ibn Mas'ūd was asked about a man who married a woman without allotting her something and had not consummated the marriage before he died. Ibn Mas'ūd said, 'She receives the like dower of other women of her class, neither more nor less. She has to observe the *'iddah* and she inherits.' Ma'qil ibn Sinān al-Ashja'ī said, 'The Messenger of Allah ﷺ gave a similar decision about Barwa' bint Wāshiq, one of our women.' Ibn Mas'ūd was very happy to hear that. At-Tirmidhī said that it is a sound *ḥasan ḥadīth*. It is also related from him by another path of transmission. This was the normative practice among some of the people of knowledge among the Companions of the Prophet ﷺ and others. It is also the view of ath-Thawrī, Aḥmad and Isḥāq. Some of the people of knowledge among the Companions of the Prophet ﷺ, including 'Alī ibn Abī Ṭālib, Zayd ibn Thābit, Ibn 'Abbās and Ibn 'Umar said that when a man marries a woman and does not consummate the marriage and has not allotted her a dower before he dies, then she inherits but has no dower and must observe *'iddah*. That is the position of ash-Shāfi'ī who said, 'If the *ḥadīth* of Barwa' bint Wāshiq is confirmed, it is argument for what is related from the Prophet ﷺ.' It is related from ash-Shāfi'ī that he retracted this position in Egypt and accepted the *ḥadīth* of Barwa' bint Wāshiq.

There is disagreement about the firmness of the *ḥadīth* of Barwa' bint Wāshiq. Qāḍī Abū Muḥammad 'Abd al-Wahhāb said in his commentary on the *Risālah* of Ibn Abi Zayd: 'The experts in *ḥadīth* and leaders of the people of knowledge reject the *ḥadīth* of Barwa' bint Wāshiq.' Al-Wāqidī said, 'This *ḥadīth* was situated in Madīnah and none of the scholars accept it.' As we and Ibn al-Mundhir mentioned, at-Tirmidhī considered it to be sound. Ibn al-Mundhir said, 'It is confirmed like the report of 'Abdullāh ibn Mas'ūd from the Messenger of Allah ﷺ. We say that.' He mentioned that it is the view of Abū Thawr and the People of Opinion. A similar position to that of 'Alī, Zayd, Ibn 'Abbās and Ibn 'Umar is mentioned from az-Zuhrī, al-Awzā'ī, Mālik and ash-Shāfi'ī. There is a third position which is that the woman has no inheritance until she has a dower. Masrūq said that.

Part of the argument of Mālik, that a marriage which is ended before any allotment does not oblige a dower, is that its basis is divorce, but if the *ḥadīth* is sound, then the analogy opposing it is unsound. Abū Muḥammad 'Abd al-Ḥamīd related from the School that which is in agreement with the *ḥadīth*. Praise be to Allah. Abū 'Umar said, 'The *ḥadīth* of Barwa' bint Wāshiq was related by 'Abd ar-Razzāq from ath-Thawrī from Manṣūr from Ibrāhīm from 'Alqamah from Ibn Mas'ūd. It says in it: 'Ma'qil ibn Sinān stood up.' Ibn Mahdī related from ath-Thawrī from Firās from ash-Sha'bī from Masrūq that 'Abdullāh said, 'Ma'qil ibn Yasār stood up' I believe that what is correct is Ma'qil ibn Sinān rather than Ma'qil ibn Yasār because Ma'qil ibn Yasār was a man of Muzaynah and this *ḥadīth* is about a woman of Ashja', not Muzaynah. That is how Abū Dāwud related it from ash-Sha'bī from 'Alqamah. He says in it: 'Some people of Ashja'.' Ma'qil ibn Sinān was killed in the Battle of al-Ḥarrah. A poet says:

The Anṣār weep for their leaders,
and Ashja' weeps for Ma'qil ibn Sinān.

In the phrase '*before you have touched them*', *mā* means 'which'. It means 'If you have divorced women without touching them.' The recitation of Nāfi', Ibn Kathīr, Abū 'Amr, 'Āṣim and Ibn 'Āmir is '*tamassūhunna*' and that of Ḥamzah and al-Kisā'ī is '*tumāssūhunna*' from Form III because sexual intercourse needs the participation of both of them. The first reading also has an associative meaning. Abū 'Alī preferred it because the verbs with this meaning normally are in Form I, but both readings are good. '*Aw*' ('or') means 'and' here, meaning, 'before you have touched them and have not allotted them.'

**But give them a gift –**

This means give them something they will enjoy having. Some, like 'Alī ibn Abī Ṭālib, al-Ḥasan ibn Abī 'l-Ḥasan, Sa'īd ibn Jubayr, Abū Qilābah, az-Zuhrī, Qatādah, and aḍ-Ḍaḥḥāk, take it as being mandatory. Others, such as Abū 'Ubayd, Mālik ibn Anas and his people, Qāḍī Shurayḥ and others, see it as merely being a recommendation. The people with the first position take it as a command and those with the second view look at the words, *'a duty for good-doers'* and '*for all who are godfearing'* (2:241) and say that if it had been mandatory, it would have been made general to all people. The first view is more appropriate because of the universal nature of the command to give and connecting the gift to them by the particle of possession in the words: *'Divorced women should receive maintenance.'* (2:241) That is more apparently an obligation than a recommendation. The second *āyah* stresses the fact that it is an obligation because everyone must have fear of Allah in respect of *shirk* and disobedience. Allah says: *'guidance for the godfearing.'*

There is disagreement about the pronoun 'them' and which women are meant. Ibn 'Abbās, Ibn 'Umar, Jābir ibn Zayd, al-Ḥasan, ash-Shāfi'ī, Aḥmad, 'Aṭā', Isḥāq and the People of Opinion say that a gift is mandatory for a woman divorced before consummation or the allotment of a dower and recommended for others. Mālik and his people said that it is recommended in every divorce even if the marriage was consummated. In the case of a woman whose marriage has been consummated and who has an allotted dower, she should receive her dower but no extra gift. Abū Thawr says she should receive a gift as well, as should every divorced woman. The people of knowledge say that in the case of a woman who has not been allotted a dower and whose marriage has not been consummated, she should only receive a gift. Az-Zuhrī said that the qāḍī decides it for her. Most people say that he does not decide it.

This consensus is about free women. If a slave-girl is divorced before allotment and consummation, then most say that she receives a gift. Al-Awzā'ī and ath-Thawrī said that she receives no gift because she belongs to her master and he is not entitled to property in exchange for the harm to his property by divorce. As for the fixed school of Mālik, Ibn Sha'bān said, 'The gift is on account of the sorrow of divorce. That is why there is no gift before or after consummation for a woman parted by *khul'*, freeing herself and *li'ān* because in that instance she is the one who chose divorce.' At-Tirmidhī, 'Aṭā' and an-Nakha'ī said that the wife should receive a gift after *khul'*. The People of Opinion said that a woman separated by *li'ān* receives a gift. Ibn al-Qāsim said that there is no gift where an invalid marriage is concerned. Ibn al-Mawwāz said, 'There is no gift in a marriage which becomes unsound after a sound contract, such as when one of the couple becomes the owner of the other.' Ibn al-Qāsim said, 'The basis of that is that Allah's words: "*Divorced women should receive maintenance/a gift*" only apply to divorce, not invalidity.' Ibn Wahb related from Mālik that a wife given a choice receives a gift which is not the case with a slave-girl who is freed while married to a slave. She has a choice about herself. Such a wife does not receive a gift. As for a free woman given a choice, or who is given authority [for divorce] or whose husband marries a slave-girl, and she chooses herself, in all such instances she receives a gift because the husband is the cause of the separation.

Mālik says that it is not specified whether the gift should be a little or a lot. People disagree about this. Ibn 'Umar said that the minimum is about thirty dirhams. Ibn 'Abbās said, 'The largest gift is a servant, then clothes, then maintenance.' 'Aṭā' said that a medium-sized gift is a dress, veil (*khimār*) and mantle. Abū Ḥanīfah said, 'That is the minimum it should be.' Ibn Muḥayriz said that anyone receiving a state pension should give thirty dinars and a slave should also give a gift. Al-Ḥasan says that it is according to ability and continued, 'One gives a servant, another gives clothes, another a garment and another money.' That is what Mālik said because the *āyah* says *'according to his means'* and there is no amount or limit specified. Al-Ḥasan ibn 'Alī gave a gift of 20,000 and skins full of honey. Shurayḥ gave a gift of 50,000 dirhams.

It is said that one considers the circumstances of the woman as well. Some Shāfi'īs said that. They said, 'If we were consider the state of the man alone, and then if he were to marry two women, one of whom is noble and the other lowly and divorce both before consummation without naming any dower, would they be equal in the gift, the lowly receiving the same as the noble woman? This is contrary to the words of Allah *"...a gift to be given with correctness."* That would oblige that when a wealthy man marries a lowly woman, he is like her because if he divorces her before consummation and allotting a dower, he is obliged to give a gift commensurate with his state and a dower suitable for someone like her. According to this, the gift would be many times greater than the suitable dower and so she would be entitled before consummation many times more than what she would be entitled to afterwards in the form of a suitable dower which is in exchange for sexual intercourse.' The People of Opinion and others say that the gift to a woman divorced before consummation is half of a suitable dower and nothing else, because a suitable dower becomes due by the contract and the gift is part of the suitable dower. Therefore it is obliged for her as the half of the specified dower is obliged when she is divorced before consummation. This is refuted by Allah's words: *'...he who is wealthy according to his means, and he who is less well off according to his means.'* This is evidence which refutes a limit. Allah knows the realities of all matters.

Ath-Tha'labī mentioned a *ḥadīth* and said that the words: *'There is nothing wrong in your divorcing women…'* were revealed about a man of the Anṣār who married a woman of the Banū Ḥanīfah without specifying a dower for her. He divorced her before touching her and the *āyah* was revealed. The Prophet ﷺ said, 'Give her a gift, even if it is your hat.' Ad-Dāraquṭnī related that Suwayd ibn Ghafalah said, "Ā'ishah al-Khath'amiyyah was married to al-Ḥasan ibn 'Alī ibn Abī Ṭālib. When 'Alī was struck down and allegiance was given to al-Ḥasan as the caliph, she said, "Congratulations on the caliphate, Amīr al-Mu'minīn!" He said, "'Alī is murdered and you make a show of gloating! Go, you are divorced three times." She wrapped herself in her garments and waited until her *'iddah* was over. He sent her 10,000 as a gift along with the rest of her dower. She said: "A scant gift from a parting lover!" When he heard what she had said, he wept and said, "If it had not been that I heard my grandfather (or my father told me that he heard my grandfather) say, 'If a man divorces his wife three times finally or three times over cycles, she is not lawful to him until she has married another husband,' I would have taken her back."' One variant has: 'When the messenger informed him, he wept and said, "If I had not divorced her finally, I would have taken her back. But I heard the Messenger of Allah ﷺ say, 'If a man divorces his wife three times with a divorce in each period of purity, or a divorce at the beginning of each month, or three times all at once, she is not lawful to him until she has married another husband.'""

If someone is ignorant about the need to give a gift, he should still give it to his divorced wife, even if years have passed and she has since married someone else, or to her heirs if she has died. Ibn al-Mawwāz related that from Ibn al-Qāsim. Aṣbagh said that he does not owe anything if she has died because it is solace for the wife on account of being divorced and that has occurred. The reasoning behind the first is that it is a right confirmed against him and it moves from her to her heirs, as is the case with other rights. This notes its obligatory nature in the school. Allah knows best.

**he who is wealthy according to his means and he who is less well off according to his means –**

This is also taken as evidence of the mandatory nature of the gift. Most recite *'al-mūsi'*, who is someone in a wealthy situation. One says, 'he spends according to his means (*qadaruhu*)'. Ibn Kathīr, Nāfi', Abū 'Amr and 'Āṣim in the transmission of Abū Bakr recite *'qadruhu'* in both places, while Ibn 'Āmir, Ḥamzah, al-Kisā'ī and 'Āṣim in the variant of Ḥafṣ recite *'qadaruhu'*. Abu-l-Ḥasan al-Akhfash said that they mean the same. Abū Zayd also related that and that is used elsewhere in the Qur'an. *'Muqtir'* is someone with little property.

**a gift to be given with correctness and courtesy:**

The words *'with correctness and courtesy'* here mean with moderation according to the Sharī'ah.

**a duty for all good-doers.**

This is further evidence for the mandatory nature of the gift. The verb *ḥaqqa* means to decide and oblige. The word 'duty' stresses it. It is also said that this means that it is for the believers because only they can be called 'godfearing' and 'good-doers'. All people are commanded to do good and be godfearing. They do good by performing the obligations of Allah and avoiding actions in which they disobey Him so that they do not enter the Fire. So it is obliged for all people to do good and be godfearing.

وَإِن طَلَّقْتُمُوهُنَّ مِن قَبْلِ أَن تَمَسُّوهُنَّ وَقَدْ فَرَضْتُمْ لَهُنَّ فَرِيضَةً
فَنِصْفُ مَا فَرَضْتُمْ إِلَّآ أَن يَعْفُونَ أَوْ يَعْفُوَا۟ ٱلَّذِى بِيَدِهِۦ عُقْدَةُ
ٱلنِّكَاحِ ۚ وَأَن تَعْفُوٓا۟ أَقْرَبُ لِلتَّقْوَىٰ ۚ وَلَا تَنسَوُا۟ ٱلْفَضْلَ بَيْنَكُمْ ۚ
إِنَّ ٱللَّهَ بِمَا تَعْمَلُونَ بَصِيرٌ ﴿٢٣٧﴾

**237 If you divorce them before you have touched them but have already allotted them a dower, they should have half the amount which you allotted, unless they forgo it or the one in charge of the marriage contract forgoes it. To forgo it is closer to taqwā. Do not forget to show generosity to one another. Allah sees what you do.**

**If you divorce them before you have touched them but have already allotted them a dower,**

People disagree about this *āyah*. One group, including Mālik and others, says that it removes the ruling of the gift in the previous *āyah* from any woman who is divorced after a dower has been allotted. Sa'īd ibn al-Musayyab said that this *āyah* abrogates the *āyah* in *Sūrat al-Aḥzāb* (33:49) because it includes giving a gift to all wives whose marriage has not been consummated. Qatādah says that it abrogates the *āyah* preceding it. I say that the positions of Sa'īd and Qatādah are debatable since the preconditions for abrogation do not exist and it is possible for it to coexist with the other *āyahs*. Ibn al-Qāsim said in the *Mudawwanah*, 'The gift is for every divorced woman in 2:241 and for any woman whose marriage has not been consummated in the *āyah* in *Sūrat al-Aḥzāb*.' So Allah excluded a woman who has been allotted a dower by this *āyah*. Here it is confirmed that she has half of what has been allotted. One group of scholars, including Abū Thawr, say that the command to give a gift to every divorced woman is universal and that this *āyah* makes it clear that a woman who has had a dower allotted to her receives half of it and the *āyah* does not mean that the gift is cancelled. Rather she receives a gift as well as half the dower.

**they should have half the amount which you allotted,**

This is mandatory. The consensus is that the allotted dower is divided equally between the man and the woman. 'Half' is the portion of something divided in two.

If a husband allots his wife a dower and then divorces her before consummation, the dower being in her possession, Mālik says that the growth of every property or slave given to her as a dower is shared between them, just as any decrease or destruction is shared between them. The woman owes nothing of it. If he gives her gold or silver and she uses it to purchase a slave or house, or she uses it to buy a share of something or buys something else like perfume, kitchen utensils or something else which she uses for her outfitting and putting things in order for remaining with him, all of that is in the position of the dower given to her and they both share in any growth or decrease in it. If he divorces her before consummation, she only keeps half of it. She is indebted to him for half of what she took from him. If she bought something personal with some or part of it, then she can be in debt to him for half of the dower that she took from him. That is also the case if she buys a slave or a house with a thousand that he gave her as a dower. If he then divorces her before consummation: she owes him half of the thousand.

There is no disagreement that if a man consummates his marriage and then dies having named something for her, she receives the total that he named for her as well as her share of the inheritance and she must observe *'iddah*.

They disagree about a man who has been alone with a woman but has not had sexual intercourse with her before parting from her. The Kufans and Mālik say that he owes the total dower and she must observe *'iddah* based on the report of Ibn Mas'ūd who said, 'The Rightly-guided Caliphs judged that when someone closes the door or lowers the curtain, she inherits and must observe *'iddah*.' It is related *marfū'* and ad-Dāraquṭnī transmitted it. It will be mentioned in *an-Nisā'*. Ash-Shāfi'ī did not oblige a full dower and says that she does not have to observe *'iddah* if there was no consummation. That is based on the apparent text of the Qur'an. Shurayḥ said, 'I did not hear Allah mention a door or a curtain in His

Book. When he claims that he has not touched her, then she receives half the dower. That is the position of Ibn 'Abbās.' What our scholars say about this will be mentioned in *an-Nisā'* (4:21).

**unless they forgo it**

This is forgoing the half they are due because of the marriage. This refers to women who have charge of their own affairs. Allah allowed them to forgo it after it has become mandatory since it is solely their due and they can see that it is carried out or they can forgo it as they like. Women in charge of their own affairs are those who are adult, sane and sensible. Ibn 'Abbās and a group of *fuqahā'* and Tābi'ūn said that it is permitted for a virgin who does not have a *walī* to do that. Saḥnūn related it in the *Mudawwanah* from other than Ibn al-Qāsim after Ibn al-Qāsim mentioned that she was not permitted to set aside the half. If she is a ward of someone or a child, it is not permitted for her to cancel the half. There is no disagreement about that as far as I know.

**or the one in charge of the marriage contract forgoes it.**

People disagree about who is meant by this. Ad-Dāraquṭnī related that Jubayr ibn Muṭ'im married a woman from the Banū Naṣr and divorced her before consummation. He sent her the full dower and said, 'I am entitled to forgo it. Allah says: *"...unless they forgo it, or the one in charge of the marriage contract forgoes it."* Therefore I am entitled to forgo it.' He interpreted the *āyah* as referring to himself in every situation before and after divorce, namely the marriage contract, since he could act on it or not. Ad-Dāraquṭnī also related *marfū'* from Qutaybah ibn Sa'īd from Ibn Lahī'ah from 'Amr ibn Shu'ayb from his father from his grandfather that the Messenger of Allah ﷺ said, 'The *walī* of the marriage contract is the husband.' This also comes from 'Alī, Ibn 'Abbās, Sa'īd ibn al-Musayyab and Shurayḥ. He said that that was stated by Nāfi' ibn Jubayr, Muḥammad ibn Ka'b, Ṭāwūs, Mujāhid, ash-Sha'bī and Sa'īd ibn Jubayr. That is also true of Mujāhid and ath-Thawrī. Abū Ḥanīfah preferred it, and it is the sound view from ash-Shafi'ī. They all say that a guardian has no control over any of his ward's dower as there is a consensus that it would not he permitted for him to absolve the husband of all the dower if there were no divorce. So the same applies if there is. They agree that a guardian does not have the power to give away any of his ward's property, and the dower is her property. They agree that guardians cannot absolve the husband, no matter whether they are nephews, uncles or fathers. Allah knows best.

Some of them say that a guardian has that right. Ad-Dāraquṭnī also has a report from Ibn 'Abbās regarding that, and it is the position of Ibrāhīm, 'Alqamah and al-Ḥasan, and others added 'Ikrimah, Ṭāwūs, 'Aṭā', Abu-z-Zinād, Zayd ibn Aslam, Rabī'ah, Muḥammad ibn Ka'b, Ibn Shihāb, al-Aswad ibn Yazīd, ash-Sha'bī, Qatādah and Mālik, and it was the old position of ash-Shāfi'ī. According to them it is permitted for a father to forgo half of the dower of his virgin daughter if she is divorced before the consummation of her marriage whether or not she has reached the age of menstruation. 'Īsā ibn Dīnār said, 'She does not have recourse to any of it from her father.'

The evidence that it is the *walī* that is meant is found in the words of Allah at the beginning of the *āyah*: *'If you divorce them before you have touched them but have already allotted them a dower, they should have half the amount you allotted.'* So He mentioned the husbands and addressed this to them. Then He says, *'...unless they forgo it,'* and mentioned women. Then a third group are mentioned: *'...or the one in charge of the marriage contract forgoes it.'* This does not refer to the previously mentioned husband unless no one but him exists. But the guardian exists and so he is the one who is meant. Makkī said that and Ibn al-'Arabī mentioned it. Furthermore, Allah says: *'...unless they forgo it,'* and it is known that a minor girl is not in a position to forgo. A young girl, and one who is a ward, are not in a position to forgo and so Allah made the two categories clear. He said: *'...unless they forgo'* when they are entitled to do that: *'...or the one in charge of the marriage contract,'* who is the *walī*: *'...forgoes it'* because he is in charge of the matter.

That is what is related by Ibn Wahb, Ashhab, Ibn 'Abd al-Ḥakam and Ibn al-Qāsim from Mālik about the father of a virgin girl and the master of a slave-girl. The *walī* is permitted to forgo when he is one of the appropriate people. He is not permitted to forgo if he is a simpleton.

If it is said that we do not agree that it is the *walī*, but rather it is the husband. He is more entitled to this title because he has more control over the contract than the *walī*, as was already stated, then we reply that we do not accept that the husband has more control over the contract than the father of a virgin girl. The father of the virgin has control of it, rather than the husband, because the object of the contract is the dower of the virgin. The husband does not have the right to contract that, but rather it is the father who does. Shurayḥ allowed the brother to forgo half the dower. That is what 'Ikrimah said: 'The one who makes the contract of marriage between them can forgo, whether he is an uncle, father or brother, even she dislikes it.'

**To forgo it is closer to taqwā. Do not forget to show generosity to one another.**

This is addressed to both men and women according to Ibn 'Abbās. Mujāhid said, 'What is best is for a man to forgo all the dower or for a woman to forgo half of it.'

**Allah sees what you do.**

This is a promise to the good-doer and warning for the one who does not do good. Nothing you do is hidden from Allah.

حَٰفِظُواْ عَلَى ٱلصَّلَوَٰتِ وَٱلصَّلَوٰةِ ٱلْوُسْطَىٰ وَقُومُواْ لِلَّهِ قَٰنِتِينَ ﴿٢٣٨﴾

**238 Safeguard the prayer – especially the middle one. Stand in obedience to Allah.**

**Safeguard the prayer – especially the middle one.**

The command is in the plural, directed at the entire Community. The *āyah* is a command to persevere in performing the prayers at their correct times with all their preconditions. Safeguarding implies constancy in a thing and perseverance in it. The 'middle' of something is the best and most balanced part of it. Allah uses the term in another place in the same way when He says: *'In this way We have made you a middlemost community.'* (2:143). A desert Arab praised the Prophet ﷺ:

O midmost of all people in praise!
Noblest of people in mother and father!

The middle prayer is singled out for mention because it is in the middle of all the prayers, to honour it. An example of this is found in Allah's words: *'When We made a covenant with all the Prophets – with you and with Nūḥ'* a(33:7) and: *'In them are fruits and date-palms and pomegranates.'* (55:68) There are various positions regarding what constitutes the middle prayer:

– One is that it is *Ẓuhr* because it is in the middle of day, according to the sound position that the day starts from dawn. We begin with *Ẓuhr* because it is the first prayer prayed in Islam. Those who said that it is the middle prayer include Zayd ibn Thābit, Abū Sa'īd al-Khudrī, 'Abdullāh ibn 'Umar and 'Ā'ishah ﷺ. One thing that indicates that it is the middle prayer is what 'Ā'ishah and Ḥafṣah said when they recited the *āyah* and said, 'especially the middle one and the *'Aṣr* prayer.' It is related that it is harder for the Muslims because it comes at a time of when it is very hot and they are distracted from it by work in their property. Abū Dāwud reports from Zayd: 'The Prophet ﷺ used to pray *Ẓuhr* at midday and he did not pray any prayer which was harder for the Companions of the Prophet ﷺ. Then: *"Safeguard the prayer – especially the middle one..."* was revealed.' He said that there are two prayers before it and two prayers after it. Mālik related in the *Muwaṭṭā'* and Abū Dāwud aṭ-Ṭayālisī in the *Musnad* that Zayd ibn Thābit said, 'The middle prayer is *Ẓuhr*.' Aṭ-Ṭayālisī added, 'The Prophet ﷺ used to pray it at midday.'

– It is said to be *'Aṣr* because the two prayers of the day are before it and the two prayers of the night after it. An-Naḥḥās said, 'Better than this is the argument that it is called "middle" because it is between two prayers. One of them is the first to be made obligatory and the other was the second to be made obligatory. Among those who said this were 'Alī ibn Abī Ṭālib, Ibn 'Abbās, Ibn 'Umar, Abū Hurayrah, and Abū Sa'īd al-Khudrī. This view is the one preferred by Abū Ḥanīfah and his people and ash-Shāfi'ī and most of the traditionists. It was the view of 'Abd al-Malik ibn Ḥabīb and preferred by Ibn al-'Arabī in *al-Qabas*. In his *tafsīr*, Ibn 'Aṭiyyah said, 'It is the position of the majority of people, and I also say that.' Hadiths transmitted by Muslim and others are offered as evidence for this position. Ibn Mas'ūd reported that the Messenger of Allah ﷺ said, 'The middle prayer is the *'Aṣr* prayer.' At-Tirmidhī transmitted it and said that it is a sound *ḥasan ḥadīth*. We dealt with more of this in *al-Qabas*, a commentary on the *Muwaṭṭā'* of Mālik ibn Anas.

– It is said to be *Maghrib*. Qubayṣah ibn Abī Dhu'ayb said that as well as others. Their evidence is that it is middle in the number of *rak'ah*s neither more nor less and is not shortened on a journey, and the Prophet ﷺ did not delay it or bring it forward. Prayers are aloud after it and silent before it. 'Ā'ishah reported that he ﷺ said, 'The best of prayers in the sight of Allah is the *Maghrib* prayer. It is not decreased for a traveller or someone who is resident. Allah began the night prayers with it and sealed the day prayers with it. If someone prays *Maghrib* and prays two *rak'ah*s after it, Allah will built him a castle in the Garden. If someone prays four *rak'ah*s after it, Allah will forgive him the wrong actions of twenty years (or forty years).'

– It is said to be *'Ishā'* because it is between two prayers which may not be shortened and it comes at the time of sleep and it is recommended to delay it, so that makes it difficult to safeguard.

– It is said to be *Ṣubḥ*, because the two night prayers before it are those in which the prayer is said out loud and the two daytime prayers after it are silent and because it is a time when people are asleep and rising for it is hard in the winter because of the cold and in the summer because the night is short. Those who said that it was *Ṣubḥ* include 'Alī ibn Abī Ṭālib and 'Abdullāh ibn 'Abbās. It is also transmitted in the *Muwaṭṭā'* and at-Tirmidhī reports it from Ibn 'Umar and Ibn 'Abbās in commentary. It is related from Jābir ibn 'Abdullāh. It is the position of Mālik and his people and ash-Shāfi'ī inclined to it according to al-Qushayrī.

The sound report from 'Alī is that it is *'Aṣr* which is related from him by a sound known path. For evidence that it is *Ṣubḥ*, they cite, *'Stand in obedience to Him,'* i.e. in it, and there is no prayer in which *al-qunūt* (standing in obedience) is prescribed except *Ṣubḥ*. Abū Rajā' said, 'Ibn 'Abbās led us in the morning prayer in Basra and did the *qunūt* in it before *rukū'*. He raised his hands and when he finished, he said, 'This is the middle prayer in which Allah commanded us to stand in obedience.' Anas said, 'The Prophet ﷺ did the *qunūt* in the *Ṣubḥ* prayer after *rukū'*.' The ruling on the *qunūt* and what scholars say about it will be found in *Āl 'Imrān*.

– Some say that it refers to the Jumu'ah prayer because one is encouraged to go to it and listen to the *khuṭbah* in it and it is made a festival. Ibn Ḥabīb and Makkī mentioned that. Muslim related from 'Abdullāh that the Prophet ﷺ said about some people who failed to come to Jumu'ah, 'I thought about commanding a man to lead the people in the prayer and then burning the houses of some men who failed to come to Jumu'ah.'

– *Ṣubḥ* and *'Aṣr* together. Shaykh Abū Bakr al-Abharī said that his evidence for that in found in the words of the Messenger of Allah ﷺ, 'The angels of the night and the angels of the day succeed one another in overseeing you.' Abū Hurayrah related it. Jarīr ibn 'Abdullāh said, 'We were sitting with the Prophet ﷺ when he looked at the full moon and said, "You will see your Lord as you see this moon without any doubt that you are seeing Him. If you are able not to miss the prayer before sunrise and before sunset, do so."' He means *'Aṣr* and *Fajr*. Then Jarīr recited, *'Glorify your Lord with praise before the rising of the sun and before its setting.'* (20:130) 'Umārah ibn Ru'aybah related that he heard the Messenger of Allah ﷺ say, 'Someone who prayed before the rising of the sun and before its setting will not enter the Fire.' It means *'Aṣr* and *Fajr*. The Prophet ﷺ also said, 'Whoever prays the two cool ones will enter the Garden.' It is confirmed in *Ṣaḥīḥ Muslim* and elsewhere. He called them that because they are done in times of coolness.

– *'Ishā'* and *Ṣubḥ*. Abu-d-Darda' said in his final illness. 'Listen and convey to your descendants: safeguard these two prayers (i.e. in the group): *'Ishā'* and *Ṣubḥ*. If you had known what was in them, you would have come to them, even crawling on your hands and knees.' 'Umar and 'Uthmān said that. The imams related that the Messenger of Allah ﷺ said, 'If you had known what was in *'Ishā'* and *Ṣubḥ*, you would have come to them, even crawling.' He said that they are the hardest prayers for hypocrites. It makes the one who prays *Ṣubḥ* in the group rise at night and *'Ishā'* is in the middle of the night. Mālik mentioned it *mawqūf*, stopping at 'Uthmān and Muslim has it *marfū'*. Abū Dāwud and at-Tirmidhī transmitted that the Messenger of Allah ﷺ said, 'Whoever attends *'Ishā'* in the group, it is as if he prayed half the night. Whoever prays *'Ishā'* and *Fajr* in the group, it is as if he had prayed the entire night.' This is contrary to what Mālik and Muslim related.

– The five prayers as a group. Mu'ādh ibn Jabal said that. That is because *'Safeguard the prayer'* includes the obligatory and the supererogatory. Then he singles out the obligatory.

– It is unspecified. Nāfi' quoted Ibn 'Umar as saying that. Ar-Rabī' ibn Khaytham said that. Allah concealed it among the five prayers as He concealed the Night of Power in Ramadan, the time of acceptance on the day of Jumu'ah and the times of the night when supplication is accepted so that people will pray at night in the darkness to converse with the Knower of secrets. Evidence for the validity of its being undefined and not specified is found in what Muslim related in the *Ṣaḥīḥ* at the end of the chapter where al-Barā' ibn 'Āzib said, '"Safeguard the prayer – especially 'Aṣr" was revealed and we recited it for as long as Allah wished and then Allah abrogated it and said, "*Safeguard the prayer – especially the middle one.*"' A man asked, 'So it is the *'Aṣr* prayer?' Al-Barā' said, 'I have informed you of how it was revealed and how Allah abrogated it. Allah knows best.' This implies that after it was specified, its specification was abrogated and made unknown. Allah knows best. This is what Muslim preferred because he puts it at the end of the chapter. More than one of the later scholars said that it is sound, Allah willing, because of the contradictory evidence and lack of preference. All that is left, then, is to persevere in all of them and perform them at their times.

This disagreement about the middle prayer indicates the falseness of the position of those who claim that the words 'and the *'Aṣr* prayer' in the *ḥadīth* of Yūnus, the freedman of 'Ā'ishah, where she told him to write out the Qur'an for her were actually part of the Qur'an. Our scholars said that it is like a commentary from the Prophet ﷺ as indicated by the *ḥadīth* of 'Amr ibn Rāfi': 'Ḥafṣah told me to write out the Qur'an for her. Part of what she dictated to me was: "*Safeguard the prayer – especially the middle one* (which is *'Aṣr*.) *Stand in obedience to Allah.*" She said, "That is how I heard the Messenger of Allah ﷺ recite it."' So her words about *'Aṣr* indicate that the Messenger of Allah ﷺ explained the middle prayer as being *'Aṣr*. Nāfi' related 'and the *'Aṣr* prayer' from 'Ā'ishah and from Ḥafṣah, but without 'and'. Abū Bakr al-Anbārī said, 'This extra word indicates that it is false, and that what is in the copy of the community of Muslims is sound.'

There is another argument which is that if someone says, 'the middle prayer and the *'Asr* prayer,' he makes the 'middle prayer' other than *'Asr*. This is refuted by the *hadīth* of the Messenger of Allah ﷺ that is related by 'Abdullāh. He said, 'On the Day of the Confederates, the idolaters kept the Messenger of Allah ﷺ from the *'Asr* prayer until the sun was yellow. The Messenger of Allah said, 'They have kept me from the middle prayer. May Allah fill their bellies and graves with fire!'

'The middle prayer' is evidence that the odd number is mandatory because the Muslims agreed that the number of obligatory prayers is less than seven and more than three, and there is only five between seven and three. Pairs have no 'middle' and so it is confirmed that the number is five. We find in the *hadīth* of the Night Journey: 'They are five and they are fifty. The word is not changed with Me.'

**Stand in obedience to Allah.**

This means in the prayer. People disagree about the meaning of the word *qānitīn*. Ash-Sha'bī said that it means 'in obedience'. Jābir ibn Zayd, 'Aṭā' and Sa'īd ibn Jubayr said that. Aḍ-Ḍaḥḥāk said, 'Every use of the word *qanūt* in the Qur'an refers to obedience.' Abū Sa'īd said, quoting the Prophet ﷺ, that the people of every *dīn* will stand as rebels on the Day of Rising, but this Community will be told, 'Stand in obedience to Allah.' Mujāhid said that it means 'in humility'. *Qunūt* means long bowing, humility, and lowering the eye. Ar-Rabī' said that *qunūt* means long bowing. Ibn 'Umar said that and he recited: '*...he who spends the night hours in prayer* (*qānit*), *prostrating and standing up?*' (39:9) The Prophet ﷺ said, 'The best prayer is the long *qunūt*.' Muslim and others transmitted it. A poet said:

Obedient (*qānitan*) to Allah, calling on his Lord
and intentionally withdrawing from people.

Ibn 'Abbās said that *qānitīn* means calling or supplicating, and it is used with that meaning in the *hadīth*: 'The Prophet ﷺ did the *qanūt* for a month, invoking against Ri'l and Dhakwān.' Some people said that it means to supplicate. Other people said that it means to stand for a long time. As-Suddī said that it means to be silent, and his evidence is that the *āyah* was revealed to forbid speaking in the prayer which was permitted at the beginning of Islam. This is sound based on Muslim and others relating that 'Abdullāh ibn Mas'ūd said, 'We used to greet the Messenger of Allah ﷺ while he was praying and he would reply to us. When we returned from the Negus, we greeted him and he did not reply to us. We said, "Messenger of Allah, we used to greet you during the prayer and you would reply to us." He answered, "One is occupied in the prayer."' It is related that Zayd ibn Arqam said, 'We used to speak in the prayer and a man would speak to the man at his side until it was revealed: *"Stand in obedience to Allah."* So we were commanded to be silent and forbidden to speak.'

It is said that the linguistic root means to be constant in a thing. Since that is the linguistic root in language, it is permitted to describe someone who is constant in obedience as '*qānit*'. That same is true about someone who stands long in the prayer, recitation, and supplication in the prayer, or has long-standing humility and silence. All of these are aspects of the idea of *qunūt*.

Abū 'Umar said, 'All Muslims agree that deliberately speaking in the prayer while knowing that one is in the prayer, when it is not to put the prayer right, invalidates the prayer. Al-Awzā'ī's position that when one speaks to revive a person or other important matters, the prayer is not invalidated by that, is logically weak since Allah says: *"Stand in obedience to Allah,"* and Zayd ibn Arqam said, "We used to speak in the prayer until Allah revealed: '*Stand in obedience to Allah.*'"' Ibn Mas'ūd said that he heard the Messenger of Allah ﷺ say, 'Allah introduced that you should not speak in the prayer.' This is when it is not a major matter which obliges that one stop the prayer and for which one must start anew. When someone does stop the prayer because of the excellence of saving a person's life, or on account of property or something similar, he should start the prayer again and not build on what he has done. This is the sound position regarding the question, Allah willing.

They disagree about someone who speaks out of forgetfulness. Mālik, ash-Shāfi'ī and their people believe that speaking in the prayer out of forgetfulness does not invalidate it. Mālik, however, said, 'The prayer is not spoiled by deliberately speaking in it when that is about the prayer and putting it right.' That is the view of Rabī'ah and Ibn al-Qāsim. Saḥnūn related from Ibn al-Qāsim that Mālik mentioned the case when an imam leads the people in prayer for two *rak'ah*s and says the *salām* out of forgetfulness and they say, '*Subḥānallāh*,' but he does not understand. So one of the men praying behind him in the prayer says, 'You have not finished! Finish the prayer!' and he turns to the people and asks, 'Is he telling the truth?' and they say, 'Yes.' The imam leads them in the rest of the prayer and both those who spoke and those who did not finish the prayer with him owe nothing. In doing that they are doing what the Prophet ﷺ did on the day Dhu-l-Yadayn spoke in the prayer. This is the position of Ibn al-Qāsim in the *Mudawwanah* and he related it from Mālik. It is the well known position of Mālik's school. Ismā'īl ibn Isḥāq imitated it and cited it as evidence in his book in which he refutes Muḥammad ibn al-Ḥasan. Al-Ḥārith ibn Miskīn said, 'All of Mālik's adherents take a different position to that of Mālik in the question of Dhu-l-Yadayn with the sole exception of Ibn al-Qāsim who took Mālik's position.

Others rejected that, saying that that took place at the beginning of Islam. Now that people know their prayer, whoever speaks in it must repeat it. That is the position of the Iraqis: Abū Ḥanīfah and his people and ath-Thawrī. They believe that speaking in it makes it unsound in every instance, whether that is deliberate or out of forgetfulness and whether it is about the prayer or something else. That is the view of Ibrāhīm an-Nakha'ī, 'Aṭā', al-Ḥasan, Ḥammād ibn Abī Sulaymān and Qatādah. The people of Abū Ḥaniḟah claimed that this *ḥadīth* from Abū Hurayrah about Dhu-l-Yadayn is abrogated by the *ḥadīth* of Ibn Mas'ūd and Zayd ibn Arqam. They said that Abū Hurayrah became a Muslim later and he has the *ḥadīth* of Dhu-l-Yadayn *mursal* as he has another *ḥadīth mursal*: 'If *Fajr* catches someone in *janābah*, he has no fast.' They said that he has many *mursal ḥadīth*s.

'Alī ibn Ziyād mentioned that Abū Qurrah heard Mālik say, 'When a man speaks in the prayer, it is recommended for him to repeat it and not build on what he has already done.' He said, 'Mālik said to us, "One day the Messenger of Allah ﷺ spoke to his Companions because they thought that the prayer had been shortened. No one is permitted to do that today."' Sahnūn related from Ibn al-Qāsim about a man who prayed alone and thought that he had finished four *rak'ah*s and a man at his side said, 'You have only prayed three.' The man turned to another and asked, 'Is what he said true?' 'Yes,' was the answer. He said that his prayer was spoiled and that he should not have spoken nor looked at him. Abū 'Umar said, 'Regarding this question, they differentiated between an imam with a group and someone praying alone. They permitted speech about the prayer for the imam and those with him, but not for someone praying alone. Other people took Ibn al-Qāsim's answer to refer to the person praying alone and to the imam and those with him, based on the disagreement about what he said about using the *ḥadīth* of Dhu-l-Yadayn as the position of Mālik on that differed.'

Ash-Shāfi'ī and his people said that whoever speaks deliberately, knowing that he is praying, should not complete the prayer and he renders the prayer invalid. If he speaks out of forgetfulness, or speaks thinking that he is not in the prayer because he has finished it, he builds on what he has already done.

The position of Aḥmad varies regarding this matter. Al-Athram mentioned that he said, 'What a person says in his prayer to put the prayer right does not invalidate his prayer. If he speaks for any other reason, it is invalidated.' This is the well-known view of Mālik. Al-Khiraqī mentioned that Aḥmad's view is that if someone speaks deliberately or out of forgetfulness, his prayer is invalid, with the exception of the imam who can speak to put the prayer right in which case his prayer is not invalidated.

Among Mālik's adherents, with the exception of Saḥnūn, if someone says the *salām* after two *rak'ahs* in a four *ra'kah* prayer, his words do not invalidate the prayer. If he says something else, then the prayer is invalidated. What is, in fact, sound is what Mālik believed in his well-known position, holding to the *ḥadīth* and taking the basic universal principles about violation of rulings and the generality of the Sharī'ah and removing what is imagined of its being specific when there is no proof of that being the case. If someone were to say that the words spoken are about the prayer and forgetfulness, the Prophet ﷺ told them, 'Saying "*Subḥanallāh*" is for men and clapping for women.' So why did not they not say '*Subḥanallāh*'? The answer is that it is possible that at that time it was not their custom, and if it is as you have said, they did not say '*Subḥanallāh*' because they thought that the prayer had been shortened. That comes in the *ḥadīth*: 'People went out quickly, saying, "Has the prayer been shortened."' That required speech. Allah knows best.

Some of those who disagree said that the words of Abū Hurayrah, 'The Messenger of Allah ﷺ led us in the prayer' can mean that he led the Muslims while he [Abū Hurayrah] was not one of them, as is seen in what is related from an-Nazzāl ibn Sabrah who said, 'The Messenger of Allah ﷺ said to us, "We and you used to be called the Banū 'Abd Manāf. Today you are the Banū 'Abdullāh and we are the Banū 'Abdullāh.' By that he meant that he said to his people. This view is unlikely. It is not permitted to say, 'He led us in the prayer' when at that time he was an unbeliever and not one of the people of the prayer, and so that is a lie. In the *ḥadīth* of an-Nazzāl, the speaker was one of the people and heard what he heard from the Messenger of Allah ﷺ. As for what the Ḥanafīs claim of it being abrogated and being *mursal*, our scholars and others, especially Ḥāfiẓ Abū 'Umar ibn 'Abd al-Barr in *at-Tamhīd*, answered their position and refuted it. He mentioned that Abū Hurayrah became Muslim in the year of Khaybar and came to Madīnah that year. He was the Companion of the Prophet ﷺ for four years and was present for the incident of Dhu-l-Yadayn. That was not before Badr as they claim and Dhu-l-Yadayn was killed at Badr. He said that Abū Hurayrah being present on the day of the incident with Dhu-l-Yadayn is preserved by trustworthy transmitters,

*Qunūt* can mean 'standing'. It is one of its possible meanings as mentioned by Abū Bakr ibn al-Anbārī. The community agree that standing in the obligatory prayer is mandatory for every healthy person who is able to stand, whether praying alone or as imam. The Prophet ﷺ said, 'The imam is appointed to be followed.

When he prays standing, pray standing.' The imams transmitted the *ḥadīth*. It clarifies the *āyah*.

They disagree about whether a healthy person should pray sitting down when he prays behind a sick imam who cannot stand. A group of scholars allow that, indeed the majority of them, based on the words of the Prophet ﷺ about the imam: 'When he prays sitting, then all pray sitting.' This is the sound position regarding this matter as we will soon explain, Allah willing. One group of scholars allow someone to pray standing behind a sick imam because each is performing his obligation according to his ability in imitation of the Messenger of Allah ﷺ who prayed sitting in his final illness while Abū Bakr was standing beside him, following his prayer and the people were standing behind him. He did not indicate to them or Abū Bakr to sit. He completed the prayer with them sitting while they were standing. It is known that that was after he fell from his horse and it is known that the later action abrogates the earlier one

Abū 'Umar said, 'Among those who took this position and argued for it were ash-Shāfi'ī and Dāwud ibn 'Alī. It is transmitted by al-Walīd ibn Muslim from Mālik. He said, 'I prefer someone to stand beside him to inform the people in the prayer.' This is an unusual (*gharīb*) transmission from Mālik. One group of the people of Madīnah and others said that, and it is sound, Allah willing, because it was the last prayer that the Messenger of Allah ﷺ prayed. What is well-known from Mālik is that someone sitting does not lead people standing in the prayer. If he leads them sitting, then both his prayer and their prayer is invalid because the Messenger of Allah ﷺ said, 'After me, no one should lead the prayer sitting down.' He said that if the imam is ill, the prayer of the imam is complete and the prayer of those following him is spoiled. He said, 'If someone prays sitting down and is not ill, he must repeat the prayer.' This is the transmission of Abū Muṣ'ab from Mālik in the *Mukhtaṣar*. So someone who prays sitting must repeat the prayer whether that is within the time or after it. It is related from Mālik that they only have to repeat it if it is within the time. Muḥammad ibn al-Ḥasan has a similar position in this to the well-known position of Mālik. He argued for his position and school by quoting the *ḥadīth* that Abū Muṣ'ab mentioned.

Ad-Dāraquṭnī transmitted from Jābir that ash-Sha'bī said that the Messenger of Allah ﷺ said, 'After me, no one should lead the prayer sitting down.' Ad-Dāraquṭnī said, 'Only Jābir al-Ju'fī related it from ash-Sha'bī, and his *ḥadīth*s are abandoned. It is *mursal* and not used as evidence.' Abū 'Umar said, 'Jābir al-Ju'fī does not have anything authoritative related from him with an *isnād*, so how much more is that the case with what is related as *mursal*?'

Muḥammad ibn al-Ḥasan said, 'When a sick imam leads the prayer sitting for both those who are healthy and other ill people who are sitting, his prayer and the prayer of those behind him who cannot stand is valid and permitted, but the prayer of those behind him who can stand is invalid.' Abū Ḥanīfah and Abū Yūsuf said that both his prayer and their prayer is allowed. They said, 'If he prays and indicates to people who are bowing and prostrating, it does not satisfy them all in their view and the prayer of the imam is allowed.' Zufar said, 'Their prayer is allowed because they prayed their obligatory prayer and their imam prayed his obligatory prayer as ash-Shāfi'ī said.

As for what Abū 'Umar and other scholars before and after him said about that being the last prayer that the Messenger of Allah ﷺ prayed, I have seen others who collected the paths of transmission of *ḥadīth*s about this and discussed it speaking about the disagreement of the *fuqahā'* regarding that. We will mention a brief summary of it so that it is clear to you what is correct, Allah willing, regarding the soundness of those who say that the prayer of someone healthy behind a sick imam is allowed. Abū Ḥātim Muḥammad ibn Ḥabbān al-Bustī mentioned in his sound *Musnad* from Ibn 'Umar that while the Messenger of Allah ﷺ was in a group of his Companions, he said, 'Do you not know that I am the Messenger of Allah to you?' 'Yes,' they replied, 'we bear witness that you are the Messenger of Allah!' He continued, 'Do you not know that whoever obeys me has obeyed Allah, and part of obeying Allah is obeying me?' They answered, 'Yes, we bear witness that whoever obeys you has obeyed Allah and part of obeying Allah is obeying you.' He said, 'Part of obeying Allah is to obey me, and part of obeying me is to obey your commanders. If they pray sitting, then pray sitting.' 'Uqbah ibn Abī 'ṣ-Ṣahbā' is in the path of transmission, and he is trustworthy as Yaḥyā ibn Ma'īn said.

Abū Ḥātim said that this report is clear evidence that following the imam praying sitting when their imam prays sitting is part of obeying Allah Almighty which Allah has commanded His servants to do. I consider it to be a sort of consensus. They agree that it is permitted because four of the Companions of the Messenger of Allah ﷺ gave a *fatwā* to that effect: Jābir ibn 'Abdullāh, Abū Hurayrah, Usayd ibn Ḥuḍayr and Qays ibn Qahd. They did not relate, from any of the Companions who witnessed the descent of revelation and sought refuge from alteration and change, anything different to what those four said, whether with a connected or broken *isnād*. Therefore it is as if the Companions agreed that when the imam prays siting down, those who follow him must also pray sitting down. That is what was stated by Jābir ibn Zayd, al-Awzā'ī, Mālik ibn Anas, Aḥmad ibn Ḥanbal, Isḥāq ibn Ibrāhīm, Abū Ayyūb Sulaymān ibn Dāwud al-Hāshimī, Abū Khaythamah, Ibn Abī Shaybah, Muḥammad ibn Ismā'īl and those of the people of *ḥadīth* who followed them like Muḥammad ibn Naṣr and Muḥammad ibn Isḥāq ibn Khuzaymah. This is the Sunnah that was related from the Prophet ﷺ from Anas ibn Mālik, 'Ā'ishah, Abū Hurayrah, Jābir ibn 'Abdullāh, 'Abdullāh ibn 'Umar ibn al-Khaṭṭāb, and Abū Umāmah al-Bāhilī.

The first in this community to invalidate the prayer of someone following an imam sitting when his imam is sitting was al-Mughīrah ibn Miqsam, the companion of an-Nakha'ī. Ḥammād ibn Abī Sulaymān took it from him, and then Abū Ḥanīfah took it from Ḥammād, and his people after him followed him. The report with the best *isnād* which they use as evidence is what is related by Jābir al-Ju'fī from ash-Sha'bī who said that the Messenger of Allah ﷺ said, 'After me, no one should lead the prayer sitting.' If its *isnād* is sound, it is *mursal.* Abū Ḥanīfah said, 'Among those I have met, I have not seen anyone better than 'Aṭā', nor among those I met any more mendacious than Jābir al-Ju'fī. I have not gone to him with anything without him bringing me a *ḥadīth* about it and claiming that he had so many thousands of *ḥadīth*s from the Messenger of Allah ﷺ that he had not uttered.' So Abū Ḥanīfah discredited Jābir al-Ju'fī and thought him a liar, differing from the position of those of his companions who adopt his position.

Abū Ḥātim said, 'Many reports, both summary and abridged, have come about the prayer of the Prophet ﷺ while he was ill. Some of them have clear details. According to some of them: "The Prophet ﷺ came and sat beside Abū Bakr. Abū Bakr followed the Prophet ﷺ and the people followed Abū Bakr." One of them has: "He sat to the left of Abū Bakr." This is an explanation.' So it says that the Prophet ﷺ prayed sitting with the people while Abū Bakr prayed standing. Abū Ḥātim said, 'In short regarding this report, 'Ā'ishah related about this prayer up to this point, and Jābir ibn 'Abdullāh has the rest of the story. He said that the Prophet ﷺ commanded them to sit in that prayer as he commanded them to do when he had fallen from his horse. Muḥammad ibn al-Ḥasan ibn Qutaybah related from Yazīd ibn Mawhab from al-Layth ibn Sa'd from Abu-z-Zubayr that Jābir said, 'The Messenger of Allah ﷺ was ill and we prayed behind him while he was sitting and Abū Bakr let the people hear his *takbīr.*' He said, 'He turned to us and saw us standing and indicated for us to sit. So we followed his prayer sitting. When he said that *salām*, he said, "You almost did what Persia and Rome did. They stood for their kings while they were seated. Do not do it. Follow your imam. If he prays standing, pray standing. If he prays sitting, then pray sitting."'

Abū Ḥātim said, 'This report provides evident clarification that the Prophet

ﷺ sat to the left of Abū Bakr and Abū Bakr moved to follow his prayer and said the *takbīr* so the people could hear it and follow his prayer. Then the Prophet ﷺ commanded them to sit when he saw that they were standing. When he finished the prayer, he commanded them to sit when their imam prayed sitting. Jābir ibn 'Abdullāh saw his prayer when he had fallen from his horse and his right side was scratched. He ﷺ fell in Dhu-l-Ḥijjah 5 AH. He witnessed this prayer when he ﷺ was ill on another occasion. He gives each report. Do you not see that he mentions about this prayer: "Abū Bakr raised his voice with the *takbīr* so that people could follow him"? When he fell from his horse, the prayer that the Messenger of Allah ﷺ prayed was in his house and there was no need to raise his voice with the *takbīr* so that people could hear it because 'Ā'ishah's room was small. He raised his voice in the Great Mosque where the Messenger of Allah ﷺ prayed when he was ill. Since what we described is not sound, we cannot make some reports abrogate others. This is the prayer to which he ﷺ went supported by two men, and he was the imam in it and prayed sitting and commanded them to sit. As for the prayer that he prayed at the end of his life, he went out to it between Barīrah and Thawbah. He followed the imam in it and prayed sitting behind Abū Bakr while wrapped in a garment.'

Anas ibn Mālik related: 'The last prayer that the Messenger of Allah ﷺ prayed with the people, he prayed wrapped in a single garment, sitting behind Abū Bakr.' So the Prophet ﷺ prayed two prayers in the mosque in the group, not one prayer. We find in the report of 'Ubaydullāh ibn 'Abdullāh from 'Ā'ishah that the Prophet ﷺ came out between two men, one of whom was Ibn 'Abbās and the other 'Alī. Masrūq reported from 'Ā'ishah: 'The Prophet ﷺ felt better and so he came out between Barīrah and Thawbah. I could see his sandals hitting the pebbles and saw the bottom of his feet.' This indicates that there were two prayers, not one prayer.

Abū Ḥātim reported from Muḥammad ibn Isḥāq ibn Khuzaymah from Muḥammad ibn Bashshār from Badal ibn al-Muḥabbar from Shu'bah from Mūsā ibn Abī 'Ā'ishah from 'Ubaydullāh ibn 'Abdullāh from 'Ā'ishah that Abū Bakr led the people in the prayer while the Messenger of Allah ﷺ was in the row behind him. Abū Ḥātim said, 'Shu'bah ibn al-Ḥajjāj differed from Zā'idah ibn Qudāmah about the text of this report from Mūsā ibn Abī 'Ā'ishah. Shu'bah had the Prophet ﷺ following in the prayer sitting while the people were standing. Zā'idah made the Prophet ﷺ the imam when he prayed sitting while the people were standing. They are both trusted custodians. How can one make one of these two apparently contradictory transmissions abrogate the previous accounts? If someone makes one of the two reports abrogate the earlier position of the Prophet

ﷺ and leaves the other without evidence that confirms its validity that allows his opponents to take what other of the two reports and leave the one he took.'

Similar to this in the *sunan* is the report of Ibn 'Abbās about the Prophet ﷺ marrying Maymūnah while he was in *iḥrām* and the report of Abū Rāfi' that states that he married her while they were both out of *iḥrām*. So the two reports are apparently contradictory about the same action while we do not think that there is any real contradiction between them. One group of *ḥadīth* scholars consider the two reports about the marriage of Maymūnah contradictory and believe in the report of 'Uthmān ibn 'Affān from the Prophet ﷺ: 'No one in *iḥrām* should marry or give someone in marriage.' They take it since it is agrees with one of the reports related about the marriage of Maymūnah and abandon the report of Ibn 'Abbas who said that the Prophet ﷺ married her while he was in *iḥrām*. Someone who does that must say that the two reports about the prayer of the Prophet ﷺ when he was ill are contradictory according to what we mentioned, and so one must take the report containing the command for the followers to pray sitting when the imam prays sitting. That view is taken, and it agrees with one of the two transmissions about the Prophet's prayer ﷺ when he was ill. He should abandon the other report as is done in the case of Maymūnah's marriage. Abū Ḥātim said, 'Some Iraqis who follow the Iraqi school say that his words, "When the imam prays sitting, then pray sitting," mean when he says that *tashahhud* sitting, all do the *tashahhud* sitting. So they twisted the report from the general meaning in the report without any evidence to support that interpretation.'

فَإِنْ خِفْتُمْ فَرِجَالًا أَوْ رُكْبَانًا فَإِذَا أَمِنتُمْ فَاذْكُرُوا اللَّهَ كَمَا
عَلَّمَكُم مَّا لَمْ تَكُونُوا تَعْلَمُونَ ﴿٢٣٩﴾

**239 If you are afraid, then do the prayer on foot or mounted. But when you are safe, remember Allah in the way He taught you when previously you did not know.**

**If you are afraid, then do the prayer on foot or mounted.**

'*Rijāl*' means 'on foot'. It is the plural of *rājil* or *rajul*. It describes a person walking on his feet. Allah commanded people to stand in the prayer with gravity and stillness and with the limbs at rest, and this applies when there is security and peace of mind. Then Allah mentions the occasional state of fear and makes it clear that this act of worship is not cancelled for His slaves in any circumstances, but in certain situations people are allowed to do the prayer while walking or on the backs of horses, camels and the like, and are permitted to pray with nods and gestures in any direction. This is the position of the scholars. This is the prayer performed by someone praying alone when he is constricted by fear for himself during fighting, or fear of a wild animal that is after him, or of an enemy who is pursing him or of a flood that is overflowing. In general, in every matter in which he fears for his life, he is permitted to do what is mentioned in this *āyah*. There is a consensus of the scholars on this dispensation when someone is acting and moving in a manner by which he thinks that he will save his life.

They disagree about exactly what constitutes the fear in which it is permitted to pray like this. Ash-Shāfiʿī said that it applies to the situation when the Muslims are actually in sight of the enemy and are not in a fortified position protecting them from being hit by arrows, or when the enemy is so close that they can strike at any time, or when someone whose information is trusted comes and tells them that the enemy is close and making for them. Otherwise it is not permitted to pray the fear prayer. If people pray it based on a report and then the enemy leaves, they do not have to repeat the prayer. Some say that they should, which is the position of Abū Ḥanīfah. Abū ʿUmar said, 'The situation in which it permitted for someone in fear to pray on foot or mounted, facing the *qiblah* or not facing the *qiblah*, is in one of intense fear. The circumstances in the reports about it are other than this.' This refers to the fear prayer with an imam and the division of people (into two groups). Its ruling is not dealt with in this *āyah*. The fear prayer behind an imam will be dealt with in *Sūrat an-Nisāʾ*. Mālik differentiated between fear of the enemy and fear of wild beasts and the like which might attack and bring about death. When it is on account of other than the enemy, it is recommended to repeat the prayer within the time if one reaches safety. Most scholars view fear as having the same ruling in either instance.

Abū Ḥanīfah said that fighting invalidates the prayer but the *ḥadīth* of Ibn ʿUmar refutes that and the evidence of the *āyah* reinforces Ibn ʿUmar's position. The literal meaning of the *āyah* is the strongest proof of it as will be dealt with *Sūrat an-Nisāʾ*. Ash-Shāfiʿī said that since Allah made a dispensation permitting the omission of some of the preconditions of the prayer, that indicates that fighting does not invalidate the prayer. Allah knows best.

The number of *rakʿah*s is not reduced in the fear prayer to below that of the travel prayer according to Mālik, ash-Shāfiʿī and a group of scholars. Al-Ḥasan ibn Abī 'l-Ḥasan, Qatādah and others said that the *rakʿah* is prayed by indication. Muslim related from Bukayr ibn al-Akhnas from Mujāhid that Ibn ʿAbbās said, 'Allah prescribed the prayer on the tongue of the Messenger of Allah ﷺ as four *rak'ahs* when resident, two when travelling and one in fear.' Ibn 'Abd al-Barr said that only Bukayr ibn al-Akhnas has this. It is more fitting to safeguard the prayer. When someone prays two *rak'ahs* when travelling and in a state of fear, he leaves disagreement in favour of certainty. Aḍ-Ḍaḥḥāk ibn Muzāhim said, 'Someone in fear of death in hand-to-hand fighting and elsewhere prays one *rak'ah*. If he is unable to do that, then he says two *takbīrs*.' Isḥāq ibn Rāhawayh said, 'If he is only able to say one *takbīr*, that is enough.' Ibn al-Mundhir mentioned.

**But when you are safe, remember Allah in the way He taught you**

This means return to the full pillars of the prayer you are commanded to do normally. Mujāhid said that it means when you are resident, and aṭ-Ṭabarī also reported this position. One group say that it means when the fear you were subject to, which made you resort to the fear prayer, is removed.

Scholars disagree about whether the person in fear builds on the prayer to complete it if the situation becomes safe. Mālik said that if someone prays one *rak'ah* in a safe situation and then fear occurs, he should mount and complete the prayer while mounted. That is the same if he prays one *rak'ah* in fear and then becomes safe: he should dismount and complete the prayer. This is also one of the positions of ash-Shāfi'ī and is what al-Muzanī said. Abū Ḥanīfah says that if someone begins the prayer safe and then fears, he starts anew and does not complete what he has done. If he prays in fear and then becomes safe, he completes it. Ash-Shāfi'ī said that the one who dismounts completes it but the one mounted does not. Abū Yūsuf said that he does not complete it in any of those situations.

The words *'remember Allah'* here mean to thank Him for the blessing of teaching you the form of the fear prayer, which satisfies the obligation of prayer imposed on us, so you do not miss any of the prayers. This is something that you did not know. The *kāf* in '*kamā*' implies thankfulness.

Our scholars say that the basis of the prayer is supplication and a state of fear is one in which supplication is most appropriate which is why the prayer is not cancelled by fear. If the prayer were to be cancelled by fear, it would be more likely to be cancelled by other things, such as illness or the like. Allah commanded us to safeguard the prayers in every situation: health or illness, at home or on a journey, in strength or weakness, fear or security. The obligation of prayer is never removed from the responsible person. The ruling of someone ill will come in *Āl 'Imrān*. It means perform the prayer as best you can. It is not cancelled in any state so that if you can only do it by indication by the eyes, then you must still do it. This is why the prayer differs from other acts of worship, all of which can be cancelled by excuses. Ibn al-'Arabī says, 'Our scholars say that this is an immense matter and the one who abandons the prayer is killed because it resembles faith in that the obligation to do it is never removed.' They said that the prayer is one of the pillars of Islam and nothing can replace it nor can it be delegated. Someone who abandons it is killed. This will be discussed in *at-Tawbah.*

وَالَّذِينَ يُتَوَفَّوْنَ مِنكُمْ وَيَذَرُونَ أَزْوَاجًا وَصِيَّةً لِّأَزْوَاجِهِم
مَّتَاعًا إِلَى الْحَوْلِ غَيْرَ إِخْرَاجٍ فَإِنْ خَرَجْنَ فَلَا جُنَاحَ عَلَيْكُمْ فِي
مَا فَعَلْنَ فِي أَنفُسِهِنَّ مِن مَّعْرُوفٍ وَاللَّهُ عَزِيزٌ حَكِيمٌ ﴿٢٤٠﴾

**240 Those of you who die leaving wives behind should make a bequest to their wives of maintenance for a year without them having to leave their homes But if they do leave you are not to blame for anything they do with themselves with correctness and courtesy. Allah is Almighty, All-Wise.**

**Those of you who die leaving wives behind should make a bequest to their wives of maintenance for a year without them having to leave their homes**

A group of commentators have said that this means that a widow should stay in the house of her husband for a year and that she is entitled to maintenance from his estate as long as she does not leave it. If she leaves, the heirs can stop the maintenance. The waiting period of four months and ten days and the maintenance were abrogated by the shares of inheritance in *Sūrat an-Nisā'*. Ibn 'Abbās, Qatādah, aḍ-Ḍahḥāk, Ibn Zayd and ar-Rabī' followed this opinion. Scholars disagree about lodging. Al-Bukhārī related that Ibn az-Zubayr said, 'I said to 'Uthmān about this *āyah* in *al-Baqarah: "Those of you who die leaving wives behind..."* which was abrogated by the other *āyah*, "Why do you write it down?" He answered, "Nephew, I will not change any of it from its place."' Aṭ-Ṭabarī said that Mujāhid said, 'This *āyah* is one of judgment and is not abrogated. The *'iddah* was confirmed as four months and ten days but then Allah gives widows a further bequest of lodging for seven months and twenty days during which they may continue to live in their husband's house if they wish or leave if they wish. That is from the words of Allah: *"...without them having to leave their homes. But if they do leave, you are not to blame."'* Ibn 'Aṭiyyah says that all this is removed by abrogation, which is agreed upon by everyone except for what aṭ-Ṭabarī said that Mujāhid said. Qāḍī 'Iyāḍ said that the consensus is that the 'year' is abrogated and her waiting period is four months and ten days. Other said that '*waṣiyyah*' (bequest) is an instruction from Allah which was mandatory for wives after the death of their husband, allowing them reside in the house for a year, and it was then abrogated.

What aṭ-Ṭabarī mentioned from Mujāhid is sound and confirmed. Al-Bukhārī transmitted from Isḥāq from Rawḥ from Shibl from Ibn Abī Najīḥ that Mujāhid said about: *'Those of you who die leaving wives behind...'*, 'A widow was obliged to spend this waiting period with her husband's family. Then Allah revealed: *"Those of you who die leaving wives behind should make a bequest to their wives..."*' He added, 'Allah then allotted a full year for her, another seven months and twenty days as a bequest. If she wished, she could stay with his executor, and if she wished, she could leave. That is from the words of the Almighty: "*...without them having to leave their homes. But if they do leave, you are not to blame.*"'

The first position is more apparent since the Prophet ﷺ said, 'It [the *'iddah*] is four months and ten days. In the Jāhiliyyah, one of you would throw a piece of dung at the end of a year.' He was reporting about the state of widows before the Sharī'ah. When Islam came, Allah Almighty commanded them to stay in their houses for a year and then that was abrogated by four months and ten days. In addition to its clarity in the firm Sunnah transmitted by single reports, it is the undisputed consensus of Muslim scholars. Abū 'Umar said that. The same is true of the rest of the *āyah*. According to the majority of scholars this *āyah* is all abrogated. Then the command to provide wives lodging for the year was abrogated except for an aberrant, avoided transmission from Ibn Abī Najīḥ from Mujāhid which is not corroborated. None of the Muslim scholars among the Companions and Tābi'ūn or those after them said that she has more than four months and ten days as far as I know. Ibn Jurayj related the like of what people say from Mujāhid. So the consensus is reached and disagreement removed. Success is by Allah.

*'Bequest'* is recited by Nāfi', Ibn Kathīr, al-Kisā'ī and 'Āṣim in the transmission of Abū Bakr in the nominative. It is possible that it means: 'they should make a bequest' and *'to their wives'* describes it. That is how it is in the reading of 'Abdullāh ibn Mas'ūd. Abū 'Amr, Ḥamzah and Ibn 'Āmir recite it in the accusative based on an implied verb: 'make a bequest'. Someone deceased does not make a bequest. It means when someone is close to death. It is said that it means: 'Allah commands" and it means to give them maintenance, so Allah has assigned that for them. It is also possible that it is in the accusative for the adverbial *ḥāl* or because it is a verbal noun. *'Matā''* here is their maintenance for a year.

*'Without them having to leave their homes'* means that the relatives of the deceased and his heirs who inherit the house should not expel the deceased's widow from it.

**But if they do leave you are not to blame for anything they do with themselves with correctness and courtesy.**

This refers to them leaving voluntarily before the year is up. Then there is nothing held against the guardian, judge or anyone else because the widow does not have to stay in the house for a whole year. It is said that it means that there is nothing wrong in cutting off their maintenance or in them looking for new husbands since that is cut off from them under the supervision of the heirs. They cannot remarry until their waiting period is finished but there is nothing wrong in them remarrying after the end of the waiting period. The words *'with correctness and courtesy'* here mean in accordance with the Sharī'ah.

**Allah is Almighty**

It entails a threat to those who oppose the limits in this case and expel the wife when she does not want to leave.

**All-Wise**

Firm in judgement (*muḥkim*) in what He desires in the affairs of His slaves.

وَلِلْمُطَلَّقَٰتِ مَتَٰعُۢ بِٱلْمَعْرُوفِ ۖ حَقًّا عَلَى ٱلْمُتَّقِينَ ﴿٢٤١﴾ كَذَٰلِكَ يُبَيِّنُ ٱللَّهُ لَكُمْ
ءَايَٰتِهِۦ لَعَلَّكُمْ تَعْقِلُونَ ﴿٢٤٢﴾

**241 Divorced women should receive maintenance given with correctness and courtesy: a duty for all who are godfearing. 242 In this way Allah makes His Signs clear to you, so that hopefully you will use your intellect.**

People disagree about this *āyah*. Abū Thawr says that it is one of the *āyahs* of judgment, and every divorced woman is owed maintenance. That is what az-Zuhrī said, adding that it even applies to divorced slave-girls. Sa'īd ibn Jubayr said that every divorced woman should receive maintenance. That is one of the positions of ash-Shāfi'ī. Mālik says that every woman divorced once or twice receives it, except in the case of a woman divorced before consummation whose dowry has been allotted; she simply receives half her dowry. If it has not been allotted, then she receives maintenance not exceeding the dower of a woman of her status. There is no definition of the amount of maintenance, as Ibn al-Qāsim said.

Ibn al-Qāsim said in the *Mudawwanah* about when the curtain has been lowered (privacy between the couple has been established), 'Allah Almighty has appointed maintenance for every divorced woman on the basis of this *āyah*. Then in the other *āyah* He makes an exception for a woman whose dower has been allotted and whose marriage has not been consummated: she does not receive maintenance. Ibn Zayd claimed that it is abrogated.' Ibn 'Aṭiyyah said, 'Ibn al-Qāsim fled from the word "abrogation" to "exception" and that is not proper in this place. It is indeed pure abrogation as was stated by Zayd ibn Aslam. When Ibn al-Qāsim makes *"divorced women"* include every divorced woman, he must then say that there is abrogation.'

'Aṭā' ibn Abī Rabāḥ and others said that this *āyah* is about previously married women who have had sex, since in another *āyah* it mentions the maintenance of those whose marriage has not been consummated. This position is about a woman who has been allotted a dower before consummation and whose marriage has not been consummated in general. That is on the basis that Allah's words in 2:247 specifies this category of women. When it is said that this is general and undefined, then that is abrogation and not specification.

Ash-Shāfi'ī said in another view that there is only a gift for a woman who has been divorced before consummation when there has been no touching or allotment, because someone who is entitled to something of the dower does not need a gift. The words of Allah about the wives of the Prophet ﷺ: *'Come and I will give you all you need'* (33:27), are taken as being voluntary on the part of the Prophet ﷺ, not mandatory, and His words: *'...there is no 'iddah for you to calculate for them, so give them a gift'* (33:49), are also taken to be not mandatory. Ash-Shāfi'ī said that when a woman has been allotted a dower, she has no gift if she is divorced before consummation, because she takes half of the dower when there has been no sexual intercourse. In the case of a woman whose marriage has been consummated, she receives a gift when she is divorced because the dower is in compensation for sexual intercourse and the gift on account of of the dissolution of the contract. Ash-Shāfi'ī obliged a gift for a woman after a *khul'* and buying her freedom. Mālik's people said, 'How can a woman who ransoms herself be given a gift when she us the one who spends? How can she then take a gift?' There is no gift due to a woman who chooses separation, whether by *khul'*, ransoming herself, buying her freedom, or by mutual agreement, *li'ān* or emancipation, when she chooses separation, whether or not it has been consummated and whether a dower has been stipulated or not.

أَلَمْ تَرَ إِلَى ٱلَّذِينَ خَرَجُوا۟ مِن دِيَٰرِهِمْ وَهُمْ أُلُوفٌ حَذَرَ
ٱلْمَوْتِ فَقَالَ لَهُمُ ٱللَّهُ مُوتُوا۟ ثُمَّ أَحْيَٰهُمْ إِنَّ ٱللَّهَ لَذُو فَضْلٍ
عَلَى ٱلنَّاسِ وَلَٰكِنَّ أَكْثَرَ ٱلنَّاسِ لَا يَشْكُرُونَ ٢٤٣

**243 What do you think about those who left their homes in thousands in fear of death? Allah said to them, 'Die!' and then brought them back to life. Allah shows great favour to mankind, but most people are not grateful.**

The literal meaning of the words '*What do you think...?*' is 'Do you not see?' but in this usage it refers to the vision of the heart and means 'Do you not know?' Sībuwayh says that the phrase is used to call attention to the story of those people.

The story behind the *āyah* is that some of the tribe of Israel suffered a plague in a town called Dāwardān and fled from it. They went into a valley and Allah caused them to die there. Ibn 'Abbās said that there were four thousand of them and they said, 'We will go to a land where there is no death,' but Allah made them die anyway. A Prophet passed by them and prayed to Allah and He brought them back to life. It is said that they were dead for seven or eight days, and Allah knows best. Al-Ḥasan said that Allah made them die before their time was up as a punishment for them and then brought them back for the rest of their lifespans. It is said that he did that to them as a miracle for one of the Prophets whose name is said to be Sham'ūn. An-Naqqāsh related that they fled from the fever.

It is also related that they fled from fighting or from *jihād*. When Allah commanded them to fight through Ezekiel and they feared death in *jihād*, they left their homes and fled from it, so Allah made them die to teach them that nothing could save them from death. Then He brought them back to life and commanded them to fight by His words: *'Fight in the Way of Allah.'* (2:190) Aḍ-Ḍaḥḥāk said that.

Ibn 'Aṭiyyah says that all these stories have weak *isnād*s. The important point about the *āyah* is that, in it, Allah informs his Prophet Muḥammad ﷺ about the importance of taking note of the mistakes of the people of the past and to acquaint him with some people who left their homes in flight from death and how Allah made them die and then brought them back to life to show them and all those after them that death is in the hand of Allah and no one else and so there is no sense in having fear of it or the delusion of being able to escape from it. Allah revealed this *āyah* before commanding the believers of the Community of Muḥammad ﷺ to fight *jihad*. This is the position of aṭ-Ṭabarī. It is the apparent meaning of the *āyah*.

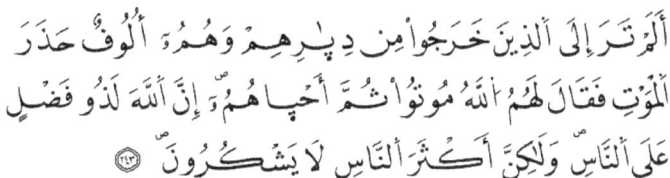

*'Ulūf'* (thousands) is the plural of *alf.* The number referred to by the word 'thousands' is said to be 60,000 or 80,000. Ibn 'Abbās said 40,000. Abū Mālik said 30,000. As-Suddī said 37,000. It was said by 'Aṭā' ibn Abī Rabāḥ to be 70,000. Ibn Jurayj related from him that it was 8,000. The sound position is that it was more than 10,000 because of the plural used for 'thousands'. It is not used for less than 10,000. Ibn Zayd said that the expression means they were united (the verbal root *alafa* has the meaning of unite), meaning that one group of their people did not leave nor was there any dissension between them, but they were united. This group then differed from them and left in order to flee from death and to seek to live. So Allah made them die in the place where they claimed that they were safe. According to this, *ulūf* is the plural of *ālif.*

Ibn al-'Arabī said, 'Allah caused them to die for a time as a punishment and then brought them back to life. This death was a punishment after which there was life. There is no life after the death which is the end of one's term.' Mujāhid said, 'When they were brought to life, they returned to their people, and they recognised that they had been dead. The blackness of death was on their faces. None of them touched a garment without it becoming a grimy shroud until they finally died at the time written for them.' Ibn Jurayj said that Ibn 'Abbās said, 'The smell remains on that clan of the tribe of Israel until today. It is related that they were in the middle of Iraq.' It is said that they were brought back to life after they were putrid. That smell exists in their descendants until today.

The expression *'in fear of death'* means in order to avoid death. It is said that two angels shouted the word 'Die!' at them, meaning that Allah said this by means of the angels, and Allah knows best.

The soundest of these positions, and best known, is that they were fleeing from the plague, as Sa'īd ibn Jubayr related from Ibn 'Abbās who said, 'They left, fleeing the plague, and died. Then one of the Prophets asked Allah to bring them back to life so that they could worship Allah, and Allah brought them back to life.' 'Amr ibn Dīnār said about this *āyah*: 'The plague broke out in their town and some people left and some remained. More left than remained. Those who left were saved and those who remained died. When it happened again, they all went out except for a few and Allah caused them and their animals to die. Then He brought them to life and they returned to their town and reproduced.' Al-Ḥasan said that they left to avoid the plague and Allah made them all die at the same moment, including their animals. They numbered 40,000.'

Rulings derive from this *āyah.* The imams related from 'Āmir ibn Sa'd ibn Abī Waqqāṣ who heard Usāmah ibn Zayd relate from Sa'd that the Messenger of

Allah ﷺ said, 'The plague was a punishment with which Allah punished some nations and some of it remained, and it comes and goes. Anyone who hears that it has broken out in a land should not go to it, and if someone is in a land where it has broken out, he should not leave it, fleeing it.' Abū 'Īsā at-Tirmidhī transmitted from Qutaybah from Ḥammād ibn Zayd from 'Amr ibn Dīnār from 'Āmir ibn Sa'd from Usāmah ibn Zayd that the Prophet ﷺ mentioned the plague and said, 'It is something that remains of a plague or punishment which Allah sent on a group of the tribe of Israel. When it breaks out in a land where you are, do not leave it. When it breaks out in a land where you are not, do not go to it.' He said that it is a sound *ḥasan ḥadīth.*

'Umar and the Companions acted according to these *ḥadīth*s when he returned from Saragh when 'Abd ar-Raḥmān ibn 'Awf informed them of the *ḥadīth*, as is well known in the *Muwaṭṭā'* and elsewhere. People dislike fleeing from the plague and a land with disease. It is related that 'Ā'ishah said, 'Fleeing from the plague is like fleeing from battle.' There is the story of 'Umar who was on his way to Syria with Abū 'Ubaydah and returned. Aṭ-Ṭabarī said, 'The *ḥadīth* of Sa'd contains evidence that a person should guard against disliked things before they occur and avoid feared things before they attack and that one must have steadfastness and lack of terror after such things occur. That is because the Prophet ﷺ forbade someone who is not in a land where the plague is to enter the land where it is raging and he forbade someone who is in the land where the plague has broken out from fleeing from it. That is what is mandatory with respect to the general ruling of everyone who fears fearful matters. In that he follows what one follows in the case of the plague. This idea is like the words of the Prophet ﷺ: 'Do not wish to meet the enemy. Ask Allah for well-being. If you meet the enemy, be steadfast.'

This is what is sound in respect of this matter and it is what is demanded by what the Messenger ﷺ said and by the action of his noble righteous Companions. When Abū 'Ubaydah argued with 'Umar and asked, 'Are you fleeing from Allah's decree?' 'Umar answered, 'Would that someone other than you said that, Abū 'Ubaydah! Yes, we are fleeing from Allah's decree to Allah's decree.' It means that the human being cannot escape what Allah has decreed for and against him. However, Allah has commanded us to be cautious about perilous matters and put energy into guarding ourselves against disliked things. Then 'Umar said to him, 'If you had camels and descended into a valley where one side was lush and the other barren, would you not graze on the lush side? Doing so is based on Allah's decree. If you were to graze them on the barren side, that is also by the decree of Allah.' 'Umar returned to Madīnah from that place.

Aṭ-Ṭabarī said, 'We do not know of any disagreement about the fact that when unbelievers or highwaymen make for a weak land whose people will not be able to resist those who are coming, they can remove themselves from them. Life-spans are decreed and can be neither lengthened nor shortened. It is said that it is forbidden to flee from the plague because the one who is in the place where it breaks out might have already taken his portion of it, since he shared with the people of that place in the cause of that prevalent illness. So there is no point in him fleeing. So he adds the hardship of travel to the first signs of the plague. Then his pains are doubled and harm increased. They will die on every road and be cast into every ravine and mountain pass. Therefore it is said that no one flees from the plague and is safe.' Ibn al-Madā'inī related that.

There is enough warning about that in Allah's words in this *āyah*. If he flees and is safe, he might say, 'I was saved because I left it,' and his belief will thereby be deficient. Generally speaking, fleeing from the plague is forbidden based on what we mentioned and also because it entails emptying the land when there are oppressed people in it for whom it would be difficult to leave. They will be harmed if the wealthy, who are the pillars of the land and support the oppressed, evacuate it. When the plague has broken out in a land, no one should go it, being cautious about harmful situations and averting ideas which disturb. There may be destruction in entering that place and it is not permitted in the judgment of Allah expose oneself to it. It is mandatory to protect oneself from what is disliked. It is feared that what someone believes will be false so that he might say, 'If I had not entered this place, that disliked matter would not have happened to me.' This is the point of the prohibition of entering a land where the plague has broken out or leaving it. Allah knows best.

Ibn Mas'ūd said, 'The plague is a trial for those who remain and those who flee. Someone who flees may say, "I was saved because I fled." Someone who stays may say, "I stayed and so I died."' Mālik indicated something similar when he was asked about disliking to look at a leper. He said, 'I have not heard that there is any dislike of doing that. I can only think that what has come about that being forbidden is out of fear of being alarmed by him or the fear that it will cause wrong thinking in a person. The Prophet ﷺ said about the plague, "When you hear that the plague has broken out in a land, do not go to it. If it breaks out where you are, do not leave it to flee from it."' He was also asked about a land in which there was death and illnesses and whether it was disliked to leave it. He answered, 'I see no harm in leaving or staying.'

The Prophet ﷺ said, 'When the plague breaks out in a land where you are, do not leave it, fleeing from it.' This indicates that it is permitted to leave a plague land if one is not fleeing from it since he is certain that what befalls him could not have missed him. That is also the ruling of someone who enters it when he is certain that entering it will not bring him anything unless Allah has decreed it for him. Then a person is permitted to enter or leave it within the parameters that we mentioned. Allah knows best.

The word for plague is '*ṭā'ūn*'. It is generally used for death from pestilence. It is related from 'Ā'ishah that the Messenger of Allah ﷺ said, 'The annihilation of my community comes about through defamation (*ṭa'n*) and plague (*ṭā'ūn*).' She said, 'We know what *ṭa'n* is. What is *ṭā'ūn*?' He said, 'It is a bubo like the ganglion of a camel in the groin and armpits.' Our scholars say that this pestilence was sent by Allah as revenge and a punishment to whomever He wishes of His disobedient and unbelieving servants. He sent it as martyrdom and mercy to the righteous. Mu'ādh said about the 'Amwas Plague, 'It is martyrdom and mercy for them and the supplication of your Prophet: "O Allah, give Mu'ādh and his family a portion of Your mercy." It appeared on his hand.' Abū Qilābah said, 'I knew what martyrdom and mercy are, but I did not know what the supplication of your Prophet meant. I asked and was told that he asked for the obliteration of his community to be by stabbing and the plague.'

Jābir and others reported that the Prophet ﷺ said about the plague, 'The one who flees from it is like someone who flees from battle. Whoever is patient is like someone who is steadfast in battle.' We find in al-Bukhārī from Yaḥyā ibn Ya'mar that 'Ā'ishah informed him that she asked the Messenger of Allah ﷺ about the plague, the Prophet of Allah ﷺ, told her, 'It is a punishment which Allah sent to those before you. He made it a mercy for the believers. There is no one who comes into contact with the plague and then remains where he is with fortitude and in expectation of the reward, knowing that only what Allah has written for him will befall him, who will receive any other reward than that of a martyr.' This explains the words of the Prophet ﷺ: 'The plague is martyrdom and the one who dies of it is a martyr.' It means someone who is steadfast in it in expectation of a reward from Allah, knowing that what afflicts him was only what Allah decreed for him. That is why Mu'ādh hoped to die in it since he knew that whoever dies in it is a martyr. The one who fears and dislikes the plague and flees from it is not included in the meaning of the *ḥadīth*.

Abū 'Umar said, 'I have not heard that any people of knowledge fled from the plague except for what Ibn al-Madā'inī mentioned about 'Alī ibn Zayd ibn Jud'ān fleeing from the plague to Sayala. He used to go to every Jumu'ah and returned.

When he went to Jumu'ah, they shouted to him, 'Flee from the plague!' He died at Sayala.' He said, "Amr ibn 'Ubayd and Rabāṭ ibn Muḥammad fled to ar-Rabāţiyyah. Ibrāhīm ibn 'Alī al-Fuqaymī said about that:

When death startled every denier,
I was steadfast, but Rabāṭ and 'Amr were not.

Abū Ḥātim mentioned that al-Aṣmā'ī said, 'One of the Basrans fled from the plague and mounted a donkey of his and travelled with his family in the direction of Safawān. He heard someone chanting behind him:

He will not outrun Allah on a donkey or on an unbeaten fast horse.
Death comes as decreed. In the morning it is in front of the traveller.

Al-Madā'inī said, 'The plague broke out in Egypt while 'Abd al-'Azīz ibn Marwān was governor. He fled from it and stopped in one of the towns of Upper Egypt called Sukar. When he had stopped there, the messenger of 'Abd al-Malik ibn Marwān reached him. 'Abd al-'Azīz asked, 'What is your name?' He answered, 'Ṭālib ibn Mudrik,' which means 'Seeker, son of the one who reaches.' He exclaimed, 'Oh! I do not think that I am returning to Fusṭāṭ!' He died in that town.'

وَقَٰتِلُوا۟ فِى سَبِيلِ ٱللَّهِ وَٱعْلَمُوٓا۟ أَنَّ ٱللَّهَ سَمِيعٌ عَلِيمٌ ﴿٢٤٤﴾

**244 Fight in the Way of Allah. Know that Allah is All-Hearing, All-Knowing.**

This is addressed to the Community of Muhammad ﷺ ordering them to fight in the Way of Allah. The purpose of this fighting is to make the word of Allah uppermost. The ways of Allah are many and varied, and the *āyah* applies to all of them. Allah says: *'Say: "This is My way."'* (12:108) Mālik said, 'The ways of Allah are many and there is not one of them which should not be fought on, in or for. The greatest of them is the *dīn* of Islam. There is no disagreement about this.'

It also is said that the people addressed are those of the tribe of Israel who were brought to life. That is related from Ibn 'Abbās and aḍ-Ḍaḥḥāk, who say that the *wa* (and) which comes at the beginning of the *āyah* connects it to the previous matter and if this is the case then something is elided and what is intended is: 'He said to them, "Fight..."'

An-Naḥḥās said that the *āyah* is a command to the believers not to flee in the face of fighting. It means, 'Know that Allah hears your words if you say the like of what those people said and He knows your intention.' Aṭ-Ṭabarī said that those who say that it is those who were brought to life who were commanded to fight have no basis for what they say. Allah knows best.

مَّن ذَا ٱلَّذِى يُقْرِضُ ٱللَّهَ قَرْضًا حَسَنًا فَيُضَٰعِفَهُۥ لَهُۥٓ أَضْعَافًا كَثِيرَةً
وَٱللَّهُ يَقْبِضُ وَيَبْصُۜطُ وَإِلَيْهِ تُرْجَعُونَ ﴿٢٤٥﴾

**245 Is there anyone who will make Allah a generous loan so that He can multiply it for him many times over? Allah both restricts and expands. And you will be returned to Him.**

**Is there anyone who will make Allah a generous loan**

Allah commanded *jihād* and fighting for the truth and there is nothing in the Sharī'ah which it is not permitted to fight for, the greatest object being the *dīn* of Islam as Mālik said. Then Allah encouraged people to spend to that end and included this in this passage about fighting in the Way of Allah. So a person spends hoping for the reward for fighting, as 'Uthmān ibn 'Affān did in the case of the Army of Hardship.

When this *āyah* was revealed, Abu-d-Daḥdāḥ set out to give all his wealth as *ṣadaqah*, seeking the reward of his Lord. The Shaykh, faqīh and imam, Qāḍī Abū 'Āmir Yaḥyā ibn 'Āmir ibn Aḥmad ibn Manī' al-Ash'arī (by lineage and school) reported to us in Cordoba in Rabī' al-Ākhir 628 AH, when I read to him from Abū Ijāzah by reading from Abū Bakr 'Abd al-'Azīz ibn Khalaf ibn Madyan al-Azdī from Abū 'Abdullāh ibn Sa'dūn from Abu-l-Ḥasan 'Alī ibn Mahrān from Abu-l-Ḥasan Muḥammad ibn 'Abdullāh ibn Zakariyyā ibn Ḥaywah an-Naysābūrī in 366 AH from his uncle, Abū Zakariyyā Yaḥyā ibn Zakariyyā from Muḥammad ibn Mu'āwiyah ibn Ṣāliḥ from Khalaf ibn Khalīifah from Ḥumayd al-A'raj from 'Abdullāh ibn al-Ḥārith that 'Abdullāh ibn Mas'ūd said, 'When: *"Is there anyone who will make Allah a generous loan,"* was revealed, Abu-d-Daḥdāḥ said, "Messenger of Allah, does Allah desire a loan from us?" He replied, "Yes, Abu-d-Daḥdāḥ." Abu-d-Daḥdāḥ said, "Give me your hand." He gave it to him and he said, "I have lent Allah a garden with six hundred palm trees in it." Then he walked to the garden where Umm ad-Daḥdāḥ was with his family. He called her. "Umm ad-Daḥdāḥ!" "At your service!" she replied. He said, "Come out. I have lent my Lord a garden with six hundred palm trees in it."

Zayd ibn Aslam said, 'When: *"Is there anyone who will make Allah a generous loan,"* was revealed, Abu-d-Daḥdāḥ said, "May my father and mother be your ransom,

Messenger of Allah! Does Allah ask us for a loan when He has no need of a loan?" He said, "Yes, He wants to admit you to the Garden by it." He said, "If I lend my Lord a loan will He guarantee the Garden for me and my daughter, Daḥdāḥah?" "Yes," he replied. He said, "Give me your hand." The Messenger of Allah ﷺ gave him his hand and he said, "I have two gardens, one at as-Sāfilah and one at al-'Āliyah. By Allah, they are all that I own. I have made them a loan to Allah Almighty!" The Messenger of Allah ﷺ said, "Make one of them for Allah, and leave the other as livelihood for you and your dependants." He said, "I bear witness, Messenger of Allah, that I have made the better of them a loan for Allah Almighty." It was a garden of six hundred palm-trees. The Prophet ﷺ said, "Allah will repay you with the Garden for them." Abu-d-Daḥdāḥ went to Umm ad-Daḥdāḥ who was with heir children in the garden going around in the palm-trees and said:

My Lord has guided me to the paths of guidance,
to the path of good and correctness.
Leave the garden at al-Widād.
It is a loan until the Meeting.
I have lent it to Allah, relying voluntarily,
not seeking a favour or its return,
Only the hope for many times more in the Hereafter.
So set out with yourself and your children.
There is no doubt that piety is the best provision
which someone sends ahead to the Hereafter.

Umm ad-Daḥdāḥ said, 'A profitable sale! May Allah bless you in what you purchased!' Then Umm ad-Daḥdāḥ answered him in verse:

Allah has given you the good news of good and joy.
A person like you settles what he owes and is faithful.
Allah has provided for my dependants
and given black *'ajwah* dates and bright flowers.
The slave strives and has what he toiled for
in the long nights and owes what he procured.

Then Umm ad-Daḥdāḥ told her children to remove what was in their mouths and what was in their sleeves and went to the other garden. The Prophet ﷺ said, 'How many heavy clusters and abundant houses Abu-d-Daḥdāḥ will have!'

Ibn al-'Arabī said, 'By the judgment, wisdom, power, will and decree of the

Creator, when people heard this *āyah*, they were separated into categories and divided into three groups. The first group are base. They said, "The Lord of Muḥammad is poor and in need of us and we are rich and independent." This is unconcealed ignorance. They are refuted by His words: *"Allah has heard the words of those who say, 'Allah is poor and we are rich.'"* (3:181) The second group preferred avarice and miserliness and desired wealth and did not spend in the way of Allah or ransom captives or help anyone, being too lazy to obey and relying on this world. The third group set out to obey Allah, choosing to respond to what they heard with haste like Abu-d-Daḥdāḥ and others, and Allah knows best.

The word used for 'loan' here is *qarḍ*. It is everything for which there is repayment. *Aqraḍa* means to advance money to someone. *Qirḍ* is used in another dialect. Az-Zajjāj said that linguistically it means a good or bad test. Al-Kisā'ī said that it is what you advance of good or bad actions. Its root means 'cutting'. The word *miqrāḍ*, meaning scissors, comes from it, because *aqraḍa* implies cutting out a piece of one's wealth which will be repaid. Another form of the word is used for when the traces of a people are cut off and they are destroyed. *Qarḍ* here is a noun but Allah could say *iqrāḍ*. The word is used to make it familiar to people in a way that they will understand. Allah is Rich-beyond-need and Praiseworthy, but He likens what the believer gives in this world in exchange for what he hopes for of reward in the Next World to a loan, as He likens the giving of lives and property in order to obtain the Garden to buying and selling, as will be discussed in *Sūrat-Tawbah*, Allah willing.

It is said that the aim of this *āyah* is to encourage *ṣadaqah* and spending wealth in the Way of Allah to help the poor and needy and to be generous with them, and 'in the Way of Allah' also means to support the *Dīn*. Allah alludes to the poor by mentioning Himself, even though He is sublime and beyond need of anything, to encourage *ṣadaqah*, as He alludes to the sick, hungry and thirsty by mentioning Himself in the famous *ḥadīth*: 'Son of Ādam, I was ill and You did not visit Me; I asked you for food and you did not feed Me; I asked you for water and you did not give it to Me.' The reply was, 'O Lord, how could I give you water when You are the Lord of the worlds?' He said, 'My slave asked you for water and you did not give it to him. If you had given it to him, you would have found that with Me.' This *ḥadīth* can be found in both al-Bukhārī and Muslim. All of this is to ennoble the person alluded to in order to encourage those who are addressed.

Someone who asks for a loan is duty bound to repay the loan and Allah has made it clear that those who spend in the Way of Allah certainly do not lose by doing so. Allah absolutely rewards it. In a *ḥadīth* we read, 'Spending in the Way of Allah is multiplied seven hundred times or more.' This will be explained in 2:261. Here Allah says: '*...so that He can multiply it many times over*'. This has no end or limit.

The reward for the loan is so large because it gives expansion to the Muslim and relieves him. Ibn Mājah related in the *Sunan* from Anas ibn Mālik that the Messenger of Allah ﷺ said, 'On the Night Journey I saw written on the gate of the Garden, "*Ṣadaqah* is rewarded ten times over and a loan eighteen times." I asked Jibrīl, "Why is a loan better than *ṣadaqah*?" He replied, "Because a beggar may ask when he has something but the one who asks for a loan only does so out of real need."'

Muḥammad ibn Khalaf al-'Asqalānī related from Ya'lā from Sulaymān ibn Yusayr from Qays ibn Rūmī that Sulaymān ibn Udhubān lent 'Alqamah a thousand dirhams to be repaid when he received his stipend. When his stipend arrived, Sulaymān demanded repayment and was hard on 'Alqamah, so he paid it. It seemed that 'Alqamah was angry. A month passed and then he went to him again and said, 'Lend me a thousand dirhams until my stipend comes.' He answered, 'Yes, and with honour! Umm 'Utbah! Bring that sealed bag you have!' She brought it and he said, 'By Allah, they are your dirhams that you paid me. Not a single dirham has moved.' He asked, 'What has made you do this for me?' He said, 'It is because of what I heard from you.' He asked, 'And what did you hear from me?' He replied, 'I heard you mention from Ibn Mas'ūd that the Prophet ﷺ said, "If any Muslim gives a loan to another Muslim twice, it is as if he had given it as *ṣadaqah* once."' He said, 'That is what Ibn Mas'ūd told me.'

A loan in the Sharī'ah is one to one, in other words, a person returns what has been lent him. Scholars agree that it is permitted to lend dinars, dirhams, wheat, barley, dates and all similar goods. The Muslims agree that stipulating an increase over and above what has been lent is usury, even if it is only a handful of fodder, as Ibn Mas'ūd said, or a single grain. It is, however, permitted to give more when repaying provided that it was not a precondition because that is courtesy and the *ḥadīth* transmitted by Abū Hurayrah reports, 'The best of you is the best of you in repayment.' The imams transmitted it: al-Bukhārī, Muslim and others. The Prophet ﷺ praised repaying well. That is undefined and not limited by any description. That is how the Prophet ﷺ repaid the loan of a young camel with a four-year-old camel. This *ḥadīth* contains evidence for the permission to lend animals. That is the school of the majority while Abū Ḥanīfah forbade that as already mentioned.

It is not permitted for someone who takes a loan to give a gift to the one who gave him the loan while it is still outstanding nor is it permitted for the lender to accept it unless that is their normal custom, and the Sunnah has brought this. Ibn Mājah transmitted from Hishām ibn 'Ammār from Ismā'īl ibn 'Ayyāsh from 'Utbah ibn Ḥumayd aḍ-Ḍabbī that Yaḥyā ibn Abī Isḥāq al-Hunā'ī said, 'I asked Anas ibn Mālik about one of our men who lent his brother some money. Could he give him a gift?' He answered, 'The Messenger of Allah ﷺ said, "When one of you gives his brother a loan and then he gives him a gift or lets him ride his animal, he should not accept and not ride unless that was the normal custom between them before that."'

A loan can be property, whose ruling we have explained, or it can be in the form of reputation. We find in a *ḥadīth* from the Prophet ﷺ: 'Is one of you unable to be like Abū Ḍamḍam? When he left his house he would say, "O Allah, I have given my reputation as *ṣadaqah* to Your servants."' It is related that Ibn 'Umar said, 'Give a loan of your reputation for day when you are poor.' He meant: 'Do not take your due from someone who insults you and do not carry out a *ḥadd* on him until the Day of Rising when there will be a full reward.' Abū Ḥanīfah said, 'It is not permitted to give reputation as *ṣadaqah* because it is Allah's right.' That is related from Mālik. Ibn al-'Arabī said, 'This is false. The Prophet ﷺ said in the *Ṣaḥīḥ*: "Your lives, property and honour are unlawful to you..." This demands that these three matters are treated in the same way: as a human right.'

Al-Wāqidī said that the word 'generous' (*ḥasan*, literally "good") means what is reckoned as good by the lender. 'Amr ibn 'Uthmān aṣ-Ṣadafī said that it means not entailing obligation or harm. Sahl ibn 'Abdullāh said, 'He does not believe that there is compensation for the loan.'

**so that He can multiply it for him many times over?**

'Āṣim and others recited '*yuḍā'ifahu*' while Ibn 'Āmir and Ya'qūb recited '*yuḍa''afahu*', Ibn Kathīr, Abū Ja'far and Shaybah recited '*yuḍa''afuhu*', and others recited '*yuḍā'ifuhu*'. This stresses the idea of great increase. Al-Ḥasan and as-Suddī say only Allah knows what this multiplication entails since He says: '*...pay out an immense reward direct from Him.*' (4:40) Abū Hurayrah said that this is about money given to help in *jihād*.

**Allah both restricts and expands.**

This is general to everything. '*You will be returned to Him*' is a threat. He will repay every action.

أَلَمْ تَرَ إِلَى الْمَلَإِ مِن بَنِي إِسْرَائِيلَ مِن بَعْدِ مُوسَىٰ إِذْ قَالُوا لِنَبِيٍّ
لَّهُمُ ابْعَثْ لَنَا مَلِكًا نُّقَاتِلْ فِي سَبِيلِ اللَّهِ قَالَ هَلْ عَسَيْتُمْ
إِن كُتِبَ عَلَيْكُمُ الْقِتَالُ أَلَّا تُقَاتِلُوا قَالُوا وَمَا لَنَا أَلَّا نُقَاتِلَ
فِي سَبِيلِ اللَّهِ وَقَدْ أُخْرِجْنَا مِن دِيَارِنَا وَأَبْنَائِنَا فَلَمَّا كُتِبَ
عَلَيْهِمُ الْقِتَالُ تَوَلَّوْا إِلَّا قَلِيلًا مِّنْهُمْ وَاللَّهُ عَلِيمٌ بِالظَّالِمِينَ ﴿٢٤٦﴾

**246 What do you think about the council of the tribe of Israel after Mūsā's time when they said to one of their Prophets, 'Give us a king and we will fight in the Way of Allah!'? He said, 'Is it not possible that if fighting were prescribed for you, you would not fight?' They said, 'How could we not fight in the way of Allah when we have been driven from our homes and children?' But then when fighting was prescribed for them, they turned their backs – except for a few of them. Allah knows the wrongdoers.**

**What do you think about the council of the tribe of Israel**

In order to encourage fighting, Allah mentions another story which concerns the tribe of Israel. The 'council' (*mala'*) are the nobles among a people. It is as if they were filled with honour. Az-Zajjāj said that they are called this because they are filled (*mala'a*) with everything they need. Here the 'council' means representatives of the people, and *mala'* can be used as the name for a group, like *qawm* and *raht*. The word also means good character. Part of that is found in a *ḥadīth*: 'Make the council good. All of you will be seen.' Muslim transmitted it.

**after Mūsā's time**

After his death.

**When they said to one of their Prophets, 'Give us a king and we will fight in the Way of Allah!'?**

It is said that the Prophet referred to was Shamwīl ibn Bāl ibn 'Alqamah who was known as 'the son of the old woman'. It is also said that it was Sham'ūn [Samuel] as as-Suddī said. It is said that he was known as 'the son of the old woman' because his mother was old and barren and asked Allah for a child. It is said that he was called 'Sham'ūn' because she prayed to Allah to give her a child and He heard her prayer and she bore a boy. Therefore she called him 'Sham'ūn' and said, 'Allah has heard (*sami'a*) my prayer.' The *sīn* becomes a *shīn* in Hebrew. He was one of the descendants of Ya'qūb. Muqātil said that he was one of the descendants of Hārūn. Qatādah said that the Prophet was Yūsha' ibn Nūn. Ibn 'Aṭiyyah said that this is weak because Dāwud was generations after Mūsā and Yūsha' ibn Nūn was Mūsā's servant. Al-Muḥāsibī mentioned that his name was Ismā'īl. Allah knows best.

This *āyah* tells us that at that time the tribe of Israel were abased and defeated by their enemies and asked for permission to fight and were commanded to do so. When the command came many were faint-hearted. A few, however, were steadfast and so Allah gave them victory. One reports states that these were the ones who were made to die and then brought back to life. Allah knows best.

**He said, 'Is it not possible that if fighting were prescribed for you, you would not fight?'**

Nāfi' reads "*asītum*' while the rest read "*asaytum*' which is the best known. The word *kutiba* (lit. written) here means 'prescribed'. When they saw the reality of fighting and thought about actually taking part in the battle, their resolve weakened.

**But then when fighting was prescribed for them, they turned their backs**

The words 'turned their backs' means that their intentions became muddled and their resolve failed. This happens with wealthy nations who incline to comfort and an easy life. When war occurs, they are reluctant to fight and follow their nature. Part of this idea is found in the prohibition of the Prophet ﷺ when he said: 'Do not wish to meet the enemy. Ask Allah for well-being. But when you do meet them, then stand firm.' The imams have related it. Then Allah reported that a small number of them remained firm on their first intention and their resolve to fight in the Way of Allah continued.

وَقَالَ لَهُمْ نَبِيُّهُمْ إِنَّ ٱللَّهَ قَدْ بَعَثَ لَكُمْ طَالُوتَ مَلِكًا قَالُوٓا۟ أَنَّىٰ يَكُونُ
لَهُ ٱلْمُلْكُ عَلَيْنَا وَنَحْنُ أَحَقُّ بِٱلْمُلْكِ مِنْهُ وَلَمْ يُؤْتَ سَعَةً مِّنَ
ٱلْمَالِ قَالَ إِنَّ ٱللَّهَ ٱصْطَفَىٰهُ عَلَيْكُمْ وَزَادَهُۥ بَسْطَةً فِى ٱلْعِلْمِ
وَٱلْجِسْمِ وَٱللَّهُ يُؤْتِى مُلْكَهُۥ مَن يَشَآءُ وَٱللَّهُ وَٰسِعٌ عَلِيمٌ ﴿٢٤٧﴾

**247 Their Prophet said to them, 'Allah has appointed Ṭālūt to be your king.' They said, 'How can he have kingship over us when we have much more right to kingship than he does? He has not even got much wealth!' He said, 'Allah has chosen him over you and increased him greatly in knowledge and physical strength. Allah gives kingship to anyone He wills. Allah is All-Encompassing, All-Knowing.'**

**Their Prophet said to them, 'Allah has appointed Ṭālūt to be your king.'**

Their Prophet responded to their request. Ṭālūt (Saul) was a water-bearer, or tanner, or a mule driver, but he was a man of knowledge and so Allah elevated him. He was from the tribe of Benjamin and not from the tribe of either prophethood or kingship. Prophethood was in the descendants of Levi and kingship in the tribes of Yahūdhā (Judah). That is why they objected. Wahb ibn Munabbih said, 'When the Council of the tribe of Israel said this to Samuel, he asked Allah to send them a king and to show him who he was. Allah said to him, "Keep an observant eye on the horn in your house. When a man comes to you at the time when the oil is bubbling up in the horn, he is the king of the tribe of Israel. Then anoint his head with it and make him their king."' He said, 'Ṭālūt was a tanner and went out looking for an animal he had lost. He went to Shamwīl to ask him to pray for him to find the animal or to find some relief and the oil bubbled up. So Shamwīl took him and anointed his head and told him, "You are the king of the tribe of Israel whom Allah has commanded to be advanced to kingship." Then he told the tribe of Israel, "Allah has appointed Ṭālūt to be your king."'

Ṭālūt and Jālūt are two Arabicised foreign names and so they are not declined. The same is true of Dāwud.

**They said, 'How can he have kingship over us**

'How can he rule us when we are more entitled to be kings than he is?' Their custom was that the Prophets would name the king by Allah's command. When they asked, 'How?' it means 'From what path when we are from the tribe of kings and he is not?' They also pointed out that he was poor, completely ignoring the strongest reason, which was the prior decree of Allah, and their Prophet pointed out this conclusive argument against them: *'Allah has chosen him over you.'* His choice is the definitive argument. He made it clear to them that that was the reason why Ṭālūt was chosen.

**He said, 'Allah has chosen him over you and increased him greatly in knowledge and physical strength.**

He also possessed knowledge, which is the basis of a person's character, and physical strength which helped him in war and fighting. This *āyah*, therefore, provides the description of what a ruler should be like and the conditions governing rulership. A ruler merits his authority on the basis of knowledge, piety and strength, not on the basis of lineage. Lineage has no real say in the matter since knowledge and virtue supersede it as Allah makes clear by informing us that He chose Ṭālūt over them on account of his knowledge and strength even though their lineage was more noble. We have already mentioned the preconditions of leadership at the beginning of the *sūrah*. This *āyah* is the basis for it. Ibn 'Abbās said, 'At the time, Ṭālūt was the most knowledgeable man among the tribe of Israel, and the most complete. His physical stature alarmed the enemy.' It is said that he was called Ṭālūt because of his height (*ṭawl*). It is also said that the increased strength took the form of great charity and courage, not actual physical strength. A poet says:

You see a thin man and think little of him
    when a bold lion is in his clothes.
You admire a handsome man and put him to the test,
    and the handsome man is not as you had thought.
A camel may be immense but lacking in heart
    and the camel has no need of its great size.

This is the meaning of the words of the Prophet ﷺ to his wives: 'The first of you to join me will be the one with the longest hand.' They used to measure their hands, and then it was Zaynab who died first because she used to work with her hands and give *ṣadaqah*. Muslim transmitted it. One of the interpreters said that what is meant by knowledge here is knowledge of war. This is making the general particular without any evidence for doing so. It is said that 'increased knowledge' refers to the fact that Allah gave him revelation, but this would mean that Ṭālūt was a Prophet.

**Allah gives kingship to anyone He wills.**

Some commentators believe that these words are something that Allah said to Muhammad ﷺ. It is also said these are the words of Shamwīl and that is more likely. He said that to them when he saw their obstinacy and argumentativeness. He wanted to conclude his words with some definitive statement which could not be gainsaid, and so he said this. The ascription of a worldly kingdom to Allah is because He owns it. Then, without them asking, he informed them that 'the sign of kingship...' It is also possible that they had asked him for proof of his truthfulness about Allah choosing Ṭālūt to be king. Ibn 'Aṭiyyah said, 'The first is more apparent based on the context of the *āyah*. The second is more in keeping with the blameworthy qualities of the tribe of Israel. Aṭ-Ṭabarī believed that.'

وَقَالَ لَهُمْ نَبِيُّهُمْ إِنَّ ءَايَةَ مُلْكِهِۦٓ أَن يَأْتِيَكُمُ ٱلتَّابُوتُ فِيهِ
سَكِينَةٌ مِّن رَّبِّكُمْ وَبَقِيَّةٌ مِّمَّا تَرَكَ ءَالُ مُوسَىٰ وَءَالُ هَٰرُونَ
تَحْمِلُهُ ٱلْمَلَٰٓئِكَةُ إِنَّ فِي ذَٰلِكَ لَءَايَةً لَّكُمْ إِن كُنتُم
مُّؤْمِنِينَ ٢٤٨

**248 Their Prophet said to them, 'The sign of his kingship is that the Ark will come to you, containing serenity from your Lord and certain relics left by the families of Mūsā and Hārūn. It will be borne by angels. There is a sign for you in that if you are believers.'**

**Their Prophet said to them, 'The sign of his kingship is that the Ark will come to you.**

It is said that the Ark (*tābūt*) was sent down to Ādam. From him it reached Ya'qūb and from then on remained with the tribe of Israel. Those who fought with it were victorious until they disobeyed Allah and the Ark was seized and then the Amalekites defeated them: Jālūt (Goliath) and his people according to as-Suddī. So the tribe of Israel were forced to surrender the Ark to them. This is the strongest evidence that disobedience is the cause of failure, and this is clear.

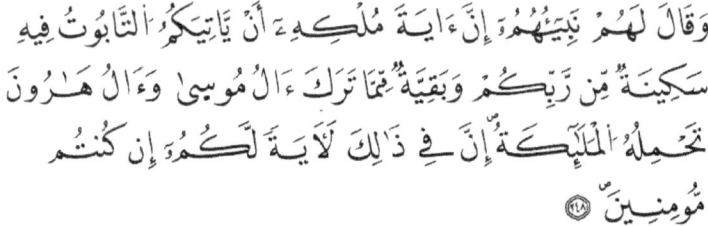

An-Naḥḥās said that it is related that the sign in the Ark was that a groan was heard coming from it. When they heard that, they went out to fight. When there was no groan, they did not go out. It is said that they used to place it at a critical place on the battlefield and they would have victory. This continued until they disobeyed Allah and were defeated and the Ark was taken from them and they were abased. When they saw this, some of them arranged for a Council and they asked the Prophet of the time for a king. When he told them that Ṭālūt was their king, they then rejected him as Allah tells us. When he gave them the decisive argument, they then asked for a clear sign of that.

We read in aṭ-Ṭabarī, 'When they asked their Prophet for the clear sign regarding what he said, he called on his Lord and, because of that, affliction descended on the people who had taken the Ark. There is some disagreement about that. It was said that they put it in a temple of theirs in which there were idols and the idols were overturned. They said, "Put it in the temple of the idols under the great idol," and in the morning it was on top of the idol. They tied it to its feet and in the morning the hands and feet of the idol were cut off and cast under the Ark. So they took it and put it in a village and those people experienced pains in their necks.' It is said that they put it in a lavatory and then they were afflicted by haemorrhoids. When the affliction was great, they said, 'It is this Ark which is the problem,' and they returned it to the tribe of Israel. They put it on a cart between two oxen and let them loose in the land in the direction of the tribe of Israel. Allah sent angels to drive the oxen until they reached the tribe of Israel who were under the command of Ṭālūt. Then they were certain of victory. The angels carried the Ark in this transmission. It is related that the angels came to carry it. Yūsha' ibn Nūn put it on the earth. It is related that they saw the Ark in the air when it descended among them. Ar-Rabī' ibn Khaytham said that. Wahb ibn Munabbih said that the size of the Ark was three cubits by two cubits. Al-Kalbī said that it was made of acacia wood from which combs are made.

**containing serenity from your Lord and certain relics left by the families of Mūsā and Hārūn.**

People disagree about the "*sakīnah*" (serenity) and the "*baqiyyah*" (relics). The word *sakīnah* is derived from *sukūn*, meaning tranquillity, gravity and serenity. So it means that the Ark was the cause of serenity in their hearts despite their disagreement over Tālūt. We find a similar use of the word when Allah says: *"Allah sent down His serenity on him"* (9:40), meaning something which made his heart tranquil. He meant that the Ark was the cause of tranquillity in their hearts. Wherever they were, they relied on it and did not abandon it when it accompanied them in war.

Wahb ibn Munabbih said, 'The *sakīnah* is a *rūḥ* (spirit) from Allah which spoke. When they disagreed about something, it clarified the matter for them, and when it shouted in war, they had victory.' 'Alī ibn Abī Ṭālib said, 'It was a wind which blew and had a face like a human being.' It is said that he said that it was a gale with two heads. Mujāhid said, 'It was an animal like a cat with two wings, a tail and shining eyes. When it looked at an army, that army was defeated.' Ibn 'Abbās said that it was a gold basin from the Garden in which the hearts of the Prophets were washed. As-Suddī said that. Ibn 'Aṭiyyah said, 'The sound view is that the Ark contained some excellent objects left by the Prophets and the hearts of the people were strengthened by that.'

We read in *Ṣaḥīḥ Muslim* that al-Barā' said, 'A man was reciting *Sūrat al-Kahf* and he had a horse with him tethered by two ropes. Then a cloud came over him and began to draw near and his horse began to shy away from it. In the morning he went to the Prophet ﷺ and mentioned that to him and he said, "That was the *sakīnah* which descended on account of the Qur'an."' We find in the *ḥadīth* of Abū Sa'īd al-Khudrī that Usayd ibn al-Ḥuḍayr was reciting the Qur'an at night in his drying-floor. In it the Messenger of Allah ﷺ said, 'Those were the angels who were listening to you. If you had continued, the people would have seen them in the morning and they would not have been concealed from them.' Al-Bukhārī and Muslim transmitted it. Sometimes the Prophet ﷺ mentioned the descent of the *sakīnah* and sometimes the descent of the angels. It indicates that the *sakīnah* was in that canopy and that it always descends with the angels. This is the argument of those who said that the *sakīnah* was a spirit (*rūḥ*) or something with a spirit because it is not valid that listening to the Qur'an be done by something that is not sentient. Allah knows best.

Several things are said about the relics (*baqiyyah*). It is said that they consisted of the staff of Mūsā, the staff of Hārūn, and fragments of the tablets because they were broken when Mūsā threw them down. Ibn 'Abbās said that. 'Ikrimah added the Torah to the list. Abū Ṣāliḥ said that it was the staff and garment of Mūsā, the garment of Hārūn and two tablets of the Torah. 'Aṭiyyah ibn Sa'd said that it was the staff of Mūsā, the staff of Hārūn, their garments, and fragments of the tablets. Ath-Thawrī said that some people said it was a measure of manna in a gold basin, the staff of Mūsā, the turban of Hārūn and fragments of the tablets. Some said that it was the staff and sandals. The meaning of this is what is related about when Mūsā came to his people and found them worshipping the Calf. He threw down the tablets in anger and they broke. He extracted from them what was unbroken and took the fragments of what was broken and put them in the Ark. Aḍ-Ḍaḥḥāk said that the word refers to *jihād* and fighting the enemy. Ibn 'Aṭiyyah said the command to do that was in the Ark, either written or by the mere fact of it being brought. They are ascribed to the families of Mūsā and Hārūn since the command comes from one people to another, all of whom were from the families of Mūsā and Hārūn. The family (*āl*) of a man are his kin.

فَلَمَّا فَصَلَ طَالُوتُ بِالْجُنُودِ قَالَ إِنَّ اللَّهَ مُبْتَلِيكُم بِنَهَرٍ فَمَن
شَرِبَ مِنْهُ فَلَيْسَ مِنِّي وَمَن لَّمْ يَطْعَمْهُ فَإِنَّهُ مِنِّي إِلَّا مَنِ
اغْتَرَفَ غُرْفَةً بِيَدِهِ فَشَرِبُوا مِنْهُ إِلَّا قَلِيلًا مِّنْهُمْ فَلَمَّا
جَاوَزَهُ هُوَ وَالَّذِينَ آمَنُوا مَعَهُ قَالُوا لَا طَاقَةَ لَنَا الْيَوْمَ بِجَالُوتَ
وَجُنُودِهِ قَالَ الَّذِينَ يَظُنُّونَ أَنَّهُم مُّلَاقُو اللَّهِ كَم مِّن
فِئَةٍ قَلِيلَةٍ غَلَبَتْ فِئَةً كَثِيرَةً بِإِذْنِ اللَّهِ وَاللَّهُ مَعَ
الصَّابِرِينَ ﴿٢٤٩﴾

**249 When Tālūt marched out with the army, he said, 'Allah will test you with a river. Anyone who drinks from it is not with me. But anyone who does not taste it is with me – except for him who merely scoops up a little in his hand.' But they drank from it – except for a few of them. Then when he and those who believed with him had crossed it, they said, 'We do not have the strength to face Jālūt and his troops today.' But those who were sure that they were going to meet Allah said, 'How many a small force has triumphed over a much greater one by Allah's permission! Allah is with the steadfast.**

**When Tālūt marched out with the army,**

The word for 'march out' (*faṣala*) means to go out with them but the verb also means 'to separate from'. Wahb ibn Munabbih said, 'When Tālūt set out, they said to him, "The water will not be enough for us, so ask Allah to make a river flow for us." He said, "Allah will test you with a river."' According to as-Suddī, there were eighty thousand soldiers. Wahb continued, 'No one stayed behind the army except for those excused by youth, age or illness. *Ibtilā'* is testing.'

*Nahar* and *nahr* (river) are two dialectical forms. The word is derived from the meaning of expansion. *Nahār* (day) comes from it. Qatādah said, 'The river with which Allah tested them was a river between Jordan and Palestine.' The reason for the test was so that Tālūt would know that those who left the water alone would obey him in respect of other things and those who were overcome by desire for water and disobeyed his command would disobey him in more important matters. It is related that they reached the river and were thirsty and the water was very sweet and good. That is why those who obeyed had an allowance of scooping up a handful to remove the pain of thirst from themselves. It is clear that a handful is to relieve the harm caused by thirst for those who are resolute and steadfast in the hardship of life and whose concern is for other than just being comfortable. It is as 'Urwah said:

Feel the purity of water, and the water is cool.

This is the sense of the words of the Prophet ﷺ, 'Enough for a person are a few morsels with which to keep his back straight.' One of those with a grasp of profound meanings said that this *āyah* is an example that Allah has made which represents this world. Allah likened the river and the one who drinks from it to someone who inclines to this world and seek to have a lot of worldly things. The one who does not drink from it is like someone who turns from it and makes do with little of it. Someone who scoops up a handful is like someone who only takes what he needs from it. These three have different states in the sight of Allah. This is excellent, although it moves from the literal to an interpretation, but the meaning is nevertheless sound.

**he said, 'Allah will test you with a river.**

Those who say that Tālūt was a Prophet take these words as a proof, since it is clear that Allah had revealed to him that this was a test from Allah for them. Those who say that he was not a Prophet say that it was Shamwīl who informed him of the revelation and then he informed the people. The test was to distinguish the sincere people from the false-hearted. Some people believe that 'Abdullāh ibn Ḥudhāfah, the Companion of the Messenger of Allah ﷺ, commanded his companions to light a fire and enter it to test their obedience, but his nature led him to make the matter he imposed harsh. This will be dealt with in *an-Nisā'*, Allah willing.

**Anyone who drinks from it is not with me.**

'He will not be one of my companions in this battle.' It was not a test of their faith so they did not become unbelievers by doing that. As-Suddī said that they were eighty thousand and so they inevitably included believers, hypocrites, and both serious and lazy people. We find in a *ḥadīth*: 'Whoever cheats us is not one of us,' meaning 'He is not one of our Companions and not following our path and guidance.' It is said:

When you try to deceive Asad by iniquity,
I am not from you and you are not from me.

This saying is used by the Arabs. If a man's son is following a different path, he may say, 'You are not from me.'

**But anyone who does not taste it is with me –**

Allah uses the verb *ṭamaʿa* (taste) rather than *shariba* (drink). Allah does not repeat the same word, because the best style in Arabic is to avoid repetition and the style of the Qur'an is the most eloquent possible. This is an aspect of that eloquence.

Our scholars use this as evidence for the principle of *sadd adh-dharāʾiʿ* because the least taste is included in the word 'taste'. When 'tasting' is forbidden, there is no way for someone to drink from what is forbidden.

The use of the word 'taste' also indicates that water is considered to be food. If it is food, it means that it nourishes and supports the body. So usury may occur in respect of it. Ibn al-ʿArabī said, 'That is sound in the School.' Abū ʿUmar said, 'Mālik said, "There is nothing wrong in selling water on the bank for water different in amount and on credit.' That is the view of Abū Ḥanīfah and Abū Yūsuf. Muḥammad ibn al-Ḥasan said, 'It is one of the commodities that are measured and weighed. According to this position, there should be no disparity in it.' He considers that to be usury because the cause with respect of it being usury is weighing and measuring. Ash-Shāfiʿī said, 'It is not permitted to sell water with different amounts or on credit.' His reason for its being usury is that water is one sort of combustible.

Ibn al-ʿArabī said, 'Abū Ḥanīfah said, "If someone says, 'If my slave so-and-so drinks from the Euphrates, he is free,' he is only free if he drinks directly from the river with his mouth. If he drinks using his hand or scoops it up with a vessel, he is not freed because Allah made a difference between drinking directly from the river and drinking with the hand."' He continued, 'This is unsound because the drinking of water is used for every form of doing so in Arabic, whether that is scooping up with the hand and drinking directly by mouth. It is one application. When he finds that water which the oath was about in language and actuality, that fulfils the oath.'

I say that the view of Abū Ḥanīfah is sounder. The people who understand language make a distinction between them as does the Book and the Sunnah. Al-Jawharī and others said that the verb *karaʿa* denotes drinking water directly from the place without using one's hands or a vessel. In the Sunnah, Ibn Mājah mentioned in the *Sunan* from Wāṣil ibn ʿAbd al-Aʿlā from Ibn Fuḍayl from Layth from Saʿīd ibn ʿĀmir that Ibn ʿUmar said, 'We passed by a pond and began to drink directly (*nakriʿu*) from it. The Messenger of Allah ﷺ said, "Do not drink directly from it. Rather wash your hands and then drink from it. There is no more sweeter vessel than the hand."' This is a text. Muslim transmitted from Layth ibn Abi Sulaym and said that he is weak.

**except for him who merely scoops up a little in his hand.'**

Scooping is taking up something with the hand or some implement. *Mighrafah* (ladle) comes from the same root. *Gharf* and *ightirāf* (scooping) mean the same. This usage means to do it once. Some say that when the word *gharfah* (Warsh) is used it means with one hand and when *ghurfah* (Ḥafṣ) is used it means with two, and some say that they both mean the same thing.

Whoever desires what is purely *ḥalāl* in these times without any suspicion or doubt should drink water with his own hands from springs and rivers whose flow is subjected by the flow at the end of the night and end of the day, seeking from Allah by that to gain good deeds, remove burdens, and join the imams and pious. The Messenger of Allah ﷺ said, 'If someone drinks with his hand while able to use a vessel, desiring to be humble by doing that, Allah will record good deeds for him according to the number of his fingers. That was the vessel of 'Īsā ibn Maryam when he cast aside the cup and said, "Uff! This is part of this world."' Ibn Mājah transmitted it from Ibn 'Umar. He said, 'The Messenger of Allah ﷺ forbade us to drink on our bellies: that is *kar'* (drinking directly from the water with the mouth). He forbade us to scoop it up with one hand. He said, "None of you should drink like a dog nor drink with one hand as was done by people with whom Allah was angry. He should not drink from a vessel at night without first shaking it, unless it was covered. If someone drinks with his hand while able to use a vessel..."' Baqiyyah ibn al-Walīd is in the *isnād*. Abū Ḥātim said, 'His *ḥadīth*s are recorded but not used as an authority.' Abū Zur'ah said, 'If Baqiyyah relates from trustworthy sources, then he is trustworthy.'

**But they drank from it – except for a few of them.**

Ibn 'Abbās said that they drank according to the degree of their certainty. The unbelievers drank eagerly, and those who were merely disobedient less than that. Seventy-six thousand of the people failed the test and only the believers remained, some of whom did not drink at all and some of whom took a handful. Those who drank were not quenched, but remained intensely thirsty. Those who completely left the water were in a good situation and were more steadfast than those who took a handful.

**Then when he and those who believed with him had crossed it,**

This means that they crossed the river. *'Huwa'* is used for stress. The verb *jāwaza* means 'to cross a place'. Ibn 'Abbās and as-Suddī said, 'Four thousand men crossed the river with him, including those who drank from it. When they saw Jālūt and his armies, which numbered one hundred thousand, all of them heavily armed, three thousand six hundred and eighty of his army left.' If this is so, the believers who had certainty in the resurrection and the return to Allah and who said, *'How many a small force has triumphed over a much greater one by Allah's permission'* were same number as the people of Badr. Most commentators say that those who did not drink crossed the river with him and some of them said, 'How can we face the enemy when they are so many!' and those with true resolve made the other statement. Al-Barā' ibn 'Āzib said, 'We used to say that the people of Badr were the same number as the companions of Ṭālūt who crossed the river him: about 310.' One variant has '313'. He added, 'Only those who believed crossed with him.'

**But those who were sure that they were going to meet Allah**

Here *ẓann* means certainty. The word can also mean doubt. It means that they thought that they would be killed with Ṭālūt and would meet Allah as martyrs. So there was uncertainty about the possibility of being killed.

**'How many a small force has triumphed over a much greater one by Allah's permission!'**

A *'fi'ah'* (force) is a group of people and section of them. It also comes from a root meaning to cut with a sword, so it is like a section cut from the rest. This statement was to encourage fighting, being steadfast and obeying those who are true to their Lord. This is how it is mandatory for us to behave. But ugly actions and false intentions have prevented that until we have reached the stage where a large number of us can be defeated by a small number of the enemy as we have seen happen more than once. That is what we have brought on ourselves!

In al-Bukhārī, Abu-d-Dardā' said, 'We fight on the basis of our actions.' In the *Musnad*, the Prophet ﷺ said, 'Are you given provision and victory except on account of your weak ones?' Now actions are false and the weak are neglected. Steadfastness is scarce, reliance on Allah is weak and *taqwā* has completely disappeared! Allah says: *'Be steadfast, be supreme in steadfastness; be firm on the battlefield; and show fear of Allah'* (3:200); *'Put your trust in Allah'* (5:23); *'Allah is with those who show fear of Him and with those who are good-doers'* (16:128); *'Allah will certainly help those who help Him'* (22:40) and: *'When you meet a troop, stand firm and remember Allah repeatedly so that perhaps you will be successful.'* (8:45)

These are the reasons for victory and its preconditions. They are lacking and do not exist with us. We belong to Allah and to Him we return! Only the mention of the word Islam remains, and only the merest trace of the *dīn*, due to the appearance of corruption, excessive transgression and lack of guidance so that the enemy has conquered the lands of the east and west, land and sea. Seditions have become widespread, and the trials are terrible. There is no protection except with the All-Merciful!

وَلَمَّا بَرَزُوا۟ لِجَالُوتَ وَجُنُودِهِۦ قَالُوا۟ رَبَّنَآ أَفْرِغْ عَلَيْنَا صَبْرًا وَثَبِّتْ أَقْدَامَنَا وَانصُرْنَا عَلَى ٱلْقَوْمِ ٱلْكَٰفِرِينَ ۝

**250 When they came out against Jālūt and his troops, they said, 'Our Lord, pour down steadfastness upon us, and make our feet firm, and help us against this unbelieving people.'**

They went out onto the field of battle. Jālūt was the ruler of the Amalekites and their king. His shadow extended for a mile. It is said that the Berbers are descended from him. It is said that he had three hundred thousand warriors. 'Ikrimah said seventy thousand. When the believers saw their numbers, they prayed to their Lord. This is like Allah's words: *'Many a Prophet fought when there were many thousands with him…'* (3:146-147) When the Prophet ﷺ met the enemy, he would say in the fighting, 'O Allah, I attack and move by You.' When the Prophet ﷺ met the enemy, he would say, 'O Allah, I seek refuge with you from their evil and put You at their throats.' At the Battle of Badr, he made supplication until his cloak fell from his shoulders, asking Allah to fulfil His promise as will be dealt with in *Āl 'Imrān*, Allah willing.

فَهَزَمُوهُم بِإِذْنِ ٱللَّهِ وَقَتَلَ دَاوُدُ جَالُوتَ وَءَاتَىٰهُ ٱللَّهُ ٱلْمُلْكَ وَٱلْحِكْمَةَ وَعَلَّمَهُۥ مِمَّا يَشَآءُ ۗ وَلَوْلَا دَفْعُ ٱللَّهِ ٱلنَّاسَ بَعْضَهُم بِبَعْضٍ لَّفَسَدَتِ ٱلْأَرْضُ وَلَٰكِنَّ ٱللَّهَ ذُو فَضْلٍ عَلَى ٱلْعَٰلَمِينَ ۝

**251 And with Allah's permission they routed them. Dāwud killed Jālūt and Allah gave him kingship and wisdom and taught him whatever He willed. If it were not for Allah's driving some people back by means of others, the earth would have been corrupted. But Allah shows favour to all the worlds.**

**And with Allah's permission they routed them.**

Allah sent down victory on them. The root of the verb '*hazamū*' (they routed) literally means to break. It also means to sink a well. Zamzam is called 'the *Hazmah* of Jibrīl,' meaning that he sunk it with his foot and water came out. Another form of the word means kindling.

**Dāwud killed Jālūt**

That was because King Ṭālūt selected him from his people to fight Jālūt. He was a short young man, sallow and sickly. Jālūt was one of the strongest and most powerful of men. He used to defeat entire armies on his own. Yet Jālūt was killed at Dāwud's hand in front of the Amalekite army. His full name was Dāwud ibn Ishā [Jesse] or Dāwud ibn Zakariyyā and he was descended from Yahudhā ibn Ya'qūb in whose line was both prophethood and kingship. He was a shepherd and the youngest of his brothers and looked after the sheep while his seven brothers accompanied Ṭālūt. When war came, he said to himself, 'I will go and see this fight.' When he started on the way, he passed by a stone and it called out to him, 'Dāwud! Take me. It is through me that you will kill Jālūt.' Then another stone called him and then another. So he took them and put them in his bag and went along.

Jālūt came forward seeking single combat. People backed away from him until Ṭālūt said, 'If someone goes out and kills him, I will marry my daughter to him and give him authority over my property.' Dāwud came forward and said, 'I will go and kill him.' Ṭālūt thought little of him when he saw him because of his youth and small size and rejected him. Jālūt called out a second and third time and Dāwud came out once more. Ṭālūt asked him, 'Have you had any experience of fighting?' 'Yes,' he replied. 'What was it?' he asked. He said, 'A wolf attacked my sheep and I hit it and then cut off its head.' Ṭālūt said, 'Wolves are weak. Have you tested yourself against anything else?' 'Yes,' he said, 'A lion came and I hit it and then took its jaws and split them. Do you think this man is stronger than a lion?' 'No,' he answered. Ṭālūt had armour intended only for the person who was to fight Jālūt. He told him about it and it was brought and he put it on. Ṭālūt said, 'Ride my horse and take my weapons,' which he did.

When he had gone a short distance, people said, 'The youth is a coward!' Dāwud said, 'If Allah does not kill him for me and help me against him, this horse and armour will be of no use to me. I will fight him in the way I am used to fighting.' Dāwud was extremely skilful with a slingshot. He dismounted and took his bag and tied it round him and took his sling and went out to Jālūt who was bristling in his armour. Jālūt said to him, 'You, lad, come out against me!' 'Yes,' he replied. 'You are scarcely even a match for a dog!' Ṭālūt said. 'That may be so,' replied

Dāwud, 'but you are less than that.' He said, 'I will feed your flesh to the birds and wild beasts today!' They approached one another. Jālūt went to seize Dāwud with his hand since he thought little of him. Dāwud took the stone, put it in the sling, said the name of Allah and slung it and it hit him on the head and killed him. He removed his head and put it in his bag. The army was defeated in the subsequent confusion. It is said that he hit at the site of his nose. It is said that it hit his eye and emerged from the back of his head and hit some of his army and killed them. It is said that the stone split up until some of it hit everyone in the army. It was the handful which the Prophet ﷺ threw at Hawāzin in the Battle of Ḥunayn. Allah knows best. People have many stories about this *āyah*. I have mentioned to you what is meant by it and Allah is praised.

The meaning of the statement of Ṭālūt, 'If someone goes out and kills him, I will marry my daughter to him and give him authority over my property,' is confirmed in our Sharī'ah. It is when the leader says, 'If someone brings a head, he will have such-and-such,' or 'If he brings a captive, he will have such-and-such.' This will explained in *al-Anfāl*.

This indicates that going out for single combat can only be done with the permission of the leader, as Aḥmad, Isḥāq and others said. What is transmitted from al-Awzā'ī varies. It is related that he said that no one should embark on that without the leader's permission. It is also related that he said that there is nothing wrong with it. If the leader forbids anyone going out to single combat, no one may do so except with his permission. One group permits going out, not mentioning whether it is with or without the permission of the leader. This is the position of Mālik. Mālik was asked about a man in the ranks who says, 'Who will come forth?' He said, 'That is up to his intention. If he desires Allah by that, I hope that there is no harm. That was done in the past.' Ash-Shāfi'ī said, 'There is nothing wrong in going out.' Ibn al-Mundhir said, 'It is good to go out with the permission of the leader, but someone who goes out without the permission of the leader does nothing wrong. That is not disliked because I do not know of any report that forbids it.'

**and Allah gave him kingship and wisdom.**

As-Suddī said, 'Allah made him the inheritor of both the kingdom of Ṭālūt and the prophethood of Shamwīl. He taught him how to make chain mail, speak the language of the birds and other forms of knowledge.' Ibn 'Abbās said, 'It is that Allah gave him a chain connected to the galaxy and celestial sphere. The end of which was at Dāwud's hermitage. Nothing happened in the air without the chain ringing so that Dāwud knew what has happening. No one with a disease touched it without being healed. The sign of his people entering the *dīn* was when they touched it with their hands and then they wiped their palms on their chests. They used to take their arguments to it after Dāwud until it was removed.'

**If it were not for Allah's driving some people back by means of others, the earth would have been corrupted.**

For the word 'driving' Nāfi' reads *difā'* while the rest read *daf'*. They are both verbal nouns as Sībuwayh said. Abū Ḥātim said that they they mean the same.

Scholars disagree about the people by whom corruption is driven back. It is said that they are the *Abdāl*, who are forty men. Whenever one of them dies, Allah replaces him with another. They will all die on the Last Day. Twelve of them are in Syria, eight in Iraq. It is related that 'Alī said, 'I heard the Messenger of Allah ﷺ say, "The *Abdāl* are in Syria and they are forty men. When one of them dies, Allah replaces him with another man. By them succour is poured forth and by them He helps the believers against their enemies and removes affliction from the people of trials."' At-Tirmidhī al-Ḥakīm mentioned it in *Nawādir al-Uṣūl.*

The following is also transmitted from Abu-d-Darda': 'The Prophets are the pegs which hold the earth in place. When Prophethood was brought to an end, Allah replaced the Prophets with some of the people from the Community of Muhammad ﷺ called the *Abdāl.* They are not superior to other people in respect of fasting or prayer, but on account of their good character, true scrupulousness, good intention, sound hearts and good counsel for all the Muslims, seeking Allah's pleasure by steadfastness, forbearance, intelligence, and humility without abasement. They are the caliphs of the Prophets, the people Allah has chosen for Himself and whom He has selected for Himself by His knowledge. They are forty true men. Thirty of them have a similar certainty to that of Ibrāhīm, the Friend of the All-Merciful. By them Allah drives away disliked things from the people of the earth and innovations which people have introduced. It is because of them that people have rain and provision. None of them dies without Allah putting someone else in his place.'

Ibn 'Abbās said, 'If it were not for Allah's driving back the enemy by the armies of the Muslims, the idolaters would have triumphed and killed the believers and ruined their towns and mosques.' Sufyān ath-Thawrī said, 'They are the martyrs who are the means by which the *dīn* is established.' Makkī related that most commentators say, 'If it were not that Allah has defended those who do not pray by those who do and those who are not fearful of Allah by those who are, people would have been destroyed for their wrong actions.' That is like what an-

Naḥḥās, ath-Tha'labī and the rest of the commentators say, 'If it were not for Allah's driving back the impious unbelievers by the pious believers, the earth would have been corrupted.'

The Prophet ﷺ is reported as saying in a *ḥadīth*, 'Allah drives the punishment away from those of my community who do not pray by those who do, from those who do not give zakat by those who do, from those who do not perform *ḥajj* by those who do, and from those who not do *jihād* by those who do. If they had all agreed to abandon these things, Allah would not put off their destruction for the blink of an eye.' Then the Messenger of Allah ﷺ recited: *'If it were not for Allah's driving some people back by means of others, the earth would have been corrupted.'*

The Prophet ﷺ also said, 'The angels call out every day: "Were it not for Allah's slaves who pray, suckling children and grazing animals, the punishment would already have fallen upon you."' Abū Bakr al-Khaṭīb transmitted the same idea from the *ḥadīth* of al-Fuḍayl ibn 'Iyāḍ. Manṣūr related from Ibrāhīm from 'Alqamah from 'Abdullāh that the Messenger of Allah ﷺ said, 'Were it not for humble men, grazing animals and suckling children, the punishment would already have fallen upon the believers.' Someone said:

If it had not been for Allah's slaves who bow
　　and orphaned suckling children,
And animals grazing in the wild,
　　the most painful punishment would have fallen on them.

Jābir reported that the Messenger of Allah ﷺ said, 'By a man's rectitude, Allah puts right his children and grandchildren and the people of his house and the houses around him and they will remain in Allah's protection as long as he is among them.' Qatādah said, 'The believers experience trials on account of the unbelievers and the unbelievers experience well-being on account of the believers.' Ibn 'Umar reported from the Prophet ﷺ, 'On account of a righteous believer Allah will drive away affliction from a hundred of the people of his household and his neighbours.' Then he recited this *āyah*.

It is also said that this driving back is by means of the laws prescribed on the tongues of the Messengers. If it were not for that, people would plunder and loot one another and be destroyed. This is an excellent statement as it is general to restraining, defence and other things. Reflect on it. *'But Allah shows favour to all the worlds'* indicates that the fact that the believers avert the evil of the unbelievers is a favour and blessing from Him.

تِلْكَ ءَايَٰتُ ٱللَّهِ نَتْلُوهَا عَلَيْكَ بِٱلْحَقِّ وَإِنَّكَ لَمِنَ ٱلْمُرْسَلِينَ ﴿٢٥٢﴾

**252 Those are Allah's Signs which We recite to you with truth. You are indeed one of the Messengers.**

Allah is informing his Messenger ﷺ that only a sent Prophet will have knowledge of these signs which He mentions.

تِلْكَ ٱلرُّسُلُ فَضَّلْنَا بَعْضَهُمْ عَلَىٰ بَعْضٍ مِّنْهُم مَّن كَلَّمَ ٱللَّهُ وَرَفَعَ
بَعْضَهُمْ دَرَجَٰتٍ وَءَاتَيْنَا عِيسَى ٱبْنَ مَرْيَمَ ٱلْبَيِّنَٰتِ وَأَيَّدْنَٰهُ
بِرُوحِ ٱلْقُدُسِ وَلَوْ شَآءَ ٱللَّهُ مَا ٱقْتَتَلَ ٱلَّذِينَ مِنۢ بَعْدِهِم مِّنۢ بَعْدِ مَا
جَآءَتْهُمُ ٱلْبَيِّنَٰتُ وَلَٰكِنِ ٱخْتَلَفُوا۟ فَمِنْهُم مَّنْ ءَامَنَ وَمِنْهُم مَّن كَفَرَ وَلَوْ شَآءَ ٱللَّهُ
مَا ٱقْتَتَلُوا۟ وَلَٰكِنَّ ٱللَّهَ يَفْعَلُ مَا يُرِيدُ ﴿٢٥٣﴾

**253 These Messengers: We favoured some of them over others. Allah spoke directly to some of them and raised up some of them in rank. We gave Clear Signs to 'Īsā, son of Maryam, and reinforced him with the Purest Rūḥ. If Allah had willed, those who came after them would not have fought each other after the Clear Signs came to them, but they differed. Among them there are those who believe and among them there are those who disbelieve. If Allah had willed, they would not have fought each other. But Allah does whatever He desires.**

**These Messengers: We favoured some of them over others.**

This *āyah* is confusing. There are firm *ḥadīth*s in which the Prophet ﷺ stated, 'Do not choose between the Messengers,' and 'Do not give preference to any of the Prophets of Allah,' meaning, 'Do not say that this one is better than that one.' They are related by trustworthy imams. Scholars disagree about this, some saying that these statements were made before there was revelation of his superiority and before he knew that he was the master of the children of Ādam and that the Qur'an abrogated the prohibition of preference with this *āyah*.

Ibn Qutaybah said that his words, 'I am the master of the children of Ādam', refer to the Day of Rising because he will intercede on that Day and he will have the Banner of Praise and the Basin. His words, 'Do not prefer me to Mūsā', are a mark of his humility, as Abū Bakr said, 'I have been appointed and I am not the best of you.' The same is true of his words ﷺ, 'No one should say that I am better than Yunus ibn Mattā.' That expresses humility. The words of Allah: *'Do not be like the companion of the fish...'* (68:48) indicate that, in fact, the Messenger of Allah ﷺ was better than him because Allah says, 'Do not be like him.' That indicates that the other statements of the Prophet ﷺ were expressing humility. It is permitted to say, 'Do not prefer me to him in action. He may be better in action than me,' or to say in affliction and trial, 'He has a greater trial than me.'

The leadership and excellence which Allah has given His Prophet ﷺ on the Day of Rising over all the Prophets and Messengers was not because of his actions, but rather because Allah preferred him and singled him out for this distinction. This is the interpretation which al-Muhallab preferred. One of them said, 'It is forbidden to delve into that because delving into that is a means leading to argumentation and that would lead to mentioning the Prophets in a way which is not appropriate and might lessen the respect due to them.' Our shaykh said that it means that one does not say, 'The Prophet is better than all the other Prophets,' which is the literal prohibition because that that might lead to deprecation of the other Prophets. The prohibition is about using the expression, not about what one might believe in that way. Allah has reported that the Prophets vary in excellence. One should not say, 'Our Prophet is better than the Prophets,' nor that he is better than a certain Prophet, in order to avoid what has been forbidden and to show proper courtesy and to act in accordance with belief in what the Qur'an contains of preference. Allah is the One who knows the realities of things.

The best that is said is that the prohibition of preference is in respect of the reality of Prophethood itself which is one trait in which there is no rivalry. Rivalry exists in increased states, election, miracles, and kindnesses, not in the fact of Prophethood itself. That is why there are Messengers and 'those with resolve', the one Allah took as a Friend, the one He spoke to, and those He raised in rank. Allah says: *'We favoured some of the Prophets over others'* (17:55) and *'These Messengers: We favoured some over others.'*

This is excellent and combines the *ḥadīth*s without need for any abrogation. Saying that some are favoured over others is based on virtuous qualities and means. Ibn 'Abbās indicated that when he said, 'Allah preferred Muḥammad over the Prophets and over the people of heaven.' They asked, 'Ibn 'Abbās, what is his being favoured over the people of heaven?' He replied, 'Allah Almighty says: *"Were any of them to say, 'I am a god apart from Him,' We would repay him with Hell. That is how We repayment the wrongdoers."* (21:29) He said to Muḥammad: *"Truly We have granted you a clear victory, so that Allah may forgive you your earlier errors and any later ones."*

(48:1)' They asked, 'What is his being favoured over the Prophets?' He said, 'Allah says: *"We have not sent any Messenger except with the language of his people"* (14:4) and He said to Muḥammad ﷺ: *"We only sent you to the whole of mankind."* (35:28) He sent him to both jinn and men.' Abū Muḥammad ad-Dārimī mentioned this in his *Musnad.*

Abū Hurayrah said, 'The best of the sons of Ādam are Nūḥ, Ibrāhīm, Mūsā and Muḥammad. They are "those with resolve" among the Messengers." These are texts from Ibn 'Abbās and Abū Hurayrah about specification. It is known that the Messengers are better than those who were not sent with a Message. The one who is sent is favoured over others by the Message while he is equal in Prophethood regarding what the Messengers encounter of their nations' denial and being killed by them. This is not hidden.

However, Abū Muḥammad 'Abd al-Ḥaqq ibn 'Aṭiyyah said, 'The Qur'an demands preference. That is in general without any specification of anyone less favoured. That is also the case in the *ḥadīth*s. That is why the Prophet ﷺ said, 'I am the most honoured of the sons of Ādam with my Lord' and 'I am the master of the sons of Ādam.' He was not specific. The Prophet ﷺ said, 'No one should say that I am better than Yūnus ibn Mattā' and 'Do not prefer me to Mūsā.' Ibn 'Aṭiyyah said, 'This is a strong prohibition against specifying the less favoured because Yūnus was a young man and caved in under the burdens of Prophethood. If the Prophet ﷺ did not express that, neither should anyone else.'

Allah willing, what we prefer is better. When Allah reported that He favoured some over others, He made some of the rivalry clear and mentioned the circumstances in which others were favoured. He says: *'Allah spoke directly to some of them and raised some of them in rank. We gave Clear Signs to 'Īsā, the son of Maryam'* (2:253); *'We gave Dāwud the Psalms'* (17:55); *'We gave him the Gospel'* (5:46), *'We gave to Mūsā and Hārūn the Discrimination and a Shining Light and a Reminder to those who are godfearing'* (21:480; *'We gave knowledge to Dāwud and to Sulaymān'* (27:15); and *'When We made a covenant with all the Prophets – with you and with Nūḥ.'* ;(33:7) So He was general and then specific. He began with Muḥammad ﷺ. This is clear.

That is similar to what was said about the Companions. They shared in being Companions of the Prophet ﷺ and then were distinct with respect to the virtues Allah bestowed on them in the form of gifts and means. By those gifts they vary in excellence although they are all Companions, upright and praised. How excellent are the words of Allah: *'Muḥammad is the Messenger of Allah, and those who are with him are fierce to the unbelievers...'* (48:29) He says: *'He bound them to the expression of* taqwā *which they had the most right to and were most entitled to.'* (48:26) He says: *'Those of you who gave and fought before the Victory are not the same.'* (57:10) He says: *'Allah was pleased with the believers when they pledged allegiance under the tree.*" (48:18) So He was general and then specific. He forbade disgrace and deprecation. May Allah be pleased with all of them and provide us with love for them!

**Allah spoke directly to some of them.**

The one to whom Allah spoke was Mūsa. The Messenger of Allah ﷺ was asked about Ādam and whether he was a sent Prophet. He said, 'He was a Prophet who was spoken to.' Ibn 'Aṭiyyah said, 'The interpretation of people regarding this is that Ādam was spoken to in the Garden and so the special quality of Mūsā remains.'

**and raised up some of them in rank.**

An-Naḥḥās said, 'Some of the commentators, including Ibn 'Abbās, ash-Sha'bī and Mujāhid, said that this refers to Muḥammad ﷺ. He said, "I was sent to the red and black (i.e. all mankind), the earth was made a mosque for me, I was helped by terror at the distance of a month's travel, booty was made lawful for me, and I was given intercession."' His marks of distinction include the Qur'an, the splitting of the moon, the tree speaking to him, his feeding a lot of people from a few dates, and his obtaining milk from the sheep of Umm Ma'bad after its milk had dried up. Ibn 'Aṭiyyah said this and added, 'He is the person with the largest community and by him all the Prophets are sealed, not to mention other aspects of the great and noble character which Allah granted him.' It is possible that it means both Muhammad ﷺ and others whose signs are great. It is possible that it refers to Allah's statement that He raised Idrīs up to a high place and to the ranks of the Prophets in the heavens as reported in the *ḥadīth* of the Mi'rāj.

**We gave Clear Signs to 'Īsā, son of Maryam,**

The clear signs of 'Īsā were bringing the dead to life, healing the blind and lepers, and creating a bird of clay as we read in the Qur'an.

**and reinforced him with the Purest Rūḥ.'**

'The Purest *Rūḥ'* is Jibrīl as already stated.

**If Allah had willed, those who came after them would not have fought each other**

By 'them' Allah means the Messengers. It is said that the pronoun 'them' refers specifically to Mūsā and 'Īsā. It is said that it is all the Messengers after them, which is the literal meaning of the *āyah.* It is said that fighting refers to what was done by people after they had all passed away but this is not the meaning. What is meant is people fighting one another after the time of the Prophet concerned. People fell into disagreement after each Prophet. Some believed, and some rejected out of rebellion, envy and desire for worldly goods. All of that is by the decree and will of Allah. If He had willed differently, whatever He had willed would have happened, but the secret in this matter is that He did not will other than what occurred.

# Table of Contents for *Āyats*


142 The fools among the people will ask... 1
143 In this way We have made you a middlemost community... 6
144 We have seen you looking up into heaven... 9
145 If you were to bring every Sign to those given the Book... 11
146 Those We have given the Book recognise it ... 12
147 The truth is from your Lord, so on no account be among the doubters. 13
148. Each person faces a particular direction... 13
149 Wherever you come from, turn your face to the Masjid al-Ḥarām... 16
150 Wherever you come from, turn your face to the Masjid al-Ḥarām... 16
151 For this We sent a Messenger to you from among you... 18
152 Remember Me – I will remember you. Give thanks to Me... 18
154 Do not say that those who are killed in the Way of Allah are dead... 20
155 We will test you with a certain amount of fear and hunger... 20
156 Those who, when disaster strikes them, say, 'We belong to Allah... 22
158 Ṣafā and Marwah are among the Landmarks of Allah... 24
159 Those who hide the Clear Signs and Guidance We have sent down... 27
160 except for those who sincerely repent and put things right... 30
161 But as for those who are unbelievers and die unbelievers... 31
162 They will be under it for ever... 31
163 Your God is One God. 'There is no god but Him, the All-Merciful... 33
164 In the creation of the heavens and earth... 34
165 Some people set up equals to Allah... 42
166 When those who were followed disown those who followed them... 43
167 those who followed will say, 'If only we could have another chance... 44
168 Mankind! eat what is good and lawful on the earth... 45
169 He only commands you to do evil and indecent acts... 46
170 When they are told, 'Follow what Allah has sent down to you'... 47
171 The likeness of those who disbelieve... 50
172 You who believe! eat of the good things We have provided for you... 50
173 He has only forbidden you carrion, blood and pork and... 51
174 Those who conceal what Allah has sent down of the Book... 65
175 Those are the ones who have sold guidance for misguidance... 66

| | |
|---|---|
| 176 That is because Allah has sent down the Book with truth… | 67 |
| 177 True goodness does not lie in turning your faces to the East… | 68 |
| 178 You who believe! retaliation is prescribed for you… | 71 |
| 179 There is life for you in retaliation, people of intelligence… | 82 |
| 180 It is prescribed for you, when death approaches one of yo… | 83 |
| 181 Then if anyone alters it after hearing it… | 92 |
| 182 But if someone fears bias or wrongdoing… | 92 |
| 183 You who believe! fasting is prescribed for you… | 94 |
| 184 for a specified number of days. But any of you who are ill… | 94 |
| 185 The month of Ramadan is the one in which the Qur'an was sent… | 108 |
| 186 If My slaves ask you about Me, I am near… | 122 |
| 187 On the night of the fast it is lawful for you to have sexual relations… | 128 |
| 188 Do not devour one another's property by false means… | 147 |
| 189 They will ask you about the crescent moons… | 150 |
| 190 Fight in the Way of Allah against those who fight you… | 154 |
| 191 Kill them wherever you come across them and expel them… | 157 |
| 192 But if they cease, Allah is Ever-Forgiving, Most Merciful. | 157 |
| 193 Fight them until there is no more *fitnah* … | 160 |
| 194 Sacred month in return for sacred month… | 161 |
| 195 Spend in the Way of Allah. Do not cast yourselves into destruction…. | 166 |
| 196 Perform the Ḥajj and *'umrah* for Allah… | 170 |
| 197 The Ḥajj takes place during certain well-known months… | 205 |
| 198 There is nothing wrong in seeking bounty from your Lord… | 211 |
| 199 Then press on from where the people press on… | 223 |
| 200 When you have completed your rites, remember Allah… | 226 |
| 201 And there are others who say, 'Our Lord, give us good in this world… | 227 |
| 202 They will have a good share from what they have earned… | 229 |
| 203 Remember Allah on the designated days… | 231 |
| 204 Among the people there is someone whose words about the life… | 243 |
| 205 When he leaves you, he goes about the earth corrupting it… | 245 |
| 206 When he is told to be fearful of Allah, he is seized by a feeling of might… | 247 |
| 207 And among the people there are some who give up everything… | 248 |
| 208 You who believe! enter Islam totally… | 249 |
| 209 If you backslide after the Clear Signs have come to you… | 251 |
| 210 What are they waiting for but for Allah to come to them… | 252 |
| 211 Ask the tribe of Israel how many Clear Signs We gave to them… | 253 |
| 212 To those who disbelieve, the life of this world is painted… | 254 |
| 213 Mankind was a single community. Then Allah sent out Prophets… | 256 |
| 214 Or did you suppose that you would enter the Garden without… | 259 |

215 They will ask you what they should give away... 261
216 Fighting is prescribed for you even if it is hateful to you... 262
217 They will ask you about the Sacred Month and fighting in it... 264
218 Those who believe and make hijrah... 264
219 They will ask you about alcoholic drinks and gambling... 273
220 ...on this world and the Next. They will ask you ... 281
221 Do not marry women of the idolaters until they believe... 285
222 They will ask you about menstruation... 299
223 Your women are fertile fields for you... 308
224 Do not, by your oaths, make Allah a pretext to avoid good action... 313
225 Allah will not take you to task for careless statements in your oaths... 314
226 Those who swear to abstain from sexual relations with their wives... 317
227 If they are determined to divorce... 317
228 Divorced women should wait by themselves for three... 325
229 Divorce can be pronounced two times... 337
230 But if a man divorces his wife a third time... 357
231 When you divorce women and they reach... 365
232 When you divorce women and they reach... 367
233 Mothers should nurse their children for two full year... 369
234 Those of you who die leaving wives behind... 381
235 Nor is there anything wrong in any allusion to marriage... 394
236 There is nothing wrong in your divorcing women... 401
237 If you divorce them before you have touched them... 408
238 Safeguard the prayer – especially the middle one... 412
239 If you are afraid, then do the prayer on foot or mounted... 424
240 Those of you who die leaving wives behind... 427
241 Divorced women should receive maintenance... 429
242 In this way Allah makes His Signs clear to you... 429
243 What do you think about those who left their homes in thousands... 431
244 Fight in the Way of Allah... 436
245 Is there anyone who will make Allah a generous loan... 437
246 What do you think about the council of the tribe of Israel... 442
247 Their Prophet said to them, 'Allah has appointed Ṭālūt... 444
248 Their Prophet said to them, 'The sign of his kingship... 446
249 When Tālūt marched out with the army... 449
250 When they came out against Jālūt and his troops... 454
251 And with Allah's permission they routed them. Dāwud killed Jālūt ... 454
252 Those are Allah's Signs which We recite to you with truth... 459
253 These Messengers: We favoured some of them over others... 459

# Glossary

**Aḍḥā**: *see ʿĪd al-Aḍḥā.*
**adhān**: the call to prayer.
**Amīr al-Mu'minīn**: 'the Commander of the Believers', the caliph.
**Anṣār**: the "Helpers", the people of Madīnah who welcomed and aided the Prophet ﷺ.
**ʿAqīq**: a valley about four and a half west of Madīnah.
**ʿaqīqah**: an animal killed in celebration of the birth of a child and *ṣadaqah* equal to the weight of the child's hair given in the way of Allah for the same reason.
**ʿArafah**: a plain 15 miles to the east of Makkah. One of the essential rites of the ḥajj is to stand on ʿArafah on the 9th of Dhu-l-Ḥijjah.
**ʿĀshūrā'**: the 10th day of Muḥarram, the first month of the Muslim lunar calendar. It is considered a highly desirable day to fast.
**ʿAṣr**: the mid-afternoon prayer.
**awliyā'**: the plural of *walī.*
**Awṭās**: a location between Makkah and Ta'if, about fifteen miles from Makkah, the site of a battle.
**āyah**: a verse of the Qur'an.
**Badr**: a place near the coast, about 95 miles to the south of Madīnah where, in 2 AH in the first battle fought by the newly established Muslim community, the 313 outnumbered Muslims led by the Messenger of Allah overwhelmingly defeated 1000 Makkan idolaters.
**baḥīrah**: in the Jāhiliyyah period, a female camel which had given birth five times, the last being a male. Its ears were slit and let free to graze.
**Bi'r Maʿūnah**: site of an expedition four months after the Battle of Uḥud where a delegation of Muslims were attacked and killed.
**ḍammah**: the Arabic vowel 'u'.

**Dār al-Ḥarb**: 'the Abode of War', the domain of the unbelievers.
**dhikr**: lit. remembrance, mention. Commonly used, it means invocation of Allah by repetition of His names or particular formulae.
**dhimmah**: obligation or contract, in particular a treaty of protection for non-Muslims living in Muslim territory.
**dhimmī**: a non-Muslim living under the protection of Muslim rule.
**Dhu-l-Ḥijjah**: the twelfth month of the Muslim calendar, the month of the hajj.
**Dhu-l-Majāz**: a market located between Makkah and 'Arafah in the territory of Hudhayl. The Arabs came there after sighting the new moon of Dhu-l-Ḥijjah and stayed for eight days. It was very popular.
**Dhu-l-Qa'dah**: the eleventh month of the Muslim calendar.
**dīn**: the life-transaction, lit. the debt between two parties, in this usage between the Creator and created.
**Fajr**: the dawn prayer.
**farḍ**: an obligatory act of worship or practice of the *dīn* as defined by the Sharī'ah.
**farḍ kifāyah**: a collective obligation, something which is obligatory for the community as a whole and is satisfied if some of them perform it.
**faqīh**: pl. *fuqahā'*, a man learned in knowledge of *fiqh* who by virtue of his knowledge can give a legal judgement.
**fatḥah**: the Arabic vowel 'a'.
**Fātiḥah**: "the Opener," the first sūrah of the Qur'an.
**fatwa**: an authoritative statement on a point of law.
**fidyah**: a ransom, compensation paid for rites or acts of worship missed or wrongly performed because of ignorance or ill health. Also the amount paid by a woman in the *khul'*.
**fiqh**: the science of the application of the Sharī'ah. A practitioner or expert in *fiqh* is called a faqih.
**fitnah**: civil strife, sedition, schism, trial, temptation, also *shirk*.
**Fiṭr**: *see 'Īd al-Fiṭr.*
**fuqahā'**: plural of *faqīh*.
**gharīb**: a hadith which has a single reporter at some stage of the *isnād*.
**ghusl**: major ablution of the whole body with water required to regain purity after menstruation, lochia and sexual intercourse.
**ḥadd**: Allah's boundary limits for the lawful and unlawful. The *ḥadd* punishments are specific fixed penalties laid down by Allah for specified crimes.
**hadith**: reported speech of the Prophet ﷺ.

**hady**: sacrificial camel.
**hajj**: the annual pilgrimage to Makka which is one of the five pillars of Islam.
**ḥāl**: In Arabic grammar, a circumstantial adverb in the accusative case which describes something happening at the same time as the action or event mentioned in the main clause.
**ḥalāl**: lawful in the Sharī'ah.
**hamzah**: the character in Arabic which designates a glottal stop.
**harām**: unlawful in the Sharī'ah.
**Ḥaram**: Sacred Precinct, a protected area in which certain behavior is forbidden and other behaviour necessary. The area around the Ka'bah in Makkah is a Haram, and the area around the Prophet's Mosque in Madīnah is a Haram. They are referred to together as al-Ḥaramayn, 'the two Ḥarams'.
**al-Ḥarrah**: a stony tract of black volcanic rock east of Madīnah.
**Hārūn**: the Prophet Aaron, the brother of Mūsā.
**Ḥarūriyyah**: the first Khārijites who separated themselves from 'Alī and based themselves at Ḥarūrā', a town two miles from Kufa.
**ḥasan**: good, excellent, often used to describe a hadith which is reliable, but which is not as well authenticated as one which is *ṣaḥīḥ*.
**Ḥashwiyyah**: a sect who took the verses of the Qur'an literally and hence became anthropormorphists. They also espoused other innovations.
**Hawāzin**: one of the large Arab tribes in the Hijaz who were part of the Qays tribal grouping.
**Ḥawwā'**: Eve, the first woman.
**Hijaz**: the region along the western seaboard of Arabia in which Makkah, Madīnah, Jidda and Ta'if are situated.
**Hijrah**: emigration in the way of Allah. Islamic dating begins with the Hijrah of the Prophet Muḥammad ﷺ from Makkah to Madīnah in 622 AD.
**Hūd**: the Prophet sent to the people of 'Ād.
**Ḥudaybīyah**: a well-known place ten miles from Makkah on the way to Jiddah where the Homage of ar-Riḍwān took place.
**ḥudūd**: plural of *ḥadd.*
**Ḥunayn**: a valley between Makkah and Ta'if where the battle took place between the Prophet ﷺ and Thaqīf pagans in 8/630.
**Iblīs**: the personal name of the Devil. He is also called Shayṭān or the 'enemy of Allah'.
**Ibrāhīm**: the Prophet Abraham.

**'Īd**: a festival, either the festival at the end of Ramadan or at the time of the Hajj.
**'Īd al-Aḍḥā**: a four day festival at the time of hajj. The *'Īd* of the Sacrifice, it starts on the 10th day of Dhu-l-Ḥijjah (the month of Hajj), the day that the pilgrims sacrifice their animals.
**'Īd al-Fiṭr**: the festival at the end of the month of fasting (Ramadan).
**iḍāfah**: a possessive construction in Arabic in which the first noun is indefinite and the second usually definite. It is used to indicate possession. The first word is called *'muḍāf'* and the second is *'muḍāf ilayhi'*.
**'iddah**: a period after divorce or the death of her husband for which a woman must wait before re-marrying.
**ifrād**: a form of hajj in which the hajj alone is performed.
**iḥrām**: the conditions of clothing and behaviour adopted by someone on hajj or *'umrah*.
**ijtihād**: to exercise personal judgement in legal matters.
**īlā'**: a vow by a husband to abstain from sexual relations with his wife. If four months pass, it is considered a divorce.
**imam**: Muslim religious or political leader; leader of Muslim congregational worship.
**īmān**: belief, faith.
**insha'llāh**: 'Allah willing'.
**iqāmah**: the call which announces that the obligatory prayer is about to begin.
**'Īsā**: the Prophet Jesus.
**'Ishā'**: the obligatory evening prayer.
**Isḥāq**: the Prophet Isaac.
**ishārāt**: allusions, hints, indications of meanings too fine to be expressed directly.
**Ismā'īl**: the Prophet Ishmael.
**isnād**: a hadith's chain of transmission from individual to individual.
**istibrā'**: the waiting period for slave-girls.
**istiḥādah**: bleeding from the womb of a woman outside her ordinary periods.
**istiẓhār**: a woman considering herself as menstruating until her situation is clear.
**i'tikāf**: seclusion, while fasting, in a mosque, particularly in the last ten days of Ramadan.
**Jāhiliyyah**: the Time of Ignorance before the coming of Islam.
**Jālūt**: Goliath.

**Jam'**: another name for Muzdalifah.
**jamrah**: lit. a small walled place, but in this usage a stone-built pillar. There are three *jamrah*s at Minā. One of the rites of hajj is to stone them.
**Jamrat 'l-'Aqabah**: the largest of the three *jamrah*s at Minā.
**janābah**: major ritual impurity requiring a ghusl: brought about by sexual intercourse, sexual discharge, menstruation, childbirth.
**jawhar**: literally 'jewel', substance, specifically the essence or the intrinsic being of a thing.
**Jibrīl**: the angel Gabriel.
**jihad**: struggle, particularly fighting in the way of Allah to establish Islam.
**jinn**: inhabitants of the heavens and the earth made of smokeless fire who are usually invisible.
**jizyah**: a protection tax payable by non-Muslims living under Muslim rule to the Muslim ruler.
**Jumāda-l-Ākhir**: the sixth month of the Muslim calendar.
**Jumāda-l-Ulā**: the fifth month of the Muslim calendar.
**Jumu'ah**: the day of gathering, Friday, and particularly the Jumu'ah prayer which is performed instead of *Ẓuhr* by those who attend it.
**Jurjān**: an area in north-east Persia.
**Ka'bah**: the cube-shaped building at the centre of the Ḥaram in Makkah, originally built by the Prophet Ibrāhīm. Also known as the House of Allah.
**al-Kadīd**: a place between Makkah and Madīnah.
**kafālah**: long-term fosterage.
**kaffārah**: atonement, prescribed way of making amends for wrong actions, especially missed obligatory actions.
**kalām**: 'theology' and dogmatics. *Kalām* starts with the revealed tradition and employs rationalistic methods in order to understand it and resolve contradictions.
**kasrah**: the Arabic vowel i.
**Khārijites**: the earliest sect, who separated themselves from the body of the Muslims and declared war on all those who disagreed with them, stating that a wrong action tums a Muslim into an unbeliever.
**khaṭīb**: an orator, someone who delivers the *khuṭbah*.
**Khazraj**: along with Aws, one of the two major tribes of Madīnah.
**Khorasan**: Persian province southeast of the Caspian Sea; a centre of many dissident movements in early Islamic history.
**khul'**: a form of divorce initiated by the wife from her husband by giving him a certain compensation, or by returning back the bride price (*mahr*) which he gave her.

**khuṭbah**: a speech, and in particular a standing speech given by the imam before the Jumu'ah prayer and after the two *'Īd* prayers.
**Khuzā'ah**: an Azdī tribe who were concentrated around Makkah.
**Kitābī**: Someone who is one of the People of the Book, i.e. a Jew or Christian.
**li'ān**: mutual cursing, a form of divorce in which the husband and wife take oaths when he accuses her of adultery and she denies it.
**Majannah**: a market located near Makkah at Marr az-Zahrān over the last ten days of Dhu-l-Qa'dah. People came to it after the end of the 'Ukāz market.
**Maqām of Ibrāhịm**: the place of the stone on which the Prophet Ibrāhīm stood while he and Ismā'īl were building the Ka'bah, which marks the place of the two *rak'ah* prayer following *ṭawāf* of the Ka'bah.
**marfū'**: 'elevated', a narration from the Prophet ﷺ mentioned by a Companion. "The Messenger of Allah ﷺ said..."
**Maghrib**: the sunset prayer; also the western part of Muslim lands. Today it means Morocco.
**Maryam**: Mary, the mother of 'Īsā.
**Mash'ar al-Ḥarām**: a venerated place in the valley of Muzdalifah where it is a sunnah to stop.
**Masjid al-Ḥarām**: the great mosque in Makka.
**mawla**: a person with whom a tie of *walā'* has been established, usually by having been a slave and then set free.
**mawqūf**: 'stopped', a narration from a Companion without mentioning the Prophet ﷺ.
**Minā**: a valley five miles on the road to 'Arafah where the three *jamrah*s stand. It is part of the hajj to spend four or possibly three nights there over the course of the hajj.
**mīqāt**: plural *mawāqīt*, one of the designated places for entering *iḥrām* or *ḥajj* or *'umrah*.
**Mizāb ar-Raḥmah**: 'the Spout of Mercy', the rainspout at the top of the Ka'bah on its northeastern side.
**mu'adhdhin**: someone who calls the *adhan* or call to prayer.
**mudabbar**: a slave who has been given a *tadbīr*, a contract that he be freed after his master's death.
**mudd**: a measure of volume. approximately a double-handed scoop.
**Mudlij**: an Arab tribe which was a branch of Kinānah.
**mufti**: someone qualified to give a legal opinion or fatwa.
**Muhājirūn**: Companions of the Messenger of Allah ﷺ who accepted Islam in Makkah and made hijrah to Madīnah.

**Muḥarram**: the first month of the Muslim lunar year.
**Muḥassir**: a depression on the way to Minā.
**mujāhid**: some performing jihad.
**mujtahid**: a scholar who is qualified to carry out ijtihād.
**mukātab**: a slave who has been given a *kitābah*, a contract to buy his freedom.
**munkar**: "denounced", a narration reported by a weak reporter which goes against another authentic hadith.
**muqallid**: a person who practises *taqlīd*, not performing *ijtihād* himself but instead following the legal opinion already arrived at by a *mujtahid*.
**Murji'ites**: the opponents of the Kharijites. They held that it is faith and not actions which are important. There is also a political position which suspends judgement on a person guilty of major sins.
**mursal**: a hadith where a man in the generation after the Companions quotes directly from the Prophet without mentioning the Companion from whom he got it.
**Mūsā**: the Prophet Moses.
**Musaylimah**: the false prophet of the Banū Ḥanīfah in Najd.
**muṣḥaf**: a physical copy of the Qur'an.
**musnad**: a collection of hadiths arranged according to the first authority in its *isnād*; also a hadith which can be traced back through an unbroken *isnād* to the Prophet.
**mustafiḍ**: hadith related by three or more transmitters, although it does not reach the level of *mutawātir*.
**mut'ah**: a temporary marriage.
**mutakallimūn**: those who study the science of *kalām*, the science of investigating theological doctrine.
**mutawātir**: a hadith which is reported by a large number of reporter: at all stages of the *isnād*.
**muzābanah**: a forbidden sale in which something whose number, weight, or measure is known is sold for something whose number, weight or measure is not known.
**Muzdalifah**: a place between 'Arafah and Minā where the pilgrims returning from 'Arafah spend a night in the open between the ninth and tenth day of Dhu-l-Ḥijjah after performing Maghrib and 'Ishā' there.
**Nafr**: the 12th or 13th of Dhū al-Ḥijjah when the pilgrims leave Minā after having complete the rites at 'Arafah, Muzdalifah and Minā.
**Nakhlah**: a place between Makkah and Ṭā'if, two days ride east of Makkah.

**Nūḥ**: the Prophet Noah.
**People of the Book**: principally the Jews and Christians whose religions are based on the Divine Books revealed to Mūsā and 'Īsā; a term also used to refer to any other group who claim to be following a Book revealed prior to the Qur'an.
**People of Hadith**: 'the adherents of Hadith', the movement who considered only the Qur'an and hadith to be valid sources of fiqh.
**People of Opinion (*ra'y*)**: a term used to describe those who use personal opinion to deduce judgement. It was a term used particularly to describe the early Ḥanafīs.
**Qadariyyah**: sect who said that people have power (*qadar*) over their actions and hence free will.
**qāḍī**: a judge, qualified to judge all matters in accordance with the Sharī'ah and to dispense and enforce legal punishments.
**Qādisīyah**: a decisive four day battle fought against the Persians in Iraq in 15/636.
**qiblah**: the direction faced in the prayer which is towards the Ka'bah in Makkah.
**qirāḍ**: wealth put by an investor in the trust of an agent for use for commercial purposes, the agent receiving no wage, but taking a designated share of the profits after the capital has been repaid.
**qirān**: performing hajj and *'umrah* simultaneously.
**qiṣāṣ**: retaliation.
**Qubā'**: a village on the outskirts of Madīnah (originally about 5 km/3 miles outside the city) where the first mosque in Islam was built, also known as the Masjid at-Taqwā (Mosque of Fear of God).
**qunūt**: a supplication said in the prayer.
**Quraysh**: one of the great tribes of Arabia. The Prophet Muḥammad ﷺ belonged to this tribe, which had great powers spiritually and financially both before and after Islam came. Someone from this tribe is called a Qurayshī.
**Quzah**: a mountain at Muzdalifah.
**Rabī' al-Awwal**: the third month of the Muslim calendar.
**Rabī' al-Ākhir**: the fourth month of the Muslim calendar.
**Rajab**: the seventh month of the Muslim calendar.
**rak'ah**: a unit of the prayer consisting of a series of standings, bowing, prostrations and sittings.
**Ramadan**: the month of fasting, the ninth month in the Muslim lunar calendar.

**Riḍwān**: the Homage of Riḍwān was a pledge which the Muslims took at Ḥudaybīyah to avenge 'Uthmān when they thought that Quraysh had murdered him in 6/628.
**rūḥ**: (plural *arwāḥ*) the soul, vital spirit.
**rukū'**: the bowing position in the prayer.
**ṣā'**: a measure of volume equal to four *mudd*s.
**Sabians**: a group of believers. It is not entirely clear who they were. Possibly they were Gnostics or Mandaeans.
**Sacred Months**: the months of Rajab, Dhu-l-Qa'dah, Dhu-l-Ḥijjah and Muḥarram in which fighting was forbidden.
**ṣadaqah**: charitable giving in the Cause of Allah.
**Ṣafā and Marwah**: two hills close to the Ka'bah.
**Ṣafar**: the second month of the Muslim lunar calendar.
**ṣaḥīḥ**: healthy and sound with no defects, used to describe an authentic hadith.
**Ṣaḥīḥ**: "the Sound", the title of the hadith collections of al-Bukhārī and Muslim.
**saḥūr**: pre-dawn meal before a day of fasting.
**sā'ibah**: in the Jāhiliyyah, a she-camel let loose to graze, usually as a result of a vow to idols.
**salām**: the expression, '*as-salāmu 'alaykum*,' or 'Peace be upon you,' used as a greeting and to end the prayer.
**sawīq**: a gruel made of wheat or barley.
**sa'y**: the main rite of 'umrah and part of hajj. It is going between the hills of Ṣafā and Marwah seven times.
**Sha'bān**: the eighth month in the Muslim calendar
**shahādah**: bearing witness, particularly bearing witness that there is no god but Allah and that Muhammad is the Messenger of Allah. It is one of the pillars of Islam. It is also used to describe legal testimony in a court of law.
**Sharī'ah**: The legal modality of a people based on the revelation of their Prophet. The final Sharī'ah is that of Islam.
**Shawwāl**: the tenth month of the Muslim calendar.
**Shayṭān**: devil, particularly Iblīs, one of the jinn.
**shirk**: the unforgiveable wrong action of worshipping something or someone other than Allah or associating something or someone as a partner with Him.
**Shu'ayb**: the Prophet Jethro.
**ṣiddīq**: a man of truth, the *ṣiddīq* is the one who believes in Allah and

His Messenger by the statement of the one who reports it, not from any proof except the light of belief which he experiences in his heart and which prevents him from hesitating and prevents any doubt entering him about the word of the Messenger who reported.

**Sīrah**: biography, particularly biography of the Prophet ﷺ.

**Ṣirāṭ**: the narrow bridge which spans the Fire and must be crossed to enter the Garden. It is described as sharper than a sword and thinner than a hair. It will have hooks over it to catch people as they cross it.

**siwāk**: a small stick, usually from the arak tree, whose tip is softened and used for cleaning the teeth.

**Ṣubḥ**: dawn prayer

**sukūn**: a diacritic mark that means that there is no vowel sound after a consonant.

**Sulaymān**: the Prophet Solomon.

**sunan**: plural of sunnah.

**Sunnah**: the customary practice of a person or group of people. It has come to refer almost exclusively to the practice of the Messenger of Allah ﷺ.

**sūrah**: a chapter of the Qur'an.

**Tābi'ūn**: the second generation of the early Muslims who did not meet the Prophet Muhammad ﷺ but learned the *dīn* of Islam from his Companions.

**tadbīr**: a contract given by a master to a slave whereby the slave will be freed after the master dies.

**tafsīr**: commentary or explanation of the meanings of the Qur'an.

**Ṭā'if**: a walled town south of Makkah known for its fertility. It was the home of the tribe of Thaqīf.

**takbīr**: saying '*Allāhu Akbar*,' 'Allah is greater'.

**takbīr al-iḥrām**: the *takbīr* which begins the prayer.

**talbīyah**: saying '*Labbayk*' ('At Your service') during the hajj.

**Ṭālūt**: Saul.

**tamattu'**: a form of hajj in which 'umrah is done first, and then the ḥājjī comes out of iḥrām before going back into *iḥrām* for the hajj itself.

**tanwīn**: nunation.

**taqlīd**: imitation; following the opinion of a *mujtahid* without considering the evidence.

**taqwā**: awe or fear of Allah, which inspires a person to be on guard against wrong action and eager for actions which please Him.

**Tarwiyah**: 'drawing water', on the 8th of Dhu-l-Ḥijjah, the day before 'Arafah when the pilgrim gather water in preparation for the days of the Hajj which lie ahead.

**tashrīq**: 'drying meat in the sun', the days of the 10th, 11th, 12th and 13th of Dhu-l-Hijjah when the pilgrims sacrifice their animals and stone the jamrahs at Minā.
**ṭawāf**: circumambulation of the Ka'bah, done in sets of seven circuits.
**ṭawāf al-ifaḍāh**: the circumambulation that pilgrims must perform when coming from Minā to Makkah on the 10th of Dhu-l-Ḥijjah.
**tawḥīd**: the doctrine of Divine Unity.
**tayammum**: purification for the prayer with clean dust, earth, or stone, when water for *ghusl* or *wuḍū'* is unavailable or would be detrimental to health.
**Tha'alibiyyah**: a Kharijite sect.
**Thabīr**: a mountain near Makkah.
**Thamūd**: a people to whom the Prophet Ṣāliḥ was sent, possibly a group of Nabateans. Madā'in Ṣāliḥ is located at al-Ḥijr in Najd about 180 miles north of Madina. The inscriptions on the tombs there date from 3 BC to 79 CE which are probably after the culture which once flourished there was destroyed.
**Thaqīf**: a tribe based in the town of Ta'if, a branch of the tribe of Hawāzin.
**'Ukaz**: the most famous and largest pre-Islamic market in Arabia. It was located to the east of Makkah, at the edge of the Ḥarām. Every region attended it.
**Umm al-Mu'minīn**: literally 'Mother of the Believers', an honorary title given to the wives of the Prophet.
**umm walad**: a slavegirl who has had a child by her master.
**Ummah**: the body of Muslims as one distinct Community.
**'umrah**: the lesser pilgrimage to the Ka'bah in Makkah performed at any time of the year.
**'Uranah**: a wadi near 'Arafāt.
**uṣūl**: plural of *aṣl*, the basic principles of any source used in *fiqh*.
**wājib**: a necessary part of the Sharī'ah but not obligatory, although it is sometimes used as a synonym for *farḍ*.
**walī**: (plural *awliyā'*) someone who is a 'friend' of Allah, thus possessing the quality of *wilāyah*. Also a relative who acts as a guardian.
**waṣīlah**: in the Jāhiliyyah, a she-camel that has given birth to two females with no male in between them. It was set loose to graze.
**wilāyah**: guardianship.
**wasq**: a measure of volume equal to sixty *ṣā'*s.
**wuḍū'**: ritual washing to be pure for the prayer.
**Yaḥyā**: the Prophet John the Baptist, the son of Zakariyyā.

**Ya'qūb**: the Prophet Jacob, also called Isrā'īl (Israel).
**Yūnus**: the Prophet Jonah.
**Yūsuf**: the Prophet Joseph.
**Ẓāhiriyya**: a school of *fiqh* which derived its judgements from the literal text of the Qur'an and Sunnah, and rejected the use of other legal principles like analogy.
**zakat**: a wealth tax, one of the five pillars of Islam.
**ẓihār**: an oath by a husband that his wife is like his mother's back to him, meaning she is unlawful for him. It was a form of divorce in the Jāhiliyyah.
**zindīq**: a term used to describe a heretic whose teaching is a danger to the community or state.
**Ẓuhr**: the midday prayer.
**Zuhrah**: a clan of the Quraysh tribe.

www.ingramcontent.com/pod-product-compliance
Lightning Source LLC
Chambersburg PA
CBHW080721300426
44114CB00019B/2447
* 9 7 8 1 9 0 8 8 9 2 7 5 1 *